What Is a Slave Society?

The practice of slavery has been common across a variety of cultures around the globe and throughout history. Despite the multiplicity of slavery's manifestations, many scholars have used a simple binary to categorize slaveholding groups as either "genuine slave societies" or "societies with slaves." This dichotomy, as originally proposed by ancient historian Moses Finley, assumes that there were just five "genuine slave societies" in all of human history: ancient Greece and Rome, and the colonial Caribbean, Brazil, and the American South. This book interrogates this bedrock of comparative slave studies and tests its worth. Assembling contributions from top specialists, it demonstrates that the catalog of five must be expanded and that the model may need to be replaced with a more flexible system that emphasizes the notion of intensification. The issue is approached as a question, allowing for debate between the seventeen contributors about how best to conceptualize the comparative study of human bondage.

Noel Lenski is Professor of Roman History at Yale University. A recipient of fellowships from the Humboldt and Guggenheim Foundations, he has published extensively on Roman imperial history, including *Failure of Empire: Valens and the Roman State in the Fourth Century AD* and *Constantine and the Cities: Imperial Authority and Civic Politics.*

Catherine M. Cameron is Professor of Anthropology at the University of Colorado, Boulder. She is an archaeologist of the American Southwest and has conducted a worldwide, cross-cultural study of captive-taking in prehistory. Cameron is the author of *Captives: How Stolen People Changed the World,* coeditor (with Paul Kelton and Alan Swedlund) of *Beyond Germs: Native Depopulations in North America,* and editor of *Invisible Citizens: Captives and Their Consequences.*

What Is a Slave Society?

The Practice of Slavery in Global Perspective

Edited by

NOEL LENSKI

Yale University

CATHERINE M. CAMERON

University of Colorado, Boulder

With the assistance of JOSHUA FINCHER

CAMBRIDGE
UNIVERSITY PRESS

CAMBRIDGE
UNIVERSITY PRESS

University Printing House, Cambridge CB2 8BS, United Kingdom

One Liberty Plaza, 20th Floor, New York, NY 10006, USA

477 Williamstown Road, Port Melbourne, VIC 3207, Australia

314-321, 3rd Floor, Plot 3, Splendor Forum, Jasola District Centre, New Delhi - 110025, India

79 Anson Road, #06-04/06, Singapore 079906

Cambridge University Press is part of the University of Cambridge.

It furthers the University's mission by disseminating knowledge in the pursuit of education, learning and research at the highest international levels of excellence.

www.cambridge.org
Information on this title: www.cambridge.org/9781316508039
DOI: 10.1017/9781316534908

First published 2018
First paperback edition 2020

A catalogue record for this publication is available from the British Library

ISBN 978-1-107-14489-7 Hardback
ISBN 978-1-316-50803-9 Paperback

Contents

Figures

Maps

Tables and Charts

TABLES

CHARTS

Notes on Contributors

Kim Bok-rae is Professor of European Culture and Tourism at the Andong National University, South Korea. She received her doctorate in history from the University of Paris I. Her interests involve comparative history among China, Korea, and Japan. She has published several articles on Korean *nobis* in comparative perspective: "Nobi: A Korean System of Slavery," in *Structure of Slavery in Indian Ocean Africa and Asia* (2003); "Korean Nobi Resistance under the Chosun Dynasty(1392–1910)," in *Slavery and Resistance in Africa and Asia* (2005); "The Third Gender: Palace Eunuchs," in *Children in Slavery through the Ages* (2009); and "Debt Slaves in Old Korea," in *Bonded Labour and Debt in the Indian Ocean Worlds* (2013).

James F. Brooks is Professor in the Departments of History and Anthropology at the University of California, Santa Barbara. He was president of the School for Advanced Research in Santa Fe from 2005 to 2013 and has held fellowships at the Institute for Advanced Study in Princeton and the Robert Penn Warren Center for the Humanities at Vanderbilt University. He is the author of *Captives & Cousins: Slavery, Kinship and Community in the Southwest Borderlands* (2002) and *Mesa of Sorrows: A History of the Awat'ovi Massacre* (2016).

Catherine M. Cameron is Professor of Anthropology at the University of Colorado, Boulder. She is an archaeologist of the American Southwest and has conducted a worldwide, cross-cultural study of captive-taking in prehistory. She is the author of *Captives: How Stolen*

People Changed the World (2016), coeditor of *Beyond Germs: Native Depopulation in North America* (2015), and editor of *Invisible Citizens: Captives and Their Consequences* (2008).

Bernard K. Freamon is Professor of Law Emeritus at Seton Hall Law School in Newark, New Jersey. His recent publications include an edited collection entitled *Indian Ocean Slavery in the Age of Abolition* (2013) and "ISIS, Boko Haram, and the Human Right to Freedom from Slavery under Islamic Law," published in the *Fordham International Law Journal* (2015): 245–306. He continues to write, consult, and lecture on the issues of slavery and slave trading in Islamic legal history.

Robert Gudmestad is Professor of History at Colorado State University and is the author of *A Troublesome Commerce: The Transformation of the Interstate Slave Trade* (2003) and *Steamboats and the Rise of the Cotton Kingdom* (2011).

Kyle Harper is Professor of Classics and Letters and senior vice president and provost at the University of Oklahoma. He is the author of *Slavery in the Late Roman World, AD 275–425* (2011), *From Shame to Sin: The Christian Transformation of Sexual Morality in Late Antiquity* (2013), and *The Fate of Rome: Climate, Disease, and the End of an Empire* (2017). His work has explored the economic, social, and environmental history of the period spanning the ancient world and the early Middle Ages.

Matthew S. Hopper is Professor of History at Cal Poly, San Luis Obispo. He is the author of *Slaves of One Master: Globalization and Slavery in Arabia in the Age of Empire* (2015), which was a finalist for the Frederick Douglass Book Prize. He was a Fulbright fellow in Tanzania and Oman, has been a visiting fellow at Yale University and the University of Cambridge, and was a member at the Institute for Advanced Study in Princeton.

Peter Hunt is Professor of Classics at the University of Colorado, Boulder. His works on ancient slavery include two books, *Slaves, Warfare, and Ideology in the Greek Historians* (1998) and *Ancient Greek and Roman Slavery* (2018), as well as contributions to *The Cambridge World History of Slavery. Vol. I, The Cambridge History of the World. Vol. 4,* and the *Oxford Handbook of Greek and Roman Slaveries.*

Noel Lenski is Professor of Classics and History at Yale University and formerly at the University of Colorado. A Humboldt and Guggenheim fellow, Lenski has published extensively on Roman imperial history, including the monographs *Failure of Empire: Valens and the Roman State in the Fourth Century AD* (2002) and *Constantine and the Cities: Imperial Authority and Civic Politics* (2016). His work on slavery stretches back more than a decade and includes seminal articles such as "Captivity and Slavery among the Saracens in Late Antiquity (ca. 250–630 CE)" in *Antiquité Tardive* (2011) and "Constantine and Slavery: *Libertas* and the Fusion of Roman and Christian Values" in *Atti dell'Accademia Romanistica Costantiniana* (2012).

Paul E. Lovejoy is Distinguished Research Professor at York University, and a Fellow of the Royal Society of Canada. His publications include *The Transatlantic Slave Trade and Slavery: New Directions in Teaching and Learning* (2013) and *Jihad in West Africa during the Age of Revolutions* (2016). Founding director of the Harriet Tubman Institute for Research on Africa and Its Diasporas and Canada Research Chair in African Diaspora History (2000–15), he has received an honorary degree from the University of Stirling (2007), the Distinguished Africanist Award from the University of Texas, Austin (2010), Life Time Achievement Award from the Canadian Association of African Studies (2011), and Graduate Studies Teaching Award from the York University (2011). He is general editor of the Harriet Tubman Series on the African Diaspora, Africa World Press.

Anthony Reid is currently Professor Emeritus at the Australian National University. He writes on Southeast Asian history, most recently *A History of Southeast Asia: Critical Crossroads* (2015). In 1983, he edited *Slavery, Bondage and Dependency in Southeast Asia.*

Aldair Carlos Rodrigues is Professor of Colonial Brazil at UNICAMP – University of Campinas, Brazil and teaches courses at the undergraduate and graduate levels. He is author of *Limpos de Sangue* (2011), and his current project about Brazil and the African Diaspora focuses on the formation of Dahomey and its impacts on political identities in the interior of Portuguese America during the eighteenth century.

Fernando Santos-Granero is a senior staff scientist at the Smithsonian Tropical Research Institute in Panama. Graduated from the London

School of Economics, he has done extensive fieldwork among the Yanesha of central Peru, as well as historical research of Upper Amazon indigenous societies and regional economies. He is the author of *The Power of Love: The Moral Use of Knowledge amongst the Amuesha of Central Peru* (1991) and *Vital Enemies: Slavery, Predation, and the Amerindian Political Economy of Life* (2009), and coauthor with Frederica Barclay of the books *Selva Central: History, Economy, and Land Use in Peruvian Amazonia* (1998) and *Tamed Frontiers: Economy, Society, and Civil Rights in Upper Amazonia* (2000).

Walter Scheidel is Dickason Professor in the Humanities, Professor of Classics and History, and Kennedy-Grossman Fellow in Human Biology at Stanford University. He is the author or editor of seventeen books, including most recently *On Human Bondage: After Slavery and Social Death* (2017, coedited with John Bodel), and has worked on premodern social and economic history, historical demography, and the comparative global history of labor regimes, state formation, and inequality.

Theresa Singleton is Professor of Anthropology in the Department of Anthropology, Syracuse University. She is the author of *Slavery Behind the Wall: An Archaeology of a Cuban Coffee Plantation* (2015).

Christina Snyder is the McCabe Greer Professor of History at Pennsylvania State University. Her books include *Slavery in Indian Country: The Changing Face of Captivity in Early America* (2010) and *Great Crossings: Indians, Settlers, and Slaves in the Age of Jackson* (2017).

Ehud R. Toledano is Professor of Middle East History and the Director of the Program in Ottoman and Turkish Studies at Tel Aviv University (TAU), Israel. With a PhD from Princeton University, he has conducted extensive research in Istanbul, Cairo, London, and Paris, and taught courses on the Middle East at TAU, UCLA, UPenn, Oxford, and other leading universities. Among the sixteen books he has written and edited is *As if Silent and Absent: Bonds of Enslavement in Islamic Middle East* (2007).

Acknowledgments

This volume was born from a conference held during September 27–28, 2013, at the University of Colorado, Boulder. The event created a tremendously stimulating atmosphere, in which our fundamental question was examined from multiple global and theoretical perspectives. The results of those discussions have developed into the chapters in this book, some of which arise from the original papers delivered at the conference, others from contributions solicited later. Although some of the original participants were unable to submit a chapter, we wish to thank them for their inspiring discussions and insights. These include Daina Ramey Berry (University of Texas, Austin), Gwyn Campbell (McGill University), Walter Hawthorne (Michigan State University), and Joseph Miller (University of Virginia). David Lewis, who attended the conference without delivering a paper, was surely one of the most helpful interlocutors. His subsequent published work has demonstrated a powerful grasp of the problems this volume poses. During fall semester 2013, we also co-taught a course at the University of Colorado entitled "Slavery: A Global Perspective," which was intended to involve students in the *What Is a Slave Society?* conference and to introduce them to the broader world of slavery, past and present. This was a wonderful group of students who challenged us to think even more deeply about the ideas we were presenting in both the course and the conference.

The conference succeeded because of the skilled and efficient work of Sandra Crowell, University of Colorado Classics Department

Program Assistant, who arranged travel, receptions, dinners, and much more for our many attendees. Lesa Morris, Anthropology Department Program Assistant, offered parallel help. During the conference, three graduate students provided enthusiastic assistance: Erin Baxter, Paxton Bigler, and Lindsay Johansson. Erin also served as videographer. The conference was funded by grants from a variety of CU entities: the Center for Western Civilization, IMPART, the Graduate Committee for Arts and the Humanities, the Vice Chancellor's Research Council, the Dean's Fund for Excellence, the President's Fund for the Humanities, the Kayden Award Committee, and Classics Department Course Fees. We are grateful for their confidence in this endeavor and pleased to offer these studies in return. The conference was also sponsored by the Department of Anthropology, Department of Classics, Department of History, and Mediterranean Studies Group. The slavery course associated with the conference was supported by a grant from the University of Colorado's Gamm fund for interdisciplinary courses.

Translating the stimulation and excitement of a conference to written form is often a challenge, but the authors of these chapters have been a delight to work with. These prominent and enormously busy scholars met all of our many deadlines without complaint, making our editorial job easy. During the course of the project, we also requested chapters from scholars who had not attended the conference but whose work, we realized, would add enormously to the resulting book. We thank Bernard Freamon (Seton Hall University), Anthony Reid (Australian National University), Aldair Rodrigues (University of Campinas, Brazil), and Theresa Singleton (Syracuse University) for crafting excellent papers that add greatly to this volume.

Noel Lenski benefited greatly from interchanges with Dan Tompkins, who was especially generous with his knowledge and materials on Moses Finley, as well as Richard Talbert, who kindly supplied his special issue of the *American Journal of Philology*, dedicated to the theme of "Moses Finley in America," immediately after its publication. David Lewis and Kostas Vlassopoulos shared valuable ideas and critical advice on both of Lenski's chapters. Lenski also delivered the paper that became the first chapter of this volume not just at the initial conference but also at conferences held at the Institute for the Study of the Ancient World and Yale University in 2014, and Washington University in St. Louis in 2015. The Yale audience, soon to be colleagues, offered invaluable advice and criticism, especially David Blight, Emily Greenwood, Ed Rugemer, and Stuart Schwartz. Blight and Rugemer as well as Eckart Frahm have been extremely helpful on questions of comparative bibliography.

At Cambridge University Press, Asya Graf, Editor of Archaeology and Renaissance Studies, encouraged us in the initial stages of developing this book project and Beatrice Rehl was equally helpful and encouraging as we moved through the remaining stages. Our thanks go to three anonymous scholars who reviewed this book's initial proposal and made important suggestions about its development, as well as the two anonymous reviewers who read the full manuscript and helped all of us to perfect our chapters. Indeed, "Reader B," whose expertise in the history of slavery globally and of Greek slavery in particular was formidable, contributed a wealth of suggestions that helped both authors and editors vastly improve their work. As this book came together, we had superb editorial assistance from Josh Fincher, who skillfully developed a referencing system for each chapter (no small task with scholars from multiple disciplines), built the bibliography, copyedited the entire document, and later produced its index. University of Colorado grad student Lindsay Johansson provided editorial assistance at the beginning of the project, and retired University of Colorado graphic artist Dave Underwood drew all the maps.

Introduction: Slavery and Society in Global Perspective

Noel Lenski and Catherine M. Cameron

What is a "slave society"? At first glance it might seem simply to be a society that allows some individuals to hold others in a position of subordination as property. Just as humans treat cattle, sheep, or dogs as their "own," some societies permit their members to treat humans by right of ownership as slaves.[1] Any society that permits this could – in a general sense – be called a slave society. For some historians and social scientists, however, the phrase "slave society" constitutes a sociologically definable class that distinguishes a select and limited group of geo-temporally delimited cultures as different in quality and quantity from the many other social contexts in world history that permit slaveholding. Such "genuine slave societies," as they have been termed, are to be distinguished from "societies with slaves," where slavery also exists, but on a smaller and less intensive scale. For this subset of scholars, "Slave Societies" (and here we begin using capitals and quotation marks to set off this specialized sense of the term, a practice maintained throughout this volume) are few in number, many would say as few as five – ancient Greece and Rome, modern Brazil, the Caribbean, and the US South. They are also thought to be

[1] Jacoby 1994 attempts to link the rise of slavery with the domestication of animals and the rise of animal husbandry. His article is useful for its collection of references to slaves as "animals" across a broad pool of (mostly Western) sources. It does not account for the fact that slaves are referred to and treated as animals (especially dogs) in societies without developed husbandry; see Rushforth 2012, 15–71. On the same theme, see also Keith Bradley 2000.

unique in history in that they alone can be said to incorporate slaves and slavery at a "structural location" central to the functioning of that society's economic and cultural elite.

This distinction between "Slave Societies" and "Societies with Slaves" was first developed by groundbreaking ancient historian and sociologist Moses Finley in the 1960s. Finley expanded on the idea in two important monographs from 1973 and 1980, and the distinction was then adopted widely by other Greek and Roman historians until it has become a virtual corollary of ancient slavery studies.[2] It has also enjoyed widespread currency among modern historians, particularly historians of the West, which – Finley posited and subsequent Western scholars have maintained – was historically exceptional in developing "Slave Societies." Yet the idea has gained purchase even beyond the study of Western history to such an extent that it affects both the discourse and the methodology of many slave studies across disciplines up to the present.

The chapters presented in this volume arose as papers presented at a conference held at the University of Colorado, Boulder, during September 27–28, 2013, under the title "What Is a Slave Society? An International Conference on the Nature of Slavery as a Global Historical Phenomenon." The conveners of the meeting and editors of this volume organized the event in order to interrogate Finley's construct. Neither is of the belief that the "Slave Societies/Societies with Slaves" binary remains useful or even tenable in light of ongoing studies of the practice of slavery in a variety of cultures across global history. Nevertheless, both are convinced that the model's supporters still have a case to make, and that those of us who would question a paradigm so widely deployed should offer a forum for debate and perhaps also an alternative for its replacement. They posed the title of the conference – and of this volume – as a question with the deliberate intent of inviting inquiry, discussion, and potential dissent.

In the same spirit, this volume, containing chapters by most of the original attendees and four further contributors, all revised in dialogue with one another, retains contrasting and at times contradictory opinions about the subject. As a collection of individual studies by multiple authors with unique perspectives, it makes no apologies

[2] Finley 1968, 1973a, 1980.

for melding a series of divergent approaches and conclusions. Each author has been invited to engage not just the theme of the conference but also the content of the other chapters. The result is thus not a coherent line of argument, let alone a continuous narrative, but rather a series of debates, or an interconnected grid of opinions about the nature of slavery and slaveholding across history. The conference thus began with a question, and the resulting volume maintains an interrogatory stance.

This book opens with a lengthy chapter on the origins of the idea of the "Slave Society" written by Noel Lenski and intended to provide background and a jumping-off point for the debate that follows. It explores the rise of the model and its subsequent effects on the study of ancient history as well as its interpenetration into fields of history, sociology, and anthropology well beyond the Classical world. The chapter then questions the tendency to restrict the "Slave Society" distinction to just five Western cultures by illustrating how five non-Western societies not mentioned by Finley and his followers seem to fit his criteria for inclusion in the club. Having indicted the model's ethnocentrism, the chapter then moves to more fundamental problems with its construction. It explores issues arising from its assumptions about fundamental similarities between ancient and modern slave systems. It then formulates a new model that attempts to measure the "intensity" of slaveholding practices by comparing them with an "ideal" form of slavery that would balance equally benefits to the master with disadvantages to the slave. This model may or may not replace the Finleyan construct, but it should at least provide a credible alternative to the black-and-white distinction it has imposed.

The thematic chapters of this volume are articulated into four parts. The first explores **Ancient and Late Antique Western Societies**. It begins with Chapter 2 on Classical Greece by Peter Hunt, which opens with the fundamental question of definitions. Hunt examines the long-standing dichotomy between "property definitions" of slavery and Orlando Patterson's subjective definition based on violent domination, natal alienation, and dishonor.[3] While acknowledging the validity of Patterson's *depiction* of slavery, Hunt argues that the notion of property is determinative of the slave state. Slave societies,

[3] Patterson 1982, 1–17.

he contends, are those that most obviously treat humans as property. In addition, he reiterates Finley's emphasis on the structural location of slavery as a matter of paramount importance: slave societies are characterized by the predominance of slaves as the primary suppliers of surplus for the elite. By this definition, Athens was by all means a "Slave Society." Slaves were held as chattels, the proportion of slaves in its population – 20–50 percent of aggregate – was large, and these provided the primary source of surplus production. Sparta, by contrast, was not, for its helots retained limited but tangible rights in property and inheritance that set them above chattel slaves.

In Chapter 3, Kyle Harper and Walter Scheidel join forces to argue in favor of the Finleyan model. They begin by situating Finley's scholarship in its historiographical context. Reacting to Marx's historical materialism and Weber's conquest thesis, the former of which argued that the ancient economy was based in a "slave mode of production" and the latter that it depended on war captives for the generation of slaves, Harper and Scheidel point out that Finley charted a new path that emphasized the property nature of the slave–master relationship: the defining feature of the chattel slave was not his universality qua laborer nor her capture in battle but rather the fact of being treated as a piece of property. Harper and Scheidel continue by inferring that Rome's heavy dependence on slave labor – and thus on commoditized laborers – may have helped propel it to economic prosperity and even toward progressive sociocultural development. They then turn to questions of scale and structural location in an effort to prove that Roman Italy in particular was home to an economy built on and by slaves who then disappeared, by and large, when that economy collapsed in the fifth century.

Noel Lenski closes the first section with a chapter that explores how Finley developed his model within his own mid-twentieth-century context. It begins by exploring the various intellectual strains undergirding Finley's thought: Marx, Bücher, Meyer, Weber, and Polanyi. From these Finley derived his assumptions that the ancient Greek, and, by extension, Roman, economies were fundamentally primitive, based in agriculture, averse to free labor, and unique in ancient world history for the intensity of their slaveholding. Early on, his desire to understand what was unique about Classical Greek slavery (by which he meant Athenian slavery) led Finley to the conclusion that Greece's invention of personal freedom necessitated the use of chattel slaves – making it the world's first "genuine slave society." He then grafted this idea onto a theory developed by István Hahn that emphasized the importance of large-scale private property holding and the availability of free-market exchange as catalysts for the growth of what Hahn termed the *Skavenhaltergesellschaft*. Lenski goes on to question the validity of Finley's model as a tool for comparing the slaveholding practices of ancient societies like Greece and Rome with the modern US South, which was always the paradigm for Finley's "Slave Society."

Part II of this book treats **Non-Western Small-Scale Societies**. In its first chapter, Catherine Cameron covers a broad spectrum of small-scale societies from across the globe, many of which fulfilled all of Finley's criteria for inclusion among the canon of "Slave Societies." Opening each section with a quotation from Finley, the chapter systematically lays out a kind of *koine* of captive-taking among these societies: they regularly raided for captives, often women and children but sometimes also men, and then detained these in subordinate statuses, sometimes over the short term but often throughout their lives and at times even across generations; they did so in numbers that varied widely from context to context but sometimes reached as high as 25 percent of the aggregate population. Their slaves were often structurally important to social differentiation, constituting the main avenue through which elite male status was expressed; they were treated as property, whether of individuals or, more commonly, male heads of household, and were gifted or exchanged for other goods. They were also economically productive, generating surplus while providing leisure for their elite owners. Ultimately, while small-scale societies display significant differences with more complex state-based social systems, in certain instances, they clearly intensified the practice of captive-taking and slaveholding to the point that they too could be considered "Slave Societies" within the terms of their own social complex.[4]

In Chapter 6, Christina Snyder explores the bewildering variety of slaveries practiced in native North America. Captive-taking and

[4] Many of these ideas are explored in greater detail in Cameron 2016a.

slaveholding on the continent preceded European contact and persisted in its aftermath, with native practices often conforming themselves to colonial patterns over time. In all instances precontact slavery was based on captive-taking, and many – though not all – native societies were "open" to the incorporation of captives into their cultures.[5] Some, however, like the Northwest Coast peoples, developed robust systems of trans-generational slavery.[6] Several – like the Cherokee or Chickasaw – merged their native traditions with colonial patterns by organizing plantations populated by African slaves, and others – like the Westos – came to specialize in slave raiding and trading as the basis of their economies.[7] Overall, Snyder argues, slavery in Native American societies was in constant flux, ever shifting in its forms, purposes, and intensity to meet changing social and economic circumstances. These insights obviously cast a shadow over attempts to view colonial New World slavery in essentializing terms, for it too developed over time and even in dialogue with the native forms – Amerindian and African – it encountered.

In Chapter 7, Fernando Santos-Granero carries the argument to tropical Native America, between southern Florida and the Gran Chaco of South America. He demonstrates the diffusion of captive-taking and slaveholding here too in the precontact period. Focusing on five societies, he shows how some of these – like the Kalinago and Conibo – practiced regular captive-taking raids and then used their victims as slaves for the remainder of their lifetimes, while others – like the Tukano, Chiriguaná, and Guaicurú – held slaves alongside serf-like or tributary dependent populations. Using three approaches, one structural, a second processual, and a third phenomenological, Santos-Granero shows that, while the groups he treats may not qualify as Finleyan "Slave Societies" for want of a "slave mode of production," they were societies structured around captive-taking and slaveholding. Thus, at least from the slaves' perspective, there would have been little difference between the level of violence and alienation imposed in these societies as compared to those that fit Finley's model more comfortably.

[5] Snyder 2010; Rushforth 2012; cf. Cameron 2011.
[6] See Donald 1997.
[7] See Bowne 2005.

Paul Lovejoy continues this section in Chapter 8 with an examination of "Slavery in Societies on the Frontiers of Centralized States in West Africa." Focusing on the interior of Upper Guinea in the eighteenth century and the Bight of Biafra in the nineteenth, when the Muslim states of Fuuta Jalon and Sokoto dominated the interior of these regions, Lovejoy draws into doubt the validity or usefulness of the Finleyan "Slave Society" even as he also questions some of the terms of discussion inherent in this volume: ideas of "statehood," of "society," of "modes of production" are none of them easily applicable to the African societies he investigates. Even so, slaves – people who could be bought and sold and who were subject to the will and whim of their masters – existed in these regions before Western contact, and societies that fit Finley's criteria for recognition as "Slave Societies" were also present and indeed common. Exploiting this situation, Aro merchants traveled the Cross and Niger Rivers collecting marketable slaves traded from the Igbo and Ibibio who were then sold to Western slavers. So too the small-scale societies surrounding the Sokoto Caliphate simultaneously retained slaves of their own and were subject to enslavement by the hulking "Slave Society" on whose frontiers they lived. In this sense, slave societies were common in this region of West Africa in the eighteenth and nineteenth centuries.

Ultimately, then, the notion of the slave society – when used as a descriptive term – remains useful as a way to identify societies that are fundamentally shaped by the institution of slavery. The chapters in this section would seem to agree, however, that the use of the notion of a "Slave Society" to establish a firmly bounded sociological category is as likely to distort as enhance interpretation. All indicate that too keen a focus on the illusory ideal of an archetypal "Slave Society" is at once overly rigid and less than productive of meaning for those seeking to explain the complexity of slaveholding systems across cultures.

Part III of this volume treats **Modern Western Societies** and offers a more sympathetic reading of the Finleyan idea. Aldair Carlos Rodrigues opens in Chapter 9 with an examination of "The Colonial Brazilian 'Slave Society': Potentialities, Limits, and Challenges to an Interpretative Model Inspired by Moses Finley." Brazil was the largest importer of African slaves in the transatlantic complex and it used these slaves to recreate a colonial version of the status regimes of the metropolis. At the start of the colonial period, slavery was still very much alive in Portugal, albeit in a system restricted to the social elite. But the New World recreation of Portuguese slavery allowed entrepreneurs and social climbers to employ slave-owning as the fundamental tool for the creation and assertion of status. This is confirmed by demographic analyses that have emphasized that slaveholding occurred across a broad spectrum of social statuses in Brazil before the end of the transatlantic slave trade in 1850, giving it a solid purchase across Luso-American society. A closer look at regional variation demonstrates that the use of African slaves predominated in coastal regions with sugar production and access to the transatlantic market, while São Paulo and Amazonia made heavier use of indigenous peoples, often as semi-servile dependents, until late in the eighteenth century. After refuting recent efforts to downplay the difference between colonial and metropolitan slaveholding, Rodrigues closes with a look at recent research that has recovered a place for slave agency in Brazil, particularly in studies emphasizing the creative adaptation of the European tradition of godparenthood and African traditions of warfare. Thus, while defending the usefulness of Finley's model, Rodrigues acknowledges the limitations imposed by its emphasis on the perspective of masters rather than slaves.

In Chapter 10, Robert Gudmestad explores the question in North America with "What Is a Slave Society? The American South." He accepts the challenge to look past the Finleyan binary and apply Lenski's new intensification model to this context. Beginning with a survey of the history of slavery in North America, he shows how the introduction of cash crops invited the intensification of African slaveholding by white colonists. Over the course of the seventeenth century, these created the normative and administrative apparatus necessary for the large-scale use of slavery out of whole cloth, for the British had abolished slavery in the metropolis some four centuries earlier. The patchwork nature of American colonial settlement and the variegation in landscape and climate led to tremendous variability in American slaveholding. This tended to be smoothed out in the late eighteenth century as slavery intensified in the warmer climates of the South even as it withered in a North active in the invention of abolitionism. Even so, Gudmestad emphasizes that the Southern states hardly used slaves in any uniform way, as regards both their demographic and their economic importance. Ultimately, the welding together of the United States after 1789 created a Manichaean political and economic system, unique in world history for the tensions it created over the question of slavery. When the country fissured in 1860, it was the level of intensification that dictated whether states would side with the Union or the Confederacy. In this sense, intensification best describes the patterns of slaveholding that emerged in some areas and the opposing trends that came to prevail in others.

In Chapter 11, Theresa Singleton introduces material culture to the debate in her exploration of "Islands of Slavery: Archaeology and Caribbean Landscapes of Intensification." After problematizing the whole notion of "the Caribbean" as a unified geographical, let alone political, space, she explores how the differential bias in Caribbean slave archaeology for larger plantations has masked the diversity in the scale and practice of slaveholding and other forms of dependent labor. She then turns to a diachronic investigation of the development of slavery, starting with *encomiendas* of the sixteenth century and moving to the large-scale plantations associated with English and French colonization in the region following the sugar revolution. Controlled by large-scale investment interests and populated by enslaved African laborers, these geo-temporal contexts did indeed give rise to structures Finley characterized as a "Slave Society" in places like Barbados, Jamaica, and St. Domingue. More difficult to explain is why these economies turned from indentured white to enslaved black labor, as is the question of why the Spanish waited to develop intensive slave-based production until the nineteenth century, a period when slave production was de-intensifying in the British and French contexts. The "Slave Society/Societies with Slaves" binary may then be useful in the broadest terms for modeling the Caribbean, but its two-dimensional simplicity falls short of offering an explanatory model for the regional variability characteristic of the Caribbean as whole.

Part IV of this book looks at **Non-Western State Societies** in a series of five chapters. The first, Chapter 12, by Matthew Hopper, covers nineteenth-century Eastern Arabia, which was home to tens of thousands of slaves who worked in the production of pearls and dates. Overturning entrenched notions that Islamic cultures hold slaves only for purposes of military or bureaucratic service, household maintenance, or sexual exploitation, Hopper elucidates a highly sophisticated, market-driven slave system that concentrated slaves from East Africa and Baluchistan on plantations and pearl fisheries. Highly elastic international demand for these commodities and intensive capital investment in the infrastructure necessary to conduct them created the perfect market environment for the intensified exploitation of slave labor. Nevertheless, this occurred on terms consonant with the environmental and social conditions in the Persian Gulf, which were, of course, markedly different from those of plantation economies. Nevertheless, excluding these Eastern Arabian states (which meet all of Finley's criteria) from the canon can only reinforce unwelcome prejudices in favor of Western agricultural economies, as if these were uniquely capable of forging "genuine slave societies."

Focusing on the East African nexus of the Indian Ocean and Persian Gulf slaving zone in Chapter 13, Bernard Freamon investigates "Slavery and Society in East Africa, Oman, and the Persian Gulf." He draws into question the implicit territoriality of Finley's "Slave Societies" and attempts to expand the definition of "society" to include the broader geographical matrix of East Africa, South Asia, and the Persian Gulf, a region interlinked by shared conditions of climate, geography, and migration patterns. Freamon shows that the traffic in slaves along routes between the Red Sea and East Africa reached back to the second millennium BCE but that it grew greatly in scale beginning in the fifteenth century CE as a function of the flourishing of Islamic empires. The growth of the transatlantic systems was paralleled in the eighteenth- and nineteenth-century Indian Ocean, influenced simultaneously by the rise of European colonial slaveries on the Mascarenes and Réunion, as well as by Islamic slaveholding on Zanzibar and Pemba. Earlier historiography has often identified the characteristics of a Finleyan "Slave Society" without making explicit reference to the model, although some have also emphasized the broader variety of status relationships and the intercultural exchange of slaves common within this geosphere.[8] After reviewing the often massive sizes of slaveholdings, particularly among Arab magnates of the nineteenth century, whose cases are well documented, Freamon concludes that the broader West Indian Ocean region spawned a kind of "Slave Society" that was transregional and transcultural.

[8] See especially Cooper 1977, 1980, and Gwyn Campbell 2004.

In Chapter 14, Ehud Toledano examines the question of slave societies in reverse – that is, from the perspective of abolition. Strongly critical of Lenski's introductory chapter, he proceeds from the assumption that, taken broadly, Finley's model is defensible and useful. To prove the point, he undertakes to demonstrate that a strong indicator that Ottoman society was a "Society with Slaves" and not a "Slave Society" is the fact that no antislavery movement arose from within it. Building on recent work by Madeline Zilfi, he shows how Islamic law and scripture provide a strong cultural and social framework for the ongoing practice of enslavement that tended to help preserve the institution in the face of Western opposition.[9] Nevertheless, argues Toledano, slavery was insignificant enough as an economic or social institution in Ottoman society that few took the trouble to oppose it.[10]

In Chapter 15, Kim Bok-rae examines Korean *nobis* in the Chosun period (1392–1910). Long considered true slaves in Western scholarship, *nobis* were indeed subject to labor for their noble masters (*yangban*), could be sexually exploited by these, and could be bought and sold independent of the land on which they labored.[11] Nevertheless, Kim argues, *nobis* differed from chattel slaves in the Western world both because of their assimilation to the Korean commoner class (*yangmin*) and because the masters' property rights over the persons of the slaves were only rarely exercised. Ownership of a *nobi* was thus ownership over his labor product more than his person. To drive home the point Kim uses the micro-historical example of a *yangmin* named Damulsari who falsely claimed to be a public *nobi* in order to *protect* herself and her children from tribute claims of the master of her husband, thus proving that *nobi* status was at times something that could be coveted. In light of this micro-historical example, Kim urges caution about the cross application of Western models of dependency to non-Western societies: ownership rights on a human do not always or easily square with Western concepts of chattel slavery.

In Chapter 16, Tony Reid then offers a contribution entitled "'Slavery so Gentle': A Fluid Spectrum of Southeast Asian Conditions

[9] Zilfi 2010.

[10] See also Toledano 1998; cf. Erdem 1996. Note that Zilfi 2010, 100, is herself convinced that slavery "was culturally and institutionally integral to both state and society."

[11] See Palais 1996, 208–70, 1998; cf. Patterson 1982, passim.

of Bondage." After opening with a critique of holistic efforts to define "the slave" in absolute and culturally neutral terms, Reid explains that the entire region was characterized by persistent and widespread systems of status inequality, even if these do not always map easily onto Western notions of chattel slavery. Europeans arrived in the region in the sixteenth century, when commerce was burgeoning and warfare common, and witnessed large-scale captive-taking by both the Siamese and Burmese states, which often resulted in the transplantation of huge population groups onto state-controlled rice plantations, as well as chattel slave raiding by entrepreneurs working among the stateless peoples in the highlands surrounding the rice-growing states. Reid then narrows the lens to cover the "Malay world" of the Peninsula and Archipelago, where we find the best documentation on the problem in Southeast Asia. There Dutch sources reveal how preexisting systems of slavery and dependency were adapted to European legal and economic frameworks even as other systems developed under indigenous, Muslim, and Chinese hegemony. The Dutch colonists of Batavia attempted to corral this ferment of slave cultures using European law and in so doing provide us with our best evidence of a Finleyan "Slave Society" in the region. By the same token, Reid counsels against Finley's oversimplified schematism in favor of more differentiated and culturally contingent approaches to the complex comparative problem of slavery and dependency.

Finally, James Brooks concludes this volume with a lyrical and highly personal look at how experiences of captivity and enslavement have shaped the cultures of the American Southwest in ways that resonate even up to the present. Building on the folksong "La Cautiva Marcelina," he shows how enslavement colors the stories humans use to structure their identities. Even up to the present, the annual processions for Santa Rosa de Lima de Abiquiú in northern New Mexico trace their roots to a Spanish settler community devastated by Comanche raiders in 1747, then rebuilt and populated with Native American *genízaros* who guarded the frontier for their Spanish captors. Rescuing their identity from this tangle of traumatic memories, the people of this tiny community represent well the long-term effects of slavery and the adaptability it imposes upon its survivors.

In the aggregate a complex picture emerges that in many ways breaks itself down along disciplinary lines. Most of those invested in the study of the Western European and colonial tradition wish to defend the Finleyan "Slave Society" model. Not only has it worked well up to the present as a conceptual and pedagogical tool, but it has also helped explain obvious similarities across the transatlantic slave systems, similarities that extend as well to ancient Greece and Rome. Those, by contrast, who work primarily on non-Western societies are much less comfortable with this construct. The basis of their dissatisfaction is twofold. First, many feel that the societies they study do meet Finley's criteria – loose as they are – for inclusion in the circle of "Slave Societies" even if the particular societies in which they specialize have often been overlooked by Western historians. Second, and more important, insofar as their disqualification has been or could be justified, the grounds for this result from the radical differences between the structures of these societies and "normative" Western slave societies like the US South.

At root, Finley's model emphasizes the crucial importance of "structural location" as the determinative factor for consideration as a "Slave Society." If slaves constitute the primary producers of economic surplus for the elite, they inhabit a "Slave Society." Detecting this has been easiest for historians among Western societies structured, like our own, around capitalist market exchange. The model is less obviously detectable among non-state and premodern state societies, the former of which lack market mechanisms and the latter of which could fairly be classed as proto-capitalist – with primitive market structures, but also severe limitations on capital investment imposed by much more circumscribed financial, technological, legal, and cultural horizons. For the model to be valid in a global historical context, however, it should be testable across a range of societies that are not Western and even those that are precapitalist. When such testing occurs, as it does in this volume, it becomes clear that Finleyan "Slave Societies" in the broadest sense do indeed arise in a variety of non-Western cultures, particularly in that period of the eighteenth and nineteenth centuries when capitalist exchange and its effects began spreading rapidly across world markets in the Persian Gulf, East and West Africa, and Southeast Asia.

Moreover, if we abide closely by Finley's criteria, we must admit that slavery can gain structurally significant importance for the creation and maintenance of the elite in a broad range of cultures that are entirely precapitalist. Some small-scale societies of Native North and South America display a widespread tendency toward captive-taking which, in some groups, developed into fully fledged and relatively large-scale slaveholding. The same could be said of some African societies even in the precontact period, and arguments have been made – though not in this volume – that the same is true in Korea and Southeast Asia. Western contact of course changed the dynamics of slaveholding in these cultures even as it changed all aspects of economy and society, but this often meant simply adapting native slave-ways to suit an environment now governed by exchanges – economic, political, and military – with the West. Seen from the broadest angle, then, "Slave Societies" come to seem much less remarkable and much more variegated than Finley has argued. Each displays its own peculiarities dictated by a set of variables unique to a given culture, and all arise from both economic and cultural tendencies that favor the intensification of slaveholding in environments that devalue the humanity of some group or class to the point that fellow people can be treated as mere chattels.

1

Framing the Question: What Is a Slave Society?

Noel Lenski

The institution of slavery is found in multiple forms around the globe, in a variety of cultural contexts, and in all historical periods up to the present. While few would deny this sad reality, Western historians and some anthropologists have long been convinced that certain societies stand out as distinctive in the scale and degree of their slaveholding practices. These perceive a line of demarcation between "Slave Societies," which are thought to be only very few in number and all Western, and "Societies with Slaves," which have been much more common across the history and geography of the planet. This binary was first proposed by ancient historian Moses Finley in the 1960s and has gained wide currency not just among ancient historians but indeed among all scholars of slavery operating in the English-speaking world, and even beyond it. The present volume proposes to interrogate this construct.

This chapter has been composed in order to open the debate. It explains the author's own difficulties with the idea of a concretely definable difference between "Slave Societies" and "Societies with Slaves." These are based on two primary concerns with the model: first its **ethnocentrism**, for all of the "Slave Societies" Finley and his followers have identified are Western; and second its **categorical imprecision**, for the division of the manifold and multifarious cultural, political, and social structures in world history into just two groups seems inherently problematic. In what follows, I treat each of these issues in turn. First, however, it is necessary to explore further the way in which the idea of the "Slave Society" arose and the degree to which it has influenced the scholarship on slavery.

GENESIS OF THE IDEA OF A "SLAVE SOCIETY"

Moses Finley (1912–86) was a brilliant ancient historian, whose rich and troubled life experience played a key role in his formation as a pathbreaking scholar. Recognized early for his genius, Finley completed a law degree at Columbia University at just seventeen years of age, but then turned to graduate work in ancient history in 1934.[1] His studies were interrupted for a decade during the latter part of the Great Depression and throughout World War II when he worked, inter alia, as an editorial assistant and translator for the Institute for Social Research in New York (Horkheimer's Institut für Sozialforschung in exile from Frankfurt) from 1937 to 1939 and for the American Society for Russian Relief (a pro-Soviet political and social action group).[2] The former steeped Finley in the most sophisticated social science research methods of the day; the latter, coupled with Finley's sympathies for Soviet Russia and Marxism more broadly, eventually led to his dismissal from his first permanent academic appointment at Rutgers University and his transfer to Great Britain in 1953.[3] There he taught ancient history, primarily at Cambridge, for some thirty years down to his death in 1986.[4] In no small part thanks to his broad training and tumultuous life experience, Finley was the first person systematically to import the formal tools of sociology into the study of ancient history and also the first to use comparative methods to inform our understanding of the premodern world. His work has had a major impact on the way ancient history is practiced up to the present, and his life and achievements were celebrated at two conferences held to honor the centenary of his birth in 2012.[5]

[1] Of the many recent studies on Finley, see especially Shaw and Saller 1981; Shaw 1993; Watson 2004; Nafissi 2005, 191–283; Tompkins 2008, 2013a, 2013b, 2016.

[2] On the importance of this period for the formation of Finley's thought on slavery, see Perry 2014.

[3] On these crucial years in Finley's development, see Tompkins 2016.

[4] More on Finley's biography at Watson 2004.

[5] Both are now published as William V. Harris 2013 and Jew, Osborne, and Scott 2016. See also the special issue of *American Journal of Philology*, which publishes a 1985

Finley first mentions the notion of the "Slave Society" in a groundbreaking survey article published in the *Encyclopedia of World Sociology* in 1968. There he writes:

> The distinction is particularly sharp as between *genuine* slave societies – classical Greece (except Sparta) and Rome, the American South and the Caribbean – on the one hand, and *slave-owning* societies as found in the ancient Near East (including Egypt), India, or China, on the other hand [emphasis original].[6]

He then elaborates the concept in greater detail in the third chapter of his groundbreaking *The Ancient Economy* (1973), where he once again lists ancient Greece and Italy as the "first genuine slave societies in history."[7] At the outset it is worth noting the repetition of the heavily overdetermined word "genuine," which has come to play an important role in the rhetoric of this construct in subsequent literature. Its implications of authenticity and verifiability lend an air of essentialism to a construct that was, of course, a creation of Finley's imagination, but that quickly gained purchase as a sociohistorical given.

The conception of the "Slave Society" comes to full fruition in Finley's widely read and deservedly acclaimed *Ancient Slavery and Modern Ideology* (1980) (hereinafter, *ASMI*). There he lays out the criteria that he considers foundational to any "Slave Society":

- Slaves must constitute a significant percentage of the population (say, 20 percent or more).
- Slaves must play a significant role in surplus production.
- Slaves must be important enough to exercise a pervasive cultural influence.[8]

The theory obviously has the virtue of laying out definable markers by which to characterize the category. It is obvious from the beginning, however, that these are quite broad in scope and lacking in precision.

interview with Finley by his protégé Keith Hopkins – also a prominent figure in this chapter – with an introduction and four essays, Naiden and Talbert 2014.

6 Finley 1968, 308; cf. 310: "What counts in evaluating the place of slavery in any society is, therefore, not absolute totals or proportions, but rather *location* and *function*. If the economic and political elite depended primarily on slave labor for basic production, then one may speak of a slave society."

7 Finley 1973a, 71, "the first genuine slave societies in history," and 93, "In Italy … where for some centuries we found genuine slave societies."

8 Finley 1980, 79–82 (reprint Finley 1998, 147–50).

Even the first, which establishes a quantifiable benchmark, was obviously a ballpark figure with no well-articulated criteria for its selection nor any firm sense that a different figure could just as easily have been used.

Already in his 1968 encyclopedia entry, Finley had sketched out comparanda to Classical Greece and Rome by listing the US South and the colonial Caribbean as further exemplars of this typology. In *ASMI* he adds a fifth, Brazil, and also canonizes his list of five in the preface when he states, "Although slaves have been exploited in most societies as far back as any records exist, there have been only five genuine slave societies, two of them in antiquity: Classical Greece and classical Italy."[9] Finley's assertion was taken up by his successor as Professor of History at Cambridge, Keith Hopkins – an equally brilliant scholar, also deeply committed to comparative methods – who stated the case even more categorically in his influential and widely read *Conquerors and Slaves* (1978):

> Only a handful of human societies can properly be called "slave societies," if by slave society we mean a society in which slaves play an important part in production and form a high proportion (say over 20%) of the population. There are only two well established cases from antiquity: classical Athens and Roman Italy ... From the early modern period, only three more cases are known, the West Indian Islands, Brazil, and the southern states of the USA. These five societies in which slaves played a considerable role in production (and in ostentatious consumption) form a distinct category of "slave society."[10]

Hopkins then offers a graphic illustration of his point by comparing the absolute and proportional numbers of slaves in these five societies in a table that helped to cement this canon of five into the purported lone representatives of the archetype. The "Slave Society" was thus a historiographical construct invented with the good intention of comparing slaveholding practices across societies that became reified into a vaguely articulated, seductively exclusive category of sociological analysis.

9 Finley 1980, 9, 80 (reprint Finley 1998, 77, 148).

10 Hopkins 1978, 99–100. Interestingly, Hopkins 1967, 172–73, quibbles with the application of the title "Slave Society" to Greece and Rome. Hopkins's argument in *Conquerors and Slaves* has been the subject of more extensive revision in recent scholarship, on which see Hin 2013.

THE IMPACT OF THE MODEL

The impact that this theory has had on ancient historians has been tremendous, so much so that the notion of the "Slave Society" can be regarded as all but totalizing in this subdiscipline. Already in 1981, one year after the publication of *ASMI*, an entire volume of studies was dedicated to Finley's approach in the new Italian journal *Opus: Rivista internazionale per la storia economica e sociale dell'antichità*, albeit with many papers critical of the new theory. Nevertheless the Finleyan model quickly took hold as a normative for scholars of Greece and Rome, particularly in the Anglophone world. Thus, in his widely used textbook *Slavery and Society at Rome* (1994) Keith Bradley devotes an entire chapter to "The Slave Society of Rome" in which he lays out Finley's theory and adduces Hopkins's catalog of five as "the only genuine slave societies to have existed in all of human history."[11] So too Cambridge's more recently published textbook on Roman slavery, *Slavery in the Roman World* (2010) by Sandra Joshel, lists these five as the only true "Slave Societies."[12] In her article on the origins of Greek slavery in the multiauthored comparatist volume *Slavery and Serfdom*, Tracey Rihll considers "Ancient Greece … the first genuine slave society," although she differs with Finley on how it came into being.[13] The model also permeates hers and several others' articles in the monumental *Cambridge World History of Slavery, Vol. I: The Ancient Mediterranean World* (2011), five of whose twenty-two chapters discuss the notion, and two of which treat it as a normative paradigm.[14] It

[11] Bradley 1994, ch. 2, esp. p. 12: "A slave society consequently is 'a society in which slaves play an important part in production and form a high proportion (say over 20 per cent) of the population.' On this test, only five genuine slave societies have existed in all of human history: Brazil, the Caribbean and the United States in the modern era, and Athens and Roman Italy (not the whole of the Roman Empire) in classical antiquity."

[12] Joshel 2010, 7–8: "Equally important is the term 'slave society' and its distinction from a society that has slaves … If the proportion of slaves is set at over twenty percent of the population, only five slave societies have existed in human history: ancient Greece, ancient Italy, and, in the modern period, the United States, Brazil, and the islands of the Caribbean."

[13] Rihll 1996, 89, 111. See also Fisher 1993, 3–4.

[14] Rihll 2011, 48 and 69–72, a section titled "Why and How Did Athens Become a Genuine Slave Society?"; Bradley 2011, 244–45: "Three conditions can be posited as necessary for the emergence of a genuine slave society … These conditions were met at Rome in all likelihood by c. 300 at the latest"; Edmondson 2011, 339; Grey 2011, 485; Morley 2011, 284–85.

constitutes the underlying model in the articles on slavery in both the *Oxford Handbook of Roman Studies* (2010) and the *Oxford Handbook of Social Relations in the Roman World* (2011).[15] In addition, the "Slave Society" has had an effect on continental European scholarship, as evidenced by the popular introductory textbook of Elisabeth Hermann-Otto, *Sklaverei und Freilassung in der grieschisch-römischen Welt* (2009) and the widely used French textbook *Esclave en Grèce et à Rome* (2006) by Jean Andreau and Raymond Descat, now translated into English: both include discussions of the Finleyan distinction between "Slave Societies" and "Societies with Slaves," although neither lists the canonical five.[16]

To be sure, most of the titles listed thus far are textbooks or handbooks and may thus be forgiven for transmitting "received" knowledge rather than challenging established paradigms, but even work aimed at pushing the boundaries of research in ancient slave studies displays a marked attachment to Finleyan orthodoxy. In the introduction to their sweeping comparative volume *Slave Systems Ancient and Modern* (2008), Enrico Dal Lago and Constantina Katsari also credit the model.[17] Similarly, Sara Forsdyke, in her widely acclaimed study of ancient Greek popular culture, *Slaves Tell Tales*, assumes the validity of the model and its five-member roster.[18] Walter Scheidel, a contributor to this volume, whose work has revolutionized much of what we think about Roman slavery, recurs to the notion several times in his studies with an emphasis that appears designed not just to highlight the exclusive nature of this club but also to glorify Rome's primacy within it.[19] So too Kyle Harper, another equally revolutionary figure

[15] Bradley 2010, 625: "Rome was a genuine slave society"; Schumacher 2011.

[16] Hermann-Otto 2009, 11–13; Andreau and Descat 2006, 23–27, esp. 26. Compare the English translation in Andreau and Descat 2011, 13–16, esp. 13. Further examples of the use of the model in francophone scholarship in Ferrer 2003; Oudin-Bastide 2005.

[17] Dal Lago and Katsari 2008b, 5: "In some respects, then, the concept of 'slave system' relies on the definition of 'slave society,' first advanced by Moses Finley." See already Cartledge 1985, 18: "Greece and Rome were indeed 'slave' societies properly so called."

[18] Forsdyke 2012, 19–20.

[19] Scheidel 2005b, 1: "How did the Greek Aegean and Roman Italy become two of the very few genuine slave societies in world history?"; Scheidel 2008, 105: "Genuine 'slave economies' ... were rare in history. Classical Greece and the Italian heartland of the Roman empire are among the most notable cases"; Scheidel 2012, 89: "Building on Greek and Hellenistic institutions, ancient Rome created the largest slave society in history ... Since the role of slavery in central productive processes

in Roman slavery studies and also co-contributor with Scheidel to this collection, builds on the premise that the Roman Empire continued to maintain its status as a genuine "Slave Society" down through the fourth century CE in his award-winning *Slavery in the Late Roman World* (2011). Indeed, the book's opening page offers an outstanding example of the ongoing vitality of claims for the unusual scale of ancient slaveholding as evidence for Rome's exceptionality – and its paradigmatic role for the future of Western civilization.[20]

Thus far we have discussed only Greek and Roman historians, but Finley's model has had a significant impact on the historiography of slavery well beyond the field of ancient Mediterranean studies. For obvious reasons, modern historians are less likely to access Finley's scholarship and thus to have occasion to build on his hermeneutic, but the theory was sufficiently broadly conceived to have gained attention beyond the halls of the Classics Department almost since its inception. To give just a few examples – and one could cite many more – David Turley's *Slavery* (2000), still one of the few textbooks widely available for comparative courses on slavery, sets out the distinction between "Societies with Slaves" and "Slave Societies" as its operative paradigm.[21] It is also present in the work of James Palais on Chosŏn Korea, which he considers another exemplar of a "Slave Society." Similar claims are made by Carl I. Hammer, who argues that the Baiuvarii of southern Germany were also *A Large-Scale Slave Society*

turned Rome into a 'slave economy,' just as the widespread domination of slaves as a primary social relationship made it into a 'slave society,' these two terms may be used interchangeably … In short, Rome was a 'slave society' to the extent that without slavery it would have looked profoundly different." Note, however, that Scheidel 2005b, 1, and 2008, 105 n. 1, already indicate an awareness that the Finleyan canon of five may be too restrictive.

[20] Harper 2011, 3: "The Roman empire was home to the most extensive and enduring slave system in premodern history. Slavery has been virtually ubiquitous in human civilization, but the Romans created one of the few 'genuine slave societies' in the western experience. The other example of classical antiquity, the slave society of Greece, was fleeting and diminutive by comparison. Stretching across half a millennium and sprawling over a vast tract of space, Roman slavery existed on a different order of magnitude. Five centuries, three continents, tens of millions of souls: Roman slavery stands as the true ancient predecessor to the systems of mass scale slavery in the New World. We cannot explain the Roman slave system as the spoils of imperial conquest. Roman slavery was a lasting feature of an entire historical epoch, implicated in the very forces that made the Roman Mediterranean historically exceptional." See further Harper 2011, 33–38.

[21] Turley 2000, 1–5.

of the Early Middle Ages.[22] So too the comparative sociological study of Alain Testart *L'esclave, la dette et le pouvoir* (2001) takes the Finleyan binary as its starting point.[23] B. W. Higman references the model in his recent essay on "Demography and Family Structures" in the third volume of *The Cambridge World History of Slavery* (2011), retaining not just the outlines of the construct but also the canonical list of five.[24] Indeed, Finley's construct is also credited and discussed in the introduction to that same volume, unsurprisingly so given that one of that book's editors, David Eltis, also upholds both the broader model and the narrower canon of five in his acclaimed *The Rise of African Slavery in the Americas* (2000).[25]

American historian David Brion Davis also employs the model in his *Inhuman Bondage: The Rise and Fall of Slavery in the New World* (2005) when he draws a link between Greco-Roman and transatlantic slave systems, building from the assumption that "Greece was probably the first genuine 'slave society' " and that modern slaveholders constructed their ideology on Greek and Roman principles.[26] The Finleyan model also forms the backbone of Ira Berlin's extremely influential *Many Thousands Gone* (1998). Berlin's primary aim becomes clear already in his table of contents, where the layout of chapters charts the divergent trajectories of the Northern and Southern halves of colonial and early US North America: both started off as "Societies with Slaves," but only the Southern states spawned "Slave Societies." As he points out early in the book:

> The transformation generally turned upon the discovery of some commodity – gold being the ideal, sugar being a close second – that could command an international market. With that, slaveholders capitalized production and monopolized resources, muscled other classes to the periphery, and consolidated their political power.[27]

For Berlin, then, the "Slave Societies" of the American South arose in response to the development of cash crops meant for exchange on the world market: tobacco in the Chesapeake and Virginia Piedmont,

[22] Palais 1996, 208–70; 1998, 23–47; Hammer 2002.
[23] Testart 2001, 28–31.
[24] Higman 2011, 482.
[25] Eltis 2000, 7–8; Eltis and Engerman 2011, 7–11.
[26] Davis 2006, 27–47, quotation at 41.
[27] Berlin 1998, passim, quotation at 9.

rice on the coastal plains and lowlands of the Carolinas, and cotton in the Deep South. Important for Berlin is thus the critical notion of *transformation* – "Slave Societies" come into being as a result of a conjunction of economic and historical forces.[28]

Both notions – the "Slave Society" paradigm and the importance of transformation – also appear in the work of Paul Lovejoy, another contributor to this volume. Lovejoy builds on the Finleyan theory in his *Transformations in Slavery: A History of Slavery in Africa*, still the most widely read survey of African slavery in print (3rd edn. 2012).[29] Of course, none of the societies Lovejoy treats was included in the exclusive canon of five, yet he adapts Finley's model to argue that various societies in African history do in fact correspond to the paradigm. One can begin to sense that the limitation of the model to five Western societies has difficulty standing up to the weight of comparative evidence. The same problem arises in the work of Orlando Patterson, who pioneered the comparative study of slavery with his *Slavery and Social Death* (1982). From the beginning of this work Patterson references Finley's "Slave Society" but distances himself from the canon of five Western societies, emphasizing instead the surprisingly high number of societies in which slavery has grown to structurally significant levels.[30] The same can be said of the most recent effort to synthesize the world history of slavery, the *Handbuch Geschichte der Sklaverei* (2013) of Michael Zeuske, which devotes considerable attention to the model but acknowledges its obvious limitations in a global historical context.[31]

The "Slave Society" model has thus been extremely influential both in ancient history circles and well beyond them. It has provided a tool that is useful to think with for those wishing to draw distinctions between the scale and intensity of slave systems in world history. Its early limitation to a canon of just five world societies has also proven serviceable, although mostly to historians of the Occident who seek both to highlight the uniqueness of Western culture and economy and to trace common threads in Western history that can be linked to an ancient European legacy. The latter concern has obviously shown

[28] Berlin 2003, passim, esp. 8–11, builds on the same paradigm in much the same terms.
[29] Lovejoy 2012a, 9–11.
[30] Patterson 1982, vii–x. See also Patterson 1991 passim; 2008.
[31] Zeuske 2013, 201–18.

signs of strain in the face of comparative evidence, but the model's now almost unquestioned acceptance as a totalizing paradigm has occasioned little reflection, let alone critique.[32]

ETHNOCENTRISM

It is striking that all five "Slave Societies" distinguished by Finley and his closest followers are Western. To some this may seem unproblematic, for it corresponds well with post-Marxist and postcolonialist assumptions about the role of Western hegemony in escalating the level of violence and domination across the globe in the modern and even ancient worlds. Of itself the circumscription of the catalog to Western societies need not be misconceived – these five may in fact define the limits of the model, which may, therefore, describe a truly Western phenomenon. But it should be kept in mind that when Finley developed his canon – and Hopkins ratified it – historians in European and American universities had not yet absorbed the full significance of global perspectives. Now that they have recognized the importance of broader social, temporal, and political settings, however, it is important to test the received canon against an expanded set of comparanda.

It is no surprise that historians of ancient Greece and Rome, alongside historians of the early modern West, have done the most to elaborate and perpetuate the canon of five. Not only does it link cultural practices shared between Western societies across the *longue durée*, it also sets the West apart as uniquely capable of systematizing the use of slavery into a social and economic driver that propelled "our" culture to the forefront of history – albeit at tremendous cost to human life and liberty. In a world more than ready to acknowledge Patterson's aperçu that slavery is no longer so much "the peculiar institution" as it is "an embarrassing institution," adherence to this list could hardly be regarded as an honor.[33] Yet even if the contemporary world considers

[32] It is noteworthy that even some studies that have explicitly distanced themselves from the model of the "genuine slave society" still incorporate its vocabulary and conceptual apparatus into their discussion, cf. Santos-Granero 2009, 126, 219. Miller 2008 is the first historian I know to have challenged the model's "static logic," and Vlassopoulos 2016 argues decisively that "the concept of the slave society should be finally dropped from the conceptual toolbox of ancient historians."

[33] Patterson 1982, ix.

recognition as a "Slave Society" *dis*honorable, it remains a distinction unto itself to be deemed "worthy" of the rubric – of making the list. One senses this particularly among ancient historians, who cherish a belief that Greece and Rome deserve a special place in history for having arrived at this level of brutal sophistication so early in the course of world affairs. The implication seems to be that Greece and Rome were the only premodern societies capable of the rationalism, efficiency, and complexity necessary to orchestrate coordinated cruelty at this level. The same sense of superiority – imbued with all due remorse – can also be found in the work of modern Western historians.[34] The unstated assumption seems to be, "the West is the best," even when it comes to being scoundrels.

If, however, we look beyond the Western canon of texts, it is difficult to avoid the conclusion that the West is not in fact unique. To be sure, modern European colonial "Slave Societies" derived a formula – based on the massive growth of investment capital, the rise of the first extensive network of global trade, the intermingling of slave labor with modern technologies (cotton gins, mechanical looms, tall ships, steamships, railroads, and the slave plantation itself), the introduction of warm-weather cash crops into the European market, and the development of race-based slavery – that elevated slavery to an industrial scale whose effects were surely more horrific for the slaves themselves than in any other place or period in history. Yet these societies were hardly alone in holding large percentages of their populations in slavery, using these slaves as the primary generators of economic surplus for the elite, or enfolding the practice and discourse of slavery into all aspects of their cultures.

In what follows I explore five new candidates for induction into this macabre hall of fame – two of them ancient neighbors of Rome, the other three from North America and Africa. These represent only some possibilities for an expanded canon. Many more could be offered, indeed, many more are explored in the remaining chapters of this volume. In fact, the primary criterion for discussion in this

[34] Eltis 2000, 8, speaks of "European exceptionalism" as regards both the slave-free dichotomy and the scale of slaveholding. See also Harper 2011, 3, quoted earlier at n. 20.

introduction is that the societies treated later are *not* explored in detail in the studies that follow.

Fourth- to Second-Century BCE Carthage

While it is not especially remarkable that Finley never devoted serious attention to the slaveholding societies of Asia, Africa, or precontact North or South America, it is more disappointing that he chose not to discuss the slaveholding practices of ancient societies in contact with Greece and Rome, especially given that many appear to have fit his criteria for a "Slave Society."[35] Among the most obvious examples is Rome's greatest rival of the Republican era, Carthage.[36] Carthage was a seventh-century foundation from Phoenician Tyre, an island city-state singled out in the book of Joel as a slave-trading center, whose servile population grew so large in the early fourth century BCE that it revolted, seized control of the polity, and succeeded in imposing a new dynasty.[37] Large-scale slaveholding was thus a foundational element of the Punic society of Carthage. Epigraphic testimonia help to differentiate a range of dependent statuses in Carthage ranging from client (*'š sdn*) to chattel slave (*'bd*), the former perhaps deriving from indigenous populations subject to Carthaginian overlordship and the latter from captivity and market exchange.[38] By the fourth century BCE, when our source reports become more abundant, we begin to catch glimpses of a highly diversified slave supply that included birth and debt bondage but also large-scale captive-taking and purchase through the greater Mediterranean slave trade. In their conflict with Agathocles of Syracuse in 310, for example, the Carthaginians brought 20,000 shackles in anticipation of securing large hauls of slaves, and in his effort to rebuild a Carthaginian navy at the end of

[35] In addition to the two ancient societies discussed here, one could also include the pre-Islamic Arabs of the third through seventh centuries (Lenski 2011), the fifth-century CE Huns (Lenski 2014), and the fifth- through eighth-century CE Germanic successor kingdoms of Western Europe (Lenski 2008).

[36] More on Carthaginian slavery at Gsell 1913–28, 1:302, 2:299–300; Matilla Vicente 1977, 99–103; Lemaire 2003; Wagner and Ruiz Cabrero 2015, 85–108.

[37] Joel 3:1–8; Justinus, *Epitome* 18.3.1–19, with Elayi 1981.

[38] Schiffman 1976. Février 1951/52 argues that *'š sdn* means, rather, freedman.

the Second Punic War, Hasdrubal son of Gisco purchased 5,000 slaves to serve in Carthaginian galleys.[39] We have epigraphic testimonia of manumissions and learn from an allusion in Plautus that Carthaginian slaves were allowed to marry.[40] Slaves were thus an integral part of Carthaginian society, so much so that in the stiff treaty terms granted by Rome to Carthage in 201, the Carthaginians were allowed to retain their slaves, and in the even more draconian negotiations following the Third Punic War in 146, we learn that the last Carthaginian commander, Hasdrubal, was allowed to keep a limited selection of 100 slaves, an indication that he originally held a massive *familia*.[41]

The Carthaginian economy was well known for its strength in manufacturing, overseas transport, and mining. We have a number of epigraphic testimonia from Carthage that indicate that industry was dominated by free laborers even if slave involvement is also attested.[42] A passage from Polybius indicates that when Carthage was captured in the Second Punic War, some 12,000 prisoners were taken of whom 10,000 were treated as free Carthaginians and not enslaved, while 2,000 "workmen" (*cheirotechnai*) were used by the Romans as public slaves during their occupation.[43] This would seem to confirm that these workers were considered semi-servile by the indigenous Carthaginians. If so, manufacturing in Carthage will have operated much as it did in Athens, involving a mix of free, semi-dependent (*paroikoi*), and servile (*douloi*) labor. The structure of Carthaginian mining labor is even more difficult to measure, but insofar as the Romans' most productive mines in Spain were taken over from Carthage, there is reason to suspect the heavy use of slave labor in these as well.[44] When we turn to agriculture, there are much stronger indications of the heavy involvement of slaves. Here it should be recalled that the Roman agricultural writers Varro and Columella, from whom we derive much of our best information on the deployment of slaves in Italian agriculture, drew heavily on Carthaginian predecessors and especially Mago, who laid the groundwork for Varro's discussion of the selection and

39 Diodorus Siculus, 20.13; Appian, *Historia Romana*, 9.35.
40 Plautus, *Casina* vv. 67–77.
41 Polybius, 15.18.1, 38.8.4. See also Appian, *Historia Romana*, 9.59, 9.93.
42 Sources at Lemaire 2003, 221.
43 Polybius, 10.17.9; cf. Livy, 26.47.
44 Strabo, 3.2.10 = Polybius, 34.9.9; Diodorus Siculus, 5.36.3–4.

management of slave overseers.[45] By virtue of our source material, our impressions of Carthage's use of agricultural slaves also come largely from a Greek and Roman perspective. We learn of Scipio Africanus encountering enslaved Roman prisoners farming the fields around Locha west of Carthage shortly after he landed in North Africa in 204.[46] Diodorus Siculus reports that, after the Carthaginians drove the Syracusan tyrant Agathocles out of North Africa in 307 BCE, they enslaved his soldiers and forced them to labor in the fields.[47] Moreover, what we can know concerning Carthaginian agriculture was that it was aimed not so much at producing staples for the population of Carthage as at the generation of economic surplus for the elite through the export of olive oil, wine, animal products, fruits, and nuts.[48] In keeping with Finley's principles for slave societies, then, slaves seem to have been deployed first and foremost to generate surplus for the enrichment of the Carthaginian elite.

The Greek and Roman sources also teach us something about the size and volatility of Carthaginian slave population. Diodorus says that after the Carthaginians suffered a major defeat at the hands of Dionysius of Syracuse in 396, their Libyan allies rose up in revolt and laid siege to Carthage in a force that had swollen to as many as 200,000 because of its recruitment of slaves.[49] Justin reports yet another uprising in the mid-fourth century when the disgraced politician Hanno assembled a force of 20,000 slaves against his city.[50] To prevent just such unrest, the Carthaginians took the decision to free all their slaves before beginning their final standoff with Rome in 148.[51] Carthage was thus awash in slaves, who penetrated all aspects of the economy and existed in numbers large enough that they could pose a threat to the capital itself when organized for revolt. Although we lack any statistical information by which to measure slave demography, it

45 Varro, *Res rustica*, 1.17.4–7; Cf. Columella, 12.4.2; Cf. Martin 1971, 37–52, esp. 41: "Le mode d'exploitation de ce territorire était, semble-t-il, esclavagiste pour l'essentiel."

46 Appian, *Historia Romana*, 9.15; cf. Sallust, *Bellum Jugurthinum*, 44.5.

47 Diodorus Siculus, 20.69. See also 14.41.1, on Siceliotai enslaved by Carthaginians.

48 Charles-Picard and Charles-Picard 1961, 83–93, 122–23, esp. 87–88: "The master lorded it at the head of his slaves."

49 Diodorus Siculus, 14.77.

50 Justinus, *Epitome*, 21.4.6; cf. Orosius, 4.6.18; Gsell 1913–28, 2:247.

51 Appian, *Historia Romana*, 9.93.

is clear from these testimonies that the percentage of slaves in the Carthaginian population was high enough to threaten the free population. There is thus every reason to assume that Carthage easily fit Finley's criteria for a "Slave Society."

Sarmatians of the Second through Fourth Centuries CE

Moving into the Roman imperial period, we encounter another group that appears to fit Finley's criteria for a "Slave Society" in the Sarmatians. These Indo-Iranian peoples, who are first attested textually and archaeologically in the territory between the Volga and Don Rivers, moved westward into the Tisza River valley (modern Hungary) in the course of the first century CE, causing violent displacements of the indigenous peoples north of the Lower Danube as they went. By the second century, they became capable of challenging Roman power along the Danube bend.[52] One way they did so was by taking captives. The historian Dio reports that in 175, having been defeated by Emperor Marcus Aurelius, the Sarmatian king Zanticus appeared before the Roman ruler to plead for peace terms but met with a cautious reply because of the Sarmatians' obvious continued strength, as attested by the fact that "they had only just returned a hundred thousand captives that were still in their hands even after the many who had been sold, died, or escaped."[53] The scale of this captive-taking as well as the fact that the Sarmatians clearly retained their captives over the long term and even sold some for profit indicates that the Sarmatians were possessed of a sizable slave culture already in the second century CE. A mid-third-century legal source confirms that they continued to hold captive slaves in this period. A Coptic text of the fourth century also portrays Sarmatians as stereotypically given to slaveholding; even as late as the late fifth century we learn that the Ostrogoths, at this point masters of Pannonia, defeated a Sarmatian

[52] It would be wrong to assert state formation, let alone political or even tribal continuity, in the territory of the Banat under discussion here. Archaeological work indicates, however, a cultural continuity among the "Sarmatian" inhabitants of the area from the first to the early fifth centuries CE; see Harmatta 1970, 41–57; Grumeza 2014.

[53] Dio Cassius, 71.16.2.

king named Babai and took as plunder the treasures and slaves he had been holding.[54]

Our most revealing evidence for their slaveholding ways comes in a cluster of sources from the fourth century reporting that when the Sarmatians were attacked by their Gothic neighbors in 334, they felt the need to arm their slaves in self-defense. Although this tactic helped them repulse the Goths, the slaves were (according to the fourth-century historian Ammianus) more numerous than their masters and were thus able to defeat them and drive them out of their homeland. We learn most about the incident from the contemporary writers Eusebius and the author of the anonymous *Origo Constantini*, who report that the emperor was willing to accept as many as 300,000 of the free Sarmatian refugees – a number in the range of the total population of classical Athens; if we assume there was an equal or greater number of slaves in Sarmatian territory before the revolt, the Sarmatians of the third and fourth centuries would have had a larger "Slave Society" than Classical Athens.[55] The free Sarmatians, referred to in our sources as the Agaragantes, were then resettled in the imperial territories of Thrace, Scythia, Macedonia, and Italy, while the former slave Sarmatians, called Limigantes in our Roman sources, assumed political control of Sarmatian territory, whence they continued to harass the Romans through the fourth century and, as we have seen, to practice slaveholding, although their power appears to have been greatly weakened by the waves of Huns and Goths who overtook the region at this time.[56] The very fact of this major fourth-century slave uprising should merit greater attention in modern historiography, for it represents one of the very few slave revolts in recorded history to have succeeded – one of which Finley appears to have been unaware. Of itself this is a strong indicator that the Sarmatians rivaled their Roman neighbors in the intensity of their slaveholding.

[54] *Codex Justinianus* 8.50.1 (222–35 CE); Ps. Basil, *Encomium on St. Mercurius*, 13–17 (*Corpus Scriptorum Christianorum Orientalium: Scriptores Coptici* 43: 6–7 = 44: 6–7); Jordanes *Getica*, 55[282].

[55] Eusebius, *Vita Constantini*, 4.6.1–2; cf. Jerome, *Chronicon*, s.a. 334; *Consularia Constantinopolitana*, s.a. 334; *Origo Constantini*, 32; Ammianus, 17.12.16, 19.11.1, 29.6.15.

[56] See, for example, Ammianus, 17.12.11, 15, 20, 29.6.7–8.

Northwest Coast Indians of the Eighteenth and Nineteenth Centuries CE

The linguistically and culturally interrelated native peoples of the Pacific Northwest also appear to fit Finley's criteria. These people, who numbered about 150,000 at the period of first contact with Europeans in the late eighteenth century, inhabited the coast of North America between the Columbia River basin and the Yakutat Bay. They coalesced into politically independent, small-scale, kin-based societies. These had sophisticated economies based in hunting, gathering, and fishing, as well as the production of practical and ritual goods. Although their political organization was fragmented and thus resistant to hierarchization, all Northwest Coast groups were marked by a tripartite social structure consisting of elite "titleholders," middling commoners, and subordinate slaves.[57] The upper caste dominated property relations and developed a sophisticated system of exchange and gift giving that entailed complex dealings in private property. Status was based on the scale of a male titleholder's property holdings and his skill and ability to redistribute them. In this scheme slaves constituted a major source of social and economic capital.[58]

Most of the slaves described in our sources for precontact and early-contact Northwest Coast societies appear to have been taken as captives. Nevertheless, slave status was heritable and could and did continue for generations. Enslavement also resulted from unpaid debt and gambling as well as the recovery of orphans.[59] All rights connected with property applied to these slaves, who could be gifted in potlatch ceremonies, traded for goods (and, after contact, money), used as laborers, abused by their owners, and killed with impunity.[60] Titleholders were householders who managed elaborate labor regimes of extraction, production, and redistribution together with their wives, often structuring work on the basis of caste and gender. Slaves, especially male slaves, were regularly deployed to cut and haul firewood, carry water, build wooden houses, construct canoes,

[57] Kroeber 1923; Drucker 1965.

[58] Mitchell 1984; Donald 1997, 87–88; Cameron 2016a, 32–35.

[59] Donald 1997, 103–20.

[60] See Donald 1997, 139–64, on how slave prices, which are both abundant and consistent, indicate a developed market; cf. Mitchell 1984, 40.

carve wooden articles, hunt and fish, gather oysters, paddle boats, and accompany their masters in war. Female slaves were used to clean fish and game, prepare food, produce clothing, and manufacture tools and ceremonial paraphernalia.[61] As with other Native American societies, slaves could also be used as ritual victims in funerals and reconciliation rites.[62] Slaves were traded over long distances, often through multiple transactions, and thus served as exchange commodities alongside obsidian and "coppers" – hammered metal plates that served as prestige exchange goods.[63]

The size of the slave population can be judged from early-contact Western observers who offer anecdotal testimonies of numbers as high as 30–40 percent.[64] This can be compared with somewhat lower numbers gathered during censuses taken by the Hudson Bay Company and other Western observers that indicate demographics hovering around 15 percent, although the numbers vary widely from less than 5 percent up to 25 percent depending on the tribe and kin group. In general, slave percentages dwindled rapidly after the 1840s, when Western contact caused native populations to plummet and also led to a decline in slaveholding as American and European agents worked systematically to eliminate slavery.[65] But for the arrival of these Western outsiders and their insistence on abolition, the Northwest Coast system of slavery would have been likely to perpetuate itself indefinitely.

Sokoto Caliphate of the Nineteenth Century

Another example of what could surely be classed as a Finleyan "Slave Society" is the Sokoto Caliphate of the Central Sudan in the nineteenth

[61] Sir George Simpson quoted at Merk 1931, 101: "Slaves form the principal article of traffick on the whole of this coast and constitute the greatest part of their Riches; they are made to fish, hunt, draw water and wood; in short all the drudgery falls on them; they feed in common with the family of their proprietors and intermarry with their own class, but lead a life of misery." On slave labor more generally, see Donald 1997, 121–38; Ames 2008.

[62] Donald 1997, 165–81.

[63] Donald 1997, 139–56; Ames 2008, 144–46.

[64] Simpson 1847, 125: "One full third of the large population of this coast are slaves of the most helpless and abject description." McIlwraith 1948, 1:158, estimates 30–40 percent of the total population.

[65] Donald 1997, 182–97.

century.[66] The caliphate was founded after 1804 as a jihad-based political movement coordinated by Usman dan Fodio, who took advantage of disruptions caused by long cycles of drought in the region to consolidate power around a new capital in the savanna at Sokoto.[67] He and, above all, his son, Muhammad Bello, established a jihadist state that ruled the region from eastern Burkina Faso to Cameroon (with one emirate as far east as Lake Chad) for a full century down to 1903. This was a region of tremendous ethnic, geographical, and climatic diversity that the caliphs united under Fulbe rule following the principles of Islam (see Map 8.3).

The initial breakneck territorial expansion of the caliphate in its first twenty years led to the creation of massive numbers of captives. Even after territorial wars declined beginning in the 1830s, the flow of captives did not cease, for the construction of fortified frontier communities known as *ribāt* created launch pads for ongoing slave raids among extraterritorial peoples.[68] Moreover, the caliphate also followed a custom particularly marked in Muslim cultures of collecting at least some of its tribute directly in slaves. In keeping with the geographical complexity of the region, the economy of the caliphate was highly diversified, with specialization in the production of shea butter in the Nupe emirates of the central Niger River basin, tobacco in the Katsina Emirate, and cotton and indigo almost everywhere. In those regions suitable to agriculture, slaves labored on plantation estates – referred to in Hausa as *rinji* – which were generally managed for their absentee landlords by slave overseers at the head of large gangs of slaves.[69] In others, slaves served as cattle herders and miners of gold and salt. In all regions, they worked as domestics, porters, cooks, and menials. Slaves also manufactured indigo-dyed cotton cloth as well as garments, mostly for export, in production centers around Kano and Zaria.

[66] Lovejoy 1979; 2005; 2012a, 195–201; 2016a, passim, esp. ch. 4. The application of the "Slave Society" model to African contexts would likely have bothered Finley if we can judge by his outburst against mid-century Africanists (especially Miers and Kopytoff) and their efforts to compel Western historians to "redefine and reclassify slaves in order to provide a place for their own pseudo-slaves" at Finley 1980, 69–70 (reprint 1998, 137–38).

[67] Last 1967.

[68] Salau 2006.

[69] Lovejoy 2005, 153–206; 2016a, 112–21; Bashir Salau 2011.

Throughout the caliphate, property tended to become concentrated in the hands of emirs and aristocrats, who established large plantations, as well as merchants. One emir of Zaria, Mommon Sani, reputedly owned 9,000 slaves, and reports of slave families ranging from the low hundreds to the low thousands are common.[70] These aristocrats relied on slave labor for the generation of surplus production whose economic benefits they used to promote their status in society. From travelers' accounts and population figures available for the mid-nineteenth century, it appears that the percentage of slaves in the caliphate's population hovered between 25 percent and 50 percent and that the absolute number of slaves in the later nineteenth century was roughly comparable with the slave population of Brazil – ca. 1,500,000 souls in 1871.[71] Sokoto was, in other words, a massive "Slave Society," operating in the modern world, but very much according to patterns akin to those governing ancient slave systems: absenteeism; slave overseers; a slave supply supplemented directly by regular hauls of war captives; a large-scale, regional market economy with well-established but limited long-distance trade; and a very high rate of manumission. The collapse of Sokoto slavery began only when the region was overtaken by the British between 1897 and 1903, but the process continued down to 1936.[72] Indeed, had it not been for British intervention, Sokoto's "Slave Society" would surely have continued indefinitely as it had for the previous century.

Dahomey of the Nineteenth Century

The West African kingdom of Dahomey rose to power out of the chaos that ensued from the expansion of the European slave trade. Located in what is today the Republic of Bénin and based at its capital of Abomey, about 100 kilometers inland from the Bight of Bénin, Dahomey responded to the increased level of violence created in the region through the transatlantic slave trade by consolidating power

[70] Smith 1960, 157–58; Ferguson 1973, 60, 233. For aggregate figures, see Lovejoy 1979, 359–62; 2005, 186–94; 2016a, table 4.2.

[71] Lovejoy 2005, 2–3; 2016a, 105–06; cf. Barth 1857, 523.

[72] See, for example, the incredible diary of Fulbe raider Hamman Yaji, who enslaved more than 2,000 people around Madagali, south of Lake Chad, between 1912 and 1920; Vaughan and Kirk-Greene 1995.

around a highly centralized monarchy.[73] By the 1720s, it had conquered its neighboring coastal territories, including the rival kingdom of Hueda, whose chief city of Ouidah served as the second largest port for the export of slaves from Africa to the New World after Luanda.[74] After consolidating this territory, the Dahomians – an ethnically Fon people – and their monarchs developed a virtual monopoly on the production of slaves from the surrounding interior – taken above all from the Aja and Yoruba peoples. These were gathered by trading, raiding, and full-scale warfare conducted by the kings and their representatives, who were supplied with money (especially cowries) and weapons (firearms) by Western merchants associated with the slave trade.[75] The actual trade in slaves was conducted through Ouidah and other coastal cities via middlemen who operated under royal concessions. Many of these impresarios were themselves manumitted slaves from Brazil, who had returned to their homeland with the cultural and linguistic ambidexterity to act as intermediaries between native and European cultures. Between 1650 and 1866, the Bight of Bénin exported more than 2,000,000 human chattels, most of them out of Ouidah, which made slaves far and away the most valuable export commodity produced in the region.[76] Dahomey was thus a state whose export economy was structured around the transatlantic slave trade, a situation characterized by some as a "slave-raiding mode of production."[77]

The peoples who inhabited this region had their own indigenous traditions of slavery that predated European contact. As with so many West African cultures, these were characterized by the use of captivity as a means to incorporate new individuals and groups into the dominant society. In this tradition, captives were treated relatively mildly, like partially disadvantaged members of a family or clan, and were usually

[73] For Dahomey, see above all Manning 1982; Law 1991. Monroe 2007 confirms the high degree of central state organization using archaeology. Interestingly, Polanyi 1966 used Dahomey as a test case for his "substantivist" theory of the existence of an "archaic economic type" between "primitive" and "capitalist" systems. This met with prompt and sustained critique that has continued up to the present; see Manning 1969; Coquery-Vidrovitch 1971; Peukert 1978; Law 1986.

[74] Law 2004.

[75] Manning 1990, 88–91.

[76] See tables 4.1 and 7.4 at Lovejoy 2012a, 78, 141; cf. Manning 1990, 91–99.

[77] Law 1991, 348, citing Elwert 1973.

assimilated into the capturing society within their own lifetimes.[78] But the Dahomians appear quickly to have adopted new modes of captive-taking and slaveholding that were much more violent and were structured around a market economy. In fact, Dahomey appears to have arisen in the early eighteenth century out of a band of slave raiders whose leaders structured their new kingdom around the principles of monarchy and militarism.[79] Dahomian kings managed a highly centralized bureaucracy that marshalled armies numbering more than 10,000 – including female "Amazon" warriors – who raided peoples beyond their territories annually in coordinated attacks.[80] Most of the resulting captives were then sold to Western traders, but many were also sacrificed in annual ceremonies, and those remaining – disproportionately females – were retained as slaves to serve as porters, manufacturers, functionaries, and also to farm plantations, whose produce fed the standing army.[81] The kingdom reached its height in the first half of the nineteenth century under King Ghezo (1818–58), who was as notorious for his brutality as he was for his political savvy. Ghezo not only fended off British efforts to curb the slave trade but also fostered solidarity among his people by redistributing much of the wealth he generated from the slave trade and from his extensive system of plantations among his citizens, and also by strictly forbidding their sale to foreign traders.[82]

Even though the British began choking off the slave trade from the 1840s until the last shipment of slaves from Ouidah in the 1860s, the Dahomians were able to retool their economy by creating massive plantations for the production of palm oil.[83] These were themselves worked by captive slaves, who were also employed to transport their produce overland from the Dahomian heartland to the coastal port at Ouidah.[84] This new system of plantation agriculture lasted down to

[78] Kopytoff and Miers 1977b; cf. Manning 1982, 7–9.
[79] Law 1986.
[80] On the "Amazons," see Bay 1998, 200–09.
[81] Law 1986, 257–58; Manning 1990, 48–50, 63–72, 115–16.
[82] Law 1986, 266–67.
[83] On the shift to palm oil production, see Coquery-Vidrovitch 1971; Law 2004, 203–30. On British pressure to end the slave trade, see Law 2012.
[84] Coquery-Vidrovitch 1971, 117–19; Manning 1982, 12–19; Law 2004, 211–14; Lovejoy 2012a, 171–76.

1892, when the French annexed the kingdom as a colony and ended slavery by statute.

Estimates of the percentage of slaves in the aggregate population are difficult to come by, but figures in the range of one-quarter to one-third in the Fon heartland during the mid-nineteenth century have been hazarded, and individual plantation owners are known to have owned *familiae* of more than 1,000 slaves.[85] Most of this enslaved population was oriented toward the production of surplus for the ruling elite, which meant especially the Dahomian kings and their dependents. Dahomey was thus a "Slave Society" operating on its own logic. Highly militarized and surprisingly centralized for eighteenth- and nineteenth-century West Africa, it was extremely adaptive to Western economic demand. Building on indigenous systems of captive-taking, it used its military prowess to supply slaves, and then slave-produced palm oil, to the West and thus built an economy on the exploitation of human bodies as generators of capital.

These five examples – fourth- to second-century BCE Carthage, the Sarmatians of the second through fourth centuries CE, the eighteenth- and nineteenth-century Northwest Coast peoples, and Sokoto and Dahomey in the nineteenth century – offer only a limited sample of the many possible examples of "Slave Societies" that could be added to the canon of five so regularly repeated in the historiography of the ancient and modern West. To be sure, no two look precisely the same, nor are any of them precise comparanda with the Western five. Each system is culturally specific, its bases founded in varying subsistence strategies, levels of social complexity, interactions with the environment, relations with other peoples or states, and periods in world history, and its contours shaped by religious, intellectual, economic, and social preconditions. As we see in what follows, however, the canonical five also display as many differences as similarities, differences that have often gone overlooked due to efforts to reinforce a picture of archetypal uniformity that does not map well onto historical reality. The one element that ties all of them together is violence and particularly violent capture. This is true not just of these five non-Western societies but also of the five from the original canon, for even the three modern transatlantic societies only succeeded in building slave

[85] Manning 1982, 192; Lovejoy 2012a, 172–74.

systems by outsourcing the necessity of violent capture to the international market – a process that shredded the populations and societies of coastal Africa in patterns of violence that affect many regions up to the present. A second commonality is the concentration of slave ownership among the elites, for although slave ownership was socially broad-based in four of these five societies – the Northwest Coast Indians being the exception – members of the elite amassed disproportionately large slave families that they then deployed to buttress their status through large-scale systems of production. Finally, all nine societies were subject to transformation. This was certainly true of the canonical five societies, each of which saw growth, efflorescence, and then decline in the use of slaves over time. It was also true of the five new inductees, even if we can no longer recover the origins of intensified slaveholding among the Northwest Coast Indians nor the Sarmatians. The intensified slave systems of Carthage, Dahomey, and Sokoto, however, both arose out of periods of militant expansion and then flourished in market conditions favoring the exchange of slaves and slave-produced goods. All five of these non-Western societies subsequently witnessed the precipitous decline of slavery, the Carthaginians and Sarmatians through violent societal collapse (in the latter instance precipitated by a slave revolt), and the nineteenth-century examples through the imposition of antislavery measures from outside the society itself. In some ways, however, the same could be said of the US South and, to a lesser degree, the "Slave Societies" of the Caribbean (St. Domingue excepted) and Brazil, which closed down slaving under intense economic and political pressure from outside the centers of slaveholding. These "Slave Societies" thus followed an internal logic that is in many ways consistent across time and place: violence and favorable market circumstances led to their growth, and external pressures to their decline.

CATEGORICAL IMPRECISION

Even if we grant that Finley's ideal type of "Slave Society" could be applied to places and periods other than the canonical five, this does not mean that the model should simply fold in new entrants and continue to win acceptance without further interrogation. In fact, there are several fundamental issues that make the construct questionable as a hermeneutic paradigm regardless of the size of the cultural set to which it is applied. These difficulties with the "Slave Society"/"Society with Slaves" paradigm number at least four:

1. *Its use of binary categories is too rigid.* By building on a bipartite distinction, the "Slave Society"/"Society with Slaves" model assumes that slaveholding praxis can be broken into just two forms. To arrive at this sharp division in the context of comparative discussions, the model must offer only vague criteria as benchmarks for inclusion. The only quantitative measure – a minimum of ca. 20 percent of aggregate population enslaved – is itself an arbitrary number that fails to take account of the vast disparity in slave demographics across even the canonical five. At the top of this scale would be some Caribbean islands such as eighteenth- and early nineteenth-century Jamaica, St. Vincent, or St. Domingue, where more than 90 percent of the population lived in slavery, and at the bottom Roman Italy, where recent estimates put the slave population below 20 percent.[86] There are obviously vast differences between the scale and intensity of slaveholding praxis in these societies, differences that stretch well beyond demographic concerns. These relate to slave supply, slave treatment and management, methods of confinement and surveillance, types of slave employment, levels of free–slave interaction, rates of manumission, levels of slave resistance, militarization of the free populace, etc. The assumption that the practice of slavery in such societies was more or less the same is thus a gross oversimplification, to put it mildly.

   The other two criteria are even less decisive. The use of slaves as the dominant producers of surplus for the elite is a commonplace across many slaveholding cultures, and this remains true even if the scale of societal complexity, the scale of surplus production, and the scale of slaveholding varies. Even in small-scale societies like those of precontact North and South America, slaves were employed to produce consumable and

[86] On the Caribbean systems, see Patterson 1982, 358–62, with references. Patterson's appendix C remains useful for demonstrating the wide-ranging demographic scope of large-scale slaveholding. On Roman Italy, see Scheidel 2005a. Contrast Lo Cascio 2002, who argues for a figure closer to the traditional 35 percent. De Ligt 2012, 190 posits 26 percent in 28 BCE.

durable goods that were exploited by their masters for the elevation of their status – sometimes through agriculture, sometimes through fishing, hunting, or herding, and sometimes through manufacture.[87] To be sure, societies in which slaves produce the majority of this surplus are fewer in number, but not negligible, and there is no obvious touchstone by which to judge the level of surplus production by slaves that would be necessary to permit qualification as a "Slave Society." The same problem applies a fortiori to the matter of the cultural penetration of the concept of slavery. Slavery becomes a significant paradigm in most of the societies where it occurs, again leaving no firm criteria by which to establish how deeply or broadly the notion of slavery must reach into a culture before it can be said to represent a "genuine slave society." Even if we take Finley's binary to mark a threshold that must be crossed rather than a border between two fully articulated and sharply demarcated types of society, it remains unsatisfactory in its simplicity and vagueness.

2. *No clear-cut boundaries can be set to the notion of "society."* Finley would have been the first to admit that "society" is hardly a category that is clearly circumscribed or easily definable. What are the temporal, geographical, political, cultural, and social limitations of a single society? In his chapter on the rise of "Slave Societies" in *ASMI*, he made explicitly clear that with "Ancient Greece" he was referring to Classical Athens and, secondarily, to Chios and Corinth and with "Roman society" to Italy and Sicily in the late Republican and early Imperial periods.[88] We are thus talking about a model that, by Finley's estimate, applies only to quite circumscribed periods and places – the ca. 300,000 people who inhabited Attica between the fifth and fourth centuries BCE, and the ca. 10,000,000 who lived in Roman Italy and Sicily in the last century BCE and the first century CE.[89] While most ancient historians follow Finley in

87 For native peoples of North America, see Snyder 2010, 130–35; Rushforth 2012, 59–71. For those of the tropical Americas, see Santos-Granero 2009, 126–46.

88 Finley 1980, 85, 113–14 (reprint 1998, 153, 181–82).

89 On these demographic figures, see Garnsey 1998, 195–200, with full bibliography for classical Athens; Launaro 2011, 184–88, with full bibliography for Roman Italy.

restricting their discussion to these periods and places, the model is often cross-applied by synecdoche to all of Classical Greece and the vast expanse of the Roman Empire over its six centuries of flourishing, although it rightly fits neither of these larger temporal and territorial agglomerations. The same could be said of the application of the model to modern transatlantic societies. Thus, for example, although we speak generically of the antebellum South as a "Slave Society," the term does not well apply to any part of Virginia before the seventeenth century, for example, nor to the Appalachian west of Virginia in any period. To be sure, the entirety of the American landscape and economy became intertwined into a single "society" by the mid-eighteenth century, but the criteria for a "Slave Society" only ever truly applied to discrete locations (all south of the Chesapeake basin) in discrete time periods (from ca. 1700–1865).[90] This applies all the more emphatically to Finley's "Caribbean," which was fragmented into an archipelago of plantation settlements controlled by the Spanish, Portuguese, English, French, Dutch, and Danish empires which were by no means united as a single "society." These were rival colonial enterprises populated by rival empires that shared only a common business model – the African slave plantation. The logic of Finley's characterization of the Caribbean as a holistic "Slave Society" is thus fundamentally flawed. Insofar as the model is used, it must therefore be used with caution: slaveholding practices were intensified in any given society because of a set of factors peculiar to that geo-cultural nexus in a specific period. While the three main transatlantic slaving systems certainly did share commonalities in terms of cultural, geographic, and economic preconditions, these varied, in degree and in kind, between all three and were hardly equivalent to those found in other times and places where intensive slaveholding arose.

3. *It is built on assumptions derived from Western social, political, legal, and economic structures.* Because of the limited number of comparative instances he applied, Finley constructed a model that fit best within Western parameters. Already in a 1959 article

[90] See Berlin 1998, passim, esp. table 1; Bergad 2007, 118, table 4.2.

and again in his 1980 book, Finley argued that Greek, and to a lesser extent Roman, "Slave Society" arose out of a political context that placed a high value on personal "freedom"; "free" citizens were obliged to live up to political and military obligations to the state and were thus compelled to turn to slave labor for the generation of economic surplus necessary to sustain these nonproductive endeavors.[91] Finley also put a premium on Western notions of private property as opposed to kin-based, collectivist, or monarchical-redistributive systems for the organization of wealth. Neither could the redistributive economies of ancient Mesopotamia and Egypt nor could the feudal economies of East Asia and Medieval Europe support large-scale slavery, for none – he felt – had well-enough-developed notions of the private ownership of land and chattels.[92] "Slave Societies" – he believed – could only arise in the presence of commodity markets through which slaves could be purchased and their surplus production sold.

All of these assumptions have been challenged on their own merits.[93] More important, none of these conditions appears necessary or sufficient for the intensified use of slaves. Finley's theory that political "freedom" is a precondition of "Slave Societies" situates his model very much within a Western discourse, for political freedom is a Western construct, or at least Finley believed it was.[94] In the global context of slaveholding, by contrast, "freedom" need not be tied to individual political rights – full adherence to the politically dominant group. Rather, freedom for a slave means adherence to the *socially* dominant group, be that politically, religiously, ethnically, or tribally defined. "Freedom" for the ex-slave means access to the rights and privileges of the society within which s/he lives – liberation

[91] Finley 1959; cf. Finley 1964, 236 (reprint 1981, 119); 1968, 308; 1980, 90 (reprint 1998, 158).

[92] Finley 1980, 70–72 (reprint 1998, 138–40).

[93] On the presence of market structures and economic rationalism in ancient Mesopotamian societies, see Gledhill and Larsen 1982. On those in ancient Greece, see Osborne 1991; Morris 2005; Scheidel, Morris, and Saller 2007, chs. 12–14. On those in ancient Rome, see Rathbone 1991; Temin 2013.

[94] Von Dassow 2011 argues that archaic Mesopotamian societies already developed articulated understandings of personal and political freedom.

from the disadvantages of servitude, not necessarily enfranchisement in the state. Slavery, and its corollary "freedom" can therefore arise and thrive independently of participatory governance, as long as the boundaries and structures of community are impenetrable enough to exclude systematically a class of outsiders who live precariously within it.[95] The oligarchic trading empire of Carthage, the kin-based chiefdoms of the Northwest Coast, the jihad-based plantations of the Sokoto Caliphate, the militant autocracy of Dahomey all spawned and sustained demographically extensive and socially intensive slave systems in the absence of participatory democracy and political autonomy.

As to private property, Finley and others are surely correct to emphasize the importance of the master's ownership claims over the slave.[96] The problem with this precondition is that, for all of its simplicity – indeed, because of its simplicity – the "property definition" of slavery is in many ways a dodge: it defers meaning by attempting to summarize a complex phenomenon (slavery) using a single word that is itself highly contested, culturally contingent, and extremely difficult to define (property). "Property" and its corollary "ownership" are constructs fraught with ambiguity and always embedded in specific social contexts – what can be owned, how it is owned, who may own it, and on what basis, all vary from society to society and shift within a society over time.[97] Insofar as Western definitions can help foster a cross-cultural understanding, the civil law notion of property as "the right to use, enjoy, and abuse" surely is descriptive of the master's power over the slave in a generic way.[98] Slaves

[95] See the related arguments at Vlassopoulos 2011 and 2016. My argument differs markedly from Patterson 1991, which itself would seem to contradict Patterson 1982, 209–39.

[96] Finley 1980, 74–77 (reprint 1998, 142–45).

[97] Kopytoff 1986; Graeber 2001, 2011; Wilk and Cligget 2007, 153–75; Cameron 2016b. See also the critique of Patterson 2017, 266–70, leveled at Lewis 2017 on related grounds – the definition of property is fraught and complex, making it only an imperfect yardstick for the identification of slavery. This is not to deny its usefulness altogether (so also Patterson 2017, 271–81; cf. Patterson 2012) but only to affirm that the notion of human property alone cannot sufficiently define the contours of slavery.

[98] Patault 1989, 22–23.

as individuals whose bodies can be freely disposed of for labor, exchange, sex, reproduction, and even wanton destruction, are hardly unique in world history and by no means peculiar to the West.[99]

Finley, of course, had emphasized *private* property, which is, to be sure, a more specific idea, yet here again, not uniquely Western. Indeed, four of the five non-Western societies described earlier (with the Sarmatians there is no evidence by which to judge) each had notions of private ownership of slaves and other chattels even if these were structured in ways not entirely commensurate with European law. Moreover, the implication that societies that structure property in collectives favoring reciprocity or redistribution (rather than capitalist exchange) cannot have practiced slavery in demographically extensive and socially intensive ways is clearly disprovable empirically. Alone, the native societies of the Mississippi Shatter Zone and the tropical Americas discussed in this volume by Christina Snyder and Fernando Santos-Granero display the practice of slavery at a level of demographic and social intensity that seems comparable to that of ancient Greek and Roman societies, yet none had capitalist economies nor Western notions of private property.[100] The fact that these were small-scale societies certainly diminishes the overall number of slaves each held and the economic and social complexity of the way these were employed and exchanged, but the impact of slavery on both masters and slaves was every bit as powerful and persistent as that more familiar from other premodern slaveholding societies.

Finley's scheme also leaves no room for the intensified practice of slavery in non-agriculturalist societies. Orlando Patterson has shown that pastoralism is the only subsistence strategy that can be correlated statistically with slaveholding.[101]

[99] I, for one, am baffled at how Finley 1980, 77 (reprint 1998, 145) might have concluded that "slavery was a late and relatively infrequent form of involuntary labour, in world history generally and in ancient history in particular."

[100] Snyder Chapter 6 and Santos-Granero Chapter 7. See also Santos-Granero 2009; Snyder 2010.

[101] Patterson 2008, 32–69.

It is thus unsurprising that some pastoral societies operating on borderlands between larger states have structured production and social relations around the taking of captives and the traffic in slaves. Many of these, including, for example, the prenomadic Arabs known in late antiquity as "Saracens" or the Comanches of the nineteenth-century Southwest, thrived on slave raiding and slave trading, so much so that it became an essential element of economic production.[102] Yet the Finleyan binary entirely ignores pastoral slave cultures, leading its adherents entirely to have overlooked the crucial importance of slavery to these – very different – slave societies.

4. *It emphasizes similarities while glossing over differences.* Above all, the "Slave Society" model is flawed because it emphasizes similarities – many of which are real – at the expense of accounting for differences – which are just as real and often more salient. The emphasis on a unique and uniquely definable category has, in other words, led Finley and his followers to assume that the rise, development, and perduration of the two ancient and three modern "genuine slave societies" must be interrelated, when in fact they need not be. This is an issue best treated in one-to-one comparisons, a task to which I return in Chapter 4, where divergences are cataloged between the US South and Athens and Rome. To summarize these results in brief here, crucial differences between American and Athenian slavery (which in many ways offer strikingly close parallels) include: 1) the lack of evidence for the significant use of Athenian slaves in agriculture; and 2) the integration of Athenian slaves into sectors of the economy and society from which they were excluded in the South. Differences between Rome and the American South are much more numerous and include: 1) slave sources, for where Rome drew heavily on captives in the period of its rise and always permitted the "extrusive" enslavement of native Romans (especially exposed infants), the US South relied on the importation of slaves through the market to get its start and then the redistribution of slaves southward, again through the market; 2) the penetration of slave labor to all sectors of the

[102] On Saracens, see Lenski 2011. On Comanches, see Brooks 2002; Hämäläinen 2008.

> Roman economy, a stark contrast with the US South, which used slaves almost exclusively for low-skill, manual labor; 3) the absence of racial slavery, a crucial structuring phenomenon in all transatlantic systems and especially the United States, even though it was entirely absent from Rome; 4) manumission rates, which were unusually high in Rome but extremely low in the American South. Scholars of slavery in Athens, Rome, and the US South would, of course, not deny these fundamental truths, yet they all too often gloss past them in the effort to fit these divergent systems into Finley's binary without attempting to understand how these crucial differences render comparison less apt than, for example, comparison with the integrative practices of captive-taking pre-state societies, the deployment of high-status and military slaves in Islamic contexts, the connection between imperial conquest and enslavement in Sokoto slavery and other jihad contexts, or even the penetration of slave labor into high-status professions in the British Caribbean but not the US South.

To summarize, the "Slave Society"/"Society with Slaves" model is based on a number of conceptual flaws that render it extremely problematic as a tool for comparative analysis. Its division of all slave systems into just two categories is too rigid to account for the vast disparities in praxis even among the canonical five "Slave Societies" listed by Finley and his followers. Its notion of "society" is too vague to provide useful parameters of analysis. It is built on assumptions that bias the model in favor of Western political, legal, and economic structures: the principles of political freedom and participatory governance, capitalist forms of private property holding, developed commodity markets, and shortages of wage labor. Not only do these automatically exclude extensive and intensive slaveholding systems from outside the Western ambit, they also, in many ways, exclude Greece and Rome. Finally, the model is misleading in that it lumps together divergent slaveholding systems as if they were interrelated and thus fails to account for major differences between systems in terms of external and internal sources of slave supply, the practice of racial slavery, extensive versus restricted practices of manumission, and broad versus narrow spheres of slave labor deployment.

A NEW MODEL

The "Slave Society" model, at least in the eyes of this author, thus turns out to be an impediment to a fuller understanding of slave systems. For all its virtues as an early example of the use of comparative sociology, it is outdated in its methodology, ethnocentric in its scope, and deceptive in its generalizations. In the face of these problems, it is worth asking whether a better scheme might be offered. Any new approach should work to derive a model that applies to differing cultures across time and space. In fact, the fundamental problem with comparative slave studies is that slavery never manifests itself in precisely the same guise and with precisely the same characteristics in any two periods or places. By extension, the word "slavery" itself can be and often is applied to a variety of forms of dependency – plantation slavery, domestic slavery, military slavery, debt slavery, wage slavery, slavery to one's passions, a network "slave server," etc. "Slavery" is, in other words, an elastic term that can be made to fit a variety of relationships of dependency along a continuum that recedes ever farther from what historians, anthropologists, or sociologists might recognize as "true slavery," or Finley's "genuine slavery," if such there ever was.

Establishing a model for comparing slave systems thus hangs very much on the definition of slavery itself. This is, of course, a long-standing issue that continues to provoke debate up to the present. Although various approaches have been developed, the main point of difference between them hangs on whether they focus on slaves as property or on slavery as a position of social disadvantage. At one end of these opposing poles is the definition offered in Article 1(1) of the League of Nations 1926 Slavery Convention:

- "Slavery is the status or condition of a person over whom any or all the powers attaching to the right of ownership are exercised."[103]

This can be contrasted with the definition derived by Orlando Patterson in his monumental *Slavery and Social Death* (1982):

[103] www.ohchr.org/EN/ProfessionalInterest/Pages/SlaveryConvention.aspx, accessed on January 30, 2017. This property definition of slavery can be traced back to Aristotle, *Politics*, 1253b 33, 1254a 14–18; cf. *Economics*, 1344a 23–26.

- "[Slavery is] the permanent, violent domination of natally alienated and generally dishonored persons."[104]

Patterson, whose definition is more elaborate and less obvious at first glance, expands on its implications at some length in ways that should be summarized to clarify its meaning. By "permanent," Patterson intends "enduring" and "transgenerational" rather than "never-ending," for slaves can and do come free from bondage through death, flight, or manumission – although in so doing, they cease to be slaves. "Natal alienation," in turn, refers to the exclusion of the slave from the community of rights derived from attachment to a family, clan, tribe, polity, or state. "Generally dishonored," for Patterson, does not deny that some slaves attain considerable prestige, but asserts only that the condition of slavery is, in and of itself, dishonorable. Insofar as some slaves have access to honor, it is only through their master, whose own honor is then parasitically increased in proportion to that of his or her slaves.[105]

Although some have insisted on one of these definitions to the exclusion of the other, the most obvious resolution to the dilemma between the two is to combine them. In fact, this move was anticipated by H. J. Nieboer in his important study *Slavery as an Industrial System* (1910), where he defines the slave as:

- "A man who is the property of another, politically and socially at a lower level than the mass of the people, and performing compulsory labour."[106]

Nieboer's definition thus combines the notion of property with that of social disadvantage, but adds to these the important concept of compulsory labor, a fundamentally Marxian idea. Nieboer's work also influenced Finley, who further elaborated its second point by introducing the idea of "kinlessness," a concept he derived from a famous article of Hénri Lévy-Bruhl that had argued that slavery was at root

[104] Patterson 1982, 13.

[105] Toledano 2017 takes umbrage at Patterson's notion of general dishonor, arguing that it cannot account for the power and prestige of Ottoman *kul/harem* slaves. Yet Patterson treats precisely such slaves at 1982, 299–342, more than answering Toledano's case thirty-five years before it was made. See also Patterson 2017.

[106] Nieboer 1910, 5.

a status defined by alienation from the enslaving society.[107] Finley's notion of "kinlessness" was in turn retooled by Patterson into "natal alienation," that is, as we have seen, the utter separation (by violence, custom, or law) from birth rights within the enslaving society.[108] The genealogy of attempts to arrive at a cross-cultural definition of slavery is thus complex and shows miscegenation between the varied – and often opposing – approaches. As with any genealogy, however, it represents a process of division and separation that has, over time, led to an artificial dichotomy between definitions based in property and those based in social disadvantage that has compromised a fuller understanding of the whole idea of slavery.

This is in part due to Patterson himself, who self-consciously omitted the notion of property from his definition, arguing that, as a relationship of domination, the property right of the master over the slave was subsumed under his rubric "violent domination."[109] In correspondence exchanged shortly before the appearance of *Slavery and Social Death,* Finley had taken Patterson to task for his omission of property from his definition, and much of the subsequent criticism of Patterson's case is related to this same concern.[110] This has been leveled in particular by advocates for the elimination of contemporary human trafficking and forced labor such as Kevin Bales and Jean Allain, both of whom regard the clear and broad implications of the 1926 Slavery Convention as crucial to their obviously worthy cause.[111] In response to these and other objections that had surfaced over the thirty years since the appearance of *Slavery and Social Death,* Patterson revised his definition in a 2012 contribution:

[107] Lévy-Bruhl 1931.

[108] Finley 1980, 76–77 (reprint 1998, 144–45) identifies three components of slavery, "the slave's property status, the totality of the power over him, and his kinlessness." These elements are already present at Finley 1968, 307–08, which cites both Lévy-Bruhl and Nieboer. For Patterson's use of Finley, see Patterson 1982, 7.

[109] Patterson 1982, 17–27. In rejecting a property definition, Patterson was following Westermarck 1906, 670–71. Kopytoff and Miers 1977b, 11–12, also bridle at the property definition. Vlassopoulos 2011 restates the importance of domination as a determinant of slave status in Greek society.

[110] Dan Tompkins kindly shared with me correspondence between Finley and Patterson beginning on July 6, 1980.

[111] Allain 2012a; Allain and Hickey 2012; cf. Allain and Bales 2012. See also Lewis 2017 for the case that a simple property definition best suits ancient Greek and Neo-Babylonian slaveries; but see the trenchant critique of Lewis's case by Patterson 2017.

- Slavery is "the violent, corporeal possession of socially isolated and parasitically degraded persons."[112]

This new definition is to be commended for the greater role it assigns to problems of property through the concept of "corporeal possession." Even so, it stops short of using the words "property" or "ownership" and in many ways seems to represent a response to the decades-long accumulation of criticism of the most insightful aspects of the original definition – criticisms that were, at any rate, inevitable given the high-profile, high-impact nature of Patterson's work. A better solution would surely be to retain much of the crispness of the 1982 definition but to concede more ground on the question of property, for complex and contingent though the idea of property is, it still captures best the essence of a master's claims over the person of a slave.

The advantage to combining Patterson's 1982 definition with that of the 1926 Slavery Convention is that such a bipartite approach acknowledges the reality that slavery is fundamentally a dialectical relationship. At root it is a legal or social construct that builds from the assumption that one person – the master – has a right to dominate another – the slave – with advantages to the former and disadvantages to the latter. In this sense, slavery is no "real" or "tangible" thing, but a fictional bond between two parties or classes of parties who nevertheless acknowledge its reality and tangibility within a given social/political context: slavery exists because, within a particular society, masters *and* slaves agree that it exists. Any definition of slavery that will succeed in crystalizing the phenomenon must therefore account for this dialectic. To do so, it must emphasize both:

1. *The benefits the slave offers to the master* – which accrue as a result of the slave's status as property: the slave can be sold, exchanged, gifted, lent, or rented; its offspring can be treated as accretions to the master's holdings; its body can be exploited for labor, sexual gratification, abuse, and even destruction; its labor product can be expropriated gratuitously.

and:

2. *The disadvantages imposed by the master on the person of the slave* – which accrue as a result of the master's violent domination over

[112] Patterson 2012, 329.

> the slave: thus the slave's kinlessness, her rightlessness, his social disability and dishonor; that is, the complex of disadvantages that Patterson aptly captures with the simple phrase "social death."

A fitting definition of slavery might thus combine existing definitions into a working whole thus:

- *Slavery is the enduring, violent domination of natally alienated and inherently dishonored individuals (slaves) that are controlled by owners (masters) who are permitted in their social context to use and enjoy, sell and exchange, and abuse and destroy them as property.*

This definition can be taken as reflective of an "ideal type" of slavery, one that has existed in specific temporal and geographical contexts across history, including the five canonical "Slave Societies," as well as the five new examples discussed earlier, and many more, some to be discussed in the chapters of this volume. These were societies in which structures of dependency were expressed most intensely, both as regards the benefit to the master and the disadvantage to the slave. In some very real sense, then, with his invention of the notion of the "Slave Society" Finley was attempting to identify those geo-temporal junctures where "ideal slavery" flourished, where structures of dependency were expressed most intensely. In addition, he was interested in contexts where "ideal slavery" was robust enough to affect demographic profiles intensively. Nevertheless, each of the five societies he mentions, indeed all slaveholding societies, only ever approached the various markers of ideal slavery by degrees. Slavery in Rome, for example, was not nearly as "permanent" or "enduring" for a given slave as slavery in the Old South. Similarly, the dishonor attached to slaves in Greece and Rome did not begin to approach the dishonor of slaves in the Old South. One could counter, however, that property control over slaves in the Old South prior to the Fugitive Slave Act of 1850 (and arguably after it) was more precarious than that in Rome because of the real possibility of flight to the free states and Canada. Roman slaves, of course, could and did flee, but they could never reach territory where slavery was forbidden, not even if they made it beyond the Roman frontiers, and masters' efforts to track them down, while limited by ancient technologies of transport and communication, were supported with the full vigor of the law as well as uniform participation from the broader society throughout the Empire.[113]

If we accept that "Slave Societies" are to be judged by the degree to which their structures of dependency approach "ideal slavery," the benchmark for comparing them would thus seem not to be Finley's tidy binary but a scale, or rather a series of scales. These might be termed *vectors of intensification*, that is, measures of the degree to which a particular "Slave Society" approaches each aspect of the ideal definition put forward earlier in this chapter. For purposes of quantification, these could be broken down according to two sets of four components each, deriving from the components of our definition.

The slave's property value, and thus benefit to the master, could be measured according to four criteria:

1. The use value of the slave as commodity – how valuable were slaves to the operation of the economy in the primary (food production), secondary (manufacture), and tertiary (service) economic spheres?
2. The exchange value of the slave as commodity – how valuable were slaves to their masters as objects of redistribution, exchange, and sale?
3. The use value of the slave's labor product – how important was slave production to the maintenance and functioning of the master's household and the broader economy?
4. The exchange value of the slave's labor product – how important was slave production to the generation of wealth through trade and commerce for the master's household and the broader economy?

By way of example, one could plot these using estimates from ancient Rome of the first century BCE and the Old South of the early nineteenth century in Chart 1.1.

Under the master's domination and thus the disadvantage to the slave could be measured:

[113] On the hunting of Roman fugitives, see Fuhrmann 2011, 21–44.

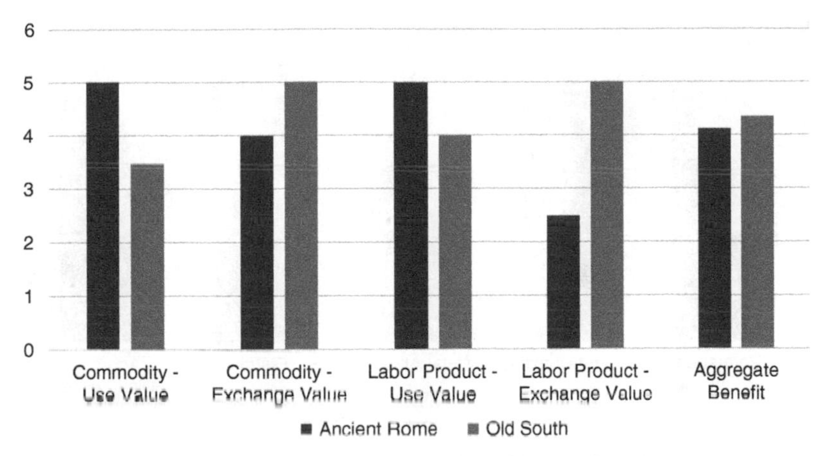

CHART 1.1 Benefit to Masters – Rome and the US South

1. The permanence of the slave condition – what were the chances for liberation of the slave from within the "Slave Society," and what were the possibilities for integration into that society for the freed slave?
2. The level of violent domination – what was the likelihood the slave would experience violence through capture, physical abuse, sexual abuse, or murder, both because these were sanctioned or forbidden by the society and because they were more or less likely to occur?
3. The degree of natal alienation – what level of physical, legal, racial, and social distance did the master class keep between itself and its slaves, and to what degree was this social and legal division maintained across generations?
4. The level of dishonor – to what degree could slaves and freedmen attain positions of honor, and to what degree did the stigma of slavery negatively affect them and their offspring?

Chart 1.2 reflects a schematic effort to plot these categories for Rome and the Old South.

The integers used in the two charts represent estimates based on my personal knowledge of both slave systems and are further elaborated in Chapter 4. One could, however, derive data-driven metrics based on quantitative values that would offer greater precision. So

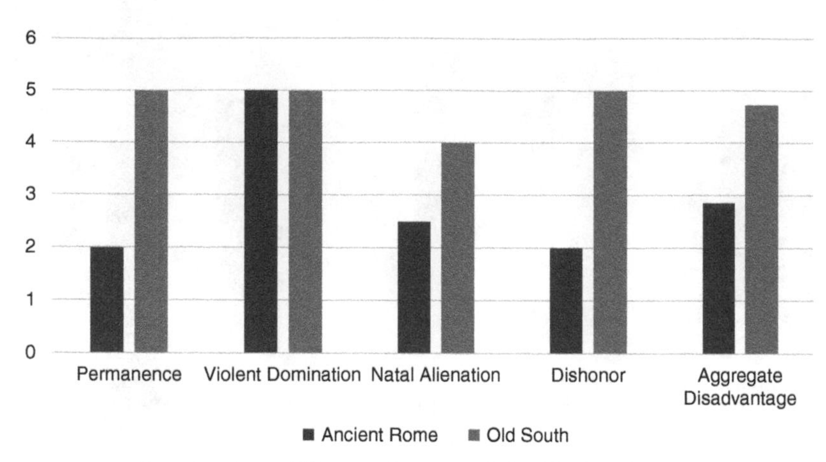

CHART 1.2 Domination of Slaves – Rome and the US South

too these categories used could obviously be further articulated, but are meant to serve here as one possible illustration of a method for measuring the intensity of slave systems comparatively across historical societies. The advantage to this method over Finley's is that it avoids facile bipartite distinctions and simple divisions into opposing categories. This permits one to account for differences in intensity between "Slave Societies" and also allows comparison with societies that use slaves in less intensive ways. If, for example, we add Siamese society of the eighteenth and nineteenth centuries (discussed in this volume by Anthony Reid, Chapter 16), Dahomey society of the nineteenth century (discussed in this chapter), along with twelfth-century Korean *nobi* slavery (discussed in this volume by Kim Bok-rae, Chapter 15)[114] we could plot the comparison with Charts 1.3 and 1.4.

Further comparison could be made by aggregating this data along a Cartesian grid charting the degree of benefit to the master (X) against the degree of disadvantage to the slave (Y). The "ideal slave society" would most closely approach the 1:1 slope as it balanced benefits to the master with disadvantages to the slave. Moreover, the grid can also chart the intensity of slaveholding in the society, which can be gauged by distance from the XY intercept. Finally, the grid can also account for the demographic significance of slavery by varying the size of the marker for each society relative to the percentage of the population

[114] See also Palais 1996, 208–70, for a somewhat different account of Chosŏn slavery.

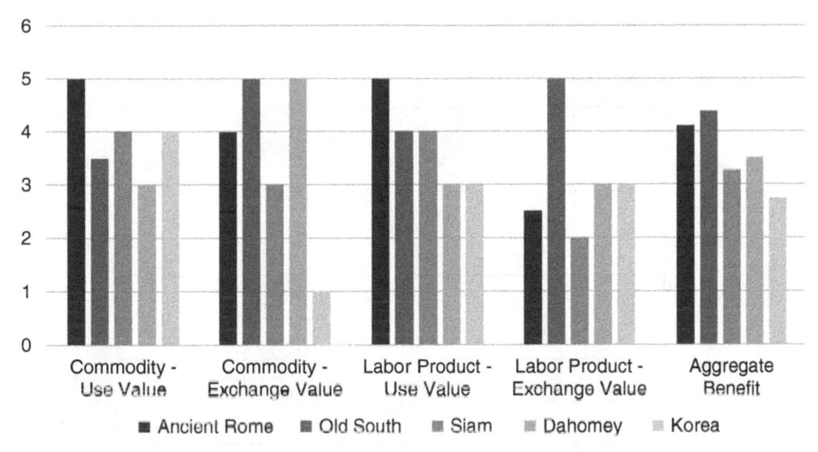

CHART 1.3 Benefit to Masters – Global

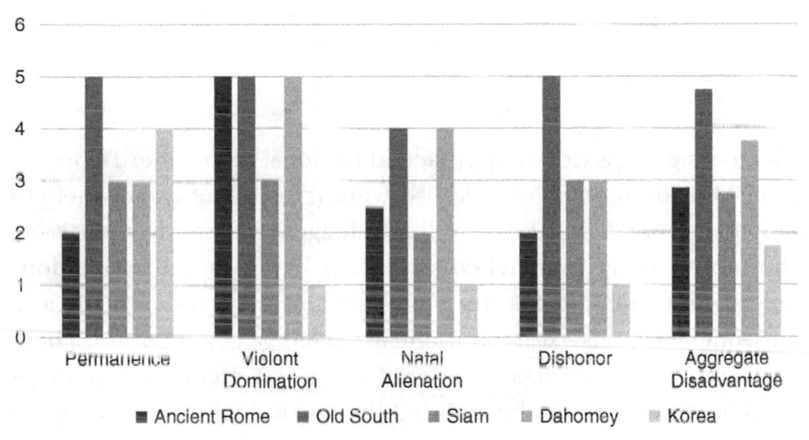

CHART 1.4 Domination of Slaves – Global

held in slavery – larger markers indicate higher percentages. Chart 1.5 offers an attempt to represent graphically the five societies used here as examples.

Chart 1.5 indicates that the "Slave Societies" of the US South and Dahomey most closely approach the ideal. The Old South system was the most intensive of the five, due to its highly developed economic structures and thus its highly efficient benefit to masters, but also due to the extreme disadvantages it imposed on slaves, who were locked tightly into a system that endured relentlessly across generations. The

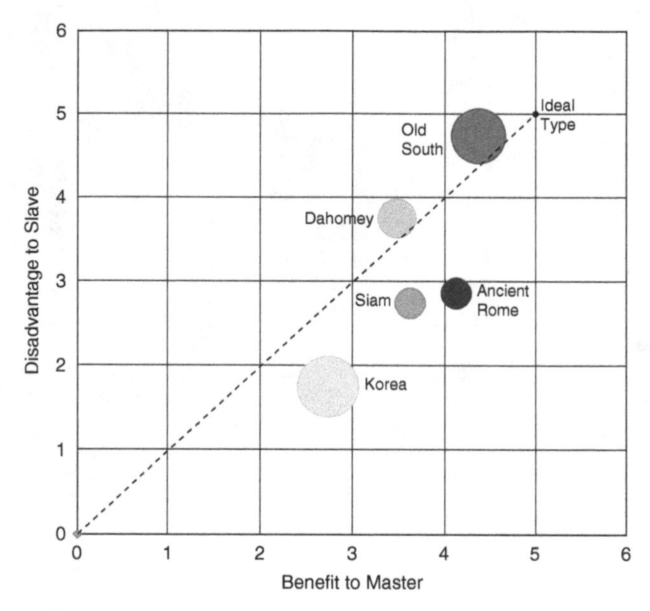

CHART 1.5 Vectors of Intensity

Roman system less closely approached the ideal than either Dahomey or the Old South, primarily because, while it too was of great benefit to masters, it operated with fewer disadvantages to slaves. Korean *nobis,* who more closely approached serfs than slaves, had a tremendous level of protection against their masters and were also – partly as a consequence of this – scarcely useful as exchange commodities. These experienced a much less intensive form of servitude and, perhaps for this reason, could be enlisted in much higher demographic percentages than "true" slaves. So too Siamese slaves, many of whom also suffered less intensive domination than Old South or Dahomeyan slaves and who constituted a lower percentage of the population than slaves in the other societies. The one factor not covered in these tables is time, which could only be added to a three-dimensional graphic and whose effects can hardly be measured for any of these societies except the Old South because of inadequate source material.

It is hoped this model may prove useful for future analysis of comparative slave systems. It is intended, as much as anything, to illustrate a methodology that accounts for both similarity and difference and that does not flatten distinctions to the point of masking the complexities of social structures across cultures. If this exercise has served any purpose, it would be first to have shown that a simple binary cannot begin to account for the variety of slaveholding practices manifested across societies in world history, and second to have demonstrated that in comparing slave systems, the central concern should always be the question of intensity. This latter is true in at least three arenas: benefit to the master class, disadvantages to slaves, and demographic significance. The most intensive "Slave Societies" are those that display the highest levels in all of these arenas, while the least intensive begin to approach forms of dependency that many would not consider slavery at all. Here again, debates over such questions of boundaries ultimately result in binary distinctions that are neither definitive nor, in many cases, even defensible. If instead we focus on the level to which systems of dependency approach a balanced dialectic between benefits to masters and disadvantages to slaves, we can begin to account for the bewildering variety of slave systems that have arisen in world history. If we measure this balance against the level of intensification in each of these two arenas as well as the demographic impact of slavery overall, we will begin to see that slave societies are many, but intensive slave societies much fewer – albeit, surely more numerous than five. In this sense we will keep alive the spirit of Moses Finley's inquiry even if we alter his terms for the debate.

PART I

ANCIENT AND LATE ANTIQUE WESTERN SOCIETIES

2

Ancient Greece as a "Slave Society"

Peter Hunt

INTRODUCTION: WEAK AND STRONG CONCEPTS OF "SLAVE SOCIETIES"

Classical Athens and arguably many of the other city-states of Classical Greece were "Slave Societies." It is hard to understand or to describe these states without invoking the concept of a "Slave Society" or some periphrasis. Another class of Greek states depended, however, on a labor force best described as consisting of serfs. Before expanding and justifying these two claims, I wish briefly to set out my understanding of the uses and drawbacks of the concept of a "Slave Society."

The concept of a "Slave Society" comes in a range of strengths. The weak end of the spectrum merely denotes societies in which the institution of slavery is crucial, usually in terms of the proportion of slaves and the role of slavery in the society's economy and culture. But some historians, such as M. I. Finley and David Turley, believe that specific and important consequences follow from the predominance of slavery in a given society and that these consequences do not follow for societies in which slaves are present but not important, "Societies with Slaves." For example, Finley held that slavery contributed to the ideal of freedom and to the equal rights of the citizen in classical Greece and Rome.[1] And Turley argues that true "Slave Societies"

[1] Finley 1959 = 1981, 115: "One aspect of Greek history, in short, is the advance, hand in hand, of freedom and slavery." On the Western ideal of freedom and the institution of slavery, see Patterson 1991 and Raaflaub 2004.

tend to possess a well-developed state and to display a starker and less porous distinction between slaves and masters.[2] The more of these consequences that are wrapped up in the definition of "Slave Society," the stronger a term it becomes – but also the more open to contestation. Although there is a long tradition in the humanities and social sciences of arguing over terminology, I believe that, whenever we can convert such a debate to one over particular propositions, we are better off. Thus I prefer a weak definition of the "Slave Society" together with additional propositions that can be confirmed, disproved, or at least debated.

Retaining the weak definition of a "Slave Society" is useful for several reasons. Most obviously, it provides the scope conditions for the further arguments of generalizing historians such as Finley: "Slave Societies" and only "Slave Societies" are generally marked by a (consequent) characteristic, X. Such arguments need to be evaluated on a case-by-case basis, but that some consequences follow from having lots of slaves is a priori likely. For example, a "Slave Society" necessarily devotes more energy to the supply or reproduction of slaves. Consider the annual importation of thousands of slaves to fifth-century BCE Athens in contrast with the sale of about a dozen slaves per year in fourteenth-century CE Florence.[3] And only in "Slave Societies" are security precautions against slaves likely to be a concern; indeed, in some "Slave Societies," they become a major preoccupation. The concept of the "Slave Society" also helps the comparative historian of slavery choose the societies and periods from which to seek arguments or merely ideas to test. For instance, the evidence for Neo-Babylonian slavery – a "Society with Slaves" – has much less to offer the historian of classical Athenian slavery by way of parallels, inspiration, or telling contrasts than do the "Slave Societies" of the New World, despite Mesopotamia's vastly greater proximity in time and space.[4]

Regardless of the extent of slavery in a "Slave Society" and its impact on the rest of that society, the "Slave Society" designation cannot be expected to tell us everything about a society: "Slave Societies" differ greatly from each other. Nor does slavery permeate

[2] Turley 2000, 62–63.

[3] Phillips 1985, 105.

[4] On Babylonian slavery, see Dandamaev 1984; Baker 2001; cf. Galil 2007.

all the parts of a state equally: large geographic or other variations in the extent of slavery are more likely than not. But these critiques of the concept of "Slave Society" as obscuring differences between and within a society, made eloquently by Noel Lenski in the introduction to this volume, strike me as too all-purpose. Similar objections can be directed against almost any of the other key concepts that historians rightly consider crucial to their craft: urbanism, agrarianism, capitalism, industrialism, the market economy, democracy, imperialism, and law. These terms are all subject to debate, but they are still valuable, almost irreplaceable, for historians, despite their inexactness and potential for abuse.

One key problem about the concept of a "Slave Society" remains: should historians simply evaluate the importance of slavery on a continuum – or the several scales that Lenski proposes – rather than trying to draw a line at any one point in a spectrum and saying, "This is a slave society; that is not"? A society with 19 percent slaves is not likely to be radically different from one with 20 percent slaves; setting boundaries is potentially arbitrary. And, unfortunately, we have trustworthy numerical data for only a small subset of the societies in which slavery is present. The traditional dichotomy may still be accurate: there may be many societies in which slaves constitute less than 10 percent of the population – often much less – and a few "Slave Societies" with 20 percent or more, with few if any intermediate cases.[5] If this is indeed the pattern, several factors may explain it. For example, slavery requires a certain infrastructure of law, coercion, markets, supply, moral acceptance, and familiarity that, once acquired, make the acquisition and profitable use of more slaves easier and cheaper.

For these reasons, I believe that the traditional concept of "Slave Society" is a crucial tool for historians, especially for comparative historians and historians of slavery. I believe that if historians decided to rid themselves of the term, they would simply have to resort to a periphrasis or new piece of jargon that would cover much the same semantic territory. And, to turn to my topic for the rest of this chapter, if I were allowed to tell a social historian of another period and place

[5] There must, of course, be transitional periods, since a society cannot go from 10 percent to 20 percent slaves instantaneously.

just two things about classical Greece, I believe that I would convey the most by saying that Athens was a "Slave Society" while the Spartans depended on serfs.[6] The rest of this chapter attempts to justify these claims about Athens and Sparta and to suggest why they are crucial to understanding ancient Greek society, politics, and culture.

THE HETEROGENEITY OF CLASSICAL GREEK SOCIETY

Classical Greece was not a single country or society but rather encompassed around 1,000 *poleis*, city-states, whose social and political structures varied greatly.[7] Theopompus, a fourth-century historian, reportedly wrote:

> The Chians were the first of the Hellenes, after the Thessalians and Lacedaemonians, to make use of slaves. However, the acquisition [of slaves] was not [made] in the same way by them. The Lacedaemonians and Thessalians will be shown to have arranged the enslavement of the Greeks who formerly occupied the territory that they now have ... However, the Chians acquired barbarians as slaves by paying a price for them.[8]

Theopompus thus defines the two types of subject populations that constitute my topic. Of the states dependent on purchased barbarian slaves, we have much more evidence about Athens than about any other – even Chios, Theopompus' archetype. Sparta's Helots are the best attested of the other type of domination, but are much less well known than Athenian slaves due to the secrecy of Spartan society, the oral nature of its culture, and the tendency of Sparta's contemporaries to idealize it in one way or another. I focus on these two cases, Athens and Sparta, but will offer reasons to believe that each is a tolerable model of a particular category of Greek societies (see Map 2.1).

Theopompus makes his distinction in terms of the origins of the two systems: who was enslaved and how. In an important article, Michael Jameson also argued for two main categories, but he connected the

[6] This is a bit of a cocktail party gambit, but many of the other obviously important features of Athenian society are things a social historian would anyway assume of an ancient society: that Athenian society was militaristic, patriarchal, (somewhat) agrarian, and emphasized honor and reciprocity.

[7] Hansen 2006, 20–21.

[8] Theopompus F 122 (a) in Shrimpton 1991 with slight alterations.

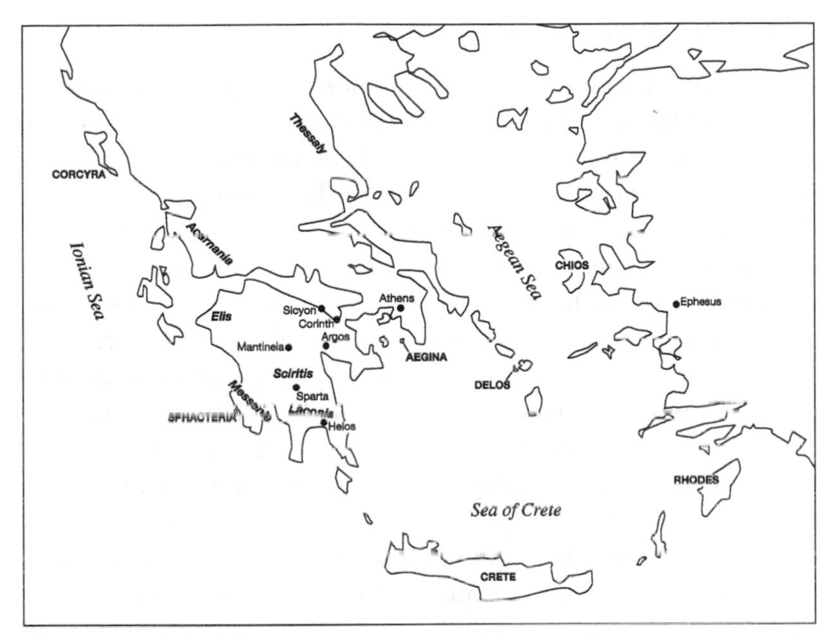

MAP 2.1 The Ancient Greek World

labor and agricultural regime in each case.[9] In some areas, often the most fertile plains that had been cultivated for the longest time, a traditional system of subsistence agriculture focusing on grain production predominated. The labor force in these areas consisted of native inhabitants reduced to a type of serfdom. In the other category, we find a more market-oriented and labor-intensive system of mixed agriculture with grain, fruit, olives, and grape vines. Here farm owners supplemented their own labor with that of imported slaves from areas bordering the Greek world, mainly north and east of the Aegean and from the Black Sea area.

Separate controversies surround the issue of whether Athens was a "Slave Society" and whether Sparta was one. In the case of Athens, the "bought barbarians" were manifestly slaves; the question is whether there were enough of them and whether they were economically important enough to make Athens a "Slave Society." In the case of Sparta, the importance of the Helots is undeniable, but whether they were slaves is debated.

[9] Jameson 1992.

ATHENS AS A "SLAVE SOCIETY"

References to slaves are extremely common throughout the extant literature of Classical Athens (ca. 500–323 BCE).[10] Most helpful are the more than a dozen comic plays set in Athens, thousands of pages from philosophers (including two treatises on household management), the three main historians whose works total 2,000 pages, and the fourteen volumes (in one collection) of Attic oratory – including speeches given for rhetorical display, before the assembly, or in the law courts, the last category of which is most helpful for the social historian. Taken as a whole, hundreds of references to slaves in these texts leave a strong, if imprecise, impression of a numerous slave population.

A few pieces of evidence or lines of inference more concretely suggest widespread ownership of slaves. In one preserved law court speech, a disabled citizen, poor enough to receive a public pension, complains that he cannot afford even to buy a slave to do his work for him: this appeal for sympathy would fail if slave ownership were confined to the rich.[11] Citizens of all classes were eligible to serve on jury panels, usually numbering in the hundreds. Nevertheless, litigants sometimes speak explicitly as if all the members of the jury had slaves.[12] This cannot have been true, but equally, it cannot be the case that only the rich owned slaves.

This inference is confirmed in another practice: citizens who armed themselves to fight as hoplites, heavy-armed infantry, came from the top third or half of the citizen body in terms of wealth; they represented a class intermediate between the leisured wealthy and the poorer *thetes*.[13] One slave attendant typically accompanied each Athenian hoplite on campaign to help carry his armor and other

[10] It is hard to define the period when Athens was a slave society. At both ends, the basic problem is that it is impossible to tell the difference between much less slavery and much less evidence. Thus, the gradual growth of slavery in the sixth century BCE is mainly an inference, likely but controversial, from its prominence in the classical period (*contra* Edward Harris 2012). More of a discontinuity in Athens's social and political structure marked the end of the Classical period, but again slavery continued and historians of Hellenistic Athens lack even the problematic Classical evidence for slave numbers.

[11] Lysias 24.6.

[12] Lysias 5.5; Demosthenes 45.86. On the social composition of Athenians juries, see, e.g., Todd 2007.

[13] I am being conservative: Strauss 1986, 78–81, has the hoplites making up more than half the population in 431 BCE and an even greater proportion after 403.

TABLE 2.1 *Estimated Demography of Athenian Slaveholding*

Citizen Class/Slave Type	Number of Owners	Slaves/ Owner	Total
Mine slaves			15,000
Household slaves of wealthy citizens	1,000	10	10,000
Farm and craft slaves of wealthy citizens	1,000	10	10,000
Slaves of hoplite class	9,000	5	45,000
Craftsmen/household slaves of *thetes*	20,000	0.2	4,000
Total slaves			≈85,000

supplies.[14] So hoplites could be expected to possess *at least* one slave, that is, more than a third of the citizen males, perhaps a half, typically owned slaves, a larger proportion than in the antebellum South.[15] The Athenian characters in Aristophanes' comic plays provide confirmation. They are in most cases represented as average citizens, often farmers; sometimes they even contrast themselves with the rich. These Aristophanic Athenians own between two and eight slaves; even Chremylus, the incarnation of poverty in Aristophanes' *Wealth*, has three slaves.[16]

It is possible roughly to quantify these impressions of numerous slaves by dividing the citizens into classes based on wealth, and, within each, multiplying the average number of slaves per adult citizen by the number of adult citizens. My mid-range estimate in that experiment comes out at about 85,000 slaves in the fourth century (see Table 2.1).

This procedure is based on a wide range of evidence but is admittedly impressionistic; for example, what do we make of the fact that Plato posits a man with fifty slaves for a thought experiment?[17] Its results, however, are consistent with two ancient estimates of subsets of the slave population. That these were indeed estimates and not the result of any sort of census deserves emphasis: the Athenian state

[14] Jameson 1992, 141, n. 41, with Isaeus 5.11; Hunt 1998, 166–68; cf. Osborne 1995, 29–30.
[15] Kolchin 1993, 180; cf. Degler 1959.
[16] Lévy 1974, 33; Garlan 1988, 61.
[17] Plato, *Republic*, 9.578e.

probably never counted slaves or total inhabitants but at most enumerated its armed forces.[18]

The first estimate comes from Hyperides, an Athenian statesman, who claimed in 338 BCE that if the Athenians had armed their slaves, they could have raised 150,000 soldiers from them.[19] This would imply a slave population, including women and children, much greater than this already substantial figure. Ancient orators could play fast and loose with facts; their scope for exaggeration was especially wide when it came to numbers that could not be checked. Thus, the safest inference is only that Hyperides did not come off as a fool or a liar since his audience, an Athenian jury, knew that there were a lot of slaves, many more slaves than male citizens.[20]

The second estimate comes from Thucydides. Earlier in the fifth century, before the plague of the 420s and Athens's defeat in the Peloponnesian War, Athens was an imperial center with a much larger population. Athens was also more prosperous, which probably meant a higher proportion of slaves. In his account of 413 BCE, Thucydides reports that when the Spartans set up a fort in Athenian territory, more than 20,000 slaves deserted, "a great part of them skilled workers."[21] Given that only some slaves were skilled and that running away required severing all bonds with friends and perhaps family for an extremely uncertain future, such a high number of fugitives is easily consistent with a large slave population and rules out low estimates of the Athenian slave population at that time. Unfortunately, these two passages provide the best ancient figures we have for the Athenian slave population.[22]

Even high estimates of the slave population are compatible with the total wealth of Athens.[23] When Athens possessed an empire, it amassed at one point a surplus of around 10,000 talents.[24] This amount could

[18] For example, Thucydides, 2.13.6–7, provides our best evidence, but its interpretation is not quite clear, e.g., Winton 2007.
[19] Hyperides, Fr. 29 (Jensen).
[20] Hansen 1991, 93.
[21] Thucydides, 7.27.5 (trans. Crawley).
[22] Hansen 1991, 93, *contra* Andreau and Descat 2011, 42–44, on the high slave numbers recorded in Athenaeus; cf. Van Wees 2011, 111–12.
[23] Compare Taylor 2001, 30–34, on the scale of mining and slavery in Athens and Thrace.
[24] Thucydides, 2.13.3. A talent contains 6,000 *drachmai*.

buy 300,000 slaves at the price of 200 *drachmai* per slave – the high average price I use in all these examples.[25] A tax on private wealth in 428 BCE yielded 200 talents.[26] We are not sure about the tax rate, but 1 percent is likely enough and implies a total of taxable wealth of 20,000 talents.[27] One hundred twenty thousand slaves at 200 *drachmai* per slave would constitute 20 percent of this total, a perfectly plausible proportion of wealth tied up in slaves, especially considering that the taxable wealth of Athens was probably considerably smaller than its full resources: for example, it did not include "invisible wealth" in bank accounts.[28] Similarly, the *minimum* wealth of the liturgical class – the approximately 1,200 rich Athenians required to pay special taxes and to render expensive services for the city – was three to four talents in the fourth century.[29] Thirty slaves might cost one talent.

Modern estimates of the total numbers of Athenian slaves range from 30,000 to 250,000.[30] Historians' estimates of the proportion of slaves vary less – from 20 percent to more than 50 percent – since high estimates of slave numbers correlate with, and partly depend on, high estimates of the total population. I find the extreme estimates implausible and favor a range from 60,000 to 120,000 (25 percent to 45 percent of the total population) in the fourth century with higher numbers in the fifth century. But, faced with a bookie with a time machine and a team of census takers, I would not bet my house (much less my life) even on this wide range. I am green with envy when I see a historian of the United States able to assert that slaves made up 57.2 percent of the population of South Carolina – even if that last digit is overoptimistic.[31] Fortunately, even the lowest estimates of the Athenian slave population imply a city-state with numbers of slaves

[25] The average price of the slaves on the Attic stele is 175 *drachmai* (Pritchett 1956, 276–77).

[26] Thucydides, 3.19.1.

[27] Meiggs 1972, 257; cf. Christ 2007. Van Wees 2011, 111–12, estimates the total wealth of Athens in 322 at between roughly 14,000 and 22,000 talents and favors a high number of slaves.

[28] Cohen 1992, 194–202.

[29] Hansen 1991, 110–15; Van Wees 2011, 112; cf. Davies 1971, xxiii–xxiv. In the fifth century, we would expect this class to be both richer and more numerous.

[30] Sallares 1991, 60 (30,000–50,000); Finley 1959 = 1981, 102 (60,000–80,000); Andreau and Descat 2011, 44 (200,000–250,000; cf. Van Wees 2011, 111–12). Hunt 1998, 11, n. 42, collects more estimates.

[31] Kolchin 1993, 100.

well beyond anything that could be called a "Society with Slaves"; judging strictly by numbers, Athens was a "Slave Society."

These high numbers strongly suggest that slaves played a significant economic role in Athens. Some Athenian slaves, of course, served to enhance the lifestyles and status of the elite, but most were productive. They played large and sometimes dominant roles in the main sectors of the economy: agriculture, clothing manufacture, crafts production, public works, and mining.

Domestic slaves are often considered nonproductive, but, especially in the case of female slaves, this view drastically underrates the proportion of time and energy devoted to preparing food and producing clothing in premodern societies. For example, a garrison of 480 soldiers left to stand siege in Plataea was accompanied by 110 slave women to bake their bread – and this in circumstances where it was crucial to minimize the number of mouths to feed.[32] A key skill that every elite girl would know by the time she married in her teens would be how to assign wool-working tasks to the slave women of the house.[33] Domestic slaves were not only an important category of slaves in Athens but also a productive one.

Outside the house, workshops of various types employed many slaves. For example, the orator Lysias and his brother owned 120 slaves, many of whom worked in their shield shop; Demosthenes's father owned a sword and a sofa workshop employing more than fifty skilled slaves in total.[34] The labor force for public works, such as the construction of the Erechtheion temple, and for manning the navy are recorded on inscriptions. These lists often include approximately equal numbers of slaves, foreigners, and citizens.[35] Silver was by far Athens's most important export, and almost all the workers in and around the mines were slaves. Their numbers varied greatly but may have reached 30,000 in some periods. Inscriptions recording mine leases suggest that more than 400 mines were being worked during some years, and each mine with its associated ore processing may have required an average of eighty slaves.[36]

32 Thucydides, 2.78.3.
33 Xenophon, *Oeconomicus*, 7.6.
34 Lysias, 12.19; Demosthenes, 27.9.
35 E.g., Randall 1953; Graham 1992, 1998; Margaret Smith 2008, 137–61.
36 Isager and Hansen 1975, 42–44; cf. Demosthenes, 37.4, 9, 12, 21, 29; Xenophon, *Poroi*, 4.1–4.33.

Thus slaves played major roles in domestic production, urban crafts, and mining, a large part of the Athenian economy. Nevertheless, full-time farmers constituted at least a third of the citizen population, yet the role of slaves in agriculture is more controversial. Much of Xenophon's *Oeconomicus* concerns farming. Its advice is addressed to a wealthy landowner and assumes a labor force consisting of slaves.[37] Other references also imply that slave laborers were the norm on substantial farms.[38] So in terms of where the elite got its wealth, one criterion of a "Slave Society," we are on strong grounds: whether a rich man's income came from craft production, mining, or agriculture, he relied on slave labor. We have seen that all hoplites are assumed to have owned slaves. Since the archetypal Athenian was a hoplite farmer, slave labor probably supplemented family labor even on medium-sized farms – an impression occasionally confirmed in our sources. In addition, slaves are laborers, who, unlike a farmer's sons, will never have any claim to the family property – a great advantage in an agrarian system like Athens with partible inheritance. Buying slaves allowed farmers to cover their labor needs at difficult points in the household life cycle without introducing another potential heir.[39]

Yet Ellen Wood has argued that most Athenian agriculture involved grain production, largely for subsistence, by small farmers. It would not make much sense for such poor farmers to buy slaves – if they could even afford them – since they would have had to feed them all year round and would only really need extra labor during sowing and harvest. Her argument that many references to "slaves" in agriculture use ambiguous terminology – particularly that the word *oiketes* can refer to a free person – has been decisively rebutted.[40] More fundamentally, the issue of slave use by small subsistence farmers has been superseded: there were probably few small farmers in Attica, and the farming there usually involved a mix of labor-intensive market crops. First of all, we find virtually no evidence of poor farmers. This is not conclusive, since the poor, especially out in the countryside, are invisible or almost invisible in our literary sources. But in a couple of

[37] E.g., Xenophon, *Oeconomicus*, 3.4, 3.10, 5.10, 5.16, 7.35, 9.5.

[38] Osborne 2010, 32, on Demosthenes 47 and Menander *Georgoi*.

[39] Osborne 1996, 66–69.

[40] Hanson 1992, 221, n. 22, and Jameson 1992, 142, n. 50; *contra* Ellen Wood 1988, 46–51.

passages, we hear "the rich and farmers" in a way that almost identifies them.[41] Second, models of the distribution of arable land in Athens agree that there does not seem to be enough land to accommodate the population of Athens in the countryside considering the probable size of farms.[42] The solution I favor is to make room in the model by reducing the number of small, poorly attested farmers. This leaves us with a less agricultural Athens and with the poor citizens living mainly in the city.

Athens was economically advanced and housed the largest concentration of population of any city in the Greek world. The city provided a market for all sorts of agricultural products. Attica itself produced grain, but cheap imports from the Black Sea area met more than half of its demand.[43] In contrast, Athenian farmers are represented in comedy as slave owners focused much more on vineyards, figs, and olives than on grain: "I had sold my grapes and had my mouth stuffed with pieces of copper; indeed I was going to the market to buy flour!"[44] The Attic countryside was dominated by intensive mixed agriculture more suited to slave labor than is growing grain. In such a system, there was agricultural work to be done for much of the year, so slaves rarely represented merely idle mouths to feed.[45] Consequently, agricultural labor in Attica fits into the familiar and plausible mold of slavery in market-oriented agriculture.

In terms of both the number of slaves and their economic role, Athens was a "Slave Society." If, as Finley posited, "Slave Societies" are few and far between, one obvious question is how and why Athens became a "Slave Society." The widespread assumption that outsiders are inferior and do not have rights is enough to explain why moral opposition to slavery was rare. Slaves who performed household or sexual services were a luxury; others displayed their owners' wealth

[41] Hunt 2010, 41, on Aristophanes, *Ecclesiazusae*, 197–98, and [Xenophon], *Constitution of the Athenians*, 2.14.

[42] Jameson 1992, 144–45; cf. Van Wees 2001, 51–54; Gallego 2010.

[43] Moreno 2007, 3–32, esp. 10, table 1, estimates that Athens imported 70 percent of its grain, and Bresson 2015, 409–10, comes to a similar conclusion, but my case does not depend on such a high figure; cf. Millett 2000, 41–42.

[44] Aristophanes, *Ecclesiazusae*, 817; Ehrenberg 1974, 56–57, collects many passages to this effect.

[45] Hanson 1999, 75–76. Slaves could also be shifted between different sorts of work at different times of year; we even hear of slaves for rent, which also makes the institution more flexible.

and status. The desire of ruling classes for luxuries and display is familiar, but for a large society to import slaves until they constitute 25–45 percent of its population requires an unusual combination of political and economic causes.

On the supply side, slaves in Athens seem to have been cheap when expressed in grain equivalent – at least compared to slaves in the Roman Empire.[46] Three factors help explain the low prices of slaves in Athens. First is geography: the Greek world had an extremely high ratio of border to area.[47] Greek cities were spread widely over the Mediterranean and Black Sea coasts. In many cases, relations between the Greek cities and the inland peoples involved trade in slaves or hostilities and slaving raids. Second, the Greeks often possessed superior armies and more highly organized societies than their inland neighbors.[48] They were more likely to enslave than to be enslaved, though both outcomes are attested. Third, the Greek world was connected by active maritime trade networks: the slaves captured when, for example, a Persian king sacked cities as he reasserted control over a rebellious western province, might quickly show up for sale in Athens. Even by sea, transportation cost something, but distance made slaves more valuable: they were much easier to control when spread throughout the Mediterranean and far from home than they would have been in a large group near to home right after capture.

So much for the slave supply. We must also explain why slave labor, that is, external labor, was required or desired. This boils down to the question of why free people, natives, were not as cheap and effective a source of labor as slaves. The answer at Athens seems to be twofold and essentially political.[49] First, even the poor were citizens. In particular, debt bondage had been forbidden since the reforms of Solon in the early sixth century.[50] By the late fifth century, poor citizens had equal political and judicial rights, which they guarded jealously. The poor at Athens could not be exploited to the extent or in the ways that

[46] Scheidel 2005b.

[47] A similar consideration may explain the high proportions of slaves among some pre-state peoples who lived in small political units close to actual or potential enemies. Compare Cameron, Snyder, and Santos-Granero in this volume.

[48] See Lovejoy this volume for parallels in Africa.

[49] Here I follow Scheidel 2008, although the general line of argument goes back to Finley 1959 = 1981.

[50] *Pace* Edward Harris 2002.

lower classes typically are, a problematic development from the point of view of the elite and one that made slave labor more attractive.

Second, Athens and other Greek city-states provided extensive military and political opportunities for, and imposed requirements on, their citizens. These interfered and competed with private employment of many free Athenians and made citizens less attractive as workers. The city, taken both as an economic and as a political entity, provided a large variety of jobs that poor Athenians could do individually – or together with a purchased slave or two. Poor Athenians were usually able to sustain themselves without entering into long-term, subordinating economic relations with the elite.

Historians sometimes invoke another factor: free Athenians found it demeaning, even slavish, to work over the long term for somebody else. This revulsion against working for another would, at least, add a premium to the cost of such labor. This mind-set was probably as much a result as a cause of the recourse to slave labor – and elite sources may give us an exaggerated impression of its strength – but it still contributed to the scarcity of cheaply available labor to which the elite could turn, whether they needed workers on their farms or in their sword workshops.

As one might expect, slavery's prominence in Athenian high culture reflected its importance to the workings of the society at large.[51] Most obviously, slaves played important roles in all branches of Athenian literature. Captured Trojan women symbolized the possibility of undeserved catastrophe in several plays of Euripides.[52] The conniving "clever slave" of Athenian comedy, who bamboozles his master, was in line with the flouting (and sometimes reassertion) of conventions and hierarchies that gave comedy much of its appeal.[53] In philosophy and political discourse, the metaphor of slavery was applied to describe and sometimes to denounce various harsh hierarchies. Both Plato and Aristotle viewed the relationship of body and soul according to the metaphor of slavery, which even played a role in Plato's cosmology.[54] Governments could be condemned for imposing slavery on

[51] Hunt 2011.

[52] Hall 1997, 111; cf. Daitz 1971. Slavery for captured males could never be quite undeserved, since men could be expected to fight to the death; cf. Hunt 2011, 26.

[53] Most recently, the articles collected in Akrigg and Tordoff 2013; cf. McCarthy 2000.

[54] Vlastos 1968; Schütrumpf 1993.

one or another group among citizens. States could be expected to resist metaphorical slavery to an imperial power. Warmongers could even describe compromise as equivalent to slavery.[55] Finally ethnic chauvinism and contempt for slaves, usually foreigners, tended to reinforce each other: to some extent, Athenians saw slaves as despicable foreigners and foreigners as slavish.[56]

The most important way that slavery affected Athens was, paradoxically, its adoption of democracy – or, to be more precise, the egalitarian ethos that made democracy possible.[57] Earlier we discussed how Athenian democracy made slave labor more attractive, but slavery may also have made democracy possible. The easy availability of slaves allowed the democratic compromise by which the rich maintained their economic superiority – for Athens avoided the redistribution of land and cancellation of debts attested elsewhere – but ceded political rights to the poor. This arrangement was palatable to the rich because they did not need the poor for their livelihood; slaves, who were bought foreigners, provided their labor force. The avoidance of subordinating economic ties – such as the patronage so conspicuous at Rome – allowed for an ideal of basic equality among the male citizens consonant with the political and juridical equality assured by the democracy.[58] Of course, this had an ideological side to it: all citizens, however rich or poor, could feel united in at least being free and not slaves. So slaves played a unifying role in ideology as the "other" that allows a group to smooth over the differences and tensions within it – with a fair degree of success at Athens.[59] In Athens, the development of democracy and of slavery each reinforced the other.

That Athens was a "Slave Society" is crucial for understanding its economy, culture, and political system. However, even if we discount Sparta and its kin, many other Greek cities were manifestly different in obvious respects from Athens, the largest of the Greek cities, democratic, substantially commercial, and possessed of rich silver mines. We can assume that other Greek cities were "Societies with Slaves" – for we would have heard of any city anomalous enough not to practice

55 E.g., Thucydides, 1.141.1, with Hunt 2010, 109–17.
56 Rosivach 1999.
57 Cf. Finley 1959 = 1981; Jameson 1977–78; and Ober 1989, 24–27.
58 Millett 1989; *contra* Zelnick-Abrahmovitz 2000.
59 Hunt 1998, 126–43; Osborne 2010, 38–39; Cartledge 2002, 118–51.

slavery – but whether they were "Slave Societies" cannot be determined from a priori considerations. When we turn to direct evidence, the first impression is of its paucity. We do not, for example, have substantial evidence from comedy or oratory from other city-states, so we lack two of the genres that, in the case of Athens, provide the strongest evidence of widespread slavery. Historical sources, which focus on war, provide our best evidence for other cities. Slavery on a large scale is clear both in references to slave members of trireme crews and to the desertion or capture of slaves when an enemy army invaded a city's territory. To take just one example, Corcyra lost the sea battle of Sybota and more than 1,000 of its sailors were taken captive. Eight hundred of these were slaves![60] We do not know how the ratios of slave and free in naval crews correspond to those in the population as a whole. Perhaps, Corcyra preferred to man ships mainly with slaves – expropriating or "borrowing" them from the wealthy – with just enough of an admixture of citizens to keep order and ensure effectiveness.[61] I would be surprised if Corcyra actually had a population that included so large a proportion as 80 percent slaves. Yet even the absolute number of slaves in this navy is significant. If slaves were even 50 percent of the total Corcyraean crews at Sybota – since the crews taken prisoner might have been atypical – there were more than 10,000 male slaves at that battle and this from a city much smaller than Athens.[62] Six years later, during the civil war at Corcyra, the democrats and oligarchs sent out heralds to the countryside and promised freedom to slaves, obviously agricultural slaves, who would help their side.[63] In the fourth century, we again have reports of the capture of large numbers of slaves in the countryside during an invasion of Corcyra.[64] Such reports find parallels in the case of other Greek states, suggesting that the countryside was full of agricultural slaves.[65]

[60] Thucydides, 1.55.1.

[61] Aristotle, *Politics*, 1327 b8–11.

[62] Thucydides, 1.47.1: 50 percent of 110 ships with 200 men/ship = 11,000. Hansen 2006, 95–96, considers 55,000 a minimum estimate for Corcyra's population based on the size of its navy.

[63] Thucydides, 3.73.

[64] Xenophon, *Hellenica*, 6.2.6, 6.2.23, 6.2.25.

[65] E.g., Acarnania (Xenophon, *Hellenica*, 4.6.6), Chios (Thucydides, 8.15.2 with 8.40.2; cf. Polyaenus, *Stratagems*, 3.9.23), Elis (Xenophon, *Hellenica*, 3.2.26), and Mantinea (Xenophon, *Hellenica*, 7.5.15).

Agriculture in some places was marked by greater concentrations of property than in democratic Athens and perhaps even greater reliance on slaves, but less urbanized city-states might not have had the numbers of slaves skilled at crafts that we find at Athens, and most lacked Athens's extensive mines.[66] Given our sparse evidence, definite conclusions are impossible, but it does not seem that Athens was exceptional in terms of its reliance on slavery. The real controversy revolves around the Spartan Helots, not their numbers, but whether they were slaves at all.

WERE THE HELOTS SLAVES?

The Helots were a group subject to the Spartans, the ruling class of a large, overwhelmingly agrarian area in the Peloponnese including Laconia and Messenia. The Helots may have constituted 70 percent of the population of the Spartan territories; in one campaign, seven Helot men reportedly accompanied each Spartan soldier.[67] All Spartan men were professional soldiers: unlike other Greek citizen-soldiers, they did not practice any other trades or farm the land themselves. Presumably, they needed to devote some of their time to managing their estates, but they were mainly at leisure to fulfill their political and military obligations because the actual farm work – and even much of the supervision – was performed by Helots.[68] Given the proportion of Helots in the population, their domination of agricultural production, and their provision of the surplus upon which the Spartans depended, Sparta and its territory would have to be classified as a "Slave Society" *if the Helots were slaves.* I do not believe they were, but I admit that at first the question looks murky indeed.[69]

Our sources usually refer to the Helots by that name, but several Greek texts refer to them as *douloi,* which is the common and usually unambiguous Greek word for slaves (*doulos* in the singular).[70] The

[66] Jameson 1992, 139–40.

[67] See Scheidel 2003, 242–43, for Helot numbers; Hunt 1997 for Helots at the battle of Plataea. A class of free, noncitizen farmers, the *perioikoi,* also lived under Sparta's rule and provided soldiers for its army.

[68] Cf. Santos-Granero in this volume on the Chiriguaná, Tukano, and especially the Guairurú.

[69] I have presented similar arguments in more detail in Hunt 2017, 61–75.

[70] Xenophon, *Agesilaus,* 2.24; *Lacedaemonians* 12.4; Isocrates, *Archidamus,* 28; Plato, *Laws,* 6.776d; cf. [Plato], *Alcibiades,* 1.122d.

Athenian oligarch and intellectual Kritias went so far as to say that at Sparta the free men were the freest and the slaves the most slavish.[71] We find this terminology also on official documents, such as Spartan treaties that specify that city-states in alliance with Sparta are to come to its aid "if the *douleia* revolt."[72] This must refer to the possibility of a Helot revolt, something that happened occasionally and that the Spartans consequently feared.

These texts were not, however, written by social historians concerned with the precise and accurate application of socioeconomic categories. The Greeks had a proclivity for dichotomies and in particular tended to assimilate those "between slave and free" to one of the two categories.[73] An ideological consideration explains why some sources went in one direction and called the Helots slaves. In the Greek world, the actual slavery of "bought barbarians" was uncontroversial, whereas any subjection of Greeks was deprecated. So to assimilate an unusual serf-like population of Greeks, the Helots, to the typically foreign *douloi* of most Greek cities was politically expedient for the Spartans. Historians need to examine the actual conditions of the Helots' oppression and to decide for themselves if they were slaves.[74]

Historians traditionally distinguish slavery from other forms of oppression according to one main criterion, that slaves are regarded as property.[75] The crucial issue, then, is whether Helots could be sold, a point on which our evidence is scanty and ambiguous. No ancient source mentions the sale of a Helot while there are many references to the sale of chattel slaves in Athens. But our sources for Spartan society are such that we would not expect to find references to selling Helots, whether this took place or not. The argument from silence is weak, so scholarly debate hinges largely on just one problematic passage, in which the geographic writer Strabo cites Ephorus (a fourth-century historian) to explain the name "Helot" in terms of the legendary conquest of Helos in the archaic period. The inhabitants of Helos were "condemned to slavery on certain terms, namely that it was not

[71] Kritias 88B37 (Diels-Kranz).
[72] Thucydides, 4.118.7, 5.23.3.
[73] Finley 1959 = 1981, 116, 119–20, 132; Lloyd 1966.
[74] E.g., Luraghi 2002; Luraghi and Alcock 2003; Hodkinson 2008; Cartledge 2011.
[75] Nieboer 1910, 7.

permitted for the holder either to liberate them or to sell them outside the boundaries."[76] Since Strabo claims that this established the system of Helotage, historians hopefully assume that the ban on sale of Helots "outside the boundaries" was also the classical practice and known to Ephorus. Nino Luraghi has argued vehemently that the natural understanding of this phrase is that sales outside Spartan territory, but not all sales, were forbidden.[77] On this reading, Helots could be sold within Spartan territory, and thus from a legal perspective they were chattel slaves. But the lack of liquidity in the Spartan economy, the apparent stability of the Helot population, and the lack of reasons to sell individual Helots had predisposed many historians to read this passage as meaning that Helots could not be sold at all. MacDowell, for example, interprets "outside the "boundaries" as referring to the boundaries of an individual Spartiate's estate.[78] Finally, archaic Helos may have had one set of boundaries, but the area under Spartan control must have had many, given its complex geography, which encompassed Messenia, Laconia, and Sciritis – not to mention the separate districts of Sparta, whose division Strabo describes earlier in our passage, and the many *poleis* of the *perioikoi*. Luraghi's arguments are strong, but agnosticism about this passage and issue is still attractive.

Even were we to accept that Spartan law countenanced the sale of Helots, drawbacks of the definition of slavery in terms of property are conspicuous in this case. For starters, curbs and limits on property rights, which differ from society to society, were particularly strong at Sparta: selling one's land was shameful; for individuals to manumit their Helots was forbidden. And ancient Sparta seems not to have had written laws in the classical period.[79] Once we are in the realm of oral law or customary practices, especially in a state such as Sparta, which drastically limited property rights, the criterion of property can become fuzzy indeed. In the case of the Helots, if land was mainly

[76] Ephorus, *FGrH* 70 F117 in Strabo, 8.5.4. Translation from MacDowell 1986, 24.

[77] Luraghi 2002, 228–29; see already Ducat 1990, 21–22. We find also limits on the selling "out of the country" of two other serf-like populations: the Penestai (Archemachos: FGrHist 424 F1) and the Mariandynoi (Poseidonios: FGrHist 87 F8). Whether we should equate "out of the country" for these groups and "beyond the boundaries" for the Helots or should understand a distinction between the two expressions is not clear.

[78] E.g., MacDowell 1986, 35.

[79] Cf. Millender 2001, 132–36.

transferred to heirs at death and almost always along with its Helots, then Helots were in practice not treated as saleable property.

It was not the position of the Helots, but more general objections to the property criterion that originally motivated sociologist Orlando Patterson's famous alternative definition of slavery: "the permanent, violent domination of natally alienated and generally dishonored persons."[80] All aspects of this definition are apt descriptions of slavery, but when it comes to demarcating slavery from other forms of oppression, that slaves were natally alienated – bereft of all the rights and bonds that come with birth within a family, clan, village, or state – seems to be the pivotal attribute.

If we apply Patterson's definition to the Helots, we find that their subjection was a permanent condition unless the Helot was freed by a special dispensation of the Spartan state. The Spartan rule of Helots was also conspicuously violent and involved dishonor, as a passage from Myron of Priene, a historian of the late third or second century BCE, makes clear:

> They impose on the Helots every outrageous practice that leads to every conceivable disgrace. For they ordered that each Helot necessarily wear a dog-skin cap and be clothed in a leather jerkin and receive a fixed number of blows each year, even when having done no wrong, so that they never forget that they are slaves. In addition, if any of them was in appearance robust beyond that which was fitting for a slave, they imposed the death penalty on them, and they fined their masters, for not having cut short their vigorous growth.[81]

Most of the details as well as the general tenor of this description are confirmed by other sources.[82]

Myron, however, also represents the Helots as sharecroppers: "And, having handed over land to them, they prescribed that the Helots always bring a share (of the harvest) to them."[83] According to earlier

[80] Patterson 1982, 13.

[81] Myron, F. 2 (Athenaeus, *Deipnosophists*, 14.74.657c–d) from the *Jacoby Online* (trans. Paul Christensen).

[82] Aristotle, *Politics*, II.1264a32–6; Theopompus, *FGrH* 115 F13; Ephorus *FGrHist* 70 F117; Plutarch, *Lycurgus*, 28.

[83] Myron, F.2, with Hodkinson 2000, 127–31; see also Hodkinson 1992, 125–29, which argues for sharecropping instead of a fixed rent in kind, which he believes is a late "invention" (126) like the equal allotments for all Spartiates. My argument here does not depend on the particular amounts or whether fixed rents or a proportion

sources, too, the Helots had to hand over half of their crops to their Spartan lords.[84] Sharecropping on explicit, public terms implies that the Helots had rights to the rest of their produce.[85] Some customary rights of possession are consistent with slave status. In Athens, for example, some slaves lived separately from their masters, to whom they paid a specified rent out of their earnings, the rest of which they kept.[86] Such persons – who are attested in many societies – were still slaves, since their masters could revoke the whole arrangement at any time and sell their slaves wherever they wanted. The sharecropping arrangements with Helots, on the other hand, do not seem to have been revocable: Plutarch even tells us that a curse was laid upon Spartans who took more than their agreed-upon portion from the Helots.[87] And apparently all Helots, not just a favored few, remained in this condition and for many generations.[88]

Continuity in the farming workforce was in the interest of the Spartiates as well as the Helots.[89] Thus, the sharecropping agreement was hereditary on both sides as new Spartiates and Helots succeeded those who died. In this sense, Helots inherited the right to farm the land they occupied upon agreed terms – and to any surplus they acquired.[90] Inheritance is, of course, the opposite of natal alienation. And inherited wealth and status – even if paltry in most cases – would make it easier to explain the social and economic distinctions

of the crop was owed, but depends only on the contractual nature, however harsh or moderate, of the Helots' obligations.

84 Plutarch, *Lycurgus*, 8.3; Tyrtaeus, F.6; Plutarch, *Customs of the Spartans*, 41 (=*Moralia* 239e).

85 The Penestai (Archemachos: FGrHist 424 F1) and Mariandynoi (Poseidonios: FGrHist 87 F8) also served on stated terms. That such people willingly agreed to a contract of servitude in the archaic period may be mythical, but historians such as Archemachos seem to have known that there were conditions and limits on their subjection in the classical period.

86 Kamen 2013, 19–20; cf. Kazakévich 2008.

87 Plutarch, *Moralia*, 239 D–E.

88 The loosely supervised slaves in the South Carolina low country, who worked according to the task system, provide a comparison: their time was their own after they had finished their tasks for the day. They began to resemble "protopeasants" (Kolchin 1993, 31–32). In the absence of the Civil War and emancipation, after a few more generations, they might not have been classifiable as slaves at all and might, in fact, have resembled serfs – or Helots.

89 Hodkinson 2000, 120–25.

90 Hodkinson 1992, 125–33, explores the complexity and flexibility that any such system required in practice.

attested among the Helots. For example, some scholars have detected references to a title, "Helot leader."[91] And Thucydides relates that in 425 BCE, the Spartans encouraged Helots to run an Athenian naval blockade and bring supplies to soldiers stranded on the island of Sphacteria. The Spartans allowed Helots who owned ships – not their Spartan masters – to register the value of their crafts so they could be reimbursed if their ships were damaged or destroyed while running the blockade.[92] This shows that some Helots owned ships, which they presumably normally used to conduct trade or to fish, and which they, in many cases, must have inherited and subsequently passed on to their children. The continuation over generations of sharecropping and inheritance – not to mention the maintenance of Helot numbers – also implies the existence of families.[93] Although we do not know whether Helot families had any official protection from forcible separation, ancient sources refer to the wives and families of Helots and most historians assume that these families were not disturbed often.[94]

Some groups are at the borderline of the definition of slaves, where the acknowledgment of family ties was neither so negligible that natal alienation was clearly in force nor so well established that a master could not separate family members if he really wanted to. That should not surprise or upset us; many definitional categories have border areas as well as central or paradigmatic cases.[95] Historical change makes this absolutely crucial: it would be ludicrous to insist that the status of a large group of people must be either that of slave or serf with no possibility of a period of transition even, say, for a couple of generations. Even those historians who regard the Helots as slaves concede that they reside on the borderline of the category: they are "helotic slaves" in Luraghi's formulation.[96] Nevertheless, I believe that it is the dominance of slave studies in the discipline of history and historiographical peculiarities in the study of serfs that has, more than anything else, convinced some historians to put Helots on the borders

[91] Ducat 1990, 63, on Hesychius.

[92] Thucydides, 4.26.5–7.

[93] Ducat 1990, 64.

[94] E.g., Luraghi 2009, 278.

[95] Patterson 2003, 291–92. See Lakoff 1987, 12–57, for an introduction to theory of structured categories.

[96] Ducat 1990, 40–44; Luraghi 2002.

of slavery, when they belong squarely and firmly in the category of serfs where other historians place them.[97]

In contrast to the investigation of slavery in various times and places, the concept of serfdom has received less attention recently as a category of social analysis for two main reasons. First, the study of serfdom has become a poor stepsister of slave studies, largely an outgrowth of the popularity of New World slavery as a field. To take but one example, an otherwise identical JSTOR search of scholarly literature for "slave" and "serf" yielded, respectively, 4,097 items for "slave" and only 71 for "serf." Second, the term "serf" is a dangerous third rail whose use can evoke harsh reactions from medievalists, Marxian historians, or their opponents. Comparative historians are aware, even if only vaguely, of these trends in historiography are understandably loath to use a term that medievalists themselves, who might appear to possess first rights, seem to be abandoning.

A definition of serfdom useful for comparative history needs to distinguish serfs from other peasants, on the one hand, from slaves, on the other.[98] For social historians, peasants are not just small farmers. They are subject to rents, be they in the form of taxes, labor obligations, payments in kind or money, or some sort of sharecropping arrangements.[99] These obligations may be more or less formal, legal, or customary, but they are defined and not unlimited, as is the labor of slaves. Serfs are a subset of peasants but endure additional constraints on their freedom: most conspicuous, they are bound either to the land or to their lord.[100] Thus, serfs are bound peasants, a mainstream definition of serfdom apt for the vast majority of medieval and modern serfs.

Helots, too, were peasants in that they worked the land they lived on. They owed labor (probably) and a rent in kind to their Spartan lords. In addition to the limits on exploitation implicit in a sharecropping agreement, Helots had property and other rights vis-à-vis the Spartans.

[97] See Hunt 2017, 71–75; contra Lotze 1959, 60–68, and Finley 1959 = 1981, 142. Helots as serfs: e.g., Jameson 1992, 135; Van Wees 2003, 33, n. 1 (hedging); Davies 2007, 353–54. Whether control or ownership of Helots was individual or communal is a related but separate question: e.g., Cartledge 2011, 80–82.

[98] Russian and medieval serfs were not all rural cultivators, but most were; cf. Bush 1996, 206.

[99] Wolf 1966, 10.

[100] E.g., Bloch 1975 (orig. 1933), 49–54.

But Helots were not simply peasants. They were bound to their Spartan lords and to their land. This explains why freedom could be a reward – given, promised, or conceded – for Helots and why they are sometimes described as running away or deserting.[101] As bound peasants, the Helots fit the category of serfs without any hedging or any need to invoke "border areas."

It was not only Sparta that depended predominantly upon a serf class rather than upon imported slaves. Crete with its *woikeis* and Thessaly with its *penestai* are the most famous other examples from the ancient Greek world.[102] Hans van Wees has also highlighted the possibility that in other places, Sicyon and Argos, serf-like classes were subjugated in the archaic period but gained their freedom.[103] At the edges of the Greek world, we again hear of the subjugation of non-Greek populations on similar terms: for example, Syracuse had its Kyllyrians and Heraclea its Mariandynians.[104] Some areas of the Greek world depended on the exploitation of people "between free and slave" in the words of one ancient second-century CE scholar – or, in our terms, serfs.[105] Historically, such societies were in decline from the late archaic and early classical periods, when several classes of serfs were liberated, through 369 BCE, when Sparta itself lost control of Messenia, its richest land and home to a large proportion of its Helots.[106]

CONCLUSION

For a society to be a "Slave Society," it must comprise many slaves. The definition both of *slave* and of *many* requires making distinctions,

[101] E.g., Thucydides, 1.103.1–2, 4.41.3, 4.80.3–4, 5.14.3, 5.34.1. G. E. M. de Ste. Croix 1981, 148, points out what was generally a corollary of this: "serfs, because they were 'bound to the soil,' could marry and have a fairly secure family life."

[102] This has been the traditional view of Cretan social structure, e.g., Willetts 1967, 15, and Gagarin 2010, but is now disputed by Link 1994, 30–48; 2001; and Lewis 2013.

[103] Van Wees 2003, 38–45.

[104] Van Wees 2003, 45–47.

[105] Pollux, *Onomastikon*, 3.83.

[106] This process may have begun earlier, in the seventh century BCE, and encompassed more of Greece; historians simply do not possess good evidence about the organization of agricultural labor that early. Even at Athens, Solon seems to have freed the *hektēmoroi*, "the one-sixth-partners," from their obligations at the beginning of the sixth century; according to one source, the poor in Attica had previously been "enslaved" to the rich. Unfortunately, almost all aspects of Solon's reforms and of the previous social structure are obscure and objects of controversy.

drawing lines, which necessarily simplify the messy world. But historians do this every time they generalize or use a category. In the case of ancient Greece, our uneven evidence adds another layer of uncertainty. In this chapter, I have defended the traditional position that Athens was a "Slave Society." Its *douloi* were obviously slaves, their numbers were more than 25 percent of the population, and slavery had a profound effect on Athens's economy, social structure, political system, and culture. Many other similar Greek city-states possessed slaves and may well have been "Slave Societies," but the numbers of slaves and a fortiori the social and cultural effects of slavery are less clearly known than at Athens.

In Sparta's territory, Helots constituted a large majority of the population. Their exploitation freed the Spartiates to focus on the military training and accomplishments for which they are celebrated. Several other states, constituting a substantial minority of the Greek world, depended on classes similar to the Helots. In the case of the Helots too, I defend a conventional view: that the Helots were not slaves, but a serf-like population of bound peasants; and that Sparta was not a "Slave Society."

Admittedly, these arguments reduce the extent of the certainly known, classical Greek city-states that can be characterized as a "Slave Society" to a single example, Athens. It is some consolation, however, that Athens was the most populous Greek city and a dominating cultural force both in the classical period and after; when we speak of classical Greek culture, we often really mean Athenian culture, the product of a "Slave Society" in both more and less obvious ways.

3

Roman Slavery and the Idea of "Slave Society"

Kyle Harper and Walter Scheidel

SLAVE SOCIETY: A USEFUL CATEGORY OF ANALYSIS?

Anyone who works on ancient Mediterranean slavery labors in the shadow of the great sociologist-historian Sir Moses Finley. There are two periods in the study of ancient slavery: before Finley and after Finley. Almost nothing written about slavery in the Classical world before his contributions of the late 1960s through the early 1980s matters today, except as handy catalogs of evidence. Most of what came before him was Marxist mythmaking, humanist apologetics, or dry positivism. Finley made ancient slavery real. To understand how he did so is to understand why the idea of a "Slave Society" mattered as a historiographical intervention. The task of these chapters, presumably, is to ask whether it is an intervention that has outlived its usefulness or if, in the full light of cross-cultural study, it remains meaningful.

The notion of a "Roman Slave Society" immediately raises a bigger question, whether the Roman Empire formed a single "society" in any meaningful sense of the term. Any premodern polities that were significantly larger than city-states lacked the cohesiveness and integration that is typical of modern nation-states, and internal social and cultural segmentation was the norm.[1] Inasmuch as something like a unified "society" existed within early empires, it would have been confined to the ruling class or other specialized groups. Roman slavery, in this

[1] Gellner 1983, 8–18, is a classic statement.

widest sense, is analogous to "New World slavery" as a phenomenon stretching across vast amounts of space with zones of intensity and underdeveloped hinterlands (although in the Roman case slavery was geographically central rather than peripheral). Exploration of the overall importance of slavery in the Roman world needs to proceed within this conceptual framework.

This is not the place to provide a general overview of Roman slavery, a topic that has been covered by several excellent recent surveys.[2] Instead, this chapter explores two questions in turn. First, where did the category of a "Slave Society" come from? The study of Classical antiquity played an important role in the development of the idea of a "Slave Society" – where (1) slaves existed in large numbers; (2) they played an important role in primary sectors of production; and (3) slavery as an institution was highly significant culturally. In a set of chapters devoted to querying its cross-cultural validity, it will be helpful to explore the background of the idea and to delineate the problems it was contrived to solve. Second, to what extent was the Roman world, over the long cycle of imperial expansion, flourishing, and dissolution, penetrated by the institution of slavery? This problem requires attention to scale, geographical variation, and the social and cultural location of slavery, as well as the long chronological sweep of the "Roman Empire."

BEFORE THE IDEA OF "SLAVE SOCIETY"

A principal merit of the concept of a "Slave Society" was that it allowed historical sociology to analyze premodern slave systems while laying aside the burdensome inheritance of Marx and Weber. Above all, it displaced and moved beyond the clunky Marxist notion of a "slave mode of production." Marx had developed the idea of a "slave mode of production" as an important part of his theory of historical materialism.[3] The concept was developed to describe the class structures of the ancient world, especially in the case of Classical Greece and Rome.

[2] Keith Bradley 1994; Joshel 2010; Bradley and Cartledge 2011, 214–509. On the economy, see now Scheidel 2012.

[3] Banaji 2010 on the concept and its fate; Marx's own thoughts on precapitalist economies are most evident in the incomplete *Grundrisse der Kritik der politischen Ökonomie*, most easily available in Marx 1964.

Marx drew from his own considerable and direct knowledge of the ancient world, and from contemporary political economy and stadial theories of history disseminated from the Scottish Enlightenment, as well as Hegel. The construct held that this phase of history was dominated by the structure of slavery. The ludicrous estimates of the Roman slave population, which are based on little that could properly be called evidence, actually go back to the late eighteenth and early nineteenth centuries, and they already undergirded Marx's idea of a "slave mode of production."[4]

The "slave mode of production" was from its genesis embedded in a narrative of ancient history that we might call "the conquest thesis." The conquest thesis is a story that derives from the ancient histories and from the way that the ancients thought about slavery. Roman ideology conceived of slavery as an artefact of war. Slaves were those captives whose lives had been spared, and the "social death" of slavery was a suspended death sentence on the field of battle. The Romans thought of war as the primary source of the slave supply, a conception that was at many points in time untrue.[5] But the story has had power in the ancient and modern worlds.

In the eighteenth century, the conquest thesis was accepted as an integral part of Roman history. In his essay "Of the Populousness of Ancient Nations," David Hume identified slavery as the "chief difference between the domestic economy of the ancients and that of the moderns." He held that there was "a perpetual flux of slaves to Italy," but "so far from multiplying, they could not, it seems, so much as keep up the stock without immense recruits."[6] Gibbon too would argue that Roman slaves "consisted, for the most part, of barbarian captives, taken in thousands by the chance of war, purchased at a vile price ... But when the principal nations of Europe, Asia, and Africa, were united under the laws of one sovereign, the source of foreign supplies flowed with much less abundance, and the Romans were reduced to the milder but more tedious method of propagation."[7]

4 Harper 2012; later in this chapter, on slave numbers.

5 *Digest*, 1.5.4–5; on the sources of the Roman slave supply, see Harper 2011, 67–99; William Harris 1980, 1999; Scheidel 1997.

6 Hume 1742[1987], 385.

7 Gibbon 1776[1995], 31.

The conquest thesis was part of the received wisdom about the ancient world by the time Marx sat down to think in depth about the role of class structure in history.[8] There are also unevaporated traces of stadial theory in Marx's grand historical architecture. Marx, writing mostly before the deep time revolution (though recognizing later in his life the importance and richness of "primitive society" as it was then being delineated by anthropologists such as Lewis Henry Morgan), thought of an originary state of primitive communism giving way to the ancient slave mode of production. The ancient slave mode would yield to feudalism, and eventually of course to capitalism. The slave mode of production was both a structure and a chronological phase.

What needs emphasis is that for Marx, *the* decisive criterion of the capitalist mode of production was wage labor.[9] For Marx, capitalism, wage labor, and modernity were covalent categories. At least in part, the rigidity of the "mode of production" as a concept in historical sociology originates in Marx's insistence that the structures of ancient slavery and medieval feudalism were distinct from modern capitalism. This is the subtle reason why the "conquest thesis" was so important. It provided a powerful enough motor to drive the ancient slave mode of production without the forces of market capitalism.[10] For Marx ancient slavery was *not* capitalist.[11] It was a system of exploitation reproduced not by the circulation of capital but by the continuous

[8] E.g., Reitmeyer 1789; Blair 1833; and esp. Dureau de la Malle, 1840.

[9] See Harper 2012. Marx and Engels 1977, 203: "The slave did not sell his labour power to the slaveowner, any more than the ox sells his labour to the farmer ... The slave himself is a commodity, but his labour-power is not his commodity."

[10] Karl Marx, *Capital*, vol. 2, part 4, chapter 20 in Marx and Engels 1997: "But the slave system too – so long as it is the dominant form of productive labour in agriculture, manufacture, navigation, etc., as it was in the developed states of Greece and in Rome – preserves an element of natural economy. The slave market maintains its supply of the commodity labour power by war, piracy, etc., and this rapine is not promoted by a process of circulation, but by the actual appropriation of the labour power of others by direct physical compulsion."

[11] See the concession Marx nearly made to Mommsen for Roman Sicily: Karl Marx, *Capital*, vol. 3, part 6, chapter 47, in Marx and Engels 1998: "A formal analogy, which, simultaneously, however, turns out to be completely illusory in all essential[s] points to a person familiar with the capitalist mode of production, who does not, like Herr Mommsen, discover a capitalist mode of production in every monetary economy, is not to be found at all in continental Italy during antiquity, but at best only in Sicily, since this island served Rome as an agricultural tributary so that its agriculture was aimed chiefly at export."

capture of new slaves. The army and the general, rather than the factory and the capitalist, were characteristic of the ancient slave mode.

In his insistence that ancient slavery was not capitalist, Marx belongs among the primitivists.[12] The debate between primitivists (who argued that premodern societies were not just underdeveloped but structurally noncapitalist) and modernists (who would describe Roman economy and society by granting high significance to markets, merchants, the middle class, etc.) was a perduring conversation across the late nineteenth and twentieth centuries. Max Weber was the arch-primitivist, and his treatment of ancient slavery – with important differences of interpretation – draws heavily from Marxist foundations. Weber's subtle treatment of ancient slavery construes it as a sort of proto-capitalist institution embedded in a thoroughly militarized society. Ancient slavery was, in his reconstruction, characteristic of "political capitalism," a category he invented to solve the problem of Roman slavery.[13] Like Marx, his narrative is founded explicitly and entirely on the conquest thesis. It is telling that the two great historical sociologists of the nineteenth century each created a major category of analysis to account for Greco-Roman slave systems – the slave mode of production and "political capitalism," respectively. Finley would feel compelled to do the same. It must be said that Roman slavery has been a fertile analytical problem.

Finley (himself a committed primitivist) intervened at a time when the study of slavery was bitterly divided between an Anglo-Germanic humanist tradition, which suppressed any deep engagement with the brutality of ancient slavery, and a doctrinaire Marxist tradition that flourished in the Communist bloc.[14] The former lacked the analytical tools for a compelling historical sociology, while the latter was committed (in the Soviet case especially) to rigid adherence to orthodoxy.[15] The idea of a "Slave Society," it is worth remembering, was invented not as an abstraction but as a means to solve a problem – the problem of Classical Mediterranean slavery. Drawing on Weber

[12] See Morley 1998.

[13] Weber (1896) 1988; Love 1986; Capogrossi Colognesi 1990; Lo Cascio 2009, 299–315.

[14] The best treatment of which is Finley 1980.

[15] The outstanding example of the former was Vogt 1953; the most outstanding contribution of Soviet scholarship was Shtaerman 1964. See Tompkins 2014 for a consideration of the origins of this Cold War divide.

and Karl Polanyi, Finley rewrote the economic history of the ancient world, delineating its structural features and prompting new and productive questions about the nature of Greek and Roman societies. A serious engagement with slavery was soon to follow.

Finley's work on ancient slavery would culminate in his book *Ancient Slavery and Modern Ideology*, but one article in particular paved the way for his distinctive approach. In his study of the "servile statuses" of the ancient world, Finley argued that dependency takes various forms and falls along a "spectrum" of freedom and unfreedom (in contradiction to the pithy but fundamental claim of Roman law that all men are either free or slave).[16] It is hard to overstate what a simple breakthrough this essay would mark. Finley's appreciation for the importance of "status" was a direct correlate of his primitivism. Ancient societies, in his eyes, were based on status, not contracts, transactions, and markets. Economic relations were embedded in society. By considering the problem of status in this way, Finley resisted the temptation to collapse relations of dependence into abstract forms like "serfdom." At the same time, the notion of a spectrum of servile status did serve to underscore the distinctiveness of "genuine chattel slavery" as a type of institution. (It is revealing that the phrases "genuine chattel slavery" and "genuine slave societies" were Finleyan locutions.) Finley would later emphasize the property relationship, the totality of the master's power and its basis in violence, and the slave's lack of access to social honor as distinguishing characteristics of genuine chattel slavery.[17]

The concept of a "Slave Society," then, at least in terms of its genesis, is dependent on a specific definition of slavery itself, and that definition emphasizes the slave's condition as a piece of property. Now, Roman law was able to define these complex relations with crystalline (and some would argue delusive) sharpness. The master was *dominus*. His power was *dominium*, a virtually absolute and exclusive power to use, abuse, and sell.[18] Slaves were the living dead. Legal status was absolute: all men are slave or free.[19] Slaves were natally alienated,

[16] Finley 1960b; see also Finley 1964.
[17] Finley 1973a, 62–94; Finley 1980.
[18] Buckland 1908 remains fundamental.
[19] *Digest*, 1.5.3 (Gaius): *Summa itaque de iure personarum divisio haec est, quod omnes homines aut liberi sunt aut servi.*

genealogical isolates. The Roman law of status codified the slave's domination, dishonor, and alienation. It is not accidental that Orlando Patterson's monumental cross-cultural study of slavery closely reflects these very notions. *Slavery and Social Death* is deeply indebted to Finley, whose analysis in turn absorbed many of the notions inherent in the Roman definition of slavery.[20]

Yet crucially, Patterson's initial move in *Slavery and Social Death* is to displace a "legal," property-based definition of slavery with a more universally valid sociological definition ("the permanent, violent domination of natally alienated and generally dishonored persons").[21] His argument is that property itself is a legal construct for organizing power relationships, so a property-based definition of slavery is culturally bound to state-based societies with a law of property; even in those societies, he would argue, a legalistic definition confuses the construct (property) for the thing itself (power). Patterson preserves the basic distinction between "Slave Societies" (slave-based societies) and "Societies with Slaves" (slaveholding societies). He was urgently concerned to reshape the definition of slavery into something broader, capable of accounting for a wider range of social formations.

Crucial and productive though it has been, we can question whether this opening maneuver was necessary.[22] It is true that property can be a legal construction of certain kinds of relationships among persons and things (exclusive powers to use, abuse, and sell), but that cluster of powers is not itself culturally bound. Property is a cross-cultural category, with all the variability of any big, important cross-cultural category. Humans were buying and selling things long before anyone had committed rules to writing.[23] More pertinently, though, it is the subjection to that particular cluster of powers, usually applied to things, that makes the slave a slave. In other words, slavery is the institution of treating humans as property.[24] Slavery is precisely equivalent, on this view, to genuine chattel slavery. It is this radical fact of commodification that accounts for the animalization of the slave (à la David Brion

[20] Patterson 1982. Bodel and Scheidel 2017 offer a critical assessment.

[21] Patterson 1982, 13.

[22] Lewis 2017.

[23] E.g., Smail and Shryock 2013.

[24] Lewis 2017 convincingly shows that property rights (in humans and otherwise) are never or rarely absolute, a fact that does nothing to diminish the connection between slavery and property.

Davis), as well as the effectively (but not absolutely) constant features like dishonor and natal alienation.[25] None of this is to diminish or discount any of the many other relations of exploitation that humans have ingeniously contrived in our short history. But not all systems of captivity are systems of slavery, nor are all serf-like relations of dependence systems of slavery, though both provide fertile ground for the emergence of genuine chattel slavery. The distance between freedom and slavery is a spectrum, with many subtle gradations between them, but the asymptotic leap to true slavery is the treatment of a human being as a piece of property.

This definition of slavery also helps to explain one of the paradoxical features of slavery as a historical phenomenon, what might be called Patterson's paradox: slavery flourished in those societies that have often been considered to mark the most advanced edge of civilizational progress, like Greece and Rome.[26] In these societies, notions of liberty were especially important; one does not have to be a Victorian liberal like Lord Acton to admit that the institutionalization of citizenship and the ideology of freedom were exceptionally prominent in Classical antiquity. Patterson explained this paradox through a Hegelian reading of ancient ideology, with its stark insistence that all men are slave or free. For Patterson, the idea and reality of freedom depended on, and developed through, an antagonism with slavery. In a material sense, for Patterson, Western freedom emerged from a peculiar experience with slavery.

While this was a rhetorically powerful counter-narrative to the triumphalist liberalism of the "Western Civ." story, it is not necessarily true. Even if it is capable of explaining the sharpness of freedom in Western cultures, it does not explain why slavery emerged in these cultures in the first place. More important, it leaves unanswered why "Slave Societies" emerged – that is, why slavery becomes unusually central in some times and places. Notably, Patterson's more recent efforts to offer a sociological explanation for the existence of slavery in some societies tries to tease out the most important variables – the prevalence of warfare, the type of marriage system, and the subsistence base.[27] His analysis demonstrates that no single pathway led to

[25] Davis 1966.
[26] Esp. Patterson 1991.
[27] Patterson 2008.

slavery (slavery can emerge in a remarkable variety of conditions; as Patterson argued, it is hardly a peculiar institution), but there are telling correlations between the existence of slavery and the incidence of militarism and polygyny. An economist might look at this same analysis and conclude that Patterson has focused on a powerful supply mechanism (enslavement in war) and a powerful demand generator (the need for marriageable women). Needless to say, these are not the only sources of supply and demand for slaves, but they are powerful enough to produce detectable signals in his analysis.

What is more interesting, though, is the framework of this study. Patterson codes for the existence of slavery as an institution, not its importance. Historians of slavery know well the sheer variety of social formations that can accommodate the institution of slavery. But what causes the kinds of transformation that turn "Societies with Slaves" into "Slave Societies"? These, we could suggest, are economic and institutional, in the sense that supply and demand (which can be culturally motivated) are primary drivers, shaped by the legal regime. This formulation, too, explains the paradox of slavery's importance along the advanced edges of social development: progressively liberal societies were, generally, the most commercially advanced societies too. Certainly, the "Slave Societies" of the ancient Mediterranean, Greece and Rome, were exceptionally developed economically and institutionally. This pattern is evident, for example, in the recent efforts of Ian Morris to define a globally valid social development index.[28] Greece and Rome were in the vanguard of Iron Age development with trade systems that outpaced anything previously seen.

On this model, slaves are human property, and "Slave Societies" emerge under conditions that accelerate and intensify the circulation of commodified human beings. This model fits the phenomenon of slavery in the case of Republican and Imperial Rome. The Romans created one of history's truly large-scale "Slave Societies"; indeed, even by the parameters of the newer wave of scholarship that lowers the estimates of the slave population, hundreds of millions of souls experienced slavery in the centuries of Roman dominance.[29] The Roman slave system was not a by-product of conquest; rather, Roman

[28] Morris 2013.
[29] Scheidel 2012.

conquest created expansive trading networks, a legal framework for property rights, and access to underdeveloped frontier regions on three continents. Here is where Marx, Weber, and Finley all went wrong. Roman slavery was not a distinctly uncapitalist phenomenon. Rather, it was an essential part of the lunge toward development that was the Roman economy.

Importantly, Finley's own reconstruction of the ancient economy was distinct from Marx's and Weber's in that his primitivist views were not inextricable from his analysis of slavery. For Marx, the "slave mode of production" was an essentially precapitalist form of production, a class structure built on something other than wage labor. For Weber, slave-based "political capitalism" was a nonrational (in his technical sense) system, doomed to inversion once the process of conquest came to an end. For Finley, the ancient economy was embedded in ancient society. But at the same time, the status of Greece and Rome in history's (obviously too narrow) selective catalog of "Slave Societies" seemed somehow to connect them more closely with the Atlantic slaveries of the modern world. Here, Finley's honesty as a historian won out over his consistency as a sociologist – a most forgivable inconsistency! The right solution is to accept his diagnosis of ancient Rome as a "Slave Society" but to reject thoroughly any form of dogmatic primitivism. Roman class structure was transformed by commerce and by slavery. Had it not been transformed by commerce, it would not have been transformed by slavery.

LOOKING FOR ROMAN SLAVERY

Discussions of "Slave Societies" have traditionally privileged the issue of slave numbers, an approach that is notoriously difficult to apply to ancient history. Moreover, it is not at all clear that clear demographic thresholds exist. An answer to the question whether slaves accounted for at least 15 percent or 20 percent of the population of certain parts of the Roman world – a share that is sometimes thought to constitute a cutoff for genuine "Slave Societies" or "large-scale slave systems" – is hard to come by and would tell us little about the Roman world as a whole. The often-cited analogy between a presumed slave share of one-third in the population of Roman Italy 2,000 years ago as well as that of the Southern United States, Brazil, and Cuba in the mid-nineteenth century is both wrong and misleading.[30] One-third of the overall population of the Old South in 1860 may have been made up of slaves, but state rates varied dramatically from a few percent to more than half. We may conjecture a comparable range of regional variation across the Roman world, with serious consequences for the significance of slavery in any given time and place.

The one thing we can say with confidence is that the whole of the Roman world was a "slave-owning society" – or a conglomerate of such societies – in that, just as in many other parts of the ancient world, chattel slavery was legal and socially acceptable everywhere. We know most of the Classical Roman doctrine that portrayed slaves as the antithesis of free persons and formally consigned them to a class of property alongside livestock and real estate.[31] Legal restrictions on owners' powers over their slaves existed and grew somewhat over time, yet remained modest overall. Under Roman law, slaves had no right to recognized kinship relations or to property, and manumission was entirely at their owners' discretion. Violent abuse was only curbed at the margins. While other legal traditions survived for a long time, Roman law eventually came to define master–slave relations throughout the empire, at least nominally if not necessarily in practice. From a legal perspective, slave ownership was unexceptional, and the same was quite consistently true of recorded philosophical and religious thought.[32] It is thus perfectly clear that the Roman world as a whole was a world with slaves, a world to which there was no practical or theoretical alternative: slavery was a basic fact of life like death and taxes.

While we cannot tell for sure which regions housed the fewest slaves, it appears that chattel slavery was particularly prominent in parts of Italy and more generally in the Aegean and in the Hellenistic cities of the eastern parts of the empire.[33] Chattel slavery had a long tradition within the territory of the Roman Republic. The evidence for the earliest stages of Roman history is so poor that we know little

[30] Threshold: Hopkins 1978, 99 (20 percent cutoff); Patterson 1982, 353 (15 percent to 20 percent). For the one-third analogy, see Hopkins 1978, 101; Finley 1980; Bradley 1994, 12, 29–30; with the critique in Scheidel 2005a, 65.

[31] The most recent survey of Roman slave law is Gardner 2011.

[32] Garnsey 1996.

[33] In what follows we draw on Scheidel 2012, which provides a fuller account.

beyond the existence of the institution: references in histories written hundreds of years later that imply a large presence of slaves may or may not be mere retrojections of later conditions. By the third century BCE, the picture becomes clearer thanks to plausible reports of mass enslavements (in the tens of thousands) and references to the drafting of private slaves for the war effort against Hannibal. In that period as well as over the following centuries, warfare was a principal source of slavery. Recorded tallies rose over time, and the total intake must have been very considerable even if we allow for rhetorical inflation. Reported capture tallies add up to some 700,000 between 297 BCE and 167 BCE, and later campaigns are associated with even larger numbers.[34] By one estimate, some two to four million slaves are likely to have entered Italy in the last two centuries BCE.[35] Military action undertaken by the Roman state was not the only source of new slaves: Roman demand for slave labor encouraged capture and sale by more geographically remote third parties.

As the slave population of Roman Italy grew, natural reproduction was bound to assume growing importance. Military campaigns were frequently associated with the enslavement of women and children, whereas men suffered more fatalities. Under Roman law, the children of slave women acquired the status of their mothers. The sources do not allow us to measure the scale of this process, but once the slave population reached into seven figures (see later in this chapter), the conclusion that slave births represented the single most important source of slaves becomes all but inevitable as alternative assumptions would imply unrealistically high rates of capture in war or domestic child enslavement.[36] Natural reproduction helped stabilize the slave system over time, even in the face of ongoing attrition through manumission.

By the end of the Republican period and the reintroduction of monarchy in the first century BCE, Italy had turned into an exceptionally slave-rich environment. Legislation addressed the possibility of slaveholdings in excess of 500, and one elite member (himself a freedman) reputedly left more than 4,000 slaves in his will.[37] Modern

[34] Scheidel 2011, 294–96.
[35] Scheidel 2005a, 77.
[36] Scheidel 2011, 306–08.
[37] Gaius, *Institutes*, 1.43; Pliny the Elder, *Natural History*, 33.135.

attempts to estimate the number of slaves in Roman Italy in this period take the form of top-down guesses that are inevitably of little value. A somewhat more promising approach is to estimate numbers from the bottom up by relating the size of the elite population to plausible slave numbers and by quantifying likely demand for slave labor, especially in farming. This conjectural exercise points to a total Italian slave population on the order of one to one and a half million, lower than earlier guesses of two or three million, but nevertheless a considerable portion of the total population, around 15 percent to 25 percent.[38] We must allow for marked variation within Italy, with strong concentrations of slave ownership in the city of Rome (with its large number of wealthy households and the imperial court) and the western central peninsula. Rural villas – large market-oriented agricultural estates that have been likened to plantations – may have housed large numbers of slaves in Tuscany and Campania, as envisioned by accounts in contemporary agronomic treatises. This concentration is also reflected in concerns about the omnipresence of freed ex-slaves and in occasional documentary sources such as a massive roster of freedmen from the smallish town of Herculaneum, who on any reading of this text must have accounted for a very sizeable share of the local population in the first century CE.[39] That slavery was apparently so strongly clustered in the center of Roman power speaks loudly to its locational significance for the ruling class.

The Greek city-state culture had long been associated with slave ownership, especially in its Aegean core,[40] and this practice appears to have persisted throughout the Roman period. The incorporation of these communities into the Roman Empire therefore increased the overall weight of slavery within the system as a whole. The scale of Greek and Hellenistic slavery generally defies quantitative assessment. For example, the existence of slave-staffed estates on some Aegean islands in the fourth century CE may be understood as a sign of long-term continuities or as the result of the late Roman reconfiguration of resources toward the Propontic region. Galen's casual claim in the second century CE that his hometown of Pergamum was inhabited by

[38] Scheidel 2005a, 66–71.

[39] De Ligt and Garnsey 2012. For the overrepresentation of freedmen in Roman epigraphy, see Mouritsen 2011, 120–41.

[40] See Hunt in this volume.

40,000 (adult male) citizens and 80,000 "wives and slaves" need not be true but at the very least indicates that high rates of slave ownership could be considered a feature of Hellenistic centers.[41] This impression is supported by other sporadic references, such as an inscription about 107 public slaves appropriated from a lesser Anatolian town, a hyperbolic invective regarding the 1,000 or 2,000 attributed to individual wealthy households farther east in Antioch, or a papyrus documenting a slave-rich household in Alexandria.[42] The best data for the Hellenistic world are preserved in the Roman census returns from Egypt in the first three centuries CE, where close to 15 percent of urban residents and some 8 percent of villagers in some areas – mostly in Middle Egypt – were slaves, compared to only 7 percent of the inhabitants of one city farther south in Upper Egypt.[43] We may think in terms of a gradient from relatively large slave numbers in Alexandria (where the record is, however, almost nonexistent) to smaller numbers elsewhere that decreased with distance, but even this rough conjecture rests on shaky ground.

Slave ownership as an elite practice also appears in the Latin West, most notably in a (stylized) reference to a Tripolitanian owner of 400 slaves.[44] More generally, elite status tended to be associated with slave ownership as a matter of course. All this supports the notion of something like a "Slave Society" that encompassed the top tiers of local communities across the empire, for whom slave ownership had become one of the shared practices that lent a measure of coherence to the empire-wide ruling class. This is not to say that the wealthy and powerful generally relied on slave labor for their income: tenancy, wage labor, and presumably also various more traditional kinds of bondage were widespread.[45] Yet the habit of elite members to be surrounded and waited on by slaves can be regarded as a distinctive feature of the Roman world, and it is telling that there is no comparable tradition of relying on hired servants, in striking contrast to later

[41] Harper 2011, 163–70; Galen, 5.49 (ed. Kühn). For slavery in the Hellenistic empires as a Greek custom, see Thompson 2011.

[42] *Inscriptiones Graecae ad Res Romanas Pertinentes*, 4.914; John Chrysostom, *Homily on Matthew*, 63.4; *Oxyrhynchus Papyri*, 44.3197.

[43] Scheidel 2011, 289–90.

[44] Apuleius, *Apology*, 93.

[45] Kehoe 2013.

European practice. This suggests elite preference for service mediated by coercion rather than contracts.

This preference is likewise highlighted by the exceptional visibility of slaves and especially freedmen in the Roman epigraphic record, well beyond Italy proper. That close to half of known individuals in the extant epitaphs of Narbo (Narbonne in Provence) were freedmen does not mean that the city was mostly populated by slaves and ex-slaves, but attests not only to their desire but also to their ability to advertise their status, an ability that was in itself a function of socioeconomic status derived from their attachment to the slave-owning ruling class.[46] The overall impression is of elite circles that heavily relied on slaves both for personal service and for commercial ventures. The use of municipal slaves by urban communities across the Roman world is logically consistent with this preference.[47]

The notion that the practice of slave ownership was a defining characteristic of elite status is also borne out by the very considerable amount of attention it attracted in the Roman legal tradition, which emanated from within and primarily catered to the imperial ruling class, and by slavery's ubiquity in the Roman literary tradition, another elite domain.[48] Across the empire, elite mentality seems to have been infused with the expectation of slave ownership.[49]

In practical terms, with respect to the production of elite wealth, the significance of slave labor probably varied greatly. Overall, slaves may have made up around a tenth of the population of the early empire (first and second centuries), which is itself highly uncertain but often put at around sixty or seventy million.[50] Unlike much of New World slavery, especially as practiced in the United States, Roman-style slavery was extremely malleable. There were hardly any constraints on the kind of occupations slaves might hold, from miners and gladiators to business managers and imperial administrators. Literary, legal, and epigraphic sources attest to their presence in a wide range of activities such as farming, service, retail, education, medicine, and

[46] Woolf 1998, 99, n. 56. For the prominence of freedmen, see earlier in this chapter.

[47] Weiss 2004.

[48] Law: Morabito 1981 has produced an exhaustive collection. On literature, see Joshel 2011, who starts with the apt observation that "slaves are everywhere in Roman literature."

[49] See also Bradley 1994, 29; Morley 2011, 284–85.

[50] Scheidel 2011, 292.

entertainment, in private as well as public settings.[51] This was made possible in no small part by legal and cultural norms that permitted both the ruthless application of coercion and pain incentives for hard and dangerous labor and the bestowal of rewards that were commensurate with skilled services that required loyalty, motivation, and trust. At least for some freed slaves, manumission was a means of transformative social mobility. Formal restrictions were modest and prejudice evanescent: in 193 CE, the son of a freed slave briefly ascended to the throne. This flexibility played no small part in slavery's capacity – potential or realized – for penetrating all spheres of life.

The importance of slavery in the Roman world continued into Late Antiquity. Although no one defends it in its orthodox form today, one of the dominant economic narratives of this period has been the story of transition "from slavery to feudalism."[52] In Marxist terms, the centuries of Late Antiquity were seen as a transitional phase between the ancient slave mode of production and the medieval feudal mode of production based on serfdom. It is always tempting to see Late Antiquity as a period of transition between antiquity and the Middle Ages, but in economic history, this has sometimes taken a rigidly evolutionary form of transition. In the case of labor relations, Late Antiquity was supposed to be the period when the "colonate," a system of tied tenant labor, displaced the slave villa as the dominant form of economic exploitation.[53] We could occupy many pages describing what has happened to this story (parts of which remain in genuine dispute), but it is notable that some of the most prominent Marxists today hold on to a narrative in which Roman slavery was real slavery (part of a slave mode of production) because slaves were exploited on plantations while late antique slavery was not true slavery because slaves were allegedly treated like tenants.[54] This neo-Marxist narrative preserves the pattern of transition from slavery to feudalism. But it fails to convince, both as a reading of the evidence and as an analytical system (which tries to squeeze Late Antiquity into a Procrustean bed of Marxist theory).

[51] Bradley 1994, 57–80; Bodel 2011.
[52] Wickham 2005, 259.
[53] Carrié 1982, 1983.
[54] Vera 1995, 2007.

There were slaves – genuine chattel slaves – throughout Late Antiquity and beyond. In so many ways, it has become increasingly evident that the socioeconomic system of the fourth century was structurally similar to the system that prevailed at the height of Roman power: imperial unity, trade, urbanism, property rights, etc., framed the circum-Mediterranean economy, including the slave system. By the end of the sixth century, the Mediterranean world was a very different place, and after the *coup de grâce* of bubonic plague, it was basically unrecognizable.[55] The concept of a "Slave Society" could help describe the crucial changes that occurred across this period, without resorting to sleights of hand, like arguing that slaves were not really slaves. Mediterranean society in the fourth century remained a "Slave Society," a late cycle of the old Roman imperial system; by the latter half of the sixth century, Mediterranean societies could be better characterized as "Societies with Slaves." For the better part of a millennium, the Mediterranean would then be ringed, with the crucial exception of Islamic heartlands, by "Societies with Slaves." In these "Societies with Slaves," slavery was principally domestic and tilted toward female enslavement, neither of which seems characteristic of Roman slavery as late as the fourth century.[56]

None of the received criteria of a "Slave Society" (numbers, primary production, cultural significance) is as clear as it might be, and none is easy to establish in the case of an ancient world where our evidence is always thinner and more ambiguous than we would like. There is tantalizing evidence nonetheless for the economic and cultural centrality of slavery across the late empire. Contemporary census registers seem to show shocking numbers of slaves.[57] Price schedules indicate the high but not prohibitive value of female and especially male slave labor, but the documents are not adequate to form reliable price series.[58] There are preachers who never cease to worry about the vulnerable bodies of slaves as a temptation to unrestrained violence and sexual laxity.[59] By the sixth century, there were clearly still slaves,

[55] The debate between "continualists" and "catastrophists" persists, but see Ward-Perkins 2005, for a synthesis of the catastrophist view; on the Justinianic Plague, see Little 2007.

[56] Harper 2011, 497–509; further substantiated by Harper 2010.

[57] Harper 2008.

[58] See Harper 2010.

[59] Harper 2011, 280–325.

but the evidence for the fundamental social importance of slavery is distinctly harder to come by. An imperial "Slave Society" had become a fragmented set of "Societies with Slaves."

Perhaps there is a parallel in the distinction between "Societies with Slaves" and "Slave Societies" and the distinction between systems of dependence and the institution of slavery. It in no way trivializes the manifold experiences of captivity or serfdom to draw a clear line between them and slavery. Captivity, of course, can be the prelude to enslavement, but also to other kinds of subjection. With the sheer, radical violence of turning a person into a piece of property, there is a change in quality – and that change is what marks the passage into slavery. Similarly, it in no way trivializes the exploitation inherent in "Societies with Slaves" to draw a line between them and "Slave Societies." When the sheer, radical violence of slavery becomes fundamental to the very organization of a society, it produces that white heat of systemic exploitation characteristic of the "Slave Society."

CONCLUSION

The category of a "Slave Society" is a tool of historical sociology. It was created to chart a way around the rigid orthodoxies of historical materialism, and, in that sense at least, it has been spectacularly successful. Whether it can withstand the full light of comparative sociology is another question; we know inconceivably more about the story of slavery in the fullness of time and space than did the progenitors of the idea of a "Slave Society." Perhaps the best criterion for defining a "Slave Society" is that in the absence of slavery, it would have looked very different, or in extreme cases might not even have existed at all (as in the colonial Caribbean). The Roman world clears this threshold in various ways. While we cannot properly measure to what extent slavery sustained Roman expansionism during the formative Republican period, it may well have been critical at times of mass mobilization wars in the third and first centuries BCE. More generally, it formed part of a system of predatory growth fueled by conquest and plunder. Just as wars mobilized monetary resources for use by the Roman state and especially by its elite, concurrent slaving mobilized labor power and increased elite wealth and autonomy. Inasmuch as the mature empire was the result of this process, slavery may justifiably be considered a driving force of political and economic development.

In terms of its intrinsic character and its structural location, slavery occupied a central position in the Roman economy.[60] By nature, empire and chattel slavery were very much alike, constituting analogous systems of violent and asymmetric domination and predatory appropriation that mobilized and allocated resources and created, sustained, and reinforced inequality and hierarchy. It was not by coincidence that slavery and empire flourished and declined together. Complementing imperial power over collectives, slavery ensured elite power over individuals. The fact that both empire and slavery were rooted in violent domination did not require violence to be continuously expressed or exercised: by necessity, state rulers and slave owners both relied on the effective sharing of claimed resources and ostensible acts of beneficence in the management of their affairs. None of this altered the essence of imperial rule or slavery, nor did it diminish rulers' and owners' entitlement to and capacity for violent intervention. The structural location of Roman slavery was not primarily a function of scale. A vital component of the households and ventures of the dominant groups (be they rulers, landowners, or even merchants), slave labor occupied a central position in the creation, management, and consumption of elite wealth and social power. Slavery and manumission enabled elite members to create distinctive networks of subordination and economic control that increased their autonomy from the free commoner population.

These mechanisms may have been most pervasive in Roman Italy but to varying degrees extended across the empire as a whole. Provincial elites reproduced this pattern contingent on local resources and incentives. In some regions, they had already operated in comparable environments, most notably in Greek and Hellenistic cities, and in others, especially in the West, they adopted Roman-style chattel slavery as an element of a more far-reaching process of culture change. While there may not have been a single "Roman Slave Society," elite circles across the empire came to embrace a distinctive culture of slavery. Roman rule created practices of slavery in some areas and maintained existing ones in others, sustaining what – in

[60] See observations along similar lines in Scheidel 2012, 106–7.

keeping with universalist Roman aspirations – we might very loosely label a "slave world."[61] Slaves did not "make" the Roman world in the same all-encompassing manner in which they "made" the colonial plantation societies of the New World. Yet without them Roman history would look rather different.

[61] We therefore share the concerns expressed by Bradley 1994, 30, and Morley 2011, 284, regarding unduly restrictive or mechanistic definitions of "Slave Society."

4

Ancient Slaveries and Modern Ideology

Noel Lenski

AN ARCHAEOLOGY OF FINLEY'S THEORY 1: THE BACKGROUND

Finley's overriding scholarly concerns, the areas of research to which he devoted much of his career, were the interrelated questions of the ancient economy and ancient slavery. One of his earliest published works was a review – none too favorable – of the magnum opus of his doctoral advisor William Westermann (a monograph-length article on "*Sklaverei*" for the German handbook known as *Pauly-Wissowa*), and Finley's last was an edited volume, published posthumously, titled *Classical Slavery*.[1] In the intervening years he published at least eleven articles or essays, one further edited volume, and one monograph dedicated to slavery.[2] As such Finley was hardly unique in his generation, for questions of the ancient economy and its dependence on slave labor had sparked debate since the late eighteenth century, and this had reached a fevered pitch by the mid-twentieth, stoked by the tinderbox of accumulated scholarly material and by the burning

[1] Finley 1935, 1987. More on Finley's career-long interest in and scholarship on slavery at Momigliano 1987; Shaw 1998; Perry 2014; Vlassopoulos 2016. Vlassopoulos's vision is the most global and traces a somewhat different trajectory than this study, especially because it is not focused so narrowly on the "Slave Society/Societies with Slaves" binary.

[2] Finley 1959; 1960a; 1960b; 1961; 1962; 1964; 1965b; 1968; 1973a, ch. 3; 1979b; 1980[1998]; 1982.

debate between Marxist and non-Marxist historians in the mid-century moment.

Finley outlines the spectrum of this earlier work on slavery in the first chapter of his *Ancient Slavery and Modern Ideology* (*ASMI*) in a survey astonishing for its breadth of learning, and its tendentiousness.[3] The argument is dismissive of earlier work, serving to highlight its inadequacy and the concomitant need for correction, which Finley then claims to provide. This brush-clearing exercise has served well to create a prevailing impression that Finley is the first serious scholar to forge a clear path into the question, an impression many have been content to take at face value. The fact is, however, that Finley's approach both in *ASMI* and in his earlier studies shows distinct traces of the earlier debate that supply Finley with most of his assumptions and insights. Four strains are particularly salient, deriving respectively from Marx, Weber, Polanyi, and the so-called *oikos* debate between Bücher and Meyer.

As mentioned in the introductory chapter, Finley maintained an active interest in Marxism in his early years, and although he abandoned any affiliations he may have had with communist organizations in the aftermath of World War II and set himself up in opposition to contemporary Marxist historians, he would have been the first to admit that Marx had an indelible impact on his thought. As he stated in a 1976 interview, "Marxism is therefore built into my intellectual experience, what the Greeks would have called my *paideia*."[4] This was of course not uncommon among mid-twentieth-century historians, ancient and modern, British and continental. The fact is that Marx had in many ways framed the debate about economic development in terms that were – and in some ways still are – difficult to escape.

Marx and his followers conceived of the ancient world as characterized by the "slave mode of production," one of five (or perhaps six – as discussed later in this chapter) stages of development in the history of material relations outlined in his theory of historical materialism: primitive communism, the slave mode of production (MOP), the serf MOP, the capitalist MOP, and socialism. According to Marx, ancient Greco-Roman labor was fundamentally the province

[3] The problems with this chapter are outlined by Nafissi 2005, 244–46; Vlassopoulos 2016, 76.

[4] Finley 1976a, 201.

of slaves, who eventually reacted against the contradictions inherent in their repression through violent revolution, and thereby ushered in a new "serf" mode that would endure up to the dawn of the capitalist world. The concept was only ever elaborated by Marx in any detail in his *Outlines (Grundrisse) of the Critique of Political Economy*, a series of notebooks written in winter 1857/1858 but first published in 1939–41.[5] Nevertheless, Marx mentions his scheme in his essay *On the Critique of Political Economy* published in 1859.[6] Moreover, the *Grundrisse* were available to Engels, who developed the theory of historical materialism in the *Anti-Dühring* (1878) and *Origins of the Family* (1884), and, through whom the scheme gained wide currency in early twentieth-century Marxist historiography.[7] Its lexicon and conceptual apparatus have influenced historiography more broadly up to the present.[8]

Meanwhile, a broader set of assumptions and methodologies pervasive throughout the corpus of Marx and Engels had worked their way into academic discourse in ways that affected Finley profoundly. First and foremost was the quintessential Marxist tenet that historical development was fundamentally a matter of material relations and relations of production.[9] Equally influential were Marx's essentially Hegelian notion of a stadial or evolutionary development in history and his belief that dialectical relationships between classes led to conflict and, through its resolution, historical progress. Marx argued that in history all such conflicts ultimately revolved around class struggle over control of the means of production, and that these resulted in crisis and revolution, overturning one system in favor of the next. Also characteristic was Marx's desire for holistic and typological categorization: entire epochs could be characterized as overdetermined by essentially uniform patterns of economic and social organization. Equally implicit was a high degree of Western ethnocentrism, for the patterns Finley identified were explicitly indicative of Western Europe, which Marx and his followers treated as the core drivers of

[5] Marx 1939–41, 375–415, most easily accessible in Marx 1964, 67–120; cf. Hobsbawm 2011, 127–75.

[6] Marx 1859, 9, with further references at Hahn 1971, 30 nn. 5–7.

[7] Engels 1878[1962], 166–71; cf. Welskopf 1957, 39–70.

[8] See, for example, Wickham 2005; Banaji 2010.

[9] Which was itself spawned by Marx's engagement with the new science of political economy, Morley 1998.

historical progress. Every single one of these assumptions affected Finley, some by creating the intellectual apparatus underpinning his own inquiries, others by providing counterpoints for the development of conclusions at variance with Marx and the Marxists.

Marx was, of course, far from Finley's only antecedent to have explored questions of economic development over the longue durée. The late nineteenth century witnessed a flourish of debates on the question, at least one of which had an equal if not greater impact on Finley – the so-called *oikos* (household) controversy. In a series of essays published in 1893 under the title *Die Entstehung der Volkswirtschaft*, political economist Karl Bücher offered a bold thesis based in contemporary anthropological debates that, as Marx had assumed, there had been no capitalist political economy prior to the modern world, but that the ancient economies of Greece and Rome had instead developed around the structures and principles of the household (*Haushaltswirtschaft*). Bücher also believed in stadial development, but his structuring principles were not "modes of production" but rather social organizational units: the tribe, household, city, and nation. In the ancient world, Bücher argued, economic relations remained fundamentally rural and rooted in patterns derived from the family, such that economic thinking simply reproduced the structures of the household in the context of material exchange. The ancient economy was thus nothing more than an extended system of autarkic households (*oikoi*), a type of unit that managed labor through the family that, as it grew in scale, included slaves. Bücher's theory had the obvious implication that antiquity witnessed no true differentiation of labor, no developed markets, and no growth in the scale and complexity of trade.[10]

This "Primitivist" thesis drew immediate criticism from ancient historian Eduard Meyer, who in two studies of 1895 and 1898, deployed his more expansive knowledge of the ancient sources to show that there is, in fact, abundant evidence for labor differentiation, markets, and long-distance trade even in much earlier economies than Greece and Rome.[11] Furthermore, Meyer argued, the rise of large-scale slavery in Classical antiquity was evidence not of economic primitivism but its

[10] Bücher 1893, republished in facsimile in Finley 1979a.

[11] Meyer 1895[1924]; 1898[1924], republished in facsimile at Finley 1979a. On the controversy, see Nafissi 2005, 17–54.

opposite: the commercial demand generated by the growth of the ancient economy in the Classical period could not be met by free labor, partly because the free poor – who had become fully enfranchised in their respective polities through the rise of democracies – were unwilling to take jobs, and partly because their labor was too expensive. Given that ancient societies engaged in regular warfare and slaves were its natural by-product, the capitalist producers of ancient cities thus turned to slave labor to meet production demands. Then, as warfare diminished under the Roman Empire and the slave supply dried up, rural landowners were forced to turn the free poor into their bound tenants toward the same ends, although demand was greatly diminished by the collapse of the ancient capitalist economy. Meyer's synthesis in many ways set the terms of the debate down to Finley's own day and was especially influential on Finley's teacher, Westermann.[12] Indeed, it has been observed that Finley borrowed a good deal of his understanding of the ancient economy and of ancient slavery from Meyer, even if he roundly criticized Meyer in print.[13]

The primitivist-modernist debate was soon joined by sociologist Max Weber, who combined a deep knowledge of the ancient sources with an uncanny eye for explanatory models. Weber's work on the ancient economy focused primarily on the Roman Empire, whose geographic and economic scale made it a better test case for the kinds of holistic arguments wagered by his predecessors than either ancient Mesopotamia or Greece. In the end, Weber came down on the side of Bücher and the primitivists, but only after conceding many of the points Meyer had irrefutably proven. Weber thus followed Meyer in accepting that Classical *civilization* was fundamentally based in complex cities (rather than the household), but he argued the ancient *economy* was anchored in the countryside, which remained the primary generator of surplus. This contradiction meant that, although antiquity witnessed the rise of markets and the development of long-distance trade, it remained fettered to a primitive locus of production.

[12] See Finley's critique of Westermann at Finley 1935, 1980, 52–55 (reprint Finley 1998, 120–23).

[13] Finley 1980, 46–47 (reprint Finley 1998, 114–17), esp. "In sum, Meyer's lecture on ancient slavery is not only as close to nonsense as anything I can remember written by a historian of such eminence, but violates the basic canons of historical scholarship." On Finley and Meyer, see Nafissi 2005, 71–72, 79–80, 191–94, 204–06, 245–51; Edward Harris 2012, 4–6.

This was above all the result of one particularly primitive obsession – warfare. The large-scale warfare incessantly engaged in by the Greeks and Romans generated a surplus of slaves who were fed into the labor stream to man the landed estates of the elite. This glut of servile labor displaced free workers even as it devalued labor as a social good, with the result that the dispossessed masses remained underemployed and restive even as the ruling class that developed the urban civilization characteristic of Classical antiquity was enriched. For Weber, then, "the civilization of antiquity was based upon slavery,"[14] for it was the slave who allowed the household of the lord to expand into a capitalist enterprise. At the same time, this very paradox – the reliance of urban civilization on slave labor – doomed the ancient economy to primitivism, for the system's most dynamic producer (the slave-driven *oikos*) kept production out of the hands of free labor and out of the centers of potential industrial development (the cities). In the absence of these (fundamentally modern) economic drivers (producer cities and an urban bourgeoisie), the ancient economy thus faltered once regular warfare dropped off in the course of the High Empire. In Late Antiquity, so Weber argued, we thus witness the rise of bound tenant laborers (*coloni*) who replace slaves as the generators of surplus for an elite who remained on the land, and we therefore move from a city-based ancient world to the estate-based Middle Ages.[15]

The last entrant into this debate to have had a major impact on Finley's thought was Karl Polanyi, the most prominent primitivist of Finley's own day and a personal friend of Finley himself. Polanyi was a one-time Marxist who abandoned his dogmatism in favor of a modified – that is to say overtly Christianized – version of socialism. In keeping with the mid-twentieth-century Zeitgeist, Polanyi expanded on the ideas of earlier primitivists by folding the work of anthropologists into his economic models for premodern societies. He too proceeded from the assumption that capitalist economic structures were a modern phenomenon not to be found in European societies prior to the nineteenth century. He argued instead that these precapitalist societies functioned with economic systems characterized not by exchange but rather by redistribution and reciprocity. There was

[14] Weber 1896[1976], 392.

[15] Weber 1891[2008], chapter 4; 1909[1976], 336–66.

no rationalist economic thought that allowed for the detachment of material relations from the social realm in the manner of the modern marketplace. Instead economic behaviors were always embedded in social and political structures that did not respond to the logic of supply and demand.[16] Like Marxism, Polanyi's theory of embedded economies was holistic, generalizable, and nomological: it explained all structures that governed economic relations across time according to crystalline, definable principles.

By the time Finley began publishing on slavery in the late 1950s, he was deeply aware of and variously informed by each of these traditions. From the Marxists he had absorbed the assumption that history was fundamentally an inquiry into material relations, that it could be explained in evolutionary terms, that it involved some version of class struggle (although, following Weber, Finley preferred to focus on status as the fundamental organizational determinant), and that it was ideally explained in terms that were holistic, generalizable, and nomological. From Bücher he drew on primitivism, but a version of it fully informed by the sorts of objections Meyer had raised from the ancient source material. Finley's primitivism was, in other words, Weberian, for in addition to his interest in status, Finley was deeply indebted to Weber for his emphasis on the predominance of countryside over city. Finley's ancient cities, like Weber's, were consumers rather than producers – in contrast with the cities of the late Middle Ages and modernity. And while Finley rejected Weber's argument that warfare drove the rise of slavery, he accepted the belief that antiquity had given way to feudalism, a shift he attributed to the economic impact of self-generating bureaucratic bloat – a Weberian mainstay – and the rise of new semi-dependent statuses like the *humiliores* and bound *coloni* of the later Roman Empire – a point emphasized by both Meyer and Weber and closely related to Marx's rise of the "serf MOP."[17] From Polanyi, Finley took the notion of an ancient economy embedded in social and political concerns and thus unable to develop in response to market mechanisms. He could not, however, abide the universalizing cross-cultural explanations of which

[16] Polanyi 1944, esp. 43–55. See also Nafissi 2005, 149–72, on the biographical background to the formulation of Polanyi's theory; cf. Wilk and Cliggett 2007, 3–15; Morley 2009, 21–49.

[17] Finley 1973a, 85–93; 1980, 123–49 (reprint Finley 1998, 191–217).

Polanyi was so fond and preferred instead to focus more narrowly on the Western, and especially the Classical world. This last reflects the final strain of Marxism evident in Finley's approach, for while he was very widely read in global history, his published work shows that he was also convinced not just of the exceptionality but also the exemplarity of the Western world. Greece and Rome were the only two civilizations before modernity to have displayed the civilizational features that would eventually take full flower in modernity, including chattel slavery.

AN ARCHAEOLOGY OF FINLEY'S THEORY 2: DEVELOPING THE MODEL

Finley had been trained as a Greek historian and it was always from this background that he approached the question of slavery. When he undertook to explore the problem more deeply, he began by writing a series of four articles on slaveholding by the Greeks. The first, published in 1959 and titled "Was Greek Civilization Based on Slave Labor?", took up this fundamental question (posed already by Meyer and Weber, among others),[18] and answered it with a resounding yes. His pathway to this answer, however, also led him into the concern that would most occupy him for at least the next several years, and arguably for the rest of his career: can we really speak of "Greek Slavery" in singular and holistic terms given that "Greek Society" consisted of more than a thousand poleis each of which manifested distinctive traditions, and most of which imposed some form of unfreedom on a sector of their populace, even if in many instances these were not nearly as restrictive as, say, the slavery of the US South? Contrary to Weber, who founded his argument for a slave-based Classical civilization on estate production, Finley chose instead to focus on political structures and in so doing followed hints laid out in Meyer, who had contended that it was the introduction of democratic governments that had insulated lower-status free men from the labor market. Following similar logic, Finley argued that Athens, the city with the most fully developed slave system, was also Greece's most advanced democracy, and he therefore

[18] Finley's title reproduces that of Zimmern 1909, although Finley makes no reference to this study.

concluded, paradoxically, that "One aspect of Greek history, in short, is the advance, hand in hand, of freedom *and* slavery."[19] The rise of Greek slavery was, in other words, to be correlated with the Athenian invention of political freedom.

Finley again took up the question of "The Servile Statuses in ancient Greece" in an article published in 1960 that explores the spectrum of statuses attested across Greek societies.[20] In it he shows how difficult it was for the Greeks to define slavery in any clear-cut fashion. Instead, he argues, the various unfree statuses of the Greeks are best categorized as the product of a bundle of privileges and powers over things like property, control of labor and movement, control of family, social mobility, and civic and religious rights. Here again he repeats the tenet: "It is a fact, I believe, that social and political progress in the Greek *poleis* was accompanied by the triumph of chattel slavery over the other statuses of dependent labour," even as he is willing to concede that this triumph only occurred in a minority – indeed a small minority – of the many civic contexts we could properly call Greek.

Some of the same ideas are aired in "Between Slavery and Freedom" (1964), although here Finley also breaks much new ground.[21] First and foremost, he introduces the fundamentally Marxist idea of revolution by arguing that the few ancient societies that did advance out of the widespread prevalence of lesser forms of unfreedom (debt bondage, helotage, serfdom) did so because of revolt on the part of those whose claims to status had been compromised. Thus the *hektemoroi* and *agogimoi* of sixth-century Athens and those bound by *nexum* in Rome were able to throw off these lesser forms of servitude, but succeeded in doing so only because they had some residual claims to status in the first place. Slaves, Finley explains, never did, with the result that in Athens they never rebelled, and in Rome they did so only during a brief window between 135 and 71 BCE. This argument was clearly a broadside at the dogmatic Marxists, for whom Rome's slave revolts were evidence of the veracity of historical materialism and the catalyst for a shift in the mode of production. The same article also first aired some of the ideas that would later become the

[19] Finley 1959, 72 (reprint Finley 1960a, 164).

[20] Finley 1960b. The question of the range of dependent statuses in Greek culture was already an important one in the work of Finley's teacher, Westermann.

[21] Finley 1964.

building blocks of his model in the *Ancient Economy* (*AE*) and *Ancient Slavery and Modern Ideology* (*ASMI*): that there were in Athens no labor activities in which slaves did not engage, but also none that slaves and only slaves performed (a case Finley himself then refutes with the mention of mining); that Classical Athens was atypical among Near Eastern and even Greek civilizations for having no semi-servile dependent statuses (a problem that worried Finley more than any other, precisely because it so obviously undercut his argument that "Greek civilization" was characterized fundamentally by "Slave Society"); and that Roman slave estates (*latifundia*) were best compared to the plantations of the US South as models of slave agriculture *par excellence* (early evidence of a bias for American slavery as the consummate paradigm for all "Slave Societies" – on which more in what follows). Ultimately, the article concludes:

> I might close with a highly schematic model of the history of ancient society. It moved from a society in which status ran along a continuum towards one in which statuses were bunched at the two ends, the slave and the free – a movement which was most nearly completed in the societies which most attract our attention for obvious reasons. And then, under the Roman Empire, the movement was reversed; ancient society gradually returned to a continuum of statuses and was transformed into what we call the medieval world.[22]

Finley's model thus owed more to Meyer and Weber than Marx, for it emphasized rise and fall rather than historical progression. But instead of putting weight on the shifting valences of warfare as the driver of slave supply and production, Finley's pure ancient slavery was thought to have been refined into its essence in the political centrifuge of democracy, which meant that it was bound to dissipate once that centrifuge had been turned off.

Finley's final exploratory article appeared in 1965 under the title "La servitude pour dettes" (reprinted in translation as "Debt-Bondage and the Problem of Slavery") which laid the final groundwork for the case he would eventually make in *ASMI*. Here he returned to the problem of semi-dependent statuses but presented new arguments based on comparative material from the ancient Near East. He began by examining loan contracts, which, he argued, were originally introduced not to garner interest payments but to secure labor through

[22] Finley 1964, 249 (reprint Finley 1981, 132).

the impressment of debt-bondsmen. Here he first airs his Polanyian conviction, crucial to *ASMI*, that wage labor was a recent invention, virtually unknown to the primitive economies of antiquity. He also posits a fundamental difference between "Western Society" and "Near Eastern Society," the latter of which, he ventured, "was always a stratified one, in which large sections of the population were never wholly free."[23] This contrasted with Greece and Rome, where the oppressed debtor classes rebelled rather than continue to abide in diminished states of unfreedom:

> The effect, in any event, was that debt-bondage was abolished *tout court*, by political action, and its return was prevented by the growing political power of the emancipated class as they became part of the self-governing community, in which they could use their position for both political and economic ends.[24]

With this, Finley had put the finishing touches on his construction of a trigger mechanism, a switch that turned on the centrifuge of freedom necessary to refine slavery down to its purest form. Solon's elimination of debt bondage in the 590s and Rome's elimination of *nexum* in 326 had foreclosed the option of enslavement for Athenian and Roman citizens and thus generated an acute need for the deracinated labor of slaves to provide for the burgeoning – if still primitive – economies of these two paradigmatic states.

THE MODEL AND ITS CONTEXT

As noted in the introductory chapter, Finley first aired the "Slave Society/Societies with Slaves" antinomy in 1968 in an entry for the *International Encyclopedia of the Social Sciences*. This new encyclopedia replaced the earlier *Encyclopaedia of the Social Sciences*, first published in 1934, in which Finley's former dissertation advisor had played a crucial role in the composition of the article on "slavery."[25] This earlier piece had been divided up among five historians, who covered, respectively, primitive, ancient, medieval, general modern, and US South slavery, and who deliberately eschewed any attempt to create a

[23] Finley 1965b, 181 (reprint Finley 1981, 164).
[24] Finley 1965b, 184 (reprint Finley 1981, 166).
[25] Knight, Phillips, Stern, Westermann, and Williams 1934. Finley himself had worked as an editorial assistant for the encyclopedia in this period.

unified model. Finley, by contrast, aimed to offer a holistic synthesis that would cover slavery as a unitary global phenomenon. To do so, he avoided fine-grained particularities and focused on definitional and universalizing criteria, above all the importance of property and what he termed the economic "location" of slave labor – concepts that would prove crucial for what would follow. The article put the Classical societies and above all the US South in the spotlight as paradigmatic while using the societies of the ancient and medieval Near and Far East as counterpoints – paradigmatic instances of lesser forms of dependency. The theory had thus been registered, but it awaited elaboration.

This first occurred in the third chapter of *AE* (first edition 1973) and was then brought to full fruition in the second chapter of *ASMI* (1980), a book that grew from a series of lectures Finley delivered at the Collège de France in 1978.[26] Because the two chapters cover much the same ground, it is most economical to treat them in tandem. Both begin with Finley's omnipresent concern over the variety of dependent statuses, which, he emphasizes, cannot be adequately described with the commonly mentioned tripartite distinction between free, slave, and serf. As he had argued in "Servitude pour dettes / Debt-Bondage," the varied forms of dependency are thus best set along a spectrum between two poles, pure freedom and pure slavery. While admitting that neither ideal type ever truly exists, he once again returns to an investigation of the pathway ancient Greece (and to a lesser degree Rome) took to arrive remarkably close to both pure slavery and pure freedom. The latter, Finley argues, was achieved through the "radical commodification" of the slave body – which entailed its treatment as property, its total subjection to the master's power, and its kinlessness. The key to the "Slave Society," Finley claims, is to understand the "social location of slavery," by which he means two things: 1) the employment of slaves (where did they work?); and 2) the social structure of slaveholding (which status groups owned slaves?). The hallmark of a "Slave Society," Finley argues, is when slaves worked in the sector most important for the generation of economic surplus (which in Finley's primitivist

[26] Nafissi 2005, ch. 10, sees the period in which *AE* and *ASMI* were written as one of retreat from bolder Weberian positions into the less defensible primitivism of Polanyi. Tompkins 2008, 130–31, challenges this.

understanding meant agriculture), and when they were owned by the elite stratum of society (which relied on slaves as the primary generators of its wealth).

In *ASMI,* he fully fleshes out his characterization of the "Slave Society" with the *criteria* mentioned in Chapter 1 of this volume: 1) slaves must constitute a significant percentage of the population (20 percent or more); 2) they must play a significant role in surplus production; and 3) they must be important enough to exercise a pervasive cultural influence. He also lays out three *conditions* for the rise of the "Slave Society": 1) the private ownership of land with significant concentration in the hands of an elite; 2) the development of commodity production and markets for surplus; and 3) the unavailability of an internal labor supply. Free wage labor, Finley once again claims with echoes of Polanyi, was a "sophisticated latecomer" that was "spasmodic, casual, marginal" in antiquity. The ancients thus needed to turn to dependent laborers to meet their productive needs. But how did it arise that the elite would turn to "chattel slaves" as opposed to other forms of dependents? Finley rejects the Weberian claim that this arose from the surplus of captives generated by conquest. Instead, he contends, Greek chattel slavery's rise was triggered by the elimination of lesser forms of dependency in the wake of Solon's abolition of debt bondage (the argument he developed in the four preliminary studies). He also contends that the same mechanism that forced the rise of pure slavery also occasioned its decline; here Finley is much more comfortable offering a straight Weberian line: the bloating of bureaucracy and taxes in the late Roman world, along with the introduction of new status distinctions applicable to free citizens, reintroduced lesser forms of dependency that could supplant chattel slavery.

Even as Finley was developing his model, debates were raging over the history and sociology of ancient slavery in both West and East. Finley was himself witness to a particularly memorable manifestation of these when he attended the Eleventh International Historical Congress in Stockholm in 1960.[27] There epic fights erupted between Eastern Bloc Marxist historians and their Western counterparts, particularly those represented by the Mainz Academy for the Study of

[27] Finley 1980, 56, 60–62 (reprint Finley 1998, 124, 128–30). On this event and its relation to Finley's historiography on slavery, see Tompkins 2014.

Slavery. The latter, founded in West Germany in emphatic response to Marxist methods, championed the empirical investigation of sources for ancient slavery while downplaying the inherent inhumanity of slave systems using the examples of Athens and particularly Rome as practitioners of a less virulent form of the institution. Finley had no patience for the apologetic aspects of the latter approach and devoted the third chapter of *ASMI* to its refutation. This was not, however, his primary concern.

Much more important for Finley were contemporary Marxist debates regarding the so-called Asiatic Mode of Production. Marx's earliest formulation of the stadial theory of historical materialism in *Toward a Critique of Political Economy* had actually listed another MOP, termed "Asiatic" – a form of material relations that was believed to have predated the development of private property and was characterized by collective exploitation controlled through a despotic political elite via taxation and corvée labor. The Asiatic MOP was thought to have been typical of the "Oriental" states of Mesopotamia and Egypt that predated Greece and Rome.[28] Because Marx later spoke of only slave, serf, and capitalist MOPs, and in this was followed by Engels, early Soviet historians questioned the validity of the Asiatic mode, and by 1934 Soviet academia had come to reject it as incompatible with Marxist orthodoxy. This was then reinforced by Stalinist state policies that bracketed the "Asiatic mode" not as one of the crucial stages of historical materialism but rather as a distinct and permanent other, an economic mode founded in Oriental despotisms that had prevailed in "Asia" down to the twentieth century – an interpretation that furnished a valuable ideological tool for an expansionist Russia promoting the necessity of intervention in revolutionary China. Nevertheless, the Asiatic MOP returned to the academic spotlight in the 1960s, as Finley was himself well aware.[29] This was particularly because of the work of eminent Assyriologist Igor M. Dyakonov, who argued for a broader definition of slavery that included all forms of subjection to forced labor, regardless of whether they entailed the control of

[28] For sources and discussion, see Welskopf 1957, 96–115; Dunn 1982; cf. Tompkins 2014, 442–48.

[29] Finley 1965a; 1968, 312, shows an early awareness of the debate in Marxist historical circles.

people as chattels.[30] Dyakonov drew criticism from within the Marxist historical community and from Finley himself, who singled him out in *ASMI* for his "rearguard" attempt to preserve the "Engelsian unilinear scheme."[31]

In his engagement with this debate, Finley was especially influenced by a brilliant article published in 1971 by Hungarian Classicist István Hahn on the subject of "The Beginnings of ancient societal formations in Greece and the Problem of the so-called Asiatic Mode of Production."[32] Hahn had also reacted against Soviet historians' efforts to broaden the definition of slavery. In order to differentiate between the manifold instances of ancient "dependency" and some purer form, Hahn outlined one negative and five positive preconditions necessary for the rise of what he termed the "Slaveholding-Society" (*Sklavenhaltergesellschaft*) – a term with wider currency in mid-century Marxist historiography that appears to have given rise to Finley's coinage "Slave Society."[33] These included: 1. The absence of developed labor-saving technology; 2. Private landownership; 3. Developed commodity production and a secure export market; 4. Suitable mid- to large-sized business interests (factories or estates); 5. High levels of economic organizational capacity; and 6. Sufficient export of enslaved laborers from underdeveloped neighboring peoples. Hahn's numbers 2. and 3. corresponded directly with two of Finley's three conditions for the rise of a "Slave Society" as laid out in *AE* and *ASMI*. So too Hahn's negative condition was included by Finley in both *AE* and *ASMI* but not listed among his three formal criteria.[34] Finley departed from his predecessor's model, however, in omitting Hahn's numbers 4–6 and substituting in their stead his own new negative

[30] Summarized at Dyakonov 1976–77.

[31] Finley 1980, 70 (reprint Finley 1998, 138); cf. Zelin 1968; Hahn 1971.

[32] Hahn 1971, cited at Finley 1980, 164, n. 12 (reprint Finley 1998, 232, n. 12).

[33] But see the argument in Chapter 11 of this volume, where Singleton notes that the term "Slave Society" was used in Goveia 1965. Finley's terminology and model are already present in the dissertation of Salem 1978. See also Hobsbawm 1971, 42: "Recently there have been important advances toward the study of certain types of society – notably those based on slavery in the Americas (the slave-societies of antiquity appear to be in recession)." Higman 2001, argues that the term "Slave Society" began formally to be used of trans-Atlantic systems in the mid-nineteenth century and entered the academy of the 1960s via two interrelated paths, one through Americanists, the other Marxists (by which he means Finley).

[34] Finley 1980, 90, 137–39 (reprint Finley 1998, 158, 205–07). See also Finley 1965c.

condition, "the unavailability of an internal labor supply." The shift is striking and requires explanation.

In a note in *ASMI* Finley openly acknowledges his debt to Hahn for the development of his theory, and he restates the same in a 1982 article written in response to reactions to the "Slave Society" theory published in the Italian journal *Opus*.[35] He does not, however, explain the reason for his divergence from Hahn's scheme, which was, it could be argued, already more developed than Finley's and more carefully rooted in economic criteria. In the absence of explicit engagement with this omission by Finley, it seems safest to assume that he sidestepped aspects of Hahn in order to preserve a place for the model he himself had already developed in his four preliminary studies of 1959–65. These, of course, had emphasized the role of political rather than economic conditions in the rise of chattel slavery in Greece. Finley thus substituted his condition, which had already been elaborated in political terms (the invention of personal freedom) for Hahn's final three (large economic concerns, economic organization, and ready supplies of slaves). In so doing, however, Finley needed to rebrand the "invention of freedom" argument as an economic matter, a shift that necessitated recourse to a primitivist economic assumption he derived from the work of Polanyi: when debt-bondage was abolished, wage labor was not available as a viable alternative, forcing Athens to turn instead to chattel slaves.

This of course means that, in retooling Hahn, Finley created what purported to be a nomological model with global implications, but its elaboration was contingent on political circumstances peculiar to Classical Athens. This flaw was already apparent in the preliminary articles and particularly "Debt Bondage and the Problem of Slavery," which had explicitly denied that any Asiatic society had been capable of refining the ideal type of chattel slavery. Here we see a Western bias characteristic of Finley's broader corpus that ultimately traces back to Marx and his mid-twentieth-century followers – the Asiatic MOP debate. For this reason, Finley's mechanism for the activation of the genuine "Slave Society," his on-off switch, cannot help but seem compromised in comparison with the more globally applicable scheme

35 Finley 1980, 167, nn. 50, 54 (reprint Finley 1998, 235, n. 50, 54); Finley 1982, 205 (reprint Finley 1998, 272).

of Hahn from which it derived.[36] Hahn's model accounts for cycles of development in which unfreedom is intensified and then abates at particular junctures in history due to strictly economic factors. His intensified *Sklavenhaltergesellschaft*, like Finley's, was a relative rarity in world history, but it was not bound to Western contexts nor was it tied to the accidents of Classical Greek (and, by extension, Western) political development. Indeed, Hahn had argued that similar ancient "slaveholding societies" had arisen not just in Classical Greece and Rome, but also in the Third Dynasty of Ur; in Hammurabi's Babylon[37]; in the great temple economies of the Egyptian New Dynasty; in the Phoenician cities of the ninth to seventh centuries BCE; and in Carthage from the fifth to the third centuries BCE.[38] Finley, by contrast, proceeded with his previously formulated assumptions that 1) political freedom and purified slavery always marched in lockstep, and therefore 2) only Western societies with evolved understandings of individual freedom were capable of evolving into "Slave Societies."[39] There is thus evidence from his first article in 1959 down to his final publications on slavery that Finley regarded all "Asiatic" societies – by which he meant not just the ancient Near East, but all non-Western societies – as a monolithic "other," incapable of pure freedom and, by extension, pure slavery.[40]

[36] Shaw 1998, 26–29, is clearly aware of the weakness of Finley's "negative condition."

[37] For a reassessment of Assyrian and Babylonian slavery, which demonstrates the intensification of slaveholding in the contexts emphasized by Hahn, see Jursa and Tost forthcoming; cf. Dandamaev 1984; Wiggerman 2000; Baker 2001; Jursa 2010, 224–28, 232–40.

[38] See Chapter 1.

[39] Finley's lifelong interest in personal freedom as a fundamentally Western – ultimately Greek – invention is attested throughout his oeuvre, e.g., Finley 1973b, 1976b; cf. Shaw and Saller 1981, xii.

[40] Finley 1959, 72; cf. Finley 1960a, 164: "The pre-Greek world – the world of the Sumerians, Babylonians, Egyptians, and Assyrians … was, in a very profound sense, a world without free men." Finley 1980, 67 (reprint Finley 1998, 135): "But the Greeks and Romans transformed this 'primordial fact' into something new and wholly original in world history (and something rare throughout history), namely, an institutionalized system of large-scale employment of slave labour in both the countryside and the cities"; cf. Finley 1980, 69–70 (reprint Finley 1998, 137–38); Finley 1960b (reprint Finley 1981, 142–43); Finley 1964, 237–38; cf. Finley 1981, 120–21. Momigliano 1987 offers a related critique of Finley's slave theory in noting the studied absence of engagement with Jewish slavery, but the most direct attempt to grapple with this weakness of Finley's approach is presented in Liverani 1982, as Finley 1982, 203–04 (reprint Finley 1998, 269–70), is well aware.

For its day, Finley's model in many ways represented a step forward. It replaced Marxist notions of "modes of production" by eschewing assumptions concerning stadial historical development and instead accounting for a spectrum of dependent statuses in antiquity – chattel slaves were only one sort of dependent laborers in a world too complex to be characterized by a single sweeping MOP. It also met the objections of modernists that slavery played varying roles in each society and that, despite their ubiquity in ancient societies, slaves were often not the most important labor source for agricultural and industrial production. What mattered to Finley were only those situations in which slaves provided the main source of surplus for the elite. Furthermore, it responded to those inclined to humanize Greco-Roman slavery by emphasizing the brutality entailed by systems of chattel servitude regardless of whether they are ancient or modern. Above all, it opened the door to comparative slave studies, for the similarities Finley identified between ancient and modern societies were both striking and useful for defining the patterns and parameters of slaveholding practice across cultures and periods.

Nevertheless, Finley's progress came with costs. The first was massive oversimplification, for even as he overturned the holistic model of the Marxists, he replaced it with an equally sweeping ideal scheme – the "Slave Society/Societies with Slaves" binary. Neither could the new model explain relationships of dependency in the less intensive "Societies with Slaves" – which it bracketed as fundamentally separate from slavery studies and, by implication, less worthy of interest[41] – nor was it precise enough to account for the massive differences between the very few "genuine Slave Societies" whose existence it conceded. Second, it sacrificed dynamism, for the establishment of a binary necessitated the creation of an activation mechanism – an on-off switch for the "Slave Society" – that turned what must have been a process (the intensification and abatement of ancient slavery) into a discrete event that could rapidly bifurcate a culture into antinomic ideal types. A society either was or was not a "genuine Slave Society."[42] Third, it implied a false equivalency between the "radical commodification" of the slave body as property and the rise of the "genuine

[41] Vlassopoulos 2016, 85–88.
[42] See especially Vlassopoulos 2016, 91–94.

Slave Society." For Finley, the conversion of the servile dependent into property, into the "means of production," was truly realized only in the "genuine slave societies," which were alone capable of bunching status at the two extremes of slave and free.[43] Yet this assumption is easily falsifiable, for countless "societies with slaves" have taken the step of radical commodification, treating some dependents as chattels even while holding other laborers (that is, other forms of laborer) in less restrictive forms of servility or even contracting with them as free laborers.[44] Fourth, the model failed to engage adequately with the historical contingency of the notion of chattel property. As noted in Chapter 1 of this volume, attempting to solve the complicated question of "what is a slave" with recourse to a "property definition" is ultimately a strategy for deferring meaning by pretending that "property" is a simple and universal category – which, as Finley himself was well aware, it is not. Finally, the new model was predicated on ethnocentrism, for the causal factors Finley established for the creation of a "Slave Society" connected it to the rise of personal freedom – in Greek and (to a lesser degree) Roman society and, by implication, the Atlantic slave societies (particularly the US South). More importantly, because Finley proceeded from the assumption – deeply ingrained in Western thought since Herodotus – that only Western societies developed notions of personal freedom while Eastern societies were by nature given to despotism, all non-Western societies were ipso facto excluded from consideration as "genuine Slave Societies."[45]

FINLEY AND THE GREEKS

Finley's model offered the obvious benefit of translating ancient slavery into a global realm, allowing it simultaneously to inform and be informed by comparison with slaveholding practices in other

[43] This is especially clear in Finley 1980, 77 (reprint Finley 1998, 145) in the paragraph beginning "Yet, for all the advantages (or apparent advantages), slavery was a late and relatively infrequent form of involuntary labour." The same equivalency between chattel slavery and the "Slave Society" is apparent in Shaw 1998, 11–24.

[44] The most obvious examples are the societies of Southeast Asia, discussed by Anthony Reid in Chapter 16 of this volume, but another excellent example would be the later Roman empire, discussed briefly later in this chapter.

[45] The notion that ancient Near Eastern societies had no concept of personal freedom is disproven in von Dassow 2011; cf. Vlassopoulos 2007, ch. 4.

temporal and geospatial contexts. This has brought tremendous benefit to the study of ancient slavery, in part by making it "relevant" to modern (that is, the majority of) historians and thus drawing the distant past into their field of view. The comparison has also shed light on ancient practices by helping ancient historians better understand our circumscribed pool of evidence through comparison with analogous modern situations.[46] Problems arise, however, with the assumption of proponents of the "Slave Society" model that the canonical five slave societies share essential similarities with one another and, by extension, operate in fundamentally different ways from slaveholding cultures deemed "Societies with Slaves." In this sense, Finley's preoccupation with holistic characterization and ideal types can distort our understanding of ancient slaveries by fostering assumptions that the scale and intensity of Greek and Roman slavery were necessarily related to the same phenomena that explain modern slavery.

Many of the problems with the model are related to the agendas that Finley set himself or the assumptions he adopted from his predecessors. Foremost among these is the belief that Athens was paradigmatic of "Slave Societies" or even of Greek society writ large. He was surely correct that Athens was a city particularly given to stark divisions between free citizens and slaves, but neither was it the only such Greek city, nor was it representative of forms of "slavery" – even chattel slavery – attested across the kaleidoscope of Greek politics. In his drive to rationalize this bewildering variety into comprehensible categories, he created two boxes into which he slotted all forms of Greek dependency – "Athens" and "other." Thus, although the definitional criteria he offers for "slaves" – deracination, treatment as property, and exclusion from access to full membership in the social, political, and religious community – were applicable to many of the dependent statuses he identified in his preliminary articles, he elided this reality in his focus on the essential slavery he identified at Athens. The same problem was then compounded when he cross-applied the Athenian model to Rome.

[46] For example, Keith Bradley's monograph (1989) on slave rebellions in Roman antiquity builds fruitfully on the problematic source record for these large-scale events using enlightening comparanda from the New World. See also Paul Cartledge's (1985) brilliant comparative study of the frequency of slave revolts.

This problem of privileging Athens and then treating it as homologous with Rome then exacerbated a second crucial error – the assumption that there needed to be some trigger that activated the centrifuge of slavery refinement. As noted, Finley believed that three conditions were necessary for the rise of a "Slave Society": 1) the private ownership of land; 2) the sufficient development of commodity production and markets; and 3) the unavailability of an internal labor supply. To be sure, the first two factors were present in Athens, but they are also well attested in other premodern societies both before and after the rise of Athens.[47] It was above all the third condition, however, that was crucial to Finley's explanation, for he assumed that the lack of alternative labor sources in Athens stemmed both from the structural absence of wage labor and the abolition of debt bondage by Solon in the 590s BCE. Here, primitivist assumptions ultimately tracing to Polanyi vitiate the argument,[48] for recent scholarship has made a strong case for the importance of wage labor as a significant element in ancient markets in both Greece and Rome.[49] Indeed, the many clear and unequivocal attestations now assembled for Greek (and Roman) wage labor beg the question, why did Classical Athens and high Roman Italy not intensify wage labor instead of turning to slaves as they witnessed commodity production and market scale increase? Moreover, an equally powerful case has been made that, while Solon did abolish enslavement for debts, he did not abolish debt bondage. Edward Harris's careful reading of the sources on the question shows that Athenians could be and still were compelled to labor for creditors until their debts had been covered, and that Solon ended only the practice of permitting such debtor-servants to be treated as chattels and sold abroad.[50] For that matter, Deborah Kamen's study *Status in Classical Athens* has emphasized that Athenian society – and the Athenian marketplace – cannot be split into two starkly divided status

[47] The Neo-Babylonian Empire of the seventh and sixth centuries BCE underwent much the same efflorescence of private property holding and increased individual prosperity experienced by Classical Greece a century later, cf. Jursa 2010, passim, summarized at 1–61.

[48] Polanyi 1944, esp. 43–55, see also Nafissi 2005, 149–72.

[49] On Greek wage labor, see Loomis 1998. On Roman wage labor, see Brunt 1980; Jördens 1990; Scheidel 1994, 151–224; Cuvigny 1996; Erdkamp 1999; Banaji 2001, 190–212; Shaw 2013; Temin 2013, 114–38; Freu 2015; Hollderan 2016.

[50] Edward Harris 2002.

groups (free and slave), but that Classical Athens manifested a "spectrum of statuses" that left various sectors of the free population open to participation in the labor market.[51] Finally, in her critique of Finley's model, Tracey Rihll has rightly emphasized that Solon's reforms also did not end the enslavement of native-born exposed infants, citizens convicted of capital crimes, women convicted of promiscuity, Greeks from other city-states, nor even the bondage of Athenians ransomed by fellow citizens who could not repay their ransom.[52] Solon's reforms did not, therefore, generate the seismic fissure in social status Finley posited as the causal mechanism for the sudden rise in chattel labor. Indeed, as several historians have since argued, slavery played a much more prominent role in Bronze Age Greece than Finley had allowed.[53] Moreover, a number of remarkable Greek epistles inscribed on lead, most discovered and published since the death of Finley, attest to the regular deployment of slaves in the northern reaches of the Hellenophone world already by the late archaic age.[54] There was thus no single operator for the intensification of the Classical Athenian slave system, both because it was relatively intensive already by the Bronze Age and because it did not witness the radical diminution in the supply of free labor Finley posited for the early sixth century BCE.

Finley's desire to generalize the argument in holistic fashion also led him to assume the experience of Athens could be cross-applied to Corinth and Chios, which are also reported to have engaged in the intensive exploitation of chattel slaves. Here too, however, we have little if any evidence for the trigger mechanism of democratization identified as crucial to the rise of the Athenian "Slave Society." Chios offers some slight evidence for an early rise of democratic structures in a fragmentary early sixth-century inscription, yet through most of its history oligarchic governments alternated with democratic. Corinth, by contrast, had only the briefest flirtation with democratic governance in the early fourth century, but was otherwise ruled by tyrants

[51] Kamen 2013.

[52] Rihll 1996, 105–06. Rihll accepts Finley's concept of the "Slave Society" but offers an entirely different explanation for how it arose that places a much heavier emphasis on violence than Finley's birth of freedom trigger.

[53] Edward Harris 2012; Rihll 1996, 90–101. Contrast with Finley 1965d, 54–59.

[54] Ceccarelli 2013, nos. 1 (550–500 BCE), 4 (530–510 BCE), 5 (ca. 500 BCE); Bravo 2013, with earlier bibliography. I am grateful to my colleague Jessica Lamont for these references.

or oligarchs in archaic and Classical times.[55] Thus, in the period when these cities were greatly expanding their use of chattel slaves, neither followed Athens's pattern of radical leaps toward political freedom. Moreover, several other Greek polities – the islands of Aegina and Corcyra, for example, and cities and islands other than Chios along the Ionian coast – also saw the intensification of slaveholding and commercialization of slave production in the Classical period, but only some of these show signs of democratic governance. Even in Sparta, a city with an entrenched oligarchy, recent reassessments have emphasized that the dependent helots forced to generate surplus for the elite Spartiates meet the basic criteria for "slaves" insofar as their status was heritable and they could be owned and even sold as private property, albeit only within the Spartiate community.[56] So too recent work on the *doloi* and *woikēs* of Crete, long likened to serfs, indicates that these also are better classed as chattel slaves, yet Crete was itself thoroughly oligarchic.[57] There is thus no demonstrable link between the rise of chattel slavery and the rise of democracy in the broader context of the Greek city-state. And Rome's situation is equally divergent, for although it did pass legislation eliminating debt-bondage in 326, its approach to the enfranchisement of its citizens was a centuries-long process that never resulted in the level of freedom or mass political equality that we find in Athens. Indeed, aware that the parallel with Rome was weak, Finley explicitly declined to attempt any proof that his model worked in its case, relying instead on the trust of his reader in the cross-applicability of his trigger theory.[58] The debt-bondage elimination trigger mechanism works for only one ancient city-state – Athens – and only in imperfect fashion.

[55] Hansen and Nielsen 2004, 466 (no. 227); 1067–68 (no. 840), with further bibliography. Aware of this weakness in the Finley model, Scheidel 2005b and 2008 substitutes for democracy the more generalizable (but much vaguer) notion of "strong commitments." See also Descat 2006, which argues (entirely in opposition to Finley) that the introduction of a monetized slave trade, first attested on Chios, provoked the need for relief from enslavement for debts in the sixth century.

[56] Ducat 1990, 19–29; Luraghi 2002, 2003. But see the contrary arguments of Hunt in Chapter 2 of this volume. I agree with Hunt's overall argument, in no small part because it demonstrates the importance of the bipartite definition of slavery I offer in Chapter 1: the helots were, *stricto sensu*, the property of their Spartiate owners and they were violently dominated and generally dishonored. They were not, however, natally alienated and as such more closely resembled serfs.

[57] Link 2001 and Lewis 2013.

[58] Finley 1980, 86 (reprint 1998, 154): "As documentation, the Roman evidence is unsatisfactory, as I have already indicated, though I myself have no doubt about the

Finley's model is also vitiated by an unstated but clear assumption that the quintessential ideal type of purified slavery was found in the US South. When Finley ideated the "Slave Society," what he meant was not so much a generalizable type instantiated across his five exemplary cultures as, simply, American slavery. This emerges from the fact that almost uniformly when he offers substantive parallels to the ancient situations, they are drawn from the US South and not the Caribbean or Brazil. This is true of his arguments on the frequency of slave sales (*ASMI* 76, reprint 1998, 144); on slave demography (*ASMI* 80, reprint 1998, 148, where Cuba and Brazil are mentioned without elaboration); on the growth of slave numbers (*ASMI* 83, reprint 1998, 151); on the profitability of slave labor (*ASMI* 91–92, reprint 1998, 159–60); on attitudes to slave labor, a point of contrast (*ASMI* 99–100, reprint 1998, 167–68); on slave–master relations (*ASMI* 104, reprint 1998, 172); on slave psychology (*ASMI* 108, reprint 1998, 176); and on public debates on slaves and slavery (*ASMI* 149, reprint 1998, 217). America is also the standard comparandum for ancient slavery in *The Ancient Economy* and the preliminary articles.[59] Much of the explanation for this stems from the fact that Finley was operating within the Anglo-American academy, and that most of the high-quality work accessible to him up to the publication of *ASMI* in 1980 concerned the US South. But these preconditions underlying his research should caution against continued acceptance of the "Slave Society" model as globally valid after so much subsequent comparative work has shown its problems. Moreover, as we see in what follows, the comparison between Rome and the United States works only in the broadest terms but comes unglued on closer scrutiny.

Nor does the America–Athens comparison work as well as Finley supposed, for a number of reasons, two of which are salient. Finley had, as noted earlier, followed Hahn in arguing for the importance of private landownership concentrated in the hands of the elite and of commodity production and markets. To be sure, private property was prevalent in Athens, but it was not highly concentrated in

chronology and the broad outlines of the development." Aware of this weakness, Hopkins 1978, 102–15 shifts the emphasis to military demands, but then overstates the level of Roman citizen service.

[59] See Finley 1973a, 71, 79, 84; Finley 1964, 238–39, 242, 246; 1968, 308, 310, 311. Finley was not the first to have drawn parallels between Roman and US South plantation slavery, see Yeo 1952, an article Finley cites in *ASMI*.

the hands of the elite. Indeed, recent studies have shown that the Athenian distribution of property and particularly of land was among the most equitable of any society in world history.[60] There is no evidence for the existence of any large-scale, monocultural, market-oriented plantations like those of the Old South. Of course, this was never Finley's argument, but in both *AE* and *ASMI* he did argue – like Weber – that the overwhelming majority of economic production in antiquity came from the land. As such he was obliged to posit – without proving – that the Athenian economy was based on agricultural production and that this was generated for the elite primarily by slaves. This stood in contrast with Bücher (as well as Finley's teacher, Westermann), who had contended that Athenian prosperity was based in industrial production or, more accurately, a mixed regime of agriculture and industry.[61] Which side was correct in this debate remains unresolved, but what we can say is that, while we have relatively frequent attestations for slave labor in industrial occupations in Classical Athens, we have very few for slaves in agriculture. Slaves are known to have served in ceramic works, building construction, weaving operations, shield, sword, sail, and furniture manufactories, and in the silver mining operations at Laureion – in massive numbers – and in the service sector as personal attendants, porters, house servants, dancing girls, and prostitutes.[62] By contrast, their attestations as field laborers are confined to spare mentions,[63] mostly found in the one Classical Greek household management manual extant (Xenophon's *Oeconomicus*), where they are discussed mainly as farm managers rather than as field hands.[64] This is not to deny that slaves labored in the fields, but the assumption that the majority of agricultural labor was performed by slaves, or even that the majority of laborers in the fields of Athenian aristocrats were slaves, is based less on evidence than on suppositions and propositions. Indeed, some have argued that the majority of agricultural production in ancient Attica was performed by the free peasantry, and even if that argument remains controversial,

[60] Ober 2010; 2015, 71–100; Kron 2011.
[61] Westermann 1955, 12–14.
[62] Garlan 1988, 60–73; Osborne 1995, 30–36 (reprint 2010, 86–92); Schumacher 2001.
[63] De Ste. Croix 1981, 140–42, 505–06; Jameson 1977/78; 1992, 142–46; Burford 1993, 208–22.
[64] Xenophon, *Oeconomicus*, 5.15–16; 7.35; 9.5; 12.2–6; 13.3, 6–12; 15.5; cf. Demosthenes 55.32, 34.

the argument to the contrary has by no means been proven.[65] If we simply follow the evidence, then, it must be admitted that Athenian slavery was more productive in industrial than agricultural sectors, making it a very different animal than the slavery of the US South.

Athenian slaves also differed from those in the US South in the degree of their integration into the economy and society. Not only did the jobs they held extend across the economic spectrum, their chances for manumission were much greater than those of US South slaves and their opportunities for economic – but not political – success considerable.[66] The anonymous author often called "The Old Oligarch" famously complained that slaves in fifth-century Athens clothed and carried themselves so much like freepersons that one would never dare strike a person behaving impudently in the streets, for it was impossible to tell a free man from a slave – a situation that never would have arisen in early nineteenth-century Charleston or Atlanta.[67] The Athenians allowed slaves to serve as bankers, some of them attaining such wealth that the slaves Pasion and Phormion could use their fortunes to gain freedom, citizenship, and the highest status in Athenian society.[68] The Athenians even deployed slave archers from Scythia as their primary police force and occasionally used slaves in their armies and navy as well.[69] None of this could have occurred in the US South, even if similar scenarios were relatively common in a number of societies that do not rate for inclusion among Finley's five.[70]

The problem with this recourse to the US South as paradigmatic becomes most apparent on the question of slave rebellions. Neither the US South nor Athens (Finley's modern and ancient paradigmatic types) witnessed major slave uprisings. In order to fit the comparative evidence to this pattern, Finley therefore also felt compelled to downplay the significance of rebellion in other slaveholding systems.

65 On peasant holders as the main source of agricultural production in Attica, see Ellen Wood 1988; cf. Ober 1989, 24–27, 270–86. Burford 1993, 264–65, n. 69, argues the contrary, but Osborne 1995, 32–36 (reprint 2010, 92–95) presents a solid case for the relative unimportance of slave labor in Classical Athenian agriculture.

66 Canevaro and Lewis 2014; Kamen 2016.

67 Pseudo-Xenophon, *Constitution of the Athenians*, 1.10; cf. Vlassopoulos 2011, 123–24.

68 See Bäbler 1998, 119–22; Cohen 1992, ch. 4; cf. Kamen 2013, ch. 2, for more on wealthy and privileged Athenian slaves.

69 Jacob 1928, 53–79; Hunt 1998.

70 Noteworthy are the slave soldiers of Arab and Ottoman Muslim societies; see Crone 1980; Pipes 1981.

We thus find arguments like "In the whole of history, there have been only four slave revolts on the scale of a genuine war," by which he means the three Roman revolts between 135 and 71 BCE and the Haitian revolt of 1791.[71] This is of course falsifiable if we think of, for example, the Tyrian slave revolt of the fourth century BCE and the Sarmatian slave rebellion of 330 CE (both discussed in the introductory chapter), of the Zanj revolt in Abbasid Iraq (869–883 CE), or even the key role Hausa and other Muslim rebel slaves played in the overthrow of the Ọyọ empire in 1817.[72] This does not negate the validity of Finley's underlying argument – that large-scale slave revolts have been rare in history – but the failure to mention these revolts (all from within "Asiatic," that is non-Western, cultures), and the effort to downplay the significance of the Haitian and Roman examples (which Finley characterizes as extensions of broader political unrest rather than slave self-assertion) reveal a bipartite agenda: first, to constrain the evidence to his model; and second, to imply its global applicability on the basis of a circumscribed dataset.

None of this is to deny the many similarities between Athenian and US South slavery. First, insofar as we can tell, the enslaved population in Classical Attica was around 35 percent of aggregate, which is remarkably close to the percentage of aggregate population enslaved in the combined states of the Confederacy around 1861.[73] Second, apart from natural reproduction, the primary source of slaves in Classical Attica appears to have been market purchase – rather than war captives, child sale, self-sale, penal enslavement, or other supply streams.[74] This can also be said of the US South, for in the last quarter of the eighteenth century internal supply networks from captive native peoples largely disappeared, making the market trade in Africans the largest supply stream by far, and even after the prohibition on slave imports in 1807, the market continued to be the primary fulfiller of

[71] Finley 1980, 114–15 (reprint Finley 1998, 182–83). More on revolt at Finley 1980, 71, 110–15 (reprint Finley 1998, 139, 178–83); Finley 1973a, 68.

[72] On the Zanj revolt, see Popović 1998; Furlonge 1999; Kennedy 2016, 153–55. The Zanj were slaves from East Africa, held in southern Iraq near Basra, where they cleared and farmed marginal land in large concentrations before rebelling under ʿAlī b. Muḥammad and seizing control of the region for more than a decade. On the slave revolt against the Ọyọ, see Law 1977, 255–60.

[73] On the slave population of Classical Attica, see Hunt, Chapter 2 in this volume. On the US South in aggregate, see Patterson 1982, 363; Bergad 2007, 118.

[74] Braund and Tsetskhladze 1989; Lewis 2011, 2016.

increased demand in the Deep South as domestically bred slaves were transferred from the Tidewater states through trade.[75] As in the US South, Athenian slaves were used to generate market surplus for the enrichment of all classes and particularly the elite, and both societies also avoided large-scale slave uprisings, although both things could be said of many other slaveholding societies. Above all, Athens was also the only "Slave Society" of antiquity that could be argued to have developed something akin to a racial ideology of slavery. This is surely at the heart of Aristotle's theory of the natural slave, which builds ethnic prejudice against those "barbarian" peoples with feeble minds (Thracians, Scythians) or weak spirits (Asians, Persians) into a justification for their bondage to those "Greek" people whose minds were assumed to be superior and thus naturally suited to holding the former in thrall.[76] Missing from Aristotle's argument is the emphasis on somatic – as opposed to psycho-spiritual – inferiority, but the subconscious ethnocentrism repackaged as a rational science of mastery offers a very close parallel to the plantation manuals and proslavery tractates of the Old South; nor was the argument unique to Aristotle, for its philosophical underpinnings are clearly traceable to Plato and its ethnocentric assumptions permeate Greek comedy, making it likely that many Athenians held similar views.[77]

Even so, the many differences between the two slaveholding systems, as well as Finley's many less defensible arguments used to bolster a case for parallelism, serve to highlight the limitations of the "Slave Society"/"Society with Slaves" binary with respect to these two foundational societies. Finley had wisely avoided the effort to design a Marxist holistic scheme generalizable across all economic systems, for the "Slave Society" pole of his binary was explicitly asserted to be a very rare phenomenon in the world history of political economy. But like the Marxists, he posited its nomological applicability across history as well as universalizing criteria for the existence of this rare and distinctive species and the peculiar circumstances under which it might arise. Because, however, he grounded his argument in the concrete historical realities of just one Greek city-state and elaborated

[75] Johnson 1999; Gudmestad 2003.

[76] Garnsey 1996, 107–27.

[77] Schütrumpf 1993. On slaves in comedy, see the essays in Akrigg and Tordoff 2013.

it using one modern comparandum, he discovered a paradigm that truly applied only to these two societies – and only in imperfect ways.

ROME AND THE US SOUTH: DOES FINLEY'S MODEL HELP?

The differences between ancient and modern slave systems are even more glaring when one compares Rome with the US South. The contrasts are legion but can be grouped under three larger structural categories: 1) differences between market conditions in the precapitalist Roman world versus the capitalist modernism of the US South; 2) the absence of racial categories as structuring components of slaveholding in Rome versus their pervasive presence in America; 3) the robust presence of mechanisms for the integration of the enslaved into Roman society that were almost entirely absent in the Old South.

As to market conditions, Finley himself was the late twentieth-century standard-bearer for the primitivist school that perceived fundamental differences between modern capitalist systems and the ancient economy: he believed that the ancient world had no understanding of economic rationalism or profit maximization; no truly free and responsive markets; no structurally significant wage labor; no organized, large-scale industrial production; and no modern sense of work ethic. Although Finley's "primitivist" economic theory has drawn criticism from many quarters in the intervening years, some of his contentions have never been successfully challenged.[78] Chief among these is the absence of evidence for a true world market, for although unregulated local markets were much more a part of the ancient economy than Finley assumed, numerous studies have shown that products and services tended to circulate in regional patterns and that "global" (in the sense of pan-imperial) exchange was neither fostered nor achieved. Insofar as global trade there was, this reflected the flow of money and provisions to finance the imperial army and the food supply of the city of Rome.[79] This stands in obvious contrast with the US South, where economic activity was entirely contingent

[78] Although the bibliography is massive, for challenges, see Rathbone 1991; Scheidel, Morris, and Saller 2007; Temin 2013. For modified defense, see Morley 2007; Bang 2008.

[79] Duncan-Jones 1994, ch. 12; Bang 2008, ch. 2; contrast Howgego 1994.

on trade between Europe, Africa, and the Americas and where it operated in an environment in which the government's role was secondary to private commerce.

This difference had a particular impact on slavery in the two contexts because, in contrast with the modern Atlantic systems – and the US South in particular – the Roman world had no obvious "cash crop" whose production was circumscribed by climate and geography and whose value depended on free trade in the manner of sugar, cotton, rice, tobacco, cacao, indigo, and coffee. It could be objected that wine was such a commodity, for its production was indeed difficult north of the fiftieth parallel, and its distribution from various production centers around the Mediterranean is well attested archaeologically. These preconditions, however, still permitted the production of wine in the vast majority of imperial territories. Although some have argued that Italian domination of wine production in last two centuries of the Roman Republic favored the rise of large estates (*latifundia*) populated by slave-producers,[80] scholars have found very little archaeological evidence to support the existence of this greatly mythologized property type.[81] Both texts and archaeology point instead to more dispersed landownership – with the wealthy holding many mid-sized farms in a broad portfolio – but not massive factory farms in the manner of American plantations or Brazilian *engenhos*. The sources also indicate that ancient estates were exploited to produce a traditional Mediterranean polyculture, in marked contrast with the monocultures characteristic of US South plantations. Some posit olive production as another parallel to the cash crops of the modern world, and in fact, the large-scale, monocultural production of olives in parts of Spain and North Africa comes as close as anything to resembling the cash crops of the modern Atlantic world.[82] Oleiculture was not, however, particularly labor-intensive, making it poorly suited to slave production. Thus textual and epigraphic evidence from North Africa indicates that tenant laborers predominated over slaves in the later Empire, when oil production reached its zenith.[83] All this means that the fundamental driver of New World slave economics – global

[80] For example, Tchernia 1983, 1986; Carandini 1985.
[81] Jongman 1988, 97–154; Marzano 2007, 129–53; Launaro 2011, 155–58.
[82] Mattingly 1988, esp. 50–52; de Vos 2013.
[83] Lenski 2017; cf. Kehoe 1988.

trade in high-profit staples – appears to have been absent from the Roman world. In fact, with the possible exception of the silver from the Laureion mines of Attica and the gold mines of Spain in the Republican era, we can find no firm evidence for the large-scale generation of any product by ancient slaves in a manner similar to what drove the slave plantations of the New World. For this reason, I have rated the exchange value of US Southern slaves' labor product at twice that of Roman slaves in Chapter 1, Chart 1.1.

Roman slaves were instead used in a much greater range of productive activities that sets them apart from their New World counterparts. This included involvement in the full range of primary production (cerealiculture, viticulture, ovicaprid and bovine husbandry, pisciculture), mining and quarrying, transport and trade, and manufacturing (textiles, ceramics, metal-casting, furniture, building trades, etc.). Slaves were also engaged in a wide variety of service tasks that integrated them into all levels of the ancient economy. This can be seen in the domestic sphere with the mind-boggling complexity of household attendants attested in both private and imperial service.[84] Roman slaves also served regularly as bookkeepers and accountants, business managers and traders, teachers and artists, doctors and bankers, eunuch chamberlains and popular entertainers.[85] And in the first century CE, imperial slaves and freedmen were also charged with managing important business of state.[86] Most all of these sectors of the economy were foreclosed to slaves in the US South. Among other modern transatlantic systems, nineteenth-century Rio de Janeiro as well as the British Caribbean offer closer parallels in the breadth of deployment of slave labor in various sectors of the economy, though never in high-level management, teaching, or medicine.[87] And the Romans' penchant for extravagant displays of household slaves and attendants as well as their deployment of slaves in political and administrative posts is much more closely paralleled in Arab and Ottoman slavery than in the slave systems of the New World.[88] For all these

84 See Treggiari 1973, 1975.

85 See, for example, Christes 1979; Kudlien 1986; Kirschenbaum 1987, 89–127; Aubert 1994, passim, esp. 114–16, 141–46, 199–200; Horsmann 1998; Andreau 1999, 64–70.

86 Weaver 1972.

87 Karasch 1987, 185–213; Katherine Smith 2012.

88 Lal 1994, 99–118; Toledano 2007a; Zilfi 2010, 100–06.

reasons, I have rated Roman slaves much higher in their use value as commodities than American slaves in Chapter 1, Chart 1.1.

The capillary penetration of slaves into all professions stemmed from several factors, all of which are characteristic of most premodern slaveries, chief among these being the absence of racial ideology. Race was, without question, the key structuring component of all transatlantic slaving systems and was nowhere as important as it was in the US South.[89] Although the Greeks did develop an ethnic ideology of slavery most elaborately articulated in Aristotle's theory of the "natural slave," the Romans were what one might term "equal opportunity enslavers." To them race and ethnicity mattered little to eligibility for enslavement.[90] Thus the Romans tended to enslave the ethnic other – often Hellenes or Syrians of the eastern Mediterranean in the early Republican period, then Celtic and Germanic peoples from the North in the late Republic and Empire – all peoples were eligible for enslavement, including native Roman offspring exposed at birth as well as adult citizens convicted of crimes.[91] And in many periods, noncitizen indigenes within the Empire and even Roman citizens could be held in a variety of semi-servile positions rendering them subject to forced labor, as *clientes, humiliores, paramonarii, paroikoi, coloni, adscripticii, gynaecarii, linyphii, barbaricarii, monetarii,* etc.[92] Ancient Romans thus differed markedly from the US South in the extent and degree of their reliance on internal sources of enslavement and other forms of labor dependency, especially because racial and ethnic characteristics were fundamentally secondary to eligibility for enslavement. For this reason I have rated the level of dishonor for Roman slaves much lower than that for US Southern slaves in Chapter 1, Chart 1.2.

The flipside of Rome's voracious appetite for slaves was its extreme liberality with manumission, a point discussed later in this chapter.

[89] On the crucial role race played in transatlantic slaving systems, see Rawick 1972, 125–60; Davis 2006, 48–103; Blackburn 2010, 307–68.

[90] On justifications for slavery in antiquity, see Garnsey 1996; cf. Ramelli 2016.

[91] On the enslavement of foundlings, see the competing arguments of William Harris 1999 and Scheidel 1997, neither of whom denies that the enslavement of foundlings happened regularly. On other forms of endogenous enslavement, see Buckland 1908, 401–18.

[92] On *humiliores*, see Garnsey 1970. On *paramonarii*, see Samuel 1965; Sosin 2015. On the colonate, see Sirks 2008. On *gynaecarii, linyphii, barbaricarii,* and *monetarii*, see Sirks 1993.

Here, however, it is worth noting that sexual relations between masters and slaves (particularly male masters and female slaves) regularly (though by no means uniformly) resulted in manumission and marriage, while anti-miscegenation laws in the US South foreclosed such marital unions and all but occluded the likelihood of manumission for females who produced offspring by their masters.[93] Thus, where the Roman system set very low bars to the social legitimation of affective unions between masters and slaves, the racial basis of US South slavery forced such unions into the realm of social deviancy. Indeed, by the late eighteenth century, race conditioned eligibility for enslavement to such a degree that African somatic features alone occasioned the presumption of servile status in courts of law.[94]

The racialization of America's slave system created a near permanent barrier to high-level economic or administrative activity for the enslaved as well as a bar to integration into society for freedmen. Rome's "color blind" system knew no such bars, allowing access to nearly all market and administrative levels and thereby exploiting slavery as a particularly violent and repressive form of social integration. This openness to slave participation in the economy was compounded by the Romans' primitive understanding of legal agency, which essentially necessitated the use of enslaved dependents for the conduct of many third-party transactions. Because third-party contracts were difficult for either the primary or third party agents to enforce or grieve, large-scale and long-distance business was largely confined to members of business owners' *familia* – their sons and their slaves, who for purposes of business transactions as indeed for much else were treated as virtual equals to the primary.[95] In the US South, by contrast, racial ideology combined with outright fear of and bars to integration to prohibit slaves from learning to read or write, condemning them to illiteracy and innumeracy and thus excluding them from participation in the economies of knowledge, money, and

[93] On Roman slave–master relations, see Hermann-Otto 1994, 83–98. On legal and moral strictures against master–slave relations in the US South, see Edmund S. Morgan 1975, 333–36; Kathleen Brown 1996, ch. 6; cf. Hodes 1997 on prohibitions against affective relations between free white women and slave men. Male slaves' relationships with their mistresses created much more anxiety for the Romans; see Grubbs 1993.

[94] Berlin 1974, 91–99; Thomas Morris 1996, 21–29.

[95] On the legal agency, see Aubert 1994, 46–116.

power. Race also produced a justification for slaveholding in a US South that found itself regularly needing to explain the contradiction between the enlightenment political principles of universal freedom and equality it claimed to uphold and the mass oppression it sustained against a significant sector of its populace. Roman society and law, by contrast, saw no strong need to justify slavery, which was treated as a universal constant across cultures, an artefact of the "law of nations" (*ius gentium*). This absence of racial criteria in Roman slavery cannot be emphasized strongly enough as a crucial element differentiating the ideology, economics, ethics, and praxis of slavery in Rome versus the modern world.

At the opposite ethical pole, because the primitive custom of captive-taking was never as far from Roman slaveholding as it was from the New World, there were aspects of Roman slaveholding that were much more barbaric – and economically irrational – than the calculating efficiencies of American slavery. This is especially evident in Rome's ceremonies of the triumph and arena, where captives and slaves were often murdered gratuitously for the delectation of the masses and the emphatic display of state power.[96] This went on continuously from the archaic period, when gladiation arose from the tradition of offering battle captives in sacrifice to the spirits of Rome's dead, into Late Antiquity when a panegyrist of Constantine could still revel in 313 CE: "What is lovelier than this triumphal celebration in which he employs the slaughter of enemies for the pleasure of us all, and enlarges the procession of the games out of the survivors of the massacre of the barbarians?"[97] This gratuitous waste of potential manpower was anything but market-oriented and would have made no economic sense to the slaveholders of nineteenth-century America. Instead, its orgiastic jouissance strikes one as having much closer connections to the ritual abuse and murder of captives attested in excavations at Cahokia or Teotihuacan than anything witnessed in the market economies of the new world. This gratuitous and ritualized violence to which Roman but not American slaves were subjected can be balanced by the more direct and regular application of violence

[96] On the triumph, see Beard 2007, esp. chapter 4; on the arena, see Plass 1995, passim, esp. 29–45.

[97] *Latin Panegyric*, 12(9).23.3.

in the workplace known from the US South to result in equally high levels of violent domination in Chapter 1, Chart 1.2.

As mentioned earlier in this chapter, one of the most distinctive features of Roman slavery was its strong propensity toward manumission. Freedmen are everywhere in Roman epigraphy, literature, and art – particularly from the city of Rome. This was in part because the avenues to freedom were many and could be relatively informal and the advancement of freedmen in Roman society relatively streamlined and rapid. Attaching statistics to this phenomenon is not, however, as easy as it first appears. In fact, the main problem is that if we take the abundant evidence of epigraphy at face value, the numbers seem impossibly high. Tombstones offer ample testimony to a robust freedman component in the population of Rome, where it appears that 70 percent to 75 percent of those commemorated in the epitaphs were freed.[98] In a similar vein, using data gathered from tombstones in cities across Italy, Geza Alföldy argued that nearly all slaves in Italian cities of the early Imperial period could expect manumission by the age of thirty. More recently, Henrik Mouritsen has shown that the heavy preponderance of freedmen in Roman funerary epigraphy is more a reflection of the Roman epigraphic habit than a statistical measure of manumission.[99] For reasons likely related to relative prosperity and the desire for self-promotion, freedmen were much more likely to be commemorated with inscriptions than freeborn members of the populace.[100] Even so, the numbers remain striking by any reckoning and surely indicate that a significant cross-section of the populace consisted of freedmen at any given time. Indeed, indications from non-funerary epigraphy also point to an astonishingly robust freedman population in Roman Italy of the early imperial period. The *collegia* inscriptions of Ostia, which list members of the city's professional guilds, record about 30 percent Greek names, a statistically reliable indicator of freedman status.[101] So too, a set of marble inscriptions from Herculaneum on the Bay of Naples records a list of what appears to be the entire male citizen body categorized by status.

[98] See Solin 1971, 135–37. Mouritsen 2004 calculates a similar percentage (69 percent) of funerary inscriptions for freedmen in Ostia.

[99] Alföldy 1972[1986] with Mouritsen 2011, 132–37.

[100] Mouritsen 2011, ch. 5, esp. 120–41.

[101] Mouritsen 2005, 42–43.

The inscriptions are fragmentary but their extensive data have allowed for plausible demographic modeling that indicates 23 percent of the city's population consisted of freedmen, which would mean that about 60 percent of urban slaves who reached the age of twenty-five must have obtained their freedom.[102] From the same city, a large cache of writing tablets deciphered by Giuseppe Camodeca indicates that 41 percent of the 370 named individuals were freedmen.[103] Finally, the columbaria inscriptions for the slave *familiae* of the Volusii and Statilii indicate that 32 percent and 46 percent, respectively, of each total *familia* had been manumitted at a given time.[104] None of these figures can be taken as equivalent to census data, but the fact that the lowest among them indicates 30 percent of an average city's populace in the first century CE was freed is nothing short of remarkable. In this sense, Rome displays similarities to the slave cultures of West Africa or many native peoples of North America that used enslavement as a means to integrate outsiders into their cultures.[105] To be sure, Rome kept in place legal, social, and economic strictures that limited the practice of manumission during the High Empire, but these did not prevent the Romans from continuing to use slavery to strengthen the reproductive capacity of the kin group and the social reproductive capacity of the citizen populace.[106]

These numbers surpass anything known from New World slave systems, and they overtop the numbers from the American South by a whole order of magnitude. By 1850 manumission rates in the Southern states of the United States stood at 0.045 percent of the aggregate slave population annually. This dismally low figure arose from extremely restrictive views and laws on manumission and resulted in a freed population that reached just 6.2 percent in the combined Southern states and a meager 1.5 percent in the Lower South in 1860.[107] The situation was more favorable to manumission

[102] DeLigt and Garnsey 2012; cf. Mouritsen 2007.
[103] Camodeca 2000, 67–68.
[104] Mouritsen 2012.
[105] See Kopytoff and Miers 1977b; Starna and Watkins 1991; Rushforth 2012; Cameron 2016a, ch. 3.
[106] On this function of slavery, see Meillasoux 1991, 23–40. Jongman 2003 argues that slaves served as the de facto replacement population for Rome and other urban centers with high excess mortality rates.
[107] Berlin 1974, 137; cf. Fogel and Engerman 1974, 150; Cole 2005.

in the French, Portuguese, and Spanish environments of Louisiana (where the 1785 census documented 3.5 percent free colored),[108] Brazil (where Rio de Janeiro in 1849 counted 5.2 percent freed, São Paulo 19 percent in 1829, and Salvador 29.8 percent in 1835),[109] Cuba (where the 1774 Havana census documented 20.1 percent).[110] The reasons for these differences were partly economic (the US system could ill afford manumission after the closure of the slave trade in 1807), but more than this, the disparity can be accounted for based on distinctions of law and culture. This reality, famously asserted in the controversial thesis of Frank Tannenbaum, has been reaffirmed in work by Ariella Gross and Alejandro de la Fuente that shows the variable effects of the sliding scales of legal restriction between American, French, Brazilian, and Spanish regimes, with the American norms, by far the strictest, resulting in the smallest freedman population.[111] Finley's canonical "Slave Societies" were thus hardly uniform in their approach to manumission, but the US South stands out as the least apt comparandum for Rome. Moreover, insofar as the Spanish and Brazilian numbers approached the Roman manumission rates, this was closely related to the genetic relationship between the legal norms of all three systems. As regards manumission, then, distinctions are more fruitfully drawn between Romanist and non-Romanist than between "Slave Societies" and "Societies with Slaves."

Indeed, for parallels with Roman society we would be just as well served by turning to Muslim societies, in which the manumission of slaves was ranked as an act of religious charity (*zakāt*) and valued to such an extent that it constituted a regular feature of enslavement and took on a rich variety of forms. The rules of manumission were extensive and highly articulated, and manumission itself established quasi-filial patron–client relations between masters and freed slaves (*mawālī*). This meant that in all periods and political contexts of Islamic history, and particularly in the Ottoman world, enslavement could best be

[108] Gayarré 1866–67, 3:170–71; cf. Dubois 2004, 73–80.

[109] Rio de Janeiro: Karasch 1987, 66, 341; São Paolo: Luna and Klein 2003, 158–79. Salvador: Nishida 1993, 365.

[110] Herbert S. Klein 1967; cf. Fuente 2008, 174–78, on free blacks in sixteenth-century Havana, who were closer to 10–15 percent of the population. More on free blacks in Spanish colonial society at Aimes 1909; Baade 1983, 51; Landers 1999, 138–44.

[111] Tannenbaum 1947; Fuente and Gross 2015; cf. Eder 1976.

described as a forced induction into the dominant society.[112] Indeed, we might also turn to the indigenous societies of precontact North America as well, for these too practiced widespread captive-taking, but often quickly converted captives who had been violently abducted into members of their own clans and tribes. Since the publication of a famous article by James L. Watson in 1980, anthropologists have long drawn the distinction between "open" and "closed" slave systems, that is, those that either allow or refuse the integration of slaves into the dominant culture.[113] Rome was very much an open slave society, which puts it at the opposite end of the spectrum from the US South and explains why I ranked it much lower on the scales of "permanence" and "natal alienation" in Chapter 1, Chart 1.2.

The degree to which this is true can also be measured in the rapidity with which former slaves were integrated into Roman society after their manumission. Roman manumission itself granted full private law rights to the freedman, who could vote, conduct legitimate business, marry, produce citizen offspring, and leave much of his property to heirs in a legally recognized testament.[114] With these rights in place, freedmen became notorious in Roman society for their rapid ascent of the economic ladder. Many had acquired education and skills to make them more useful and profitable to their masters that could be converted into economic benefits following manumission. Although such figures, classically parodied in Petronius's Trimalchio, were often the butt of jokes for being uncouth arrivistes, their economic power and pride in their accomplishments were real and are well attested in the many monuments they have left to the archaeological record.[115] Furthermore, the children of freedmen were eligible for full participation not just in the economy but also in the politics of Rome. Indeed Emperors Macrinus and Diocletian are reputed to have been the sons of freedmen, and Vitellius was said to have had slave ancestry as well.[116] None of this was conceivable in the US South, where legal restrictions based in racist ideology foreclosed any possibilities for

[112] Toledano 2017. See also the essay of Freamon, Chapter 13 in this volume.
[113] James Watson 1980a.
[114] The laws are summarized at Alan Watson 1987, 23–45; cf. Mouritsen 2011, 66–119.
[115] Joshel 1992, passim esp. 25–61; Lauren Petersen 2006; Mouritsen 2011, 206–47.
[116] Macrinus: *Historia Augusta, Life of Macrinus*, 4.3. Diocletian: *Epitome de Caesaribus*, 39.1; Eutropius, 9.20. Vitellius: Suetonius, *Life of Vitellius*, 2.1.

political achievement to former slaves. This disparity, combined with differences in the level of professional training and responsibility accorded to Roman slaves, led me to rank them much lower on the scale of dishonor than their US South counterpart in Chapter 1, Chart 1.2.

Finally, Roman and US South slavery diverged entirely on the degree to which the institution of slavery itself acted as a driver of political economy. Walter Johnson's monumental *River of Dark Dreams* has hammered home the degree to which notions of empire, economy, and slave society were interlinked in the US South.[117] There planters not only fought tooth and nail to guard their right to hold slaves and to protect their human property from threats posed by flight and the forces of abolition, they also schemed to spread their Cotton Kingdom across North America and even overseas. Theirs was thus a fully articulated ideology of slavery, equipped with a planned economic model based in slave production, a political shibboleth trumpeting the righteousness of race-based slavery, and an imperialist strategy organized to spread a consciously articulated way of life across the Western Hemisphere. None of this can be demonstrated for Rome. To be sure, the agricultural manuals of Cato, Varro, and Columella outline the manner in which slaves should be best exploited, but in them we sense more concern with minimizing risk than maximizing profit, and we can also trace an awareness that grows over time of the importance of free labor, while none offers an ideological justification for the use of slave labor as a positive economic or societal good. Rome's empire was by all means an instrument of enslavement, but we have very little evidence that imperial campaigns were undertaken with the explicit aim of enslaving the enemy and none at all that Rome's object in expanding its empire was to spread its "Slave Society." For the Romans, surrounded as they were by other slaveholding cultures, there was no need for such a crusade. In fact, this is precisely the point: far from being unique in world history as one of the first two "genuine Slave Societies," Rome was entirely typical in its world. Slavery was not a site of moral, political, or economic contestation in antiquity. It was taken for granted, by Rome and its neighbors, and as such it evolved according to a very different logic from the market-based, societally closed, and politically defensive slavery of Dixie.

[117] Johnson 2013.

To be sure, the scale and intensity of Rome's slaveholding increased rapidly in lockstep as the scale and reach of its empire grew. But after the acquisition of that empire, scale and intensity subsided as tenancy as well as free labor replaced slavery as the primary source of manpower for the landed elite.

CONCLUSION

Finley's "Slave Societies"/"Societies with Slaves" binary represented an important step in the process of comparative slave studies. It grew out of a lifelong passion for the topic that stemmed from Finley's enduring interest in late nineteenth- and early twentieth-century sociology – Marx, Bücher, Meyer, Weber, and Polanyi. Like all of these predecessors, Finley strove to derive holistic models applicable across world history, but like all but Polanyi, his dataset was primarily Western. Ultimately he walked a middle ground between all of them, taking from Marx the central importance of property relations and revolutionary struggle and the assumption that only Western societies merited serious discussion, from Bücher and Polanyi primitivist assumptions about the functioning of the ancient economy and its absence of capitalist structures or rationalist economic thought, from Weber the primary importance of agricultural production and the belief that slavery was eventually overtaken by less binding forms of dependency in Late Antiquity, and from Meyer the assumption that the growth of democratic freedoms necessitated the turn to slave labor in Classical Greece. It was ultimately this last idea that proved most important for Finley's own contribution to the debate. Explored in a series of articles published from 1959 to 1965, Finley expanded upon this notion to explain how Athens seemed to distinguish itself from previous Greek city-states in bunching status at just two poles, chattel slave and free citizen. Influenced by the seminal work of István Hahn on the rise of the *Sklavenhaltergesellschaft*, Finley rounded out his model by introducing the importance of private-property holding and commodity production for the market as the other two decisive factors in the rise of the ideal type "Slave Society."

The problem, as has become clear, is that both the exclusivity and the simplicity of the binary model render it less than helpful in comparing the variety of slaveholding societies across human history. This is true even when one compares the three societies on which Finley focused most of his attention – Athens, Rome, and the US South. While all share similarities, their differences are just as notable – particularly as regards Rome and America. Thus both Athenian and Roman societies knew no truly integrated world market and no high-revenue staple production like those that drove the rise of plantation culture in the US South. Both witnessed a much wider and deeper penetration of slaves into all levels of market production, and Rome in particular saw slaves climb remarkably high on the social ladder, very much in the manner of Islamic slaveholding societies. This was facilitated in both instances by the absence of racial slavery, a factor with a huge impact on Rome, which drew only very weak links between race, ethnicity, and enslavability. This allowed manumission to be much more streamlined and common in the Roman system, which used enslavement in some ways as a violent means of societal integration. As such, Rome came much closer to the transatlantic systems of the Spanish Caribbean or Portuguese Brazil (which borrowed Roman legal structures) than to the US South. Indeed, there are aspects of Roman manumission culture that begin to look more like the captive-taking societies of precontact North America. The same primitive strain can be seen in the retention of captives for ritual slaughter by the Romans in arena sports, which never abandoned connections to their origins in captive-taking throughout their history. Finally, neither Rome nor Athens witnessed the interpenetration of slaveholding into the political economy in the manner of the Old South, for they considered slavery a cross-cultural given and saw no need to promote it actively as a social or economic institution.

In his *Handbuch Geschicte der Sklaverei* (2013) Michael Zeuske has described the development of world slavery in terms of "plateaus and processes." In his scheme, slaveholding has undergone a sort of evolution throughout history, beginning with kin-based forms, developing into large-scale collective forms, then imperial forms undergirded by codified law (in the manner of Greece and Rome), which gave way to modern slaveries constructed out of these preexisting forms to suit capitalist market conditions and rationale. This last phase, which he terms "the second slavery," never existed in the ancient world, when slavery often assumed large-scale proportions but retained commonalities with prehistoric slaveries, especially a more pronounced tendency toward enslavement as an integrative structure.[118] Slavery was used to fold newcomers violently into the hegemonic group and, as such, differed from modern plantation slavery, a form first pioneered in Sao Tomé in the sixteenth century that then gradually spread across the Atlantic world. This first occurred in enclaves generally located on islands or in coastal regions down to the late eighteenth century. Only with the rise of the global industrial economy in the nineteenth century did mass-scale industrial slavery take off. With the cross-application of technologies like the steamship and railroads, industrial slavery could penetrate deeper into colonial territories and its products could be shipped across the planet to satisfy a burgeoning – uniquely modern – market demand. This "second slavery" was a phenomenon best known from the three colonial contexts Finley listed as his modern "Slave Societies" – the US South, Brazil, and the Caribbean (insofar as this last can be considered a single "society"). In fact, however, it was a form that cropped up nearly simultaneously elsewhere in societies Finley politely ignored: African societies, such as Sokoto, Dahomey, Fuuta Jalon, and Zanzibar; Middle Eastern societies, such as Egypt and Oman; Indian Ocean societies, such as the Mascarenes, Java, and the Philippines. And many more could be listed. Moreover, this industrial wave of "second slavery" was both quantitatively and qualitatively different from any form of ancient slavery, including Greece and Rome. According to Zeuske, these forms continue to develop, for abolition was never an event but a process, and the norms, concepts, and vocabulary it introduced have simply been worked around or bypassed to create a "third slavery" that endures up to the present.[119] In light of the work of Zeuske and others, the time for comparative slave studies has surely come, and the Finleyan model, for all that it brought the dialogue forward in the mid-twentieth century, is now preventing it from making further progress.

[118] See also Laviña and Zeuske 2014.
[119] See more at Bales 2000; Allain 2012b.

PART II

NON-WESTERN SMALL-SCALE SOCIETIES

5

The Nature of Slavery in Small-Scale Societies

Catherine M. Cameron

What, in other words, brought about the transformation from the "primordial fact" of individual slaves to the existence of slave societies, and what subsequently brought about a reversal of that process?

(M. I. Finley)[1]

Moses I. Finley's influential binary "Slave Society" and "Society with Slaves" was clearly directed at complex, state-level societies. While he acknowledges slavery as a "primordial fact," he bestows "Slave Society" status upon only five societies that were among the most highly developed of their time (ancient Greece and Rome, the US South, and colonial Caribbean and Brazil, the last three as extensions of European economies).[2] Finley was uninterested in small-scale societies, and even if he had been interested, there were few studies of slavery among such groups at the time he wrote. In fact, he dismisses the indigenous people of the New World as "insufficient, when not useless" with respect to their potential as slaves, never recognizing the fundamental importance of slaveholders and slaves in many of these groups.[3] The surge in studies of slavery among small-scale societies in the past decade allows us to reassess just how exclusive Finley's five "Slave Societies" really were.[4] This chapter stresses that slavery can

[1] Finley 1980, 77.
[2] Finley 1980, 88.
[3] Finley 1980, 88, 130.
[4] Brooks 2002; Cameron 2008; Donald 1997; Gallay 2002, 2009; Ekberg 2010; Ethridge and Shuck-Hall 2009; Rushforth 2012; Santos-Granero 2009; Snyder 2010.

be a basic structural element of societies, even those at simple levels of social development. The three chapters that follow this one (by Snyder, Santos-Granero, and Lovejoy) explore slavery in small-scale societies in the American Southeast, tropical America, and western Africa.

This chapter is part of a long-term exploration of captive-taking and enslavement in small-scale societies worldwide.[5] The larger project is aimed at archaeologists and intended to inform studies of the prehistoric past. It uses ethnohistoric and historic data, especially accounts made prior to the extensive transformations that resulted from European contact. The small-scale groups examined range in scale from semi-sedentary hunter-gatherers, pastoralists, and horticulturalists, to land-based and maritime chiefdoms. These are not societies with cities, formal governments, or large, dense populations. They might occupy villages or towns of a few hundred (or sometimes less) to a few thousand. Social relationships are based primarily on kinship (real or fictive) rather than class. Yet surprisingly, even some demographically very small groups can have relatively rigid systems of social stratification in which slaves occupy the bottom rung. Slaves are mostly captives taken during raids or warfare and are excluded from societal membership specifically because they are outsiders who lack a kinship relationship with other members of the group.

The focus of this chapter, as well as the three chapters that follow it, is on small-scale societies, yet warfare, captive-taking, and enslavement were activities that involved societies at a variety of social levels, with more complex groups generally preying on their less developed and less populous neighbors. Moreover, relationships between slave-raiders and their prey were not static. Changing social or environmental conditions could allow victims to become victimizers.[6] The volatile interactions among indigenous people and European colonizers in many parts of the world often resulted in increases in indigenous warfare and led to dramatic transformations in indigenous power dynamics. The size and instability of small-scale societies means that such political reversals were likely also common in the past.

[5] Cameron 2008, 2011, 2013, which inform the monograph Cameron 2016a.

[6] Lenski, this volume, Chapter 1; Lovejoy, this volume, Chapter 8.

What follows is an overview of several topics important to a consideration of slavery in small-scale societies. It begins by exploring the social location of captives and slaves in such groups. Their sometimes ambiguous social location mirrors many of the same complications that make slavery so difficult to define in more complex societies. A survey of slave numbers in small-scale societies establishes that it was not just the occasional unlucky wretch who fell into the hands of an enemy; slaves could make up a substantial proportion of these groups. I examine the ways warfare and captive-taking functioned in the creation of social status and how the presence of slaves operated to create an elite class even in societies that might be assumed to have been free of social stratification. Finally, I examine the slaves' role in economic production and show how the products of slave labor created wealth for their masters in addition to giving them a source of labor that was free of the obligations of kinship. Nevertheless, slaves were not valuable only economically; a gift of slaves also symbolized efforts to create social ties among groups.

WHO WAS A SLAVE?

This totality of the slaveowner's rights was facilitated by the fact that the slave was always a deracinated outsider – an outsider first in the sense that he originated from outside the society in which he was introduced as a slave, second in that he was denied the most elementary of social bonds, kinship.[7]

Kinship was the fundamental structuring principle of small-scale societies, and uprooted captives had no kin. In many cases, because they lacked kin, captives were not considered human, although most small-scale societies had procedures that would allow them to be integrated into the dominant group and thus to become human. Enslavement of captives was a selective process, and in most societies, not all captives became slaves. In a minority of cases, for example, the Northwest Coast, captives were permanently enslaved, and slave status was passed down through the generations. In the majority, however, enslavement might be temporary, and generational transmission of slave status was limited. While we might speak of manumission for slaves in Greece, Rome, or the South, there was no formalized path

[7] Finley 1980, 75.

to "freedom" for slaves in small-scale societies, only inclusion into or exclusion from the kinship network of their captors.

The majority of captives taken in small-scale societies were women and children.[8] This was partly because adult males were difficult to subdue and harder to control once warriors returned home. Women were valued as sexual partners, and their reproductive abilities could increase group size. Women and children were also easier to incorporate. Women could become concubines or primary or secondary wives. Captive children were highly malleable and could be trained into a slave role from a young age. Both women and children could be adopted, usually occupying marginal and low-status social locations, but sometimes becoming a full member of the group.[9] Factors determining how a captive was to be incorporated included age and sex, but might also involve their personality and skills. A captive among the Comanche who readily learned their language and social practices would more rapidly emerge from the ranks of the enslaved, and some of these former slaves could even gain some measure of social standing, although their slave status was never completely forgotten.[10] In some societies, a captive woman who bore her master children could increase her social standing.[11]

Where a variety of social locations were open to captives, the sorting process often began when warriors returned home with their captives. In the American Southeast, it was the privilege of high-status women (called "beloved women") to determine the fate of captives.[12] Some would be tortured and killed to compensate for the death of the captor group's warriors,[13] some would be adopted, and others would be enslaved. Among the Kalinago of the Caribbean, female captives became concubines and household servants. Men were used as sacrificial victims and boys were raised as slaves with this ultimate fate in mind. In many groups, captives initially went through a severe hazing as their prior identity was erased and their new identity in captor

[8] Also true in Classical societies. Finley 1954, 49–50.

[9] Cameron 2011.

[10] Rivaya Martínez 2012.

[11] Similarly, in ancient Mesopotamia: the Laws of Hammurabi (119, 144, 146, 147, 170, 171, 175, 176a) indicate that slave women who bore children for their masters could no longer be sold.

[12] Snyder 2010, 93; see also Snyder in this volume, Chapter 6.

[13] Also a practice in Classical Greece, *Iliad* 23.175–76.

society was established (ritualized "social death").[14] Captives who faced their torture bravely were sometimes able to negotiate a better social position for themselves – if they survived.[15]

In most small-scale societies, even where incorporation seems to have occurred, the social position of the captive often remained marginal. "Adoption" might be a familiar term in Western societies, but it had a different meaning in the *Pays d'en Haut* (the upper country of New France). "Even captives themselves ... found their relationship with adopted relatives hard to comprehend, not familial in any sense that they recognized yet still expressed as kinship."[16] When food was in short supply, adopted kin were the first to be denied access to sustenance. Among the Iroquois, a man might "marry" a female captive, but the marriage was not officially sanctioned and the woman's position was much like that of a slave.[17] Bowser describes the uncertain status of captive women among the Tupinamba, a group who, at the time of contact, lived in palisaded villages at the mouth of the Amazon River.[18] They became wives but occupied a very different social location than native-born Tupinamba wives. Many were eventually sacrificed, and when they died, their skulls were crushed, a burial practice accorded to slaves. "Thus, captive wives did not achieve full rights of social personhood but were categorized as captives in perpetuity, even in death."[19]

The ambiguity of a captive's status raises the long-standing debate on where to draw the line beyond which a marginalized individual can be classed as a slave. Many scholars define the slave as property, while others, following Patterson, emphasize the relationship of the slave to her master as one of subordination and dishonor.[20] These definitions are not necessarily incompatible, but they have been the subject of some debate.[21] While Marx might have argued that small-scale

[14] Patterson 1982, 51–62.

[15] Rivaya-Martínez 2012.

[16] Rushforth 2012, 47.

[17] Starna and Watkins 1991, 51.

[18] Bowser 2008, 272.

[19] Bowser 2008, 272.

[20] Patterson 1982, 13.

[21] Patterson 1982, 21–27, has argued that the concept of property was too open-ended to specify a particular category of person. Lewis (2017), on the other hand, believes that the Patterson critique was aimed at a limited and incorrect view of the concept of property.

societies do not have concepts of private property, anthropologists today recognize the multitude of ways in which property is conceived, even in Western societies, and this is evident in a consideration of who owned slaves in small-scale societies.[22] Among the Comanche, "Captives belonged to their captors, who sometimes gave them away to a relative or sold them to non-kin."[23] Similarly, among the tribes of the *Pays d'en Haut*, "The warrior who captured each slave exercised mastery over the person as a private possession and any family wishing to kill or adopt a slave would have to negotiate terms with the original master."[24] In other small-scale societies, while a slave might be "owned" by an extended family, larger kin group, or clan, in practice, the activities of the slave were often directed by a household head or his spouse. The prestige of slave ownership also predominantly accrued to that individual. For the Chilkat, a Northwest Coast group, "slaves were the common property of the house group and the head of the house group managed all of the house group's property, including slaves, on behalf of and for the benefit of the entire group."[25]

Although the status of incorporated captives could be ambiguous, many small-scale societies had a well-defined slave status about which there is little ambiguity. Among Northwest Coast societies, the slave could be given away, exchanged, or sold; she could be killed without any social sanction; could be required to do any task at her master's whim and could not refuse; and the master could exercise all of these rights additionally over the slave's children.[26] The same was true for captives among the Chiriguaná of southeastern Brazil, where masters had the power of life or death over their slaves; they could sell them and demand any sort of work from them, including sexual favors.[27] The nature of slave labor in many small-scale societies also underscores the status of the slave. On the Northwest Coast

[22] Donald 1997, 69–70; Wilk and Cliggett 2007, 166.

[23] Rivaya-Martínez 2012, 49.

[24] Rushforth 2012, 46.

[25] Donald 1997, 88. Early Roman households also managed property in this same manner through the *paterfamilias*, and this method of property management continued to affect property relations into the sixth century CE (personal communication, Noel Lenski, March 2015).

[26] Donald 1997, 72.

[27] Santos-Granero 2009, 159.

slaves undertook a wide variety of tasks, especially drudge labor such as hauling water and wood and most household tasks. They were involved in almost all areas of food production, including taking and preparing salmon. They built and repaired houses, made temporary huts when traveling, made nets and baskets, and might even be required by their master to assault an enemy.[28] Similarly, slaves among the Chiriguaná accomplished most of the farming for their masters. Captive women were forced to do the most demanding household chores and captive men and boys the heaviest agricultural work.[29] Chiriguaná men, apparently, did little other than fishing, hunting, and waging war.

NUMBERS

It is conventional to begin the analysis by what I have repeatedly called the "numbers game."[30]

Many small-scale societies contained more than just a few slaves. Often their proportions rivaled or exceeded current estimates of slaves in Classical Roman Italy.[31] Of course, scholars of small-scale societies have as much difficulty estimating the size of slave populations as Classical scholars do, but the results suggest significant percentages. In parts of island Southeast Asia, slave numbers ranged between 10 and 30 percent of the population.[32] Among the hunter-gatherers of North America's Northwest Coast, slaves could constitute between 5 and 25 percent of the inhabitants; proportions averaged 20 percent in communities at the mouth of the Columbia River.[33] Similarly, in the southern Plains, the Comanche held a slave population that ranged between 10 and 25 percent of the group.[34] As much as 10 percent of the tiny Tutchone Athapaskan population of the Yukon were slaves.[35] In South America and adjacent regions (defined as "tropical America"

[28] Donald 1997, 127–28. Slaves in state-level societies could also be forced into combat; see Brown and Morgan 2006.

[29] Santos-Granero 2009, 136–37.

[30] Finley 1980, 79.

[31] See also Lenski, this volume, Chapter 4.

[32] Reid 1983b, 161–62.

[33] Ames 2008; Donald 1997, 182–97.

[34] Hämäläinen 2008, 250.

[35] Legros 1985, 50.

and extending from southern Florida to the Gran Chaco of South America), Santos-Granero reports slave proportions in indigenous horticultural and hunter-gatherer groups that ranged around 5 to 10 percent or more, but this percentage could be much higher when the territory of an entire group was annexed and its residents attached as "servant groups."[36] Although estimates of numbers of slaves held in the precontact Cauca Valley of Columbia are not available, they are reckoned to have been "substantial."[37]

WARFARE, CAPTIVE-TAKING, AND THE CREATION OF STATUS

To take a largely economic approach to Roman slavery, then, diverts attention from the broad cultural significance slavery held in Roman society at large ... Once Roman slavery is approached as a social institution in which the economic aspect, though important, was subsidiary, it becomes possible to appreciate the vast amount of time and space in which the Romans themselves were conscious of the presence of slavery among them and of the impact slavery made upon their culture.[38]

Slavery, however, has never existed in a social vacuum. Like all enduring social relationships, it has existed only with the support of the community ... And it has been shown, elsewhere, that the peculiar symbolic conceptions of the slave and the slave relationship were shared by all members of the community.[39]

The importance of slaves to the social structure of small-scale societies begins with the role of warfare in the creation of social status.[40]

[36] Santos-Granero 2009; see also Santos-Granero, this volume, Chapter 7.

[37] Carneiro 1991, 177.

[38] Bradley 1994, 15–16.

[39] Patterson 1991, 10.

[40] Over the past two decades there has been a debate among anthropologists concerning the prevalence and frequency of war in small-scale societies. Some scholars have argued that European intrusion and the introduction of new trade goods, diseases, and other disruptions created a "tribal zone" of warfare among previously peaceful small-scale societies throughout the world (Ferguson and Whitehead 1992). However, archaeologists have uncovered extensive material evidence for prehistoric warfare among such groups, including war-related iconography, weapons of war, defensive structures, and bodies showing evidence of violent death (for a small sample of such studies in the New World, see Chacon and Mendoza 2007a, 2007b; Dye 2004; Haas and Creamer 1993; Keeley 1996; LeBlanc and Register 2003; Lekson 2002; Martin and Frayer 1997; Schwitalla et al. 2014). There can be no doubt, however, that the

Warfare and captive-taking were common social activities in many, perhaps most, small-scale societies in the past and were often the primary avenue to social status for young men. Status is a quality that requires recognition by others. As Patterson observes in the quotation cited earlier in this chapter, the master/slave dyad emerged only when this asymmetrical relationship was acknowledged and validated by the larger social group. I have argued elsewhere that archaeologists should abandon their perception of small-scale societies as largely "egalitarian" and recognize that members of these groups were highly alert to differences in social status.[41] The existence of slaves in these societies was as accepted a part of the social landscape as it was in ancient Rome or early nineteenth-century Savannah, Georgia. This section uses ethnohistoric examples to highlight the centrality of warfare and captive-taking and the importance of the resulting slaves to social construction in small-scale societies.

Ethnohistoric and other accounts of warfare establish that, although enlarging territory and controlling natural resources or trade routes could be causes for war, the most powerful motivations were male desires for status and prestige, the imperative to respond violently to the death of kin, and especially the aspiration of gaining access to a supply of women beyond those produced in one's own society.[42] This latter motivation explains the high frequency of female captives in many groups. Motivations for war on the Northwest Coast, for example, included protection of status, revenge for the loss of status and other grievances, the desire for slaves, and disputes over women.[43] Warfare here was especially closely tied to status, and the taking and enslavement of captives was an important part of status building. Raiding and captive-taking were a direct way for men to

incidence of warfare was significantly increased in many parts of the world after European contact and that, because of their need for labor, Europeans encouraged the taking and selling of captives for the slave trade (e.g., Lovejoy 2012, 73–75). This pattern was not unique to postcolonial times, however. In a study of the greater Mediterranean region from Classical antiquity to the early modern era, Fynn-Paul (2009) shows increases in indigenous warfare and slaving occur in areas adjacent to state-level societies because of the state's demands for slaves.

[41] Cameron 2016b.

[42] Chagnon 1988; Maschner and Reedy-Maschner 1998; see also Bishop and Lytwyn 2007 for band-level societies.

[43] Ames and Maschner 1999, 195–99; Donald 1997, 105; Mitchell 1984; see Kan 1989, 222–23 for the Tlingit.

achieve wealth that they could convert to prestige through the hosting of feasts and other ceremonies, including the well-known potlatch.[44]

Captive-taking and the high rank that accrued to successful raiders were an integral part of the ethos of many small-scale societies. The centrality of these cultural attitudes not only fueled raiding and warfare but validated the taking and keeping of captives. For example, in the *Pays d'en Haut* "No honor was more important to a young man than capturing slaves. His success was celebrated in public ceremonies, etched into his war clubs, and displayed on his body with tattoos representing each enemy he had captured."[45] The high status that derived from success in warfare and captive-taking was often enshrined in local legend, myths, or sagas of the exploits of warriors. In the coastal chiefdoms of the Philippine Islands during the twelfth to sixteenth centuries, the social value and importance of warfare and raiding were bolstered by an ideology presented through epic tales in which elite warriors attacked their enemies and returned with many captives and other valuables.[46] In fact, the taking of captives was more highly valued than killing enemies.

As in ancient Rome, slaves in small-scale societies were owned primarily by an elite stratum.[47] Recognized leaders funded, organized, or led raids or war parties and generally took the bulk of the booty, including captives, although they might distribute some to successful warriors. In other cases, the young man who took the captive remained her master, and the captive was generally a major first step on the captor's road to social and economic success. Among the Kalinago, at the end of a raid, female captives were kept by war captains, while male captives were divided among the war captains and warriors. In the Cauca Valley of Columbia, paramount chiefs decided when to go to war and led warriors, and they received the bulk of the plunder, including captives. Other men who succeeded in war also acquired captives. "The braver the warrior and the more prisoners he took, the higher the status he could reach ... a warrior could become a war captain in this way."[48]

[44] Mitchell 1984; see also Donald 1997.
[45] Rushforth 2012, 4.
[46] Junker 2008, 119.
[47] Finley 1980, 82.
[48] Carneiro 1991, 177. Comparison could be made to Homeric society, *Odyssey* 14.199ff.

Simply by their presence, slaves created a stratified social order with the relationship between master and slave at its center. As Hajda notes for Northwest Coast groups, "The wealthy and slaves – polar opposites – depended on each other for their status ... The highest social evaluation, in short, rested on possessing others with the lowest. The degradation of one person raised the status of another."[49] Patterson made this point more than three decades ago (although he used the term "honor").[50] Discussing small-scale societies in places as diverse as Iceland and sub-Saharan Africa, he shows that a master's power and status derive from power over slaves. In ancient Iceland, "The class of the lowly is the source from which the master class draws its livelihood and leisure."[51] Among the Fulani of western Africa, "the strong image that the Fulani have of themselves is negatively defined largely in relationship to their stereotype of the despised *maccube* (slaves) and ex-slaves."[52]

Power in small-scale societies accrued to those with the most followers, and captives were instant followers whose owners had none of the obligations to them that they owed to their kin. Scholars of African slavery have argued that ownership of slaves was as empowering there as ownership of land might be in China or Europe.[53] Where captives became wives or concubines, their reproductive abilities could also increase the size of the group and the numbers of followers their master could claim.

The status of their master was also enhanced by his ability to distance himself from daily labor. Slaves in many small-scale societies did all the drudge work, hauling wood and water, paddling canoes, working hides, and so on. Masters in many such groups did little or no work, except that of a managerial type. In fact, much like the ancient Greeks and Romans, work was treated with disdain; manual labor was slavish.[54] Although a leisure class seems antithetical to our common ideas of egalitarian small-scale societies, slaves served as retainers, at the beck and call of their master or mistress, a daily public display of the

49 Hajda 2005
50 Patterson 1982, 81–85, drawing on Finley 1964; cf. Finley 1973a, 41–44.
51 Carl O. William 1937, cited in Patterson 1982, 81.
52 Patterson 1982, 83.
53 Thornton 1999; see also Isaacman and Isaacman 1977, 117.
54 Patterson 1982, 34, 84–85.

master's power and status. The Makú captives of the Tukano (Amazon region), among their many duties, had to hold their master's large cigar while he smoked, female captives breastfed their mistress's baby while the mistress lounged in her hammock, and captives prepared the coca powder for their master's use.[55] Chiriguaná chiefs traveled with many followers, including sons, warriors, and captives. "The conspicuous display of a large number of servant-concubines, captive-soldiers, and children attendants was apparently an important way to build up and consolidate Chiriguaná leadership."[56] On the Northwest Coast, a titleholder did almost nothing beyond the management of his household. Titleholders scorned work. "A high-born Tlingit does little outside ceremonial activities other than amuse himself. He will scarcely speak to anyone but his equal. Common labor is quite impossible if he wishes to maintain his prestige. *Anyeti* [titleholder] women are not taught the common art of weaving ... In fact, girls who have never worked are considered special prizes to be won in marriage."[57]

Sacrifice was perhaps the ultimate symbol of the master's power over the slave. Slaves were not infrequently sacrificed at public ceremonies, displaying the owner's extraordinary wealth, which was so great that he could afford to destroy his most valuable possessions. Sacrifice was also common at the funeral of an important person to accompany the dead into the afterworld. When chiefs in the Cauca Valley died, "Their rich funerary accompaniments included their gold and feather adornments, weapons, and jars of food and fermented drink, as well as wives and war captives, who were sacrificed to serve as chiefly burial retainers."[58] Slaves among the Germanic societies of northern Europe prior to the end of the fifth century CE were sacrificed to gods, often by drowning.[59] Among the Calusa of southern Florida, "they took captives to sacrifice during annual fertility rites."[60] One

[55] Santos-Granero 2009, 133.

[56] Santos-Granero 2009, 137. This can perhaps be compared with the way in which the Romans displayed their captives in great triumphal processions as generals returned from war or paraded their slaves in the funeral corteges of prominent people (Bradley 1994, 24–25).

[57] Oberg 1973, 87, cited in Donald 1997, 124.

[58] Redmond 1994, 32.

[59] Lenski 2008, 94–95. Archaeologists have documented sacrificed slaves in European Neolithic graves beginning as early as 6000 BCE; see Testart et al. 2012.

[60] Santos-Granero 2009, 86.

European explorer explained that Calusa gods demanded these sacrificial victims.[61]

Slaves were significant actors in the social structure of many small-scale societies. Young warriors gained praise and acclaim when they returned with a captive and the captive was often an initial step up the social ladder for the young man. In small-scale societies, just as in complex states, slaves were owned primarily by the wealthy who used them in public displays of status. The rich often did no real work, but let the community watch as their slaves waited on them, labored for them, followed them about, or were sacrificed to serve their masters in the afterworld. The master and his family gained immeasurable status from this relationship to the slave, a constant reminder of the superiority of one and the servile and wretched condition of the other. Far from being part of a social dynamic important in only five "Slave Societies," as suggested by Finley, slaves could exercise a pervasive cultural influence that permeated small-scale societies too.

THE SLAVE ECONOMY IN SMALL-SCALE SOCIETIES

> No one will deny that the American slave states were slave societies: given the presence of enough slaves, above an undefinable minimum, the test is not numbers but social and economic location ... By "location" I mean two interlocking things, location in employment (where slaves worked) and location in the social structure (which strata possessed and relied on slave labor).[62]

> What [Thomas] Jefferson set out clearly for the first time was that he was making 4 percent profit every year on the birth of black children ... slavery presented an investment strategy for the future.[63]

Finley argues against slaves as a social class in Rome because their masters could force them into any sort of labor, from mine work to craft production.[64] Although the range of productive activities (also the scale of productive activities) is far more limited in small-scale societies, masters exercised the same power over their slaves, who were also fungible laborers for the very reason that they lacked personhood in the enslaving society. In addition to drudge work, slaves

[61] Santos-Granero 2009, 86.
[62] Finley 1973a, 71–72.
[63] Wiencek 2012, 44.
[64] Finley 1980, 77.

paddled canoes, processed fish and animal hides, tended domestic animals, worked in agricultural fields, made crafts, cared for small children, and served as general gofers. While the economic systems of small-scale societies were nothing like those of Finley's five "Slave Societies," the labor of slaves in these societies was nonetheless used to enrich their masters. The work of slaves allowed masters to accumulate surplus food and other goods that could be given away in status-enhancing public ceremonies or as wealth in power-generating systems of trade.

In horticultural societies, women did much of the agricultural work, and captive women could add significantly to the labor force. In Africa, for example, women's labor involved intensive hoe agriculture and captured women could add significantly to output.[65] In fact, the increase in production that captive women permitted may have played a role in the development of state-level societies in fifteenth-century Uganda.[66] In South America, slaves and servant groups produced an agricultural surplus for the Tukano and Chiriguaná and other groups.[67] Early European explorers reported that Chiriguaná gardens were highly productive and great stores of food were evident, including fermented drinks.[68] This high productivity was the result of captive labor. In the Northwest Coast, slaves were involved in almost all areas of food and craft production.[69] Women there processed salmon, and the addition of captive women to the group could allow production of a surplus.[70]

The economics of small-scale societies operated largely (although not exclusively) through gift exchange, and status accrued to the person who could give the most.[71] Gift-giving was often undertaken as part of elaborate ceremonies or occasions that have been called "competitive feasts."[72] These occasions offered males in small-scale societies an avenue for the conversion of surplus food into social status

[65] See papers in Robertson and Klein 1983a, especially Meillassoux 1983, 49–50; Robertson and Klein 1983b, 9–10.
[66] Robertshaw 1999.
[67] Santos-Granero 2009.
[68] Santos-Granero 2009, 136.
[69] Donald 1997, 127–28.
[70] Donald 1997.
[71] Mauss 1925[1990].
[72] Hayden 1996.

and power. Accruing and preparing large quantities of food and other goods to be given away at such events was an enormous undertaking, one that only the wealthiest men could attempt. Captives not only produced excess food, but also labored to prepare it. In many groups beer or other alcoholic beverages were critical to the success of the event, yet time-consuming to produce.[73] The addition of captives to the labor pool could ensure the event was successful. For example, among the Conibo of the Amazon, DeBoer argues that men sought female captives specifically for their labor in both agricultural production and in the production of beer, which was used in status-enhancing feasts.[74] Raiding and status were intimately connected by a desire for labor.

Masters in small-scale societies relied on their slaves for the production of durable goods. Treated bison hides were the currency for the bison hunters of the proto-historic southern Great Plains and these groups were "highly specialized commodity producers whose economy focused on the intensive exploitation, processing, and exchange of bison products."[75] Tanned hides especially seem to have become status items, and their quantity and quality were a measure of a man's social position.[76] Female labor was essential for the laborious task of hide production, and captive women, often taken from adjacent Puebloan groups, supplied labor needs. The man with many women could significantly increase his production of hides and thus his status. The durable good of most value among the Comanche was horses, and the vast herds of horses that the Comanche amassed in the eighteenth and early nineteenth centuries required a small army of horse tenders. For this purpose, the Comanche captured young boys, often taken from isolated farms and ranches in northern Mexico.[77] In island Southeast Asia, chiefs and other elite men undertook slave raids to acquire laborers, many of whom were set to the production of craft goods for trade.[78] Female slaves produced both pottery and textiles, which significantly enhanced their masters' economic power.

[73] Jennings et al. 2005.
[74] DeBoer 1986.
[75] Habicht-Mauche 2008, 185.
[76] Habicht-Mauche 2008, 193.
[77] Hämäläinen 2008.
[78] Junker 2008.

Slaves offered another advantage to men in search of prestige. In these kin-based societies, men who needed labor generally had to rely on the help of kin, to whom they were then obligated. Slaves, who were by definition kinless, provided labor without obligation. In other words, men who had slaves could develop a power base independent of other kinship groups, a significant factor in their development of power. For Africa, "the use of slaves to supplement the labour power of younger kinsmen, also amounted to the strengthening of a particular kind of socio-economic order, as much as the control of slave labour by a ruling class consolidated an opposed kind of order."[79]

Slaves themselves were objects of wealth and were widely traded in small-scale societies. They were high-value objects that often circulated in a "prestige goods" economy or as gifts in intergroup interactions. At the time of European contact, the Northwest Coast had well-documented corridors along which slaves and other goods were moved, and these trade routes have been traced well into the precontact period.[80] An account from the early nineteenth century, reconstructed from the documents of the Hudson Bay Company, illustrates the role of the slave trade in the acquisition of wealth and prestige:

> Tsibasa [a local titleholder] raids the Nawitti for people to enslave, trades the slaves for furs, and the furs, in turn, for goods from the [European] fort. With his new wealth, he then holds a potlatch and thus substantially completes the conversion of slaves into prestige and status, and he does all this within a matter of months.[81]

The Conibo of eastern Peru also engaged in extensive trade of captives, primarily newly captured individuals who were often traded for iron tools.[82] Among the Kalinago, the trade in slaves was so common that early explorers documented fixed exchange rates for them.[83] Prices for slaves were similarly fixed in the Germanic tribes during the first to fifth centuries CE and mirrored those in Roman territory at the same time, an indication of commerce in slaves between the two regions.[84]

[79] Cooper 1979, 115.
[80] Ames 2008; Donald 1997, 1939–64; Mitchell 1984.
[81] Mitchell 1984, 41.
[82] Santos-Granero 2009, 154.
[83] Santos-Granero 2009, 151.
[84] Lenski 2008, 98. Consider also the ancient Greek trade of salt to the Thracians in exchange for slaves (Alexianu 2011).

In the Americas, the exchange of slaves was often a powerful symbol used to create productive bonds between groups. In the Northeast, a gift of captives signaled the end of warfare, smoothed over antagonisms that had developed between allies when a raid or murder had occurred, and served as an offering intended to initiate trade relationships.[85] "Both practically valuable and symbolically potent, captives often passed from village to village through overlapping systems of captive exchange, journeying hundreds or even thousands of miles from their birthplace."[86] During the eighteenth century, the Wichita of the southern Plains used women they had captured from other tribes as important elements in trade alliances with Caddo groups as well as with the French.[87] "Taking lessons learned in French markets about European desires for enslaved women, Wichita diplomatic overtures were made to Spaniards in the form of captive women."[88]

CONCLUSIONS

"Slave Societies," according to Finley, are different from "Societies with Slaves" in fundamental ways.[89] In his "genuine Slave Societies," slaves constituted a considerable proportion of the population (around 20 percent or more), they had significant involvement in surplus production, and they were a pervasive cultural element of the societies. This brief survey of slavery in small-scale societies suggests that these same three elements can be found in many such groups. Small-scale societies are nothing like ancient Greece or Rome in terms of social organization, the organization of labor, or the level of production they achieved. Yet warfare and captive-taking were common and often formed the central idiom around which male power was built. Not all captives were enslaved, but even those adopted often lived marginal lives not much different from those of slaves.

In many small-scale societies slaves were as demographically significant as in ancient Classical societies and sometimes even reached the numbers found in the industrial slave states of the American South.

85 Rushforth 2003, 785–86.
86 Rushforth 2003, 787.
87 Barr 2007, 250.
88 Barr 2007, 250.
89 Finley 1980, 79–82; see Lenski, this volume, Chapter 1.

There is no doubt that slave labor in small-scale societies in many parts of the world provided a labor force that produced surplus goods. That surplus supported an elite stratum not unlike that found in more complex societies. Partly because of its association with warfare and partly because of the numbers of slaves found in small-scale societies, slavery was an integral component of these societies. Slaves' presence created hierarchy, and their daily debasement as well as their labor created status and wealth for their masters. While individual slaves might have yearned to be returned to the society of their birth and may have silently despaired of their cruel treatment and daily indignities, neither slave nor master thought the relationship unjust. The slave almost certainly had been familiar with other slaves from birth; she had just not experienced the social situation herself. Slavery in small-scale societies was not just pervasive, it was a fact of life.

This volume includes chapters that support Finley's categorization and others that do not. What I wish to emphasize is that Finley's criteria for "Slave Society" status also fit many small-scale societies. I join those voices that encourage scholars of slavery to look for new methods of analysis that will help us understand slavery as a multidimensional phenomenon that took on different forms through time and across the world, forms that cannot so easily be squeezed into two categories.

6

Native American Slavery in Global Context

Christina Snyder

In 1495, Christopher Columbus shipped 550 Caribbean Indians to Spain. In the cramped quarters of Columbus's caravels, 200 of them died, and the survivors were sold as slaves. To attract potential Spanish buyers, Columbus drew on his experience in the African slave trade, claiming that Indian slaves would be even more valuable than "black slaves from Guinea." Over the next four centuries, millions of Indigenous peoples from the Americas shared the fate of these Caribbean Indians. As Columbus implied, colonialism forced Native Americans and Africans alike into a global economy that valued coerced labor. Native American slavery had much in common with bondage in other times and places, yet most modern scholarship ignores the indigenous side of the story. This oversight, I argue, has less to do with the historical record than with scholarly paradigms. A foundational work in the comparative study of slavery, Moses Finley's *Ancient Slavery and Modern Ideology*, asserts that Indians of the Americas played no meaningful role in this history. Finley mentions them briefly only as potential slaves, but dismisses the significance of their enslavement, writing, "native Indians ... proved insufficient, when not useless." According to Finley, Indians were too vulnerable to European diseases and too unaccustomed to hard labor to make effective slaves.[1]

[1] Reséndez 2016, 23–24 (Columbus quoted on p. 24); Finley 1980, 9, 88, see also 130.

Such claims were hardly new: Finley merely reiterated stereotypes that had circulated in the Atlantic world since the eighteenth century and would be repeated after him. The most significant legacy of Finley's book, developed in this same volume, was his conceptual distinction between "Societies with Slaves" and "Slave Societies." Most societies throughout history, Finley argued, could be characterized as "Societies with Slaves," a condition he also called "primordial" slavery. Slavery was flexible, and slaves were considered kinless, a form of property. But Finley stressed the individualized, isolated nature of enslavement in these contexts, claiming that slavery did not shape society as a whole, in contrast to conditions in "Slave Societies." Finley developed three criteria that distinguished "Slave Societies": they held at least 20 percent of their population in slavery, they relied on slavery economically, and they were profoundly ideologically influenced by slavery, so much so that it represented a constitutive cultural metaphor. According to Finley, only five societies in global history met these criteria: ancient Greece and Rome, and three modern American societies – Brazil, the Caribbean, and the American South. Flattening differences among such diverse cultures, Finley argued that these five "Slave Societies" were qualitatively distinct from all others. For later scholars, slavery as practiced in these five societies – all Western – became a kind of conceptual norm, the "real" slavery, from which all others deviated. While it marginalized the vast majority of slaveholding societies in global history, Finley's model retained a seductive utility that appealed to anthropologists, historians, and sociologists seeking to synthesize slavery's great diversity and variability over time. Finley's work, which has little room for Indian slaves, much less Indian masters, has profoundly influenced the field.[2]

As one of the five prototypical "Slave Societies," the American South has dominated the historiography of slavery in the United States and, indeed, much of the world. Even some ancient historians, who have far less source material with which to work, shape their analyses to fit evidence coming out of the study of the American South.[3] Until the 1970s, most Americanists narrowly focused on plantation slavery in the antebellum period, presenting this model as stereotypical,

[2] Hopkins 1978; Finley 1980; Berlin 2000; Turley 2000; Davis 2008.

[3] For a critique, see Lenski, Chapter 4 in this volume; cf. Scheidel 2005a, 65.

even monolithic. In his pathbreaking *Black Majority*, however, Peter Wood argued that colonial slaving practices were much more fluid and diverse.[4] Since Wood's revelation, early American scholarship has moved away from an Anglo-centric, teleological narrative that anticipated the rise of the United States and toward a more critical look at the competing aims and visions of diverse groups of Africans, Europeans, Indians, and creoles in early America. Many of these studies have located slavery in surprising places: colonial Santa Fe, Ivy League campuses, St. Louis trading posts, Montreal kitchens, and Cherokee plantations.[5]

This chapter focuses on the Native North Americans' experiences with slavery. I begin by exploring the meaning and nature of slavery in indigenous North America, then consider these practices in global context, and conclude by exploring new directions for the study of slavery. I argue that Finley's schema creates dangerous historical blind spots that obscure both the diversity of global unfreedoms and the links that connected slaveholding societies.

INDIGENOUS SLAVING PRACTICES

To understand Native North American practices, it is useful to distinguish "captives" from "slaves." While I critique Finley's "Slave Societies/Societies with Slaves" paradigm, his monographs offer more nuanced frameworks for understanding bondage, and that analysis is useful here. Drawing on his research on ancient Greece and Rome, Finley understood captivity as the broader category, while slavery represented one "extreme pole" on this continuum. Finley also noted the intimate relationship between warfare and captivity in various historical contexts. He wrote, "war … produces captives, not slaves; captives are transformed into slaves by the consumers." Warfare forged grossly hierarchical relationships and displaced conquered peoples, who often suffered captivity in place of death. Some of those captives were integrated into their captors' societies, while others endured Finley's "extreme pole" – slavery.[6]

4 Wood 1974.

5 See, for example, Perdue 1979; Brooks 2002; Gallay 2002, 2009; Barr 2005, 19–46; Miles 2005; Conrad 2011; Wilder 2013.

6 Finley 1980, 68–86; quotations on 68, 86.

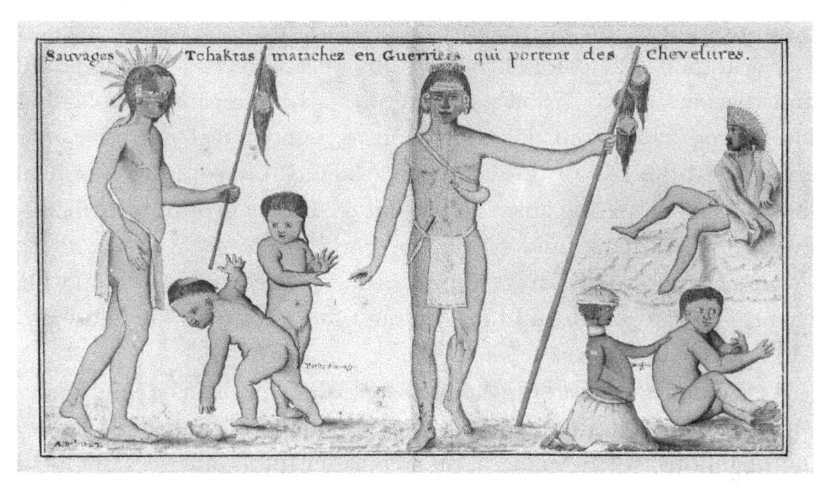

FIGURE 6.1 "Choctaws Painted as Warriors Who Carry Scalps," by Alexander de Batz (1732), illustrating how Choctaws used diverse forms of captivity. The scalps represented conquered enemies whose deaths compensated for fallen kin. The Natchez war chief depicted at top right has a blackened face, denoting his impending execution. An African boy – perhaps a slave, perhaps an adopted captive – is at the bottom right wearing a headdress and skirt. Courtesy Peabody Museum, Harvard University.

In broad detail, Native North America shares much with Greece and Rome. On the eve of European colonization, America north of the Rio Grande held five to ten million people who spoke more than 300 different languages. While practices varied, captivity was probably universal. Captives were usually acquired through war or trade, though we know from the early documentary record that some were runaways or refugees from other societies. Captives endured a range of fates: they might be executed, adopted, or enslaved. Slaves were distinguishable from other captives by the extremity of their alienation from captor society. However, the ways in which the distinction between captivity and slavery manifested depended on historical and cultural contexts (Figure 6.1). In indigenous North America, kinship organized Native societies, and anyone who lived outside the bonds of real or fictive kinship was a potential captive. Among Native Americans, slavery was distinct from captivity (or any other social relationship) in three major ways: masters deemed slaves kinless, exploited them to enhance their own power, and marked them as different.[7]

[7] Snyder 2010, Introduction; Snyder 2013.

FIGURE 6.2 Conquering warrior effigy pipe (1100–1200 CE), made at Cahokia and later traded to the Spiro site in what is now eastern Oklahoma, where it was recovered by archaeologists. Depicts a bound captive at a warrior's feet. Smithsonian Institution, National Museum of the American Indian.

Of all the privations that distinguished a slave, the most consequential was her kinlessness. In a world where kin ties were the font of power, obligation, and protection, the violent severance of those ties left slaves "without any rights, even the right to live," as Theda Perdue argued in her groundbreaking study of Cherokee slavery. Slavery probably originated as a substitute for death in war. Several pre-Columbian pipes recovered from the Midwest and Southeast depict conquering warriors looming over bound captives, depicting the coercive transfer of power from captive to captor (Figure 6.2). Historian Brett Rushforth has argued that this initial violent, humiliating moment of capture stained slaves for life.[8]

[8] Perdue 1979, 12; Rushforth 2012, 65.

Language used to describe captives also commemorated conquest. The Kwakiutl, who lived on the Northwest Coast, used a term for slaves drawn from the root *q!ak*, meaning "to cut off the head." In the Great Lakes region, Iroquois captives were known as *we-hait-wat-sha*, "a body cut into parts and scattered around." In the Southeast, the Muscogee-speaking Creeks and Natchez referred to a portion of their own population who descended from captives or defeated enemies as *estenko*, or "worthless hand." This usage seems to reflect the violent dismemberment of captives from their natal society through warfare. Such conquered people could then be forced into the societies of foreign captors.[9]

All captives faced a kind of social death – the ceremonial extinction of their natal ties – but at times captors extended new kin ties to those they selected for adoption. Slaves in Native American societies were distinguished by their *persistent* lack of kin ties.[10] Nevertheless, some scholars have questioned the level of transformation available through these adoption rituals, pointing out that the kinship terms applied to adopted captives could suggest "closeness of a relationship" but also "authority and subordination."[11] The documentary record reveals that female adoptees sometimes became "chore wives," who were distinguished from social insiders who had married voluntarily. Chore wives were overworked, abused, and socially marginalized.[12]

Other evidence suggests Native societies strongly believed in the transformative power of adoption rituals and were quite successful at integrating foreign captives. In 1742, Cherokees captured a French trader named Antoine Bonnefoy, buried a lock of his hair to signify the death of his old life, requickened him through a ritual at the council house, purified Bonnefoy by washing him, and adopted him into their nation. This is particularly remarkable because Native societies, like most others across space and time, deemed men dangerous and untrustworthy captives, and they rarely sought to incorporate

[9] Patterson 1982, 39–40; Leitch Wright 1986, 18; Richter 1992, 66.

[10] Here I challenge Patterson 1982. Native North American practices support Orlando Patterson's argument that violent natal alienation was a shared feature of disparate global unfreedoms. However, I argue that such a definition applies more broadly to all war captives, including those who were eventually incorporated into the captor society.

[11] Cameron 2011, 183.

[12] Rushforth 2012, 48–49, 60.

them into their societies. After Bonnefoy's adoption, his new brother "told me that the way was free before me," and Bonnefoy was fed, dressed, and treated like other Cherokees. While Bonnefoy was lucky, he was by no means exceptional. Through adoption, captives gained kin ties that afforded them a measure of security, a means of redress, and entitlement to a portion of resources. Meanwhile, slaves endured a kinless, liminal state.[13]

While adoptees were usually addressed through the language of kinship, slaves were distinguished by derogatory names. Cherokees, whose language is in the Iroquoian family, called slaves *atsi nahsa'i*, meaning "one who is owned," and their Muscogee-speaking Creek neighbors similarly dubbed slaves *este vpuekv*, roughly "owned person." Both the Cherokee and Creek terms for "slave" are closely related to those they applied to domesticated animals. According to English trader John Lawson, who visited the coastal and piedmont regions of the Carolinas in 1701, Siouan speakers there employed the same term to describe human chattel and tame beasts: "So when an *Indian* tells us he has got a Slave for you, it may (in general Terms, as they use) be a young Eagle, a Dog, Otter, or any other thing of that Nature, which is obsequiously to depend on the Master for its Sustenance." A thousand miles away, in the midcontinent, Illinois Indians employed dozens of terms to describe slaves and slavery, most of which likened slaves to dogs or other subservient animals. Despite the diversity of Native languages, vocabularies of bondage were united in pointing out how the kinlessness of slaves made them liminally human.[14]

Denied the kin ties that empowered cultural insiders, slaves became flexible mediums of power whom masters exploited for their own benefit. Many masters forced slaves to work. Members of Hernando de Soto's expedition, who traversed the Southeast from 1539 to 1543, saw "many Indians native to other provinces who were held in slavery." They were put to work "cultivat[ing] the soil" and "in other servile employments." Soto's men made special note of such slaves at two Mississippian capitals, Cofitachequi, in what is now central South Carolina, and Pacaha, along the Mississippi River in

[13] Mereness 1916, 244–47, quotation on 246.

[14] Perdue 1979, 4; Martin and Mauldin 2000, 141, 313; Lawson 1967, 210; Rushforth 2012, Appendix A.

present-day Arkansas.[15] Mississippians lived in complex, multi-village polities and depended on agricultural surpluses (especially maize) to feed their large populations. The archaeological record demonstrates that warfare was common among Mississippian societies, whose chiefs vied for control of trade routes, land, and other resources, including labor. Warfare escalated with the onset of the Little Ice Age, beginning around 1300 CE, which produced cooler, drier weather, lower agricultural yields, and increased competition over resources. Slave labor helped offset the costs of climate change, thus maintaining the power of the chiefdom.[16]

In addition to toiling in the fields, masters may have forced slaves to labor on public works. Evidence from early colonial sources suggests that slaves generally belonged to chiefs, leading warriors, and other elites, the very leaders who depended on monumental architecture to demonstrate and confirm their power. Archaeologists have long debated whether coerced labor was used to build some of North America's most spectacular sites, including the twelve great houses and hundreds of unit pueblos that composed the city at Chaco Canyon or the massive earthworks of the Mississippi and Ohio Valleys. Historian Daniel K. Richter cites an oral tradition among the Navajo "that a figure named Noquilpi, or the Great Gambler, lived at Chaco Canyon and, having enslaved all of his neighbors by winning games of chance, made them build him a massive house." New geoarchaeological evidence from pollen analysis reveals that some of eastern North America's largest mounds, including Mound A at the Angel Site, were built in ten years or less, a much shorter timeframe than previously suspected. While it is unclear whether slaves helped build these sites, someone was coordinating hard labor on a large scale.[17]

The complex economies of agricultural societies were not the only ones that employed slave labor. Álvar Núñez Cabeza de Vaca, a member of the 1528 expedition of conquistador Pánfilo de Narváez, was taken captive by hunter-gatherers living along the Gulf Coast of present-day Texas. Cabeza de Vaca recalled how his masters demanded exacting labor from him: "Among many other tasks, I had to dig the roots to eat out from under the water and among the rushes where

[15] Garcilaso de la Vega 1605[1993], 2:312, 400, 439.
[16] Richter 2011, 31–35, 52–53; Krus 2013.
[17] Richter 1992, 19–20; Monaghan and Peebles 2010, 935–53.

they grew in the ground. And because of this, my fingers were so worn that when a reed touched them it caused them to bleed, and the reeds cut me in many places because many of them were broken, and I had to enter into the thick of them with the [few] clothes I have said I was wearing."[18]

Slaves throughout Native North America fetched wood and hauled water. Cabeza de Vaca and another captive from the Narváez expedition named Juan Ortiz were assigned these chores. Ortiz's master, who was a chief, forced the Spaniard to supply wood and water for every household in the village, which Ortiz characterized as "continuous and unceasing labor."[19] As Ortiz suggested, these tasks, which may seem simple, were quite a burden. Because they used wood for building houses, palisades, boats, and tools and often cleared nearby plots of land for agriculture, Native communities deforested much of their immediate surroundings. In older or more populous communities, this effect was even more pronounced. The Creek town of Tuckabatchee, for example, had been continuously occupied since 1400, and by 1799 one observer noted, "the wood for fuel is at a great and inconvenient distance."[20] Fresh water was often, though not always, closer. Still, because beasts of burden were not native to North America (though Indians began to domesticate them in the seventeenth century), both tasks were time-consuming and back-breaking. Moreover, Native masters considered these menial tasks "beneath a man," according to the Chickasaws, and Anishinaabe women would do them only "if they have no servants in the house," according to a French observer. Thus, in addition to their economic benefit, assigning menial tasks to a slave and thereby freeing oneself from low-value work enhanced the status of a master, plus his family, or even his entire village.[21]

So ancient and widespread was the association between slavery and the hewing of wood and drawing of water that reference to these menial tasks became a metaphor for slavery itself. In 1772, tired of hearing Georgia colonists' demands for additional Creek land, leading chief Emisteseguo responded angrily to William Gregory,

[18] Cabeza de Vaca 2003, 96.

[19] Cabeza de Vaca 2003, 2:105, n. 3; quotation from De la Vega 1605[1993], 103.

[20] Foster 2003, 30s.

[21] Moore 1988, 48; Nicolas Perrot quoted in Rushforth 2012, 60.

asking the trader, "Would you like it if I should come to fetch you wood and water?"[22] Did Emisteseguo know that this metaphor resonated with the Anglo-American trader and, indeed, with millions of other people around the world who associated these tasks with servile status? It appears several times in the Bible, perhaps most famously in Joshua's condemnation of the Gibeonites: "Now therefore ye are cursed, and there shall none of you be freed from being slaves, and hewers of wood and drawers of water for the house of my God."[23] With the help of a translator, the Nyinba of Nepal would have caught Emisteseguo's meaning as well.[24]

Outside of the fields and forests, slaves served in their masters' homes, temples, and council houses. The female chief of Cofitachequi, a polity that once covered much of South Carolina, commanded several enslaved women who, according to what Hernando de Soto's men saw, acted as body servants. Spanish slave Juan Ortiz spent his days fetching wood and water for Ozita's subjects and his nights guarding the village charnel house, once fighting off a scavenging wolf. In 1550, teenager Hernando de Escalante Fontaneda of Cartagena de Indias, shipwrecked in Florida en route to Spain, became the slave of a Calusa chief known to the Spanish as "Carlos." While Carlos executed many other Spanish captives, he valued Fontaneda's linguistic skills – the boy quickly learned Calusa and then three other Native languages – and retained him as an interpreter. Fontaneda remained at Chief Carlos's side for seventeen years until he was ransomed at the age of thirty.[25]

As Fontaneda's story suggests, slaves also had exchange value. In the pre-Columbian era, Native Americans developed transcontinental trade networks, and slaves were among the commodities that traveled these paths. When the first Europeans arrived, many Native leaders, seeking to cement alliances through gifting, offered the newcomers slaves. These leaders were drawing on preexisting diplomatic protocols that valued slaves as status-conferring commodities. Many

[22] "Deposition of Joseph Dawes, August 4, 1772," quoted in Piker 2004, 190. Note: I modified the pronouns to reflect Emisteseguo's original question.

[23] King James Bible, Joshua 9:23, slightly modified.

[24] Levine 1980, 210.

[25] "The Account by a Gentleman from Elvas," in Clayton, Knight, and Moore 1993, 1:86, 62; Hudson 1997, 81, 492, n. 53; "Memorial of Hernando Escalante Fontaneda," ca. 1575, in Quinn 1979, 5:7–14.

Native American cultures saw the acquisition of foreign objects – rare and exotic jewelry, artwork, or weaponry – as evidence of a leader's control of foreign and even otherworldly realms. As living, flexible mediums of power, slaves may have been the most valuable sort of prestige good, tangible evidence of a leader's mastery of distant places and peoples. In the case of *caciques* of southern Florida such as Carlos, who traditionally commanded fewer resources than inland chiefs because their soil could not support agriculture, captives proved to be an economic and social boon. According to Pedro Menéndez de Aviles, who ransomed dozens of Spanish captives, the chiefs of coastal Florida "consider it a great glory and victory for them and that the other caciques of the interior may hold a high opinion of them and they may triumph, saying that they live on the seashore and are the masters of the Christians and hold them as slaves." In diplomatic contexts, the gifting of slaves was perhaps the most potent overture of peace, for, in Brett Rushforth's words, it "signified the opposite of warfare, the giving rather than the taking of life." Human spoils of war demonstrated that a leader and his people could be "a powerful ally" or "a dreaded enemy."[26]

In Native North America, as in many African societies, wealth and power flowed primarily from control over people rather than control over land. With the exception of the Northwest coastal region, where families owned specific fishing sites and other land-based resources, territory was deemed the collective property of communities or nations. In this context, slaves were particularly valuable. Chiefs with large retinues of slaves could produce more food, sponsor lavish feasts, and even give away slaves to valued subordinates or alliances – all of which bound beneficiaries of his generosity in a web of obligation.[27]

While slaves had undeniable worth as laborers and potential commodities, their social and political value mattered just as much and perhaps more. Historian Theda Perdue argued that one of the primary functions of the Cherokees' indigenous system of retaining kinless *atsi nahsa'i* was to underline the significance of the clan system that bound

[26] Helms 1992, 185–94; Brooks 2002, 15; Snyder 2010, 26–27; Pedro Menéndez de Aviles to Phillip II, 1572, in Quinn 1979, 2:589; quotation from Rushforth 2003, 785; Rushforth 2012, 34.

[27] For African comparison, see Goody 1971; Shepherd 1980, 85–86. On land, see Shoemaker 2004, 15–17.

all Cherokees into one nation. Among Indians of the Great Lakes, "political and cultural imperatives" outweighed economic incentives. In the Southwest, "desire for prestigious social units" outweighed "demand for units of labor." The public roles played by slaves in diplomacy, feasting, and even the rituals of everyday life demonstrate the intertwined nature of their social, political, and economic value.[28]

In addition to kinlessness and exploitation, slaves were marked with external signs of their condition. As has been true of cultures around the world and throughout history, Native Americans expressed identity through their hairstyles. Because they traveled abroad more frequently for warfare, trade, and diplomacy, men, in particular, dressed their hair in elaborate styles "according to difference in nationality," in the words of one French observer.[29] For many Native groups, the focal point of a man's hairstyle was his scalp lock, a tuft of hair drawn upward from the crown and adorned with jewelry, feathers, or ochre. The exquisite detail in which Native artists rendered hairstyles and scalp locks are indicative of the importance of these ethnic markers. An engraved shell cup dating from the fourteenth century recovered from the Spiro site in eastern Oklahoma depicts eight warriors' heads, seven of which have necks with saw-toothed marks suggesting that they were severed. Each of the hairstyles is distinct, suggesting that they represent vanquished warriors from different polities. The emphasis placed on hairstyle – and scalp locks in particular – explains why scalps were the most important war trophies across Native North America. With a glance, the Native eye could tell not only how many a warrior had slain but also the nation to which each had belonged.[30]

Captives entered Native communities possessing hairstyles that marked them as foreign, and thereafter those who were not adopted or enslaved were forced to maintain this difference (Figure 6.3). Natchez women wore long hair with short bangs, but they cut female slaves' hair "extremely short." Meanwhile, male slaves of the Calusa had to wear their hair long and unstyled, as opposed to other men of that society who cut it shorter and wore scalp locks. Global studies of captivity and slavery reveal that captors often manipulated the

[28] Perdue 1979, 16–18; Brooks 2002, 34; Rushforth 2012, 29.

[29] Patterson 1982, 60; Dumont quoted in Swanton 1911, 51.

[30] Snyder 2010, 17, 36–37, quotation on 17.

FIGURE 6.3 "Eight Heads: No Two Alike," shell cup engraving from Spiro (1100–1200 CE).
Reprinted by permission from Philip Phillips and James A. Brown, *Pre-Columbian Shell Engravings*, Part 2, Peabody Museum of Archaeology and Ethnology, Harvard University (Cambridge, MA, 1984), plate B-17.

hairstyles of their prisoners, especially to mark the transition from free to enslaved. This signaled a slave's distance from a captor's society but also symbolically cut his natal ties. Moreover, preventing a man from assuming the cut of warriors or shearing a woman's locks compromised a slave's gender identity.[31]

Some slaves received more permanent marks of their condition. When Hernando de Soto and his men saw slaves cultivating the fields of their masters at Pacaha and Cofitachequi, they noticed that some

[31] Du Pratz in Swanton 1911, 51, 131; "The Narrative of Le Moyne," in Bennett 1968, 104.

of the male slaves had one lame foot. To prevent escape, masters had cut "the nerves above the instep where the foot joins the leg, or just above the heel."[32] A century and a half later, in the Carolinas, English trader John Lawson observed a similar mutilation – masters cut off male slaves' toes and a portion of their forefoot. Lawson noted that if these slaves did try to escape, "the Impression of their Half-Feet mak[e] it easy to trace them."[33] In all of these cases, the slaves described were men, a fact that reveals Native peoples' anxiety about capturing would-be warriors, but also their readiness to employ them as slave laborers. Many Native oral traditions include cautionary tales about the dangers of capturing and detaining men, who were known to kill in the night or escape and return to their captors years later for vengeance.[34] Early colonial records confirm that Native captors preferred to take women and children, while captured men were in the minority. Disabling male slaves was a way of compromising their power and safeguarding against escape or assault. Fieldwork, in particular, was likely odious to male slaves because in Native North America agriculture was strongly gendered female. When Iroquois and Cherokee warriors taunted one another on the battlefield, they threatened to make captive men "beat corn."[35]

The manipulation of slaves' hair and bodies was part of a broader process of degendering that seems to be a transhistorical, cross-cultural aspect of slavery. Captors in eastern North America made good on their promise to send warriors into the cornfields. In the words of a mid-eighteenth-century male slave among the Creeks, "I made fences, dug the ground, planted corn, and worked hard." Elsewhere in Native North America, male slaves did other womanly work, including serving food, tending to guests at feasts, dressing animal hides, and processing and drying fish. In the colonial and antebellum American South, masters forced African American women to do heavy agricultural labor, work that was considered inappropriate for white women. West Africans categorized carrying wood and water as female work, but they forced their male slaves to do it. Male slaves

[32] De la Vega 1605[1993], 2:312, 400.

[33] Lawson 1967, 59, 208.

[34] On cautionary tales, see, for example, "Escape of the Seneca Boys," in Mooney 1992, 359; "The Captive Alabama," in Swanton 1995, 157.

[35] McDowell 1970, 2:436.

among the Nyinba in Nepal also carried wood and water, and they even sat in the women's section of the temple.[36]

EMANCIPATION

Though indigenous slavery could be exploitative and dehumanizing, it was usually a short-lived condition. Slaves could shed their degraded status by marriage or adoption into their captor's society. When he visited the Creek town of Apalachicola in the mid-eighteenth century, naturalist William Bartram noted the presence of several emancipated slaves, explaining that they had married locals and become "Free Citizens" who "enjoy equal privileges with the Indians." Most accurately, these former slaves had transitioned from kinlessness to belonging. And, even if a slave failed to escape slavery during her lifetime, her condition rarely passed to her children. Instead, descendants of slaves were adopted into the clan or lineage of the captor. In Native North America, the only exception to this rule seems to have been the Northwest Coast, the most highly stratified indigenous society north of Mexico. There, captors practiced transgenerational bondage and developed a clearly demarcated class of slaves, though, over the course of several generations, many of the slave class were absorbed into captors' societies as commoners.[37]

Although William Bartram documented this important path to emancipation, he was perhaps too optimistic in assuming that former slaves "enjoy[ed] equal privileges." Other sources speak to a lingering memory of slave ancestry. In 1771, a Chickasaw named North West told a visitor that his nation had warred so often and taken so many captives that most of his people were "of a slave race"; North West took pride in counting himself an exception.[38] From what he observed among the Creeks two decades later, Caleb Swan concluded, "many individuals, taken in war, are slaves among them; and their children are called, of the slave race, and cannot arrive to much honorary

[36] Dumont in Swanton 1911, 71; Goody 1971, 38–40; Perdue 1979, 15; N. Levine 1980, 210; Donald 1983, 112–14; Townsend 1983, 125; Waselkov and Braund 1995, 62; Brown 1996; quotation from Rippon 1793, 474.

[37] Waselkov and Braund 1995, 156; Donald 1997.

[38] Romans 1999, 125.

distinction in the country on that account."[39] On the Northwest Coast as late as the 1950s, according to anthropologist Leland Donald, Makahs used charges of "slave blood" ancestry to discredit one another at council meetings. While Native societies often aimed to assimilate the descendants of slaves, some stigma may have remained.[40]

With their continuum of captivity that extended the possibility of inclusion even to slaves, Native North Americans maintained an open form of slavery that provided many routes to freedom. Open systems of slavery have been common in global history in cultural contexts as varied as early modern Islamic societies, nineteenth-century Africa, medieval Scandinavia, and ancient Mesopotamia. Adoption, in many societies, was a gradual process that took place over a few generations, though, just as in Native North America, "the blemish of having a slave ancestor" often lingered.[41] However, the possibility of inclusion – indeed the ultimate *goal* of including at least succeeding generations – may have "moderated some of the worst abuses latent in slave systems," as James Brooks has argued.[42] In contrast, closed practices of slavery entailed few manumissions and little hope of escape, even over the course of generations. Atlantic slavery as practiced in many regions of the Americas, including two of Moses Finley's "Slave Societies" – the antebellum US South and the Caribbean – was the most closed form of slavery the world has ever known, "remarkable for targeting people of African descent almost exclusively and for freeing so few of them."[43] Even Finley's other three "Slave Societies" – ancient Greece and Rome and colonial Brazil – offered much more room for advancement during one's lifetime or inclusion over the course of generations. According to Keith Hopkins, a confidant of Finley, "there was in the ancient world no clear cut-off point between dependent and independent or between slave and free," a characterization that is more reminiscent of Native Americans' captivity continuum than the closed nature and rigid hierarchy of Finley's transatlantic "Slave Societies."[44]

[39] Swan 1855, 5:260.
[40] Donald 1997, 246–49.
[41] Patterson 1982, 232–34, quotation on 234.
[42] Brooks 2002, 364.
[43] Snyder 2010, 7. See also Patterson 1982, 262–73.
[44] Hopkins 1967, 167.

COMPARATIVE AND GLOBAL PERSPECTIVES

Moses Finley found that only five societies in history – all Western – met his criteria for "Slave Societies": the enslaved represented at least 20 percent of the population; slaves were a major force in the economy; and slavery was so important that it represented a constitutive cultural metaphor. Most Native American societies do not qualify for "Slave Society" candidacy. Though even rough estimates are difficult, few Native societies included high percentages of enslaved people (though I do note some exceptions in what follows). Moreover, the emphasis that Native Americans placed on the extra-economic value of slaves distinguishes them from "Slave Societies" in the West, where the institution is deemed a primarily economic one. Seeking a more universally applicable definition, Orlando Patterson interpreted slavery "as a relation of domination" – a condition that extended outside of the economic realm to empower masters in other ways. Historian of African slavery James Watson also noted that slaves in many societies consumed more than they produced; that is, they were valued more as status symbols than as laborers. This could be true even in the antebellum US South, where planters signaled and enhanced their social and political capital through practices of conspicuous consumption. As for the third criterion – slavery as a constitutive cultural metaphor – I would argue that slavery shapes all societies where it is present in profound ways, even if there are only small numbers of slaves therein (see Santos Granero, Chapter 7 in this volume). The Cherokees' conception of *atsi nahsa'i* as social deviants, charges of "slave blood" ancestry among members of the Makah Council, and Muscogee whispers about their Hitchiti-speaking *estenko* countrymen all point to the ways in which slavery shapes notions of work, status, nationhood, even of self and other.[45]

Despite the fact that Native societies largely fail to conform to Finley's criteria, the differences between "Slave Societies" and "Societies with Slaves" (or between Western and non-Western slaveholding) are not sufficient to label them as discrete phenomena, and I argue that doing so produces dangerous historical blind spots. As Julianna Barr has explained, "Slavery in North American has been cast as a monolithic, chattel-oriented system of coerced labor," and practices that do

[45] Finley 1980; Watson 1980; Patterson 1982, 334.

not adhere closely to that conceptualization are "often perceived to be more benign."[46] In other words, other forms of enslavement were not "real" slavery. In Finley's stereotypical view, Indians – as historical actors and even as laborers – lay outside the development of a modern global economy, and thus their perspectives and experiences are easily ignored.[47]

In recent decades, scholars have revised our understanding of American slavery, arguing that it is more complex, diverse, and dynamic than previously acknowledged. Though they carried nascent racial prejudices with them, the first European invaders did not bring a robust system of slavery, and, in fact, they themselves arrived in various states of unfreedom: as indentured servants; Moors enslaved during the *Reconquista*; convicts sentenced to hard labor or military stints; petty thieves or prostitutes forced to resettle in underpopulated colonies. Europeans' broad and dynamic practices of unfreedom met indigenous practices that were equally so: sometimes they clashed; sometimes they reinforced one another; often they grew closer together over time. To ignore the connections between Western and non-Western slaveries is to ignore a historical record in which they are inextricably bound.

The melding of disparate slaveholding traditions in colonial North America created a patchwork of slaveries that varied over time and from one place to another. In the Southwest, as James Brooks has demonstrated, Spanish colonizers and indigenous people "shared patriarchal structures of power and patrimony" that prized masculine honor accrued through war, a circumstance that entangled all peoples of that region in a complicated system of captive exchange. Colonists in New France, reluctant to be drawn into alliances with their Indian neighbors, initially hesitated to accept Indian slaves as gifts. Desirous of bonded laborers but unable to access the Atlantic slave trade, French colonists soon embraced the domestic indigenous slave trade, though their demands expanded and even warped previous indigenous practices in that region. Even in the colonial South's "Slave Society," early planters relied on a variety of bonded labor, including Indian slaves acquired from allied indigenous middlemen.

[46] Barr 2005, 46.
[47] Finley 1980, 9, 88.

In 1708, one in every four slaves in South Carolina was an Indian, and colonists exported untold others to English colonies in the Northeast and the Caribbean. Over the course of the eighteenth century, much of eastern North America and the Gulf South turned almost exclusively to transgenerational African American bondage, though Indian slavery (both indigenous practices and the enslavement of Indians by Europeans) persisted in the West and Alaska until the late nineteenth century.[48]

Throughout the Americas, the combination of preexisting captivity practices and Europeans' demand for bonded labor created an explosive trade in Indian slaves that began in the late fifteenth century and lasted 400 years. During this period, between two and half and five million Indian slaves were traded by European colonizers. As Brett Rushforth argues, "slavery took many forms in the early modern Americas, and this variety persisted in both indigenous and colonial settings long after the African slave trade overshadowed other slaving cultures."[49] The Indian slave trade began when indigenous groups extended preexisting diplomatic protocols, including the gifting of slaves, to European newcomers, but in time the demands of an emerging global economy that valued Indian slaves as both laborers and export commodities amplified the trade exponentially.

Some Native groups who acted as middlemen in the Indian slave trade became militaristic slaving societies, and they had much in common with "Slave Societies." Although they probably did not retain high numbers of slaves themselves, the export of slaves was a major source of economic production and engagement with slavery altered their societies in profound ways. Before the late seventeenth century, when the Chickasaws formed an alliance with South Carolina, they had a dual system of government: the civil chief governed internal affairs and managed peaceful diplomacy, while the war chief led the military and took over governance during wartime. As the Chickasaw became major slavers, the power of the civil chief eroded. In fact, Fattalamee, the acting civil chief, decided to give up his position. He told an English trader why: "Finding that the warriors had the best time of it, that slave Catching was much more profitable than

[48] Snell 1972, 61, n. 19, Appendix 1; Donald 1997; Brooks 2002, 34; Rushforth 2012; Snyder 2010; Reséndez 2016, Appendix 1.

[49] Rushforth 2012, 8–9.

formall haranguing, he then turned Warrior too, and proved as good a man hunter as the best of them."[50] In the early nineteenth century, Chickasaws recalled the stories they had heard about the violence of the slave trade era: "There was nothing but war. All nations were at war. The Chickasaws were at war with all nations – this scene of war they remembered to continue for a long time."[51]

Taking a cue from Eric Wolf, Robbie Ethridge has identified the Indian slave trade as a central feature of North American "shatter zones": "large regions of instability from which shock waves radiate out for sometimes hundreds and hundreds of miles." Indians did not need to reside in Southern "Slave Societies" to experience their impact; as middlemen and victims in the slave trade, their societies, even those far away from colonial plantations, were altered in profound ways. In fact, the trade in Indian slaves was continental in scope. James Brooks has postulated that, on the eve of European colonization, the Pawnees lived at the center of a vast captive exchange network, and that this trade intensified with the advent of colonialism. From early documents, we know that Illinois warriors took captives from the central and southern Plains and traded them to Lake Superior, and that Ottawas raided the Southwest and sold the victims in what is now Ontario.[52]

A few Native nations met all of Finley's criteria for "Slave Societies." Comanches, like other Native societies, had a long history of flexible captivity practices: they seized and killed enemy men to accrue war honors; traded other captives; and incorporated women and youths, a trend that became more pronounced in the 1770s and 1780s after a drought and a smallpox epidemic had thinned their population. By 1800, Comanches were the most powerful nation on the southern Plains, and the horse herds they had acquired through raiding and breeding had become so vast that they needed more laborers. Turning to slaves, Comanches conducted raids in Texas and northern Mexico to acquire new captives. By the early nineteenth century, slaves accounted for 10 to 25 percent of the total population of Comacheria, according to the estimate of historian Pekka Hämäläinen.[53]

[50] Moore 1988, 39.
[51] Jesse Jennings 1947, 52.
[52] Wolf 1982; Brooks 2002, 15; Ethridge 2006, 208; 2009, 1–62; Rushforth 2012.
[53] Brooks 2002, 68–69; Hämäläinen 2008, 240–65.

During the same period, four of the South's major Indian nations – the Cherokees, Creeks, Chickasaws, and Choctaws – developed forms of slavery that closely mirrored that of their white neighbors. Seeking to diversify their economies, a class of Native elites began to hold African Americans in transgenerational bondage, forcing them to work on commercial ranches and plantations. Drawing on – and reinforcing – an emerging racial ideology, their national governments began in the 1810s to codify the disenfranchisement of African Americans, while outlawing the enslavement of foreign Indians captured in war. Slavery was still loosely a kin-based practice; Southern Indians, drawing on nativist ideology popularized during an eighteenth-century anticolonial movement, extended metaphorical kinship to embrace other Native people, but distanced themselves from people of African descent. Slaveholding, though still a mark of prestige, became an almost purely economic practice and a closed one as well; only a minority of masters sought to incorporate their enslaved partners or children into their societies. This shift toward racial slavery was controversial, slow, and uneven. In 1830, African American slaves composed only 3 percent of the Choctaw population but 19 percent of the neighboring Chickasaw Nation. Slaves accompanied their masters on the Trail of Tears. The institution of slavery grew in Indian Territory, persisting until 1866, more than a year after Robert E. Lee's surrender at Appomattox, because, as sovereign nations merely allied with the Confederacy, Southern Indians had to sign separate treaties with the US government.[54]

CONCLUSION

To relegate non-Western slaveries to a qualitatively different category is to ignore the connections between disparate forms of slavery in the historical record. Native North Americans practiced diverse forms of bondage, and after Europeans invaded, a multitude of different slaveholding traditions met and, over time, blended. Indigenous and European cultures hardly represented neat binaries, and one slaveholding tradition did not give way to the other in any

[54] Snyder 2010, chapters 6–8. For enslaved population figures, see the 1832 Census of Creek Indians taken by Parsons and Abbott 1832; Baird 1972, 45–46; Doran 1975, 492–515; Littlefield 1980, 10; Bolt 1987, 152; Russell Thornton 1987, 114–18.

simple teleological way. Rather, all the practices involved were fluid and dynamic, and, throughout the colonial era and well into the nineteenth century, a motley patchwork of slaveries extended across North America. In the past decade, scholarship in early American history and Native American studies has stressed the permeability of cultural borders as well as adaptation, hybridity, and movement. Prominent among these works is Andrés Reséndez's *The Other Slavery*, which argues that by disregarding indigenous experiences with slavery we fail "to grasp the common threads running through all these institutions and gain a better appreciation of their combined scope."[55] To understand slavery's breadth and complexity, historians must move beyond a dualistic model. We might instead liken slavery to a virus with varied strains that mutate as they move across both time and space.

Moses Finley sought to provide scholars with a paradigm for understanding slavery in comparative context, but the discipline of history has changed significantly in the past four decades, now encompassing the study of a much broader range of peoples and places, most of whom practiced some form of slavery. Finley's neat schema cannot bear the weight of recent historiography: it fails to capture slavery's diversity and dynamism. If we can agree that history is the study of the human past[56] – not just the story of Europeans and their descendants – we must extend our gaze to disparate global unfreedoms, some of which will challenge us to consider new methodologies or rethink familiar categories of analysis, even those as basic to Western thought as "freedom," "citizenship," and "property." The stakes are high, for this is not just a question of historical practice. As a human rights issue, the danger of defining slavery too narrowly is to dismiss practices that do not conform to archetypes and to overlook its persistence in our own societies up to the present.

[55] Reséndez 2016, 8–9.
[56] Ogundiran 2013.

7

Slavery as Structure, Process, or Lived Experience, or Why Slave Societies Existed in Precontact Tropical America

Fernando Santos-Granero

In a recent book on indigenous forms of extreme dependence in precontact tropical America I argued that native slavery was not, as some authors have suggested, a "colonial product."[1] I asserted that slaves unquestionably existed before Europeans arrived in the American continent and concluded:

> If we take the notion of slavery to mean the condition originating in the violent capture and removal of people from their families and societies – a condition entailing their subjection to ritual processes of desocialization and depersonification, their compulsory inclusion into the society of their captors marked as inferior people without rights, and their total subjection to the power and personal whims of their masters to whom they owe their lives and who can dispose of their life and limb – then slavery was indeed present in native tropical America.[2]

I was more tentative, however, as to the existence of "Slave Societies," preferring instead to talk about "capturing" or "slaveholding" societies. The first term allowed me to underscore the idea that these societies were actively engaged in what I call the Amerindian "political

[1] Santos-Granero 2009, *contra* Whitehead 1988; Langebaek 1992; Taylor 1999.

[2] Santos-Granero 2009, 227. By tropical America I understand not only the hot lowlands between the Tropics of Cancer and Capricorn but also those areas outside the tropics yet close enough to them to have tropical climates. This vast region stretches from southern Florida in the north, to the Grand Chaco in the south, and from the piedmont of the Andes and the Central American mountain ranges in the east, to the Antilles and the coast of Guiana and Brazil in the west.

economy of life," a political economy in which life is the scarcest resource and where participant societies are involved in mutual predation with the aim of appropriating as many potentialities of life from their enemies as possible. The second expression drew attention to the fact that some of these societies constituted an extreme instance of capturing societies, as they had stretched the notion of vital capital – generally encompassing souls/vitalities, bodily trophies, magical objects, ritual paraphernalia and sacred effigies appropriated from the enemy – to include actual living people, especially young women and children. Moreover, by using these terms I was able to avoid the thorny subject of what exactly is a "Slave Society," an issue that I did not want to address at the time in order not to make matters even more complicated.

I did, however, make a passing mention of the subject. Having in mind Finley's (1980) and Meillassoux's (1986, 1991) understandings of slavery, I claimed that "in native tropical America, there were no 'genuine slave societies' in the sense of societies based on a slave mode of production."[3] But that was as far as I went. This, therefore, is a welcome opportunity to discuss a question that I left unanswered and that is still central to slavery debates. I examine this issue using historical information gathered on five tropical American slaveholding societies, to wit: the Kalinago of the Lesser Antilles, the Tukano of Northwest Amazonia, the Conibo of eastern Peru, the Chiriguaná of eastern Bolivia, and the Guaicurú of the Grand Chaco (see Map 7.1). At the time of contact – which varied between the fifteenth and eighteenth centuries – none of these societies had the kinds of institutions that underpinned state formations such as those of the Maya, Aztec, and Inka. But neither were they egalitarian societies concerned with issues of personal autonomy and averse to vertical forms of authority like those characteristic of present-day tropical America. More importantly, they all had developed, or were in the process of developing, supra-local forms of authority, often under the guise of hereditary paramount or regional chiefs. All of them practiced large-scale forms of captive slavery, but whereas among the Kalinago and Conibo slavery was the main and only form of extreme dependency, among the Tukano and Chiriguaná it was combined with the subjugation and

[3] Santos-Granero 2009, 219.

MAP 7.1 Location of Tropical American Slaveholding Societies

attachment of servant groups. Among the Guaicurú it coexisted with the subjection of neighboring peoples as tributary populations.

There are at least three ways to determine whether a given society is, or is not, a "Slave Society." One can adopt an economic perspective and attempt to identify the structural elements that define "Slave Societies" at a given point in time. This was the path followed by Moses I. Finley in his *Ancient Slavery and Modern Ideology* (1980) and, shortly after, by neo-Marxist French ethnologist Claude Meillassoux in his *Anthropologie de l'esclavage* (1986). Advocates of this approach are interested in structure rather than organization. They privilege a synchronic stance, viewing slavery as "being" rather than "becoming" and are fundamentally interested in the economic factors determining slavery. Alternatively, one can assume a more historical perspective and focus on the processual aspects of slavery, the making and unmaking of slaves. By adopting a diachronic perspective and placing emphasis on organization rather than structure and on slavery as "becoming," followers of this second way, such as Igor Kopytoff and Suzanne Miers (1977b), sought to determine the extent to which a society conformed to predominant notions of chattel-like slavery by focusing on status transformations and the ultimate fate of slaves. These two stances are obviously not exclusive; they are a matter of emphasis rather than definition.

There is, however, a third way to assess slavery, one that, unfortunately, has elicited little attention among scholars of slavery. This third approach adopts a phenomenological perspective, focusing on slavery as "lived experience." Developed by feminist anthropologists, this notion concerns how members of oppressed groups find themselves in the world, make sense of the world, and through their actions actively shape their world. By placing emphasis on "structures of experience," or the way people experience things and situations, such a phenomenological approach strives to reinstate the individual and his or her perceptions, feelings, and emotions at the center of social action. In this chapter I propose to examine the aforementioned slaveholding societies from these three perspectives with the aim of determining whether "Slave Societies" existed in native tropical America at the time of contact with Europeans.

SLAVERY AS STRUCTURE: THE ECONOMIC PERSPECTIVE

In his celebrated analysis of slavery in the ancient world, Finley defined slavery as "an institutionalized system of large-scale employment of slave labour in both the countryside and the cities."[4] Although

[4] Finley 1980, 67.

not a Marxist himself, in order to make what he meant even plainer, he added a quote from Marxist historian and political essayist Perry Anderson's *Passages from Antiquity to Feudalism*: "in Marxist language, Finley asserted, 'the slave mode of production was the decisive invention of the Graeco-Roman world.' "[5] Following the same line of thought, Meillassoux defined true "Slave Societies" as those based on a "slave mode of production." In his words, "Slavery, *as a mode of exploitation*, exists only where there is *a distinct class of individuals*, with the same social state and *renewed constantly and institutionally*, so that, since this class fills its functions permanently, the relations of exploitation and the exploiting class that benefits from them can also be regularly and continually reconstituted."[6] Both authors distinguished slavery as an occurrence, or an isolated event, from slavery as a structural feature of society. Following Fustel de Coulanges, Finley claimed that slavery was a "primordial fact,"[7] a phenomenon that existed since the origins of society, whereas "Slave Societies" were unique and few in number. Meillassoux was even more laconic, stating that "one captive does not make slavery."[8]

So, what is it that makes "Slave Societies" different? Finley argued that there are three necessary conditions for the emergence of "Slave Societies."[9] First, ownership of land must be private, and must be concentrated to such a degree that it cannot be put into production with only the labor force of the nuclear or extended family. Second, commodity production must be the main form of production and markets the main form of exchange. Finally, the need for labor cannot be satisfied by means of internal sources, compelling employers to turn to outsiders, namely slaves captured in war or acquired from other slaveholding societies. According to Finley, in such societies, slaves accounted for 30 to 35 percent of the total population.[10] They "provided the bulk of the immediate income from property" and, as such, were "the basic source of elite income."[11] Thanks to slave production,

[5] Finley 1980, 67, quoting Anderson 1974, 21.
[6] Meillassoux 1991, 36 (author's emphasis).
[7] Finley 1980, 67.
[8] Meillassoux 1991, 35.
[9] Finley 1980, 86.
[10] Finley 1980, 80.
[11] Finley 1980, 82.

members of the elite were freed from performing productive activities, and could devote their time to other social, economic, or political pursuits.[12] Finley concluded that this particular "location" of slavery was found in only five societies, which for this reason could be considered the only "genuine Slave Societies": fifth-century BCE Greece, first-century BCE Italy, and the nineteenth-century American South, Caribbean region, and Brazil.[13]

Do tropical American slaveholding societies conform to Finley's and Meillassoux's conditions? The straightforward answer would be yes and no. Certainly, none of the societies discussed here complied with the three conditions Finley posed as being indispensable for the emergence of "Slave Societies." In native tropical American societies, ownership of land was not private, and there was no concentration of land, no commodity production, and no lack of internal sources of labor. There existed, however, important intra- and intertribal commercial networks in which captive slaves were one of the most important prestige products exchanged. Such networks were based on established rates of exchange for captive slaves of different ages and sexes. Among the Kalinago, an adult slave, male or female, was worth a *caracoulli*, a crescent-shaped large pendant made of an alloy of gold, copper, and silver, considered the most important male ornament.[14] Among the Tukano, the price for a captive woman was an *uhtabú*, a white cylindrical quartz pendant, eight to ten centimeters long, a sign of bravery and leadership among Tukano men.[15] Tukano also exchanged captive slaves for other highly valued native objects such as weapons, feather headdresses, ceremonial staffs, and jaguar teeth necklaces.[16] Among the Guaicurú, captives were traded internally, as well as with neighboring peoples.[17] In colonial times, slaves were exchanged either for native products, such as *urucú* (*Bixa*

[12] Finley 1980, 88.

[13] Finley 1980, 9.

[14] Breton 1665, 106; Labat 1724, 1.2: 8 (testimony from 1705). To help readers keep track of the period to which the sources used here correspond, I have included in the references not only the year of publication of the edition consulted, but also [in square brackets] the period in which the author witnessed or reported the events described. All translations of quotes in languages other than English are mine.

[15] Kok 1925–26, 2:922.

[16] Wallace 1853, 288, 300; Goldman 1963, 105–06.

[17] Lozano 1733, 67.

orellana) paste, or for European items such as guns, oxen, or horses.[18] It is reported that after a victorious raid, Chiriguaná warriors used to gamble some of the prisoners they had captured, particularly "old women, children and infants less than seven years old, and a few girls for whom the master has no need."[19] That in all these societies captive slaves were exchanged for highly valued native products confirms the theory that the indigenous commerce in slaves preceded the European conquest and continued to thrive independently of the demands of the colonial markets long after Europeans settled in America.

Although I have found no evidence in these particular societies of the existence of permanent markets or periodic fairs in which members of different groups came together to exchange slaves for other products, these institutions have been reported in many areas of precontact tropical America. One such market, located close to the mouth of the Orinoco River, was described by Sir Walter Raleigh as a "chiefe towne" where there is a "continuall market of women for 3 or 4 hatchets a peece."[20] Here, there was an active commerce of slaves, fine ceramics, green stones, golden ornaments, hammocks, canoes, textiles, and poisons.[21] Similar markets were reported for Cumaná on the Venezuelan coast, where the locals exchanged large quantities of lime powder, used to chew coca leaves, for golden ornaments, maize, and slaves brought in by mainland traders.[22] In the area of Cartagena, Colombia, coastal peoples took salt, salted fish, and hot pepper to inland markets to exchange for maize, cotton, gold jewels, river pearls, emeralds, and slaves.[23] Given this evidence, it seems quite probable that similar markets existed in the societies discussed in my sample.

More significantly, slaves represented a large proportion of the total population in some of these societies. Together with other subordinates, they often provided the bulk of production destined for the subsistence and reproduction of their masters. According to my estimates, the proportion of captive slaves in four of the societies

[18] Boggiani 1945, 133 [a. 1892].
[19] Nino 1912, 279.
[20] Raleigh 1596, 72.
[21] Barrère 1743, 175.
[22] De las Casas 1992, 3: 1493 [a. 1566].
[23] Benzoni 1967, 127 [a. 1565].

under discussion fluctuated between 5 and 19 percent of the total population: Kalinago (5 percent), Tukano (8 percent), Conibo (10 percent), and Guaicurú (19 percent).[24] Based on impressionistic evidence, I would say that the proportion of slaves among Chiriguaná resembled that found among the Guaicurú. These percentages are certainly lower than those Finley estimated for his five "genuine Slave Societies": 30 percent in Classical Athens, 35 percent in Classical Italy, 33 percent in the American South, and around 31 percent in Brazil and the Caribbean region.[25]

If, however, we add members of servant groups and tributary populations to captive slaves, the relative weight of subordinates increases considerably in the societies of my sample. The combined population of captive slaves and attached servant groups represented 28 percent of the Tukano population and between 20 and 80 percent of the Chiriguaná population.[26] In turn, the joint population of war captives and tributaries in Guaicurú society represented between 42 and 61 percent of the total. Even if we were to accept only the lower end of these ranges, this would still mean that in societies combining captive slavery with other forms of servitude, the proportion of subordinates could be as high as 20 to 40 percent of the total population, a range that resembles that found in Classical "Slave Societies."

Although captive slaves did not always free their masters from the need to work, this very much depended on the diverse regimes of servitude and the demographic weight of subordinates that existed with respect to the total population in this region of the world.[27] Among societies where the holding of captives as slaves was the only form of servitude and subordinates represented no more than 10 percent of the total population (Kalinago and Conibo), captives worked alongside their masters. One source notes that the Conibo used to assign their slaves the heaviest household chores but that they used to work side by side with them, so that captives "served them more as companions than as slaves."[28] In contrast, where captive slaves

[24] Santos-Granero 2009, chs. 2–4.

[25] Finley 1980, 80; but see Harper and Scheidel, Chapter 3 in this volume, who argue that the percentage of slaves in ancient Rome was not as high, oscillating between 15 and 25 percent.

[26] Santos-Granero 2009, 227.

[27] Santos-Granero 2009, 219.

[28] Figueroa 1986, 292 [a. 1661].

coexisted with servant groups and represented more than 20 percent of the population (Tukano and Chiriguaná), subordinates did most of the work, while their masters did almost none. One source reports that the Tukano of the Tiquie River were "laid-back lords ... who barely knew the way to their gardens [since] they had Makú slaves who did all the work."[29] Finally, in societies in which war captives and tributaries represented at least 40 percent of the total population (Guaicurú), members of the chiefly and warrior strata were exempted from productive tasks. It is said that, among the Guaicurú, captive slaves were in charge of almost all productive activities, while "their masters sleep, get drunk or do other things."[30]

So, yes, some native tropical American societies had a large percentage of slaves and other kinds of subordinates who provided most of the subsistence needs of their masters, freeing them from the need to work in productive activities and allowing them to devote their time to other pursuits, namely, waging war and capturing more slaves. In none of these societies, however, were slaves engaged in the production of commodities or in producing a surplus beyond what was necessary to reproduce their own and their masters' families. Rather than producers of wealth, captive slaves were themselves items of wealth. So, no, although from a structural point of view these were societies based on "large-scale employment of slave labour," they could hardly be defined as being based on a "slave mode of production," and thus as "genuine Slave Societies," at least not in Finley's terms.

SLAVERY AS PROCESS: THE HISTORICAL PERSPECTIVE

Critics of the structural approach to slavery argued that defining slavery in economic terms, and from a synchronic perspective, provides a distorted view of this institution. It offers only a static image of how a "Slave Society" looks at a certain point in time, telling us little about the social dynamics of slavery and, more particularly, about changes in the slave condition. Kopytoff and Miers were the most vocal advocates of the processual approach to slavery. In their view, slavery should not

[29] Koch-Grünberg 1995, 1: 276 [a. 1909].
[30] Sánchez Labrador 1910–17, 1:251 [a. 1770].

"be defined as a status but rather as a process of status transformation which may last over a lifetime and spill over into the following generations."[31] Slavery is not so much a matter of "being" as a matter of "becoming." Based on data from African slaveholding societies, these authors suggested that the status of slaves was seldom fixed and permanent. Usually, slaves begin as total outsiders under chattel-like conditions. However, they undergo a process of incorporation that turns them gradually into insiders, first as quasi-kin and eventually as real kin.[32]

Rather than trying to come up with a universal definition of slavery or to identify the elements that make "real" "Slave Societies," Kopytoff and Miers propose that in Africa slavery "is simply one part of a continuum of relations, which at one end are part of the realm of kinship and at the other involve using persons as chattels."[33] This process of transformation of the slave status is what these authors designate as the "slavery-to-kinship continuum." By adopting this position both authors opposed Finley, who claimed that in real "Slave Societies" the slave's loss of control over his or her person "extended to the infinity of time, to his children and his children's children," unless his or her owner "broke the chain through unconditional manumission,"[34] and Meillassoux, who claimed that "slavery is *the antithesis of kinship*" and that in such societies the slave condition was irreversible and slaves could never be assimilated as kin.[35]

Tropical American slaveholding societies were similar to the African societies Kopytoff and Miers analyzed in that they present a broad scope of subordinate relations that range from chattel slavery to mild forms of servitude and even clientship. They were also similar in that the status of captive slaves was seldom permanent. However, this condition was highly variable. Among the Kalinago, for instance, the fate and status of individual captives varied widely according to age and gender. Adult male captives were tormented, executed, and eaten in cannibalistic celebrations shortly after their capture.[36] Boys

[31] Kopytoff 1982, 221.
[32] Kopytoff and Miers 1977b, 23.
[33] Kopytoff and Miers 1977b, 66.
[34] Finley 1980, 75.
[35] Meillassoux 1991, 40, 35.
[36] Du Tertre 1654, 450–51.

were emasculated and raised as household servants.[37] Young captive women could be kept as concubines by their captors, or given as maidservants to their wives.[38] In contrast, older women were always destined to be drudges, forced to perform the heaviest field and household tasks.[39]

In general terms, in Kalinago society, war captives – whether male or female – were never fully assimilated during their lifetime. Captive boys had little hope of ever being integrated; instead they were destined to be executed and eaten in cannibalistic ritual celebrations as soon as they reached adulthood.[40] Captive women taken as concubines could be greatly loved by their masters, but all sources indicate that they were "still accounted Slaves," bearing the marks of their slave condition – short hair and a lack of leg ligatures.[41] The fate of children born from unions between Kalinago men and captive concubines varied according to sex.[42] Whereas girls were raised to marry Kalinago men, boys were kept as sacrificial victims to be ritually eaten when they reached adulthood.[43] In other words, in Kalinago society the slave status was irreversible in the case of men – always destined to be ritually cannibalized – whereas it could be altered, more or less rapidly, in the case of women.

Captives in Conibo society also had little chance of being fully assimilated during their lifetimes. Captive children soon learned Conibo language, aesthetics, and social etiquette.[44] But in spite of their prompt cultural integration, they were not considered fully Conibo because they had not undergone head elongation and, in the case of girls, circumcision – traits that, from a Conibo point of view, signaled their condition as true "civil" people.[45] Captive girls

[37] Alvarez Chanca 1978, 31 [a. 1494]; De las Casas 1986, 1:370 [a. 1560]; F. Columbus 1992, 117 [a. 1539]. These cultural practices are well attested by a variety of independent sources. The fact that these allegations were not directed at any other indigenous people within the region, except for the Kariña of coastal Guiana, who were related to the Kalinago by cultural and linguistic ties, undermines the notion that the Spanish conquistadores made such accusations to demonize indigenous peoples and justify their subjugation and enslavement.

[38] Coma 1903, 251 [a. 1494].

[39] Anghiera 1966, 3r [a. 1555].

[40] Anonymous 1988, 187 [a. 1620]; Labat 1724, 2.4: 108 [a. 1705].

[41] Du Tertre 1654, 421; 1667, 379; Rochefort 1666, 332 [a. 1658].

[42] Du Tertre 1667, 379.

[43] Alvarez Chanca 1978, 31 [a. 1494]; Anonymous 1988, 187 [a. 1620].

[44] Girbal y Barceló 1924, 282 [a. 1794].

[45] Stahl 1928, 161–64 [a. 1895]; Morin 1998, 390–91.

and young women were usually taken as concubines or were raised to become future concubines for their captors' sons.[46] Those female captives who were not taken as concubines by Conibo men were given to male captives, preferably of their same tribe.[47] Under no circumstances, however, were female captives assimilated as proper wives. They always retained their status as servants, obliged to perform the most exhausting tasks.[48] Male captives were also kept as servants and assigned the heaviest chores. Few prospects to improve their status were open to them, since marriages between captive men and Conibo women, described as extremely proud "of the purity of the race," were very rare.[49] Only captive men who stood out because of their good behavior and great valor were given Conibo wives.[50]

Among the Conibo, nevertheless, the general tendency was for captives to marry other captives, preferably from their own society of origin.[51] Captive couples continued to live together with their masters, as members of the latter's households. The children born from such unions were subjected, however, to head elongation and female circumcision, and were raised as "legitimate" Conibo.[52] Having been marked as true Conibo, these children were allowed to take Conibo spouses, and were entitled to all the rights enjoyed by free Conibo. As a result, in the lapse of two generations the descendants of captive slaves became part of the general Conibo population.[53]

The marginality and exclusion of Makú captive slaves in Tukano societies was the most extreme among the five societies of the sample. Although one author reports that Makú captives were regarded and treated as "members of the household,"[54] most sources agree that they were not allowed to live in their masters' *maloca*.[55] They were expected to eat in their own houses, apart from their masters,[56] and were not allowed to participate in the final stages of cooking, or to serve food

[46] Stahl 1928, 150 [a. 1895]; Anonymous 1905, 261 [a. 1826].
[47] Fry 1907, 474 [a. 1888].
[48] Ordinaire 1887, 307.
[49] Fry 1907, 477 [a. 1888].
[50] Stahl 1928, 150 [a. 1895].
[51] Fry 1907, 474 [a. 1888].
[52] Stahl 1928[1895], 164.
[53] Girbal y Barceló 1924, 282 [a. 1794].
[54] Goldman 1963, 105.
[55] Koch-Grünberg 1995, 1:276 [a. 1909]; McGovern 1927, 248; Giacone 1949, 88.
[56] Knobloch 1972, 105.

to their Tukano masters.[57] By avoiding commensal relations with their Makú slaves – relations that in tropical America are the basis of indigenous notions of kinship[58] – Tukano masters made clear that they had no intention of establishing any kind of kinship relationships with them, making the process of assimilation of Makú captive slaves nearly impossible.

Given the almost universal Tukano refusal to marry Makú people, female Makú captives were rarely taken as concubines, serving mostly as household servants.[59] They, however, had to be sexually available to all the men of the *maloca*.[60] If these furtive relationships led to pregnancies, the children of such unions were not recognized as legitimate Tukano and could be ceded or sold to third parties without hesitation.[61] Makú male captives had even fewer chances of being assimilated through marriage, for no Tukano woman would marry a Makú man. As a result, Makú captives married among themselves in most cases. Whether captured in war, or born to Makú captive parents, Makú children retained their parents' slave status and were regular items of commerce.[62] If they were not sold or given away as presents, the children of Makú captive couples were inherited by the children of their captor.[63] Thus, in Tukano society, the only chance that Makú captives had of overcoming their slave condition was through manumission, which was a rare event.[64]

Among the Chiriguaná, the incorporation and assimilation of war captives varied through time. During the first stage, beginning around 1470, when the Tupi-Guarani ancestors of the Chiriguaná invaded the eastern slopes of the Bolivian Andes and were still not very numerous, they increased their numbers by taking local captive

[57] Jean E. Jackson 1983, 155.
[58] Gow 1989, 1991; Belaúnde 2001.
[59] McGovern 1927, 148; Terribilini and Terribilini 1961, 39; Silva 1962, 408–09.
[60] Koch-Grünberg 1995, 1:277 [a. 1909]; Goldman 1963, 96.
[61] Stradelli 1890, 433.
[62] Wallace 1853, 300–01; Coudreau 1887, 179; Stradelli 1890, 433.
[63] Ramos, Silverwood-Cope, and Oliveira 1980, 174.
[64] McGovern 1927, 177. Members of Makú servant groups performed the same duties as captive slaves, but they were allowed to retain their families, kinship networks, and traditional leaders. More importantly, after undergoing a more or less prolonged process of Tukano-ization, Makú servant groups were often incorporated to the Tukano phratric system as low-status exogamous patri-sibs (Koch-Grünberg 1995, 2: 91–92, 99 [a. 1909]; Nimuendajú 1950, 165 [a. 1927]; Silverwood-Cope 1990, 74 [a. 1968]).

women – generally Chané – as their wives or by giving their daughters in marriage to Chané captive boys who had proven their courage as warriors.[65] The children of these mixed marriages were immediately assimilated as fellow tribespeople, giving rise, with the passage of time, to the Chiriguaná as a separate ethnic group.[66] In contrast, captive men were mostly destined to be eaten in cannibalistic rituals.[67] As the intensity of the invaders' attacks increased, and with it the number of Chané people taken as captives, it became more difficult for these to become rapidly assimilated into the emerging Chiriguaná society.

In this second stage, beginning sometime in the sixteenth century, Chané women continued to be taken by Chiriguaná men, but this time as concubines (*guasá*) rather than wives (*emirekó*), retaining their status as captive slaves.[68] The fate of male captives also changed. Instead of being ritually eaten, they became the object of an intensive slave trade with the Spanish.[69] A few captive children were adopted by their captors, but most were kept as slaves. They were raised as Chiriguaná but were seldom allowed to take Chiriguaná spouses, being forced to marry among themselves instead. Children of captive couples retained the status of *tapui*, "real or potential captives"; they were considered "like objects," remaining the property of their masters as long as they lived under their domination.[70] The children of mixed unions were also considered *tapui*, but they stood a better chance of becoming assimilated than did the children of captive parents.[71] At least some captives – probably those directly captured in war – could be inherited by the children of a deceased master, who could then sell them to whomever they wished.[72] In brief, assimilation of captive slaves in this second stage was often not achieved until the third generation. It depended very much on personal attributes, such as beauty in the case of women and fighting skills in the case of men.[73]

[65] Polo de Ondegardo 1991, 138 [a. 1574]; Suárez de Figueroa 1965, 404 [a. 1586].
[66] Díaz de Guzmán 1979, 72–73 [a. 1617].
[67] Garcilasco de la Vega 1963, 322 [a. 1609].
[68] Lozano 1733, 58; Susnik 1968, 38.
[69] Matienzo 1918–22a, 54 [a. 1564].
[70] Giannecchini 1996, 328 [a. 1898].
[71] Métraux 1930, 328.
[72] Susnik 1968, 35.
[73] During this period, the invaders not only took captives from their neighbors but subjugated entire Chané local settlements, which they attached as servant groups. These subordinate groups underwent a prolonged process of Chiriguaná-ization

War captives were assimilated into Guaicurú society considerably faster than into any other society in the sample. Attractive captive girls and boys were usually adopted by their captors and cared for as if they were their own children.[74] When these adoptive children grew up, they were considered fellow tribespeople, enjoying full rights, including the right to inherit their adoptive parents' possessions.[75] Other types of captives, however, were not assimilated quite as swiftly. Attractive young women could be taken as concubines. This exempted them from being treated as drudges, but they retained their servile status throughout their lifetimes.[76] Homely children and ugly women were kept as slaves and assigned to perform the roughest chores, with few possibilities of being assimilated into their captors' society during their lifetimes.[77]

Persons not assimilated as adoptive children or as concubines retained their slave status. They were married to other captives so that, we are told, "they would produce more hunters, fishermen, and servants."[78] At the death of their masters, they could devolve to their masters' children or to other close relatives.[79] One of the few doors to social mobility open to captive slaves was prowess in war. Young captive men who displayed fighting abilities were soon incorporated as warriors and allowed to keep whatever they pillaged.[80] They maintained, however, their status of *nibotagi* or "war captive." In some cases, captive warriors were allowed to marry Guaicurú women, an expeditious means for becoming fully assimilated into Guaicurú society.[81] Emancipation of faithful captives was also possible.[82] With the passage of time, however, even the children of captive couples were assimilated "without distinction into the main body of the Guaicurú."[83]

that was completed by the late 1700s. It is said that by then, the Chané spoke, acted, and behaved in everything "almost identically to the Chiriguaná" (Mingo de la Concepción 1981[1797], 116–17).

74 Serra 1850, 372 [a. 1803]; Serra 1845, 206 [a. 1803].
75 Méndez 1969, 62 [a. 1772].
76 Sánchez Labrador 1910–17, 2:28–29 [a. 1770].
77 Serra 1850, 372 [a. 1803]; Serra 1845, 206 [a. 1803].
78 Serra 1850, 356 [a. 1803]; also Boggiani 1945, 135 [a. 1892].
79 Serra 1850, 372 [a. 1803].
80 Serra 1850, 371–72 [a. 1803].
81 Boggiani 1945, 163 [a. 1892].
82 Boggiani 1945, 117 [a. 1892], 186; Prado 1839, 32 [a. 1795].
83 Serra 1850, 372 [a. 1803].

If the measure of true slavery and genuine "Slave Societies" is the fixed and irreversible nature of the slave status, it is clear that none of the aforementioned, native tropical American societies can be considered as such. However, the fact that the slave status could be passed on to the children and even the grandchildren of captive slaves demonstrates that captivity in these societies was not a temporary condition, as was the case in some late nineteenth- and early twentieth-century indigenous societies.[84] The capture of strangers was not simply a rapid means of solving the problem of scarcity of women or of increasing the numbers of a decimated group. Captive slavery in these societies was highly institutionalized, a fact reflected in the existence of a rich vocabulary revolving around notions of servility, standardized markers of servitude, clear sets of prescriptions and proscriptions ruling the behavior expected from captive slaves, explicit forms of punishment of recalcitrant captive slaves, and accepted norms for the transfer and inheritance of slaves. And yet, in tropical America, like in Africa, the outsider condition of captive slaves was seldom as absolute as it was in the American South. Although in all of these societies war captives were regarded as uncivilized, less than human, and inferior, slavery was understood as a "civilizing" process through which total aliens could eventually be turned into close kin. Therefore, if we were to assess tropical American slavery only from a processual perspective, we would necessarily have to conclude that, whereas there is no doubt that slavery existed in indigenous societies, these societies cannot be characterized as real "Slave Societies."

SLAVERY AS LIVED EXPERIENCE: THE PHENOMENOLOGICAL PERSPECTIVE

Although the structural and processual approaches to slavery seem to diverge, they do so only insofar as they look at the social facts of slavery from either a synchronic or a diachronic perspective. Both, however, share a positivistic perspective on slavery, regarding human behavior as a product of the forces, factors, or structures – whether internal or external – that act on people to generate particular outcomes. As a result, both these approaches have paid little attention

[84] Erikson 1986; Menget 1988; Fausto 2001.

to the personal or human aspects of slavery. This seems to be what Patterson had in mind when he noted: "One of the problems with many anthropological accounts of slavery in kin-based societies is that the emphasis on the structural aspects of social life often leads to a neglect of the purely human dimension."[85]

Here, I would like to bring to the fore the human dimension of slavery by adopting a phenomenological perspective. Such an approach posits that the study of social behavior is "the study of human lived experience and that human experience is rooted in people's meanings, interpretations, activities and interactions."[86] Placing emphasis on the structures of experience, that is, on conscious subjective experience, this approach seeks to understand how people experience "things" – objects, events, situations, and interactions – and how in the process they attach meaning to things. The notion of lived experience has been used successfully by feminist anthropologists to develop new insights on gender relations and the constructed nature of gender.[87] In their use, however, lived experience is not equivalent to truth. Rather, as Maynard proposes, written or oral accounts of lived experience provide "the basis from which to address both the similarities and the contradictions in women's lives and to develop theories as to how these might be understood collectively."[88] Some feminist anthropologists, like Avtar Brah, go even further, distinguishing between the "everyday of lived experience," related to the more biographical or personal aspects of lived experience, from "experience as a social relation," which refers to collective histories and the perception of how a given group is positioned in social structural terms.[89] In this view, lived experience is mediated not just through discourse and the text – accounts of lived experience – but also through material structures and relationships – the conditions of production of such accounts.[90]

Here, I am interested in both senses of this notion, proposing to look at the lived experience of indigenous slavery from both a

85 Patterson 1982, 64.
86 Prus 1996, 9.
87 Collins 1990; Brah 1992.
88 Maynard 2006, 440.
89 Quoted in Maynard 2006, 440.
90 Maynard 1995.

biographical and a collective perspective. Unfortunately, the historical sources on native tropical American forms of slavery lack the kind of richly detailed first-person accounts of the slave experience that are available for other times and places, such as the Southern United States.[91] There are, nonetheless, numerous short accounts and much anecdotal evidence about how particular indigenous men and women endured slavery. Although mostly produced by non-slaves, these accounts furnish important clues as to how captive slaves experienced their condition. When matched with indirect evidence, such as slave reactions to different aspects of captivity, this evidence provides us with a first, rough draft of how captives felt the weight of slavery in precontact tropical America. Despite its roughness, this first sketch has the benefit of calling attention to the human dimension of slavery and, thus, contributes new elements to determine whether "Slave Societies" existed in this part of the world.

The story of an Akawaio boy captured by raiders from the island of St. Vincent during the first half of the seventeenth century provides one of the few accounts in existence of the trials and transformations war captives underwent in Kalinago society.[92] The boy, called Alayoühlé, was captured somewhere along the upper Mazaruni River in the Guyana interior.[93] He was eight or nine years old when his village was attacked and burned and his family massacred, and he was taken to St. Vincent, 420 nautical miles away from his home. Since Alayoühlé was a mainland dweller, he probably had never seen the sea. The long trip from Guyana to St. Vincent in a heavy Kalinago war canoe full to the brim with captives and pillage must, therefore, have been a severe ordeal for him.

Since he was not an adult yet, Alayoühlé was not killed immediately after arriving in the village of his captors for the purpose of being eaten in an inter-village victory ritual, as the Kalinago used to do with all adult captive men. But he probably had to withstand the abuse, beatings, and insults heaped upon all war captives when they

[91] Douglass 1845; Roper 1848; John Andrew Jackson 1862; or in the West Indies, Prince 1831; Strickland 1831.

[92] Chevillard 1659, 115–19.

[93] The following accounts are based on information presented by a specific source. Whenever additional information is used to clarify or complement the main source, the sources are duly acknowledged.

first arrived in the village of their captors.[94] He must have also been forced to witness the killing of whatever adult males were captured with him, including perhaps close male relatives such as his father or older brothers. If so, he probably saw his captors butcher them, throw the innards of the killed captives to the dogs, roast and eat choice parts of their bodies, and keep some of their fat in small gourds for later consumption on ritual occasions.[95] Fortunately for Alayoühlé, by the time he was enslaved the Kalinago no longer emasculated captive boys, a practice well documented during the late fifteenth and early sixteenth centuries.

Shortly after the victory ritual was performed, Alayoühlé's master changed the boy's name to Païaca, an act meant to deprive him of his past identity and impose upon him a new slave identity. Most Kalinago children in the village, however, called him *libelé lixabali*, "my roasted meat," since the fate of captive boys in Kalinago society was that of being ritually eaten as soon as they became adult (around sixteen). His master must have also cut his hair to impose on him a visible mark of his captive slave status.[96] Never again was Païaca allowed to grow his hair long, as both Kalinago men and women normally wore it. Like all war captives, the Akawaio boy was not considered worthy of touching a Kalinago and thus could have physical contact only with other captives. He was also kicked in punishment for minor faults. After several years working for his master doing menial tasks, Païaca was given as a present to another warrior in St. Vincent as part of a marriage agreement between the warriors' families. His new master, described as possessing an "extremely sweet nature," was soon pressed by family and friends to organize a large drinking party to sacrifice Païaca, who by then must have reached adulthood. Fortunately for Païaca, his new master was reluctant to do so. To avoid killing him, he gave the boy as a present to a Kalinago man who was known for being friends with the French. This man smuggled Païaca to Guadeloupe, where he was adopted by the missionaries of the Order of Preachers and eventually converted to Christianity.

The only life story about a captive slave among the Conibo that I know of is that of an Amahuaca boy, recounted by French nobleman

[94] Du Tertre 1654, 450; Labat 1724, 1.2: 11 [a. 1705].
[95] Rochefort 1666, 330 [a. 1658]; Labat 1724, 2.4: 108 [a. 1724].
[96] Anonymous 1988, 187–88 [a. 1620].

Laurent St. Cricq, better known by his *nom de plume*, Paul Marcoy.[97] While traveling along the upper Ucayali River in 1847, Marcoy met a young Amahuaca captive slave in a small Conibo village two days upriver from the mouth of the Pachitea. The boy, who by then was around ten years old, had been captured by the Conibo a year earlier in a raid against his village, located on a right-bank tributary of the Ucayali River. Conibo raiders used to attack enemy villages at night, killing the old people and adult men, and taking with them only the women and children.[98] So, it is more than probable that the little Amahuaca boy witnessed the killing of many of his relatives and neighbors before he was carried off by the Conibo.

Like all war captives, the Amahuaca boy must have been marked as a slave as soon as he arrived at the village of his captors. His hair was cut short, and his bangs were cut a little above his eyebrows to distinguish him from Conibo men and women whose bangs reached their eyebrows.[99] Marcoy reports that when he met him, the boy was "naked as a worm," a feature that distinguished him from Conibo males, who usually wore long tunics and were very modest about exposing their genitals. This suggests that he was still in the early stages of the process of incorporation, for the Conibo usually forced their captives to wear cotton tunics as a sign of modesty and civilization. By then, however, he had learned Conibo, and after one year of living with his Conibo captors, it is reported that "he pretended to have forgotten his place of birth and spoke with disdain about his family of origin."[100] Such wholesale adoption of Conibo language, customs, and points of view did not, however, deceive the Conibo, who regarded Amahuaca captives who attempted to "pass" as Conibo as "savages masquerading as civilized people."[101]

The boy's master must have liked the little captive very much, for he had given him a silver nose-ring that the boy wore with much pride. This, and the fact that the boy was treated as a family member, did not prevent his master, however, from selling the boy in exchange for three knives to one of the leaders of Marcoy's expedition. The

[97] Marcoy 1869, 1:629–33 [a. 1847].
[98] Raimondi 1905, 217 [a. 1862].
[99] Roe 1982, 84.
[100] Marcoy 1869, 1:269 [a. 1847].
[101] Roe 1982, 86.

boy was greatly upset when he learned that he had been sold to the white foreigners and even more so when he was forced to leave the village with his new master. He cried nonstop during the first day of navigation downriver, and at night, when he saw the cook lighting a fire and placing an iron pot on the fire, he started trembling and crying even harder – perhaps, as Marcoy speculates, because he thought he was going to be cooked and eaten. The boy was so frightened that he refused to eat, spending all that first night whining in a rhythmic tone. Marcoy reports that two days later, however, the boy had become so used to his new captors that when it was time to dine he approached them "like a puppy," sat between the legs of one of the men, and grabbed bits of food from their hands. By the time the expedition arrived to the mission of Sarayacu, he was so used to his new circumstances that he had even learned a little Quechua, the *lingua franca* of the Ucayali River.

William McGovern's account of the life of a Makú slave emancipated by his master in the early 1900s is one of the few slave accounts we have for the Tukano.[102] The Makú slave had been captured as a boy by a Desana shaman-chief in the remote headwaters of the Makú Igarapé, a tributary of the Papurí River. Unlike other slave-raiding peoples, the Tukano used to capture not only children but also adult men and women.[103] So, it could be possible that the Makú boy was spared from seeing his parents killed by the raiders. Lacking, like all Makú, ornaments and bodily paintings, the boy must have presented a strong contrast with the highly ornamented Tukano children when he arrived at his captor's *maloca*. This sign of his captive condition was later reinforced by a strict prohibition on wearing feather headdresses and cylindrical quartz pendants, the most valued ornaments of male Tukano, as well as a prohibition on participating in Tukano rituals.[104]

Like most captive children, the Makú boy must have been charged with the care of one of his master's younger sons.[105] He would have followed his little charge wherever he went, done whatever he wanted, and withstood whatever abuse his little master decided to heap upon

[102] McGovern 1927, 177–86.
[103] McGovern 1927, 248.
[104] McGovern 1927, 248.
[105] Koch-Grünberg 1995, 1:276 [a. 1909].

him.[106] In addition, he must have been required to perform a variety of menial chores. Being a captive boy he must have lived in a separate hut with other Makú slaves and servants and eaten apart from his masters. However, despite being well treated and well fed in accordance with the "patriarchal bonhomie" characteristic of Tukano masters,[107] he was considered no more than a "particularly useful sort of dog," except that, as McGovern notes, "the Tukano children frequently played with the dogs, [whereas] a Tukano mother thought it very degrading if her offspring played with the Pogsa [Makú] youngsters."[108] The Makú boy must, therefore, have grown up in a highly segregated setting. His master must nevertheless have appreciated his services, for unlike other captive children, he was not sold, as was often the case, to other Tukano people or, worse still, to local white bosses.[109]

When the Makú slave grew up and became a young man, he started accompanying his master on his hunting expeditions. On one such occasion, the Desana chief had an accident that would have cost him his life were it not for the Makú slave's assistance. As a reward, the Desana chief freed him. The emancipated Makú returned to his land of origin where he settled down with other fellow tribespeople, probably long-lost relatives. When McGovern visited him, together with the Desana chief and four of his warriors, he noticed that the emancipated Makú continued to display a subservient attitude toward his former master. The Desana chief ordered his former slave to go hunting and bring back game. When the emancipated Makú brought two monkeys and had them cooked, he and his family had to wait until the Tukano men finished eating before they sat down to eat the leftovers. The following day, before leaving, the Desana chief told the "poor frightened" Makú that he and his men would leave them in peace provided they assisted him in clearing a new garden. According to McGovern, the emancipated Makú rapidly acquiesced "lest a worse evil befell them."

One of the earliest slave narratives among the Chiriguaná is that of a brother and sister captured by a Chiriguaná chief in the Bolivian

[106] Giacone 1949, 88.
[107] Kok 1925–26, 1:628.
[108] McGovern 1927, 248.
[109] Koch-Grünberg 1906, 877.

highlands in the mid-sixteenth century.[110] The siblings were said to be Christianized Indians who lived in a highland area close to the territory of one of the Chiriguaná chieftainships. They were probably Chicha, an Andean ethnic group that was often the target of Chiriguaná raids.[111] When the siblings were captured they were still children. They probably saw their parents and other adult relatives killed by the raiders, for Chiriguaná warriors very rarely captured adults to keep as slaves. If their father was killed in the raid, they would have also witnessed how his captors beheaded him and took his head as a trophy to his village.[112] If he was captured alive, they would have seen how their father was tied up, dragged to the village of their captors, killed, and eaten in a large victory festival.[113]

During the first years of their captivity, the siblings must have served their masters as personal attendants, doing all kinds of minor household chores. As soon as the girl became nubile, her master must have taken her as a concubine, for ten years later it was reported that she had borne him two sons. Her brother was either sent to work the fields or trained as a hunter and warrior. According to Arriaga, the girl had always wanted to go back to her land "to live among Christians." At some point, she started having a secret affair with a captive slave of her same nation, and it was with him that she planned to escape. Taking advantage of a visit by a passing group of Spanish traders, the lovers eloped with them. The woman did not take her children with her, suggesting that she viewed them as more Chiriguaná than Chicha or perhaps she wanted to spare them from the afflictions of a fugitive life.

As soon as they escaped, the Chiriguaná chief sent the woman's brother, together with a group of warriors, to track her down and bring her back. On their way to the Andes, the fugitives met two Jesuit missionaries to whom they explained their situation. The priests decided to marry the couple on the spot, asking the Spanish traders to take them safely back to the Andes. When their Chiriguaná pursuers caught up with the group of traders, its leader hid the fugitives and claimed that they did not know their whereabouts. When the woman's brother came back to the Chiriguaná village empty-handed, his master

[110] Arriaga 1974, 63–64 [a. 1596].
[111] Matienzo 1918–22b, 271 [a. 1573].
[112] Díaz de Guzmán 1979, 80 [a. 1617].
[113] Díaz de Guzmán 1979, 78 [a. 1617].

was so angry that he cut him down with a sword, causing him to die shortly after.

The brief tales of two female captives among the Guaicurú – a Paraguayan girl of peasant stock[114] and a Chamacoco woman[115] – present a good example of the divergent fates of captives in this society. The Chamacoco woman, known as Joaquina, must have already been a young woman when she was captured by Queimá, the great paramount chief of the Ejué-os, one of the three chieftainships into which the Guacirurú were divided in the late eighteenth century. She must have also been beautiful, for Queimá immediately took her as his wife. Such captive wives often enjoyed great prestige by virtue of their close relation to a great chief or a renowned warrior. They were regarded, nonetheless, as being of inferior stock for having been captured in war.

Children of mixed marriages between Guaicurú men and captive women were treated as if they were full Guaicurú and could occupy the highest positions in Guaicurú society. When Queimá died in 1797 fighting against the Spanish in Paraguay, Catharina, his daughter by his Chamacoco captive wife, inherited her father's position and became head of the Ejué-os. Dona Catharina, or Lady Catharina, as she was known among the Portuguese, was so proud of her Guaicurú chiefly parentage that when, in 1801, she was invited to visit the Portuguese commander of Cuyabá, she declined the invitation, arguing that since she was single, the commander would of needs want to marry her, something she could not accept because she was a high-born lady, daughter of the great chief Queimá, and thus much superior to him in rank.

The story of the Paraguayan captive girl could not contrast more with that of Joaquina. The girl was captured when she was four or five years old during the War of the Triple Alliance against Paraguay, sometime between 1864 and 1870. She was probably the daughter of a peasant family of European ancestry, for she was described as having curly, blondish hair. She must not have been very pretty, though, for her captor, Capitãozinho, headman of the settlement of Nalique,

[114] Boggiani 1945 [a. 1892].
[115] Serra 1845, 207–09; 1850, 349–50, 372, 383 [a. 1803].

neither adopted her nor took her as a wife or concubine once she became nubile. This seems to be confirmed by Boggiani, who, when he met her in 1892, asserted that she had "grown to be a large and strong woman," but mentioned nothing about her beauty. Her parents and other relatives were doubtless killed during the raid, for there is no mention of them. As a result, the Paraguayan girl grew up as a household slave, serving her master and mistress in all sorts of chores, especially cooking. When she became an adult, her master gave her as wife to one of his most faithful slaves, described as "a sturdy and quiet old man, hardworking and especially apt for work in the fields." When Boggiani met her, she must have been around twenty-four years old. He said that by then the girl had developed a deep affection for her masters, and, although she could have gone back to Paraguay if she had wanted to, she had decided to stay with them.

DISCUSSION

These accounts show that the fate of war captives in native tropical American societies varied greatly, even after dismissing gender and age differences. In some societies, war captives had the chance of being integrated quite rapidly, either as adoptive children or as spouses; in others, they had no opportunity to be assimilated during their lifetimes and could only hope to see their children or grandchildren integrated sometime in a distant future. In still other societies, like the Tukano, assimilation was simply not an option, at least at the individual level; the only possibility for war captives to shake off their yoke was through emancipation. In certain cases, captive slaves were treated as cherished family members, and their lifestyles were practically indistinguishable from those of their masters; in other instances they were treated kindly, but were segregated physically and emotionally from their captors' society. In still other cases they could be subjected to different degrees of maltreatment.

Captive slaves reacted to their subordinate condition in very different ways, depending partly on the circumstances of their subjection and partly on their character traits. Some accepted their situation with resignation, leading a life of silent submission; others were quick in adopting the language and mores of their new masters. There were even those who embraced the values of their new masters so wholeheartedly that they spoke with disdain of their people of origin. In contrast, others longed to be reunited with their people, rejecting assimilation and attempting to escape. Some captive slaves developed strong emotional ties with their masters to the point of declining to leave them even when they were given the opportunity; others proved extremely loyal to their masters even in circumstances in which they did not have a close relationship with them. Some, however, refused to allow such ties to hinder them from pursuing a life of freedom, to the point of leaving behind the offspring born to their masters when they escaped.

Despite the great diversity of situations, two elements are constant in these accounts. First, all captives were violently uprooted from their land, their families, and their own people. Second, all of them were treated as objects and, as such, were subjected to their masters' whims, having no control whatsoever over their lives and destinies. This, as Testart has argued, is the crux of the slave condition: "No profession, no social role, no task, no mode of life is typical of the slave condition: that which is typical is neither what slaves do, or how they live, because that depends on the good will of their masters; it is neither what the master does to his slaves, but rather that he can do whatever he pleases, that he has the right to do whatever he pleases."[116] Unquestionably, all captive slaves in the foregoing accounts experienced the total power that their masters exerted over them, as there can be no doubt that all of them experienced a total lack of control over their lives and persons. This is true even of the emancipated Makú, who even after being freed continued to fear his former master and feel the control that the latter still held over his life.

As mentioned earlier, Meillasoux claimed that "one captive does not make slavery," by which he meant that the existence of one slave does not make a "Slave Society."[117] Here, I would like to advocate the opposite view, namely that one slave is enough to make a "Slave Society." If instead of focusing on the structural or processual aspects of slavery we consider slavery as lived experience, it becomes quite apparent that more than a social institution, slavery is an existential condition. It is abundantly clear that the captives featured in

[116] Testart 1998, 32.
[117] Meillasoux 1991, 35.

these accounts experienced feelings of extreme uprootedness, discrimination, powerlessness, and degradation. They underwent radical processes of depersonification and desocialization, even those who were treated more kindly than most captives in their enslaving societies, leading to what Patterson characterized as a state of "social death."[118] Some of these captives might have internalized or embraced the mores and values of their captors to the point of not wanting to abandon their masters or being proud of their newly acquired identity. But even they would – if reminded of how they were captured and turned into slaves – acknowledge the extreme violence, abuse, and coercion characteristic of the slave-making process. For such captives, I would imagine, a true "Slave Society" is neither one based on a slave mode of production, nor one where slaves produce the bulk of production, nor where the slave status is fixed and irreversible, but one in which their enslavement became possible, and in which they were forced to experience the slave condition. For this reason, I would contend that any society that approves or condones the existence of slaves – people deprived of their identity, social connections, and rights, and thus subjected to the total power of their masters – is a "Slave Society."

This would be true both of those societies where slavery is an accepted institutionalized practice and of those in which, although not legally accepted, slavery is implicitly permitted by the authorities and where the general public is aware of its existence but chooses to turn a blind eye.[119] This seems to be the case of at least some contemporary societies. In his 2009 *Global Report on Trafficking in Persons*, a crime that involves "slavery or practices similar to slavery," the executive director of the United Nations Office on Drugs and Crime reports that between 2007 and 2009, two out of every five countries covered by the report had not recorded a single conviction for slave trafficking, which led him to conclude somewhat sarcastically that: "Either they

[118] Patterson 1982.

[119] To account for both types of situations, Kevin Bales has recently proposed a more inclusive definition of slavery as "the control of one person (the slave) by another (the slaveholder or slaveholders). This control transfers agency, freedom of movement, access to the body, and labor and its product and benefits to the slaveholder. The control is supported and exercised through violence and its threat. The aim of this control is primarily economic exploitation, but may include sexual use or psychological benefit"; see Allain and Bales 2012, 4.

are blind to the problem, or they are ill-equipped to deal with it."[120] Thailand, for instance, has been repeatedly denounced for doing too little to put a stop to human trafficking and the subjection of victims to modern forms of slavery such as child prostitution.[121] Of 305 cases reported in 2012, only 27 were prosecuted, and of these only 10 resulted in convictions. Mauritania presents a similar situation. Although it abolished slavery in 1981 – it was the last country in the world to do so – this practice was not criminalized until 2007.[122] Since then, only one slave owner has been prosecuted. In a country where 10 to 20 percent of the total population is estimated to live under "real slavery" conditions, this is a clear indication of the tolerance slavery enjoys as a clandestine institution.

It could be argued that by focusing on slavery as lived experience I am replacing an economic definition of slavery with a moral one, and that by asserting that it takes only one slave to make a "Slave Society," I am depriving the definition of any sociological value that it might have had. I confess to being guilty, but only on the first count. I think that if we define slavery only in economic terms, as Finley and Meillassoux do, we run the risk of underestimating, dismissing, or even trivializing slavery as it is practiced in societies that are not considered "genuine Slave Societies." In fact, the elements that Finley takes into account to define his "genuine Slave Societies" are ultimately quite arbitrary. How do we define societies, like eleventh-century England, in which 10 percent instead of 30 percent of the population was made up of slaves? How do we define societies in which slaves provided a substantial proportion of the elites' income, but whose total economy was not dependent on slave labor, such as Egypt under the New Kingdom (sixteenth to eleventh centuries BCE)? And how do we define societies engaged in slave trafficking, whose economies benefited greatly from such trade but who did not keep slaves themselves, as was the case of the Netherlands in the seventeenth century?

What I propose to do in this chapter is to replace the economic paradigm of slavery with a new paradigm, one based on slavery as lived experience. Under this new paradigm, one slave is enough to

[120] UNODC 2009, 6.
[121] Higgs 2013.
[122] Sutter 2013.

make a "Slave Society," provided that the society in question tolerates this situation and does little or nothing to eliminate it. This is not to say that all "Slave Societies" are equal. Under the moral paradigm, "Slave Societies" can be classified on a continuum according to the degree in which the slave practice is institutionalized, approved of, and enforced. At one end of the continuum are those societies where slavery is highly institutionalized to the point of being legally normative. In such societies, slavery is regarded as morally acceptable; it is practiced openly, and slaves have little possibility of shaking off their condition. On the other end are those where slavery is nominally forbidden, but people are ambiguous about the morality of the practice and authorities tolerate it or are even complicit in maintaining it. In such societies, slaves have better chances of reversing their situation since there is no legal apparatus enforcing their enslavement. In this new perspective, precontact tropical American capturing societies were undoubtedly "Slave Societies." Slavery in such societies was strongly institutionalized and was regarded as morally acceptable insofar as it involved wild, uncivilized war captives. As soon as captive slaves or their descendants were thought to have attained a civilized status, their enslavement was regarded as morally untenable, and they could be integrated into their masters' society as fellow tribespeople, with all the rights such status entailed. In the slavery continuum advocated here, such societies occupied a middle position between Finley's "genuine Slave Societies" and contemporary societies, such as Mauritania and Thailand, where slavery is forbidden but ultimately tolerated.

8

Slavery in Societies on the Frontiers of Centralized States in West Africa

Paul E. Lovejoy

The identification of "Slave Societies" revolves around the internal characteristics of a social formation and its political economy, including the proportion of slaves in the population, their role in the economy, and their status as outsiders and marginalized dependents.[1] According to Finley's conception, a "Slave Society" is one in which 1) a significant percentage (above 20 percent) of the population is enslaved; 2) slaves are involved in a major way in production; and 3) slavery permeates social relationships as reflected in constitutive cultural metaphors. On the basis of these criteria, there were many "Slave Societies" in Africa, all associated with states and permeating many so-called stateless societies as well. Although Finley made an important contribution in recognizing the similarities of slavery in the Classical world with slavery in the Americas, he overlooked the ubiquity of slavery in other places and at other times, particularly in respect to Africa, from where many of the enslaved who were sent to the Americas actually came.[2] I argue here that the distinction between "Slave Societies" and "Societies with Slaves" often emphasizes a dichotomy that distinguishes centralized states from the so-called

[1] I wish to thank Catherine Cameron and Noel Lenski for their comments on various drafts of this chapter. The research for this study was done under the auspices of the Canada Research Chair in African Diaspora History with the support of the Social Sciences and Humanities Research Council of Canada.

[2] Finley's classic work informed my definition of "slave" and my synthesis of various studies that revealed the extent to which slavery has been important in African history. See Finley 1968, 307–13; 1964, 233–49; 1973a; 1979, 247–61; 1980.

stateless societies from where many of the enslaved came. Such an approach challenges Finley's pioneering insights in his identification of "Slave Societies" by examining the links that crossed the boundaries that marked the frontiers between states and stateless societies. The distinctions between states and stateless societies, on the one hand, and "Slave Societies" and "Societies with Slaves," on the other, are false dichotomies. This chapter specifically questions the relationship or lack of relationship between states and stateless societies with respect to the issue of slavery.[3]

This study examines slavery in societies on the frontiers of centralized states in West Africa during the era of the transatlantic slave trade and the corresponding period of jihad in the interior of West Africa in the late eighteenth and nineteenth centuries. In the first instance, the focus is on the interior of the Bight of Biafra in the eighteenth century, where it is generally considered that there was no centralized political authority and no Islamic influence, and in the second, the focus on the areas bordering the Muslim states of West Africa that were founded through jihad in the eighteenth and early nineteenth centuries. In the first case, the Igbo and Ibibio regions were heavily populated and linked through a shared commercial network dominated by Aro merchants that originally came from the town of Arochukwu near the Cross River. The second case involves the numerous small-scale societies on the upper Guinea coast that formed a cultural mosaic on the frontiers of Fuuta Jalon, wedged between the interior highlands and the coast, while the third case categorizes the numerous small-scale societies in hill retreats adjacent to the Sokoto Caliphate that served as a reservoir that was frequently assaulted in the quest for captives.[4] By examining societies in West Africa usually considered "stateless," I focus on communities that were not subject to a centralized political authority or a set of laws that were enforced beyond political jurisdictions wider than hilltop retreats, coastal mangrove swamps, and forested areas where it proved difficult to establish centralized governance.

These historical contexts allow a consideration of how slavery was situated on the periphery of states. In keeping with a critique of

[3] For the Africanist debate over stateless societies and slavery, see Kopytoff and Miers 1977b.

[4] See Lovejoy 2016a.

Finley's seminal study, I am arguing that useful models for the analysis of slavery must transcend the distinction between "Slave Society" and "Societies with Slaves" in order to take into account the states in Africa that had large numbers of slaves, often proportionately more than Finley's model of slavery in Classical civilizations, and in a regional context in which politically centralized states cannot be separated from their frontiers. Small-scale societies, even if the numbers and proportions of slaves were relatively low, were often contiguous to states in which slaves were numerous and essential to economy and social formation.

SLAVERY AS A MODE OF PRODUCTION

Theoretically, the Marxist model of "modes of production" provides a framework in which to view the relationship between the stateless societies on the frontiers of states and the formation of "Slave Societies." The idea of a mode of production based on slavery extends Finley's argument of what constituted a "Slave Society" by recognizing three components of slavery, viz., the use of slaves in productive activities to such an extent that economic relationships became dependent on slavery; the mechanisms of supplying slaves for such a social formation because in general "Slave Societies" did not reproduce themselves biologically but rather did so through the continuous introduction of slaves through enslavement and trade; and third, the mechanisms for the enslavement of people, which usually involved the forcible incorporation of people from outside the state. Sometimes biological reproduction within the state successfully maintained the enslaved population, as in the case of the Southern United States, but this did not happen in Africa, where "Slave Societies" invariably relied upon newly enslaved individuals who almost always came from beyond the frontiers of the states that incorporated them.[5]

The approach to slavery as a "mode of production" addresses much larger issues than the idea of a "Slave Society." Although Marx's concept of "modes of production" foreshadowed and may have influenced Finley's concept of "Slave Society," it was the attempt in the

[5] For an elaboration of this argument, see Lovejoy 2010. A preliminary discussion was presented in Lovejoy 1979, 19–83, with commentaries by Igor Kopytoff and Frederick Cooper.

1970s to understand slavery as a pervasive institution shaping society and economy in Africa that elaborated Marx's insights.[6] Catherine Coquery-Vidrovitch asked whether many parts of Africa, particularly in the Savanna and Sahel, had a "mode of production" that can best be compared to what seems to be implied by Marx's "Asiatic mode of production."[7] Others thought the nature of dependency and exploitation was more akin to serfdom. In addition to Coquery-Vidrovitch, Emmanuel Terray, Jean-Loup Amselle, Martin A. Klein, and especially Claude Meillassoux were among those who debated the nature of "Slave Societies" in Africa, particularly in West Africa.[8] Meillassoux's analysis expanded on the Marxian approach, in many ways summarizing the dynamic collective of anthropologists and historians who had become transfixed by the ubiquity of slavery in Africa and attempting to flesh out Marx's understanding of slavery.[9]

If societies were "stateless," that is, did not have centralized and hierarchical political and judicial institutions, they still had to be governed, and governance had to be legitimated.[10] The historian's task is to figure out how this was done, what changes occurred, and when. What we know about societies that lacked state structures suggests that they frequently seemed to have had a relationship to a state, whether through the threat of invasion, through trade, or through shared institutions, at least in historical contexts where these societies were in proximity to states. My aim is to demonstrate how slavery functioned beyond the borders of states in areas that often can be viewed as reservoirs of potential slaves for the "Slave Societies" that predominated wherever there were states. Instead of trying to find isolation and static social contexts, my intention is to show that the binary of "Slave Society" versus "Societies with Slaves" is not useful because slavery was important everywhere that we have historical documentation, albeit in ways that differed but that were often linked. Slavery was a significant social and economic reality across entire

[6] Marx 1964. Also see Hindess and Hirst 1975; Seddon 1978.

[7] Coquery-Vidrovitch 1975.

[8] Meillassoux 1960, 38–67; Terray 1974, 315–45; 1975, 85–134; Amselle 1977; Bazin and Terray 1982. Martin Klein organized a series of informal seminars in Toronto that led to numerous publications, including, ultimately, Martin Klein 1998.

[9] Meillassoux 1978a; introduction to Meillassoux 1975, 18–21; 1978b, 117–48; 1986; 1991. Also see Lovejoy 1991; Joseph Miller 1989.

[10] Horton 1976; Person 1992; Wondji 1992.

regions that were shaped in specific ways depending on political and economic structures.

Let us begin by considering how slavery in societies without states related to the defensive confinement of small-scale societies on the periphery of states. Suzanne Miers and Igor Kopytoff offered a solution by deploying an anthropological approach that defined slavery in terms of "rights in persons" as opposed to the proprietary rights also inherent, even implicit, in slavery.[11] The intensity of research since the 1970s has revealed variations that challenge an interpretation that there was a dichotomy between state and stateless and even the idea of a theoretical or conceptual progression from societies without states toward centralized states with a corresponding increase in the incidence of slavery.[12] Both Walter Hawthorne and Martin Klein have emphasized stateless, small-scale societies in their work, as have the recent collections edited by Klein together with Alice Bellagamba and Sandra Greene.[13] There is no question that the study of small-scale societies represents important work, but in my opinion the analysis has to be placed in the context of states. In fact, it is necessary to explain the dichotomy of states versus stateless and ask how areas that were not subject to states were governed and how those areas may have related to states, both directly and indirectly, through economy, politics, and often religion.[14]

From the perspective of the slave, the difference between being in a state and being in a society in which there was no state could be significant. If "Slave Society" also implies a subcommunity of slaves who could congregate and had an existence beyond the direct view of the masters, then most "stateless" societies did not have the social conditions that allowed such fraternity. When slaves were present only in small numbers, it was difficult, but not impossible, for personal relationships among them to develop. In some situations, cohabitation or conjugal relations might be allowed. However, the nature of

[11] Kopytoff and Miers 1977b; Meillassoux 1975; Robertson and Klein 1983b.

[12] The extent of publication is enormous; see entries in the annual bibliography published in *Slavery and Abolition* and the many edited collections, such as those in the Harriet Tubman Series on the African Diaspora, Africa World Press. Also see Manning 1990; Stilwell 2014.

[13] Hawthorne 1999, 2001, 2003, 2010; Martin Klein 2001; Bellagamba, Greene, and Klein, eds. 2013, 2017.

[14] Baum 1999; Hawthorne 2010; Rosalind Shaw 2002.

gender relations and the availability of slaves militated against liaisons among slaves that might preclude or limit sexual and other exploitation. Personal relationships between masters and slaves were inevitably too close. However, if slaves were wanted as sacrificial victims for funerals or religious rituals, then the scale of society and the incidence of slavery did not much matter for the individual. Incorporation into a "Slave Society" might be preferable if someone wanted to stay alive.

Nonetheless, there were clear distinctions between slavery and other social and personal relationships of dependency in societies that might have relatively few slaves. These included structures of kinship, marital arrangements, indentures, and pawnship, in which individuals were held as collateral for debts.[15] The power of masters over slaves was based on the existence of these other relationships and was reflected in personal clientage, gerontocracy, gender, and the concentration of political and military influence. In stateless societies, so-called secret associations, often of men only, governed how relationships were interpreted and whether a person was protected from enslavement and how that protection was enforced. These associations were secret only in the sense that rites of passage and knowledge of a coded language determined who could be members, who could not, and at what grade of membership. In the studies of slavery and society in West Africa, it is clear that pawnship and slavery were distinct and were subjected to the close scrutiny of such secret associations. While kidnapping, raiding, and warfare might be the major mechanisms of enslavement that supplied states with large numbers of slaves, interpersonal relationships in small-scale societies tempered slavery, although always allowing for alienation through sale.

As far as historical documentation allows us to reconstruct the history and presence of slavery, it seems clear that neither the institution of slavery nor the incidental practice of slavery were "borrowed," unlike many other institutions and practices that clearly were shaped by outside influences and pressures. The institution of slavery seems to have existed almost everywhere. The enslavement of individuals, their sale, distribution, and acquisition meant that individuals usually crossed cultural, societal, and political frontiers but the concept of slavery, which seems to be as old as recorded history, pervaded both

[15] Lovejoy 2013a; Lovejoy and Falola 2003.

sides of frontiers. However, how slaves were treated, the opportunities individuals faced, and the degrees of exploitation varied from society to society and indeed changed over time. Legal and customary provisions for slaves were contested and changed as well, whether or not codified in written texts and laws or through customary practices, and the extent to which such practices and norms were honored of course varied with time, place, and circumstance.

In addressing the issues related to what constitutes a "Slave Society" in the context of small-scale societies in Africa, it is useful to examine several examples of slavery in societies without states in West Africa, specifically the interior of the Bight of Biafra and the areas on the frontiers of the states established through jihad in the eighteenth and early nineteenth centuries. As to the question what or who was a slave, the answer is always tied to local language and particular customs and practices that define insiders as citizens and outsiders as aliens. In all cases that have been examined in detail in West Africa, slaves could be bought and sold, treated according to the will of owners, and were exclusively subjected to locally accepted norms. If such norms were violated, individual slaves were not usually in a position to defend themselves because of the absence of kinship and the lack of legal, religious, and moral recourse. Because slavery was embedded in culture and society, cross-cultural definitions and comparisons are always in danger of generating misunderstanding, speculation, and consequently poor analysis. Cultural differences inevitably meant that slaveholding practices were contingent on actual situations, the incidence of slavery, and the extent to which societies were stratified. I am only examining so-called stateless societies on the basis of documented information, which inevitably limits the time period under examination. I avoid speculation based on abstractions of slavery in societies in undefined periods of the past and in situations for which there is no evidence.

THE BIGHT OF BIAFRA HINTERLAND

The analysis of slavery in the interior of the Bight of Biafra in the middle of the eighteenth century focuses on a society where there were apparently no centralized states or any of the institutions normally associated with the structures of states. There is sufficient documentation on the nature of slavery in the region to make a number of important observations, nonetheless. This area was not on the periphery of a major state, or at least did not border any state within West Africa, the nearest states being the Kingdom of Benin to the west of the lower Niger River and the small states of the Niger–Benue confluence region, such as Idah and Nupe, to the north. Despite the absence of centralized states, the interior of the Bight of Biafra, particularly the Igbo and Ibibio communities, became a major source of slaves for the Americas, particularly in the eighteenth century and continuing into the early nineteenth century. Hence, it can be argued that the mechanisms for supplying labor to the European colonies in the Americas, and especially British America, placed the region in proximity to states that were part of the Atlantic world and specifically the European countries and colonies with which they were entangled.

The historical evidence for the Bight of Biafra for the eighteenth century indicates that an elaborate commercial network developed under the leadership of the Aro, who initially came from the town of Arochukwu on the escarpment overlooking the Cross River but subsequently established satellite communities throughout much of the Igbo and Ibibio lands of the interior of the Bight of Biafra (see Map 8.1).[16] Through this commercial network, the region connected to the Atlantic world at the port of Calabar, located on the Cross River and historically known as "Old Calabar," and at Bonny, which was situated at the entrance to a major estuary in the delta of the Niger River. Because of the importance of these two ports in the regional economy, we can say that the Igbo and Ibibio countries were on the periphery of a state, in this case most notably Britain, the predominate European trading partner from ca. 1700 to 1807. During this period Calabar and Bonny together provided the overwhelming majority of slaves sent to the Americas from this region. British ships carried more than 85 percent of the slaves from the Bight of Biafra before 1807, mostly on Liverpool, London, or Bristol ships.[17] The elites of these two ports were educated in England, and there is proof of an extensive correspondence between merchants that dates to as early

[16] On Arochukwu, see Bentor 1990; Nwokeji 2010. Also see Bentor 1995; Northrup 1978.

[17] Lovejoy and Richardson 2010.

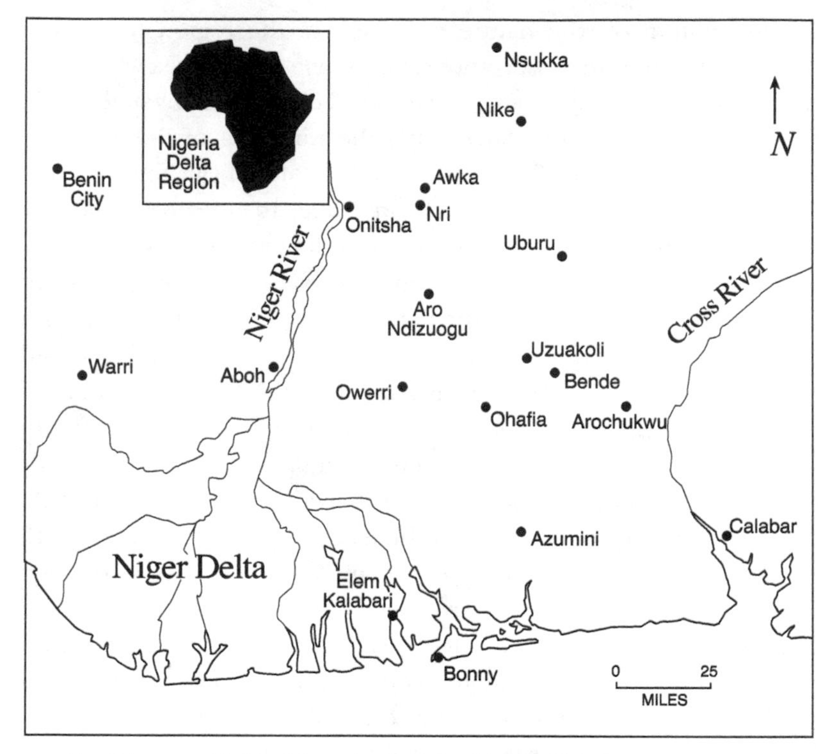

MAP 8.1 Igbo and Ibibio Hinterland of the Bight of Biafra

as 1751.[18] That is, the mercantile elite in Calabar and Bonny were fluent in English and were literate. A large bell, which according to its inscription seems to have been cast in England in 1696, is still

[18] Evidence of William James in Lambert 1975, 69:49. Also see Adams 1823, 42, 144. Adams, who was at Calabar in the 1790s, observed that "many of the natives write English." According to Adams, literacy in English was "an art first acquired by some of the traders' sons, who had visited England." William Earle noted that he had received only one of several letters that Duke Abashy had written; see February 10, 1761, William Earle to Duke Abashy, Merseyside Maritime Museum Archives, Liverpool, Earle Papers, Letter Book of William Earle 1760–61. Evidence of John Ashley Hall in Lambert 1975, 72:537. The connection between King George's son and Lace was made by those questioning Hall; Hall himself denied firsthand knowledge of the connection. Ambrose Lace claimed to have spent £60 on young Robin John Otto Ephraim; see Lace to Thomas Jones, November 11, 1773 in Gomer Williams 1897, 541–42; Hallett 1964, 195; Clarkson 1788, 125–26; "Letter from the Delegates from Liverpool, in answer to the Enquiry made by the Committee respecting the Natives of Africa who have been sent to England for Education, addressed to John Tarleton Esquire" in Lambert 1975, 69:83–86.

to be found at Arochukwu, where it can be said to symbolize the relationship of this network with Britain.[19] There is every reason to believe that the bell has been in Arochukwu since the end of the seventeenth century, although it is impossible to prove this conclusively. Nonetheless, the power of British trade and credit penetrated inland to the headquarters of the Aro commercial network. Anyone who was a slave in the interior potentially could have been sold to an Aro merchant and thereby could have been taken to either Calabar or Bonny and almost certainly from there to British territory in the Americas. The bell symbolized the relationship between the Aro and the British. The Aro communities that were scattered throughout the interior thereby organized the slave trade for Calabar and Bonny as a means of supplying labor for British colonies and through re-export to other colonies, including the Hispanic mainland.

The Aro staged caravans that passed through a country comprised of small clusters of villages that shared a common, local allegiance but could easily be in conflict with neighboring sets of villages. Without a centralized state, the Aro merchants relied on other mechanisms to guarantee their own personal safety and their ability to trade over considerable distances. They relied on certain widely known principles, including severe retribution for the shedding of Aro blood. These mechanisms included the employment of mercenary "head hunters" that guaranteed that Aro merchants were not harassed in the interior and were allowed to pass freely along trade routes. Brutal justice was left in the hands of mercenaries such as the Abam, Abriba, Ohafia, and Edda. In addition, the widespread belief that an oracle at Arochukwu had supernatural powers provided added security for Aro travelers. The Aro were easy to recognize because when traveling through the countryside they covered themselves with camwood powder, a cosmetic that gives a reddish hue to the skin. Aro merchants established formal relationships with the different sets of villages, frequenting periodic markets that were held every four days and concentrating their trade at monthly fairs at Bende, Uburu, and elsewhere. The Aro settlement at Arondizuogu became particularly important by the middle of the eighteenth century, as the work of

[19] For the bell at Arochukwu, see Lovejoy and Richardson 2010, 22; it was photographed by Richardson and Lovejoy in 2010.

Ugo Nwokeji has demonstrated.[20] The enslaved victims were taken to riverside markets where merchants from Calabar and Bonny and to a lesser extent, Elem Kalabari, also in the Niger delta, came in large riverboats that were capable of carrying dozens of people and armed with small cannons mounted fore, aft, and sometimes on a swivel in the middle. The boats traveled in groups, amounting to a small navy, which ascended upriver to purchase slaves from the Aro in exchange for imports from Europe, dried fish, and sea salt.

The Igbo and Ibibio region was densely populated; the terrain was not characterized by defensible features, but had sets of towns organizing markets in rotation every four days, where councils of senior males oversaw intercommunity relations and guaranteed basic peace and safety, but only locally. Without a state structure, an all-male secret society that had several grades of seniority undertook the task of regulating social relations, economic contracts, and unexplained events and happenings. When discipline and retribution were necessary, the "secret" society, to which free adult males belonged, was responsible for administering justice or punishment, which could be extreme. The most important of these societies was the *ekpe* society, also known in Igbo as *odonko*, to which only males could belong and which expressed itself through the personification of the leopard. It acted by invoking a masquerade of a human leopard as its public persona that undertook collective and arbitrary enforcement of the decisions of the senior *ekpe* members.[21]

How did slavery fit into this dispersed and fragmented social framework, divided by two languages, whose social significance and place in the political economy hardly made a difference as far as language and culture were concerned? Igbo and Ibibio might intermarry along border communities such as at Arochukwu itself, or they might intermingle through slavery since slaves were traded across the linguistic border, as the account of Gustavus Vassa attests. Vassa, whose childhood name was Olaudah Equiano, came from an Igbo village but passed through Ibibio territory on his way to the coast for passage to Barbados and then to Virginia.[22] Vassa's personal testimony confirms

[20] Nwokeji 2010.

[21] On *ekpe*, see Lovejoy 2013b; Röschenthaler 2011. Also see Ivor Miller 2012; Smalligan 2011.

[22] Lovejoy 2012b; Vassa 1789.

this interpretation that the interior of the Bight of Biafra was politically fragmented with no centralized state. While the *ekpe* society did provide a mechanism to enforce justice, however arbitrary, whether this can be thought to constitute a legal structure or political organization is subject to dispute; the usual interpretation is that there was no state.[23]

A substantial portion of the population at the port of Bonny was not native Ijaw but consisted rather of Igbo immigrants who had arrived in Bonny through enslavement. Similarly, the other major port, Calabar, comprised many ethnic communities, not just Ibibio, or as the local residents preferred to call themselves, Efik, to distinguish themselves from other Ibibio who inhabited the interior and were subjected to enslavement. By defining their identity as distinct, the Efik dominated the commercial wards at Creek Town, Old Town, Duke Town, and Henshaw Town on the Calabar River tributary of the Cross River and the connecting Creek River that constituted the port of Calabar. These wards were located on rivers that provided mooring for slave ships piloted upstream from the sea. The merchants at Calabar dominated the *ekpe* society and imposed a mafia-style system of law and order in Calabar. At Bonny, the leading merchants ruled through a supreme political authority, the *amanyanabo*. Often called in European documentation "king," *amanyanabo* was one of several titles associated with the *juju* shrines that supplemented the *ekpe* society as a mechanism for social control and legitimization of commercial domination.[24]

Statelessness was reflected in the way the merchants of Calabar, Bonny, and the Aro network worked through control of *ekpe* and *odonko*. The secret society was graded, and only the upper grade, which consisted of the leading merchants who had paid the necessary entrance fees to advance all the way through the ranks and benefit fully from the control of power. This inner *ekpe* council met in special *ekpe* lodges to oversee what was transpiring in the community and arrange punishments or dispense retribution that was deemed necessary; these decisions were carried out by the masked leopard. This form of self-regulation lacked legal recourse; punishment was often

[23] Afigbo 1981; Brown and Lovejoy 2010; Northrup 1978; Nwokeji 2010.

[24] For a discussion of Bonny political structure, see Lovejoy and Richardson 2004, 2010. For contemporary descriptions of Bonny town, see Adams 1823, 136–37; R. M. Jackson 1934, 68, 143–44.

collective and severe, affecting not only a specific person but kin as well. In the absence of a state, this method of determining justice and inflicting penalties might appear arbitrary to European observers but in fact guaranteed the supply of slaves and the operation of trade. The mechanisms of enforcement also protected pawns, that is, those who were being held as collateral for debts incurred by others, usually relatives, and who remained under the control of the pawn holder during the period of pawnship, i.e., until the debt was repaid. Pawns could not be sold into slavery, although violent disputes indicate that they sometimes were. At Calabar, pawns were even held on board slave ships as collateral for merchandise that had been advanced to local merchants on credit. Appeal to the *ekpe* guaranteed that pawns were not sold into slavery, sacrificed, or sexually abused because of the protection of relatives. On the infrequent occasions when slave ships sailed with pawns on board, *ekpe* decrees and corresponding boycotts of ships usually assured that pawns were brought back to Calabar.[25]

Pawnship and slavery were different by definition. Under pawnship there was legal recourse to town councils and village elders that was not available to slaves, who could even be sacrificed at funerals and festivals. Men could take slaves as wives, and since they had no rights to their own labor, the wives were entirely dependent on their husbands and their dictates. Women even could take slave "wives" who were expected to perform all the nonsexual roles of wives so that their owners could pursue careers, usually in trading, which could make them wealthy enough to buy more slaves. Given these peculiarities, it would be hard to imagine Igbo or Ibibio society without slavery. It is impossible to know the percentage of slaves in the region, but we do know that in the period before British abolition, more than one million people were transported from Calabar and Bonny as slaves. There were no major wars or natural disasters in this region during the eighteenth and nineteenth centuries, but it can be assumed that the domestic slave population was substantial. We know that there were whole villages of slaves, although in many cases these may date only to the nineteenth century. There is no possible way at present to determine if the slave population was 10, 20, or 30 percent, or even more, of the whole, but it was certainly substantial. Vassa's family, for

[25] On pawnship, see Lovejoy 2014b; Lovejoy and Falola 2003.

example, owned slaves, and his sale to several masters on his route to the coast was to individuals who owned other slaves.[26] Certainly the proportion of slaves at the two ports, Calabar and Bonny, was considerable. At Calabar, there were plantations of slaves outside the town as well, and many of the canoe boys on the riverboats were slaves. Moreover, slaves at these trading centers were also sacrificed at funerals and religious rites on occasion, which also attests to their ubiquity as well as their symbolic value.

There were two types of slaves in Igbo and Ibibio society, or at least a distinction was made between *osu* and *ohu*, with *osu* being attached to religious shrines and *ohu* belonging to individuals or kin groups. As noted, there was also a clear difference between these forms of slavery and pawnship. Moreover, while some individuals were exposed to arbitrary kidnapping, the seizure of people was also practiced as a form of retribution known as *panyarring* that was characteristic of the actions of the *ekpe* society. The complexity of these institutions and the pivotal role of slavery should be noted.[27] Slavery was a factor in local production, the rituals of social relationships and religious practice, and the sale of enslaved individuals into the transatlantic trade. The history of the Bight of Biafra interior cannot be conceptualized without recognizing the distinction between *ohu* and *osu*, the role of the *ekpe*, the prevalence of human sacrifice at funerals and festivals, and oracular consultation that relied on enslavement. The ultimate fear of any slave was sale, because sale could lead to sacrifice or deportation. The accounts are replete with information on suicide, fear of cannibalism, physical abuse, evidence of trauma, and emotional separation from kin and loved ones. Stateless or not, these societies experienced the realities of slavery.

Gustavus Vassa left the Bight of Biafra in the mid-eighteenth century and later provided accounts of what slavery was like in the interior. Vassa also described various rituals including *ichi* scarification and circumcision that were used to establish citizenship and supposedly provided protection from enslavement and collective punishments such as seizure for wrongdoing attributed to individuals and even relatives.[28] Vassa provides an assessment of slavery in Igbo society in

[26] Vassa 1789, 33, 36–40, 46–53.

[27] See, for example, Lovejoy and Falola 2003.

[28] Many details of Vassa's account of his homeland have been challenged, some doubts arising from efforts to discredit his claim of being born in Africa and others relating

the mid-eighteenth century and how he was introduced to the British colonial world via the movement of unfree labor from the frontiers of the British Empire to be settled on lands in the Caribbean, North America, and even Central America on the Mosquito Shore. Slavery from the interior of the Bight of Biafra was thereby a feature of the enforced colonization of empire. As with other enslaved Africans, Vassa was not free to return home, but instead was destined to live a life of servitude in a colonial context that was not being developed through free labor but rather through violent incorporation. Vassa's father had owned slaves, and Vassa observed the nature of slavery on his way to the slave ship. His rendition of this experience ranged from the naive belief that he was being accepted into a new family to fear of serious retribution for his mistakes and misdeeds that might have resulted in his sacrifice. Vassa never mentions what was surely the most terrifying prospect of being sold in the interior of the Bight of Biafra, which was the possibility that he might be killed at a funeral or religious ritual requiring sacrifice. Sale foreshadowed that outcome. Vassa avoided another serious prospect locally, which was attachment to a shrine as an *osu* slave, which entailed permanent banishment, the usual fate for women who gave birth to twins and for others who were subjected to arbitrary punishment for crimes that were determined through poison ordeals. Because Vassa was kidnapped, he was sold into slavery, which in his case ultimately meant that he reached the British colonies in the Americas.

In historical context, Vassa's account is not divorced from "state" societies, for in this case his relationship to Britain was established when he boarded ship and was taken to Barbados before passing to Virginia and then to Guernsey. Vassa's travels into and through the

to specific details and descriptions. Hence, the presence of women warriors, which Vassa describes in some detail, is considered nonsense and contrived. His idyllic view of his village, its setting, and some of the customs that he mentions seems generic, perhaps taken from other accounts, even if also true. The only problems with the charges of plagiarism or admitted borrowing is that the descriptions seem generally accurate, and Vassa usually identifies his source, whether Quaker Anthony Benezet or his own memory. There is nothing in Vassa's description of geography or general sense of community that was not true for his homeland or his birth town, whether that was Issieke, Usaka, or somewhere else in the interior of the Bight of Biafra. However, various details have been overlooked or dismissed that attest to Vassa's authenticity. See Lovejoy 2011, 2012b; and the website *Equiano's World*: http://equianosworld.tubmaninstitute.ca. I am currently completing a biography, *Equiano's World: The Interesting Narrative of Abolitionist Gustavus Vassa, c. 1742–1897*.

British Empire allowed him to emerge as one of its most articulate spokespersons and critics of slavery. He came to see himself as Igbo or, as he wrote it, Eboh, which in his childhood meant all neighboring peoples other than the members of his own village. He transcended a depiction of the "other" that was implicit in his native land to accept the label as inclusive of himself, which was indeed a breakthrough conceptually and culturally. However, his personal transformation and increased consciousness did not reflect the emergence of a community of diaspora Igbo. Vassa did not espouse an Igbo identity for purposes of mobilizing individuals into a collective entity or communal action but rather as a means of expressing opposition to the slave trade and support for the abolition movement. He was not instrumental in establishing a pan-ethnic label, as some commentators have claimed.[29] Based on available information and close reading of the sources, Vassa used his Igbo/Eboh identity to establish his Africanness, not a relationship with a specific ethnic formulation as a political goal. He also identified himself as Libyan, Ethiopian, and simply as African for the same purpose. Vassa in effect moved from a stateless society across a frontier into the slavery of colonial empire.

SLAVERY ON THE FRONTIERS OF THE JIHAD STATES

The interior of West Africa, the lands known in the Islamic world as the Bilad al-Sudan, "the land of the blacks," consisted of numerous states from medieval times until the European conquest of the region from the middle of the nineteenth century and continuing into the early twentieth century. In the sixteenth century, the empires of Songhai and Borno dominated most of the interior, and from the last third of the eighteenth century and especially after 1804, the region was transformed through jihad that consolidated a series of militant Muslim states that were responsible for the enslavement of those who resisted the call to jihad, especially on the frontiers of the states that were established. The relationship between the jihad states and their frontiers was based on perpetual hostility that isolated many small-scale societies, maintaining a slaving frontier that resulted in the incorporation of hundreds of thousands of people as slaves and inevitably placed constraints on the frontier communities and small states

[29] For the claim that Vassa promoted Igbo identity, see Chambers 1997.

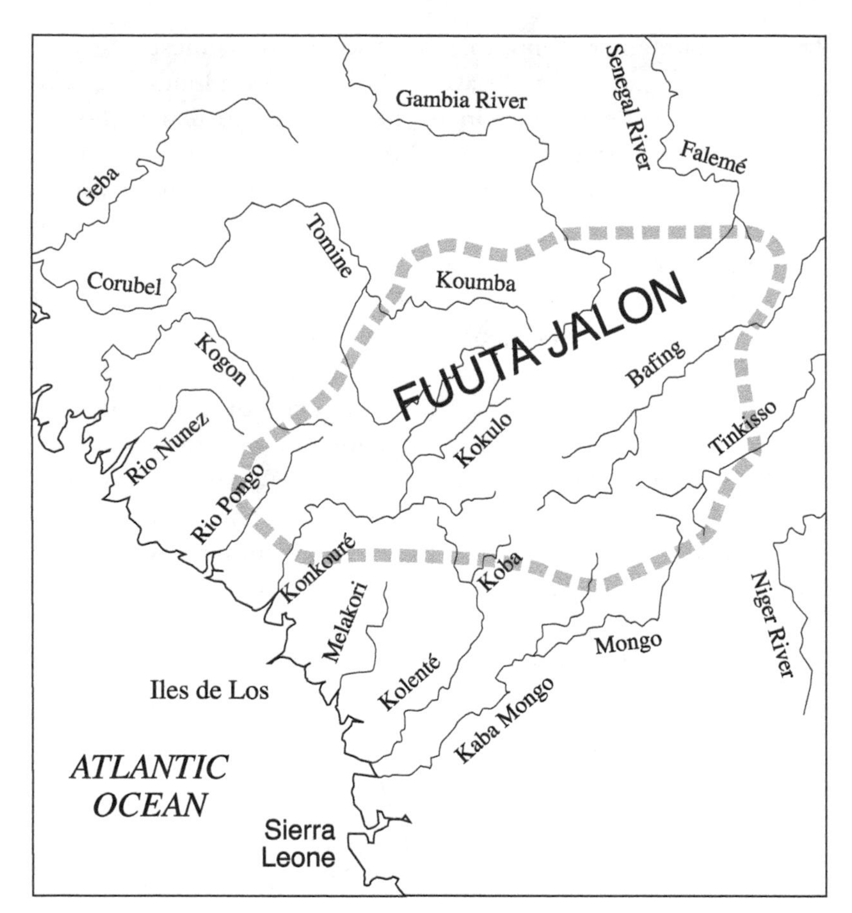

MAP 8.2 Fuuta Jalon and the Upper Guinea Coast, ca. 1800

that affected the nature of slavery within their boundaries. A consideration of slavery in this context suggests a parallel to the interior of the Bight of Biafra, which was virtually unaffected by the jihad movement. As has been argued for the Biafra hinterland, slavery has to be understood to have existed in a larger context than local society.

The upper Guinea coast from Senegambia southward to the Sierra Leone River was on the frontier of Fuuta Jalon, Fuuta Toro, and other states, such as Kaabu, that managed to survive the jihad movement (see Map 8.2).[30] The littoral of the upper Guinea coast from the

[30] See Hawthorne 1999, 97–124; 2001, 1–24; Lovejoy and Schwarz, eds. 2013; Mouser 2013, 1973, 2010.

Gambia River southward as far as Cape Mount, which is roughly the border between modern Sierra Leone and Liberia, was heavily involved in the transatlantic slave trade and hence wedged between the Muslim state of Fuuta Jalon in the interior and the transatlantic colonies of the Americas via the presence of slave ships. By contrast, the frontiers of the Islamic Sokoto Caliphate in the nineteenth century, particularly the numerous stateless societies on the Jos Plateau and in the hills of Adamawa, were largely unaffected by the Atlantic world. The small-scale societies in these two parts of West Africa were adjacent to belligerent states that had been founded through jihad, one that was on the coast but between Muslim states in the interior and therefore under the influence of the transatlantic slave trade, and the other that was far from the Atlantic and was more heavily connected with the jihad states and ultimately the trans-Saharan slave trade. Although Islam was dominant in the interior of the upper Guinea coast, there were non-Muslim coastal enclaves where trading "barracoons" were located that managed trade with European ships. Intermarriage between European slave traders and coastal families produced elites that served as intermediaries between ship captains and Muslim merchants from the inland caravan routes. Defined as stateless because these societies were autonomous one from another and not part of the Muslim states, analysis has emphasized ethnicity and language as distinguishing features of territorial occupation and access to land on which rice was grown, salt produced, and fish dried for sale inland. Although lacking substantial states, the social formation of this area related to control of trade and production and was inevitably associated with slavery. The basic premise was that the societies near the coast were not Muslim, but the stateless littoral depended on the wider Senegambia region, the Muslim state of Fuuta Jalon, and the network of Muslim towns radiating from the upper Niger River basin throughout Senegambia to the coast, and from the Gambia River southward to the Sierra Leone River. Despite the presence of stateless societies, it is impossible to conceptualize the region without reference to the state of Fuuta Jalon and indeed to the other Muslim states of the broader region.

Jihad became particularly important after 1804 with the establishment of the Sokoto Caliphate in the interior of the Bights of Benin and Biafra (see Map 8.3). While never affecting the Igbo

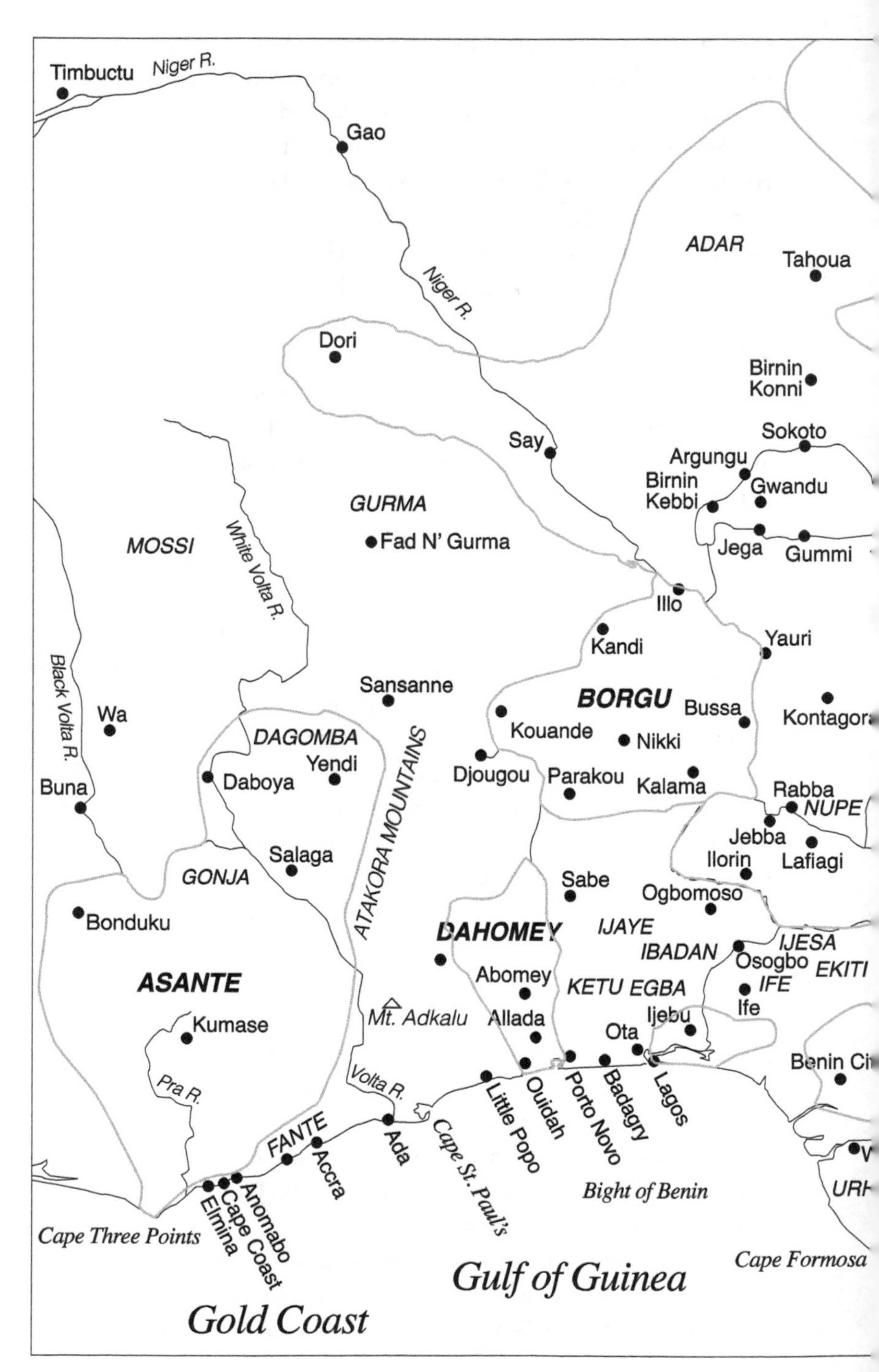

MAP 8.3 Sokoto Caliphate and Frontiers, ca. 1850

Air Massif
Agadez
ASBEN
Damergu
GOBIR
Mao
KANEM
Maradi
Zinder
MUNIYO
LAKE
CHAD
Katsina
MANGARI
Kukawa
Chari R.
Hadejia
Komadugu Yo R.
Sokoto R.
Kano
Katagum
BORNO
BAGIRMI
Kura
Azare
MANDARA
SOKOTO CALIPHATE
Gongola R.
Mt. Oupay
Zaria
Birnin Gwari
Bauchi
Gombe
Marua
MANDARA
MOUNTAINS
JOS
PLATEAU
Muri
Wase
Yola
Benue R.
Bibemi
Keffi
Muri
ADAMAWA
Nassarawa
Benue R.
Wukari
JAKUN
Taraba R.
ADAMAWA
PLATEAU
IGALA
Iga
IDOMA
TIV
Ngaundere
Akapa
Nsuka
Banyo
Tibati
BAMENDA
Mt. Oku
Onitsha
Owerri
IBIBIO
Mt. Mekua
IGBO
Arochukwu
Calabar
Mt. Kupe
IJAW
Bonny
Mt. Camaroon
Bight of Biafra

and Ibibio regions and the dominance of Aro merchants and the *ekpe* society, the Sokoto jihad affected most of the rest of the interior. Stateless societies became defined as the non-Muslim enclaves in the hills far from the walled towns and cities of the Muslim emirates. As I have argued elsewhere, the jihad movement transformed not only West Africa but ultimately the region as far as the Nile valley and the Red Sea.[31] The survival and shape of statelessness was frequently tied to the jihad movement and the eventual consolidation of the Sokoto Caliphate from Hamdullahi in the region between Timbuktu and Jenne in the middle Niger basin in the western Sudan as far east as the headwaters of the Ubangi and Shari Rivers south of Lake Chad, although Hamdullahi asserted its independence in 1817. The Sokoto Caliphate in particular became the location of a huge slave population that was on the scale of slavery in the Southern United States on the eve of the American Civil War and larger than Cuba and Brazil combined. As in the settlement of new areas of production in the Southern United States in the nineteenth century, the Sokoto Caliphate relied on the occupation of territory through military conquest, land acquisition, and the settlement of slaves for the production of agricultural commodities, including cotton. An understanding of slavery in the societies on the frontiers of this militant, expansive state has to include the fate of those individuals who were removed as slaves and colonized within the territories of the Caliphate. Slavery in the stateless societies of the Jos Plateau, the mountains and highlands of northern Cameroon, and the Atakora hills of northern Togo and Benin has to be conceptualized within this broader regional nexus.

In order to establish context, it is necessary to understand the history of the jihad movement and the attack on non-Muslim communities that jihad involved. The nature of warfare focused on enslavement and the resulting isolation of communities because of the slave trade. Hence, communities became isolated for political reasons because of the insecurity imposed by jihad. Commercial exchange in the region depended upon the movement of caravans over long distances that required self-regulating Muslim commercial networks, often characterized as trading diasporas. The only barrier to trade was the insecurity of passing through stateless areas on the frontiers of Muslim

[31] See Lovejoy 2014a and especially Lovejoy 2016a, 2016b.

states, where bandits were common. There were no natural barriers other than the Sahara in the north and the rainy season that inhibited travel southward for several months of the year depending upon the latitude north of the Equator. Muslim merchants could and did operate in stateless societies, and they crossed political frontiers, thereby providing interregional linkages that counterbalanced the dichotomy between states and stateless societies. The functioning of these networks relied on the ubiquity of walled towns, literacy in Arabic, and the leadership of Muslim scholars, jurists, and statesmen whose discussion of issues around slavery and state generated an extensive literature in Arabic. The dichotomy between Muslim states and stateless societies was reinforced through the brutality of enslavement and slavery. In conflicts between states and the societies on their frontiers, elders and infants were often killed or abandoned to suffer or even die. Women and girls were highly prized, while many boys died from the loss of blood after castration; only one in ten boys survived the operation.[32] Effectively, populations were removed from the frontier regions for settlement as slaves in the Muslim states, while survivors from raids and warfare were forced to relocate. In effect, statelessness was continuously reinvented and reinforced.

Stateless societies were found on the borders and frontiers of the Sokoto Caliphate, almost by definition a feature of jihad. The Sokoto state, established after 1804, emerged within a couple of decades to form thirty-three emirates and thereby became the largest state in Africa since the collapse of Songhai in 1591–92. Its consolidation affected much wider regions and can be credited with revolutionizing western Africa and eventually having a similar impact as far east as the Nile valley. The Caliphate reinforced its control of territory through the construction and enlargement of defensible, walled towns, of which there were several hundred by the third decade of the nineteenth century. The proportion of slaves in the population was considerable. While there are no censuses, the size of the slave population can be gleaned from circumstantial evidence, including travelers' observations during the nineteenth century, estimates of the slave trade, the numbers of slaves who ran away at the time of the British, French, and German conquest at the end of the nineteenth

[32] David 2012; Hogendorn 1999; Vaughan and Kirk-Greene, eds. 1995.

century, and court records and legal documents from the early colonial period. The stateless societies that provided the recruits for the enslaved population of the Caliphate were thereby connected to the Islamic state.

Dozens of independent small polities, stateless societies, ethnic groups, and geographically defensible communities were found along the long frontiers of the Sokoto Caliphate, stretching from Burkina Faso and northern Benin as far as Cameroon and the Central African Republic. Such communities were common from the Mandara Mountains just south of Lake Chad through Adamawa as far as the Bamenda Plateau in Cameroon. People who succeeded in maintaining their independence from the Sokoto Caliphate and resisted conversion to Islam were found in hilltop communities and remote mountainous districts from the Jos Plateau to the highlands of Adamawa.[33] Anthropologists and historians have studied many of these communities that European travelers, merchants, and diplomats visited during the era of the European scramble for Africa, and their reports are invaluable evidence for what societies were like during the period of caliphate hegemony. For the Sokoto Caliphate, one of the largest "Slave Societies" in history, slavery was a central institution, sanctioned in law, political ideology, military commitment, judiciary enforcement, and economic gain through trade, production, and services.[34] The purpose here is not to explore slavery in the Sokoto Caliphate, only to note that anyone who belonged to one of the small stateless societies along its frontiers was subject to enslavement or death during raids that were consciously planned and directed at enslaving non-Muslims or those accused of being apostates. Enslavement was not random but organized at the highest political levels, with commercial arrangements already secured for the disposition of captives and intended quotas set aside for distribution among participants for eventual use in agriculture and distribution to harems. Moreover, there is little doubt that the inhabitants of these frontier communities and settlements were aware of this fate.

In all cases of which I am aware, these non-Muslim stateless settlements and communities on the frontiers of the Muslim states

[33] The literature on this region is extensive; see Barkindo 1989; Burnham 1980, 43–72; MacEachem 2011, 109–24; Melchisedek and Dujok Alexandre 2015; Séhou 2010.

[34] For recent discussion, see Lovejoy 2015; 2016a, ch. 4; 2016b.

understood what slavery was; indeed there were slaves in all these communities, with each language displaying its idiosyncratic terminology for slavery and enslavement. However the social and juridical relations were defined, these were slaves who could be bought and sold and who did not have any personal rights over their own bodies or the tasks that they had to perform. Communities on the frontiers were not wealthy, so there were not many slaves. Nonetheless, if individuals were able to acquire any surplus, they built more and larger granaries so that they could speculate in trade, raise more goats and chickens, or till more land in areas where land was often exceedingly scarce and not that productive, it being necessary often to terrace and fertilize. Communities inevitably took risks by farming valleys that were exposed to slave raiders on horseback. Far from being egalitarian, these communities evinced degrees of relative wealth and carefully defined methods of acquiring assets that incorporated slavery, and often pawnship, as mechanisms of social control and interaction. These were "Societies with Slaves" in a wider world of slavery, and in that context they were part of the larger "Slave Society" that the Sokoto Caliphate dominated. To imagine their condition and the relative importance of slavery in many of these places before the nineteenth century is illusory. There are virtually no documents or oral traditions that speak to the issue. Yet there is no reason to believe that the first references to slavery tell us anything more than that slavery was well established by the nineteenth century.

What were the characteristics of "Slave Societies" in terms of the experiences of slaves? What difference could it make to an individual if he was a slave in a "Society with Slaves" that was fundamentally connected with the perpetuation of slavery and where slavery was widespread and economically important, as in the case of the centralized states, or if one was a slave in a society where funeral sacrifice was common, as it was in many stateless societies? In both cases the sale to the Americas or across the Sahara was a possibility. The Tuareg nomads of the Sahara lived across state boundaries and did not form states themselves, but they carried goods for merchants who were also operating across international frontiers and between states, and they managed agricultural estates farmed by slaves, some of which were located within states. The societies of the Sahara among which the Tuareg were prominent, recognized clan leadership, a common law, and a respected court system that extended beyond political frontiers. The possibility of state enforcement of legal decrees, however, was remote if not impossible. Rather, society operated on the basis of trust that was enforceable from within the group and required at least tacit approval over a wide region to avoid potential conflict, which nonetheless was a constant danger. How does one delimit social boundaries in this case, when Tuareg crossed into the Sokoto Caliphate and maintained extensive agricultural estates farmed by slaves and where they could water their herds in the dry season? The Tuareg clearly operated between and beyond states and invested heavily in slavery, even raiding for slaves, depending on circumstances and alliances.[35] Theirs was decidedly a "Slave Society," based on Finley's definition, which was buttressed by Islam and tenuous but real relationships with states, especially the Sokoto Caliphate.

CONCLUSION

The interior of the Bight of Biafra did not have state structures that might have approved, promoted, or resisted a policy that led to the deportation of a substantial enslaved population. The region simply emerged as a labor reserve for the New World, particularly for British America. As in the case of the societies that were on the periphery of the Sokoto Caliphate, the interior of the Bight of Biafra was associated with the British world, and a portion of its population was transported to the colonial lands of the Americas through enforced migration. The differences between the peripheral societies of the Sokoto Caliphate and the Igbo and Ibibio and how they peopled the Americas relates in part to the scale of each society. By comparison, enclaves in and around the Sokoto Caliphate were often very small and were not united but inevitably competed with one another for scarce resources and the control of defensible terrain.

This discussion addressing the prevalence of "Slave Societies" asks whether so-called stateless societies can be included. Certainly "Slave Societies" did not exist only in Western civilizations or antiquity, as the evidence on slavery elsewhere in Africa reveals. States like Asante, Oyo,

[35] Bernus and Bernus 1975; Bonte 1975; Bourgeot 1975; Lovejoy and Baier 1977, 1975; Rossi 2015.

and Dahomey had substantial slave populations relative to their size at levels certainly comparable to the incidence of slavery in many parts of the Americas. The Sokoto Caliphate had more slaves than Brazil in the nineteenth century, perhaps on the same order of magnitude as the United States around 1860, and more slaves than the whole of the Caribbean at any time in history. Certainly Finley's criteria for a "Slave Society" apply in terms of the scale of slavery, the use in productive activities, and the impact on society. The slave population constituted anywhere from a quarter to half of the total population, which is admittedly only an impression in the absence of census of material before early colonial rule after ca. 1900. Slaves were used extensively in production, both in agricultural output and in other sectors of the economy. The presence of slaves in society affected the way people thought and how they related to one another, and in these states, the enslaved were always perceived as outsiders who in fact came from frontier regions and stateless societies. The concept of "Slave Society" as a useful hermeneutic in light of historical and anthropological inquiry can be challenged, although as a description, many societies were fundamentally shaped by the institution of slavery.

A paradigm that sees "Stateless Societies" on the periphery of states is a theoretical construct that includes both areas that supplied labor for European colonies across the Atlantic, as in the case of the interior of the Bight of Biafra, and for the jihad states of West Africa, as in the case of the Sokoto Caliphate; sometimes this paradigm applies to both transatlantic colonies and interior Muslims states, as along the upper Guinea coast. More pertinent is a distinction between places in which slaves were more or less likely to be found and an investigation of why this might have been. The question of whether a society that lacked a centralized political forum, even if it operated within an institutional framework that transcended local interaction, was truly "stateless" depends on one's interpretive framework. Although modern scholarship has alleged that Igbo and Ibibio were stateless, it has been claimed in Arochukwu that in the nineteenth century, "we were the government; we were the state."[36] Perhaps the confederation that the Aro dominated was a state in all but name. There was a mechanism of judicial assessment under the guise of appeals to oracles

[36] Interview at the museum in Arochukwu in 1976.

and a well-regulated commercial system based on rotating markets every four days and larger fairs every twenty-eight days. A common cosmology featured worship at shrines and a belief in personal deities (*chi*) underpinned social relationships. Abam and Ohafia mercenaries acted as a police force under the supervision of Aro merchants. There were two common languages, Igbo and Ibibio, which were by and large geographically separated, but in most other respects, and certainly culturally, there were scarcely major distinctions between the two. The region constituted a common cultural complex that emerged as a reservoir for labor to be forcibly moved largely into the British Empire in the Americas and to a lesser extent to the French Caribbean and Cuba.

Rather than develop new paradigms for cross-cultural investigation of slavery that take account of cultural differences, it would be better to apply sound historical methodology based on documentation, linguistic analysis, and cultural understanding. Sound historical scholarship requires documentation, the ability to evaluate sources of information for any particular case study, and reevaluates research already done on the subject. I contend that an attempt to explore the dichotomy between state and stateless then breaks down. Rather than a distinction between political structures or their absence, the questions that need to be asked are "where is the state" and "what is the state." The Igbo interior of the Bight of Biafra may not have been part of the British Empire, but the people who came from there colonized Tidewater Virginia, Jamaica, and Barbados, and were at least as numerous as the white Britons and others who controlled these places. Eventually, the interior of the Bight of Biafra became part of the British state as a protectorate until Nigeria became independent in 1960. Similarly, the various non-Muslim societies along the upper Guinea coast remained independent of Fuuta Jalon and the other Muslim states inland, but like the Bight of Biafra hinterland, its population provided labor for the Americas. Hence the coastal zone was on the frontiers of both the Muslim interior and the European empires of the Atlantic world. The Sokoto Caliphate thrived off the societies on its frontiers, incorporating great numbers of people into its political economy as well as supplying the markets of the Sahara and sending some of its victims across the desert to the Ottoman Empire. An emphasis on the productive uses of slaves, the enslavement of people on the frontiers of Islamic states and the Atlantic market, and the means of distribution of the enslaved population reveals an interrelated system of slave supply and slave use that can be considered a mode of mobilization that linked frontiers with concentrations of slaves in states where they were used in production. The recognition of modes of production based on slavery focuses on processes that reveal how stateless societies were connected to states, whether within West Africa, across the Sahara, or in the Americas.

PART III

MODERN WESTERN SOCIETIES

9

The Colonial Brazilian "Slave Society": Potentialities, Limits, and Challenges to an Interpretative Model Inspired by Moses Finley

Aldair Carlos Rodrigues

Finley's interpretative model of the "Slave Society," deeply influential for the global history of slavery, began to be shaped in the 1950s and was consolidated in 1980 with the publication of *Ancient Slavery and Modern Ideology*. The theory used the concepts of the "Slave Society" and "Society with Slaves" to measure the scope and the degree of the penetration of the institution of slavery in different societies over the centuries, although the book focuses mainly on ancient slavery. The construct was utilized to understand the continuities and ruptures in the evolution of slaveholding.

The main criteria Finley used to define a society as a "Slave Society" were: slaves should be at least 20 percent of the population; they should play an important role in the production of economic surplus; and they should be numerous enough to exert a marked cultural influence on the society.[1] According to the Finleyan canon, there were five ideal "Slave Societies" in history: ancient Greece (except Sparta), Rome, the American South, the Caribbean, and Brazil. This thesis soon achieved consensus on an international stage, and in Portuguese-language scholarship the situation was no different. Because Brazil was taken by Finley as a "Slave Society," the historiography followed suit, and the term started to be employed more widely.

Recent estimates indicate that during the era of the transatlantic slave trade Brazil was the largest recipient of enslaved Africans in the

[1] Finley 1980, 147–50.

Americas, taking in, according to Richardson and Eltis, 41 percent of the twelve million people trafficked between 1519 and 1867. Second came British America, receiving 29 percent of that volume.[2] It is not easy to obtain consistent estimates of the percentage of enslaved people in the total population of Portuguese America. Maria Luisa Marcílio tabulated data for the early nineteenth century that indicate the general demographic profile of that time: enslaved blacks and mulattoes, 38.5 percent; whites, 28 percent; free blacks and mulattos, 27.8 percent; and Indians, 5.7 percent.[3] Therefore, Brazil easily fits within the demographic criterion of Finley's classification of a "Slave Society."

In this volume, the interpretive model formulated by Finley has been challenged, particularly in Lenski's introductory chapter, which draws it into question in part, at least, on a charge of ethnocentrism. Narrowing the concept of slave societies to the five historic formations identified by Finley obscures the relevance of slavery, for example, in African states, a point also argued in Lovejoy's chapter, Chapter 8 in this volume. Even though many societies on the African continent would meet Finley's criteria for "Slave Societies," these became invisible in the global history of the phenomenon.

Although Finley's paradigm allows a comparative and global history of slavery, we cannot find a long tradition in Lusophone scholarship of studying slavery by comparing it with the rest of the world and inserting it into the global history of slavery as an institution. Perhaps this is due to the sheer size of the country: studying Brazilian slavery as a whole is a demanding task, given the amount of evidence, not to mention the problems of regional variations over a long time span. African slavery started becoming important in Brazil as early as the late sixteenth century, in contrast with the United States, where it started gaining significance at the end of the seventeenth and in the early eighteenth centuries. More recently the comparative study of slavery has gained more traction, as we can see, for example, in the works of Laird Bergad and R. B. Marquese, who compare Brazil with the Caribbean.[4] The historiography of Brazilian slavery that was inspired by the Finleyan model, however, has focused on the territories of the

[2] Eltis and Richardson 2003, 17. See also Eltis and Richardson 2010.

[3] Marcílio 2000, 118.

[4] Bergad 1999, 2007; Marquese 2004; Marquese, Parron, and Berbel 2016.

Portuguese monarchy, within which Brazil could be considered a "Slave Society" and Portugal a "Society with Slaves."

For example, according to Manolo Florentino, the Portuguese started trading Africans around 1000 CE, and the process intensified from around 1440 onward in the context of expansion in the Atlantic. Citing Finley, Florentino characterized the society resulting from the introduction of captives into Portugal as a "Society with Slaves," in opposition to the "Slave Societies" that were formed in Brazil, the American South, and the Caribbean. The enslaved population in Portugal through most of this time oscillated between 5 and 10 percent of the total in some regions.[5] Even if the slave population had reached higher percentages, Portugal would have remained a "Society with Slaves." The differentiating factor was not merely statistical but sociological. In Florentino's words, "in Portugal the exploitation of black slave labor never constituted an essential condition for the establishment of differentiation between the upper social strata and other free men."[6] To define social status, one needed to refer to the categories and divisions of the slave system (as was true in Brazil), but the process of social mobility did not necessarily depend on slaveholding.

The wider dissemination of the concept of "Slave Society" throughout the historiography on Brazilian slavery can be credited to two influential authors who developed a more robust theoretical reflection about Brazilian social formations: Florestan Fernandes and Stuart Schwartz. Fernandes is part of a Marxist intellectual current ranging from Caio Prado Júnior to Fernando Novais that frames the colonization of Portuguese America within the broader dimensions of the formation of merchant capitalism.[7] Their focus is the role played by colonization within the framework of the primitive accumulation of capital in Europe. In the chapter titled "A sociedade escravista no Brasil" ("The Slave Society in Brazil," which is part of his book *Circuito Fechado*), Fernandes emphasized the patrimonial logic that connected colonists to metropolitan interests and its role in the process of draining resources from Portuguese America to its metropolis. Slavery furnished the basis for the process – the feet and

[5] Lahon 1999; Fonseca 2010.

[6] Florentino 1999, 8.

[7] Prado Júnior 1942; Novais 1979.

the hands – and it extended universally over the colonial territory, in contrast with the North American colonies, where it was more firmly rooted in the South. From Fernandes's point of view, Brazilian social formation was profoundly connected to an agro-exporting economy based on slavery and large landed properties. The dynamics related to this process allowed the formation of a colonial nobility, originally from the Portuguese lower social strata, that grew rich in the colony and attempted to deploy slavery to recreate the principles of stratification found in the metropolis within the colonial context.[8]

The description of a colonial slave society that had roots reaching deeper into the historiography was developed by Stuart Schwartz in his *Sugar Plantations in the Formation of Brazilian Society*. The ninth chapter, entitled "A Colonial Slave Society," analyzes the complexity of the social impact of slavery in Brazil on the basis of an extensive empirical dataset, making the core of the argument very current. Schwartz's Marxian-inspired theoretical model analyzed the social structure of colonial Brazil from the angle of the social relations of production (what Marx called "the inner secret" of society). Schwartz emphasizes that "Brazilian slave society was not a creation of slavery but the result of the integration of plantation slavery into preexisting European social principles."[9] The legal framework that separated persons who were free from those who were slaves was initially the same both in Brazil and Portugal. The difference was that in Portugal the slave component was a minority; it did not have the potential to transform the criteria and principles that structured the social order as a whole. In Portuguese America the opposite was true: the number of slaves was immense, and this fact exerted a decisive influence on the structuring of social relations. In addition to the legal separation of society into free and bond, the key criterion for social distinction rested on skin color or phenotype. This led to an extraordinarily complex set of principles for social stratification. For example, in addition to the dichotomy between free/slave, Brazilian society also recognized the condition of "*coartado*," in which a person remained in a transitional legal status between slavery and freedom while paying for freedom in installments. The concession of manumission, an important element

[8] Fernandes 1976, 33–95.
[9] Schwartz 1985, 251.

for the maintenance of slavery (particularly with regard to social control and the encouragement of productivity), ended up generating a huge contingent of former slaves and free people of color as well as their descendants.

Another element that produced a unique dimension in Brazil (although some areas of Spanish America were similar) was miscegenation on a large scale. The degree of acculturation also played its role in classifying people of color as *ladino* (acculturated) or *boçal* (newcomer). Another element in this complex socioeconomic hierarchy, according to Schwartz, was the slave-peasant figure, that is a slave who, in his condition as a captive, generated agricultural produce for his own subsistence and for the market, but whose accumulated funds could be used to purchase his freedom. On the opposite side, we have the peasant-slave, that is, individuals who, although free, lived under the patriarchal influence of a patron and worked under mandatory conditions, getting a miserable income or none at all. Yet another type in this slave regime were *negros de ganho* (slaves for hire),[10] who were common in urban areas. This matrix of types interacted and overlapped in such a way that it came to define the place of each person within the social hierarchy. Its incidence varied according to the context, but, due to the high penetration of slavery into the social fabric, the result was that no one could define his social status without reference to one of the stratification criteria created and recreated by the system of slavery.[11]

Fernandes (in an impressionistic fashion) and Schwartz (through a theoretical model supported by empirical evidence), aiming to analyze the complexity and specificities of the social and structural aspects of the slave system in Portuguese America, reframed the concept of the "Slave Society" and generalized its usage in scholarship about Brazil.

SLAVEHOLDING PATTERNS AND "SLAVE SOCIETY"

The advances made in understanding the demography of colonial Brazil, and particularly its slave demography, tend to support its

[10] Algranti 1988.
[11] Schwartz 1985, 245–64.

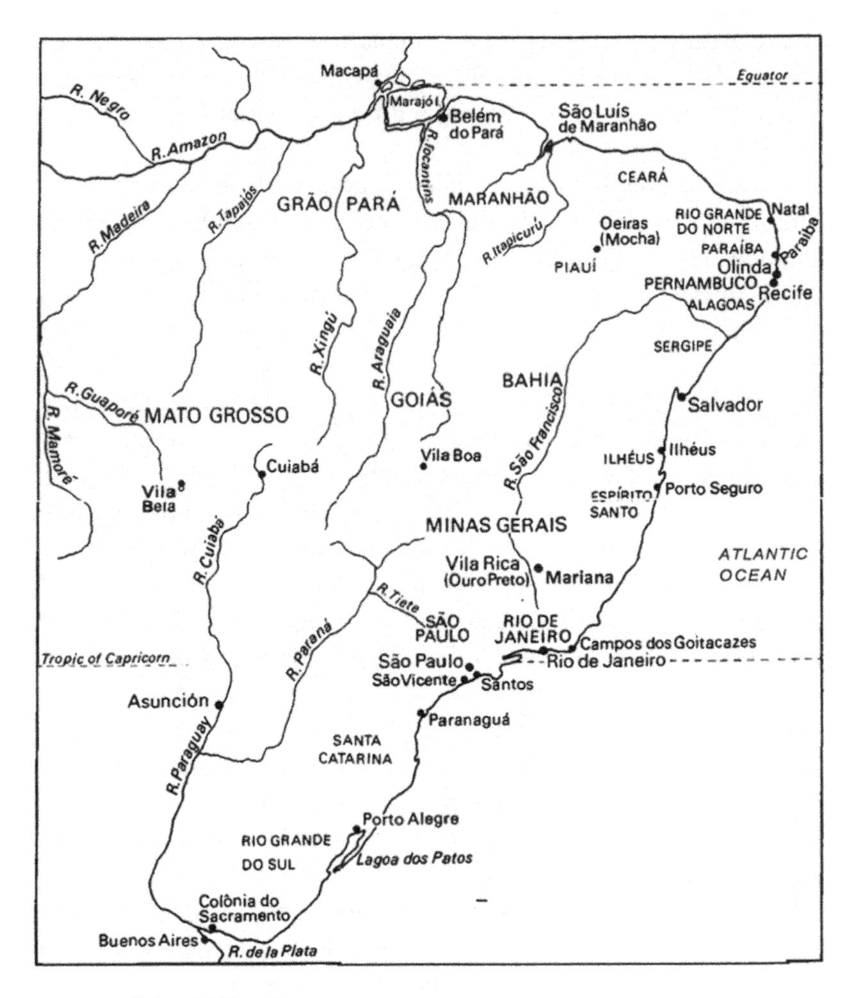

MAP 9.1 Colonial Brazil
Adapted from Leslie Bethell, *Colonial Brazil* (Cambridge: Cambridge University Press, 1987, P. 68).

classification as a Finleyan "Slave Society." As several studies have shown, slavery as an institution was socially pervasive in Portuguese America, especially at the smaller scale. We can cite, for example, some important studies about two colonial areas profoundly influenced by slavery: the captaincies of Bahia and Minas Gerais. The former was one of the main sugar-producing areas in the world, and the latter became one of the main gold and diamond exporters during the eighteenth century. Due to their different economic features, those captaincies have the potential to reveal how slaveholding patterns might vary according to context.

Data collected and analyzed by Stuart Schwartz show that the Gini Index regarding slaveholding practices in late colonial Bahia (1816–17) was 0.59. In the parishes of Recôncavo (a sugar-oriented area), 25 percent of the masters held between one and nine slaves, while in the zones where there was economic diversity the percentage of slaveholding in the same range rises to 36 percent.[12] In general, the majority of slaves lived in groups composed of ten to 100 slaves (the situation among 80 percent of slave owners). Of the sugar mills, only 15 percent held more than 100 bondsmen and only one of them owned more than 200.

Schwartz also found that sugar mill owners constituted less than 10 percent of all slave owners. The main point here is that slaveholding was widespread throughout a heterogeneous social spectrum, ranging across ex-slaves, itinerant tobacco planters, urban service workers, port workers, merchants, and businessmen.[13]

In Minas Gerais, based on the tax rolls for gold (*quinto* tax) collected in Pitangui, Serro do Frio, Sabará, São Caetano, and Vila Rica between 1702 and 1804, Vidal Luna and del Nero da Costa found, surprisingly, that 70 percent of slave owners controlled five or fewer slaves. The authors thus concluded that big mines based on huge slave forces might have been the exception and not the rule in gold mining that used slave labor.[14]

Bergad, working with a solid and extensive dataset compiled from estate inventories, found similar trends for the gold mining region over a greater span of time. He claims that "The predominance of slaveholders who owned five or fewer slaves was the most salient feature of slaveholding patterns throughout the history of Mineiro slavery."[15] Between 1720 and 1888, almost two-thirds of the slave owners held ten or fewer bondsmen, as illustrated in Table 9.1. The pattern remained the same even when the economy of Minas Gerais was becoming increasingly complex and diverse. However, Bergad

12 Schwartz 1985, 439.
13 Schwartz 1985, 439.
14 Luna and Costa 1982, 40.
15 Bergad 1999, 210.

TABLE 9.1 Patterns of Slaveholding in the Brazilian Gold Mining Area – Minas Gerais, after Bergad 1999, 208

Number of slaves	Slave owners	%	Slaves	%
1–5	4,573	45.8	12,510	11.2
6–10	2,188	21.9	16,855	15.1
11–20	1,792	18.0	26,153	23.4
21–50	1,143	11.5	34,864	31.2
51–100	247	2.5	16,734	15.0
101+	36	0.4	4,762	4.3
Total	9,979	100	111,878	100
Gini: 0.53				

warns, the fact that slaveholding was quite widespread does not mean that slaves, taken as a whole, were mostly in the hands of smallholders. The bottom two tertiles of the slaveholding population (who held one to five and six to ten slaves) controlled just 26 percent of the slaves (15 and 11 percent, respectively), while the next largest 18 percent, which held slave families of eleven to twenty members, controlled another 23 percent of the slave population. Masters who controlled more than twenty slaves held more than half of the enslaved population. The Gini Index in Minas Gerais was 0.53, slightly lower than in Bahia (0.59). Bergad does not indicate the percentile of the families who owned slaves in the eighteenth century, but shows that in 1830 one-third of all households held slaves.[16]

Even in places where slavery was less intense, such as in São Paulo, where less than one quarter of all households held slaves, slaveholding tended to follow these patterns. The data analyzed by Vidal Luna for 1777, 1804, and 1829 indicate that the owners of five or fewer slaves accounted for 65 percent of all owners in his sample, and 80 percent of the slave owners had a slave force of ten or fewer slaves.[17]

A large number of monographic studies dedicated to more local approaches – a prevalent characteristic of recent Brazilian historiography about slavery – point to the persistence of a high percentage of smaller-scale slaveholding among the population. These reinforce the

[16] Bergad 1999, 204–14.
[17] Luna and Costa 1982, 211–21.

picture of a social base committed to slavery in Brazil that was broad and heterogeneous. The strength of the slave system was founded on its great capacity for penetration deep into the social fabric.

Seen from the *longue durée*, the practice of slaveholding described earlier in this chapter underwent a drastic change only after 1850, when the slave trade between Africa and Brazil was finally closed. From that point until abolition in 1888, the trend became the concentration of slaves in the coffee-producing center in the south through the draining of the enslaved population of the north and northeast via interregional traffic. In this context the price of slaves skyrocketed. These factors together had a structural impact on slaveholding patterns high prices resulted in the concentration of ownership in the hands of large landowners, especially coffee producers who could afford it. In other words, the social base committed to slavery shrank sharply, and this eventually favored the dismantling of the institution in 1888.[18]

The scholarship on the dynamics of the slave trade has also presented important evidence indicating the way in which the commerce in slaves played a role in the making of the colonial elite, especially in port cities. Using the tools of prosopography, social historians have shown that an important segment of the Salvador and Rio de Janeiro elites who controlled local institutions had important connections with the slave trade.[19] The market for slave redistribution in the gold mining area also played a role in the formation of the socially predominant segments of the Minas Gerais society.[20] Therefore, besides the broad social base committed to slavery through slaveholding, the slave trade also created an important socioeconomic base devoted to the institution of slavery. Although not widespread, that commercial sector was important in the formation and social reproduction of the elites, especially in the final decades of the colonial period.

CHALLENGES TO FINLEY'S PERSPECTIVE: SÃO PAULO, THE AMAZON, AND INDIGENOUS LABOR

It is difficult to construct an analytical pattern that applies to all of Brazil throughout almost four centuries of slaveholding. The colonization

18 Castro 1995.
19 Fragoso 1992; Fragoso and Florentino 1993; Ribeiro 2009, 185–230.
20 Furtado 1999; A. C. Rodrigues 2009.

process operated within a hugely diverse range of degrees of penetration into the territory, differing economic arrangements, varied kinds of terrain, different degrees of exposure to the slave trade, different dynamics of cultural interaction, etc. The regions where the *crioulos* (Brazilian-born slaves of African descent) predominated demographically had features distinct from those where the sex ratio deeply affected the formation of families and the natural reproduction of the enslaved population. The slave trade also oscillated over time due to internal factors within the African continent and the economic demands of Portuguese America, and in response to the geopolitics of Africa's ports and the way they connected to Brazilian ports. The ethnic characteristics of the African population and the dynamics of interaction between those who were in more advanced stages of cultural adaptation (speaking Portuguese, for example) and the newcomers also influenced the process. All these factors influenced Brazilian "Slave Society." Despite all these variables, which challenge attempts to summarize what happened in a territory of continental dimensions, some basic features and trends stand out over time: the predominance of adult male slaves, sizable imbalance in the sex ratio, and low rates of slave reproduction. This last factor, compounded by the fact that traders in Brazil obtained slaves with relative ease through the exchange of goods produced in Brazil (as, for example, *cachaça* traded between Rio and Angola or tobacco and gold traded between Bahia and Costa da Mina) contributed to the formation of an economic system in Portuguese America that constantly needed to import a slave labor force from Africa.[21]

However, not all Brazilian regions based their economic system on an African slave labor force. The use of indigenous workers through different strategies and arrangements (predominantly coerced work, but also wage labor and coerced tutelage) in two different regions of Portuguese America challenges the hegemonic narrative about the transition from American Indian slavery to black slavery.

There is general consensus that the development of the sugar industry in the northeast, Bahia, and Pernambuco during the second half of the sixteenth century was based initially on an indigenous

[21] Some general trends in slavery in Brazil can be seen in Schwartz 1985; Florentino 1997; Herbert S. Klein 1999; Alencastro 2000.

workforce, but during the first half of the seventeenth century Africans came to predominate through a gradual transition process completed in the 1650s.[22] However, Monteiro's book about the Paulista plateau has added nuance to this narrative, arguing that African slavery made most sense in the plantation regions deeply connected to international markets, especially those involved in sugar production. In São Paulo, Indian slavery was important until the end of the eighteenth century, when the transition to an African slave labor system took root in the region due to the growth of the sugar industry there. The height of the use of indigenous laborers happened in the second half of the seventeenth century, when they were used in the production and transport of wheat from the Paulista plateau to the coastal ports of Santos and São Vicente. A decline in wheat production in the late seventeenth century impeded the transition to African slavery because in the early eighteenth century there was massive inflation in Brazil due to the gold rush in Minas Gerais and the consequent rise in the demand for slaves. As the prices for black slaves skyrocketed, they became unaffordable to all but an elite in São Paulo. Monteiro also highlights the social and political impacts in the region related to the use of native laborers, especially through the ambiguous institution of *adminstração* (administration), which was theoretically a temporary bonded status, but amounted to an alternative form of slavery. The elite, who dominated the town council (*câmara municipal*) of São Paulo, was made up of settlers who controlled the indigenous population, whose economic power they appropriated in such a way that they were able to solidify their own status and power. Despite tensions and disputes between the Paulistas, the Crown, and the Jesuits (who acted as defenders of indigenous freedom) over access to and control of the labor of the natives, the Portuguese institutional apparatus only took deeper root in the region after the discovery of gold in the neighboring Minas Gerais. In that context, the Crown started interfering more heavily in the local sovereignty the Paulistas exercised over the Amerindians.[23]

In the Amazonian region, several authors have shown the importance of the indigenous labor force in a multiplicity of economic

[22] Schwartz 1985, 51.
[23] Monteiro 1994.

activities. Chambouleyron, for instance, analyzes the use of natives (both free and enslaved) and its geopolitical consequences, especially on the control of frontiers and disputes for territories between Portugal and Spain. One of his arguments is that indigenous labor, coerced or not, and African slavery should not be understood as dichotomous since both interacted and intertwined with one another in complex economic arrangements that unfolded over the course of the seventeenth and eighteenth centuries in industries ranging from extraction to agriculture.[24]

In summary, Monteiro and Chambouleyron make us reflect on the limits of the "Slave Society" model, which was conceived to describe regions and contexts where African slavery predominated and where connections to the transatlantic slave trade were stronger. The situation that took shape in colonial areas where the indigenous labor force played a key role in colonization (São Paulo and Amazonia) does not conform to a theoretical framework that emphasizes a "Slave Society" based on an African labor force.

AN ALTERNATIVE MODEL FOR THE SOCIAL FORMATION OF COLONIAL BRAZIL

An alternative theoretical framework for understanding the social formation of Brazil has gained force in recent years under the influence of Portuguese historian Antonio Hespanha. He proposes a model that emphasizes the continuities between Portugal and Brazil. In his words, he is more interested in the "permanences in the colony of the social models known in the metropolis and in the representations connected to it."[25] Hespanha contends that slavery in Brazil could not transform the principles underlying the social stratification of the Portuguese *ancien régime*: "Slavery thus marks a difference only quantitatively; it already had its doctrinal justification and institutional position at the level of representations of corporate society."[26] Slaves lived under the domestic sovereignty (*casa*) of the *paterfamilias* alongside

[24] Chambouleyron 2010, 2015, 54–71. See also Gomes 2010.
[25] Hespanha 2007, 15.
[26] Hespanha 2007, 15: "a escravidão apenas quantitativamente marca uma diferença, pois, no plano das representações da sociedade corporativa, encontrava já a justificação doutrinal e o lugar institucional."

other members of the familial group and servants who owed him subordination.[27] From this perspective, slavery was just one form of dependency and personal subordination inscribed amidst others within the domestic (family) sphere.

Therefore, if the predominant hermeneutic current in the historiography of Portuguese America seeks to emphasize the new society ("Slave Society") resulting from the combination of the Iberian principles of social stratification with the social dynamics arising from the ubiquitous presence of slavery, the new historiographic perspective proposed by Hespanha highlights and lays emphasis on the continuities between continental Portugal and Luso-America – the Antigo Regime nos Trópicos (the *ancien régime* in the Tropics).[28] It is argued that there was no innovation in the juridical and social order since slavery already existed in Portugal and was already legitimized by its legal apparatus. Relations between masters and slaves were subsumed within the domestic sphere of the *paterfamilias*' dominion, as predetermined by the corporate principles by which society was structured. Customary practices and traditions from the *ancien régime* would be used to mediate conflicts and tensions arising from the development of slavery on tropical soil.

However, the evidence for the social history of Portugal does not appear to support this emphasis on continuity. Black slavery did not play a crucial role in the formation and reproduction of the upper social strata in the metropolis. The nobility did not obtain its economic resources directly from economic systems based on slavery, nor did it depend on slaveholding to exhibit and display its dominant social status or its exercise of privileges related to that status.[29] Local political power in Portugal was not in the control of slave owners, as occurred in Brazil.

The Portuguese upper classes relied more on servants, and even though these were in a socially submissive position, they were not

[27] Hespanha 2007, 15.

[28] Bicalho, Fragoso, and Gouvêa 2001, in which see, for example, Mattos's chapter, 141–162. On the other side of this debate, Laura de Mello e Souza 2006 addresses Hespanha's influence on this historiographical current and insists on the importance of slavery in the historic formation of Brazil in the first chapter of her book.

[29] We do not deny the role the urban slave played in a variety of economic activities in Lisbon and other regions of the country, as pointed out by several authors, for example, Lahon 1999, 2007, 73–100; Reginaldo 2009.

considered chattels. In Brazil, the lowest rung of the social hierarchy consisted primarily of enslaved people, who were considered property, and their descendants as well. On the macro level, from a relational perspective, the consequences of this phenomenon on the formation of society were totally different. Therefore, we continue to believe that Portugal was a "Society with Slaves" in Finley's terms.

AGENCY AND AFRICAN DIASPORA

Slavery is one of the most vibrant and well-studied topics in the historiography of Brazil. A massive number of books and articles has been published on this subject.[30] From the 1980s onward, a group of scholars, most of them based in the Department of History at UNICAMP (Universidade Estadual de Campinas), started constructing a new historiographical agenda, less devoted to the macro and structural aspects of slavery, within which the "Slave Society" paradigm is less important. They were more interested in themes related to slave agency. They therefore tended to draw information from primary sources more pertinent to daily life (for example, court records, police records, etc.) in order to capture how people experienced enslavement and the strategies they adopted to resist and endure bondage. In some cases the slaves were able to negotiate and build a degree of autonomy within their enslavement. This new perspective also outlined the multifaceted implications of freedom and its meanings in different contexts. Overall, what has emerged from this historiographical current is a less unilateral image of slavery, especially regarding issues related to master–slave relations.[31]

An important new current in slavery studies in recent years has emphasized the connections between Brazil and Africa. The prominence of historiography on the African diaspora no longer permits us to study the process of Brazilian social formation without investigating how Africans and their descendants experienced its dynamics with reference to the African roots of their cultural background: their understanding of social hierarchies, political power, ethnicity, kinship, dependency, subordination, concepts of territory, etc. The

[30] There are several essays evaluating historiography on slavery in Brazil, including Schwartz, 1988; Lara 2005; Herbert S. Klein 2009.

[31] Lara 1988; Chalhoub 1990; Slenes 1999.

role the African background played in the process of "adjustment" within the diaspora, the contact with the values of the Portuguese, and the dynamic of interaction and transformation that occurred in Brazil have to be taken into account. To offer only a glimpse into this historiographical current, we cite studies on godparenthood and the experiences of the enslaved population with the sacrament of baptism and the formation of spiritual kinship. Maia has analyzed 1,631 baptismal records of adult slaves (48.7 percent of all records) who received the sacrament in the parish of Vila do Carmo, Minas Gerais, between 1715 and 1750.[32] He points out that 1,351 adult Africans out of that total were male, and from these the majority, 1,227 (90 percent), had godfathers who were also enslaved. Among the 280 enslaved women, 180 (64.2 percent) had slave godfathers[33] (see Table 9.2).

Another very surprising trend found by Maia relates to the godfathers' place of residency: the majority of them were chosen from beyond the residencies of their owners. Only 402 belonged to the same slave estate, while 997 belonged to another household. In the case of the godmothers, only 131 of them belonged to the same owner as their godchildren, while 570 were from another estate.[34] The author explains this as the result of the predominance of small slaveholdings in Minas Gerais, which might have necessitated that godfathers and godmothers be sought from those outside the estate of the protégé. He also suggests, reasonably, that the slaves themselves played a role as agents in choosing their own godfathers in order to create ritual kinship relations. The slaveholders appear not to have interfered strongly in the process of choosing the godparents of the enslaved population. Therefore, paternalism and patriarchy were not unilateral or insuperable forces underlying the dynamics of godparenthood. Maia also hypothesizes that African ethnicity played an important role in the process, as he found slaves of the same origin being godparents of each other, as, for example, in the case of the Courá nation.[35]

[32] Of the children baptized, slaves accounted for 1,125 (34 percent) of the records while those born to freeborn and freed mothers amounted to 581 (17 percent): Maia 2013, 42.

[33] Maia 2013, 50.

[34] Maia 2013, 153.

[35] Maia 2013, 153.

TABLE 9.2 Godfathers of Adult Slaves Who Were Baptized, after Mariana (1715–1750)

Slave Gender	Godfathers – statuses										
	Slave	%	Free	%	Freed (*forro*)	%	Brazilian born of African descent (*crioulo*)	%	Unknown	%	Total
Male	1,227	90.8	83	6.1	21	1.5	0	0	20	1.4	1,351
Female	180	64.2	75	26.7	16	5.7	2	0.7	7	2.5	280
Subtotal	1,407	86.26	158	9.6	37	2.2	2	0.1	27	1.6	1,631

Note: Data assembled from Arquivo Eclesiástico da Arquidiocese de Mariana (AEAM), Livros O-2, O-3, O-4, O-5, *Registros de batismo de escravos adultos da Matriz de N. S. da Conceição de Mariana* in Maia 2013, 51.

The situation in Vila do Carmo parish as described by Maia had such significant consequences in Minas Gerais that in 1719 the governor of the gold mining area (1717–21) began to write about the issue. As part of his larger mandate to establish the Portuguese ruling apparatus in that difficult region as it was being occupied in the wake of the gold rush, he became concerned about the fact that enslaved Africans were serving as godparents of Africans newcomers. For him this was an issue of social control which he attempted to impose with the following ordinance:

> Among *negros* there will not be any kind of subordination from one to another, as has happened so far, because the majority of the *negros* that were baptized used to take as godfathers the same persons that they would later revere and whom they would blindly obey, despising the punishment of their masters.[36]

From his point of view, baptism was creating ties of dependency and subordination among the Africans that undermined the master's authority and may have eventually resulted in alliances that would promote revolts or the formation of maroons. He was also worried about the question of doctrine, for he believed that Christians of longer standing would better teach proper Catholicism to the enslaved population. In the face of these perceived threats, he imposed measures to try to avoid the creation of such hierarchies among Africans. He commanded priests to prohibit the practice of blacks choosing blacks as godparents in baptisms and marriages. White godparents should be chosen instead. However, the parish records of several villages indicate that such measures had little, if any, effect.[37]

In Bahia, Recôncavo, an important sugar plantation area, Schwartz and Gudeman studied records from 1723 to 1816 and verified that in 70 percent of cases the slaves' godfathers were also enslaved and in 10 percent they were ex-slaves. The masters were never adopted as godfathers or godmothers.[38] In São Paulo, where slavery was less

[36] Arquivo Publico Mineiro, (APM), Seção Colonial, Códice 11, Registro de cartas do governador a diversas autoridades, ordens, instruções e bandos, 1717–1721. Bando do governador, op. cit., fls. 282v–284 in Maia 2013, 47–48. Original in Portuguese: "que entre negros não haja subordinação alguma de uns para outros, como até agora houve, porque a maior parte dos negros que se batizaram tomavam por seus padrinhos os mesmos que depois reverenciavam e aquém obedeciam cegamente chegando aqui desprezando o castigo de seus senhores."

[37] Maia 2013, 47–48.

[38] Schwartz and Gudeman 1984.

pervasive in the social fabric, the tendency was the opposite: godfathers were free men in the majority of the records (60.55 percent), although here too masters did not serve as godparents.[39]

The data from regions deeply marked by slavery (such as Bahia or Minas Gerais) show a surprising and important trend in the creation of social hierarchies and subordination ties among the enslaved population from yet another perspective.

Africans in these regions used the Christian ceremony of baptism to develop unique conceptions of ritual kinship and its consequences for the creation (or re-creation) of hierarchies and solidarity networks that had little to do with the way European populations conceived of baptism. While using the European tradition of Christian baptism to interpret and reinterpret the social impact of ritual kinship in a new context, they participated in the creation of social hierarchies.

There was always the possibility of manipulating the Catholic sacrament to form alliances with those better positioned in the social hierarchy (people of Portuguese descent or free people of color) as a strategy for obtaining protection, a better life, or social mobility. We do not deny that master–slave power relations could play a role as well in that process, but certainly it did not happen with the frequency and intensity that we might expect considering the role godparenthood played in the logic of the *ancien régime*'s social hierarchy, especially given the purported sovereignty of the *paterfamilias* in the domestic realm.[40] The heads of households would be expected to serve as godparents to their subordinates, creating forms of dependency through ritual kinship, or, alternatively, a person from a socially inferior position would choose as godparent another who held higher social status.

Many questions about the godparents of enslaved Africans remain to be answered. Did differing conceptions about kinship among the various ethnic groups play any role in these dynamics? How? Did

[39] Rodrigues Neves 1990, 242–43.

[40] Here we differ on the question of godparenthood from Hespanha 2007, 15: "Sendo o apadrinhamento o equivalente a uma paternização espiritual, os afilhados aproximam-se da casa, ficando obrigados às fidelidades deveres mas também aos benefícios que essa inclusão comporta. A estrutura do modelo da "casa" – européia ou tropical–, bem como o seu caldo ideológico – a constelação de sentimentos que embebiam a sua representação mental –, eram os mesmos. Nem a existência dos escravos parece modificar substancialmente o modelo."

cultural and linguistic affinities influence the formation of ritual kinship? To what extent?

Another vibrant field of study that has emphasized cultural and political influences of the African past in Portuguese America's colonization are slave rebellions and the formation of maroon communities. Reis, in his oft-cited works, has discussed the ethnic dimension of the slave rebellions that erupted in Bahia in the early nineteenth century, stressing Haussa and Nago influence in the riots, as well as the role Islamic religion and jihadism played in the movement.[41] Barcia has continued this line of interpretation and compared the wave of slave revolts in Bahia with its Cuban counterpart, framing both as part of a broader process connecting West Africa and the New World through the Atlantic. He argues that prior military experience in Africa and the culture of warfare inculcated in African captives influenced the way the slave rebels used weapons, developed guerrilla tactics, and applied their prior military culture in other ways to fulfill their objectives.[42]

With respect to maroons, new studies have emphasized the impact of the warrior experience and military culture of people from West Central Africa on the formation and functioning of the longest legendary maroon community in northeastern Brazil: Quilombo de Palmares. Schwartz suggested the influence of the Imbangala warriors and institutions on the dynamics of its formation as well as on the very word used in Portuguese for maroons, *quilombo*.[43] Recently, Hunold Lara used the political culture of West Central Africa to inform our understanding of Palmares and how the Africans there challenged and in some respects shaped the colonial government while dealing with the maroons.[44]

The society formed in Brazil was not a mere extension of Portugal, but a new society, influenced by Portuguese culture but also profoundly shaped by slavery and its dynamics. To understand Brazilian social formation we can no longer ignore the historical agency of the enslaved population. The fact that the white local elites insisted on associating themselves with Portuguese values and principles of

41 Reis 1993.
42 Barcia Paz 2014.
43 Schwartz 1970; 2001.
44 Lara 2008.

stratification does not mean that enslaved Africans and former slaves did not create, recreate, and maintain aspects of their background in the formation of social hierarchies, especially when we consider the demographics of the latter. Therefore, considering colonial society as a whole from a relational perspective, there is no way Brazil's "Slave Society" could be a simple extension of Portugal because the new context contained too many new points of reference. Brazil was not just Portuguese but also African.

The Finleyan concept of the "Slave Society" does not ignore the importance of culture in its formulation, for it assumes that the massive presence of slaves in a certain context exerts a cultural influence on the society of the slaveholders. However, by focusing mostly on the economic importance and the social effects of the presence of slavery in social formations (through slaveholding practices), it leaves little room for explaining how the enslaved perceived, manipulated, and shaped the configuration of the mechanisms that organized the social fabric. The masters' perspective is emphasized at the expense of that of the slaves.

CONCLUSIONS

Finley's model, as convincingly argued by Lenski in his introductory essay and by several other authors in this volume, has limitations and overshadows the incidence of the institution of slavery in various societies. In light of this, we should be careful about taking Finley's proposition as a universal paradigm for studying slavery as a global phenomenon. This chapter was written with full consciousness of its constraints as a tool for understanding the impact of slavery on those societies.

The "Slave Society" and "Society with Slaves" framework has been successfully integrated into the scholarship on Brazil because its creative reformulations have been used to address and explain the complexities of slavery in Luso-America. Finley's concept found great acceptance because it recognized the importance of slavery to the economy and labor system and particularly because it allowed for the differentiation of the social formation of Brazil (a "Slave Society") from the social structure of Portugal (a "Society with Slaves"). We do not believe that Finley's theory has been applied in an oversimplified or monolithic way to the scholarship on Portuguese America. On the contrary, it inspired reflections about the specificities and complexity of slavery in Brazil within the larger picture that was European expansion to the New World with its attendant consequences. In general, authors directly or indirectly inspired by the "Slave Society" concept were more interested in understanding the importance of slavery in the process of colonization and its role in the formation of Brazilian social hierarchies.

In short, despite the limitations and challenges of Finley's paradigm, in the case of Brazil and Portugal the distinction between a "Slave Society" and a "Society with Slaves" remains productive. Nevertheless, the limitations of the model should be recognized as it is applied to historical circumstances in Portuguese America where indigenous labor (free and slave) continued to be important much later into the colonial period. The construct also should be more open to the way enslaved Africans themselves had an impact on social formations through their experiences and background. The agency of enslaved Africans as transformers of slavery and its consequences played a key role in the making of colonial society. They and their descendants were a major element, even the majority of the population in many of the key places foundational to the establishment of colonial society. Their perceptions and influence in Brazilian history matter.

10

What Is a Slave Society?: The American South

Robert Gudmestad

Ira Berlin is the historian who popularized the use of the "Slave Society" paradigm to understand the American South. Many historians of American slavery accept Berlin's broad characterizations: slaves constituted a significant portion of the population, the economy was based on slave labor, and slaveholders held an inordinate amount of power in society and government. The concept of differentiating between a "Society with Slaves" and a "Slave Society" is a useful characterization but is somewhat reductionist. A better way to understand the influence of slavery in the American South (and the United States) is to use a continuum between freedom and extreme enslavement. Slavery intensified – in proportion, influence, power, and violence – as it moved along the continuum. Thus Finley's idea of a "Society with Slaves" would occupy a position somewhere between freedom and a "Slave Society." This new conceptualization can take into account how and why slavery changed in society while still permitting a comparison between societies where slavery was present. This chapter will move away from the simple binary of "Societies with Slaves" and "Slave Societies" and rely on the notion of intensification along a continuum to chart the rise and fall of American slavery.[1]

As far as historians can divine from the existing records, the first African slaves in mainland North America arrived in Spanish Florida in the mid-1500s. An expedition under the command of Pedro

[1] Berlin 1998, 8–9; 2003, 9–10.

Menéndez de Avilés established St. Augustine in 1565. Thirty years later the Spanish founded Pensacola on the opposite side of Florida, but neither outpost flourished. Migrants brought relatively few slaves to Florida because there was no incentive to do so. With no gold or silver to mine and, as yet, no ability to grow labor-intensive cash crops, large numbers of slaves in Florida did not make economic sense.[2]

The lower Mississippi River Valley was equally lackluster in its enthusiasm for slavery. No real European colonization took place until 1718 with the founding of New Orleans. The region, which included present-day Louisiana and the southern portions of Mississippi and Alabama, demanded more labor than Florida. The French government responded by chartering the Company of the West and the Company of the Indies to bring African slaves to the New Orleans area. These slaves originally labored alongside whites and Native American slaves but slowly began to supplant the other groups as the main labor force. The toll on the Africans was immense. Only 700 of the first 2,000 slaves to enter the colony survived more than a few years in the "New World." Fresh imports augmented Louisiana's slave population but the region remained a "Society with Slaves" through the end of the eighteenth century.[3]

In both Spanish Florida and the lower Mississippi River Valley, there were noticeable acts of resistance to enforced servitude. The presence of a relatively untamed frontier just south of the English colonies led to the flight of slaves. Spanish authorities encouraged this process by promising liberty and protection to those runaways who managed to make it to Florida. In 1738 a black militia captain named Francisco Menendez helped thirty-eight fugitives establish a free black town about two miles south of St. Augustine. Far from acting based on motives of goodness and mercy, the Spanish were shrewdly trying to undermine society in South Carolina. Indeed, many slaves who arrived in Florida ended up being sold on the slave market and going to Cuba. Spanish disingenuousness aside, Florida did become the destination for untold numbers of Carolina slaves. One of the largest challenges to slavery in North America – the Stono Rebellion of 1739 – was itself an attempted mass exodus of Carolina slaves.[4]

[2] Davis 2006, 124.
[3] Berlin 1998, 82; Powell 2012, 92–128.
[4] Berlin 1998, 72; Landers 1999, 29–60.

Runaways in the lower Mississippi River Valley were even more successful. Slaves could turn the difficult nature of south Louisiana's environment to their advantage. The area had a larger and more active runaway, or maroon, community than any of the British colonies in North America. Runaways could typically count on assistance from friendly Native Americans, but as whites slowly claimed more and more Indian land, the escape opportunities for slaves narrowed. As options dwindled, Native Americans became more desperate and allied with slaves to attack French settlements. Ten years before Stono, for instance, an alliance of slaves and Natchez Indians killed more than 200 French settlers. The French response was predictable, swift, brutal, and effective. The savagery of the French response is a poignant reminder that slavery was typically upheld by force.[5]

The English, of course, also turned to slavery in order to build their colonies. It happened first in the Chesapeake. In 1619 John Rolfe – who would later become more famous for marrying Pocahontas – purchased twenty Africans from a Dutch captain of a man-o'-war that sailed up the James River. Rolfe was not the first Englishman in North America to purchase slaves (nor would he be the last), but his transaction was somewhat surprising. When Rolfe handed over the coins, credit, or commodities that he used to buy the Africans, England had been without slaves for 400 years. The early years of slavery in the Chesapeake, moreover, were more protean than later years. Historians have found numerous examples of Africans who purchased their freedom, bought considerable plots of land, established large farms, and even bought slaves or white servants. Anthony Johnson was one such man. Johnson arrived as a slave in Jamestown in 1621 and worked on a plantation. He eventually acquired his freedom, married, established a plantation of at least 250 acres, and owned several slaves.[6]

Johnson was certainly the exception. Most Africans who came to the Chesapeake died as slaves or servants rather than as free people. They perished after years of cultivating tobacco. It was tobacco that converted the struggling colonies of Virginia and Maryland into economic forces. The crop also intensified slaveholding in the region.

[5] Berlin 1998, 88.

[6] Edmund Morgan 1975, 334; Breen and Innes 1980, 9–17, 73–75; Kulikoff 1986, 37–42.

In the 1670s, a time when white servants outnumbered black slaves four to one, fewer indentured servants chose to migrate to the region. Landowners turned to slave labor to fill the gap, and between 1690 and 1700 they purchased 100,000 Africans. By 1700 the ratio of white servants to black slaves had been reversed. The importation of slaves leveled off once the black population began to increase rapidly by natural means in the early eighteenth century. As the black population grew, so did white fears of rebellion, and authorities in the Chesapeake implemented ever more rigorous laws designed to codify racial slavery. Historians have found examples up until the 1740s of the court system treating blacks and whites roughly the same. As the need to codify slavery grew – there was no basis for bondage in English common law – punishment for blacks and whites began to separate. For instance, when John Punch, an indentured servant of African descent, ran away with two white indentured servants, he became a slave for life. His accomplices merely had to serve four extra years of servitude. Colonial authorities also whittled down black rights. At one time, free blacks could vote, hold office, own guns, and serve in the militia. This ceased. Repressive legislation against people of African descent became one of the pillars that upheld slavery in Chesapeake society.[7]

A renewed emphasis on tobacco cultivation nurtured and sustained this turn toward a more repressive slavery. Ambitious whites pushed the plantation system further into the backcountry while their established counterparts, who grew tobacco or rice, built luxurious mansions along the rivers of Virginia and South Carolina. The men who ran the plantations also ran the government, and they envisioned their colony as one that privileged whites and that excluded the free black class from sharing power. Virginia came to define all people of African ancestry as Negroes and therefore inferior. This black–white duality gradually became common in British North America and stood in stark contrast to many of the Caribbean "Slave Societies." The elites in the Chesapeake also consolidated their power to such an extent that they developed an ideology that lumped whites into one class and Indians, mulattoes, and blacks into a "single pariah class." In

[7] Schwarz 1988, 72–82; Betty Wood 1997, 68–93; Berlin 1998, 29–46, 109–28; Wright 2000, 59–71. There is substantial evidence that Punch was an eleventh-generation maternal grandfather of President Barack Obama (Stolberg 2012).

another context, an historian has deemed this concept "herrenvolk democracy" (master race democracy) and has argued that the ideology nourished a sense of paternalism that could never admit equality between the races. The growth of slavery nourished an ideology that defended the peculiar institution.[8]

Slaves who worked on tobacco plantations tended to live in small clusters rather than large communities, a situation that inhibited the development of a slave culture. They also labored as part of the gang system where they rose at dawn and worked until sunset. Either the owner or his overseer directed the labor of various slave groups. Moreover, when Thomas Jefferson wrote the Declaration of Independence, more than 90 percent of Virginia's slaves had been born in North America. Chesapeake slaves lived in small cabins that had dirt floors and few windows. Most cabins contained rudimentary furniture, although bondservants on some of the larger plantations acquired tables and lamps. Slaves ate corn, yams, salt pork, and biscuits. The rations were minimal at best, forcing bondservants to supplement their diets with vegetables from their own gardens or fish, fowl, or rabbits that they captured.[9]

If slavery stumbled ahead in the Chesapeake, it stampeded forward in South Carolina. Settlers from Barbados moved to the area by 1690; not only did they bring slaves with them, they also brought their harsh slave code. For their part, Africans provided crucial knowledge of what would become South Carolina's cash crop: rice. South Carolinians imported slaves from African rice-growing regions and forced them to be tutors to their chattels who did not know how to cultivate the crop. African techniques like building dikes, turning soil with special tools, using mortar and pestle to husk, and winnowing with woven baskets became standard in South Carolina. Other planters learned to grow indigo, another plant that demanded a huge expenditure of labor.[10]

As the demand for labor in South Carolina became more intense, Charles Town (later Charleston) became an important entry point for the importation of Africans into British North America. White South Carolinians bought so many Africans (many of whom died in the rice

[8] Edmund S. Morgan 1975, 386; Greene 1994; Davis 2006, 131–35. The concept of "herrenvolk democracy" can be found in Fredrickson 1981.

[9] Philip D. Morgan 1998, 61; Wright 2000, 70.

[10] Peter H. Wood 1974, 55–62; Carney 2001, 69–106.

paddies) that blacks outnumbered whites by about 1720 in the low country along the coast. The size of slaveholdings grew accordingly. It was common for masters to direct plantations of fifty or even 100 slaves. More precisely, they paid someone to manage their plantations so that they could travel to Charles Town during the malaria season. More than any other region of North America, South Carolina spawned large numbers of absentee owners.[11]

The peculiar labor demands of rice cultivation helped create a new type of labor organization: the task system. Unlike the gang system, where the bondspeople labored in specific groups from sunup to sundown, slaves in the task system had a specific goal for the day. Once the bondservants had sowed the requisite number of rows or cleaned out the assigned portion of the ditch, they could do their "own" work of tending gardens or raising livestock. As slaves nourished this "informal economy," they were able to accumulate a noticeable amount of private property.[12]

But this informal economy was not allowed to develop unregulated. South Carolina adopted what was arguably the most stringent slave code in North America. Modeled after the code in Barbados and stemming from fears of a slave insurrection, South Carolina instituted harsh punishments for slaves. Members of the "Negro Watch" could administer twenty lashes to any slave caught off a plantation and even kill suspected runaways. Punishments for lesser offenses were no less brutal: castration, splitting the nose, chopping off hands or ears, branding, and burning at the stake. Unofficial punishments were probably even more barbaric. Like other "Slave Societies," South Carolina developed a coterie of masters who dominated politics and culture to such an extent that the exploitative slave code caused neither dissent nor notice.[13]

Across the southern colonies, African slaves retained significant aspects of their culture in the face of crushing oppression. Bound up in the international slave trade, these people brought with them different languages, cultural practices, prejudices, and social customs. However, they shared enough in common that they were able to mingle many aspects of their cultures into a distinctly African-American way

[11] Peter H. Wood 1974, ch. 12; Berlin 1998, 142–52.
[12] Betty Wood 1995, 105–07.
[13] Berlin 1998, 150.

of being. For example, the African practice of naming an individual for the day of the week on which he or she was born persisted in North America. A particular form of construction called "tabby" originating in Africa also appeared on the other side of the Atlantic, where it influenced the shape of slave dwellings. The most extreme form of African persistence is perhaps found in the Gullah region of South Carolina where speech patterns and cultural practices with African origins persist to this day. Slaves mixed these Africanisms, as historians call them, with English cultural practices and thus created a veritable stew of culture.[14]

Slaves also resisted bondage in multiple ways. The largest episode of rebellion, the Stono uprising mentioned earlier, happened in South Carolina in 1739 when about twenty native Africans attacked a shop that sold firearms. After killing two shopkeepers, they armed themselves and marched toward the Edisto River shouting, "Liberty!" The group was probably headed for Florida in the hopes of securing their liberty in the Spanish colony. A group of whites quickly mobilized and quashed the rebellion. Stono was the exception. Most slaves understood that they faced long odds in their struggle for freedom and resisted in more prosaic ways. Permanent escape was difficult but not unknown. Slaves established maroon communities in swamps or overgrown forests, often living for years beyond the reach of white authority. Other enslaved Americans attacked their owners, malingered, or otherwise worked as slowly as possible.[15]

Slavery was not only firmly established in what would become the American South but it also thrived in the northern colonies. When New Amsterdam became New York in 1664, it had more slaves than any other city in North America. As the thirteen colonies along the Atlantic seaboard were more closely drawn into the imperial economy, the importance of slavery in the north increased. When colonists fired the first shots at Lexington, slaves were about 12 percent of New York's population. Northern slaves tended to work as day laborers, servants, tradesman, and artisans. The nature of bondage in the northern colonies took on a different form as well. Slaves in New York could own

[14] Joyner 1984; Midlo Hall 1992, 41–95; John K. Thornton 1998, 206–34; Wright 2000, 104.

[15] Peter H. Wood 1974, chs. 11–12; John K. Thornton 1991.

their own property and sometimes selected their owners. Slaves were also important to the rural economy.[16]

The northern colonies never intensified the practice of slaveholding because there was no primary industry or staple crop with a voracious appetite for labor. Most farms were of the small or middling type, and slaves were not central to rapid economic expansion. Slaveholders, moreover, were powerful but did not monopolize the halls of power. There is no better testament to this situation than when it came time to consider proposals of emancipation in the North, as slaveholders were not politically powerful enough to squelch these plans. Even though the North eventually shed slavery, it did not stop profiting from the institution. Northern banks, insurance companies, ship captains, manufacturing companies, and textile factories directly benefited from slavery. Thus while slaves themselves became localized in one portion of the country, the benefits of slavery as an institution reached across North America through the Civil War.

By 1775, slavery was well established in what would become the United States. The American Revolution exposed the obvious contradiction of fighting against political tyranny while simultaneously accepting racial and economic subjugation. Perhaps the intensity of slavery in the various colonies can be seen most clearly in responses to the enlistment of African Americans in the Continental Army. Northern colonies moved forward with enlistment but had to back off in the face of pressure from powerful figures in the southern societies, including George Washington. Eventually the army became so desperate that it authorized the enlistment of southern slaves, but only on the condition that the slaves who enlisted would become free and their owners compensated. Few bondservants enlisted in the American cause. Instead, four times as many fought for the British since they saw, with much justification, an English victory as potentially more destabilizing to slavery.[17]

As it was, the American Revolution changed the nature of slavery in what would become the United States. In the Chesapeake and South Carolina, the peculiar institution received a challenge but was not fundamentally changed. Perhaps 80,000 to 100,000 southern

[16] Nash 1988, 9–11; Berlin 1998, 47–59, 177–81.
[17] Davis 2006, 141–48.

bondservants, including thirty owned by Thomas Jefferson, left with the British at the end of the war. Countless other slaves used the chaos of war to seize their own freedom. This dislocation was only temporary. The southern states took decisive steps to shore up slavery's foundations, including codifying bondage in the constitutions and statutes of the new states. The northern states, where slavery was not as intense, took steps to begin the eventual eradication of the peculiar institution. In 1777 Vermont outlawed slavery, and most of the other New England colonies/states followed suit. The colonies/states in the mid-Atlantic, where slavery was more important to the economy, typically enacted gradual emancipation laws, by which the newborn children of slaves became free. To soften the blow, they had to work for their masters until their twenties. The more a society intensified its slaveholding practices, the more difficult it was to uproot the peculiar institution.[18]

At the same time that the northern states were taking steps to free their slaves, freedom also expanded in the Chesapeake. Tobacco had leached the nutrients out of much of the soil, and planters turned to less lucrative and less labor-intensive farming, like wheat production. The lower profitability of slavery took the sting out of freedom for some owners; they had less to lose when they emancipated some or all of their slaves. Some owners freed their slaves out of a spirit of generosity, while others dangled emancipation as a carrot for good behavior in the hopes of staunching the flow of runaways. As more and more slaves became legally free, a growing number seized freedom for themselves. As the population of free blacks grew, portions of the Chesapeake de-escalated slavery. The process was most pronounced in Baltimore, which had a mélange of forced and free labor. All such arrangements, however, were done at the behest of private citizens rather than imposed by the state government. Slavery thus remained very much alive in the Chesapeake.[19]

Many masters in the Chesapeake sold their slaves rather than free them. The result was the beginning of a great internal migration of bondservants out of the Chesapeake and into emerging areas of the American South. Perhaps one million slaves were forcibly

[18] Quarles 1961, ch. 10; Zilversmit 1967, chs. 5–8; Berlin 1998, 228–39; Davis 2006, 150–56.

[19] Berlin 1998, 256–85; Rockman 2009, 46–72.

removed from the region between 1780 and 1860 in the Second Middle Passage. Enslaved Americans were originally compelled to move to Kentucky and Tennessee, but increasingly ended up moving to a region known as the "Black Belt," a swath of fertile land that stretched across Georgia, Alabama, Mississippi, and Louisiana. Slave traders, professionals who bought slaves in the Upper South and sold them in the Lower South, drove coffles (slaves manacled together in pairs and then connected by a common chain) in a four-month land journey. These "nigger traders" also transported slaves on coastwise ships, flatboats, steamboats, and railroads, and built slave jails in all the major cities of the South. This burgeoning slave trade was crucial for the South's economy because it readjusted the slave population to shifting labor demands. The trade wreaked havoc on slave families, as it sundered up to one-third of slave marriages in the Upper South and tore children from parents in equal measure.[20]

The interstate slave trade and the spread of cash crops intensified slavery across much of the American South. Slaveholders put pressure on the federal government to purchase Louisiana and Florida, suppress the 1811 Louisiana slave revolt, and force the removal of the Cherokees, Chickasaws, Choctaws, Creeks, and Seminoles from valuable land. These aggressive actions of the federal government to promote and develop slave-based agriculture encouraged cotton production to take root in the Black Belt. Sugar also became an important commodity, particularly in the "sugar bowl" of southern Louisiana, where the "sugar masters" valued male workers.[21]

Technology also played a key role in the consolidation of slavery in the American South. The cotton gin, a new type of loom, steamboats, and railroads solidified slavery in the Old South because they increased the value of slave-produced crops and thereby enhanced the value of land and slaves even as they allowed staple crop producers to tap into a broader market. The natural increase in slave populations also generally fueled the expansion of bondage. The net result was that slavery grew in importance, and slaveholders consolidated their economic, social, and political power.[22]

[20] Tadman 1989, 3–11; Johnson 1999, 45–58; Berlin 2003, 161; Deyle 2005, 94–104.
[21] Baptist 2002, ch. 4; Follett 2005, 49–54; Berry 2007, ch. 2.
[22] Lakwete 2003; Downey 2009, 93–101; Marrs 2009, ch. 3; Gudmestad 2011, 141–45.

The production of staple crops surged in the South, with cotton leading the way. By the time of the American Civil War, cotton was the single most valuable commodity in the world and ignited industrial revolutions in England and the United States. American exports of the white gold rose from next to nothing in the 1790s to about 60 percent of all US exports in 1860. Moreover, about two-thirds of Southern slaves were forced to cultivate cotton. Plantation agriculture was the South's economic lodestone; white Southerners channeled their money into land and slaves. Broadly speaking, slavery was profitable and even brought economic benefits to non-slaveholding whites. Southern yeomen paid relatively low taxes, sold provisions to their wealthy neighbors, and often received discounted services from masters.[23]

These changes would not have been possible without the growth of the slave population. In 1790 there were about 700,000 slaves in America; in 1860 there were 3.9 million. Three-quarters of these people were agricultural laborers and tended to live on plantations. Other enslaved Americans worked as domestic servants, carpenters, and blacksmiths. A declining number of slaves lived and worked in Southern cities and generally did the work that immigrants did in the North. Many of these bondservants were hired out for specific periods of time and often made their own housing arrangements. If nothing else, the rental market for slaves made the peculiar institution flexible enough to meet many of the Southern economy's demands.[24]

Slaves responded to the consolidation of slavery and the intensification of slaveholding practices in the South in numerous ways. Some engaged in self-mutilation or suicide in order to diminish or destroy their value. Others ran away, although the percentage of runaways from American slavery is surprisingly small. Most bondservants, though, grudgingly accepted the condition of servitude and creatively subverted white authority. Many created fictive kin in much the same way that their ancestors bound up in the Middle Passage created new relationships. They also pursued the "informal economy" of hunting, fishing, gardening, and selling items. In this way they joined family and economy together in a powerful way that provided

[23] Schoen 2009, 1–10, 121–26; Coclanis 2013, 70–73.
[24] Wade 1964; Dew 1994; Jonathan D. Martin 2004, 72–77.

a counterargument to the slave owners' insistence on denying human and property rights to bondservants. Slaves also created a "rival geography" in which they could create spaces beyond the normal gaze of whites. The slave quarters, woods, swamps, and unoccupied land provided refuge from the oppression of slavery. Slaves tried to move beyond the geography of containment that white authority tried to impose on the land and on the slaves themselves.[25]

This resistance to slavery, whether conscious or not, was part of a process whereby small numbers of American slaves carved out niches of mobility and privilege. Men rather than women tended to work in situations where they could use their laboring conditions to inch toward a tenuous type of freedom. When enslaved Americans were hired to work on Mississippi River steamboats, they could roam from Louisville to New Orleans. Many of these workers, most of whom were male, made their own arrangements with boat owners. They were outside the control of their putative masters for months at a time and normally kept a portion of their earnings to themselves. Maritime workers on North Carolina's outer banks displayed a similar degree of mobility. Even slaves in small Southern villages, if the research of David Paterson is correct, had surprising amounts of autonomy. Paterson's close examination of a small Georgia village reveals that rural slaves commonly ran errands for their owners, earned small portions of cash, and generally supported the local economy. Slaves on sugar plantations in Louisiana and bondservants who cut wood along the Mississippi River became economic agents when they were paid for their overwork.[26]

The vast majority of Southern slaves, however, had no such privileges. They labored in miserable conditions for long hours, and faced brutal punishment. Masters deliberately withheld food and clothing from their slaves in order to increase dependency. As one historian has written, whites "converted black hunger into white supremacy." Punishments for slaves often took the form of whipping. In a typical episode, the slave would be stripped to the waist (women included) and tied to a post or tree. The master would gather the

[25] Norrece T. Jones 1990; Franklin and Schweninger 1999; Greenberg 2003; Penningroth 2003; Camp 2004, 6; Kaye 2007; Rivers 2012.

[26] Dew 1994; Cecelski 2001, 44–53; Buchanan 2004, 89–92; Follett 2005, 130–31; Paterson 2009; Gudmestad 2011, 155.

other slaves, and then the driver or overseer would flay the supposed offender. Often, the episode concluded with a dousing of salt water across the open wounds. Other punishments might be more creative; there are documented cases of slaves having to drink urine, eat tobacco caterpillars, and wear leg chains. Whites not only disregarded black bodies, they abused them. The high level of sexual exploitation of slave women was an open secret in the antebellum South. Indeed, when Thomas Jefferson initiated a long-term sexual relationship with his slave Sally Hemings, this was probably the norm rather than the exception.[27]

In the face of this unremitting dehumanization, enslaved Americans crafted a vibrant culture. Folktales whose origins lay in Africa celebrated the triumph of the weak but clever animal over its stronger opponent. Christianity also became a source of support for enslaved Americans. Southern congregations had segregated seating, but blacks could often partake in communion and even be buried in the same cemetery as whites. Pious owners held church services for their slaves, with the messages usually stressing the need for slaves to obey their masters. Bondservants preferred to organize their own religious services, and the results were very different than most whites would have liked. Slave preachers emphasized how Moses delivered the Israelites from slavery. Music was emotional, boisterous, and enthusiastic. These services featured singing, dancing, and shouting. Slaves commonly blended folk beliefs like potions and charms with more traditional elements of Christianity.[28]

While slaves created an interesting culture, Southern whites crafted an elaborate justification for their oppression of another race. A variety of men, from church leaders to amateur anthropologists, argued for the superiority of white over black. A supposed hierarchy of the races emerged from the "Curse of Ham" as outlined in the book of Genesis. From there, preposterous ideas like Africans being created with larger muscles and smaller brains so that they could be better slaves filtered through the South. Slavery, then, became God's plan for the world, and slaveholders were obligated to provide a modicum of protection for their bondservants and teach them about

[27] Baptist 2001; Rothman 2003; Buchanan 2004, 55; Gordon-Reed 2008; Johnson 2013, 187 (quotation); Baptist 2014.

[28] Levine 1977; Raboteau 1978; Roberts 1989; Frey and B. Wood 1998.

Christianity. In this strange way, the concept of paternalism, or the notion that masters had certain obligations to their slaves, took root in the South. And as slaveholders prospered, it was a sign of divine favor because God rewarded piety with material success. Perhaps the most unusual manifestation of the South's "Slave Society" was this tortured ideology that, to a certain extent, survived in the postwar Lost Cause creed.[29]

While most of the American South intensified the practice of slavery, there were notable exceptions. Wide swaths of the Upper South resisted the turn, mainly because geography limited the expansion of staple crops. Missouri, for instance, had only a small region known as "Little Dixie" where there was a significant percentage of slaveholders. Slaves in the rest of the state tended to work in small groups. Their relative isolation created a different type of servitude that was no more benign than plantation slavery even though it failed to reach the same levels of demographic significance. For instance, a great number of Missouri slaves was involved in a "marriage abroad" where one of the partners (usually the man) lived apart from the spouse and children. This near-constant separation created a new kind of stress for slave unions. The contours of slave life were similar in Kentucky, Maryland, and Delaware. Slaves were never more than a quarter of Kentucky's population, the number of slaves in Maryland declined starting in about 1830, and less than 2 percent of Delaware's residents were slaves in 1860. These states, which became known as the border states during the Civil War, never saw the intensification of slavery on the scale that matched the rest of the South. Slaves were only about 10 percent of the population, the economy of only a few counties depended on slave labor, and slave owners could not achieve dominance in state politics. The slaveholding leadership in these states could not squelch dissent as it did in the Deep South. Active and noisy antislavery societies agitated for change up until the time slavery was abolished by federal fiat in 1865.[30]

The corridor along the Appalachian Mountains also did not intensify the practice of slavery. Eastern Tennessee, western Virginia, western North Carolina, and portions of Georgia and Alabama

[29] Jenkins 1935; Genovese 1974, 3–7; Faust 1981; Daly 2004; Ford 2009, 144–62.
[30] Fields 1985; Burke 2010, ch. 2; Grivno 2011; Astor 2012.

were too mountainous to accommodate plantation culture. Indeed, the western portion of Virginia even pressed for gradual statewide abolition in 1831. The dominant slaveholders, though, controlled Virginia's legislature and made sure that the debate went nowhere. Other subregions within the Southern states shaded back and forth along slavery's continuum. In Texas, the practice of slavery was more intense in the cotton-growing eastern portion of the state than in the western region, where the society was relatively disconnected from slavery. A similar situation prevailed in Florida, where the slavery was more prominent in the northern part of the state but did not spread past the middle of the state.[31]

As a whole, then, American slavery in 1860 was in a curious position. The percentage of slave owners had decreased from about 36 percent of the Southern white population in 1830 to about 25 percent in 1860. Slave prices were increasing, just like in Cuba and Brazil, and the rental market for slaves was thriving. Slave owners in the Deep South, who felt increasingly under siege since slavery in the Western Hemisphere was slowly being outlawed, craved new land for the expansion of the peculiar institution. They even went so far as to launch filibustering expeditions into Mexico, Nicaragua, and Cuba. The worldwide demand for cotton was strong, ensuring profits for planters of that crop. The same cannot be said for the other staple products, however. Rice production was increasingly uncompetitive, but planters in South Carolina had a difficult time divesting themselves of their slaves because they were seen as too specialized. Rice slaves could not plow, did not know how to pluck cotton, and were seen as tainted from living in a malarial environment. American sugar plantations remained profitable thanks to tariffs on foreign sugar. Tobacco, too, had lost its competitive edge thanks to other varieties of the weed that were cultivated elsewhere and were superior in flavor.[32]

And then the war came. While the end of American slavery is outside the scope of this chapter, it is useful to frame the ways in which slavery affected the American Civil War. The control of slave labor enabled

[31] Goodyear Freehling 1982; Randolph B. Campbell 1989; Baptist 2002, 88–95; Randal L. Hall 2012, 57–71.

[32] May 2002, 111–12; Jonathan D. Martin 2004, 188–89; Rugemer 2008, ch. 3; Coclanis 2013, 69, 72, 76, 78; Johnson 2013, 305–21.

the Confederacy to mobilize a greater proportion of its white male population (by some estimates up to 80 percent of Southern white men of military age) but also caused instability on the home front. Enslaved Americans left their plantations, sabotaged Confederate military activities, and provided useful information to Union armies. The dislocation was so powerful that one historian has even characterized the Civil War as the world's largest slave rebellion. When runaway slaves escaped to Northern armies, they forced the federal government to make a decision about whether to return them to their masters. The massive movement of slaves away from plantations put pressure on Abraham Lincoln to issue the Emancipation Proclamation and clarify the war's meaning. Southern slaves also served in the Union military. Approximately 180,000 African Americans (about 80 percent of them escaped slaves) wore blue uniforms. This infusion of manpower came at a crucial time in the contest and helped revive the Northern war effort. Slavery legally ended with the adoption of the Thirteenth Amendment in 1865.[33]

Even though slavery ceased to exist in a legal sense, it still influenced the South. It is perhaps in the aftermath of bondage that we can clearly see the flaws in the dichotomy between a "Slave Society" and "Society with Slaves." Unlike freed slaves in Greece and Rome (which are normally classified as "Slave Societies"), former slaves in the American South suffered in horrible conditions after slavery's demise. Southern state governments codified racism through the Black Codes, the convict lease system, and the Mississippi Plan. Terrorist organizations like the Ku Klux Klan intimidated African Americans and tamped down the black vote. African Americans were, arguably, not much better off as free people and significant change would only happen because of the Civil Rights movement of the mid-twentieth century. The long reach of slavery also stultified Southern economic development after 1865. The population (certainly African Americans but also many whites) was mainly uneducated, the money tied up in slaves vanished, and wealth remained inequitably distributed. Things were so bad that fully seventy years after Appomattox, income levels in the South were barely half that of the United States as a whole. Most of these

[33] Glatthaar 1990; John David Smith 2002; Steven Hahn 2003, ch. 2; Brasher 2012, 27–32.

deleterious effects can be traced to the racial dimension of American slavery.[34]

This chapter has argued that it is time to reconsider whether the concept of a "Slave Society" is useful for understanding American history. Recasting the intensification of slavery as one that moves along a continuum helps us comprehend why slavery withered away north of the Mason–Dixon line. The agricultural and labor environment in the northern colonies/states did not favor the intensification of slaveholding, which permitted an opening for antislavery ideas to take hold. Northern owners had not consolidated their power, there was no way to effectively squelch dissent, and slavery was not economically central enough to stave off elimination. Southern states, by contrast, continued to orient their society, culture, and economy around slavery. The Deep South, which was furthest along the slaveholding continuum, encouraged the greatest growth of slavery, particularly viewed the election of an antislavery president with great alarm, and decided to separate from the threat. They seceded from the rest of the country in the hopes that they could secure the future of slavery within a government that was, in the words of the Confederacy's vice president, dedicated to the proposition that there was fundamental inequality between the races. Tennessee, Arkansas, Virginia, and North Carolina, with their nominal "Slave Societies," took longer to cast their lot with the hard-core secessionists. The border states could not take the ultimate step to protect slavery and refused to secede. In a very real sense, our narrative of the secession crisis revolves around the level of intensification of slaveholding in any given region of the American landscape. Those regions with intensive practices were willing to defend the slave system through secession, and those with less intensive practices were unwilling to run the risks of breaking away from the union.

The level of intensification in the practice of slavery *within* the Confederacy also explains the outcome of the war. The Confederacy was hardly united, and white Southerners disagreed with each other over important military and social matters. West Virginia became the thirty-fifth state when it seceded from Virginia. That it did so is largely explained by the fact that it was less committed to slavery. The

[34] Coclanis 2013, 78.

leaders of West Virginia's statehood largely relied on free labor and had long resented the leadership of Virginia's tidewater planters. Other portions of the South where the practice of slavery was not as intense also resisted the Confederacy. Eastern Tennessee is the most notable example. Men from the region were more likely to volunteer for the Union than for the Confederacy. Those left behind by war in areas with a low population of slaves were also quite likely to shelter Confederate deserters and thus undermine the Southern war effort.

Finally, the ability to place the development of slavery along a continuum also brings the concept of environmental history to the foreground. Although more implicit than anything else in this chapter, an appreciation for the environment is crucial for understanding the growth and development of American slavery. In those parts of North America where slavery became more prominent, certain environmental preconditions had to be present. The long growing season that made cash crops possible, fertile soils, and access to water transportation were all necessary components of a "Slave Society." Environmental factors, in other words, created conditions under which the concentration of chattel labor was possible. The absence of these factors – coupled with the lack of gold and silver – meant that slavery was less likely to establish deep roots in the North. However, the mere presence of these environmental factors did mean that the American South was destined to emphasize the growth of slavery. The intense demand for labor could be offset with technological advances, and the government had to be relatively permissive when it came to established legal precedents for slavery. Environmental factors were important but not determinative.

Viewing the development of slavery in what would become the United States as a process of intensification, and sometimes de-escalation, solves a number of problems that Moses Finley's initial paradigm cannot address. It is a more flexible model that incorporates important factors such as economic demand, environmental conditions, and racial considerations. Our view of the past becomes clearer, and more complex, once we get past the binary distinction of "Slave Societies" and "Societies with Slaves."

11

Islands of Slavery: Archaeology and Caribbean Landscapes of Intensification

Theresa Singleton

INTRODUCTION

As the recipient of approximately 42 percent of the total disembarked victims of the transatlantic slave trade, and maintaining slave populations that consistently exceeded the 20 percent threshold set by Finley, the Caribbean region comfortably qualifies for his category "Slave Society," and indeed was ranked by Finley as one of the canonical five slave societies in world history.[1] But the intensity and scale of Caribbean slavery varied from island to island and from district to district on each island. Temporality also played a role in the scale and intensity of slavery. Finley defined the Caribbean as a "Slave Society" based on its most intensive period in the deployment of African labor from the mid-seventeenth through the nineteenth centuries. During that time, the "sugar revolution" – an array of events and circumstances – resulted in a sugar monoculture that was generated with black slave labor.[2] Nevertheless, the initial enslavement of Amerindians, and shortly thereafter of Africans, began in the sixteenth century in the Spanish Antilles, although the numbers were considerably smaller than in later periods. The Spaniards utilized various forms of labor (conscripted, enslaved, tenants) in their conquest

[1] See "Trans-Atlantic Slave Trade Database" for numerical estimates of specific and general points of disembarkation in the Caribbean, http://slavevoyages.org/tast/assessment/estimates.faces.

[2] For discussion and critique of the term "sugar revolution," see Higman 2000, 213–36; Menard 2006.

of the Antilles, and this practice set the precedent for the later colonization of the Caribbean by other European powers.

The terms Finley proposed, a "Society with Slaves" and a "Slave Society," are ingrained in the historiography of Caribbean slavery but are rarely attributed to him. They are now concepts that are taken for granted, accepted as common knowledge in Caribbean studies.[3] Scholars of the Caribbean, however, appear not to draw on Finley's usage, but on the works of scholars, some of whom were contemporaries of Finley. A classic example is Elsa Goveia's *Slave Society in the British Leeward Islands*, 1965, based on her doctoral dissertation completed in 1952 at the University of London. Her study details how the British colonies of Antigua, St. Kitts, Nevis, Montserrat, Barbuda, Anguilla, and the British Virgin Islands established slavery during the second half of the seventeenth century for economic purposes. By the end of the eighteenth century, however, slavery was not just an economic institution but the basis on which society was organized, both socially and politically. She argues that slavery was so entrenched in these insular island communities that it was believed indispensable to maintaining the existing social structure, even as slavery was becoming unprofitable.[4]

This chapter considers the usefulness of the Finley model to Caribbean slavery from the vantage point of archaeology. As an archaeologist who has investigated slavery in both North America and the Caribbean, I have referred to Finley's terms to characterize the larger sociohistorical contexts of the plantations that I investigated. Following the work of historians of Cuba, I characterize Cuba as a "Society with Slaves" prior to the nineteenth century before the massive importation of Africans to Cuba, and as a "Slave Society" from 1800 to 1866, when approximately 710,200 African victims disembarked on the island.[5] From a broad demographic perspective, this simple binary works, yet it does not permit an understanding of how slavery was deployed in local settings for the kinds of microhistorical analyses most archaeological studies yield. In this chapter, I evaluate where Finley's model offers possibilities to frame or interpret the

[3] For recent examples using the terms a "Society with Slaves" and a "Slave Society" in Caribbean studies, see Palmié 2011, 142; Ferrer 2014, 17.

[4] Goveia 1965, 151.

[5] Singleton 2015, 26.

archaeology of slavery, and where it may impede rather than enhance our understanding of slavery at specific sites and local settings.

ARCHAEOLOGY OF CARIBBEAN SLAVERY

The Caribbean is a very diverse, complex region that is variously defined from geographical, cultural, historical, or political perspectives. It encompasses the islands and the associated mainland areas that span from the Florida Keys to northern South America. Even though the Florida Keys, Bahamas, Barbados, Guyana, Suriname, and French Guiana do not have shorelines on the Caribbean Sea, they are included in the Caribbean region. On the other hand, Mexico, Belize, Guatemala, Honduras, Nicaragua, Costa Rica, and Panama all border on the western edge of the Caribbean Sea but are not always included or thought of as part of the Caribbean region. Furthermore, the diverse geographies, histories, peoples, languages, and political regimes constrain comprehensive treatment of the region as whole, making any synthesis of Caribbean slavery a formidable task.[6]

Archaeological study of Caribbean slavery is uneven as it has only been undertaken in the past thirty years. Most investigations focus on the Antilles rather than the mainland areas, and some of the islands that are the smallest and least representative of broad historiographic schemes, such as Dominica, Montserrat, and Saba, are the ones that have been subjected to archaeological investigation.[7] The former British colonies and present-day English-speaking islands have received the greatest attention, but archaeological investigations of slavery have been initiated on at least one or more islands of each former European colonial power in the Caribbean (Denmark, England, France, the Netherlands, and Spain). Where little or no archaeological study exists, efforts directed toward recording standing ruins of plantations and other sites once associated with slavery have taken place in recent years. Many of these preservation efforts are the direct consequence of the UNESCO Slave Route Project launched in 1994 that has as one of its goals to encourage its member states to

[6] For a comprehensive history of the Caribbean region, see Palmié and Scarano 2011.

[7] For Dominica, see Lenik 2011, 51–71; Hauser 2015, 143–65; for Monteserrat, see Howson 1995; for Saba, see Espersen 2017.

"inventory, protect and promote" memorial sites and places related to slavery.[8]

Plantation slavery is the predominant theme, but explorations of slavery in urban, military, and industrial settings have also received attention.[9] While many, if not most, of the plantations investigated were formerly sugar plantations, a significant number of the plantations studied produced coffee, cotton, or other cash crops.[10] Archaeologists have also studied mission plantations established for the purpose of converting Amerindians and enslaved Africans to Christianity. Excavations at two eighteenth-century French Jesuit plantations, one on the island of Dominica in the eastern Caribbean and the other in French Guiana, indicate ways in which the Jesuits implemented spatial practices dissimilar from those of many secular Caribbean plantations. Such differences may be related to different modes of surveillance and social control of the enslaved.[11] Thus the archaeological study of Caribbean slavery seeks to examine diverse plantations and not just those associated with the metanarrative of sugar and slavery.

Most plantation research enhances our understanding of everyday life in the slave quarters, particularly the activities that took place within slave dwellings and associated yard areas. Excavations yield evidence of living conditions such as the types of slave housing, foodways, personal hygiene, or health care practices, but also reveal the kinds of objects enslaved peoples acquired, made, used, traded, and discarded. Specialized analyses of pottery made by enslaved and free blacks provide insights into the production, consumption, and exchange of a particular commodity, most notably in Jamaica, as well as on other islands. So too imported, non-provisioned, mass-produced items recovered from slave quarters point to the objects enslaved people purchased with money they earned from their independent production – economic activities enslaved peoples pursued

[8] For information on the Slave Route Project, see www.unesco.org/new/en/culture/themes/dialogue/the-slave-route/.

[9] For urban slavery, see Frederick Smith and Watson 2009, 63–79; Armstrong 2014, 226–27; for slavery in the military, see Beier 2014; for industrial slavery, see Goucher 1999, 143–56.

[10] For coffee plantations, see Delle 1998, 2014; Singleton 2015; for cotton, see Wilkie and Farnsworth 2005.

[11] Lenik 2011, 65–66.

for their own benefit. Archaeological findings also suggest some of the diversions of enslaved peoples when they were not engaged in the production of plantation crops, such as smoking, playing games, making music, and preparing and drinking alcoholic beverages.

Archaeology can also be used to examine the effects of an event on plantation landscapes and slavery. For example, Holly Norton conducted a spatial analysis of the 1733 slave rebellion on St. John, US Virgin Islands, using archaeological survey, historical sources, and Geographic Information Systems (GIS). She traced the movement of the rebellion during its eight-month duration, and she also examined how planters rebuilt and organized their plantations in ways that tightened their surveillance of the enslaved after the rebellion.[12] In another study on the French island of Guadeloupe, Kenneth Kelly found that the short-lived abolition of slavery granted under Victor Hughes, the commander of French Republican forces in 1794, and the reinstatement of slavery by Napoleon Bonaparte in 1802, produced archaeological signatures. The reinstatement of slavery required some renegotiation between planters and the emancipated laborers forced back into slavery. To avoid potential slave uprisings and other forms of resistance, planters made concessions to slave laborers that included the elimination of night work in sugar mills, protection of free days, and access to markets. Archaeological research indicates that along with these concessions, makeshift slave houses of the eighteenth century were replaced with the construction of new masonry slave houses at the beginning of the nineteenth century. Additionally, while eighteenth-century slave sites contained few artifacts, artifacts recovered from those in the early nineteenth century were plentiful. The nineteenth-century abundance of artifacts is most likely related to greater access to markets now enjoyed by slave laborers.[13]

Yet despite efforts to focus on diverse plantations and topics found on islands of all sizes, large rather than small plantations are the most often studied. This bias stems from two factors: first, many large plantations were formed from smaller landholdings. For example, once sugar took root, plantations and farms that produced cotton, indigo, or tobacco were often converted into sugar plantations, or the

[12] Norton 2013.

[13] Kenneth Kelly 2011, 200–02.

planter elite acquired the productive units of smaller-scale planters and combined them into large plantations. Sometimes traces of these earlier productive units are identified through excavations, but, in many cases, the consolidation and redesign of the more recent, larger plantation obliterates evidence of earlier use. Second, large plantations with impressive, extant ruins usually indicate that their buried archaeological resources are well preserved, and these sites are more likely to be investigated than sites lacking above-ground remains. It is therefore not surprising that on some islands, the plantations with the largest slaveholdings have been archaeologically studied while smaller plantations have not. This focus on large Caribbean plantations, however, overemphasizes the planter elite and unfortunately masks the gender, ethnic, and class diversity of slaveholders.[14] It also, unintentionally, reinforces the stereotype that most Caribbean slaveholders possessed large slaveholdings, which was not necessarily the case on many islands. As archaeologists expand the scope of their studies, however, these biases will be addressed. The following discussion organized around the temporal development of Caribbean slavery considers the conditions that gave rise to Caribbean slave societies, a major concern of Finley,[15] and how archaeology contributes to interpretations of slavery during each period.

ORIGINS OF CARIBBEAN SLAVERY, 1500–1650

In the early days of Spanish conquest, the Spanish Crown established *encomiendas* or *repartimientos*, an institution that allotted a Spaniard a group of indigenous people for labor and tribute in exchange for religious instruction and protection. While not enslaved, these indigenous laborers were conscripted for a set time period for agricultural and mining operations and returned to their village homes and traditional practices once their yearly service was completed. Sued-Badillo argues, however, that famine was prevalent during these rest periods because little food was available in their villages.[16] Analysis

[14] Shephard 2002, 1.

[15] Finley 1980, 77–86.

[16] This summary on *encomiendas* looks specifically at this institution in the Spanish Antilles and not mainland Spanish America where the institution endured longer; see Guitar 2011, 115–29; Sued-Badillo 2011.

of food remains at the site of En Bas Saline in northern Haiti, one of the few Caribbean sites associated with the *encomienda* system that has been studied archaeologically, does not provide evidence of famine. In fact, feasting rituals similar to those practiced prior to European contact continued in this Taíno town after Spanish domination.[17] This finding provides insights into how an institution like the *encomienda* or slavery operated in specific localities, as does archaeological study in general.

Archaeological study of *encomiendas* in the Spanish Antilles, however, remains very preliminary up to the present. Researchers identified and examined the locations from which the Amerindian conscripts were drawn and that they occupied during their rest periods. In addition to the site of En Bas Saline, archaeologists working in Cuba have identified and studied portions of the *encomienda*, La Loma del Convento, associated with cleric Bartolomé de las Casas, who later became an outspoken advocate for indigenous Americans. Las Casas accompanied Diego Velázquez, the first governor of Cuba, in the Spanish conquest of the island, and was granted an *encomienda* in 1514. But Las Casas later renounced it in 1515 to protest the maltreatment of indigenous Americans under Spanish rule.[18] At another excavated sixteenth-century site, a sugar factory in Sevilla la Nueva, the capital of Spanish Jamaica, conscripted native laborers supplied one of several forms of labor for the operation of the factory. These native laborers were most likely obtained from three known Taíno villages located in the nearby hills. As Jamaica lacked the rich alluvial gold deposits found in Hispaniola, and to a lesser extent, Puerto Rico and Cuba, native labor became the primary resource Spaniards exploited on the island.[19]

As the numbers of conscripted native laborers declined due to introduced diseases, harsh working conditions, and underfeeding, the enslavement of indigenous peoples became increasingly important to Spanish colonists. Thousands of enslaved natives were taken from the Guianas to present-day Columbia and from Costa Rica to Florida between 1510 and 1542 to work in mines, sugar works, pearl diving, and other enterprises. Their Spanish captors justified enslaving these

[17] Deagan 2004, 597–626.
[18] Vernon Knight 2010, 26–46.
[19] Woodward 2010, 22–40.

native Caribbean peoples, labeled "Caribs," a term the Spaniards used to denote cannibals, because they resisted Spanish domination and Christianity; therefore, enslaved natives were deemed a menace to peaceful natives and Spanish rule.[20]

Pressure from opponents of the *encomienda* system, particularly from the Dominican Order of Friars, persuaded the Spanish Crown to abolish the *encomienda* system in 1542. By that time, Africans had begun to trickle into the Antilles and eventually replaced enslaved natives. In the early years, Africans worked alongside enslaved natives on agricultural operations and in mines, and forged various relationships with natives. Sometimes Africans allied themselves with natives against the Spaniards; in other cases, they allied themselves with the Spaniards against natives. They also escaped enslavement with natives and formed runaway slave communities. Because the initial imports of Africans were numerically small and they suffered high mortality, the cultural impact of Africans in the sixteenth- and early seventeenth-century Caribbean was minimal compared to that of later centuries when the transatlantic slave trade accelerated.[21]

Spaniards introduced the enslavement of indigenous Americans and Africans to labor in mines, sugar operations, and other economic activities in the Caribbean. Although the initial exploitation of Amerindians and Africans in the Spanish Antilles in the sixteenth century did not result in what could be considered a "Slave Society," slave labor played a major role in these early enterprises. Unfortunately, we know very little from archaeological study about slaves' lives in the sixteenth-century Caribbean.

By the end of the sixteenth century, the Spaniards' initial economic ventures in the Antilles declined as they became more interested in exploiting mainland America. In the seventeenth century, the English, French, and Dutch heightened their interests in the Caribbean and established permanent settlements there; they escalated the importation of enslaved Africans to produce sugar and other staple crops. Their colonies, most of which were located in the Lesser Antilles, replaced the prominent position the Spanish Greater Antilles held in the sixteenth century.

[20] Sued-Badillo 2011, 105.
[21] Sued-Badillo 2011, 107–10.

THE SUGAR REVOLUTION AND THE INTENSIFICATION OF AFRICAN SLAVERY, 1650–1800

England founded its first permanent Caribbean settlement of St. Christopher, known today as St. Kitts, in 1624. But it was Barbados, colonized in 1627, that became England's richest Caribbean colony of the seventeenth century on the basis of slave-produced sugar. The settlement of Barbados initially followed a pattern similar to Virginia, with colonists receiving land grants and employing the labor of white indentured servants. White indentures included both voluntary workers who came with the hope of acquiring land upon the completion of five- to seven-year contracts, and involuntary workers (convicts, prisoners of war, vagrants, and paupers) deported by English authorities, who were required to work for ten years.[22] White indentures worked alongside small numbers of enslaved Africans and indigenous Americans on tobacco and cotton plantations until 1645 when sugar planting proliferated. Sugar culture transformed Barbados within a very short time from a colony with landholdings of varied sizes that include a white yeomanry, mixed agriculture, and a predominant workforce of white servants to a colony of large sugar plantations, owned by sugar barons, and worked by black enslaved laborers. Between 1645 and 1650, the African population doubled, while the white indentured population decreased significantly after 1650.

The rapidity of this transformation makes Barbados "the archetype of the sugar revolution."[23] More significantly, Barbados became known as the "first slave society in the Americas." Although it was not the first to import thousands of enslaved Africans, it was the first "to institutionalize slavery as the basis of all economic production and civil society reproduction."[24] Hilary Beckles's assertion that the notion of a "Slave Society" in Barbados refers not just to an economic institution but also to a system fully integrated into the reproduction of the social relations, echoes Goveia's analysis of the Leeward Islands (which does not include Barbados). Barbados provides the earliest case to illustrate Finley's distinction between a "Society with Slaves" and a "Slave Society" in the Caribbean, and this notion, if not directly

[22] See Eltis 2000, 44–52; Beckles 2011; Palmié 2011, 131–147.
[23] Higman 2000, 224.
[24] Beckles 2011, 206–07.

referenced, in discussions on the labor transformation in Barbados, is at least implied. Yet, while the Finleyan model appears applicable to Barbados, it cannot explain why the transition from indentured to slave labor occurred. Indeed, the answer to this question remains unclear.

Explanations for the transition from indentured to slave labor in Barbados have been debated for decades. Early arguments, now dismissed, by Vincent Harlow in his *History of Barbados* (1926) and Lowell Ragatz in *The Fall of the Planter Class in the British Caribbean, 1763–1833* (1928) proposed that the climate made white labor unsuitable for sugar culture.[25] At present most scholars generally agree that economic rationales account for this transition, but noneconomic factors are posited as well.[26] David Eltis argues that by the early modern period (1500–1800) Europeans did not enslave other Europeans, and slavery had long disappeared from northwestern Europe when the transatlantic slave trade exploded and became significant to the colonization of the Americas.[27]

On the other hand, Beckles claims white indentures were temporary chattel used and abused like enslaved laborers. According to Beckles, "sugar planters would enslave labor from any source," and "servants were bought, sold, taxed as property, mortgaged, used as collateral, transferred, and alienated as chattel in much the same way as enslaved Africans."[28] He argues further that discussions of servitude and enslavement should not rely entirely on legal criteria for what constituted a servant versus a slave without considering the lived experience of workers. Using seventeenth-century accounts, particularly those from servants who documented their experiences, Beckles supports his argument that servants performed the same kinds of labor, and were treated just like the enslaved. To explain the shift from servants to slaves, Beckles discusses how a multitude of internal

[25] Harlow 1926; Ragatz 1928. Barry Higman discusses how eighteenth- and nineteenth-century writers of the slaveholding planter tradition regarded the climate of the West Indies as an obstacle to white labor and that professional history writers of the early twentieth century uncritically accepted the climate explanation. Even as late as the 1970s, the climate explanation or variations on it could be found in some history writing. See Higman 1999, 174–76.

[26] See Higman 2000, 224; Beckles, 2011, 208.

[27] Eltis 2000, 58–63. See also Eltis 2007.

[28] Beckles 2011, 212.

and external factors went against planter efforts to convert servitude into slavery, including the servants' ambition to participate in colonialism on their own terms in order to acquire the wealth they desired. With enslaved Africans, planters had more freedom to control them violently and to suppress resistance without scrutiny from colonial authorities or other sympathetic observers. Allan Kulikoff argues similarly that Chesapeake planters disciplined their enslaved laborers more harshly than indentured servants because, unlike the enslaved, indentures upon the completion of their contracts would become small independent tobacco farmers with whom planters would most likely have future business dealings.[29] Africans initially provided a feasible substitute for servants, both in Barbados and in the Chesapeake, but after the white servant pool dwindled and prices for servants rose substantially in the mid-1660s, enslaved African labor became more cost-effective than servants.[30]

Ongoing archaeological investigations in Barbados should yield empirical data on the lived experiences of white servants and enslaved blacks even as it offers the possibility of assessing the relevance of Finley's concepts of "Societies with Slaves" and "Slave Societies" to archaeology. Douglas Armstrong excavated a plantation that spans the entire period of servitude and slavery from the 1620s to 1834. He has identified discrete archaeological contexts associated with the predominance of white servants during the pre-sugar phase (1627 to 1640s), the transition to a sugar/slave economy (1650s to 1720s), and the exclusive use of enslaved labor from the 1720s onward.[31] Archaeological analysis can provide insights into the material differences of these time periods and address the differences in the living conditions of the servitude period versus those of the slavery period. At the same time, this research has the potential to examine the applicability of Finley's model to archaeology by providing empirical data from a case study when the enslaved population comprised a small portion of the workforce and when the entire workforce was enslaved.

Similar patterns of plantation settlement that witnessed the transition from servant to slave labor can be traced on other English islands

[29] Kulikoff 1986, 43.
[30] Beckles 2011, 210–14.
[31] Douglas Armstrong, Syracuse University, personal communication, September 2015.

such as St. Kitts, Antigua, and Montserrat, as well as on the French islands of Guadeloupe and Martinique, although this transformation was not as rapid as on Barbados. When the English took control of Jamaica in 1655 and the French established Saint-Domingue (Haiti) in 1697 on the western third of Hispaniola, plantation slavery was instituted from the beginning.[32] Jamaica and Saint-Domingue on the Greater Antilles possessed greater capacities to produce sugar and other staples than colonies in the Lesser Antilles. During the eighteenth century, they received the largest numbers of enslaved Africans to disembark in the Caribbean, 857,203 in Jamaica and 767,810 in Saint-Domingue, which made the slave populations at their peak 80 to 90 percent of each colony's total population.[33] Both became eighteenth-century centers of sugar production.[34] Saint-Domingue excelled in its production of sugar and coffee, so much so that by the eve of the Haitian Revolution (1791–1804) that ended slavery and French colonization on the island, it had gained recognition as the world's leading producer of both staples. Although little archaeological research on plantations has been undertaken in Haiti, many of its former plantation sites are protected and recorded through its national office of historic preservation, the Institut de Sauvegarde du Patrimoine National (ISPAN).[35]

In contrast with Haiti, Jamaica has developed as a center for archaeological research into slavery over the past three decades. Perhaps, more than for any other Caribbean island, Jamaica's former plantation complex has been approached from a variety of archaeological perspectives, including both terrestrial and maritime archaeology.[36] In addition to the investigation of slave communities, sites of slave runways (maroon communities) have received considerable attention.[37] Archaeologists have examined a wide range of

[32] Palmié 2011, 146–47.

[33] For Saint-Domingue, see DuBois 2012, 50; for Jamaica, see Mulcahy 2014, 73.

[34] See www.slavevoyages.org/tast/assessment/estimates.faces.

[35] See www.bulletindelispan.ht.

[36] Books and monographs on the archaeology of Jamaican slavery and plantations include Armstrong 1990; Higman 1998; Hauser 2008; Delle, Hauser, and Armstrong, eds. 2011; Delle 1998, 2014. For a maritime archaeological study of Jamaica's plantation economy, see Cook and Rubenstein-Gottschamer 2011.

[37] Kofi Agorsah is a pioneer in the archaeological study of maroons in both Jamaica and Suriname. His publications related to Jamaica include Agorsah 1993, 1994; Goucher and Agorsah 2011, 144–60.

topics: plantation landscapes, the use of domestic space, foodways, pottery production, slave markets, independent production, slave burial practices, and, recently, slave religiosity.[38] Archaeological research into slavery in Jamaica has yielded detailed analyses of plantations and related sites that provide a holistic understanding of slavery, resistance, and the early years of emancipation.

Slave labor was deployed in Jamaica from the beginning of English colonization; consequently, it quickly developed into a "Slave Society." But the term "Slave Society" may not be useful to understanding the social dynamics or the deployment of labor at all Jamaican sites. Candice Goucher investigated Reeder's Foundry, an ironmaking and brass casting operation of the late eighteenth century (1772–82), located in the town of Morant Bay, Jamaica. The workforce consisted of 267 laborers, including enslaved, maroon, and free black workers that the owner, John Reeder, apparently selected for their metalworking skills. Goucher, an Africanist who specializes in the study of African ironworking technologies, sought to find evidence of African iron-making technology, but the hearth and forge she uncovered were more closely related to English ironworking traditions than to those of Africa. After the demise of the Reeder Foundry in the early nineteenth century, Morant Bay became a powerful African spiritual center that Goucher suggests may have absorbed many of the foundry's iron experts given that iron objects remain important in the present-day religious rituals in the area.[39]

Without a doubt the seventeenth-century "sugar revolution" transformed many previously colonized Caribbean islands from societies with various forms of labor into "Slave Societies" and contributed to the establishment of "Slave Societies" on other islands from the beginning of colonization. Some islands, however, proved too dry, too mountainous, or too small to sustain plantation agriculture. And this is where archaeological research on specific plantations and islands can address how or perhaps even why these operations failed. On other islands and some of the adjacent mainland Caribbean areas, slavery was utilized to produce commodities other than sugar. A few

[38] Archaeological studies of slave religiosity in Jamaica include Reeves 2014, 176–96 and Saunders 2014, 2015.

[39] Goucher 1999, 150–51; Goucher and Agorsah 2011, 151.

islands had to wait until the nineteenth century to prosper from sugar and slavery.

SECOND SLAVERY IN THE CARIBBEAN, 1801–1886

The abolition of the transatlantic slave trade in Britain in 1807 paved the way for slave emancipation in the British Caribbean in 1838.[40] Ten years later, France abolished slavery. Yet, as slavery declined in the former seventeenth- and eighteenth-century colonial zones of the English and French, the importation of enslaved Africans to the Spanish Antilles, most notably to Cuba, accelerated. This nineteenth-century resurgence of the slave trade and intensification of new zones of slave-produced commodities is increasingly referred to as "second slavery." The new production zones and commodities of second slavery include: cotton in the Southern United States, coffee in southern Brazil, and sugar in Cuba. Slavery thrived in each of these zones in spite of considerable efforts to suppress the slave trade and abolish slavery altogether.[41]

In the nineteenth century, Cuba became the major locus of disembarkation for enslaved Africans in the Caribbean, but prior to 1800, the island had one of the smallest slave populations in the region. Although Spain introduced African slavery to the Caribbean, the Spanish Crown restricted the numbers of enslaved people that could be imported into its Caribbean colonies. Consequently, between 1650 and 1800, when Britain imported more than two million enslaved Africans to the region and France more than one million, fewer than 80,000 Africans disembarked in Cuba and Puerto Rico.[42] Under the Spanish Bourbon monarchs Carlos III (1759–88) and Carlos IV (1788–1808), however, this situation changed with the passage of several reforms designed to make the Spanish Antilles profitable. The last reform, promulgated in 1789, opened up the slave trade to designated Spanish colonial ports in Cuba, Puerto Rico, Spanish Santo Domingo, and Caracas for any Spaniard to purchase enslaved

[40] The British Slavery Abolition Act went into effect in 1834, but many enslaved people in the British Empire did not become fully free until 1838 after a period of forced apprenticeship following the passage of the British Slavery Abolition Act.

[41] Tomich and Zeuske 2008, 91–100.

[42] See http://slavevoyages.org/tast/assessment/estimates.faces.

Africans free of duty. In addition, the Haitian Revolution greatly facilitated Cuba's meteoric rise to a plantation colony and "Slave Society" because it ended the prominent position Saint-Domingue held as the leading producer of coffee and sugar. Within a relatively short period, Cuba seized the opportunity to fill this void in the world market and to develop an economy based upon slavery comparable to those established earlier by the English and the French.[43]

Prior to second slavery, Cuba had approximately 60,000 enslaved men and women mostly based in urban areas, with the remainder scattered on small farms or modest-sized plantations that produced tobacco or sugar, or raised livestock. The historiography of pre-nineteenth-century Cuban slavery indicates that enslaved people had greater opportunities for manumission and social mobility than slave workers in nineteenth-century plantations. But historian Evelyn Jennings found this was not the case for those workers that the king of Spain enslaved to work on defensive projects after 1763, the year the Seven Years' War ended. In Havana, many slave laborers worked for the Spanish state building fortifications that involved the heavy work of digging, hauling, construction, quarrying and cutting stone, and building batteries. Jennings posited that the work regimes, living conditions, and perhaps mortality rates for these slave laborers were comparable to those found on nineteenth-century plantations.[44]

No archaeological research into slavery in Havana has been reported or published. In many urban settings, identifying spaces exclusively occupied by enslaved residents who lived with their owners or other free residents on the same city lots poses a challenge to current archaeological methods because separating the archaeological materials belonging to the enslaved from those of other people occupying the same spaces is difficult, if not impossible. Archaeological contexts associated with urban slavery may have been excavated through the long-term, ongoing archaeology program of Havana undertaken by the Gabinete de Arqueología based in the Office of the Historian for the City of Havana.[45] Archaeologists Karen Mahé Lugo Romera

[43] Ferrer 2014, 25–37.

[44] Jennings 2002, 151–82.

[45] The Gabinete de Arqueología, established in the late 1980s, undertakes archaeological investigation on sites located in the historic districts of Havana that are designated for restoration or threatened with destruction because of new construction. Over the years, spaces occupied by enslaved residents in Havana most likely were

and Sonia Menéndez Castro of the Gabinete de Arqueología, however, conducted excavations in a neighborhood of Old Havana that had a large population of Amerindians from the Yucatán. Known as Yucatecos in Cuba, they lived in the Barrio de Campeche and arrived in Cuba in several waves from the late sixteenth through the late eighteenth centuries. They were not enslaved, but they came to Cuba involuntarily and therefore composed a coerced immigrant population that worked on public works projects, similar to the enslaved population. The archaeological study, however, focused on Yucatán pottery found throughout Old Havana to determine whether it was crafted in Cuba, imported from Yucatán, or both. Analytical sourcing studies directed toward determining where the pottery recovered from sites in the Barrio de Campeche was made proved inconclusive. Despite this drawback, the investigators posit that Yucatecos were responsible not only for introducing this pottery but also for Meso-American ways of preparing food as seen in the recovery of food preparation equipment characteristic of the Yucatán found in the excavations of colonial period houses in Old Havana.[46]

Slavery in nineteenth-century Cuba is seen as the final phase of the Caribbean "sugar revolution."[47] While sugar did drive the Cuban slave trade and the vast majority of enslaved workers labored on sugar plantations, slavery played a major role in the coffee, tobacco, and urban economies as well. Recent studies on the Cuban coffee and tobacco sectors dispel unfounded generalizations and mischaracterizations about slavery in the production of these secondary staples. For example, it is often assumed that enslaved workers on coffee plantations were treated better than those on sugar plantations. Sugar plantations in nineteenth-century Cuba are notorious for subjecting the enslaved to harsh working and living conditions with very strict policing. But similar practices prevailed on coffee plantations as well. Cuba's tobacco economy, by contrast, is frequently depicted as a small-scale, family-farm enterprise confined to free laborers with only nominal participation of enslaved workers.[48]

excavated, but it is often difficult to attribute specific archaeological materials to slave laborers in urban settings with certainty.

[46] Romera, Mahé, and Menéndez 2003, 17–46.

[47] Higman 2000, 230–31.

[48] Ortiz 1995.

But this interpretation is unsupported by historical records, and slave labor was always a major component of tobacco operations of all sizes.[49]

Archaeological study of Cuban slavery has thus far only examined second slavery on both sugar and coffee plantations. Although plantations are the focus of the archaeological study of Cuban slavery, this research is much less developed than work conducted in Jamaica or for that matter, on some of the islands of the Lesser Antilles. Cuban studies conducted from the 1960s to the 1980s focused on extant ruins rather than on excavations of areas where enslaved people lived or worked. Studies of slave quarter ruins known as *barracones*, however, have contributed to our understanding of slave living conditions on Cuban plantations and the methods of surveillance used to control the slave laborers. Lourdes Domínguez examined a large *barracón* at Taoro, a sugar plantation located about ten miles southwest of Old Havana. She estimates it housed as many as 300 residents: 224 slave laborers, some Chinese indentured laborers, and other plantation personnel such as slave overseers or plantation cooks. She found that the rooms were poorly ventilated with small windows and doors, and a turnstile was installed at the main entrance to monitor who was coming in or going out.[50]

Most enslaved Cubans, however, lived in detached houses known as *bohíos*. These slave houses were constructed of various kinds of materials, including bark, wattle (woven twigs and plant fibers), wooden boards, or mud. At the Santa Ana de Biajacas coffee plantation, the most extensive archaeological investigations of a slave settlement to date, the slave laborers lived in earthen slave houses with palm-thatched roofs, but the slaveholder enclosed the entire slave settlement, an area measuring 1.7 square acres, within a massive masonry wall. Based on what we know from nineteenth-century planter essays and slave codes, slaveholders locked enslaved laborers in these enclosures or *barracones* at night to prevent them from running away and participating in nocturnal activities in nearby taverns and shops. Archaeological excavations within the enclosure at Santa Ana de Biajacas revealed that the practice of locking enslaved people at night

[49] For slavery and Cuban coffee, see Van Norman 2013; Singleton 2015; for tobacco, see Morgan 2013.

[50] Domínguez Gonzáles 1986, 274–78.

did obstruct the slave community's ability to obtain goods from local establishments, for the enslaved people possessed very few objects when compared with the nineteenth-century plantations excavated on Guadeloupe or the eighteenth-century plantations of Jamaica.[51]

The owner of Biajacas, Ignacio O'Farrill y Herrera, was a member of the planter elite.[52] His siblings also owned numerous plantations with sizable slaveholdings in the same vicinity as Biajacas. In addition to the coffee plantation, Ignacio O'Farrill, a Catholic priest, owned two sugar plantations and approximately 350–400 enslaved persons at the peak of his slaveholding. His estate records clearly indicate that his plantations and the enslaved workers who labored on them comprised his personal property and not the corporate property of a religious order, as was the case with the Jesuit mission plantations previously described.

Matanzas jurisdiction, where the coffee plantation was located, had a very high concentration of enslaved laborers, and a high slave-to-non-slave ratio when one looks at the population statistics for the entire jurisdiction. Yet, when one looks at the specific district where Biajacas was located, the enslaved workers were concentrated on eleven sugar plantations and nine coffee plantations in 1822. The remaining agricultural properties belonged to non-slaveholders who lived on fifty-nine small farms that produced food crops, and another twenty-nine households' rented lands. Forty years later after Biajacas was abandoned and the land was subdivided into thirty-three food crop farms, the district contained a total of eight sugar plantations, two coffee plantations, and 285 subsistence and larger farms (including the thirty-three food crop farms carved from the lands formerly belonging to the Biajacas coffee plantation).[53] Although enslaved Cubans outnumbered free Cubans, there was a significant population of free, non-slaveholders in many districts. The term "Slave

[51] Singleton 2015, 91–115, 151–87.

[52] Richard O'Farrell (O'Farrell was later Hispanicized to O'Farrill), progenitor of the Cuban O'Farrills, was Ignacio O'Farrill's grandfather. Richard was born to Irish parents on Montserrat in the eastern Caribbean. He came to Cuba in 1715 and married into the Spanish colonial elite.

[53] Archivo Nacional de Cuba, Gobierno Superior Civil, legajo 871, no. 29460 "Expediente Sobre Las Ordenanzas Municipales Y Plan Describiros Del Pueblo De Madruga," 1822; Archivo Nacional de Cuba, Gobierno General, legajo 434, no. 21052, "Resumen de las fincas rústicas con expresión de los partidos a que pertenecen, clases de ellos, renta líquida e impuestos que satisfacen, 1862."

Society" (as defined by Finley) does not exclude non-slaveholders, but it sometimes obscures the role of non-slaveholders. Matanzas jurisdiction was densely populated with slave laborers, but the percentage of enslaved laborers varied according to the district from 46 percent to 90 percent in 1841 when Biajacas was still functioning as a coffee plantation.[54] While the term "Slave Society" is appropriate for the study of Biajacas and other plantations located in Matanzas jurisdiction, the term may not be useful to characterize all districts in Cuban jurisdictions containing considerably lower percentages of slaves. Nineteenth-century Cuba was a "Slave Society," but this was not reflected everywhere.

CONCLUSION: FINLEY'S OR GOVEIA'S "SLAVE SOCIETY"

In the introduction of this chapter, I pose the possibility that when Caribbeanists invoke the terms "a Society with Slaves," and a "Slave Society" they may not be referencing Finley, but other scholars of the Caribbean such as Elsa Goveia. In the preface to *Slave Society in the Leeward Islands,* Goveia states that "Slave Society" refers to "the whole community based on slavery, including masters and freedmen as well as slaves." She describes the objective of her study as "to study the political, economic, and social organization of this society and the interrelationships of its component groups and to investigate how it was affected by its dependence on the institution of slavery."[55] Goveia's approach demonstrates the strong influence of social anthropology – a subfield of anthropology that is concerned with how societies are organized – in Caribbean studies that began taking shape after World War II with publications such as that of Julian Steward with his students, *The People of Puerto Rico: A Study in Social Anthropology* (1956). Anthropology, as well as sociology, has played a major role in the study of plantation America, the African presence in the Americas, and race relations in the Caribbean and Latin America since the 1920s. Anthropologist Kelvin Yelvington discusses how several social scientists of Afro-America established an "intellectual social formation," a group of international researchers who sought with

[54] Bergad 1990, 33–34.
[55] Goveia 1965, vii.

broadly similar theoretical lenses to investigate issues related to blacks in the Americas. Yelvington focused on Melville Herskovits and his associations with Fernando Ortiz in Cuba, Jean Prince-Mars in Haiti, and others who were interested in the study of African survivals – cultural practices of African origins – found among present-day black communities in the Americas.[56] A claim can also be made that another intellectual social formation developed among scholars who sought to understand the effects of slavery and race relations in the Caribbean societies that included scholars such as Sidney Mintz, Michael G. Smith, Raymond T. Smith, and Harry Hoetink, among others. Both approaches have strongly influenced studies of Caribbean slavery. It is not surprising, therefore, that Goveia's book on "Slave Society" was published in a book series edited by Sidney Mintz that included books authored by social scientists of the Caribbean. Finley may have coined the term "Society with Slaves," but the concept of a "Slave Society" within the context of Caribbean studies appears to have predated his usage.[57]

In archaeology, a field that has been deployed in the study of slavery only relatively recently, the term "Slave Society" may be useful in some contexts but not in others. It depends on the scale of archaeological analysis, and how slavery is defined. Slavery is increasingly defined in archaeology as any form of coerced labor or captive-taking.[58] When slavery is defined in this way, the term "Slave Society" takes on a different meaning than those of either Finley or Goveia, such that one could say that the first "Slave Societies" associated with European colonialism emerged in the Caribbean during the early Spanish conquests. The line that Finley drew between "Societies with Slaves" and "Slave Societies" may thus need revision for some archaeological studies. Barry Higman stated, "slavery took a variety of characteristic forms, dependent on the type of economic activity in which the enslaved were employed."[59] Archaeology strives to understand the characteristic forms of slavery, and it is best suited for analysis of slavery in local settings.

[56] Yelvington 2006, 67.
[57] Higman 2001.
[58] Marshall 2015.
[59] Higman 1984, 396.

PART IV

NON-WESTERN STATE SOCIETIES

12

Was Nineteenth-Century Eastern Arabia a "Slave Society"?

Matthew S. Hopper

By the end of the nineteenth century, the eastern coast of Arabia (forming the western shore of the Arabian – or Persian – Gulf) had become home to tens of thousands of slaves, many of whom worked in the production of commodities for export to global markets. Many of these slaves were imported directly from Africa or Baluchistan specifically to work in labor-intensive industries such as pearl diving and date production, which had expanded dramatically in the second half of the nineteenth century. Slave labor was essential to the economy of the region in which demand for manpower exceeded supply and commodities were driven by demand from faraway places. Testimonies of runaway slaves who sought manumission from Western consuls, agents, military officers, and missionaries often recounted brutal treatment by masters. Moreover, slaves made up a significant portion of the Gulf's population. If Western observers are to be believed, enslaved Africans and their descendants made up between 15 percent and 20 percent of the population of coastal Arabia between Muscat and Kuwait by the turn of the twentieth century.[1] But was nineteenth-century eastern Arabia a "Slave Society"?

As described in the introduction to this volume, the argument that certain societies employed forms of slavery that differed qualitatively (not quantitatively, i.e., the degree of severity, demographic ratios, economic necessity, etc.) from forms of slavery in other societies

[1] Lorimer 1908, 238–41, 489–90, 1058–77, 1382–1451.

owes its popularity, in large part, to the work of Moses Finley. His classic *Ancient Slavery and Modern Ideology* (1980) argued that slavery in Europe of Classical antiquity (Greece and Rome) and in later European colonies in the Americas (Brazil, the Caribbean, and the US South) shared fundamental characteristics that made them distinct from all other societies that practiced slavery. By Finley's argument, examples of genuine "Slave Societies" could be found in five cultures (all of them Western) in world history – a claim that depended on a narrow definition of "Slave Societies." Finley's five "Slave Societies" practiced forms of slavery in which owners' rights were near total, slaves were deracinated and kinless outsiders, and slaves were divisible into hierarchies of subtypes that did not constitute a cohesive social class. Finley argued further that "Slave Societies" developed late and relatively infrequently in world history and were distinguished by recognizable features such as: a proportionally large slave population (more than 20 percent) and an economy in which slave labor constituted the major source of elite income.[2] Such economies emerged as the result of certain necessary and sufficient conditions including: demand for slave labor preceding supply of slaves, private ownership of land in sufficient concentration in some hands to need "extra-familial labour for the permanent work-force," the development of commodity production and markets, and the unavailability of an internal labor supply "compelling the employers to turn to outsiders."[3] Finley goes on to demonstrate how these conditions were met in Greece and Rome in Classical antiquity, and in select European colonies in the New World. His rigorist definition appears at first glance to eliminate all but the narrow set of Western examples he selects from world history. However, some societies in the modern Middle East or North Africa at times came close to meeting Finley's definition, and the nineteenth-century Arabian Gulf may offer one potential example of a non-Western "Slave Society." This chapter seeks to answer whether the nineteenth-century Arabian Gulf would qualify as a "Slave Society" according to Finley's definition and whether, in light of the answer to this question, Finley's qualitative distinction of Western "Slave Societies" as a classification all its own is merited.

[2] Finley 1998, 140–50.
[3] Finley 1998, 154.

BACKGROUND

Demand for slave labor across the Indian Ocean world grew for a host of reasons in the nineteenth century, most notably the expansion of commodity production for global consumption and the global spread of capitalism. On the East African coast, growth in demand accompanied the development of a massive plantation complex that produced cloves, coconuts, grain, copra, oil, and sugar for both domestic and global consumption.[4] Likewise, in Arabia and the Gulf, the rise in demand for slave labor accompanied the expansion of the production of commodities for global markets. Between the 1860s and the 1920s, two industries in particular – dates and pearls – underwent rapid growth and created new demands for labor. In the late nineteenth century in particular, the Gulf economy expanded dramatically. The growth of the slave trade in the Gulf was a reflection of an economy that – like its predecessor in the Atlantic – was influenced by global economic forces. Old patterns of Gulf slave ownership for conspicuous consumption endured, and the employment of slaves as elites (soldiers, concubines, retainers) and as domestic servants persisted, but, as described in other chapters of this volume, a fundamental shift in the use and acquisition of slaves accompanied the spread of global capitalism in the Indian Ocean and Middle East in the nineteenth century.

Historians of the Middle East, led above all by scholars of the Ottoman Empire, have recently presented sophisticated histories of slavery in the region that demonstrate how methods of enslavement, sources of slaves, and the use of slave labor differed widely throughout Ottoman history and within the empire's vast territory.[5] Elite slavery and domestic slavery typified the slave experience in some but not all of Ottoman history (see Toledano, Chapter 14 in this volume). At various times, slave labor was employed in agriculture and industry.[6] Taken in conjunction with recent research by historians of Indian Ocean slavery, it is now clear that for much of the region's

[4] Alpers 1975; Cooper 1977; Sheriff 1987; Glassman 1995; Richard B. Allen 1999; Campbell 2005.

[5] For an excellent overview of the development of this historiography, see Toledano 1998, 135–68; 2000, 159–75;.

[6] Erdem 1996; Toledano 1998, 2007a; Trout Powell 2006; Zilfi 2010, 96–152; Walz and Cuno, eds. 2010.

history slaves in the Middle East were drawn largely from Eurasian populations, were predominantly female, and were probably engaged primarily in domestic labor or were acquired as "symbols of conspicuous consumption, to reflect the power and wealth of slave owners." But dramatic quantitative and qualitative shifts in slavery occurred in the nineteenth century as a result of a confluence of economic forces.[7] By the late nineteenth century, slavery in the Arabian Gulf was typified not by Eurasian female domestic servants or concubines, but by African males laboring in pearling and date farming. Older modes of slavery persisted, but they were augmented or overwhelmed by new ones. As the Middle East, including the Gulf, was drawn into an expanding global economy in the nineteenth century, dependence on global markets subjected the Gulf economy to the whims of international consumer tastes and the demand these generated.[8] At the same time, residents of the Gulf seized opportunities presented by expanding markets by harnessing the resources of their environment using their own and imported labor.

In the nineteenth century, the Gulf experienced a boom in date exports, fueled in part by new markets in North America and Europe. The lucrative American date market grew as Salem (Massachusetts) and New York merchants expanded American trade in the Indian Ocean at cities like Muscat, Zanzibar, Mokha, and Aden.[9] Likewise, the pearling industry expanded dramatically as the fashion for pearls experienced a revival in Europe and new markets opened in North America. Pearl exports skyrocketed in the first decades of the twentieth century as the desire for pearls spread beyond royal and aristocratic classes in Europe and North America. As early as 1863, Sheikh Muhammad bin Thānī of Doha, Qatar, could remark to traveling British scholar William Palgrave, "We are all from the highest to the lowest slaves of one master, Pearl." The sheikh lamented the growing dependence of the region on the caprice of global markets.[10] An often overlooked irony of the period is that some of the same countries that were pushing for the abolition of slavery and the spread of liberal

[7] Campbell 2004, xix–xx (quote at xix); 2010, 56–61.

[8] Wallerstein, Decdeli, and Kasaba 1987; Owen 1993, 180–88; Gelvin 2005, 35–46, 73–87.

[9] Hopper 2006, 101–61, and now Hopper 2015.

[10] Palgrave 1883, 387.

ideals globally were also the largest consumers of commodities produced by slave labor in other parts of the world.

The labor-intensive date and pearl industries required a massive workforce, and the Gulf's relatively sparse population incentivized importing slave labor. In the nineteenth century, the primary (although not exclusive) source of this labor became East Africa. Arabia's long-standing trade connections with coastal East Africa facilitated early Arab participation in indigenous slave-trading networks in the Mozambique Channel, Madagascar, and the Indian Ocean islands. Mariners from the Gulf helped supply African captives to French planters on the Mascarene Islands in the eighteenth century and witnessed rising demand for East African laborers from Atlantic powers like Portugal, Brazil, and the United States in the early nineteenth century. The collapse of extensive European demand following British abolition, the Napoleonic Wars, and Atlantic anti-slave-trade measures drove prices down and encouraged Arab traders to begin employing large numbers of enslaved Africans on plantations of their own on the coast of East Africa and its nearby islands and transporting others to Arabia.[11] By the 1820s, European visitors described sizable populations of enslaved Africans in Gulf port cities.[12] By the turn of the twentieth century, the African diaspora in the Gulf was clearly visible. In 1905, Africans reportedly accounted for 11 percent of Kuwait's population, 22 percent of Qatar's population, 11 percent of Bahrain's population, 28 percent of the Trucial Coast's population (today's United Arab Emirates), and 25 percent of Muscat and Mutrah's population. J. G. Lorimer estimated that Africans made up roughly 17 percent of the total population of coastal eastern Arabia between Muscat and Kuwait[13] (see Map 12.1).

But was Eastern Arabia, with its sizable, foreign slave population engaged in production of commodities for export markets, truly a "Slave Society"? Finley did not count it among his examples, and a more fully developed theory of "Slave Societies" proposed by David

[11] Sheriff 1987, 48–49, 64–69; Richard B. Allen 1999; Vernet 2003.

[12] See, for example, Mignan 1820, 240–45; Keppel 1827, 19–23.

[13] Lorimer 1908, 238–41, 489–90, 1058–77, 1382–1451; Jayakar 1876–77, 96–102. Gibson and Jung 2002. By contrast, African Americans accounted for 10 to 12 percent of the US population in the censuses of 1900 and 1910. Available at: www.census.gov/population/www/documentation/twps0056/twps0056.html (accessed Oct. 8, 2008).

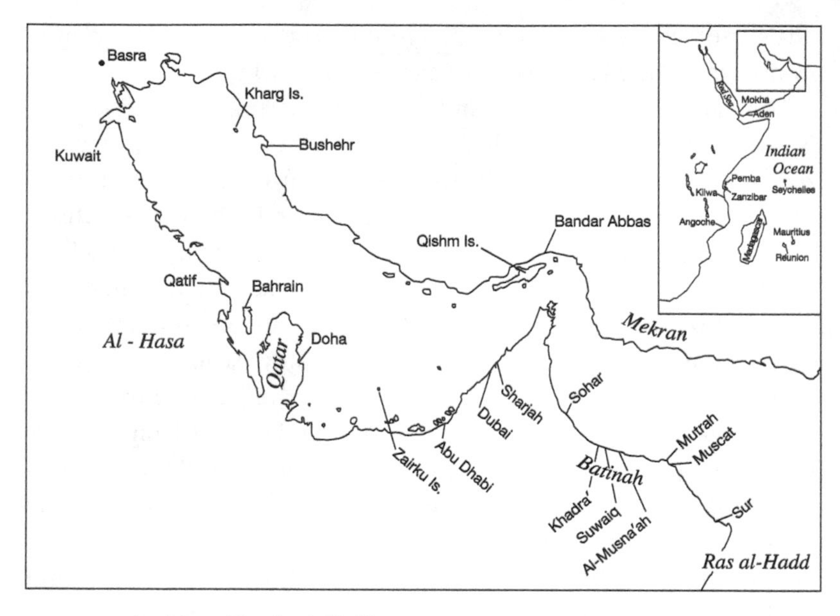

MAP 12.1 Arabian (Persian) Gulf

Turley in *Slavery* (2000) explicitly denies "Slave Society" status to the nineteenth-century Gulf. In Turley's words:

> The Persian Gulf … illustrated ways in which slave labour could be quite extensively employed without a slave society fully emerging. Omani Arab merchants supplied slaves to the gulf to work in agriculture, shipping, military and commercial activity. But the very malleability of slavery … told against the establishment of a full slave society. Bodies of slave workers were deployed to fill temporary shortfalls in labour in different sectors without transforming any of them. Where other kinds of labour performed adequately slaves did not penetrate. In the Gulf they were not associated with new or newly desired commodities and new markets.[14]

For Turley, a "Slave Society" requires a convergence in the same period and the same area of several separate factors including: "an organized system of slave supply, insufficient controllable and affordable labour of other kinds, resources of capital attracted to invest in the slave system and commodities able to be produced for which there was an elastic demand."[15] Only in such conditions could slaves play

[14] Turley 2000, 76.
[15] Turley 2000, 76.

major productive roles. Many, arguably all, of these necessary features appear to have been present in the nineteenth-century Gulf. The rest of this chapter explores whether coastal Eastern Arabia might qualify as a "Slave Society" according to the standards of Finley and even the more rigorous requirements of Turley.

ECONOMIC CONDITIONS

Both Finley and Turley acknowledge that slavery is a malleable institution that was employed in numerous societies around the world throughout history. Yet both reserve the status of "Slave Society" – as opposed to "Societies with Slaves" – for those formations that employed the strictest forms of chattel slavery under unique conditions. We can divide these conditions, roughly, into two categories: economic and social. Because the social conditions emerge largely from the compulsion of the economic, let us begin with the economic conditions. Among the economic factors necessary to produce a "Slave Society," both scholars insist on two requirements: (1) "the unavailability of an internal labour supply, compelling the employers of slave labour to turn to outsiders," as Finley put it, or, in the words of Turley, "insufficient controllable and affordable labour of other kinds"; and (2) "a sufficient development of commodity production and markets," in Finley's words, or for Turley, "resources of capital attracted to invest in the slave system and commodities able to be produced for which there was an elastic demand."[16] To these factors, Finley adds (3) "private ownership of land, with sufficient concentration in some hands to need extra-familial labour for the permanent workforce," and (4) demonstration that slaves provided "the bulk of the immediate income from property ... of the elites, economic, social and political." Although Turley does not list these two factors, he does require (5) "an organized system of slave supply."[17] I argue that the available evidence suggests that the nineteenth-century Gulf met all five of these requirements. Let us begin with the essential factors on which Finley and Turley agree: commodity production for markets and labor shortage.

[16] Finley 1998, 154; Turley 2000, 76.
[17] Finley 1998, 150; Turley 2000, 76.

A leading archeologist of the Gulf, Robert Carter, has demonstrated that, with the exception of Bahrain and Julfar (Ras Al-Khaimah), the permanent settlement of coastal Eastern Arabia between Hormuz and Kuwait was extremely limited prior to the eighteenth century. New permanent population centers like Abu Dhabi, Qatar, Dubai, Sharjah, and Kuwait developed only after the Safavid Empire lost control over the Gulf pearl fisheries in the eighteenth century, freeing hitherto mostly nomadic Arab populations to exploit the pearl beds for cash profits and thereby "override environmental constraints on permanent settlement."[18] Most of the nineteenth-century urban centers of Gulf pearl production were recent creations, having developed out of temporary encampments inhabited seasonally (if at all), and were modest towns with small populations almost wholly dependent on revenues provided by the exportation of pearls and dates. As markets for these two commodities grew, so too did demand for labor to produce them. Reports of foreign observers in the nineteenth century almost universally attest to the Gulf's dependence on pearl and date revenues to accommodate for the importation of staples like rice from India. Rice accounted for a major portion of the diet of coastal populations in Arabia, although it could not be produced in any quantity locally.[19] New settlements such as Abu Dhabi developed rapidly around the turn of the nineteenth century and quickly expanded their pearl fleets to take advantage of the opportunities presented by access to the pearl banks unrestricted by taxation or state control. Estimates by foreign observers as to the size of the total Gulf pearling fleet leap from 2,000 to 3,000 boats in the early nineteenth century to 4,000 to 5,000 boats at the end of the century. Wellsted (1838) remarked that the entire population of the "Pirate Coast" (today's UAE) was engaged in pearling except for "children, females, and men who are too aged to follow this pursuit," and Lorimer (1905) estimated that more than three-quarters of the male population of Abu Dhabi was engaged in pearl fishing.[20] At its height in 1915 more than 64,000 men worked in the Gulf pearling industry during an era in which the combined estimated populations of every urban center in

[18] Carter 2009; see also Carter 2011.
[19] See, for example, J. B. Kelly 1968, 36–37.
[20] Cited in Carter 2009, 276.

Eastern Arabia totaled 309,000 residents.[21] The Gulf's relatively small population may have provided labor sufficient to exploit the region's resources to the degree necessary to meet immediate needs for survival, but when regional markets for Gulf dates and pearls expanded to include new, far-flung global markets, the rising value of these commodities created new opportunities for the exploitation of pearls and dates with an expansion of the workforce (particularly the male workforce).

In the Gulf, as in many parts of the Middle East, the expanding global economy absorbed and augmented trade that already existed on a regional level. Date growers between Muscat and Basra shared similar conditions to those affecting producers of silk and tobacco in Anatolia, grain in Iraq, olives in Tunisia, oranges in Palestine, and cotton in Egypt and Sudan.[22] At the turn of the twentieth century, more than half of the world's estimated ninety million date palms grew in the countries touching the Arabian Gulf, with an estimated thirty million grown in Iraq alone. Oman's share of the world's date palms was relatively small, perhaps four million trees,[23] yet it was Oman that contributed the most to the creation of global markets for dates in the nineteenth century, particularly the lucrative market in the United States. American ships carrying cotton cloth from Massachusetts mills visited Omani-controlled Zanzibar annually beginning in the first years of the nineteenth century and within a few decades came to dominate international trade to that island.[24] Following the seasonal monsoon winds of the western Indian Ocean, American ships visited Arabia on these voyages to exchange cotton cloth, piece goods, and specie for coffee, hides, and dates.[25]

Muscat was the center for Arabian date exports, and Oman was home to particularly hardy varieties of dates, which could survive lengthy sea voyages and ripened earlier than most dates on account of Oman's southern latitude and intense summer heat. The *fardh* variety of dates would ripen in August, which would allow American

[21] Lorimer 1915; I.D. 1129 1919 (*Geographical Section of the Naval Intelligence Division, Naval Staff, Admiralty* [1919]), 239–96.

[22] Roger Owen 1969, 1993; Issawi 1993; Bernal 1995, 96–118; Morilla Critz, Olmstead, and Rhode 1999.

[23] Popenoe 1926.

[24] Norman Robert Bennett 1965; Sheriff 1987; Gilbert 2004, 33–36; Prestholdt 2004.

[25] Bhacker 1992, 109–13, 136–37.

ships enough time to load dates at Muscat, trade at Zanzibar, catch the monsoon winds, and make the 100-day journey home in time for the winter holidays. As American ships frequently returned from their voyages in the autumn, the arrival of Arabian dates in New York before Thanksgiving became an American tradition.[26] With the advent of steamships in the mid-nineteenth century and the opening of the Suez Canal in 1869, the voyage from the Gulf to New York was cut to sixty days, and merchants began to add varieties of dates from Basra to their annual imports of *fardh* dates from Muscat. By 1885 Americans imported more than ten million pounds of dates annually, valued at $382,267.[27] A British observer in Oman noted that it was "from the labors of the date cultivator that the country derives most of such wealth as it has."[28] American date imports grew from an average of ten to twenty million pounds annually between 1893 and 1903 to an average of twenty to thirty million pounds between 1903 and 1913. Date imports soared to nearly seventy-nine million pounds by 1925.[29]

The growth of the date industry sharply influenced labor demands in the Gulf. The primary area of nineteenth-century date expansion in Oman, Batinah – the 150-mile stretch of coast on the Gulf of Oman north of Muscat – became home to a large population of enslaved Africans. As the densest area of vegetation in Eastern Arabia, Batinah had a bigger population and more agricultural production than any other part of the Arabian Gulf south of Iraq. But Batinah differed from the other date-producing areas in the region in that it required intense human effort to irrigate the palms. Although it has some of the richest soil in Oman, Batinah receives no consistent flow of water from the inland mountains and relies entirely on well water for irrigation.[30] Batinah farmers employed the *zijrah*, a massive wooden framework with a crossbar holding a pulley wheel called a *manjūr*, connected by rope to a bull to lift water from twenty feet below the surface using leather bags, which poured into cement-coated holding tanks, which further drained into irrigation channels, *aflāj*, to water several acres of date palms (Figure 12.1). The labor-intensive process used one male

[26] Calvin Allen 1978, 140–56.
[27] Riggs 1886, 599.
[28] Thomas 1931, 142.
[29] Yearbook of the US Department of Agriculture 1894–1935.
[30] Wilkinson 1977, 47–51.

FIGURE 12.1 Reenactment of an Omani *zijrah* (elevated water well), Muscat. Photograph by Matthew Hopper (2005).

laborer, called a *bidār*, working in shifts around the clock in order to water approximately every 100 trees (Figure 12.2). The work of irrigation frequently fell on the shoulders of enslaved Africans.

By 1927 it was estimated that there were at least 15,000 wells of this kind operating in Batinah.[31] Bertram Thomas, who worked as *wazīr* (minister) of finance under Sultan Taimur bin Faisal in Oman between 1925 and 1930, estimated that there were "tens of thousands of oxen daily" working these water wheels in 1929.[32] Thomas added that runaway slaves were often punished with long hours in chains working in irrigation: "The metallic chink of ankle-chains, heard, perhaps, from the bull-pit of a well within the date grove, is an indication of some such ill-fated escapade."[33] Slaves ordinarily worked unchained but could be placed in fetters as a punishment. Date palms also have to be pollinated by hand, offshoots (suckers) removed, dead

[31] "Report of Mr. Dawson, American Manager of the Iraq Date Company Following a Visit to the Batina in 1927," IOR R/15/1/460. See also Limbert 2001, 35–55.

[32] Whitehead Consulting Group 1972, Appendix II.

[33] Thomas 1931, 238.

FIGURE 12.2 Air route to Baghdad via Amman and the desert. Tigris River. Groves of countless palm trees fringing the river's banks (ca. 1932). G. Eric and Edith Matson Photograph Collection. Library of Congress, Prints & Photographs Division [reproduction number LC-DIG-matpc-15948].

branches cut off, extra date bunches removed, stocks kept clean, and – when the fruit is ripe – there is the enormous task of harvesting (Figure 12.3). Dates also needed to be packed or pressed and conveyed overland or by sea to ports of export. Palm frond bags had to be woven to hold the dates, and they had to be loaded onto boats and conveyed to their destination. Much of this work was performed by enslaved East Africans.[34]

With the extra labor required for date production, Batinah became the primary destination of slaves in the Gulf in the late nineteenth and early twentieth centuries and was home to Oman's largest population of enslaved Africans and their descendants.[35] In 1885 S. B.

[34] Hopper 2015, 51–79.

[35] Secretary to Government of Bombay to Political Resident, Persian Gulf (Oct. 31, 1889), IOR R/15/1/200; Maj. Saddler, "Report on visit to Sur" [April 1895, no. 5–11] quoted in J. A. Saldanha, *Précis of Maskat Affairs, 1892–1905*. Part I. p. 53. IOR, L/PS/20/C245.

FIGURE 12.3 Men pollinating date palm, Oman (1912). Courtesy American Heritage Center, University of Wyoming. Paul Popenoe Collection, Box 177, Folder 2.

Miles noted that in Batinah slaves were "in high request," and consequently most slaves were eventually landed there.[36] In 1930, the British consul at Muscat remarked that "apart from the Batinah Coast, the method of irrigation does not demand slave labour."[37] The testimonies of enslaved Africans who received manumission certificates at British consulates and agencies in the Gulf between 1907 and 1940 almost universally describe a period of at least three years in Batinah prior to being sold to final destinations elsewhere in the Gulf. For young African boys, who made up a considerable percentage of those imported in the late nineteenth century, the time that passed between arrival in Batinah and eventual sale was often equal to the time required to mature to the age (early teens) at which they could be employed in the region's other key industry – pearl diving.[38]

Even more lucrative than the date industry was the Gulf's pearling enterprise. Arabia was only one of many regions that experienced a boom in the export production of pearls between the last quarter of the nineteenth century and the first quarter of the twentieth, but it

[36] S. B. Miles to E. C. Ross (Dec. 7, 1885), IOR L/PS/20/C246.

[37] Political Agent, Muscat, to Political Resident, Persian Gulf (Jan. 21, 1930), IOR R/15/1/230.

[38] Hopper 2006, 162–218.

was the world's largest pearl producer. By the turn of the twentieth century, the value of Gulf pearls was greater than that of all other regions combined.[39] As global demand for pearls increased in the late nineteenth century, prices rose, and production expanded from Venezuela and Mexico to Australia, Ceylon, and the Philippines. In the Gulf, the value of pearl exports rose steadily throughout the last quarter of the nineteenth century. Between 1873 and 1906, the value of pearl exports from Bahrain increased more than 800 percent.[40]

The rise in pearl production required additional labor and made the importation of enslaved laborers highly profitable. Originally these came from East Africa; later they were also drawn from Baluchistan and Persian Mekran. In the late nineteenth century, slave traders increasingly exported young boys from East Africa for work in the pearl industry. By the 1870s the ratio of male to female slaves among captured slave *dhows* on the Arabian coast reversed historical trends, shifting overwhelmingly in favor of young males. In 1872 the HMS *Vulture* captured a large slave *dhow* at the entrance to the Gulf of Oman carrying 169 captives from Pemba (the island was used as both a source of slaves and as a trans-shipment point) to Sūr and Batinah; 124 were males and forty-five were females, and the majority were children.[41] The HMS *Philomel* captured a *dhow* bound for Batinah in 1884 that had seventy-seven men, fourteen women, fifty-one boys, and twelve girls aboard (Figure 12.4).[42] In November 1885 the HMS *Osprey* captured a forty-two-ton *dhow* around Ras Madraka in Oman bound from Ngao in East Africa to Sūr with forty-nine male and twenty-four female slaves (eight men, twelve women, forty-one boys, and twelve girls).[43] In the last quarter of the nineteenth century, it is difficult to find any evidence of *dhows* captured off the Arabian coast carrying more female captives from East Africa than males. Slave

[39] Kunz and Stevenson 1908, 80.

[40] Hopper 2006, 195.

[41] Senior Naval Officer in Persian Gulf (and Commander HMS *Vulture*) to Rear Admiral Arthur Cumming, Commander in Chief, East Indies (Sept. 10, 1872), PRO ADM 1/6230; Lt. C. M. Gilbert Cooper, "Capture of a Slave Dhow: Or the Vulture and Its Prey" (n.d.), Lt. C. M. Gilbert-Cooper Papers, National Maritime Museum, London (NMM) BGY/G/5.

[42] Commander HMS *Philomel* to Commander in Chief, East Indies (Oct. 15, 1884), PRO ADM 1/6714.

[43] Herbert W. Dowding, Commander HMS *Osprey*, to Rear Admiral Frederick W. Richards, Commander in Chief, East Indies (Sept. 19, 1885), PRO ADM 1/6758.

FIGURE 12.4 Slaves rescued from Arab *dhow* near Zanzibar, [HMS *Philomel*, April 1893], unknown photographer.
Courtesy Beinecke Rare Book and Manuscript Library, Yale University. The Land of Zenj Photograph Collection. General Collection, Box 6, Folder 41, Image #4.

imports overwhelmingly favored males over females, and labor clearly focused on production.

During the annual diving season, enslaved divers labored alongside free divers and spent months away from shore engaged in extremely difficult work.[44] Typical dives would take a diver to depths of between fifty and eighty feet and would last between one and two minutes (Figure 12.5). For as long as he could hold his breath, the diver collected oysters and placed them in a basket tied around his waist. Divers would rest for only a few minutes before repeating the process.[45] The annual season continued for 130 days, and divers were exclusively male.[46] In the pearl industry – just as in the date industry – free men and slaves worked side by side, but while free divers kept

[44] Lorimer 1915, 2227.
[45] E. L. Durand, *Administration Report of the Persian Gulf Political Residency and Muscat Political Agent for the year 1877–78*, 32. PRO FO 78/5108; Lorimer 1907; Villiers 1940.
[46] Belgrave 1960, 43.

FIGURE 12.5 Pearl divers at work, Persian Gulf (ca.1903), *London Magazine*, Vol. XI (Jan. 1904): p. 717.

the proceeds from each pearl season, enslaved divers surrendered all of their earnings to their masters. Enslaved Africans and free men of African ancestry accounted for a large portion of Gulf pearl divers. Captain E. L. Durand in 1878 noted that, while most haulers in the Gulf were Bedouins or Persians, the divers were generally "sedees" (Africans) and sometimes "sedee domestic slaves."[47] J. G. Lorimer, in his comprehensive gazetteer of the Gulf in 1907, stated that the divers were "mostly poor Arabs and free Negroes or Negro slaves; but Persians and Baluchis are also to be found among them, and in recent years, owing to the large profits made by divers, many respectable Arabs have joined their ranks."[48]

By the conclusion of the nineteenth century, the Arabian Gulf had undoubtedly satisfied Finley's and Turley's economic conditions of a "Slave Society." The Gulf had generated both extensive commodity

[47] E. L. Durand, *Administration Report of the Persian Gulf Political Residency and Muscat Political Agent for the year 1877–78*, 32, PRO FO 78/5108. On the use of the word "Sidi," see Ewald 2000, 83.

[48] Lorimer 1907, 2228.

production/markets and "resources of capital attracted to invest in the slave system." Moreover, the major commodities in the Gulf – dates and pearls – had elastic demand. The relatively small population of coastal Eastern Arabia, the assignment of certain kinds of labor as exclusively male, and the expanding value of Gulf commodities at a time when increased production of those commodities required a larger labor force, created conditions that incentivized the importation of outsiders. Turley's requirement that a "Slave Society" have an organized system of slave supply is more than satisfactorily met as well, as indicated by his own account of slavery in the Persian Gulf. Finley's argument that landownership be consolidated in fewer hands so as to require extra-familial labor requires further exploration in the Gulf context. Gulf pearl banks were not subject to private ownership, but the boats used to extract pearls were, and the larger date gardens of Oman's Batinah Coast and Semail Valley, although divided among individual families within a broader tribal context, may approach Finley's definition. Lenski correctly notes in the first chapter of this volume that Finley's requirements of landownership inherently privileges agricultural societies over nomadic or semi-nomadic peoples, who were often slaveholders. Nevertheless, broadly speaking, the nineteenth-century Gulf appears to have met the economic conditions of both Finley's and Turley's definitions of a "Slave Society."

SOCIAL CONDITIONS

Finley's requirements for a society to qualify as a "Slave Society" also include conditions that may generally be labeled as social. These include: that the slave owners' rights over their slaves be near total; that their slaves be deracinated (uprooted) and kinless; that they be divided into internal hierarchies; and that they account for a proportionally large percentage of the population.

The very limited demographic data unfortunately do not allow us to determine any precise ratios between slave and non-slave populations in the Gulf (although the paucity of sources for Greece and Rome did not stop Finley from including demographics in his formulation), but the observations of Western travelers and officials indicate that enslaved Africans accounted for significant portions of the workforce in both the Gulf pearl banks and date gardens. Manumitted Africans (former slaves) and their descendants made up a significant portion of the Gulf population, as did Baluchis (both free and enslaved). Perhaps our best estimates come from Western observers of the Gulf pearl banks. American missionary Paul W. Harrison recalled in 1924 that many divers on the Trucial Coast were slaves, but "they do not number over one-half the divers." "Most of these slaves are Negroes from Africa," he explained. "A few are Baluchees from the Makran coast between India and Persia."[49] Charles Belgrave, the advisor to the rulers of Bahrain, recalled that while most divers abstained from eating much during the dive season and were relatively gaunt, "the pullers were stalwart specimens; many of them were negroes with tremendous chest and arm development."[50] In 1929 the British senior naval officer in the Gulf estimated that there were 20,000 slave divers (roughly a quarter of the total) diving in the Gulf in each season.[51] Also in 1929, British diplomat and scholar Bertram Thomas reported that a fifth of the "army" of thousands of divers that Batinah sent to the diving banks each year were enslaved.[52] These may not have approached the scale of slave ratios that Finley used for Roman Italy or Brazil, but they were significant (perhaps 20 percent but not 30 percent). Moreover, these populations stood out to foreign observers because they were recognizable as outsiders, another of Finley's qualifying features. At any rate, as Harper and Scheidel demonstrate in Chapter 3 of this volume, Finley's figures for Rome reflect higher estimates than current analysis of the sources will allow, so the Gulf's numbers may actually have been closer to the classic Roman example.

Testimonies preserved in British manumission records indicate that slaves in the Gulf were treated as the exclusive property of their owners and lived in constant fear of being sold away from their loved ones. Slave owners controlled both the bodies and the reproductive lives of their slaves. When a female slave born in his house came of

[49] Harrison 1924, 88.

[50] Belgrave 1960, 44.

[51] Senior Naval Officer, Persian Gulf Division, HMS *Triad*, to Commander in Chief, East Indies Station (Sept. 12, 1929), No. 27G/56/1, IOR L/PS/12/4091.

[52] "Notes on the Slave Trade by Wazir Thomas, August 1929," P. 7418/29, IOR L/PS/12/4091.

age, her master was entitled to take her as his concubine or marry her to one of his male slaves or the slave of someone else. In some cases masters availed themselves of all these options. Hilaweh bint Rashid, who was born in her master's house on Za'ab Island around 1907, was married to Nubi, one of her master's male slaves, when she was fifteen years old. She gave birth to a son and a daughter, but in 1938, when her daughter was a year old, her husband died. Her master then took her as his concubine for two years before marrying her to a man from Batinah.[53] Masters could sell away a slave's spouse as easily as marrying slaves to one another. Faraj bin Sulaiman, born on the coast of East Africa around 1905, was kidnapped as a child by a man who took him to Sūr and after a year sold him to 'Isā bin 'Ali on Za'ab Island. 'Isā worked Faraj as a diver for four years before marrying him to a slave woman named Latīfah. Three years later, despite the fact that Latīfah had given birth to a child, 'Isā sold her to Bedouins.[54]

A slave's marriage was no guarantee against sale, and enslaved men and women were frequently sold away from their families by the master. This was the case, for example, with Sadullah bin Salīm, who was born a slave in Yemen, had been kidnapped by men from 'Asīr and brought to Qatar via Hasa in the late nineteenth century, and wound up as the slave of Sheikh Qāsim bin Muhammad Al-Thānī, the ruler of Qatar. When Sadullah reached maturity, he was married to Mabruka, one of the sheikh's female slaves. The couple had three sons and two daughters, but only the daughters survived childhood. At the time of Sadullah's manumission, one of them was married to the slave of another member of the royal family and the other was fifteen and unmarried. When Sheikh Qāsim died in 1913, Sadullah and his family passed to 'Abd al-'Azīz bin Qāsim, but 'Abd al-'Azīz subsequently sold Sadullah away from his family to a man in Sharjah who sent him diving.[55] In some cases, masters of male slaves paid dowries to the owners of female slaves in order to contract a slave marriage,

53 Statement of Hilaweh bint Rashid, born in Za'ab Island, aged about thirty-five years (Feb. 18, 1942), IOR R/15/1/207.

54 Statement made by Faraj bin Sulaiman, aged thirty-four years (Oct. 10, 1939), IOR R/15/1/207.

55 Statement of slave Sadullah bin Salem, aged about forty-five years (Jan. 25, 1927), IOR R/15/1/204.

although the slave couple often continued to work for their respective masters.[56]

Slaves imported directly from East Africa undoubtedly qualify as deracinated and kinless by Finley's definition, particularly those who were kidnapped as children. Children in Zanzibar were especially vulnerable to being kidnapped and exported.[57] Arab traders from Trucial Oman would arrive annually, procure houses in Zanzibar, and purchase or kidnap slaves (both domestic and newly imported) to bring back to the Gulf. In 1839 the Omani sultan, Sa'id b. Sultan, complained to the British resident that vessels "belonging to the Arabian Ports in the Persian Gulf lying between Resel Khyma and Aboothabee" carried off "by force or fraud three or four slaves for every one purchased" from his dominions in East Africa.[58] A report from the British native agent at Sharjah confirmed that men of that district go to Zanzibar "solely for the purpose of stealing slaves." He outlined some of the tactics these men used: "One plan, I am informed, is as follows: on their arrival ... they draw up their vessels on shore and hire houses in the island ... accompanied by many slaves formerly belonging to that part of the world." He continued:

> These spread themselves through the place and, forming acquaintance among the slaves of the Island, persuade them to come to their own houses where they entertain them with dates, sweetmeats etc. ... This of course establishes an intimacy, and the intercourse continues until, a favorable opportunity offering, they are seized and detained in the house.

Other tactics he recorded included kidnapping slaves who had been hired to carry goods purchased in the market and mixing kidnapped slaves with slaves purchased in the slave market and embarking them to their ships at night in small boats owned by merchants from Sūr.[59] By the 1860s there were even reports of Suri slave traders "carrying

[56] See, for example, Statement of Marzook bin Hassan, aged about twenty-seven years (Oct. 22, 1927), IOR R/15/1/204.

[57] Akins Hamerton to Commr. William Smyth HMS *Grecian* (Dec. 5, 1841). ZNA AA 12/29.

[58] S. Hennell, Resident, Persian Gulf, to Chief Sec to Govt of Bombay, from Muscat Cove, Dec. 17, 1839. ZNA AA 12 / 29 Correspondence of Atkins Hamerton, British Consul at Zanzibar, 1841–57.

[59] A Report from (Moollam Houssain) Native Agent at Shargah, Oct. 21, 1846. ZNA AA 12 / 29 Correspondence of Atkins Hamerton, British Consul at Zanzibar, 1841–57.

kidnapped children through the public street in large baskets during the day, their mouths being gagged to prevent them from crying out."[60] On arrival in the Gulf, enslaved Africans were typically disembarked at Sūr and transferred in smaller craft to Batinah or shipped directly to ports on the Batinah coast. From there they could be sold and resold several times and were often shipped further north in the Gulf. Boys in particular were commonly sent to the coastal communities surrounding the pearl banks.

Once settled in the Gulf, the kinlessness and deracination of enslaved Africans was secured. Most of the enslaved men and women in the Gulf who received manumission from British authorities in the first half of the twentieth century did not express a desire to return to their home countries in east and northeast Africa. Some were one or two generations removed from their African homes. Others were kidnapped when they were so young that they had little or no connection to their former homes. Several of those who were old enough to recall the details of their former homes expressed a fear of being re-enslaved if they were to be repatriated.[61] Still, among the enslaved community, there is evidence that many people retained a fondness for their former homes in Africa and a longing for home or at least a curiosity about the prospect of returning to Africa.[62] When British officials granted manumission certificates, they commonly encouraged freed men and women to settle in Muscat or Bahrain, where they believed they would find the safest homes (as these were regions with large populations of freed slaves and could offer a degree of anonymity for the newly freed). Although few former slaves made the journey back to their home countries, there is evidence that some did. Juma' bin Raihan, who was born in Bagamoyo around 1871, kidnapped when he was fifteen, and brought to Wudam in Batinah, worked in the pearling industry for forty years. In 1926 he was about fifty-five years old and was too old to continue working as a hauler. He had a

60 Rigby to Secretary of Bombay Gov't (Mar. 30, 1860), ZNA AA 12/2.

61 See, for example, Statement of Medinah daughter of Wekayu of Selali in Abyssinia, aged about twenty (Nov. 16, 1925), who stated: "I do not want to go back to my country, Abyssinia, lest slave traders will re-kidnap me." IOR R/15/1/208.

62 See, for example, the case of Juma' referenced in Telegram from HMS *Hastings*, Henjam Radio, to Political Resident, Bushire, No. 1350 (Apr. 2, 1931), IOR R/15/1/209. See also Alpers 2000, 83–99.

wife and three daughters and decided that he wanted to return to East Africa. He fled to Muscat, seeking a British manumission certificate with the hopes of bringing his family with him to Africa.[63]

Finley's final social condition requires further investigation. Evidence for internal hierarchies among slaves in the nineteenth-century Gulf is difficult to detect. Most slaves could be distinguished from the free population by dress. All slaves were identifiable in that they were required to go around barefoot. In date-producing regions of Oman and in the city of Muscat, male slaves generally wore only a loincloth. But elite slaves (particularly soldiers and concubines) could be extravagantly dressed. One clear form of hierarchy between slaves existed aboard pearling vessels, where pullers and divers received different shares of the pearling crew's bounty for the season, although enslaved divers and pullers were obligated to return all or most of their earnings to their masters, and in many cases masters received these earnings directly from their slaves' captains (or sent agents to escort their slaves to and from the pearl banks and recover their earnings). Hierarchies among enslaved Africans in the Gulf undoubtedly existed, although the extent of their significance demands further research.

With respect to social conditions, the Gulf appears, at least in general terms, to meet the qualifications of Finley's and Turley's "Slave Society." Slaves indeed accounted for a proportionally large percentage of the population. They were treated as property, "the slave owner's rights over which were total." Slaves in the Gulf were clearly deracinated (uprooted) and kinless, and they may also have been divided into internal hierarchies. Thus, Finley's social and economic requirements for a "Slave Society" seem to be met in the Gulf, and even Turley's more rigid requirements satisfied.

CONCLUSIONS

Finley and Turley did not include examples from the modern Middle East in their lists of genuine "Slave Societies," but by definition the nineteenth-century Arabian Gulf would appear to qualify as a "Slave

[63] Statement made by Juma' bin Raihan, Negro, aged about fifty-five years, Suwahili, slave of Rashid bin Khalifah Suwaidi of Khan near Dubai (Nov. 29, 1926), IOR R/15/1/216.

Society." Yet the expansion of the list of "genuine Slave Societies" only serves to highlight the problem of whether the bifurcation between "Slave Societies" and "Societies with Slaves" represents the best way for historians to address the varying expressions of slavery in world history. The heuristic desirability of a neat division between "Slave Societies" and "Societies with Slaves" is self-evident, but an alternative approach, offered by Orlando Patterson and implicit in the work of Miers and Kopytoff (and others) views slavery as a spectrum of servitude and dependency, along which one can identify a multitude of forms. The notion that "genuine Slave Societies" were qualitatively different from "Societies with Slaves" is challenged by examples like the nineteenth-century Gulf, in which slave-society-like attributes can be detected even in a non-Western context that differs tangibly from European Classical antiquity and New World plantation slavery. In the final analysis, some supposedly qualitative differences between these societies appear after all to be quantitative differences. Traits such as the relative proportion of slave population, the degree of concentration of private landholdings, and the sophistication of slave markets and investment may be measured quantitatively, and may, therefore, make comparing slave systems more amenable to comparison along a spectrum rather than by means of division into two bounded and mutually exclusive categories. What, if anything, separates Finley's classic examples from the nineteenth-century Gulf in qualitative terms? Slavery in the Gulf appears to differ from slavery in Classical antiquity and New World plantations in degree rather than in kind. These differences are of social and economic structures: slaves were used in different industries than in the New World or in Classical antiquity, and traditions of law surrounding slave ownership differed, as did the religious context. These are differences to be considered alongside long-standing variations between sedentary and nomadic societies, and between planter societies in the Old World and the New World. Such differences are masked by the artificial bifurcation between "Slave Societies" and "Societies with Slaves."

In the first chapter of this volume, Noel Lenski argues convincingly that Finley's "Slave Society" model is outdated in its methodology, ethnocentric in its scope, and deceptive in its generalizations, and that it serves as an impediment to a fuller understanding of slave systems. Lenski also provides four non-Western examples of potential "Slave

Societies" to illustrate the ethnocentrism and categorical imprecision of Finley's model. To this list we may add another contender – the nineteenth-century Arabian Gulf. Indeed, the existence of even one non-Western example of a "Slave Society" raises important questions about categorization and the utility of the Eurocentric binary model. An alternative and perhaps more productive method to distinguish between the various expressions of slavery in world history would be to divide between societies in which slavery was influenced (or not influenced) by capitalism. Walter Johnson's recent powerful examination of slavery and cotton production in the nineteenth-century Mississippi Valley demonstrates that, in the nineteenth-century United States, increased global connectivity promoted slavery and the slave trade just as it spread free markets.[64] In the Gulf, expanding global markets for Arabian products like dates and pearls fueled demand for slave labor. The story of the nineteenth-century Gulf's experience of slavery may prove as intimately connected to the history of the global expansion of capitalism as that of the American South. The potential for dialogue between historians of slavery in the Atlantic and Indian Ocean worlds may prove even more productive than the dialogue between historians of Classical antiquity and American slavery encouraged by Finley's arguments for a shared heritage of distinct "Slave Societies." Lenski's proposed alternative model presented in this volume takes an important first step toward this dialogue. It is a discussion worth having, even if it presents more questions than answers.

[64] Johnson 2013.

13

Slavery and Society in East Africa, Oman, and the Persian Gulf

Bernard K. Freamon

INTRODUCTION: THE EMERGENCE OF A TRANSOCEANIC, TRANSCONTINENTAL "SLAVE SOCIETY"

When we seek to understand the reach of Moses Finley's conception of a "Slave Society," we note that Finley's view of "society" and the "social formations" to which he referred were situated in very specifically defined locations, regions, or territories. The "American South," the "Caribbean," or "Brazil" are the Finleyan examples that come to mind, but other societies would also readily fit his conception such as "West Africa" or "Southeast Asia," although those territories may not have qualified as "Slave Societies" in his view. If we employ Finley's conception of society, it would be rare to encounter a "Slave Society" that simultaneously occupied more than one shore of an ocean or a sea, or that spanned more than one continent. Of course, the truth of this statement depends in part on how one defines "society." Finley did not explicitly define the term in his writings on slavery, but it appears that he accepted definitions of society that were widely agreed upon when he wrote. In contemporary scholarly usage and indeed in common usage, a society "is a system for facilitating interdependent social relationships according to the values, norms and ideologies of a shared culture."[1] In other words, a society is a human grouping assumed to have three fundamental characteristics: (1) "readily discernible territorial borders"; (2) a structural and cultural

[1] Pfaffenberger 2008, 650.

distinctiveness; and (3) an objective existence that is "independent of the wills or actions" of its individual members.[2] In our view, a "society" is a human grouping with a great number of social and cultural commonalities involving a complex of shared ideas by which members define who they are and how their lives are organized, as well as a shared ideological or cultural vision and a "collective consciousness," sometimes embodied in a master narrative, expressing the purposes that bring the group together.[3]

Finley's list of "genuine Slave Societies" – Greece, Rome, the American South, the Caribbean, and Brazil – are all societies that were located in well-defined territories or geographical regions and encompassed many of the features we have described. They were also almost always located within a juridical and internationally recognized state or a set of closely related states. Even when we look at Finley's "Societies with Slaves," we still think of societies that are situated in specific, well-defined locations. Thus, what emerges from the Finleyan conception of a "Slave Society" is a socio-spatial paradigm that appears to be dominated by the Western historiography on slavery and slave trading. That paradigm posits the existence of a "Slave Society" or a "slave-owning" society that is bounded by one place or region and shares many of the commonalities we have identified.

Finley acknowledged that these societies needed to establish efficient means for the procurement of more slaves and, in human history, such means sometimes devolved into destructive incursions into neighboring or even distant societies. Most often such incursions were imperialist and involved war or slave raiding, but they frequently also involved the payment of tribute or commercial and transport arrangements wherein one society supplied captive human beings to another in well-organized schemes. The transatlantic slave trade is the best example, but it was by no means the only one.

This chapter argues that the socio-spatial paradigm that underpins Finley's "tidy binary," to use Lenski's description,[4] does not fit or clearly explain the history of slavery and the slave trades in the societies that occupied the western Indian Ocean littoral, that is the East African coast and southern Arabia, particularly Oman and the Persian Gulf.

[2] Pfaffenberger 2008, 650. We exclude from this definition small-scale societies.
[3] Greenwald 1973, 187–88.
[4] Lenski, Chapter 1 in this volume.

An examination of the history of slavery in the western Indian Ocean shows that the paradigm is largely inadequate because it does not take account of factors like climate, geography, and migration patterns, which in the case of the western Indian Ocean were quite important to the understanding of global history and the role of slavery in the development of that history. Recent scholarly criticism of the classical sociological conception of society, which assumes boundedness and territoriality, bears out this conclusion.[5]

Our argument is supported by the fact that the historiography of slavery in the western Indian Ocean has largely avoided the use of a Finleyan analysis in its treatment of the history of slavery and the slave trade in the region. It recognizes slavery as it existed in East African society, but it also recognizes that a similar form of slavery involving the same actors and relationships extended its reach contemporaneously to communities along the western Indian Ocean littoral, particularly in Oman and along the shores of the Persian Gulf. There seems to be general agreement among historians that a "Slave Society" existed along the western Indian Ocean littoral in the nineteenth century, but their attention has focused on the existence of a whole host of other factors – religion, culture, climate, and geography – that tended to bind the communities along the littoral into a single society despite the absence of geographical contiguity. It took some time for the scholarship to recognize this, but, beginning in the mid- to late twentieth century, historians began to use a relational approach to discussions of slavery and the slave trade in the western Indian Ocean. More than fifty years ago, George F. Hourani observed that: "[t]he western half of the Indian Ocean, from Ceylon round to East Africa, forms a cultural unity, which has to be treated as a whole."[6] Relying on this relational approach, we show that there were unmistakable geographical and climatic connections and cultural, social and economic ties that bound slavery on the East African coast with slavery in Oman and, to a somewhat lesser extent, in the Persian Gulf. This chapter argues that, consistent with this relational approach, slavery in the region should be seen and treated as one socio-spatial unit. It explains why this is so and it contends that the region should qualify as a

[5] Gregory 1982; Pred 1984; Gregory and Urry 1985; Claval 1993; Emirbayer 1997; Pfaffenberger 2008, 652; Steinberg 2009.

[6] Hourani 1995[1951], 88.

"Slave Society" although one much different than the societies Finley envisioned. It concludes that this "Slave Society" in fact extended well beyond eastern Africa to include locations in the western oceanic littoral and in the Persian Gulf. In charting the rise and development of this extensive and relational slave system, it also explores the role that non-coercive human migrations and climatic phenomena played in the unfolding of this history.

TRANSFORMATIONS IN SLAVERY IN AFRICA AND THE INDIAN OCEAN LITTORAL

Lovejoy, in his seminal *Transformations in Slavery: A History of Slavery in Africa*, now in its third edition, argues that slavery in many places in Africa underwent a "transformation" from a marginal place in African society to the status of a central institution. This transformation involved the establishment and consolidation of modes of production in African societies that were largely based on slavery (and slave trading) and on economic and political institutions centered on slavery. There were many reasons why this occurred, but two focal points in Lovejoy's analysis are important for our purposes. The first is his recognition of Finley's conclusion that some societies evolved from circumstances where slaves were only incidentally present to societies whose circumstances showed economic and social structures that included "an integrated system of enslavement, slave trade and domestic use of slaves," circumstances where "maintenance of the slave population was guaranteed." These circumstances bespoke the kind of transformation Finley recognized as essential to the development of a "Slave Society." Lovejoy demonstrates – and there can be no serious disagreement with his conclusion – that many African societies, especially those in the Sahel, and along the Red Sea and East African coasts, had experienced this transformation by 1400 CE.[7] In these societies slaves came to perform a great many functions – productive, social, and sometimes symbolic – and the fabric of relationships between the enslaved and the free or partially free was tightly woven into all of the important structures in the society, including kinships systems, legal relationships, systems of property ownership, market

[7] Lovejoy 2012a.

relationships, and political and military hierarchies.[8] Lovejoy's reliance on the Finleyan analysis is central to his thesis.

Second, Lovejoy recognizes that, even though the transformation he identifies was pan-African, there were qualitative differences in its nature between Muslim and non-Muslim areas on the continent. He describes the reason for these differences as "the Islamic factor," a set of rules, customs, norms, and religious and cultural practices in Islamic territories that caused slavery to manifest itself in ways that were dissimilar to slavery in Christian and animist areas.[9] He ascribes some of the differences to the demand for slaves arising from Islamic societies in North Africa and the Middle East, but there was also an Africanization of the Islamic religion that tended to foster the acceptance and expansion of slavery and slave trading.[10] This recognition of a tangible and sharply demarcated dichotomy between Islamic and non-Islamic slavery in the history of Africa permeates Lovejoy's entire analysis and is also important for our inquiry. Interestingly, Lovejoy concludes that in both cases the facts show that the actions of the non-Muslim and Muslim enslavers created "Slave Societies" and a profound transformation in the nature and function of slavery.

Because Lovejoy's focus is on Africa, he does not directly consider the full territorial reach of the "Slave Societies" that he identifies. In the case of the Muslim "Slave Societies" along the East African coast, we suggest that the geographical and territorial definition of those societies is larger than Africa and reached far across the Indian Ocean. If we consider the impact of the "Islamic factor" this should not surprise us, because Islamic religious ideology and the Islamic worldview does not recognize political or territorial borders, particularly those created in the Westphalian sense.[11] In the classical Islamic formulation, the world is divided into two spheres, the *dar al-Islam* (the "abode of Islam") and the *dar al-harb* (the "abode of war"). The

[8] Lovejoy 2012a, 8–11.
[9] Lovejoy 2012a, 15–18.
[10] Lovejoy 2012a, 29–36.
[11] The 1648 Peace Treaty of Westphalia, between the Holy Roman Emperor and the king of France, created the Western European concept of sovereignty in that it recognized the equality and independence of territorially defined nation-states in international law and practice, Acharya 2013. Classical Islamic law and conceptions of society do not necessarily recognize borders drawn in the sense used in the treaty, likely viewing them as nationalistic and perhaps artificial.

Swahili coast and the nations and communities along the shores of the Persian Gulf were clearly within the *dar al-Islam.* But this ideological construct is not the only factor that tends to make East Africa, Oman, and the Persian Gulf a single "Slave Society." The geographically distinctive territories were joined by climatic, geographical, migratory, and cultural factors that tended to make it into one socio-spatial unit. Before detailing the facts that show the creation of this transoceanic, transcontinental "Slave Society," it is useful to review briefly the historiography of slavery and the slave trade in the western Indian Ocean region.

THE HISTORIOGRAPHY OF EAST AFRICAN AND INDIAN OCEAN SLAVERY AND ITS EVOLUTION

The historiography of slavery and slave trading in the Indian Ocean is ancient, rich, vast, and colorful. In spite of this pedigree, it remains greatly undertheorized, in need of vigorous non-comparative analyses, and is often ignored by historians trained in the Atlantic world. This is amazing given the fact that "the Indian Ocean is by far the oldest of the seas in history, in terms of it being used and traversed by humans."[12] It is also the site of the world's first efforts to globalize economic and commercial relationships between diverse groups of human beings.[13] The region was described by Chittick as "the largest cultural continuum in the world during the first millennium and a half A.D.,"[14] and it is also probably the oldest of those continuums. The historiography of slavery in the region reflects all of these facts.

It could be said that the historiography begins with reliefs found on a terrace wall of an ancient Egyptian architectural marvel, the Mortuary Temple of Hatshepsut in Luxor, Egypt. Built in the fourteenth century BCE and spectacularly set into a breach in the Theban Hills hiding the fabled Valley of the Kings, the temple's columned, modernistic terraces rise majestically against a craggy limestone backdrop. The eponym of the temple, Queen Hatshepsut, ruled Egypt as pharaoh for twenty years, between 1478 and 1458 BCE. During her reign Egypt experienced an extraordinary period of economic

[12] Pearson 2003, 3.
[13] Pearson 2003, 3–4.
[14] Chittick 1980, 13.

prosperity and political stability, and she is said to have been the most successful of Egypt's queen–pharaohs. Senenmut, Hatshepsut's architect and perhaps her lover, determined that he should depict the prosperity of her reign in murals on the temple. These beautiful masterpieces of bas relief have justly become world renowned. The most famous depicts Hatshepsut's maritime expedition to a land the Egyptians called "Punt," located somewhere in East Africa.[15] Historians suggest that Punt is probably in present-day Somalia, although some arguments would locate it in modern Yemen, Ethiopia, or even as far south as Kenya, Uganda, Tanzania, or Zanzibar. Hatshepsut's expedition to Punt was not the first to this area by the ancient Egyptians, as other Egyptian records and inscriptions show evidence of contact between the two civilizations occurring as early as 2400 BCE.[16] The paintings on the mortuary temple wall show a great trading enterprise, with the Egyptians going south in cargo boats carrying fish and other Mediterranean goods and returning north with incense, gold, ebony, ivory, leopard skins, large animals, and slaves.[17]

The wall painting suggests that, since the earliest days of recorded history, traders were interested in procuring slaves from the ranks of the people of East Africa and marketing or distributing them to buyers and users in the region that we would today call the Middle East. The historiography also suggests that traders from India and China showed a similar interest. This trade developed over thousands of years and eventually became a triaxial affair between the coast of East Africa and three areas to the north and northeast of the Arabian Sea. Hourani and other historians have shown that from as early as the first century CE, traders began traveling to and from East Africa along these three axes in large, oceangoing sailing ships (mistakenly called "dhows" by Westerners) which depended upon the predictable

[15] Much of this narrative comes from Brunson 2002[1991], 161.

[16] Wicker 1998, 155. Wicker (160–61) argues that the mariners for Queen Hatshepsut probably used the Nile rather than the Red Sea.

[17] Wicker 1998, 157. According to Wicker, the inscription in the upper left register of the relief says: "The loading of the cargo boats with great quantities of the marvels of the land of Punt, with all good woods of the divine land, heaps of gum of *anti* (incense) and trees of green *anti*, with ebony, with pure ivory, with green (pure) gold of the land of Amu, with sandalwood, cassia wood, with balsam, resin, eye paint, with monkeys, greyhounds, with skins of panthers of the south, with inhabitants of the country and their children (slaves). Never were brought such things to any king since the world was."

Indian Ocean monsoon winds for propulsion.[18] After arriving on the East African coast with pottery, Chinese porcelain, dates, spices, perfumes, and cloth, they would return to their home port with ivory, animal skins, cloves, foodstuffs, and slaves. The three axes ran north along the coast and then through the Red Sea to Arabia, Egypt, and the Mediterranean; northeast across the ocean to the ancient seafaring ports of Sur, Qalhat, Muscat and ports in the Persian Gulf; and east–northeast to India and from there on to ports east of the Indian Peninsula.

Greco-Roman geographers' accounts and related travel literature similarly contain references to Red Sea and Indian Ocean trading that encompassed East Africa and appears to have involved a trade in slaves. The most frequently cited account is the *Periplus of the Erythraean Sea*, an anonymous guide for mariners probably authored by an Alexandrian Greek from the first century CE. The author reports:

> Ommana [Oman or the Hadramaut or perhaps the entire southern Persian Gulf] also takes frankincense from Kanē and sends out to Arabia its local sewn boats, the kind called *madarate*. Both ports of trade export to Barygaza [in India] and Arabia pearls in quantity but inferior to the Indian; purple cloth; native clothing; wine; dates in quantity; gold; slaves.[19]

Other Greco-Roman geographers and travel writers, including Strabo and Pliny, make similar references to a trading relationship with East Africa and occasionally mention the purchase and transport of slaves. Although the sources are meager, Chinese travel accounts contain similar reports. Ogot tells us that Duan Chengshi, a Chinese scholar writing in the middle of the ninth century, "refers to slave exports from Po-pa-li which, according to Oriental scholars … is in Somalia."[20]

Beginning in the ninth century CE there was an explosion of Arab and Persian travel writing and literature on the geographical environs surrounding the newly established Arab Muslim caliphate. Many of these writers focused their attentions on trade routes, geography, climatology, and maritime activities in the Indian Ocean, and a fair amount of this attention centered on East Africa and its

[18] Hourani 1995[1951], 79–84; Sheriff 2010.
[19] *Periplus Maris Erythrae* 36, translated at Casson 1989, 73.
[20] Ogot 1979, 176.

relationship to the Arab and Persian worlds. It seems that some of these writings served the commercial, naval, and trading interests of the Abbasid Caliphate, but it is also true that the geographers seemed genuinely interested in improving knowledge of ports and other geographical and climatological features of the region. Hourani points out that after the rise of Islam, the Mediterranean became a frontier, a "sea of war" between the two rival faiths of Islam and Christianity, and, given this development, the Indian Ocean became much more attractive to Muslim Arab and Persian merchant-traders as a "sea of peace."[21] The Indian Ocean became an "Islamic lake."[22] Geographer Ya'qubi, writing in the ninth century, colorfully described the caliph al-Mansur's delight at the economic advantages of seating the new caliphate in Baghdad because of the tremendous opportunities it presented for trading between Iraq, Syria, and cities on the Persian Gulf; Oman; and ports in the Indian Ocean and the Far East.[23]

Ya'qubi's accounts were soon followed by the important works of a number of other travelers and scholars, who are generally described in the historiography as the "Arab geographers."[24] They mapped the Indian Ocean and its coasts and they focused on ports and ethnographic details that they thought would be of interest to mariners and other explorers. Their descriptions of East Africa included Zanzibar and Pemba and cities as far south as Sofala in Mozambique. Ibn Battuta visited East Africa in the fourteenth century. He began his visit with a trek across the Red Sea from Mecca to seaports in Sudan, then traveled south to Adulis, Zeila, and Mogadishu, and then on to locations on the Swahili coast, most notably Kilwa. Although other sources make clear that slave-trading emporia existed in Somalia at that time, Ibn Battuta does not mention these markets. He does make

[21] Hourani 1995[1951], 52, 61.
[22] Sheriff 2010, 12.
[23] Hourani 1995[1951], 64.
[24] Not all of them were Arab. Among the most important are Istakhri, ibn Khurdhabih, Mas'udi, Ibn Hawqal, Maqdisi, and Yaqut. A Persian seafarer, Burzurg ibn Shahriyar, also made important contributions that are replete with accounts of slave trading with East Africa, including a remarkable narrative of an East African king who was captured, transported to Arabia, and sold into slavery in Basra, only to escape and make his way back to East Africa where he was reinstalled as king and later, in ironic fashion, arranged the capture of his enslavers when they returned to the region. He graciously permitted them to return to Arabia, citing his conversion to Islam as the reason. Richard Hall 1996, 16–18.

several brief references to the presence of slaves in Kilwa, remarking that the sultan frequently raided the interior for slaves and observing that "ten head of fine slaves" were awarded by the sultan to him as compensation for an importunate slight visited on him by a poor *faqir*.[25]

These fleeting references to slavery from ancient and medieval sources suggest that, while there was a slave trade between East Africa and the Arabian coast during that time, it did not involve great volume. As we pointed out, Lovejoy has convincingly argued that, only in the fifteenth century was there a transformation in the nature of slavery and slave trading in the African territories on the frontiers of the Islamic world, and this certainly would have included the East African coast. We know from the Islamic sources that great slave markets came into being in Cairo, Mecca, Baghdad, Damascus, Istanbul, and Tunis with the imperial expansion of Islam. Partially because of the liberal rules governing the emancipation of slaves in Muslim societies, these markets generated a constant demand for fresh, new slaves. Consequently, the trade in slaves between societies in East Africa and societies in the Middle East and India rapidly expanded during this time, although it remains a difficult proposition to identify all of the factors that would adequately explain why this happened.

Michael Fisher notes that in the fifteenth century the Christian Ethiopian kingdom frequently raided the Ethiopian highlands for slaves "whom it sold to pay for imports brought by merchants sailing across the Indian Ocean." During this time, Muslim Arabs also hunted the highlands for slaves. He notes that between the fifteenth and eighteenth centuries, "slave takers forcibly exported 10,000 to 12,000 slaves annually from highland Ethiopia."[26] This phenomenon produced the celebrated emancipated slave Malik Ambar, originally called Chapu, who, after being sold and resold many times, ended up in Baghdad, where he was sold to the chief minister of the Ahmadnagar Sultanate in India, also a former Ethiopian military slave. After the death of his master, Ambar rose to become sultan and took the title of Malik. He ruled for almost twenty years, commanding a military force of 50,000

[25] Ibn Battuta 2005, 25; Sheriff 2010, 229. A *faqir* is an itinerant Muslim preacher or religious scholar.

[26] Fisher 2014, 56, citing Eaton 2005, 105–28.

men, including 10,000 other Ethiopians, some enslaved, others free or emancipated.[27]

It is important to note that European slave trading played an important role in spurring the tremendous upsurge of slavery and slave trading that occurred in the Indian Ocean beginning in the eighteenth century. Recent scholarship has shown that 160,000 slaves were transported from various locations to the Mascarenes and more than 200,000 slaves reached Réunion between the late seventeenth and early nineteenth centuries.[28] Writing in the early 1970s, Edward Alpers argued that European trading to the Mascarenes was a major factor in the explosion of the Southeastern African and East African slave trades in the late eighteenth century.[29] He contended that the French merchants from the Mascarenes aggressively sought a regular supply of slave labor for a growing plantation economy based on coffee and sugar.[30] Writing at the same time and relying on French consular and commercial records, C. S. Nicholls confirmed this assessment.[31] Richard Allen has recently observed that too much attention is paid to slave trading and slavery in the northwest Indian Ocean, which was dominated by the Omani Arabs. He points out that European slave trading played as important a role as the Arab slave trade. He emphasizes that Africans were not the only objects of this trade and that Indians and Southeast Asians also formed part of what ultimately became a great migratory stream.[32]

It is well known that there was a parallel and simultaneous explosion of slave trading across the Atlantic conducted by Western European actors, and this gave rise to the emergence of a vocal and ultimately effective antislavery movement in northwestern Europe and particularly Britain. Initially the antislavery movement did not focus on slave trading and slavery on the East African coast and around the shores of the western Indian Ocean, but, by the mid-nineteenth century, there was a great increase in public and official attention to the issue, with the British government formulating a vigorous antislavery naval

[27] Fisher 2014, 56–57.
[28] Richard Allen 2008, 44 citing, inter alia Filliot 1974.
[29] Alpers 1970, 80–124.
[30] Alpers 1970, 82.
[31] Nicholls 1971, 201.
[32] Allen 2010.

and foreign policy, in no small part as a way of asserting its maritime supremacy.

The fervor created by Britain's nineteenth-century effort to suppress the East African slave trade and to bring Christianity to Africa generated the publication of a number of firsthand accounts of slavery and the slave trade in East Africa that are still useful today. Their publication also quenched a thirst in England, Europe, and the United States for tales of white heroism, naval supremacy, and evangelical success in Africa. There is a large body of this literature, and it tells us much about the nature and character of slavery in East Africa and Arabia, even if readers must keep in mind that one of its purposes was to rouse European public opinion in opposition to the practice.[33]

In the late 1930s two publications appeared that would have an even more important impact on the historiography of slavery and slave trading in East Africa. In 1938, Reginald Coupland, the Beit Professor of Colonial History at Oxford, published his *East Africa and Its Invaders*, an account of the history of Zanzibar and the coast up until the death of Saʿid bin Sultan, the Sultan of Zanzibar and Oman, in 1856. A year later he published *The Exploitation of East Africa: 1856–1890*. Both books were monuments to an imperialist conception of the problem of slavery and the slave trade in East Africa, which he maintained ran like a "scarlet thread" through 2,000 years of the region's history. Coupland sought to blame the Arabs for the underdevelopment of the Swahili civilization and to champion the anti-slaving efforts of the British. The titles of both books, describing East Africa as "invaded" and "exploited," are important clues to his perspective. The publication of these two books did not represent Coupland's first encounters with the problem of slavery, as he had previously chronicled Sir John Kirk's travels with David Livingston along the Zambezi River, and he had also published a small laudatory monograph on the British antislavery movement.[34] In spite of his imperialist perspective, which some historians have derided, Coupland's contributions were well researched, and they were the first to offer a comprehensive view of the relationship between East Africa, Zanzibar,

[33] W. F. W. Owen 1833; Burton 1872, 1894; Columb 1873; Sullivan 1873; Elton 1879; Lyne 1905.

[34] Coupland 1933[1964], 1938, 1939.

and Oman. Coupland argued that the Omani Sultan, Saʿid bin Sultan, who moved the sultanate from Muscat to Zanzibar sometime in the late 1830s, was almost singularly responsible for the establishment of a thriving clove plantation industry on Zanzibar Island, the import of Indian bankers and financiers, the exploitation of the hinterland for slaves, and the establishment of Zanzibar as the commercial engine for the entire East African coastal economy.[35] Historians have subsequently chiseled away at this thesis, but there is no question that Coupland's account establishes that, with the advent of the economic and political unity of Zanzibar and Oman in the late 1830s, a "Slave Society," in the classic Finleyan sense, was established on the islands of Zanzibar and Pemba and on the mainland. Coupland did not offer any substantial discussion of circumstances in Oman and the Persian Gulf, and he wrote well before Finley put forward his theory, but his contributions are important building blocks in the development of the historiography. Indeed, his contributions, later supplemented by those of subsequent historians of slavery and antislavery, represent the beginning of a trend that Christopher Leslie Brown has called the "humanitarian narrative" in British history, a perspective that sees the British antislavery initiative as a positive, civilizing force that justified imperial involvement in the region.[36]

It is fair to say that Coupland's histories provided the standard account of slavery and the slave trade in the region until the 1960s, when a change in scholarly approaches to African history swept through the academy, stimulated in part by the American civil rights movement, the emergence of independent states in Africa, and African Americans' demands for a more critical and Afrocentric view of their history.[37] The scholarly output produced in the wake

[35] Coupland 1938, 300: "It was trade, then, above all else, that drew Said to Zanzibar, and Said drew with him from Muscat not only many of his own Omani subjects who were of little use for trade but many also of those Indian merchants and bankers and shopkeepers who from time immemorial had been the mainstay of all oversea trade in the Indian Ocean." 310: "The Arabs were evidently making money. Snay-bin-Amir himself was a notable example of the profit to be won in East Africa ... The house he had built at Tabora and the guesthouse, the storehouses of 'currency goods' and ivory, the slave-compound – it was a village in itself."

[36] Christopher Leslie Brown 2006.

[37] It is important to note that Eric Williams, the author of *Capitalism and Slavery*, first published in 1944 and the subject of revived interest in the 1960s, had been a student of Coupland's at Oxford and, in his PhD dissertation that was the basis for

of this shift is well known, but it is important to note that it occurred even as Moses Finley was grappling with the problem of comparative slavery. His main contributions were in the field of Classical studies, but many scholars of African history adopted his approach in their discussions of the problem of slavery and the slave trade. A series of major treatments of African history appeared beginning in the early 1960s. In their discussions, they overwhelmingly focused on the Atlantic, although there was some discussion of East Africa and the Middle East. At the same time, a number of scholars began to focus specifically on the problem of slavery in Muslim Africa.

It was at about this time that Edward Alpers, Frederick Cooper, and Abdul Sheriff obtained their PhDs and began publishing treatments of East African slavery and the slave trade that focused on the commercial, religious, and social relationships between East Africa and societies on the Arabian Peninsula. Alpers published his *The East African Slave Trade* in 1967 and followed it with a series of articles and another book, *Ivory and Slaves: Changing Pattern of International Trade in East Central Africa to the Later Nineteenth Century* (1975), in which he suggested that slavery and slave trading in East Africa were part of a larger pattern of international commerce, trade, and migration that extended across the Indian Ocean. He did not rely on Finley.[38] Cooper published two very important monographs, *Plantation Slavery on the East Coast of Africa* (1977) and *From Slaves to Squatters: Plantation Labor and Agriculture in Zanzibar and Coastal Kenya, 1890–1925* (1980) that are both still very useful to scholars and students.[39] In the introduction to *Plantation Slavery*, which seeks to compare East African plantation slavery to other similar situations in history, Cooper accepts Finley's conception of the slave as an "outsider," and he seems to suggest that it applied to slaves on plantations in East Africa, particularly the slaves who worked the clove plantations in Zanzibar. Writing as he did, however, before the widespread promulgation of Finley's theory in *Ancient Slavery and Modern Ideology* (1980), he makes no attempt to determine whether East African society would fit within

the book, sought to refute Coupland's view of the history of Britain's antislavery efforts. These arguments were revived with the renewed interest in Williams's theses in the 1960s.

[38] Alpers 1967, 1975.

[39] Cooper 1977, 1980.

Finley's definition of a "genuine Slave Society." He does make many comparisons to the plantation economy in the American South and concludes, quite forcefully, that because of Islamic rules requiring humanitarian treatment of slaves, Omani attitudes toward wealth and luxury, weather, and other factors unique to the culture of the region, there was not the same degree of cruelty that one often saw in the American South.

In 1981, Abdul Sheriff was asked to contribute to the UNESCO *General History of Africa* on East Africa. He argued that "one of the main features of the history of the East African coast over the last 2,000 years has therefore not been isolation but the interpenetration of two cultural streams to produce a new amalgam, the coastal Swahili civilization."[40] Using a Braudelian approach and turning back to the historiography of Greek, Roman, and Arab geographers, Sheriff suggested that there was, beginning in the tenth century CE, a realignment of East Africa's external relations, such that it might be seen as an important participant in a developing commercial milieu that included the Persian Gulf and India.[41] Soon thereafter Sheriff published *Slaves, Spices & Ivory in Zanzibar: Integration of an East African Commercial Empire into the World Economy 1770–1873* (1987), a groundbreaking analysis of the economics, demographics, geopolitics, and ethnography of the rise of an Omani-Zanzibari "compradorial" state that transformed the practice of slavery and the slave trade in the region and integrated the Swahili merchant class into the larger Indian Ocean economy.[42] There was no discussion of the Finleyan paradigm and no effort made to compare the Zanzibari system of slavery with that found in the Western Hemisphere.

All of these authors viewed the involvement of the Omanis and certainly the Portuguese as interventional and invasive, as had Coupland, but there was a subtle but definite recognition of an ancient, transoceanic and transcontinental interdependence that stretched beyond the imperialist/capitalist narrative that tends to explain such events as a bluntly materialist search for labor and markets. Only Cooper's work engaged Finley's scholarship, and this

[40] Sheriff 1981.
[41] Sheriff 1981, 566.
[42] Sheriff 1987.

may have been because Cooper sought to compare the East African plantations with those found in the American South.

Soon thereafter, historian Gwyn Campbell began publishing important and original accounts of the southeastern African slave trade with Madagascar, Mauritius, and Réunion and slavery on those islands, eventually turning his attention to the larger Indian Ocean milieu and its relationship to East African slavery and the slave trade. In a series of important edited collections that contained contributions by Alpers and Sheriff, a new view of slavery and the slave trade in the western Indian Ocean began to emerge. The contributors saw the problem as extending beyond the realm of African history, suggesting that understanding world migrations, climatic influences on human behaviors, and the cross-border, transoceanic influence of religion was crucial to informing our understanding of Indian Ocean slavery. In Campbell's first edited collection on the Indian Ocean system, entitled *The Structure of Slavery in Indian Ocean Africa and Asia*, he sought to distinguish Indian Ocean slavery from the transatlantic paradigm, arguing that there were many more varieties of unfree labor, that the slave trade was multidirectional and multiethnic, that religion played a completely different role in the regulation of slavery and in the lives of the slaves, that there were elaborate structures for the assimilation of slaves into the larger society that did not exist in the West, and that there was not the level or quantity of violence found in the Atlantic. While acknowledging that "outsider" status was common among slaves, he suggested that this was not a universal phenomenon and varied from system to system and between communities.[43] Many of the essays in that collection made similar points, and none, as best we can determine, employed a Finleyan analysis. It is instructive to note that the opening essay was by eminent historian of African history Suzanne Miers, who sought to review the definitional issues in the Indian Ocean context. She too does not refer to Finley's approach.[44]

In a small but important pamphlet entitled "Afro–Arab Interaction in the Indian Ocean: Social Consequences of the Dhow Trade," published in 2001, Abdul Sheriff drew upon Fernand Braudel's thesis

[43] Campbell 2004, xii–xix.
[44] Miers 2004.

in support of his argument that there is an economic, social, and cultural unity of the Indian Ocean, driven in large part by the pattern of monsoons.[45] In his view, the monsoons supply "the motive power for communication over the broad ocean to redistribute the products, agricultural and industrial, and its people."[46] As part of the project, Sheriff had occasion to interview residents of Sur, an ancient slave-trading port in Oman. He reported:

> Quite a large number of the people [of Sur] are of very dark complexion: some were sons of Suri parents who had married slave or free African women, while others were apparently of slave origin; but they are all Arabic-speaking and have all adopted the local tribal surnames. As one of them said, four generations of his family were born in Sur, but the fifth was from Africa. "All the people here were from Africa," he said. "After two or three generations they were considered Omani; even half the government was African – the mother was African and father was Omani. But all are Arab."[47]

These observations were consistent with conclusions reached in a still-burgeoning literature on the presence of Africans in Indian Ocean societies outside the continent of Africa. This research is still in its infancy, but it may bear fruit in assisting historians in understanding the nature of Indian Ocean slavery and the slave trade, its relationship to larger patterns of migration, and how these relationships have changed over time.

In a 2008 essay in Simpson and Kresse's *Struggling with History: Islam and Cosmopolitanism in the Western Indian Ocean* (2008), Gwyn Campbell argued that the dominance of Islam in the western Indian Ocean and the relationships between the various communities that inhabited the region presented a new paradigm for Islamic history, breaking down traditional geographical and political divisions and allowing for "a radical, more holistic assessment of the historical role of Islam both within Indian Ocean Africa and the wider Muslim community of the Indian Ocean World."[48]

[45] Sheriff 2001. The pamphlet apparently became the basis for a series of publications by Sheriff, culminating in Sheriff 2010. The argument expands upon the observation first made by Hourani in 1951.

[46] Sheriff 2001, 2.

[47] Sheriff 2001, 11, citing interviews conducted in Sur in November–December 1997.

[48] Campbell 2008, 54.

In similar fashion, Sheriff began staking out the parameters of the relationship between East African society and societies in the Persian Gulf.[49] In 2010, he published *Dhow Cultures of the Indian Ocean: Cosmopolitanism, Commerce and Islam*, seeking to bring much of this new approach to the historiography of Indian Ocean societies, slavery, and the slave trade.[50] An even more recent iteration of Sheriff's effort to craft this new approach is found in Sheriff and Ho's *The Indian Ocean: Oceanic Connections and the Creation of New Societies* (2014). Growing out of an important conference sponsored by Sheriff's Zanzibar Indian Ocean Research Institute (ZIORI) and held in Zanzibar in 2008, the collection contains a number of contributions that greatly advance the historiographical inquiry we have described. Sheriff, in an introductory chapter, emphasizes the importance of Pearson's argument that littoral societies create a continuum, a band of relationships and connections that can extend for thousands of miles along the shore and into the hinterland, making boundaries, borders, and continental divides porous, elastic, and (in some cases) even nonexistent. As a number of historians, including Alpers, Ewald, Ho, Freitag, Bang, and Sheriff, have shown, this is exactly what happened in the western Indian Ocean, particularly with respect to the enslaved.[51] The societies involved literally blended into each other, and slavery and slave trading were essential to that blending. This provides a much sounder basis for concluding that we are dealing with one society in a unified socio-spatial context.

Sheriff's essay "Social Mobility in the Indian Ocean: The Strange Career of Sultan bin Aman" continues in this same vein.[52] It documents the early twentieth-century travels and travails of a Zanzibari freedman who books passage as a hired seaman across the Arabian Sea to the Persian Gulf and then is involuntarily sold into slavery by an unscrupulous Omani *nakhodha* (sea captain), who forces him to spend sixteen years as a slave, albeit with some privileges, in Dubai.[53] Similarly, there are a number of instances of enslaved persons moving from the Indian subcontinent west to East Africa, often with sojourns and

[49] Sheriff 2005.

[50] Sheriff 2010.

[51] Alpers 1975 2008; Freitag 1997, 2003; Anna K. Bang 2003; Ho 2006; Ewald 2010, 2013; Sheriff 2010, 2013.

[52] Sheriff 2013.

[53] Sheriff 2013, 145.

hiatus in the Persian Gulf or on the Arabian Peninsula.[54] Ewald's recent accounts of the lives of enslaved and free seamen traveling back and forth across the western Indian Ocean coast describe a similar phenomenon.[55]

Campbell has argued that Indian Ocean slavery was qualitatively different from that seen in the Atlantic, that slaves were much more willing participants in a "hierarchy of dependency" that might in some cases lead to a high-status position or even a "non-slave status," and that much of this was because of the different nature of society in the Indian Ocean.[56] Almost none of these discussions engages Moses Finley's dichotomy. The authors either regarded it as irrelevant or they made a tacit assumption that, even if the societies they were discussing might have qualified as "Slave Societies" in the Finleyan sense, the binary described by Finley was not complex enough to take account of the many layered structures of dependency they described.

SLAVERY AND SOCIETY IN EAST AFRICA, OMAN, AND THE PERSIAN GULF

What, then, can we say about the main questions posed in this volume: was there a "Slave Society" in the western Indian Ocean? The following description of the Persian port of Lingeh appears in an excerpt translated by Svat Soucek from Kazaruni's history of the Gulf during the reign of Muhammad Shah Qajar, the king of Persia (1834–48):

> There is an abundance of female and male slaves in this port, so much so that each household has ten to twelve such boys and girls – so many that the language most commonly spoken there is Sudanese ("*zaban-e Sudan*": this could also simply mean "language of the Blacks").[57]

If we examine firsthand descriptions of slavery on the East African coast, we see very similar accounts. For example, Nicholls tells us that

54 Freamon 2012, 130–31, recounting the travel of an Indian female, Fatima, who was sold into slavery by her father in India, resold by various merchants and dealers trading across the southern Arabian and East African littoral, and ultimately rescued by John Kirk, the British consul, in Zanzibar.

55 Ewald 2010, 2013.

56 Campbell 2014, 148–49.

57 Soucek 2008, 164, citing and quoting, in translation, Nadiri 1367[1988].

in the early years of the nineteenth century there was a great rise in demand for slave labor in Zanzibar to clear and plant clove plantations established by Syed Saʿid and the Omani commercial and landowning elite.[58] Saʿid eventually owned forty-five plantations and at least 12,000 slaves himself.[59] In 1811, Smee observed that "many Arabs possessed 800 or 900 slaves each."[60] By the 1830s many ordinary people owned slaves. Ruschenberger reported that some Zanzibaris owned as many as 2,000 slaves each, and "[t]he British consul reported that by 1841 almost every one of the Sultan's subjects owned slaves, the poorer about five, and the wealthier from 400 to 1,500."[61] The estimates of the number of slaves imported into Zanzibar beginning in the 1840s vary considerably, but they never fall below 7,000 a year, and some sources report the number to be as high as 20,000 a year.

The demographic situation in Oman and, to a lesser extent, throughout the coastal city-states on the Persian Gulf, was quite similar. Although the British began to take measures against the slave trade along the East African coast and between the coast and the Mascarenes, Nicholls makes the important point that the trade between Zanzibar and Oman and the Persian Gulf continued unimpeded for at least another twenty years. Again, the estimates vary but Hamerton estimated that 13,000–15,000 slaves per year were exported from Zanzibar to the Red Sea, Arabia, the Persian Gulf, and India.[62] Sheriff and other historians have questioned the higher of these figures as exaggerations, but there is no doubt that slaves made up a significant portion of the population on the Swahili coast and the Arabian Peninsula. Sheriff has estimated that Africans were 22 percent of the population in Qatar, 28 percent of the population along the Trucial Coast, and 25 percent of the population in Oman in 1904.[63] It is difficult to say what percentage of this population was enslaved, but it certainly was not insignificant. Hopper tells us that Salil bin Razik's *History of the Imams and Seyyids of Oman* reports that

58 Nicholls 1971, 203, citing Ruschenberger.
59 Nicholls 1971, 203–04, citing Reute 1907 and Bombay Office Records.
60 Nicholls 1971, 203–04, citing Smee's description of the island of Zanzibar in the India Office Records.
61 Nicholls 1971, 204, citing Hamerton's reports to the Bombay Secret Committee.
62 Nicholls 1971, 204, citing Hamerton's reports and acknowledging that he had difficulty getting correct information.
63 Sheriff 2005, 111, Table 7.4.

eighteenth-century Ya'rubi Sultan Iman Saif bin Sultan I owned 1,700 slaves, a large number given the population of Oman, and a later sultan, Ahmed bin Said, purchased 1,000 slaves in a single transaction and commanded an army that contained 1,100 African slaves and another 1,000 free Africans.[64] John Malcolm, a Scottish "diplomatist" posted to Persia at the beginning of the nineteenth century, described the Omani port of Muscat as a " 'great mart' for slaves."[65]

Consistent with this report, Muscat assumed great importance in the slave trade and the transportation of slaves to other parts of the Indian Ocean littoral, and this continued even after Sa'id bin Sultan relocated the Bu Sa'idi capital to Zanzibar, although it led to the decline of Muscat's commercial importance. The relocation of the capital changed "the orientation" of the Omanis and "strengthened the Omani connection with East Africa and deeper penetration into that continent's interior."[66] Again Hopper tells us, citing population estimates of the British government's resident surgeon as well as those in J. G. Lorimer's Gazetteer, that in 1876 one quarter of Muscat and Matrah's 40,000 residents were "Negroes," with half the remaining population of "mixed race," and by the turn of the century, Africans made up between 11 and 28 percent of the populations of all of the major eastern Arabian ports, with an overall average of 17 percent.[67] Earlier British consular reports confirm that there was a tremendous and continued influx of slaves into the Persian Gulf from East Africa and from points east. One consular report completed in 1842 estimated that Muscat was receiving at least 20,000 slaves a year and that the sultan was unable to slow the tide.[68] Another reported some fifty years later that the traffic had slowed, but slavery remained a challenge, particularly because of the noncooperation of Persian government officials.[69]

In considering whether these slave systems in East Africa and the Persian Gulf would qualify as a "Slave Society" we might conclude that a static and territorially based analysis might very well suggest that the East African coastal slave societies or the instances of slavery and slave

64 Hopper 2014, 330.
65 Hopper 2014, 330–31.
66 Peterson 2014, 160.
67 Hopper 2014, 329.
68 Burdett 2006, vol. 1, sec. 1.5.
69 Burdett 2006, vol. 2, sec. 2.2.

trading in the Persian Gulf did not, in and of themselves, represent "Slave Societies." The new historiography we have described, however, suggests that we should look at these contexts through a very different lens, one that would focus on the relation between the extraordinary transoceanic, transcontinental milieu in which slavery and the slave trade developed in the region, a new set of factors that are not necessarily beyond the ken of a Finleyan approach.

Perhaps the most significant of these new factors were the social phenomena caused by climatic factors and related population movements. There were, of course, the regular migrations that took advantage of the cyclical Indian Ocean monsoons. It is also likely that famine, disease, and drought were important determinants of the rise and fall of slaving activity in East Africa and Arabia.[70] A number of scholars have also pointed to the devastating economic effect of the 1872 hurricane in Zanzibar and the increase in illegal slave trading that followed that event.[71]

As to Finley, first, it does appear that there were large numbers of slaves in the transcultural oceanic society that we have described, particularly if we take into account the geographical setting in which slavery and slave trading took place. This is particularly true of the Persian Gulf region. Further, not all of these slaves were African, for slaves often came from the East as well. The Gulf area is sparsely populated, and large areas are inhospitable. What is more important is that we are dealing with a *maritime* culture, not one that is exclusively land-based. Consistent with a Braudelian approach, slavery looks somewhat different if we recognize the importance of the ocean to the enterprise rather than focusing strictly on land-based modes of production. Of course, even this viewpoint must be qualified in light of Cooper's study of the role of plantations, but we should recognize that even here we are concerned with island and littoral economies.

Second, slaves were significantly involved in surplus production, although here Lenski's point about ethnocentrism is well taken.[72] Slavery in Indian Ocean societies did not have the same place that it did in the Western societies that occupied Finley. Many historians have noted that in Islamic and other non-European societies,

[70] Hartwig 1979.
[71] Clarence-Smith 1989, 136; Bird 2010, 295; McMahon 2013, 44.
[72] Lenski, Chapter 1 in this volume.

slaves performed a variety of different functions, including serving in the military and navy, living with masters as concubines, and performing other elite functions. These roles do not fit neatly into Finley's paradigm. If we exclude them, we run the risk of being shamelessly ethnocentric. For example, it is said that Sultan Saʿid bin Sultan, the most famous and successful of the sultans of Zanzibar, owned hundreds of concubines. How is this to be factored into the analysis of surplus production? We encounter the same problem in trying to assess the importance of military slaves. Both kinds of slavery existed on the East African coast and in the Persian Gulf, and there was an interdependence between the two functions that extended transcontinentally. On some level, these slaves were also significantly involved in surplus production insofar as their military and reproductive labor contributed to the overall economic and demographic output of the societies in which they functioned.

Third, Finley required that the slaves present a "pervasive cultural influence" in the larger society. On this issue, there is no doubt that slavery and slave trading in the western Indian Ocean qualified. Indeed, slavery was a central feature in the economy, as well as in family life, in military and naval affairs, and in religious discourse on both sides of the ocean and up and down the coast.

Patrick Manning, an important scholar in the development of African history, has argued that movement is just as important in understanding social formations as focusing "in a static fashion on centers, kingdoms, empires, temples and great markets."[73] By this view, Indian Ocean slavery is directly related to the history and culture of migratory patterns in the region, and it draws its characteristics from those linkages, as well as from more traditional markers, such as empire and the quest for profit. This is different from the transatlantic experience, which is arguably monocausal and unidirectional to a great extent. Nonetheless, the confluence of population movements, empire, climatic factors, religion, and culture all combined to make East Africa, Oman, and the Persian Gulf in the nineteenth century into one greater "Slave Society."[74]

[73] Manning 2013, 90.

[74] See Hoerder 2002, confirming the view of East Africa as a "sociospace" intensively involved in the Indian Ocean trade emporia.

14

Ottoman and Islamic Societies: Were They "Slave Societies"?

Ehud R. Toledano

INTRODUCTION

The "comparative turn" in enslavement studies, more visible over the past decade or so than before, has – inadvertently – invited scholars with theoretical inclinations to offer models for explaining the many varieties of human bondage in history. The latest volumes of the *Cambridge World History of Slavery* opened up the field for work on the wide range of unfreedom in societies across the globe from antiquity, through medieval times, to the early modern and modern periods.[1] It is not surprising, therefore, that we are also witnessing a spike in new overarching theories that seek unifying models. To be sure, there were earlier waves of competing models, going back to the Nieboer-Domar hypothesis,[2] Alfred Zimmern's "self-manumission,"[3] Gilberto Freyre and Frank Tannenbaum on Brazil–US comparative post-emancipation realities,[4] and Moses Finley's "Slave Societies,"[5] to name just a few.

[1] These volumes have been edited by Stanley L. Engerman, David Eltis, David Richardson, and others. Volume 3 on the early modern period was published in 2011, volume 4 on the modern era is in press, and volume 2 on the medieval period is in the advanced stages of preparation.

[2] Nieboer 1910; Domar 1945, 18–32.

[3] For some interesting comments on which, see Findlay 1975.

[4] Hébrard 2013, 50–53.

[5] For the basics of the Finley model, see Finley 1980, 147–50. For a thorough critique of the model, see Lenski, Chapter 1 in this volume.

Later attempts included the social anthropology/sociology-driven models of Claude Meillassoux[6] and Alain Testart,[7] followed by the influential sociological model of Orlando Patterson.[8] More recently, the debate about the Atlantic model versus the Indian Ocean model has gained traction, and the current comparative phase in enslavement studies is producing at least three new attempts to offer comprehensive models. Among these, perhaps the most noteworthy are Dale Tomich and Michael Zeuske's "second slavery,"[9] Jeff Fynn-Paul's "slaving zones,"[10] and Noel Lenski's "intensification model."[11] If most models in the past, as the more recent ones by Tomich-Zeuske and Lenski, emphasize quantitative economic elements, Meillassoux, Testart, Patterson, and Fynn-Paul stress "softer" components drawn from anthropology and sociology, such as identity and ideology, or "system of meaning," in Clifford Geertz's language. But, for historians, all past and present models pose a major difficulty, which of course goes well beyond enslavement studies.

Induction-driven as we are and enslaved to our temporally and spatially contingent evidence, we historians have been reluctant to adopt comprehensive models lock, stock, and barrel. Instead, open-minded scholars have been inspired by parts of models, mainly those that analyze the *problematique* and offer possible explanations to the issues tackled in case research. Unlike deduction-guided social scientists, historians have, for the most part, rejected models as panaceas; it would be inconceivable for a dissertation advisor to ask a doctoral student to interrogate an historical case study against an existing model. Thus, arguably, the most successful models among historians of enslavement over the past several decades have been Finley's "Slave Societies" and Patterson's "social death."

[6] Meillassoux, 1986. See also Martin A. Klein 1986, 693–97.

[7] Testart 2001, 28–31.

[8] Patterson 1982. For critique by historians of Patterson's model, see the essays in Bodel and Scheidel 2017, which also includes my own view of the model's applicability to Ottoman enslavement.

[9] For various aspects of this model, see Kaye 2014; Tomich 2014; Zeuske 2014.

[10] An outline of the model appeared in Alan 2015, published on *H-SLAVERY*, November 13, 2014. The volume based on that conference is Fynn-Paul, Pargas, and Fatah-Black 2017. See also Fynn-Paul 2009.

[11] Lenski, Chapter 1, in this volume.

The reason for that, I would argue, is that both models are fairly simple to apply, offering the kind of concise and effective language that can be deployed in historical explanations. Finley's is not too demanding or overly pretentious in its supposed *rigueur intellectuelle*; it simply "does the job" of clarifying some of the points that an historian would seek to make about a given enslaving society. Patterson's model is, however, too rigid in its notion of "dishonor," failing to explain elite enslavement such as the Ottoman and Qajar *kul/gholam* system, or the parallel phenomenon in India, as Indrani Chatterjee has pointed out. Patterson has recently stuck to his argument in that respect, suggesting in response to Chatterjee's criticism and mine that we need to rethink whether *kul/gholam* were indeed slaves, which betrays his uninformed and ill-conceived view of the history of enslavement in Muslim societies.[12]

It is with this limited view in mind that I use Finley's model in this chapter. As an historian of Ottoman and Islamic enslavement in the early modern and modern eras, all I want from that model is the pure and simple way it enables me to distinguish enslavement in these societies from the better known, more familiar, Atlantic world societies. *By and large*, enslavement in Atlantic societies – intuitively accessible to the readers' mind – was numerically larger, economically more important, and socially more central. The distinction between "Slave Societies" and "Societies with Slaves" is also useful to me because it is very familiar to scholars working on other enslaving societies. Whether the model is applicable to *all* such societies – to be sure, it is not – or whether Finley's observations are correct across the board – quite clearly they are not – is much less of a concern to me. Insofar as theories and models are concerned, historians are eclectic and non-committal; as an historian, I take what I find useful and drop the rest.

Therefore, the kind of "demolition job" to which Noel Lenski subjects Finley's model somewhat misses the point.[13] This is mainly because historians do not expect models to work in all places and at all times, and counter-evidence does not invalidate what the model is supposed to do for us, i.e., tighten the analysis and render accessible new explanations. Inductive work, from the evidence to the

[12] For my criticism of Patterson on this, see Toledano 2017. See also Chatterjee 2017 and Patterson 2017 for a response.

[13] Lenski, Chapter 1 in this volume.

generalization, assumes that there will always be "exceptions to the rule"; we do not work with governing laws, notations, or equations. All models are "constructs" derived from empirical studies done by historians, and the notion of the "Slave Society" was, in Lenski's words, "invented with the good intention of comparing slaveholding practices across societies."[14] For the many historians, past and present, who have found Finley's model "useful," Lenski's assertion that it "became reified into a vaguely articulated, seductively exclusive category of sociological analysis" has not been a major concern, even if we accept much of the criticism Lenski levels at the ways it was applied to specific enslaving societies.

Most societies in the Ottoman Empire, many Islamic, and not a few Indian Ocean ones as well, practiced enslavement for much of their history in meaningfully different ways from most modern Atlantic world societies. Others in the Atlantic world during certain periods of time enslaved and treated bonded persons in ways that were similar to Ottoman, Islamic, and Indian Ocean societies. And conversely, during certain periods of time, the latter – e.g., the African ones mentioned by Lenski – practiced enslavement in ways that were similar to those that prevailed in the Atlantic world. Finley's "Slave Societies" versus "Societies with Slaves" has captured that distinction quite succinctly and effectively for many historians, warts and all. In fact, even historians who find Finley's model useful for drawing large-scale distinctions among societies that practiced enslavement, often, as I have done too, replace its bipolarity with a *continuum* of degrees of bondage.[15] Finley himself argued that "the ancient world was characterized by a continuous spectrum of various degrees of bondage," in a way that tempers what Lenski sees as the model's rigid dichotomy between slavery and freedom.[16]

Although Lenski deconstructs the Finley model, leaving no stone unturned, what he offers as an alternative is, indeed, a revised and corrected version of its main building blocks. Thus, his "intensification model" suggests two sets of four components each, in order to classify societies according to their "intensity" degree in relation

[14] Lenski, Chapter 1 in this volume.

[15] For example in Toledano 2000.

[16] Finley 1964.

to the "true slavery," or "ideal-[type] slave society" that he defines.[17] No doubt, this is a thoughtful method of measuring the variables, or aspects of enslavement, for both "master" and "slave," which in turn place each given society on comparative charts. These are ultimately collapsed into a "Cartesian grid" that reflects their relative standing to the ideal-type and to each other. The Lenski model, therefore, builds on and improves Finley's, rather than supplanting it altogether. By Lenski's own admission, intensification "keep[s] alive the spirit of Moses Finley's inquiry" while "alter[ing] his terms for the debate."

Accordingly, what Lenski provides is a "benchmark for comparing" structures of dependency that is not "a binary but a scale, or rather a series of scales," in his terms *vectors of intensification*. What this does is to apply the same analytical device used for quite some time to study enslavement *within* societies to a comparative study *across* enslaving societies. For *graded continuums* of enslavement, and their more recent extension to *graded continuums* of freedom, are analytically quite akin to Lenski's set of *graded scales* that measure all enslaving societies throughout the ages by the yardstick of an ideal-type, freshly defined "true slavery." For many historians who are interested in what models have to offer, "intensification" might comprise a bit too many variables and parameters, putting forth a matrix that requires extensive quantification, far more complex to apply in comparison to Finley's or Patterson's models. Especially where data are scarce, inaccessible, or unreliable, simplicity and clarity are a real virtue for scholars working in such challenging environments.

In classifying enslaving societies according to most models, the common parameters that have been considered are the size of the enslaved population, its importance within the workforce, the centrality of slavery in the economy in general and for capital accumulation of the ruling class, and the ability of the enslaved to integrate into the enslaving society.[18] Peter Hunt argues that the existence of agricultural slavery is crucial to the definition of "Slave Societies," and the diversity of tasks performed by enslaved people, and the range of treatment options, are important to the concept as well. If slavery is

[17] Lenski, Chapter 1 in this volume.

[18] These are also the basics of the Finley model well synthesized in Lenski, Chapter 1 in this volume. On the importance of capital accumulation in Rome, see, for example, Harper and Scheidel, Chapter 3 in this volume.

the essence of society, it is a "Slave Society."[19] Lenski and Snyder stress the crucial role of warfare in the "production of slaves" both in antiquity and in indigenous North American slavery, while Lenski argues further that the presence of violence is underestimated as a defining feature of "Slave Societies."[20]

To all these elements, I would add a sociocultural dimension and in so doing pose the following research question: how vital a factor was enslavement to the belief system – religious or otherwise – and to what extent did it anchor society and the social order? This is mostly because a sociocultural reading of history, I would argue, tends to "soften" the interest-driven, instrumental analysis based on political and economic factors, which has been, until the current cycle in enslavement studies, the predominant analytical and interpretative approach. It remains the foundation stone of most enslavement models in circulation. What I am suggesting is in some ways akin – though not similar – to studying enslavement as a "lived experience," in what Fernando Santos-Granero calls a "phenomenological approach."[21]

A recent contribution to the comparative approach, and hence to the "Slave Societies" debate, has been offered by David Eltis and Stanley Engerman in the "Introduction" to the third volume of *The Cambridge World History of Slavery*.[22] They stipulate several conditions for the term to be justifiably applied to societies: "Systems of slavery dedicated to the extraction of labor," they write, "whether for public projects or for the production of export crops organized for the benefit of private individuals, are normally associated with stratified societies that have moved some distance beyond the agricultural revolution. When these appear," they conclude, "it is possible to think in terms of 'slave societies' instead of 'societies with slaves.'" To Eltis and Engerman, this is the type of slavery the classical social science theorists and "most people" have in mind when they talk about slavery. "Slave Societies" were a small minority in history, and they appeared only late in human evolution, in the imperial and "human progress" age, these two leading scholars of slavery assert.[23]

[19] Hunt, Chapter 2 in this volume.
[20] Snyder, Chapter 6 in this volume.
[21] Santos-Granero, Chapter 7 in this volume.
[22] Eltis and Engerman 2011. The following quote is from page 10.
[23] On this, and an alternative to such thinking about enslavement, see Miller 2012, 2–12.

While expanding the criteria required for a society to qualify for membership in this category, Eltis and Engerman seem to play down some of the previously accepted variables. But, they remain within the same methodology of setting up a model and then assessing societies according to its parameters. Although there is nothing fundamentally flawed in such an approach, it might be interesting to try and think outside that box and do something a bit different. Thus, the working hypothesis in this chapter is that "Slave Societies" – in the limited sense I use it in this chapter – produced a different type of transition from enslavement to freedom than did "Societies with Slaves." In other words, most "Slave Societies" developed robust antislavery discourses, which later produced strong abolitionist movements, whereas practically all "Societies with Slaves" formulated weak, if any, antislavery ideology and feeble, gradualist abolitionism. This approach might be termed "analysis in reverse," where we look at the way an institution was defeated in order to understand its earlier, pre-demise nature. The basic assumption here is that later historical realities undeniably contain vestiges of past practices that enable us to better understand those earlier practices and realities.

Thus, when we look at the emergence of antislavery discourses, we need to examine where they originated – inside or outside the enslaving society, that is, whether they were a product of thinkers from the core of the cultural canon, from its periphery, or were imported from an outside source. The question here would be whether the antislavery discourse generated was indigenous and authentic, or foreign and alien to the enslaving community. The other, very much related, issue would be the nature of the processes of abolition, that is, if it was forced from the outside upon reluctant enslaving elites or driven by abolitionist elements within those elites. Also relevant would be the kind of interaction that occurred post abolition between emancipated communities and the former enslaving majority. These can be expected to be indicative of preexisting relations within that society and assist in understanding whether it was a "Slave Society" or a "Society with Slaves."

Communities of enslaved and freed persons have been studied in recent years as diasporic communities formed as a result of coerced migration, that is, the slave trade.[24] The forced displacement of

[24] See, for example, Toledano 2011a. See also the survey of the main contributions to that literature in Toledano 2007a, 38–47.

enslaved populations was a traumatic experience, which individuals and communities confronted by frequent and intense recourse to components of their culture of origin as they entered the enslaving societies that absorbed them. The interaction between freed diasporic communities and the "host" society often reflected the kind of relationships that had existed prior to emancipation and abolition. The sociocultural mechanisms deployed by the enslaved and the formerly enslaved in order to cope with their life experiences afford a view of the measure of host society tolerance and acceptance of difference. This, in turn, enables the examination of identity politics and group narrative construction that led to the emergence of rights discourses in post-enslavement societies, indicating their nature as either "Slave Societies" or "Societies with Slaves." Here too the present and what immediately preceded it can tell us a great deal about the past.

Specifically in our case, it seems fairly well accepted that modern – eighteenth- to twentieth-century – Islamic societies were closer to "Societies with Slaves" than to "Slave Societies." This view has been formed on the basis of the standard parameters mentioned earlier – the small size of the enslaved population, the relatively minor economic significance of their work within the labor market, and the high integrative capacities of the enslaving societies, which regularly depleted the enslaved population through manumission and concubinage, thereby putting pressure on the slave supply. According to Eltis and Engerman's criteria, modern Islamic societies would not be considered "Slave Societies"; the few that would qualify were medieval and early modern powers, and only segments of their economies and specific regions within them can be considered in that category

One of the main differences between the Atlantic and the Mediterranean-Indian Ocean worlds is the significant presence of Islamic societies in the latter, and the relatively small impact of Islamic practices in the former. The Ottoman and the Qajar (Iranian) empires dominated vast territories in Eastern Europe, the Middle East, North Africa, and the northeastern shores of the Indian Ocean, while the Mughals ruled significant parts of India. The largest Muslim populations in the world are still located today on lands stretching from the Indian subcontinent to Indonesia. Following the demise of these three last Muslim empires, all successor states, with the exception of Israel and India, are Muslim-majority. The culture-specific types of enslavement and, ultimately, abolition, in those societies may justify and explain their classification as "Societies with Slaves."

A related consideration in this regard is the fact that Islam, as the belief system defining those societies, sanctioned and regulated enslavement, which inhibited antislavery thinking and impeded abolition to a large extent. At the same time, Islamic societies showed a greater tendency to allow cultural retentions by enslaved and freed diasporic communities, which was instrumental and conducive to integration, rather than secessionist-separatist.[25] Except on rare occasions, such retentions were not seen by the majority culture as threatening to its value system or predominance. The ensuing *créoelité* does not necessarily reflect resistance to incorporation, as Lovejoy rightly observed. Lovejoy suggests that strong resistance creates "separate subcultures" that are "impervious to creolization," whereas the emergence of "creole cultures" implies a certain measure of assimilation, integration, and acceptance of the dominant culture.[26]

Thus, despite a prevailing sense among formerly enslaved African communities of shared victimhood and a heritage of exploitation and discrimination, the dual experience of colonialism and the rise of nationalist movements challenged the stability of those collective identities. The establishment of modern nation-states in the Mediterranean and Indian Ocean worlds during the second half of the twentieth century tested such identities by converging processes of nation building, state consolidation, labor migration, armed conflict, the evolving struggle between democracy and authoritarianism, the rise and suppression of civil society and local communal organizations, and the challenges of an emerging globalization. Within the Ottoman Empire, similar processes were occurring among Ottoman-Local elites, albeit with a distant and weak link to former military-administrative enslavement (the *kul/harem* system).[27]

[25] See, for example, Toledano 2007a, chapter 5. Also, on theory and another case study, see Gans 1997 and Sela-Sheffy 2006.

[26] For a succinct treatment of the terms "creole" and "creolization," see Lovejoy 2000, especially 13–19. For the basic concept of creolization used here (with which Lovejoy disagrees), see Mintz and Price 1976. The quotation from Lovejoy is in Lovejoy 2004, 8.

[27] See Toledano (forthcoming).

This chapter then argues that from both perspectives of post-enslavement societal situations – that of the abolitionist transition and that of the interaction between ex-enslaved communities and host societies – we can better classify and analyze a given society as a "Slave Society" or a "Society with Slaves." The Islamic societies of Ottoman and Qajar times in the Middle East would be classified through such a prism as "Societies with Slaves," which they would also be under the prevailing parameters generally accepted in enslavement studies and mentioned briefly earlier. As Hopper suggests,[28] certain regions of the Ottoman Empire can arguably be considered "Slave Societies," specifically Zanzibar and the Red Sea Persian Gulf space that surrounded it. To that one may perhaps add the Egyptian cotton economy in the 1860s, where Sudanese agricultural slaves labored in the fields to fill the supply gap created in global markets as a result of the American Civil War.

According to our "analysis in reverse" approach, the following pages demonstrate that Islamic societies, whether Ottoman, Qajar, or Mughal, did not develop internal antislavery discourses, nor did they produce effective abolitionist movements.[29] Instead, both antislavery discourse and abolitionism were interjected from the outside, mostly from Britain, and were adopted only reluctantly and after much political pressure, at least as far as enslaved Africans were concerned. This argument seeks to explain the absence of antislavery discourse and abolition movements in "Societies with Slaves," rather than assert mechanically that "Slave Societies," where slavery played a major economic role, necessarily developed abolitionism as a matter of course.

It also needs to be stressed in this context that instead of a sharp enslaved–free dichotomy, "Societies with Slaves" displayed a spectrum of slave types, ethnically and functionally, and allowed a relatively high degree of integration of ex-slaves into the enslaver society. In the modern era, enslavement in Ottoman and Qajar societies was mostly – though certainly not exclusively – African, female, and

[28] See Hopper, Chapter 12 in this volume. The same argument can be put forth with regard to agricultural enslavement in Arabia, as a recent study convincingly documents, Reilly 2015.

[29] This runs contrary to the argument in Clarence-Smith 2006. See my review article of the book, Toledano 2007b. Further arguments are presented here as reproduced in part from Toledano 2013b.

domestic, where the intimacy of the elite household mitigated certain aspects of harsh, physical enslavement, while at the same time exacerbating others, such as the sexual and psychological dimensions.[30]

Particularly relevant to our approach is the heritage of coerced migration of enslaved persons who found themselves living in foreign, often inhospitable, and exploitative societies. Not only the enslaved migrants themselves, but their children and grandchildren, well past manumission, had to cope with social, economic, and political disabilities sanctioned by law and embedded in practice. Generations after emancipation, descendants of enslaved Africans in formerly Ottoman and Qajar societies were – and still are – compelled to negotiate their own identities and to confront discrimination by the state and from other social groups. However, the processes of identity formation occurred late and were different from those that have taken place among emancipated African minorities in formerly "Slave Societies." The successor nation-state that replaced the Islamic empires effectively inhibited the awareness of difference and its sociopolitical implications. Only in recent years do we hear of African-Turkish, African-Iranian, and African-Arab activism in the eastern Mediterranean and western Indian Ocean regions.[31]

ANTISLAVERY ISLAMIC SOCIETIES OF THE MIDDLE EAST: HISTORY AND DISCOURSE

One of the main points of departure in the analysis offered in the following is that the suppression of the slave trade and the abolition of slavery were a type of social, economic, political, and even cultural reform.[32] A necessary precondition for introducing a policy of reform is a broad-based recognition that something is either morally wrong or not working, and hence in need of repair. This is, however, not a sufficient condition; one needs also the will, the support, the tools, and the perseverance to push through effective change. Whereas in non-Western societies, reform was often initiated by rulers and governments, that is "top down," public support, or at least the lack of strong and committed opposition, was also required. In Europe

[30] On this, see Toledano 2007a, Introduction.
[31] On this, see Toledano 2013a, 2007a, 50–52.
[32] The following draws in part and with revisions on Toledano 2017.

and the United States from the eighteenth century onward, many changes – including the abolition of slavery – originated in the "marketplace of ideas" and fed on public debate and grassroots organization in emerging civil societies.

Within the unwritten pact between rulers and ruled in the Ottoman Middle East and North Africa, reformers needed to test the views of their loyal elites before taking action. Without elite support and public acquiescence, plus conviction and determination on the part of the leadership, attempts at reform were all too often foiled by conservative, anti-reform groups. In the absence of real domestic backing for abolition, Ottoman reformers had to rely on outside pressure even for the limited program to suppress the trade in African slaves. Suffice it here to note that from fairly early in the European drive to put an end to Islamic slavery, enslavement and the slave trade had to be dealt with separately. The first attempts by the British to persuade the Ottoman sultan and his ministers to abolish slavery were rebuffed around 1840, and consequently, London's efforts were redirected toward the suppression of the slave trade.[33] What followed in the rest of the century was an ongoing campaign to set up treaties in order to prohibit human trafficking from Africa and from the Caucasus into the Ottoman Empire. Success was registered only with regard to the trade in enslaved Africans, which was prohibited in 1857 by an imperial edict.

However, that British achievement did not result from bringing the Ottomans to the view that slavery was wrong. Contrary to the acrimonious antislavery discourse in Europe and the United States, there was almost no Ottoman "marketplace of ideas" where enslavement was hotly contested. In fact, the decision to prohibit the slave trade from Africa was extracted from the Ottoman government through sustained diplomatic pressure. Yes, humanitarian arguments were used in the debate with Ottoman decision makers, but viziers and provincial governors did not have to face public demands to stop the slave trade; rather the reverse occurred, for in the slaving provinces there was strong opposition to suppression. In other words, putting an end to the slave trade from Africa into the Ottoman Empire depended

[33] For British attempts to intervene against Ottoman enslavement, see Toledano 1982, 91–147, 193–237, 249–78.

on government-to-government negotiations and was not predicated upon an ideological switch, sudden or gradual, to antislavery thinking within civil society.

Thus, in the Ottoman Empire, abolition – or rather suppression – occurred *in the absence* of an antislavery movement. An antislavery discourse as we know it in the Atlantic context never reached a *masse critique* in the Ottoman public sphere. A few individuals expressed disapproval of enslavement, but even toward the last quarter of the nineteenth century, no organized abolitionist lobby emerged, and Ottoman opponents of slavery were not present in any "abolitionist spaces," where "abolitionist spatial practices" occurred.[34] However, an active abolitionist community with an interest in the Ottoman Empire did exist, though it operated outside the Empire and very rarely engaged, let alone recruited, Ottoman interlocutors and supporters. Moreover, contrary to other situations, where abolitionists encountered opposition from enslavers but also support from pro-abolition groups, the foreign monitors in the Middle East and North Africa were surrounded by a hostile environment that tried to obstruct their efforts, conceal information, and even physically attack them.

Well into the last decades of the nineteenth century, Ottoman elite public opinion, in general, rejected Western abolitionist rhetoric and the notion that Ottoman enslavement was wrong, inhuman, or immoral. That view, writ large, was also shared by the public in general, so that enslavement and – to a somewhat lesser degree, also the traffic that sustained it – continued to be socially shielded and morally nourished. Hence it is not surprising that, whereas in almost all cases of abolition in the Atlantic world the role of the private clearly outweighed the importance of state action, it was overwhelmingly the reverse in the Ottoman Empire. This almost total silence concerning enslavement among intellectual, theological, economic, or political elites prevailed not only in the Ottoman world but also in the two other great Muslim empires of the time, for which separate and specific studies are still required.

[34] See, for example, the case of the Atlantic abolitionist movement, as reflected in call for papers in a special issue of the *Journal of Atlantic Studies* (Spring 2011) on the topic "Abolitionist Places," posted to *H-SLAVERY*, 20 January 2010, by Martha Schoolman.

There seems to be a wall-to-wall agreement among scholars that enslavement per se did not create any significant discomfort in Ottoman and other Islamic societies, nor did it give rise to any dissonance in their thinking or self-perception. One dissenting view, however, belongs to William Gervase Clarence-Smith, whose highly problematic book, *Islam and the Abolition of Slavery*, appeared in 2006.[35] I have no intention in this chapter of delving into his flawed propositions and arguments, which I have done elsewhere at some length.[36] Suffice it here to lay out very briefly what he maintains in this regard and then to adduce some of the views to the contrary. We need to do so in order to substantiate our proposition that "Societies with Slaves" – at least the Islamic ones reviewed here – do not produce strong antislavery and abolition movements.

In a nutshell, what Clarence-Smith is trying to do is to reverse the argument. he is not disputing the fact that in practice, abolition occurred in "Islam" – or Islamic societies, as he should have put it – only very late, that is after the rise of nation-states in Muslim-majority countries. Muslim writers, he contends, "often display intense unease that Islam accepted slavery for so long, without any mass movement emerging to advocate abolition." However, as he is keen on absolving Islamic law and theology of legitimating – hence endorsing – enslavement, he needs to argue that there was an active, vibrant antislavery discourse among Muslim thinkers and theologians, and that the formative texts of Islam contain at least seeds of opposition to human bondage. Clarence-Smith does admit, nonetheless, that all that "unease" failed to affect the "social realities of servitude," and that slavery lingered on in some Islamic societies even after secular laws had been enacted to abolish it, because the practice was socio-religiously acceptable.

Clarence-Smith actually goes even further when he states that "Islamic abolitionism," whatever that is, was not a response to Western pressures, but rather "home-grown" and rooted in classical Muslim scriptures.[37] He then allows himself to interpret Islamic sources and assert that "the foundations of slavery in the original texts were weak,"

[35] Clarence-Smith 2006.

[36] Clarence-Smith 2006, 1. For "Muslim writers," he cites two examples of works dated 1998 and 2000.

[37] Clarence-Smith 2006, 19.

and that "slavery ... was the clearest negation of a socially egalitarian vision of the faith." Moreover, Clarence-Smith reaches the unfounded conclusion that "a permanent tension between religious belief and social reality" existed, and that "many of the faithful" were embarrassed by slavery. This supposedly gave rise to a "rich diversity of debates and interpretations." One would be hard-pressed to find any substantial, serious evidence to support such claims; needless to say, had that been true, the sources would be replete with cases of rulers and slaveholding elites being constantly admonished by outraged *ulema* and their mass followers.

However, it is not a great surprise that one can easily find traces of antislavery thinking in Islamic scripture, as one surely can in scriptures of any other major religion. In and of itself, this does not challenge the fact that all major exegetic traditions within Islamic thought actually followed the opposite course and defended enslavement. Nor can those few antislavery traces mitigate the historical reality that social practice in all Muslim societies accepted enslavement and retained it long after most other societies had already rejected it. It is certainly true that Islam, as a system of belief, meaning, and law, sought from its inception to mitigate enslavement and limit its scope, but practice and custom prevailed, and the very existence of human bondage was never seriously challenged. In other words, no cognitive dissonance befell the system by the supposed tension between theology and practice. Positioned in between, Islamic law ensured the resilience of enslavement.

To further substantiate this point, we should note an even greater paradox. In modern times, governments in Muslim-majority countries – bowing to European pressure or acting to serve their own interests – worked to stop the slave trade and gradually phased out enslavement. Nonetheless, at the same time, literal, conservative interpreters of Islamic law and dogma continued to support enslavement as divinely ordained. These were the dominant forces within elite thinking in all Muslim-majority countries; antislavery voices were few and weak. Clarence-Smith needs to migrate his discussion to the Indian subcontinent in the late nineteenth century in order to find the first outspoken antislavery texts. Even then, these come from the likes of Sir Sayyid Ahmad Khan (died 1898), clearly reacting to British abolitionist rhetoric. He then leaps well into the second quarter of the twentieth century in search of writings by non-*ulema*, that is state reformers, acting outside the realm of Islamic law and tradition, or make do with Abdallah b. Nabitan, "an Arab resident in Java," in the early 1930s.[38]

More representative of attitudes to enslavement in Islamic societies were, of course, the Ottomans. Their huge empire contained the largest number of enslaved persons, whose functions and origins spanned the entire spectrum between agricultural, military-administrative, and domestic enslavement.[39] To understand Ottoman and Arab view of the institution, let us turn now to three Ottomanists who work on enslavement, Hakan Erdem and Madeline C. Zilfi, and to Amal N. Ghazal, who has studied the Arab debate over slavery and abolition.[40] Their findings represent the consensus in the literature that deafening silence shrouded the issue of enslavement in those societies.

In her recent book, *Women and Slavery in the Late Ottoman Empire*, Madeline C. Zilfi takes a harsh and highly critical view of Ottoman and Islamic enslavement.[41] She points to the earliest attempt to abolish slavery in Tunisia, where the Ottoman governor-general, Ahmet Bey, outlawed enslavement in 1846. Despite *ulema* support, the prohibition was ineffective *á la longue*, and the practice resurfaced later and persisted well past Bey's reign in that Ottoman province.[42] Zilfi believes that slavery was inextricably intertwined with the very foundation of the Ottoman Empire as a Muslim, *Şeriat*-bound entity, which the *ulema* endeavored to preserve intact. The fact that neither an abolitionist movement nor an antislavery discourse emerged in the Empire, she argues, is explained by the intransigence of the imperial establishment over enslavement. The legal distinction between slave and free was fundamental to *ulema* thinking and worldview, but higher-ranking members of that group were also personally implicated in actual slave owning, often on an excessive scale.[43]

[38] Clarence-Smith 2006, 211–15.
[39] For this see Toledano 2000.
[40] A fuller account of their relevant studies is in Toledano 2013b.
[41] Zilfi 2010.
[42] Zilfi 2010, 220. On this, see also Montana 2013.
[43] Zilfi 2010, 222–23.

Thus, the proslavery stance of that key group of political and social actors, in Zilfi's view, was predicated on a vested socioeconomic interest in opposing abolition, in addition to a religious and legal justification. Other large groups also benefited economically from slavery and the slave trade, e.g., "drovers, dealers, and the infrastructure of slave transport," who "joined forces with the theological and cultural opposition in standing against abolition."[44] To this, she adds the vocal and often violent opposition to the suppression of the slave trade in the slaving ports of North Africa and the Arabian Peninsula, asserting that the Istanbul elites could not ignore them even if they themselves were less adamant in their support of enslavement and the traffic. Since enslavement was sanctioned by Islamic law and dogma, and figured in the life of the Prophet, overt rejection of it would have played into the hands of the rigid opponents to the nineteenth-century reform movement (*Tanzimat*).

Zilfi uses the term "anti-abolitionism" to describe the discourse that permeated Ottoman elite circles. Furthermore, in accord with the research and scholarship on enslavement and abolition in the Ottoman Empire and other Muslim-majority countries,[45] she shows that the main obstacle to abolition was that slavery was anchored in Islamic socio-legal and sociocultural tradition. Since enslavement was part of the Ottoman social order, it was shielded by "the moral authority of Islam and tradition."[46] This is fully supported by Hakan Erdem's evaluation of Ottoman abolitionism and antislavery.[47] Erdem's contribution is important in a number of ways, but most of all in conveying a clear sense, gleaned from the sources, that Ottoman efforts to bring an end to enslavement lacked conviction and sincerity. Instead, they were more often a ploy to achieve another end, or serve another interest, than a reflection of genuine and honest commitment to abolitionism.

Erdem points out the fact that all the leading *Tanzimat* reformers, including grand viziers such as Reşit, Ali, and Fuat Paşas, owned slaves, and in many cases married enslaved Circassian women. Even the most open antislavery advocate, Grand Vizier Midhat Paşa, who pushed for

[44] Quotes in this paragraph are from Zilfi 2010, 224.
[45] For similar arguments, see Toledano 1998, 112–34, and Erdem 1996, 125–88.
[46] Zilfi 2010, 226.
[47] Erdem 1996.

abolitionist legislation in 1877 – which Sultan Abdülhamit II rejected – was himself implicated in the practice. He purchased his own wife, and in 1879, when governor-general of Syria, allegedly bought two Circassian women and sent them as gifts to an official whose influence he needed to court.[48] I have elsewhere shown that as late as the 1890s, the imperial court was still recruiting Circassian girls for the Istanbul harems, implicating in that activity senior officeholders and sending traders to procure young women in the Caucasus.[49]

To that posture, Erdem adds that even the Young Turks, who were keen to project a liberal, modern, Western-leaning image of their regime, could only improve on the preceding Hamidian government by prohibiting the slave trade in Circassians.[50] Concerned to cut public expenditure, they reduced the size of the imperial household and drastically cut the number of eunuchs; but they too did not feel they could tamper with the Islamic legality of enslavement itself. The Young Turks evoked the established notion that "in the House of Islam, freedom is the basic principle" (*Dar-ül İslam'da hürriyet asl olmasıyla*), conceding that the presumption of freedom (*al-asl huwwa 'l-hurriyya*) is the basic principle in scripture and law. Nonetheless, their government had to yield to the *Şeyhülislam*'s insistence that "slavery as an abstract, legal notion (*rıkk*, and *rıkkıyet*) was inviolable."[51] This meant that "wholesale abolition," in Erdem's words, would not be a viable option. Thus, despite such a seemingly powerful principle of law and tenet of faith, ways were always too easily found to skirt and interpret it away so that slavery would persist.

In the post-Ottoman Arab Middle East, the lines were being redrawn between a conservative majority and a modernist minority. Amal Ghazal rightly believes that rather than generating their own antislavery discourse, Islamic thinkers were responding to "European criticism of slavery in Muslim societies and of the alleged role that the *Sharīʿa* had played in perpetuating and legitimizing slavery."[52] Examining the debate over slavery between the Salafi modernists and the traditionalist conservatives at the turn of the twentieth century, she

[48] Erdem 1996, 128–32.
[49] Toledano 1982, 184–91.
[50] Erdem 1996, 147–51.
[51] Erdem 1996, 150, and also 188.
[52] Ghazal 2009, 139–54.

shows how modernist *ulema* in Egypt – men like Muhammad Abduh, Rashid Rida, and Syrian-born Abd al-Rahman al-Kawakibi – tried to change Islamic law and thinking by innovative reinterpretation of the scriptures (*Ijtihad*). However, they were vehemently opposed by the majority of jurists and theologians, who clung to the literal understanding of the formative texts of Islam (*Taqlid*). The issue of enslavement was but one apple of discord in a long litany of disputes over modernity.

The modernists were willing to recognize the value of European civilization and, therefore, went through some self-criticism with regard to enslavement. To conservatives, asserts Ghazal, "Europe was a wholesale evil; assimilating aspects of its modernity was to make a deal with the devil."[53] They believed that attempts to interfere with the legality of slavery in Islamic societies stemmed from the West's desire to weaken Islam and deprive it of the large number of converts produced through the slave trade. Such proslavery advocates brought up some incredible arguments in its defense, one being that bondage is economically, socially, and spiritually beneficial to the enslaved. The Muslim identity of the enslaved was all-important, squashing their unfreedom; conversion was a God-sent blessing to those heathens and a "ladder for spiritual and social satisfaction," in Ghazal's words.[54] Government and court-enforced manumission was, thus, a curse that only worsened the lot of freed slaves. The basic concept of one of the leading anti-abolitionists, Yusuf al-Nabhani, was that God, "in his great knowledge about the affairs of the world," allowed Muslims to own slaves "for reasons that might not be known to human beings."

Islamic reformists, on the other hand, embraced the Western human rights discourse and tried to anchor it in a developing and evolving reinterpretation of the scriptures and the law.[55] Thus, for example, Kawakibi, who migrated to Egypt and was active there in the reformist camp, condemned the Ottoman government for dragging its feet regarding the suppression of the slave trade and urged European powers to step up pressure on the Ottomans to stop what remained of the traffic. Citing what is widely believed

[53] Ghazal 2009, 141.
[54] Quotes in this paragraph are from Ghazal 2009, 143.
[55] Ghazal 2009, 146–50.

to have been a learned opinion by renowned modernist authority Muhammad Abduh,[56] both scholars come down on the side of abolition. Still, they too recognize that, given the Islamic legal and theological sanction that shields slavery, only a gradualist approach would be effective. The idea was to use the notion of Islamic humanism and build upon the mechanisms of manumission formulated and encouraged by Muslim law.

But such theological scholars also realized that without sustained foreign, European pressure, the Ottomans and other Muslim rulers would not act decisively to uproot slavery. Thus, Kawakibi urged Western nations to exert their influence and make specific abolitionist demands on such rulers. Muhammad Abduh's most prominent disciple, Rashid Rida, added another argument to the discussion: "Had Muslims and their rulers ... followed the rules of the *shari'a*," he asserted, "slavery would have been abolished in the first century of Islam."[57] Hence, Rida seems to absolve Islam – as an ethical and moral value system – from the blemish of enslavement, but he does that by putting the blame at the doorstep of Muslims. In other words, there was nothing wrong with theory and everything wrong with practice.

At this point, we are still left with the need to explain why serious antislavery discourse and abolitionist movements never emerged in the socioculturally sophisticated urban centers of the Ottoman Middle East and North Africa, or for that matter anywhere in the Islamic world. I have already offered my own take on that matter elsewhere,[58] so what is needed here is to make the connection between the absence of abolitionism and my proposition that Islamic societies were of the kind that does not generate substantive antislavery discourse; they were, in other words, "Societies with Slaves." The *problematique* here is therefore, why is this so, what are the reasons that induce such societies to resist abolition, then to adopt it as an imported product from abolitionist "Slave Societies," and finally to phase out slavery gradually, not with one decisive stroke of the pen or the sword?

[56] Ghazal 2009, 146–48.
[57] Ghazal 2009, 149.
[58] Toledano 2013b, 132–35.

CONCLUSION

The linkage between the nature of enslavement in a given society and the resistance to or support for abolition seems to me quite strong and logical. In the Ottoman Empire, as in other contemporary Islamic societies, the size of the enslaved population was rather small – about 5 percent in the Empire at large, close to 8 percent in the imperial capital, Istanbul. As for how central and crucial slavery was in society, opinions vary, but not to such a great extent. Madeline Zilfi believes that slavery was a fundamental institution in Ottoman society, deeply entrenched in its social, political, and economic fabric. She is, therefore, hardly surprised to see how strong the resistance to abolition was. Enslavement, she writes, "was culturally and institutionally integral to both state and society," and the ruling elites, like in the United States, were the main enslavers.[59] Hence, Zilfi concludes, "its legitimacy was defended and its demise resisted, at least in some quarters, until the empire's end."

Tunisian scholar Abdelhamid Larguèche asserts that Ottoman-Tunisian enslavement survived for so long because it was a constitutive part of elite lifestyle.[60] Indeed, there can hardly be any doubt that among the elites of the imperial capital, as among the Ottoman-Local elites that imitated their lifestyle in the provinces,[61] keeping enslaved persons was an important status symbol and a conspicuous stratifier of elite households empire-wide. The ubiquity of enslaved servants in these households – as opposed to the more than 90 percent of the population who did not acquire them – was a means to convey opulence to one's social peers. Harem slavery, including the limited and prestigious employment of eunuchs, facilitated the gender segregation that marked and reinforced the hierarchical order in Ottoman households. In stressing the role of slavery as *mainly* a sociocultural resource in Ottoman societies, Larguèche plays down the economic value that is central to Zilfi's argument.

A closely related issue in our discussion of the nexus between being a "Society with Slaves" and producing next to no abolition is the much debated question of whether enslavement in the Ottoman Empire

59 Zilfi 2010, 100.
60 Larguèche 1990, 37ff.
61 For the emergence of Ottoman-Local elites and elite households, see Toledano 2012.

and other Islamic societies was "mild." My own view has evolved over the past quarter-century from acceptance – with definite caveats – of the view that Islamic slavery was mild to rejection of that contention.[62] Zilfi is critical of the "soft" approach to Ottoman enslavement, not making allowances for either *kul/ harem* or domestic forms of the practice.[63] This would defeat the argument that the mild nature of enslavement can explain the absence of opposition to it and the lack of strong demands for abolition. In support of the view rejecting the argument that slavery in Islamic societies was mild, one can adduce cases from Moro enslavement in the Philippines under US rule, to enslavement of Africans in French-controlled North Africa, and to communities of enslaved Africans in the Indian Ocean world.[64] In all these cases, the colonial authorities chose to accept the "mild treatment" contention, in order to avoid confronting local elites with abolitionist demands, which could cause friction with a colonized population that could deteriorate into violence.

The purported mild nature of Muslim enslavement was as far from realities in the Muslim-populated regions of the Philippines or in the Algero-Sahara as it was in the Ottoman Empire. However, in polemic discourse, when Muslim writers defended enslavement in their societies, they sought to project a totally different image of the realities that enslaved persons had to cope with.[65] They emphasized domestic, household, mainly female slavery as the predominant form of bondage, and depicted that as being "part of the family," a benign form of patronage. The practice of concubinage, common in elite households, was portrayed as an intimate arrangement that enabled enslaved women to join good Muslim families and be integrated, together with their offspring, into secure and respectable households.

Muslim defenders of slavery not only denied any resemblance between the Atlantic model and Islamic realities, they even rejected the use of the term "slavery" in reference to their societies. The wall they thus erected served to repel foreign pressures as violations of the

[62] On that "evolution," see Toledano 2007a, 15–23; 1998, 14–19, and my review of Zilfi's book at Toledano 2011b.

[63] Zilfi 2010, 115–20.

[64] For these examples, see Toledano 2013b, 127–30, citing Salman 2001, 59–119; and Brower 2009, especially 174–85.

[65] For a discussion of this and related issues, see Toledano 1998, 112–34 (chapter 4: "Slavery and Abolition: the Battle of Images").

privacy and intimacy of the Muslim family. It also effectively helped prevent the emergence of home-grown abolitionist movements and stifled antislavery discourse.

To conclude, we might consider that when consciousness of the injustice of enslavement was raised within "Slave Societies," its harshness and centrality were more likely – though by no means always or automatically – to be met by intense antislavery debates, and robust abolitionist movements often emerged. However, "Societies with Slaves" almost without exception defended their alleged "mild" forms of enslavement, and consequently inhibited the rise of effective abolitionism. In Islamic societies, especially those subjected to colonialism, criticism of enslavement by Western powers was seen as part of a general assault on their Muslim identity and value system, which further blocked any internal attempts at reexamination and reform.

15

A Microhistorical Analysis of Korean *Nobis* through the Prism of the Lawsuit of Damulsari

Kim Bok-rae

INTRODUCTION

Korean premodern society was made up of three social classes: *yangban* (noble), *yangmin* (commoner), and *nobi* (often referred to in English as "slaves"). The last was subdivided along two vectors: public/private *nobis* and/or resident/nonresident *nobis*, the last of whom lived away from their masters. Under the Chosun dynasty (1392–1910) and especially during the fifteenth and sixteenth centuries, the most common type of civil suit concerned *nobis*. For that reason, the laws governing *nobis* were developed in minute detail regarding ownership, the law of succession, inheritance, etc. Although *nobis* were recognized as human, they were the object of purchase, sale, lease, donation, and succession. Their dualistic character (half-man/half-thing) has led to discussion among scholars, but the question of their status remains unresolved. Can they best be classed as slaves, serfs, or occupants of some status not adequately characterized by either concept?

The aim of this chapter is to explore the dual identity (half-man, half-thing) of Korean *nobis*, using as a microhistorical test case, the lawsuit of Damulsari. This trial was held at the Naju government office in the nineteenth year of King Seonjo (1567–1608) in 1585.[1] The male *yangban* Yi Ji-do was plaintiff and the female *yangmin* Damulsari was

[1] This litigation was unearthed by Lim Sang-Hyuk, who worked in the Presidential Truth Commission on Suspicious Death; Lim 2010.

defendant.[2] In contrast with other *nobi* lawsuits, the accused *yangmin* Damulsari insisted that she was in fact a *nobi*. The plaintiff Yi countered that the defendant Damulsari was a commoner but that she lied about her status to put her daughter Ini under the control of the government office as a public *bi* (female *nobi*). The case sheds light on the complexity of the *nobi* system by showing that *nobis* came in a variety of types and that status as a *nobi* was not universally regarded as unbearable.

The *nobi* class formed 30 to 40 percent of the total population of Korea in the seventeenth century.[3] On the basis of these figures and his choice to liken *nobis* to Western slaves, James B. Palais considered Korea during the Koryo (910–1392) and Chosun dynasties a "genuine Slave Society."[4] However, most Korean scholars regard resident *nobis* as slaves but public and nonresident *nobis* as serfs. Nonresident and/or tribute-paying *nobis* not only had a solid claim to family but managed small and independent businesses. They were also treated as members of one homogeneous community with rights before the law, making them something other than "socially dead" – to use Orlando Patterson's phrase from his monumental *Slavery and Social Death*.[5] This chapter argues that Western categories are not entirely apt for an institution that shared qualities of "slaves" and "serfs" while manifesting peculiar qualities of its own.

Slaves or serfs? This question is also closely related to the traditional Western tripartite periodization – ancient, medieval, and modern. Yet, in spite of the trend toward the emancipation of slaves in the Western world, the Chosun ruling elite (*yangban*), who were the largest owners of *nobis*, stuck to the *nobi* system, which they called a traditional and respectable one that existed for a good reason, until the end of the nineteenth century. The *yangban* always sang the praises of Chinese law codes, but they refused to shift their hereditary *nobi* system fully to the hired labor regime, called *gugong* in Chinese and *gogong* in Korean, which appeared in the Ming dynasty (1368–1644).

[2] A Korean name consists of a family name followed by a given name. Thus, Yi is his family name and Ji-do is his given name. Damulsari is her given name.

[3] After having reviewed several documents, analysts estimate respectively the total population at four to five million and the private/public *nobis* at one and a half million; Rhee 1998, 305–06.

[4] Palais 1998, ch. 2.

[5] Patterson 1982, 5–7.

A pioneer of Korean Practical Science (*silhak*), Yu Hyong-won (1622–73), also criticized the Korean *nobi* system for its hereditary basis in his *Pan-Gye Surok* (*Essays on Social Reform*). Yu argued that Chinese penal *nubis* could be emancipated by special amnesty, and even though they were in lifetime bonded service, their servile status was not inherited by their progeny. The Korean *nobi* status, by contrast, was passed from generation to generation, regardless of guilt or innocence. Certainly, this hereditary rule was not applied in the Chinese system, but it was preferable for *nubi* children, who had no means of self-support, to serve the masters of their parents. In China, the *nubi* system reached its zenith during the Tang dynasty (618–907) and was at its ebb tide after the Song dynasty (960–1279).[6] By contrast, the expansion of the Korean *nobi* system operated in the inverse direction between the Koryo and Chosun periods. In Japan, the *nuhi* system (Japanese slavery) was abolished in 900 CE, but another form of lower class called *genin* lasted until the emancipation act of 1871. The Korean *nobi* system came to an end in 1894, while its Chinese counterpart was abolished in 1909.

THE SOCIAL AND LEGAL DISADVANTAGE OF THE *NOBI*

In the early Chosun period, the number of *nobis* was considered an "index of wealth" (Figure 15.1). In his *Journal and a Description of the Kingdom of Korea* (1653–66), Dutch traveler Hendrick Hamel wrote that the main source of income of *yangban* families was through the possession of land and *nobis*.[7] According to Hamel, some *yangbans* possessed as many as 2,000–3,000 *nobis*. It seems likely that he saw many nonresident *nobis* of the same family scattered over several villages.[8]

Nobi is itself a composite word for both male (*no*) and female (*bi*) servant. Another term for *nobi* was *chang-juk*, an abbreviation for *chang-du-juk-gak*. The term *chang-du* (*no*) + *juk-gak* (*bi*) was derived

[6] *Nubis* seem to have made up no more than 1 percent of the total population even at the time when the institution was most fully developed during the Han dynasty; Wilbur 1943, 241.

[7] Hendrick Hamel (1630–92) was the first Westerner to write and experience Korea firsthand in the Chosun era (1666); Hamel 1994, 52–53.

[8] Kim Jong-sung 2013, 177–78.

FIGURE 15.1 *Nobi* document with a hand shape rather than a handwritten signature reflecting the illiteracy of the signatory. Seoul Museum of History, *nobi* document code: seo 19261.
Courtesy Seoul Museum of History.

from the custom of the Han dynasty to distinguish a male slave (*nu*) with a blue headband. The *changdu* had a "blue head" because he had a shaven head, while the *jukgak* indicated the "red legs" of a female *bi*. Women's bare legs implied "doing dirty work" or "being of low birth." Chosun women of low birth could not completely cover their calves with skirts. Originally, women's legs and feet symbolized their sexuality. Prostitutes, called *gisaeng*, were even forced to take off their traditional socks (*busuns*) in public as a severe punishment. A *yangban* lady is even known to have committed suicide because her calves were accidentally seen by others.

In an era when society was rigorously ruled by neo-Confucian principles, a *bi* who walked barefoot through the street was thus considered an insignificant being without shame. It is also not unusual to see both poor female *yangmins* and *bis* showing their naked breasts in Korean genre paintings from the eighteenth century onward, as well as in photo albums in the later Chosun period (Figures 15.2–15.3). Generally, the *nobi* had an ordinary given name without a family name. They were sometimes just called "little boy" or "little girl." Some *bis* actually had ornamental names, such as "rose" or "parrot," and like *gisaengs*, some public *bis* belonging to the local government office had elaborate names such as "white *ume* flower" or "scent of chrysanthemum." By contrast, private *nos* (male *nobis*) usually had humble names taken from lowly animals (dog, pig, toad, etc.) or wicked ghosts. Similarly, private *bis* were often given embarrassing names like "yellow dog" or "toilet."[9]

[9] Jung 2001, 15–16.

FIGURE 15.2 Young woman with a water jug wearing the Korean white traditional jacket (*jeogori*) that reveals her breasts. Japanese postcard, ca. 1900. Courtesy of Kwon Hyu-khee.

In the spiritual world of Buddhism, the official ideology of the Koryo dynasty, the chance of becoming a Buddha and attaining salvation was open to all, including the *nobi* class. According to tales included in the *Samguk Yusa* (*Memorabilia of the Three Kingdoms*), a temple *bi* was considered a *bodhisattva*, and a private *bi* called Yukmyon attained Buddhahood after having cultivated her religious senses and virtue. In the Chosun period the image of Buddha disappeared and with it the legal status of *nobis* declined. *Nobis* were equated with domesticated animals (cows, horses, and dogs), excretions, or farm tools,

FIGURE 15.3 Chosun *gisaengs* (courtesans) bathing in a river during the Dano festivals. The woman carrying a big bundle on her head and with an exposed breast was a *bi* (farthest to the right). Painted by Shin Yun-bok (1758–1813). Courtesy Kansong Museum, Seoul, Korea.

while their base names became typical symbols of their low birth. But it is not possible to find another indication of *nobis* or nobization, except their demeaning names.[10]

In cases of beating or violence between *yangmins* and *nobis*, the latter were in a considerably less favorable position. If a *yangmin* were beaten and left disabled or impossible to treat, his *nobi* assailant was to be hanged. In the event of the former's death, the *nobi* was decapitated. By contrast, when a *yangmin* beat a *nobi*, the punishment was mild. Interestingly, if the former was a close relative of the injured *nobi*'s master, no charges were pressed unless the victim's bones were broken.[11] The *nobi* system was thus weighted heavily in favor of *nobi* owners and even *yangmins*, while for *nobis* themselves it represented the bonds of oppression.

[10] Rhee 2006, 24–25.
[11] Kim Jong-sung 2013, 188–89.

All of this leads one to wonder why the eighty-year-old Damulsari took refuge at the government office in Youngam in July 1584 and proclaimed, "I am a *nobi*." Her father was a petty bureaucrat of Naju; therefore, Damulsari must have had *yangmin* status. She had been married to a private *no* named Yunpil. Such a mixed marriage between a *yangmin* and a *nobi* was not uncommon in this period. Indeed, Yunpil seems to have made a fortune despite his status as a nonresident *nobi*. According to a testimony of the *yangban* plaintiff Yi Ji-do and other recorded information, Yunpil was rich enough to have a big house and even a concubine. When Yi went to the house of Yunpil, he had been repudiated by Yunpil's own house *nobi* at the door. Yi's family, by contrast, had lost its wealth in his father's generation. Yunpil was thus richer than his master, but the fact remains that his offspring belonged to the latter. In cases of mixed marriage between a male *no* and a female *yangmin*, their offspring should belong to the male *no*'s master. In cases of intermarriage between *nobis*, their children belonged to the female *bi*'s master according to the matrilineal *nobi* law in force at the time.

THE MATRILINEAL SUCCESSION LAW OF THE LOWBORN CLASS

During the Chosun period, the multiplication of the *nobi* class to its high point of more than 30 percent of the total population was facilitated through the manipulation of regulations regarding the mixed marriage of *yangmins* and *nobis*. Some slaveholding societies proscribed marriage between slaves and free people or denied marriage to slaves altogether. The Koryo dynasty also prohibited mixed marriage between *yangmins* and *nobis*, a prohibition that was consistently observed until the late Koryo period. The early Chosun dynasty took even more extreme action by imposing divorce on mixed couples. However, in 1405, this traditional ban on mixed marriage was abandoned in the interests of the *yangban*. As the Chosun period progressed and the government gradually strengthened private property ownership, there was a steady increase in the demand for *nobi* laborers to cultivate land, the main source of tax revenues in the premodern period. For *nobi* owners, the legal sanctioning of *yangmin*/ *nobi* mixed marriages permitted a marked increase in the number of *nobis*.

As we see in what follows, many of them discouraged intermarriage between *nos* and *bis* while encouraging mixed unions. During the fifteenth and sixteenth centuries, the rates of mixed marriage increased to more than 50 percent, as attested in documents for the division of property in *yangban* families.[12] According to family registers, in the early seventeenth century such mixed marriages reached as high as 70 percent.[13] As a result, the number of *nobis*, who were exempt from duties of tax payment and military service, increased tremendously, while the number of *yangmins* fell sharply. This represented a great loss to the government's finances. During the late Chosun period, the number of *yangmins* further dwindled due to the lax enforcement of the social status system. As economic power came to be more highly valued than social status, mixed marriages rose, especially between wealthy *nos* and female *yangmins*.

In feudal Japan (1185–1868) instances of marriage between *genins* (low people) and free persons were not uncommon, but mixed marriage did not create a channel to multiply the number of *genins*. By contrast, in medieval Korea the principle of *deterior condicio* (*jong cheon bob*) established by the Koryo king Chungryol (1274–1308) in 1298, continued to be applied to Chosun society with the result that mixed marriages greatly swelled the number of *nobis*. By this principle, if either of the two parents was of low birth, the offspring would follow the status of the parent with the lower status. Chosun landowners could thus supplement their labor force by birth, that is, by managing the conjugal unions of their *bis* rather than by other forms of recruitment. The more children female *bis* had, the greater the benefit to *nobi* owners. Thus, most *nobi* owners wished their *bis* to have as many sexual relationships as possible, giving rise to the proverb "fornicating with a female *bi* is as easy as mounting a resting cow." The crassness of this saying reflects well the wretched condition of the *bi*, whose chastity was at risk from her master and from all other males. She was an available partner for all sorts of men and an open object of sexual pleasure (Figures 15.4–15.6).

In keeping with neo-Confucian moral teachings, the Chosun dynasty dealt harshly with those who committed sexual crimes. Under

[12] Kim Sung-woo 2001, 130–44.

[13] Han 1977, 177–97.

FIGURE 15.4 A young *bi* carrying a tray with wine and food dishes stops when she sees two pairs of shoes, male and female, on the floor in the back garden. Painted by Shin Yun-bok (1758–1813).
Courtesy Photo Gallery of National Museum of Korea.

the Ming code in force under the Chosun dynasty, the punishment for adultery was eighty lashes in cases of fornication, ninety for a married adulterer, and 100 in case of adultery after kidnapping. A person who committed rape was condemned to execution by hanging. Female *bis*, however, were considered outside the sphere of sexual honor. This is illustrated in a famous episode under the reign of King Taejong (1367–1422). The king's trusted sixty-year-old retainer and right-hand man Yi Suk-bun (1373–1440) attempted to rape a fifteen-year-old *bi*. Yi was seriously injured on the forehead with a knife wielded by the young *bi*. At the royal court, a great controversy arose over the level of punishment that should be meted out to her. Eventually the poor *bi* was acquitted on the grounds that she had acted in self-defense, but

FIGURE 15.5 "Nothing happened in a *gisaeng*'s house," an ironic title. After returning home, a *gisaeng* sees her boyfriend with her young *bi* covering their bodies with a thick blanket even on a hot summer day to hide their adultery. Painted by Shin Yun-bok (1758–1813).
Courtesy Kansong Museum, Seoul, Korea.

no further charges nor even criticisms were lodged against the (mis) behavior of her master, Yi.[14]

In general, Chosun *nobis* are said to have been more respectfully treated than Western slaves. For example, a third party could not infringe on the matrimonial relationship of a *nobi* couple. A *yangban* was even badly beaten for raping a married *bi*. This prohibition did not, however, apply to the masters, who had life-and-death authority over their own *nobis*. As far as masters were concerned, the chastity of a *bi* was not worth protecting. The aforementioned proverb signifies the arbitrary domination of masters over the sexuality of their *bis*.[15] It was an eccentric cultural landscape at the end of the fifteenth century

[14] Jung 2001, 37.
[15] Rhee 2000, 102–04.

FIGURE 15.6 "A boy picking a red flower." The red flower means a *bi* in straw shoes being seduced by her *yangban* playboy master with a long tobacco pipe in his left hand, inside the spring garden. Painted by Shin Yun-bok (1758–1813).
Courtesy Kansong Museum, Seoul, Korea.

where a master could toy with his *bis* with the tacit approval of his legitimate wife. The Chosun dynasty claimed to support monogamy, but in fact the system tolerated polygamy for men while enforcing monogamy for those women who belonged within the circle of honor. By contrast, the distinction between wives and concubines was strictly enforced to protect legitimate marriages arranged by respectable *yangban* families. According to an old proverb, "men are heaven, women are earth," a clear reflection of the non-egalitarian Confucian worldview. Men were considered the generating force behind all things in the universe while women were their earthbound inferiors.

In principle, the dominant–subordinate relationship between masters and *nobis* was "private," but the Chosun dynasty gave it official recognition in accordance with political need. In China and Korea, it was believed that both *nubis* and *nobis* originated as criminals.

The oldest document on Korean *nobis* was the "Penal Code of Eight Provisions" attributed to the mythical Chinese sage-hero Kija. By its account, thieves were to become the *nobis* of the families they had robbed. They were not only considered the descendants of criminals, but also the public property of the government hierarchy. After the fifteenth century they became private property. For this reason, the clause on *nobis* in *Gyeongguk daejeon* (a comprehensive law code) was not to be found in the civil, but in the penal code. Whether *nobis* were in fact originally the descendants of criminals is doubtful, but this narrative played a major role in justifying the hereditary system of *nobis* and their cruel treatment.

During the Chosun period, the relationship between masters and *nobis* was often compared to that between parents and children. The analogy was used to domesticate the *nobi* population and bring it under the umbrella of the guiding principles of Confucianism, the so-called Three Bonds (ruler–minister, parent–child, and husband–wife) and Five Relationships (ruler to ruled, father to son, husband to wife, elder brother to younger brother, and friend to friend). If a son sued his father, he was to be sentenced to 100 lashes and three years of prison labor. By extension, if a *nobi* proceeded against his master, he would be sentenced to death by hanging.[16]

According to historical documents, the law only intervened in the relationship between masters and *nobis* in instances where the former killed the latter. By contrast, a *nobi* was permitted to bring legal action against his master only in cases where the master rose up in revolt against the state. As in the case mentioned earlier in which Yi Suk-bun attempted to rape his *bi*, a master was not brought to justice for exploiting his own private property. Not only could the master enjoy the sexuality of his *bi*, regardless of her marital status, he could also force her not to sleep with her husband. However, lowborn *bis* were not generally attractive sexual partners for male *yangbans* – especially in comparison with *gisaengs*, who were accomplished in feminine arts and able to communicate in sophisticated poetry and prose. *Bis* were, however, relatively easy to take as concubines. For this reason, instances of sexual relations between masters and *bis* are commonplace in the *Gogum Sochong* (*Collection of Old and New Chosun Peculiar*

[16] Kim Jong-sung 2013, 171.

Stories). As a result, many *nobis* never knew with certainty the names of their fathers.[17] We can assume many were illegitimate children born of adulterous relationships with their masters. Such children would have been *nobis*, regardless of their fathers' status.

In *yangban* relationships of concubinage, the birth status of children varied according to the condition of the mother. A *yangban*'s children by a *yangmin* concubine should live as *yangmin* bastards. The children of a *yangban* and *bi* could become *yangmins* but only by emancipation from their father's authority. Yu Hee-chun (1513–77), the author of the *Miam Diary* (1566–77), had a number of children by an unofficial concubine of *nobi* origin over a period of eight years. When he emancipated all of them, he is said to have exclaimed, "I'm so glad to liberate my four daughters born of a mean concubine!"[18]

Sexual unions between masters and *bis* were common, but only a *bi* who gave birth to a child would be raised to the status of concubine. There were impediments to the establishment of official concubinage between a *bi* and a *yangban*. This was less the case in relationships with one's own *bi*, although problems remained for the offspring of such unions, whose lives were burdened with stringent social restrictions and a relationship of subordination to any siblings by a lawful wife. In the case of a *bi* of another master, the situation was much more complicated because the *bi* had to be acquired by the male *yangban* before she could be emancipated into *yangmin* status and made a concubine. Often a pregnant *bi*'s master would refuse to sell her or would set an exorbitant price. For example, the cousin of Yu Hee-chun raped another man's *bi* then eagerly wanted to make her his concubine. In the end, he gave up because the *bi*'s master demanded too high a price. Indeed, a concubine, once taken, was no longer just a sex object but became a family member that needed to be fed and taken care of. In *Eou's Unofficial Histories*, Gang Soo-gu said, "my best wish is to have a beautiful concubine whom I do not need to feed or clothe."[19] Concubinage was thus an expensive game for *yangbans*.

For a period, a "patrilineal *nobi* law" under which lowborn children followed their fathers' status reversed the earlier principle whereby the children of mixed marriages followed the status of the mothers.

[17] Jung 2001, 37–38.
[18] Yu 1936, 230.
[19] Lee 2007, 12.

King Taejong introduced this provision in the fourteenth year of his reign (1414) in order to increase the number of *yangmins* and thus increase the number of citizens liable for taxes and state labor/military service. As a result, the number of public *nobis* decreased, but greedy masters of private *nobis* simply ordered their male *nos* to violate female *yangmins* and thereby increase their wealth. As can be imagined, this patrilineal law also caused enormous trouble in the propagation of *yangban* private property even as it led to the debasement or "yangminization" of the lowest people. All of this meant that it was soon replaced with the old matrilineal law. Its introduction nevertheless shows how laws were manipulated in order to regulate the number of *nobis*: the patrilineal law was used in an effort to decrease the number of *nobis* and the matrilineal law to increase it. The patrilineal law is often called a "special law" because of its brief period of enforcement. It was not profitable for the state to increase indefinitely the number of nontaxable *nobis*, but it was not easy for the state to abolish the *nobi* system itself under the Chosun hierarchy. In fact, the state had its own interest in maintaining the system, for it was the greatest proprietor of (public) *nobis*.

THE LAWSUIT OF DAMULSARI

With this background in mind, we return to the case of Damulsari, who brazenly asserted her status as a *nobi* before the district court of Naju in 1585 (Figure 15.7). As stated earlier, her husband was a private *nobi* belonging to the father of the plaintiff, Yi Ji-do. Yi Ji-do thus rightly insisted that Yunpil's children should be owned by his family. To counter this, Damulsari maintained that she was the daughter of a public *bi* named Gilduk. According to the matrilineal law in force at the time, in the case of two parents of low birth, children were to follow the status of their mother, which would have meant that Damulsari's children were public *nobis*. But Damulsari was lying about her true status in order to make her offspring public *nobis*, which would have allowed them to live in a better condition than private ones.[20] Some of these differences can be summarized schematically (see Table 15.1).

[20] According to *Sungho-sasul* (*Miscellany of Sungho*, 1740) of Yi Ik (1681–1763), the labor service of private *nobis* was heavier than that of public *nobis*. No one was more miserable than a private *nobi* in Chosun; J. Kim 2013, 79–81.

FIGURE 15.7 The process of trial at the government office. Published at 韩国写真帖 [Korean Photos], by the Japanese Government General of Korea, 1910, freely available at http://dl.ndl.go.jp/info:ndljp/pid/766841.

Sometimes poor *yangmins* also sold themselves to powerful *yangban* families as *nobis* because they wanted to lean on rich or influential men to save themselves from starving to death in times of famine. This voluntary self-sale (or self-nobization) was called *tutak* and was strictly prohibited by law in the Chosun period. Nevertheless, from the *yangban*'s point of view, it was an easy means to gain wealth and labor services, which explains why it continued despite its prohibition. It certainly did not permit *yangmins* to choose freely between *yangmin* and *nobi* status or to maximize their own class interests.

At the time of the trial, Damulsari was an eighty-year-old woman. Why at this age did she take the risk of committing herself to the status of a public *bi*? In a lawsuit disputing status, it was normal for the accused to claim, "I am not a *nobi*!" Why did she dare to fight against the lawsuit of Yi Ji-do by essentially committing herself to *nobi* status through *tutak*?

TABLE 15.1 Public and Private *Nobis*

Public *nobis*[a]	Labor and/or military service *nobis*	Engaged in miscellaneous work in the central government or local government office; received a salary
	Nonresident or tribute-paying *nobis*	Lived in the province; engaged in farming; paid a certain amount of tax to the government office
Private *nobis*	Resident *nobis*	Under the direct control of nobles or temples
	Nonresident *nobis*	Engaged in agriculture while living far from their master; engaged in trades like butchering; could lead an independent economic life; could improve their social status through meritorious service in war or the *napsok* system[b]

[a] They could receive a labor service exemption at sixty.

[b] The *napsok* system was one of the financial policies of the government. In this system, the government gave an official post to anyone who offered any sort of goods in times of war and famine as a reward in proportion to the volume of his offering. If he was a *nobi*, the government permitted him to be emancipated from his low status or to be exempted from public labor service. This system was not enforced continuously but only occasionally, when need arose.

Behind the whole affair was the husband of her only daughter, Ini, a man named Guji. Guji and Ini had six children who should by rights have been private *nobis* under the direct control of Ini's master, Yi Ji-do. Like Damulsari's husband, Yunpil, however, Guji was rich and powerful in his hometown. Thus, Guji was attempting to give his children by Ini an advantage by making them public *nobis* using his fortune and personal relations. In connivance with another public *no* (an employee of the Youngam government office), Guji found records of a now deceased public *bi* named Gilduk, who had no living friends or family recorded in documents. He falsely reported to the Youngam government office that Damulsari was Gilduk's daughter, which would have made her a public *bi*. For masters of private *nobis*, it was not easy to win a suit against the government. In such cases, the government played the roles of both judge and defendant, so the verdict would be predictably one-sided. In this sort of case, most masters would not have proceeded, but Yi Ji-do was desperate. Under these circumstances, with his family's fortune on the wane and his pride injured through the mockery of his *nobis*, Yi Ji-do pressed his suit.

After surrendering herself to the Youngam government office as a public *bi*, Damulsari offered tribute to the government office and

FIGURE 15.8 Rice threshing. A man lying idly supervises farm tenants. Painted by Kim Hong-do (1745–ca. 1810).
Courtesy Photo Gallery of National Museum of Korea.

refused to pay tribute and labor service to Yi's family. When Yi Ji-do came to collect her overdue tribute payment, he was threatened at the door by her stick-wielding son-in-law, Guji. It was this that provoked Yi Ji-do to bring a civil suit against Damulsari at the Youngam government office. Because, however, the conspiracy had been hatched in Youngam, he secretly requested a change of venue. The court transferred the case to Naju, where the governor, Kim Sung-il (1538–93), was renowned for his ability to detect forged documents and artful intrigues. Kim launched a new investigation of the case in which the following assertions were made.

The Case of Yi Ji-do

The private *no* Jusan was the *nobi* of my father Yi Yu-kyum. Yunpil is the son of Jusan (private *no*). He married Damulsari, the daughter of Yi sun (*yangmin*). Damulsari gave birth to a daughter called Ini. Ini was married to Guji (private *no*) living in Youngam. Ini has six children. She paid tribute and labor service to my family, but then began refusing to pay in 1584. Thus, I ordered an old private *no* to arrest her, but Guji beat him with a wooden stick and kicked him out. Furthermore, in connivance with a public *no* of the Youngam government office, Guji tempted Damulsari to declare herself to have been the daughter of the now deceased Gilduk, and to enroll herself as a public *bi* in the register of the Youngam government office. My father was wrongly charged for murder ten years ago, and now he is on the run. I am a young student of Confucianism. My mother, Mrs. Suh, is a weak married woman. I am outraged that Damulsari and Guji hatched a plot to take advantage of my family's plight. Damulsari described herself as a public *bi*, but she surrendered herself to the government office only after several years. Everyone knows that she was born in Naju, so she was lying when she claimed that she was born in Youngam.

The Case of Damulsari

My father Jongsan died when I was young, so I scarcely knew his name. At thirteen, I was married in Naju to Yunpil, now deceased, but I do not remember the date of his death. After a hard life, I was able to live in the house of my son-in-law Guji. In the meantime, the Youngam government office enrolled my name as a public *bi* and collected the tribute of my grandchildren (Bongwha, Bongse, Inhwa, Bonsun, Bongik, and Bongi). My late husband Yunpil was the *nobi* of Yi Yu-kyum (Yi Ji-do's father). After realizing that my daughter Ini has many children, Yi's family deliberately registered me on their family register

TABLE 15.2 The Family Tree According to the Persons Directly Involved

Assertions of the plaintiff Yi Ji-do	Assertions of the accused Damulsari
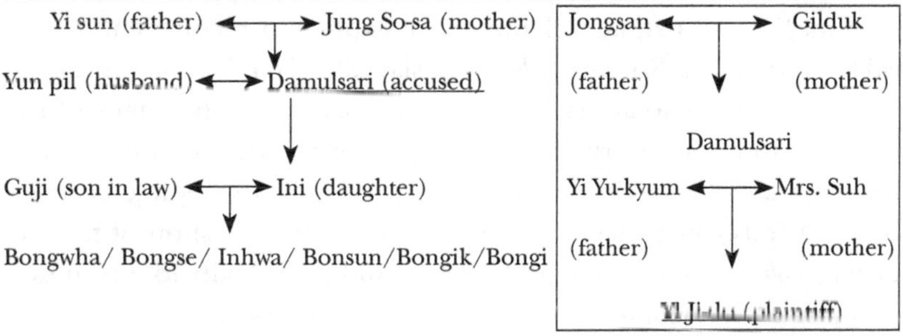 Yi sun (father) ↔ Jung So-sa (mother)	Jongsan (father) ↔ Gilduk (mother)
↓	↓
Yun pil (husband) ↔ Damulsari (accused)	Damulsari
↓	
Guji (son in law) ↔ Ini (daughter)	Yi Yu-kyum (father) ↔ Mrs. Suh (mother)
↓	↓
Bongwha/ Bongse/ Inhwa/ Bonsun/Bongik/Bongi	Yi Ji-do (plaintiff)

as a *yangmin*, but my mother Gilduk was a public *bi*. The truth will be revealed if you investigate the register of *nobis* in the Youngam government office. I am not of the Chosun people (*yangmin*) but am a public *bi*![21] (see Table 15.2).

In the course of the lawsuit, Yi Ji-do astutely revealed that Damulsari was inconsistent in her testimony, while Damulsari appeared in court only reluctantly after refusing to answer several summons and even when she came repeatedly replied, “I do not know because I lost my parents so early in life,” or “I have never heard of this.” On April 19, 1586, the verdict of the Naju governor, Kim Sung-il, was at last issued:

> First, the name of Gilduk’s father was Jongsan; Jongsan would therefore have been Damulsari’s grandfather. Nonetheless, Damulsari insisted that Jongsan was her father, but she claimed she did not know the name of her grandfather. It does not make sense even for an ignorant *bi* not to know her grandfather’s name. Second, Damulsari maintained that she was registered as a public *bi* on the Youngam government’s civil register, but this registration was forged and had no government authentication. At the moment of her *tutak* to the Youngam government office, she stated that her mother Gilduk died when she was 5 years old, but Gilduk died in 1536, and Damulsari was born in 1507. Thus, her statement does not agree with the facts … For all the above reasons, there is no way that Damulsari is Gilduk’s daughter. She betrayed her master and surrendered herself as a public *bi*. She deserves a flogging, but she is more than seventy years old. Therefore, I will exempt her from punishment, but I will give her daughter Ini and her six grandchildren to Yi Ji-do and his mother Mrs. Suh.[22]

[21] Lim 2007, 7–8.
[22] Lim 2007, 183–86.

NOBIS IN A BROADER PERSPECTIVE

Having examined the case of Damulsari, it is time to turn to two broader issues concerning the history of this oppressed class in Chosun Korea. First, we will attempt to explain or reconcile the dualistic character of Korean *nobis*: half-slave/half-serf? Economically, a *nobi* seems closer to a serf; institutionally, *nobi* status fits many of the characteristics of slavery; and socially, a *nobi* is closer to a peasant of lower status. This section of the chapter attempts to mediate between these various categories. Second, we turn to the question of tribute-paying *nobis* in an effort to add nuance and complexity to our understanding of the characteristics of the Korean *nobi* system.

Half-Slave/Half-Serf

The identity of Chosun *nobis* is often viewed as a mixture of half-man, half-thing. Physiologically the *nobi* was obviously a human being, but his body itself was owned by another person. During the fifteenth and sixteenth centuries, the *nobis* became private property, but it is not reasonable to call them "chattel slaves" *en bloc.* As stated earlier, the ban on the mixed marriage of *yangmins* with *nobis* (the greatest channel of *nobi* reproduction) was lifted, which allowed between one-third and one-half of the aggregate population to become *nobis.* Patterson called Chosun Korea "a large-scale slave system outside the mainstream history of slavery."[23] Given that *nobis* comprised about 30 to 40 percent of the population, the question arises whether it is in fact right to call Chosun Korea a "genuine Slave Society."

According to Korean scholars, the demographic statistics in the *Annals of the Chosun Dynasty* are not entirely reliable. First, there was no institutional method for taking a census with the level of accuracy possible today. The Chosun census data were based on the family register, which the government drew up every three years on the basis of a collection of reports submitted by each householder to the government office. The possible range of error in this self-reporting system was plus or minus 30–35 percent. Second, the family register gave priority to taxable individuals. Thus, only sixteen- to sixty-year-old men were included, while children, men over sixty years old, women,

[23] Patterson 1982, 2.

and *nobis* were regularly excluded. Third, it was likely that some individuals were deliberately omitted in the register for the purpose of tax evasion. Using data aggregated from Ulsan in the southeast of the country, Rhee Young-hoon has analyzed various census data for each period, from the village documents of 695 CE to family registers that reach as late as 1867. According to his data, the *nobis* comprised merely 5 to 6 percent of the population of this region, at least before the advent of the Chosun dynasty. This numerical figure obviously falls far short of the threshold for a "Slave Society."[24]

Numbers aside, the question remains whether *nobis* can truly be considered slaves. The main reason that Western scholars consider Chosun *nobis* slaves is that they were the object of purchase, sale, donation, and inheritance. The League of Nations Charter definition of a slave is as follows: "the status or condition of a person over whom any or all the powers attaching to the right of ownership are exercised." With such a simple definition, it is almost impossible to explain all different forms of human bondage in world history. For example, how does it account for very rich slaves or people who are sold and purchased without legally being considered a slave? Difficulties arise in the instance of Chosun *nobis* because, despite their salability, their market function was only rarely activated. Thus for example, only 10 out of about 9,000 *nobis* were traded in the Dansung family register (0.1 percent) during the eighteenth century, and the percentage of donated *nobis* was even lower.[25] Since the late eighteenth century, the *nobi* markets also shifted structurally from a primary concern with hereditary *nobis* to a much stronger concern with *yangmins* who sold themselves as *nobis*. Moreover, in the late Chosun period, several anti-*nobi* policies, enforced by the state to strengthen royal authority, made it easier for *nobis* to free themselves through flight or marriage with *yangmins*. All these phenomena led to a marked decrease in commercial transactions involving *nobis*.

Nobody denies that *nobis* were the object of property rights. Their price was publicly announced by the state, just as today the National Tax Service fixes official land values. The declared value of *nobis* was not appraised for taxation but as a basis for adjustment if disputes

[24] Rhee 2007, 144–59.

[25] The Dansung family register for 1678–1780 was published in two volumes by the Academy of Korean Studies in 1980.

arose by the concealment of *nobis* or their flight. The legal price of *nobis* – based on their expected lifetime labor capacity – was cheaper than that of horses and oxen. As human rights conditions improved for *nobis* during the late Chosun period, their real prices seem to have fallen. The legal price of *nobis* corresponded to sixty to eighty straw bags of rice, but they were actually traded at a cheaper price, with wide variations: younger, healthier, and more beautiful *nobis* were, unsurprisingly, more expensive. Why was the legal price of *nobis* higher than their real market price? It was apparently due to the Chosun government's efforts to restrict the trade in *nobis* and "keep them in one place," so that they could be more profitable to the state's agrarian economy. From the first half of the eighteenth century into the second half of the nineteenth, *nobis* were sold at two to twenty-seven straw bags of rice. Just before the abolition of the *nobi* system in 1894, they sold at only two straw bags of rice.[26] The primary reason for this drastic decline in prices and for the dissolution of the *nobi* system altogether was the rise of *gogong* hired laborers, who gradually supplanted the *nobis* beginning in the seventeenth century.

The hard-luck story of Damulsari and Guji reflects well the cruelty of the Chosun hereditary *nobi* system. Thirty to forty percent of Chosun people were *nobis.* They were locked in relationships of dependence with their *yangban* overlords, who tended to be reluctant to rent their holdings to *yangmin* tenants. The Chosun ruling class considered the heaven–earth-like relationship of master and *nobi* fundamental to the stability of society. After the Japanese invasion of Korea in 1592 and the Manchu War of 1636, dissent against the *yangban* was rampant, and secret organizations were formed in protest. However, society was so overdetermined by the mighty weight of social reality that restive *nobis* chose flight rather than revolt. In fact, the problem of *nobi* flight predated this period of political unrest. Han Myeong-hoe (1415–87), a Korean politician and soldier, remarked in 1484 that roughly 100,000 out of the total number of public *nobis* (450,000) were on the run, and he estimated the total number of runaway *nobis* (public and private) at one million.[27] In the early Chosun

[26] Kim Jong-sung 2013, 128.
[27] Rhee 1998, 365.

period, runaway *nobis* had few places to flee, but in the late Chosun period, due to changing socioeconomic conditions they could make their way to islands, mining towns, farms, ranches, commercial cities, or the remote northwest region. They were able to find jobs as hired laborers or in commerce in order to earn a living. They pretended to be *yangmin* or descendants of ruined *yangban* families if they had economic success.

In general, the flight of *nobis* was a passive form of resistance, but the loss of "two-legged property" created major difficulties for the *yangban*. Thus, the masters began looking for substitutes for their *nobi* laborers. That is why the hired labor system (*gogong*) came to prominence. After recognizing the difficulty of keeping people as slaves for their lifetime, the masters turned to laborers they could hire and fire at any time. The rise of *gogong* labor was thus a matter of convenience for both parties. From the point of view of *nobis*, the switch to hired labor allowed them to break away from the yoke of their hereditary bondage. For fugitive *nobis* in particular, this was the only way to make a living in a place far from home. It was also easier for masters to deal with occasional laborers than *nobis* watching for an opportunity to flee. Thus as the *gogong* system came to prevail, the *nobi* system faded until it was officially abolished in 1894. In effect, however, by this point the old institution was little more than an empty shell.[28]

Tribute-Paying *Nobis*

As to the question of tribute-paying *nobis*, in the thirteenth and fourteenth centuries, most *nobis* were publicly owned, but in the Chosun period, the ratio of private *nobis* became preponderant. Along with the large-scale privatization of *nobi* ownership, structural changes occurred in the modes of exploitation of *nobi* labor. A new form of tribute-paying *nobis* arose that paid a fixed annual tribute to their master while living separately as independent small farmers. The *nobis*' property rights were guaranteed by law, so it was illegal for even high-ranking *yangban* masters to take away their nonresident *nobis*' property arbitrarily. While it was difficult for resident *nobis* living under the

[28] Kim Jong-sung 2013, 266–67.

same roof with their masters to accumulate a fortune, nonresident *nobis* were in a more favorable position to accumulate wealth, as the case of Damulsari's husband, Yunpil, confirms. They amassed wealth through hard work, collected the tribute of other *nobis*, engaged in long-distance trade as their masters' proxy, etc.

To avoid heavy state taxes, many Koryo *yangmins* had surrendered themselves (through *tutak*) to temples as *nobis* and were required to pay tribute to the temple to which they were attached. During the early Chosun period in the early fifteenth century, such tribute-paying *nobis* were also used as public *nobis* and were distributed among the royal family and meritorious subjects who contributed to the foundation of the dynasty. This is the historical origin of Chosun tribute-paying *nobis*. For *nobi* masters in the fifteenth and sixteenth centuries, when the *nobi* system reached its zenith, there was no limitation on the ownership of *nobis*. A *yangban* could own hundreds or thousands of *nobis*, as Hamel described in his journal on the Hermit Kingdom. This was possible because of the existence of a large number of tribute-paying *nobis*, to whom the masters did not need to distribute land and whose labor they did not need to mobilize. Their management costs were thus negligible. Tribute-paying *nobis* did have to be registered on the official family register, and, like *yangmins*, they were burdened with public taxes (land tax, labor service, and tribute). They were exempt only from military service. For this reason, they were required to offer tribute to their masters. We can observe their existence already in historical documents of the late fourteenth century.

Because tribute-paying *nobis* were former *yangmins*, there were fewer constraints on their intermarriage with *yangmins*. The extensive deployment of these half-public and half-private tribute-paying *nobis* motivated the Chosun dynasty to relax the ban on mixed marriages between *yangmins* and *nobis* formerly upheld by the Koryo dynasty. The proportion of tribute-paying *nobis* in the fifteenth and sixteenth centuries was almost half of the total *nobi* population. There was thus a gulf between resident *nobis* and nonresident *nobis* that must be taken into account in any attempt to understand the Chosun system of bound labor. In fact, there was little clear differentiation between *yangmins* and tribute-paying *nobis*, except the payment of tribute collected by the master or his proxy. Since the 1990s, Korean scholars have begun a more systematic study of tribute-paying *nobis* in the documents for the division of *yangban* family property that should now play a more important role in Western scholarship.[29]

On the other hand, it is interesting to note the mutual relationship between the *kye* master and *nobis*, as an example of cooperation, if not a social integration, between two classes. The *kye* is a kind of traditional private fund popular among Koreans, whose members contribute a modest amount of money and take turns receiving a lump-sum share. The *yangban* Yi Hee-sung formed the *kye* in partnership with his ten *nobis* in 1801, at the moment of the abolition of public *nobis* by the state. Both parties went half and half in the funding of four straw bags of rice. The purpose of this cooperative *kye* was to protect both the *yangban* and the *nobi* classes. In the mid-eighteenth century, some impoverished *yangbans* could not feed, lodge, and clothe their *nobis*, so they really needed to cooperate with the latter. This relationship reflected well the change of social status system and socioeconomic circumstances in the late eighteenth century.[30] The social dissolution is represented in Chart 15.1. The number of *yangban* increased to 70 percent, while that of *nobis* decreased to 5 percent.

From the point of view of socioeconomic history, the character of *nobis* could be differentiated according to their modes of existence. However, all kinds of *nobis* under the Chosun legal system were uniformly treated without distinction and enjoyed the same status with the exception of the official division of public and private *nobis*. They had the right to litigate and enter into a lawsuit by proxy for their masters. To be sure, this was an active and articulated legal system. For reference, King Taejong ordered the installation of a large drum called a *sinmungo* in front of the royal palaces in Seoul for anyone involved in unjust situations to make a direct appeal to the royal court. However, when there were too many *nobi*-related petitions, the king prohibited ringing a *sinmungo* in cases involving *nobis*.

CONCLUSION

The saga of Damulsari shows the difficulty of considering *nobis* socially dead. Her willingness to declare herself falsely a public *nobi*

[29] Rhee 2006, 8–10.
[30] Yong-man Kim 1996, 329–30.

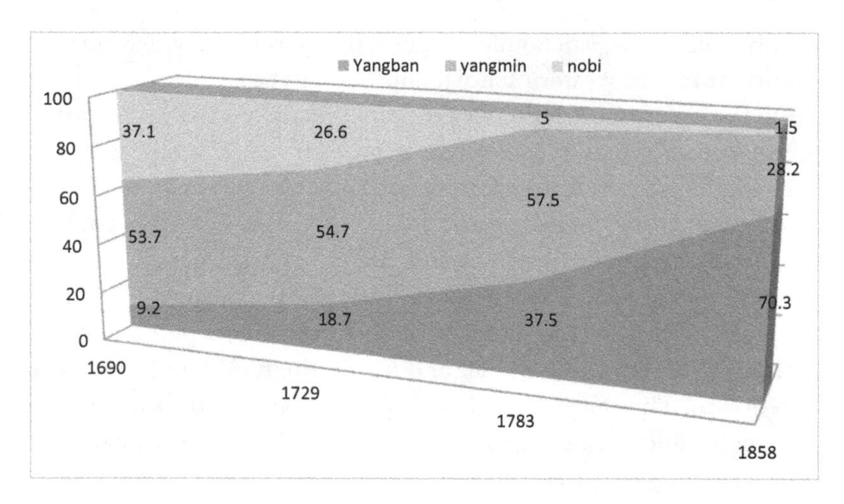

CHART 15.1 The Dissolution of Social Class, based on Shikata Hiroshi *Research on the Chosun Economy 3* (1938).

demonstrates that the title was not in itself considered abominable. As we have seen, *nobis* came in a variety of forms that fit into the social hierarchy ranging from public to private and nonresident to resident. Only the last of these – private, resident *nobis* – experienced particularly high levels of repression. Apparently for this reason, there was no great rebellion of *nobis* in the late Chosun period, even if a considerable number of *nobis* attempted to escape from the domination of their masters through flight. As Damulsari's case proves, however, *nobis* claimed some agency in efforts to improve their status, and they did so through the manipulation of the hierarchies just described by attempting to improve their standard of living through hard work as tribute-paying *nobis*, through the donation of personal property to their master, through the *napsok* system, through flight, and even through litigation and the fabrication of forged pedigrees. The lawsuit of Damulsari failed, but it helps show the complications of a system that was far from monolithic. Even though the state and the *yangban* clung to the status quo, the situation shifted as its complications led it to falter in the wake of increasing commercialization and the social and economic impoverishment of the *yangban* class in the nineteenth century. Even so Chosun *nobis* themselves helped perpetuate the system by continuing to operate within its institutional framework. As a result, vestiges of the hereditary *nobi* system, officially abolished in

1894, survived until the Korean War of 1950–53, especially with the support of the Japanese occupation.

Contemporary Koreans no longer remember that their ancestors might have been of the *nobi* class in the past. Little more than a century earlier, however, the life of a *nobi* was commonplace in this *Gemeinschaft* society. In the lawsuit of Damulsari, the fundamental cause of the legal and social conflicts was the *nobi* system itself as it remained an essential tool underlying *yangban* economic and cultural hegemony. Thus, searching for the historical underpinnings of the *nobi* system through cases like that of Damulsari should constitute a new mission for Korean historians in their efforts to recover the life of past people and share sympathy with this repressed class.

Modern economic history has been based on European models; therefore, its methodology and epistemology are inevitably Eurocentric. Many Asian scholars regard slaves in ancient Greece and Rome and serfs in medieval Europe as archetypes or paradigms of social unfreedom in their research on premodern bonded labor. Yet Western models are best not taken as universal. The variety of forms of servitude can better be understood as spectra formed by rays of light passing through a prism. This is well illustrated in the enigmatic case of Damulsari, who wanted to be a *nobi*. Her case can be taken as indicative on a microhistorical level of a broader historical truth: it is risky to neglect the diversity of global systems of servitude by attempting to lump them together under a single concept of unfreedom. In the case of *nobis*, it is not a simple matter of choosing whether they were slaves or serfs. If European slaves and serfs are to be taken as normative, *nobis* showed characteristics of both and neither and should therefore be investigated in studies of unfreedom on their own terms.

16

"Slavery so Gentle": A Fluid Spectrum of Southeast Asian Conditions of Bondage

Anthony Reid

The dual character of the slave as property and yet a person, a trusted intimate[1] and yet demeaned, makes for endless ambiguity. It also confers on slavery a peculiar importance for the historian, for it was the slave's character as property that produced the documentation that has allowed an important section of the otherwise mute underclass to emerge as individuals with voice, feelings, and agency. Despite the slippery ambivalences of the terms for slave, bondsman, serf, and servant in the countless vernaculars of the world, collectively they render one of the most critical transcultural concepts. Yoruba ideas of slavery may have differed from those of Virginia in the early nineteenth century, just as those of Balinese or Torajan society differed from Dutch-ruled Batavia (Jakarta), but many individuals experienced in their own lives the transition from one of these cultures to another. In analyzing one of the most important means by which people were torn from one society and thrown into another, we cannot retreat into a refusal to make comparisons or draw wider conclusions.

The question of a "Slave Society" raises the issue, however, of the level of that comparison. Moses Finley, like many other Marx-influenced scholars of the period, sought a broad category of social evolution, which might be imported from European history to apply to stages of evolution elsewhere. In the 1950s and 1960s there was

[1] Compare the dichotomy between the trusted slave/servant with the mere hireling in the biblical Old Testament and in John 10:13.

considerable interest in India and China (though much less in Southeast Asia) in locating in their histories a "slave mode of production," which must necessarily precede a "feudal mode." Such broad-brush, one-size-fits-all categorizations fell decidedly out of fashion among global historians of more recent times. The more we know about non-Western societies, the more absurd it appears to fit them into a Western-derived mold. The distinction remains significant between near-universal domestic or patriarchal slavery and the much rarer "industrial slavery," which made possible large-scale production systems that could not have been achieved by individual independent producers. There are cases in Asia, as we see in this chapter, where factory-like production, large-scale public works, and the opening of agricultural frontiers were made possible for brief periods by a kind of slavery. But these apply in specific times, places, and conditions, each illustrating the dependence of different systems on different conditions.

A book like the present enterprise, where the center of gravity is outside Europe, should indeed encourage a similar approach to the old issues of slavery in the ancient world. The Roman Empire may indeed have had commonalities of legal and military administration even amidst the great cultural diversity it embraced. But it is difficult to see that Greek city-states should all be categorized in the same way as regards systems of production.

Southeast Asia alone offers a very wide spectrum of types of slavery. In terms of harshness, there were a number of societies in Borneo, Sulawesi, and elsewhere where slaves were routinely sacrificed at the funerals of their masters or for some other key ritual, even into the nineteenth century. Yet it was the mildness of Southeast Asian slavery that first entered the Western literature through Montesquieu, arguing that this might be a feature of despotic situations.[2] As La Loubère put it of the Siamese capital in the 1680s, "tho' some may report that slaves are severely beaten there (which is very probable in a country where free persons are so rigidly bastinado'd) yet the slavery there is so gentle, or, if you will, the Liberty is so abject, that it is become a Proverb, that the Siamese sell it to eat of a … Durian."[3]

[2] Montesquieu 1949, 239.
[3] Loubère 1691[1969], 77.

Rather than harsh or mild, I have found it more helpful to use James Watson's distinction among African cultures, between "closed" systems, in which slaves were seen as forever kinless, despised outsiders, and "open" ones that incorporated outsiders into the dominant group within two or three generations. The former were characteristic of relatively static wet-rice-growing societies, often in the highlands, where emphasizing the distinctive apartness of slaves was a means to preserve their labor as essential to production. Open societies were, however, more dominant in expansive cities in the "age of commerce" (sixteenth–seventeenth centuries) and as an ongoing (through the nineteenth century) strategy used by stronger lowland polities to incorporate labor and population from stateless highland societies.[4]

Another source of diversity was the extent to which slavery was legally enforced by an overarching authority. Stateless societies were particularly widespread in upland Southeast Asia, where slavery was enforced only by custom and oral tradition within localized groups. The possibility of escaping to the forest or to another community provided the most effective check on brutality. At the other extreme were the stronger river-valley states of Burma and Siam, where a substantial proportion of the population was obliged to labor as state slaves, some having this legal status tattooed on their person. The most highly developed legal enforcement occurred in the multiethnic port cities, where slavery was regulated either by Islamic *sharīʿa* law or by the well-documented courts of the Dutch-ruled enclaves.

To clarify my use of terms at the outset, I believe a pattern of obligation to labor without wages for a patron, lord, creditor, or king was very widespread in Southeast Asia, as in much of the less densely populated preindustrial world. I will call this broad pattern "bondage." "Slavery" proper certainly existed within that broad category, though we should not accept at face value every use of the term either in European or Asian language sources. Many of those terms, such as *hamba*, *ata*, or *kawula* in the Malay world, could be rendered as "slave," "subject," "serf," "vassal," "bondsman," "dependent," or "servant," depending on context. I will limit the term "slave" to a person held to be saleable property, of low social status, and obliged to perform labor and other

4 Reid 1983b, 156–58.

services for a superior without payment. This chapter focuses primarily on the "Malay world" of the Peninsula and Archipelago, which offers the best documentation of any of these societies and is of itself extremely diverse.

PATTERN OF DEBT AND OBLIGATION

Early modern Southeast Asia was surprisingly underpopulated, in comparison with Northeast or South Asia or Europe at the time, despite its favorably warm, humid climate. There were no more than twenty-five million people in Southeast Asia around 1600, with population density only one-sixth that in China, Japan, or India.[5] Population was dispersed; state power was ephemeral, personalistic, and derived from sacred charisma rather than law. Control of people was everywhere the key to power. Landownership was ill defined and capital could be secured only if one had manpower to defend it. Wars were fought to acquire manpower rather than land (see Map 16.1).

The social system was based less on tying peasants to land, as in feudalism, than on binding people to their masters or patrons. Many outsiders shared the view of a Persian visitor in the 1680s, that "in 'Below the Winds' [Southeast Asia], the natives reckon high rank and wealth by the quantity of slaves a person owns."[6] Speaking of the pre-Spanish Philippines, De Morga similarly insisted that "These slaves constitute the main capital and wealth of the natives of these islands, since they are both very useful and necessary for the working of their farms. Thus they are sold, exchanged and traded, just like any article of merchandise."[7] A feature of Southeast Asia by comparison with other parts of Eurasia was the relative shortage of capital and the lack of security for it. Manpower was necessary to protect what capital one had, making wealth in people and goods interdependent.

The sources of slavery might be dichotomized in terms of debt and warfare, both seen as rooted in the forfeiture of the life of the enslaved. Judicial punishment can be seen as a variation on debt, since unpaid monetary fines would lead to enslavement. As the Batak saying had it, "Whoever has a debt pays; if he can make no payment it

[5] Reid 1988–93, 1:13–15.
[6] O'Kane [Ibn Muhammad Ibrahim 1688[1972], 177. See also Reid 1983b.
[7] Morga 1609[1971], 274.

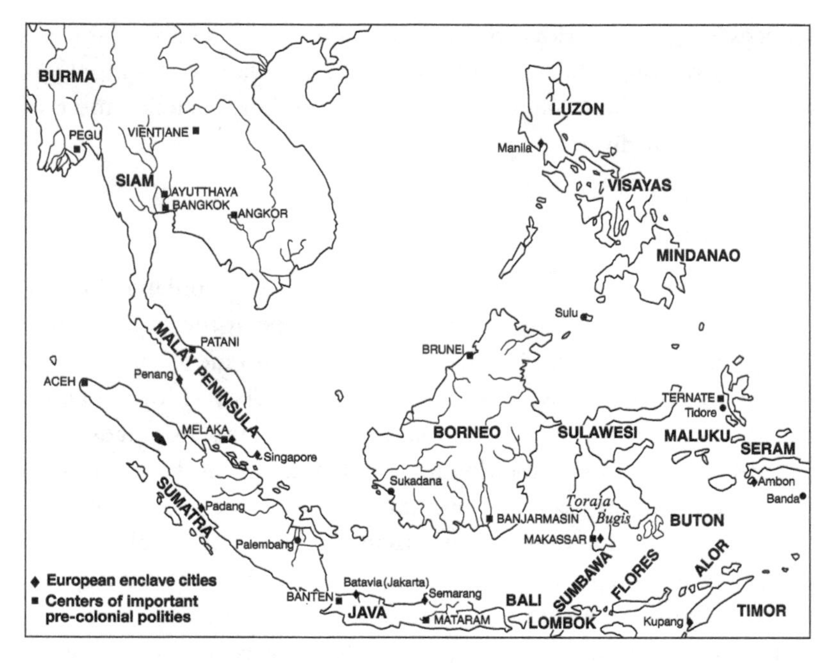

MAP 16.1 Southeast Asia in the Early Modern Period

is paid with the head." Similarly those facing death in a famine would readily sell themselves or their children into slavery in exchange for saving their lives by obtaining food. The large nineteenth-century slave population of Sumbawa in the Lesser Sunda island chain derived almost entirely from the massive eruption of the Tambora volcano in 1815 that destroyed crops throughout the island.[8] The beneficiaries in these cases were wealthy individuals to whom debt was owed. In war, on the other hand, the unfortunate conquered populations could become state slaves of the king, though he might in turn present some of them to meritorious commanders or others whose loyalty he needed.

Reformers from the seventeenth to the nineteenth centuries sought to subdivide categories of bondage with the aim of rescuing most from the horrors of the slave trade. Franciscan Juan de Plasencia, for example, insisted that Filipino field slaves (*alipin namamahay*) working the land could not be sold, whereas household slaves (*alipin sa gigilid*)

[8] Reid 1983b, 159.

could be. Most other commentators disagreed, however, and even Plasencia admitted that in practice unscrupulous people often sold even their field slaves.[9] As slavery became ever harder to defend in European terms, a similar distinction was sought between debt-bondsmen and slaves captured in war, whereby the former could not be bought and sold on the market. In reality, however, precolonial societies appeared not much concerned to make such distinctions either in their languages or their customary law. In practice many slaves were so integrally tied to their masters or their role in society that sale was unthinkable, but this was not part of a systematic legal framework as in ancient Rome or the New World.

A better Western analogy to the universality and centrality of unequal dyadic ties is the patriarchal Judaic world of the Old Testament. A great range of types of servitude is there described by the one word *'ebd* (cognate with Arabic *'abd*), including devotion to God, servitude within the patriarchal clan, or the bondage of the Israelites in Egypt. Southeast Asian languages often used similar terms for slaves and for familial dependents. In some societies wives were referred to as "bought," while husbands unable to pay the bride-price to their in-laws would be seen as "enslaved" to them. In this world equality appeared the more problematic and dangerous relationship, while intimacy was most often expressed in the language of inequality and dependence. Southeast Asian languages prioritize vertical relations in their careful use of the first- and second-person pronouns. Even today the most common words for "I" are former everyday words for slave – Malay *saya*, Javanese *kula* or *kawula*, Thai *kha*, etc. Much ink has been spilled by social scientists in describing a system of vertical dyadic ties, from the mystical unity of servant and master (*kawula-gusti*) in older Javanese thinking, to the patron–client systems of contemporary social analysis.[10]

INCORPORATION OF LABOR INTO EXPANDING CITIES

Perhaps the demographically dominant form of an "open" slavery system, and certainly the best reported, was that which provided

[9] Reid 1983b, 164.
[10] Scott 1972; Reid 1983a, 3–8.

a labor supply to the richest cities of Southeast Asia at the time of the first European descriptions. The early modern period was the region's "Age of Commerce" (roughly 1500–1650), a time of greatly expanded trade wealth, new gunpowder technologies, and changing religious norms. Cities such as Ayutthaya (in Siam), Pegu (then the Burmese capital), and, on the Islands, Aceh, Banten, and Makassar, grew rapidly in population through foreign conquests and purchase. Sultan Iskandar Muda of Aceh (1607–36) reportedly brought 22,000 captives to his capital as slaves from his raids on the Malay Peninsula in 1612–19. He used them as unpaid labor on his construction projects, and avoided even their maintenance costs by allowing them time off to earn their own subsistence.[11] The numbers of captives taken in the repeated wars of expansion of the Burma and Siam (Thailand) monarchies were reportedly even larger – tens of thousands when Burma conquered the Siamese capital in 1569 and 1767, or when Siam conquered the Lao capital in 1827.

Even into the nineteenth century Siam was punishing rebellious Malay tributaries in the Peninsula by massacres, by destruction of property, and, above all, by carrying those captured alive back to Bangkok to help in construction works and plantations. Crawfurd noted 10,000 such captive slaves in the capital in 1828. In the 1786 conquest of Patani it appeared to be mainly younger women who were taken to Bangkok as captives rather than killed, but when the punishment was repeated in 1832, some 4,000–5,000 of every age and gender were reportedly taken away to Bangkok.[12] In 1827 the whole surviving population of the Lao capital of Vientiane was removed across the Mekong into territory controlled by Siam, though their obligation to labor for the king thereafter may be better considered corvée than slavery.

A pattern of raiding for slaves can be distinguished from warfare proper by being practiced against relatively defenseless, typically stateless, people. There are documented examples as far apart in time as Chinese trader Zhou Daguan's description of Angkor's incorporation of "savage" upland peoples as slaves in the 1290s,[13] to numerous British descriptions of nineteenth-century Malay hunting

[11] Beaulieu 1622[1996], 214, 224–25.

[12] Francis Bradley 2013, 153–57.

[13] Zhou 1297[2007].

of stateless aboriginal inhabitants in the Peninsula. Malays targeted particularly younger women and children for slavery, whereas adult men were considered untamable and sure to try to run away, so it was better that they simply be killed or chased away.[14] While this border raiding against stateless hill peoples may be considered an endemic feature of settled rice-growing communities, raiding became a way of life for some only in response to the profits of the long-distance slave trade, discussed later in this chapter.

While the Dutch East India Company or Vereenigde Oostindische Compagnie (VOC) enclave cities of Batavia (Jakarta), Semarang, Makassar, and Melaka are the best-documented examples of purchasing slave labor from poorer and weaker societies, there are also numerous indigenous examples. Until Chinese migrants became numerous enough in the nineteenth century to furnish the beginnings of a labor market, there were no independent workers selling their labor in a free market. The poor were necessarily attached to a patron in some bond of obligation, and only on this basis would they take part in larger labor projects. "Wage rates" reported by the earliest European sources were about thirty times the value of a daily rice subsistence, because in reality they represented the cost to slaveless outsiders of hiring less valued slaves from their owner/patron. "It is their custom to rent slaves. They pay the slave a sum of money, which he gives to his master, and then they use the slave that day for whatever work they wish."[15] The economic motivation to buy one's own slaves, rather than renting them at exorbitant rates, was therefore high.

Aceh is again one of the best documented in its purchase of Indian slaves in the seventeenth and eighteenth centuries, and later of nearby Nias slaves. Whereas the king and his favored commanders might have abundant captured slaves at their disposal, wealthy merchants needed to buy them. The rice growing that today decorates the valley of the Aceh River behind Banda Aceh appears to have been developed in the second half of the seventeenth century by slaves rescued from famines on the Tamil coast of Southeast India and brought for sale in Aceh. A Dutch visitor noted seven English and Danish-flagged ships arriving from Madras and Tranquebar in the month of July 1689

[14] Endicott 1983, 221–36.
[15] O'Kane [Ibn Muhammad Ibrahim 1688] 1972, 177–78. See also Reid 1983b, 168.

alone, all carrying some slaves for sale.[16] One Danish Company ship was still conducting this trade in the 1730s.[17]

These wealthy cities operated explicitly "open" slave systems. The local-born children of slaves were still juridically slaves, but passed by acculturation into a more privileged form of bondage to their masters, as newer arrivals without the local language arrived to do the heavy labor. There was no category of free wage labor to move into, and dyadic ties to a master remained, though in attenuated forms. "Neither can a Stranger easily know who is a slave and who not amongst them, for they are all, in a manner Slaves to one another," a puzzled visitor reported of Aceh.[18]

SLAVE TRADE

A glimpse of the pattern of the pre-Dutch slave trade is provided by Cornelis Speelman, the Dutch conqueror of Makassar in the 1660s. He showed Makassar as already a major slave entrepôt before the Dutch conquest, with local craft bringing slaves to it from a large area of the eastern islands, including Timor, Flores, Tanimbar, Alor, Buton, Mindanao, and Sulu. They were then exported by Malay and Chinese vessels to the wealthier cities and pepper-exporting areas further west, including Banjarmasin, Palembang, Jambi, Aceh, Johor, Sukadena, and Dutch Batavia. Some had been acquired by slave-raiding expeditions, some by sale on the part of port rulers or chiefs willing to define their bondmen as saleable slaves.[19]

By the eighteenth century the ports controlled by the VOC were the wealthiest remaining cities of the Archipelago, and thus the principal markets for this kind of slave import. Since they are also the best documented, they provide many insights into the way an older system of dependent labor incorporation may have worked. Like Asian-ruled Aceh, Patani, Banten, or Makassar, the VOC cities were wealthy,

[16] 'Memorandum about the appearance of and trade in Aceh in 1689 by the commander of the civilian yacht *Den Arend* about the City of Aceh in 1689'; extract from the *Batavia Daghregister* for November 2, 1689, folios 807–18 ANRI Arsip VOC Hoge Regering 2505, transcribed and translated by Risma Manurung and Hendrik E. Niemeijer in *Harta Karun* dokumen 2. See also Reid 2006, 6–7.

[17] Krieger 2008, 133–34.

[18] Dampier 1699 [1931], 98.

[19] Speelman 1670.

and their largely migrant elites were disproportionately male and in need of both male labor and female sexual and domestic services. Since their women were local-born, the Dutch elite adopted many Southeast Asian domestic patterns, including the need to display one's status through a slave retinue. "When a lady [of Batavia] goes out, she has usually four, or more, female slaves attending her."[20] In the legal enforcement of slave status discussed in what follows, however, the Dutch cities parted company from their Asian predecessors.

As newcomers without existing sources of clients or bondsmen in a world without a market for paid labor, the Dutch relied heavily on slaves for essential tasks of construction and port services. The initial Javanese population of the city appears to have fled when the VOC took charge in 1619, and the Javanese were regarded as too dangerous to be used in the first century of Batavia. Initially labor was acquired from southern India, where there was already a market to supply wealthy cities like Aceh. At the 1632 enumeration there were 2,724 slaves in Dutch Batavia, a third of the population, in addition to 495 *Mardijkers*, or freed slaves.[21] Most slaves then belonged to the VOC, working in the warehouses and on building sites, but already there were 735 belonging to Dutch citizens. From the 1660s, when the VOC took over the Sulawesi port of Makassar, slaves were traded through that city, particularly from its East Indonesian hinterland. About 500 slaves a year were brought to Batavia between 1660 and 1690, and the number rose to about 4,000 a year during the eighteenth century. Despite enormous mortality and the manumission of a high proportion of second-generation slaves, slave numbers in the city were more than 30,000 in 1729 and remained at between a third and a quarter of Batavia's population until the demise of the VOC in 1799.

A slave register compiled for the temporary British masters of Batavia in 1816 showed that 43 percent of the 20,000 slaves were born in Sulawesi (primarily Bugis), 20 percent were born in Bali, and more than 13 percent were from the Lesser Sundas (primarily Flores, Sumbawa, and Timor). Only 16 percent were born in Batavia, indicating high rates of both death and manumission. More than a quarter

[20] Stavorinus 1798[1969], 1:322.
[21] Raben 1962, 85–86.

of the Europeans in the city then owned slaves, having an average of fourteen slaves each.[22] Other centers were even more dependent on their slaves. The Makassar population in 1676, less than a decade after its establishment as a Dutch city, was 55 percent slaves and 10 percent *Mardijkers.* At the peak of its history as a slave market in 1730 slaves had grown to 71 percent of the now much larger town.[23] Lesser Dutch cities – Melaka, Semarang, Ambon, Kupang, and Padang – did not have the resources for such extravagance, but slavery was a feature everywhere.

The key axis of the eighteenth-century slave trade between Makassar and Batavia was largely in Dutch hands and could not continue once the slave trade was declared illegal by the postwar Congress of Vienna in 1815. It was consequently banned in Dutch colonies in 1818. The supply from Bali was largely conducted by Chinese traders, however, and may indeed have disproportionately provided Chinese in Batavia with their wives and domestics. The terrible eruption of the Tambora volcano (Sumbawa, Lesser Sundas) in 1815 reduced the population of Bali, Lombok, and Sumbawa to beggary, forcing them into slavery in order to avoid starvation after their crops were destroyed. In the period 1810–30, when the booming sugar estates of Mauritius and Réunion (in the western Indian Ocean) sought slave labor from sources the British could not interdict, the slave traders from there discovered Nias, Toraja, Bali, Sumbawa, and Sulu slaves from Southeast Asia. Two or three of their ships regularly anchored at Kuta, Bali, taking away an average of 500–600 slaves every year in this period.[24]

The most important indigenous center for slave raiding and marketing in the long term was the small island of Sulu, positioned strategically between the Spanish sphere in the Philippines and those of the Dutch and British in the Malay-speaking world. Adopting the Islam of the traders relatively early, Sulu became the great scourge of the Christianized Philippines in the late sixteenth century. As a commercial center, Sulu became the financier and market for Balangingi raiders from nearby islands, who would pick off vulnerable coastal settlements, notably in the Visayas (central Philippines). Already in

[22] Abeyasekere 1983, 288–96.
[23] Sutherland 1983, 268–69.
[24] Van der Kraan 1983, 332.

1637 the bishop of Manila estimated they had taken about 1,000 a year over the previous thirty years.[25]

Sulu's economy boomed after 1770 as an alternative base for supplying sea produce such as tortoiseshell, pearls, and sea slugs to Chinese traders wary of the European-dominated ports. Economic success increased the demand for slaves, so that in the following century 2,000–3,000 per year were taken to Sulu from the Christian Philippines or animist Borneo.[26] They supplied "big men" outside the European enclaves with slaves for show, labor, or warfare, but also provided women to VOC cities with heavily male-dominated Euro-Chinese populations. To these were added the British settlements of Penang (1786) and Singapore (1819), where slavery was never legal. Female slaves were nevertheless smuggled in, which one British official described as "of immense advantage in procuring a female population for Penang." The 1830 Singapore census revealed that the "Bugis and Balinese" category contained 4,421 women and only 1,048 men, with most of the former serving as wives or concubines of Chinese. Critical Dutch sources suggest that several thousand Batak and Nias slaves were being smuggled every year into Penang and the Chinese tin-mining communities in the Peninsula. Most of this contraband trade was carried out in small Indonesian or Chinese vessels and was not policed rigorously by the colonial powers even in the nineteenth century.[27]

Vertical bonds of obligation and patronage continued to be markedly strong and the wage economy relatively weak through much of the twentieth century. The colonial government in Indonesia belatedly adopted a rhetoric of suppressing slavery but achieved this in practice by increasing its control of the population sufficiently to impose a huge burden of corvée for all its public works. Perhaps a quarter of all Java's labor time in the nineteenth century was absorbed in government corvée, while in the early twentieth century it was the turn of the labor-scarce Outer Islands to undergo this burden. The slaves in many areas opposed reforming officials' attempts to "free" them by compensating slave owners, fearing "that in buying them the 'Company' [Dutch Government] will use them for still harder labor

[25] Reid 1983a, 32.
[26] Warren 1981, 180.
[27] Reid 1983a, 30–31.

than they now suffer from."[28] Convict labor was still more useful for unpleasant tasks like coal mining, with an average of 26,000 convict laborers being deployed at any one time in 1880–1900.[29] As in many other situations, in other words, it was the rise of the absolutist state, later in Southeast Asia than in Europe, which provided the necessary condition and cause for the abolition of systems of private slavery.

LEGALISM AND THE RISE OF THE "OUTSIDER" SLAVE

Modern definitions of slave status tend to include an element of outsider-ness, whereby slaves were different in language or culture and could not have the same kinship systems, marriage, and property rights as non-slaves.[30] That such outsider-ness could be found in early Southeast Asia is clear, but always as part of a spectrum of conditions with boundaries between them that were much less clear. In thirteenth-century Angkor, Chinese visitor Zhou Daguan described what appeared to be a clear case of outsider slaves who were:[31]

> captured in the wild mountainous regions, and are of a wholly different race called *Chuang* [brigands] ... So looked down on are these wretches that when, in the course of a dispute, a Cambodian is called a *Chuang* by his adversary, dark hatred strikes to the marrow of his bones ... If by chance a Chinese ... should assuage his appetite with one of the women slaves ... the owner would refuse to be seated in the presence of a man who had defiled himself with a savage.

Slaves had no civil status and would be tattooed if they showed signs of running away, according to Zhou. Yet the abundant inscriptions of the period use a range of Khmer terms that have been translated as "slave" but in other contexts can mean simply man, woman, or young person. Ian Mabbett suggests that the relation between master/owner and slave was in reality "a network of claims and relationships."[32]

The universalist outlook of Islam and Christianity served to systematize the association of slavery with outsiders. Islamic law as

[28] Versteege, June 4, 1877, in Mailrapport 1877/456, Batavia to Ministry of Colonies, Algemene Rijksarchief, The Hague.
[29] Reid 1993, 72–77.
[30] Finley 1968; Patterson 1982.
[31] Zhou 1297[2007], 21.
[32] Mabbett 1983, 46.

it entered Southeast Asia in the fifteenth century defined slaves as saleable property in a host of regulations about injury, theft, and sexual misdemeanors. Injury to a slave was considered a lesser kind of injury to his/her owner, with the compensation required generally half of what was paid for a freeman. Islam also encouraged (but did not usually require) the idea that only unbelievers should be enslaved. One Bugis text explained that the Muslim apostle credited with the conversion of South Sulawesi taught that "God would reward those who freed their slaves" when the slaves accepted Islam like their masters.[33] Christian canon law did not regulate slaves-as-property in the same way, but shared the clear discouragement of enslaving fellow Christians. The Spanish outlawed slavery among the Filipinos they Christianized and found their labor supply in state corvée, locally called *polo* (no doubt often more onerous) rather than slavery.[34]

From the seventeenth century the VOC provides for the first time in Southeast Asia a stream of laws and promulgations about slavery, and the definition of slaves as outsiders becomes clear. In the rough early decades the Portuguese and Spanish were the archenemies, and Catholic captives could be put in chains to be reduced to the most servile category of galley slaves. The "insider" category was for some purposes restricted to Dutch-German Protestants, who could acquire former Portuguese slaves even if Christianized. The earlier ordinances did encourage Dutch slave owners to Christianize their slaves, as the Portuguese had done, but by 1700 very few were doing so because of the expectation that Christian slaves should be freed.[35] Most slaves and ex-slaves eventually assimilated into the Muslim rather than Christian population of Batavia. Conversion into the Dutch-speaking Calvinist church instead became the essential gateway to officially sanctioned marriage between European men and Asian women, ex-slave or otherwise, as opposed to "dishonest unions, hated concubinage and God-grieving adultery."[36]

The Indonesians brought as slaves to Dutch-ruled cities experienced a slave system different in two vital respects from the spectrum of dependent conditions from which they were transported. First,

33 Reid 1983b, 169.
34 Phelan 1959, 99–102.
35 Fox 1983, 249–55.
36 Eric Jones 2010, 73.

they were permanent outsiders from the viewpoint of the governing establishment, both ethnically and religiously, with no chance of eventual assimilation into it except by the rare conversion and marriage to a Dutchman. Second, they faced a tightly regulated legal system enforced by state authority and minutely described in thousands of legal decrees and court judgments. The VOC enforced the condition of slavery, captured and punished runaway slaves, and carefully regulated the way they could be treated and punished when they transgressed. Only in this area do we have enough documentation to be confident that we are seeing a fixed and permanent category of saleable slaves-as-property. This rich source of information has also made possible some creative studies illustrating the dynamic world of this one section of the Southeast Asian underclass.[37]

WERE THERE "SLAVE SOCIETIES" IN THIS SPECTRUM?

The simple answer to Finley's question is yes. If "society" is understood to include small polities and relatively self-contained social systems at particular points in time, then there were a number of clear "Slave Societies" by Finley's definition in Southeast Asia of the early modern period. But the attempt to extend a simple characterization to complex geographic areas like Southeast Asia, India, Mesoamerica, or Mesopotamia in long periods of history can only succeed through simplifications based on massive ignorance. A great historiographical industry arose from attempting to apply Marx's simple progressive schema – slavery, feudalism, capitalism – to parts of the world of which the literature of the day knew little. It was innovative in its time because it crudely broke down the barriers that had isolated European, Chinese, Japanese, Vietnamese, and Indian historiography from each other, and insisted on making analytic comparisons. But the categories did not withstand historical scrutiny. Feudalism and capitalism have already needed so much subdivision and nuance to make sense outside medieval Europe – and even within it – that they hardly survive as useful global categories.

It is high time that the intense variety of political, economic, and social conditions in which slavery is a useful category is also made

[37] Notably Fernando 2006; Ward 2009; Jones 2010.

clear. That nuancing in turn exposes variety wherever there was no overarching legal authority to enforce a particular definition. Even in such "classic" cases as the Greek-speaking world of antiquity, great variety is inescapable. Rather than attempting to categorize "Slave Societies" in this broad but crude manner, as if the American South and the Roman Empire really had significant commonality, we might be better to develop a range of terms that are globally applicable to particular situations. "Slave production" might be one such term, though already inviting subdivision into "slave agricultural production for the market," "slave factory production," and so forth.

Let me try to illustrate the point by running through the Southeast Asian cases that would pass Finley's test as "Slave Societies" in declining order of documented clarity.

The various VOC-enforced systems are much the best documented, and of these the seven small, volcanic, nutmeg-producing islands of the Banda Archipelago are the clearest case of highly profitable slave production. Southeast of Seram, Banda was until the 1760s the sole source of the world's nutmeg and mace and a great object of desire in the "spice race" of the sixteenth and seventeenth centuries. A republican oligarchy of hybrid Muslim traders had governed the island before the Dutch advent, welcoming all traders but fiercely resisting Dutch attempts at monopoly or control. The VOC brutally "won" this race in 1621, when Governor-General Jan Pieterszoon Coen ordered the conquest of the islands and the massacre or enslavement of its population of some 15,000 people. The island was then repopulated by sixty-eight Dutch *perkeniers* (production-masters) each controlling a *perk* of more than one hectare of nutmeg trees and the slaves necessary to work them. Most slaves were imported, though some 500 Bandanese slaves had to be sent back to the islands to explain how to care for the trees. Slaves formed the majority of the 5,000 inhabitants for the two centuries following this conquest, and their labor permitted probably the most profitable "Slave Society" in history. The VOC purchased the islands' whole product of nutmeg and mace (the spice derived from the fiber surrounding the nut proper) at fixed low prices and sold it in Amsterdam at more than twenty times the price. This was the most absolute of the VOC monopolies, and its huge profits kept the VOC afloat for much of the seventeenth century. It seemed a good bargain in 1669 to let the English have New York in return for finally surrendering their claims on one of the tiny Banda islands.[38]

There were a number of other examples of slave agricultural production of cash crops for the world market, but none as enduring or well documented as the two centuries of slave production on Banda. The Dutch-Bugis conquest of Makassar (Sulawesi) also resulted in the massacre, flight, or enslavement of virtually the whole population of the rice bowl to the north of the city. The so-called *Noorderdistricten* (today's Maros area) were then farmed by a slave population that produced a sufficient rice surplus to feed Dutch posts in most of eastern Indonesia. The 1851 census of the region lazily listed the whole 95,000 population of the *Noorderdistricten* as "slave," although under local Bugis chiefs they must have become ever less like saleable property over time.[39] The same probably applies to the Indian slaves mentioned earlier, who were used to develop a marketable surplus of rice in the river valley behind Banda Aceh. For its frontier pepper plantations, Aceh used laborers from long-cultivated parts of Aceh, bonded by debt to the entrepreneur who provided the necessary capital to see them through the four years before the vines became productive. Seventeenth-century Banjarmasin (south Borneo), on the other hand, imported from Makassar "male and female slaves fitted for labour in the pepper gardens," according to one account.[40]

What of the "open slave systems" of the flourishing urban centers, acquiring their manual labor through conquest or purchase from weaker or poorer neighbors? There are certainly accounts that suggest that Aceh, Makassar, and Banten in the seventeenth century had very high proportions of slaves in their populations, and that they did all construction work, port labor, and much of the production of textiles, ceramics, and the like. Most slaves in construction, however, appear to have been state slaves acquired by conquest, who were not marketable as property in the same way as private slaves. In Aceh, Beaulieu described the "great number of slaves" who built all the public works for the sultan in the 1620s. He gave them nothing for subsistence, but allowed them four days in every eight to work for their own subsistence. The more skilled and successful managed to earn enough

38 John Villiers 1981, 723–50; Loth 1995, 13–35.
39 Sutherland 1983, 268, 275.
40 Speelman 1670.

to buy themselves out of further days of forced labor at a fixed rate per day. The truly successful could even buy their liberty for around forty Spanish reals, though more for the most valuable.[41] There was no comparable discussion of a busy slave market, however, and one must doubt whether these state slaves were truly saleable.

The VOC enclaves such as Batavia (Jakarta) and Makassar had a clear-cut and enforced pattern of saleable slaves-as-property and enough documentation to be confident in categorizing them. Other than Banda, however, they were not truly dependent on slave labor for their existence and productivity. These cities lived by trade, and they needed slaves not for this essential lifeblood so much as for the comfort of the ruling classes. They certainly displayed a social system based on slavery, but not always the critical role in production that Finley sought. It would be easy to argue, however, that Batavia and Makassar were at least as "pure" examples of the genre as similarly trade-based Greek city-states in antiquity.

When turning to the Southeast Asian indigenous systems, we will always be handicapped by the absence of state legal absolutism. Without this the "open" systems of the cities appeared less systematic and more flexible than would satisfy any pure model of a "Slave Society." State labor mobilization of conquered captives and condemned criminals on the one hand, and of peasants on the other who may over the generations have merged with the former, will always be in a borderland between slavery and serfdom. Angkor (Cambodia) of the tenth to twelfth centuries is debated in these terms, as is ancient Egypt, but this will be impossible to resolve in the absence of further sources.

"Slave Society" has, I think, been shown to be more useful as a provocation than as a global category of analysis. The way forward is to understand slavery proper as one among many systems of servile labor exploitation and not necessarily the most cruel or inhumane. At a popular level it may long be necessary to remind undergraduates to rid themselves of the notion that the nineteenth-century American South is in any way typical or normative. Global history has moved on from such simplistic notions, and also from the Marxist pursuit of a "slave mode of production" as an historical stage. Slavery remains critical as a tool of comparative analysis not because it is uniquely evil

[41] Beaulieu 1622[1996], 214–15.

or particularly pervasive, but because it is the form of labor mobilization that could transfer humans drastically and involuntarily from one culture to another. In this role the contradictions inherent between human being and property become especially poignant, as no two cultural systems or moments saw the institution in quite the same way.

Conclusion: Intersections: Slaveries, Borderlands, Edges

James F. Brooks

I am grateful for the invitation from Noel Lenski and Catherine Cameron to offer some reflections on these sixteen fine chapters and hope that my own particular perspective as an ethnohistorian of indigenous and colonial slaveries in the Southwest borderlands of North America might provide a few points of illumination. It is a halting effort, lent grace only by an audio recording that rendered the haunting music and lyrics to an *indita* that comes down to us across several centuries of reciprocal slave raiding in the greater Southwest.

In "La Cautiva Marcelina" we hear the voice of a Spanish colonial woman captured by Plains Indian slave raiders and forced to witness the death of her father, husband, and children. Traveling at brutal pace on horseback from watering place to watering place, we can see her eyes cast back to the *querida patria* (beloved homeland) she left behind and know that her suffering henceforth would be sustained by only *carne de yegua* (mare's meat) and perhaps the tissues of her broken heart. Despite its regional particulars, the "unbearable pathos" of the *indita* felt universal to the "natal alienation" experienced by the victims of slavery we see in myriad detail throughout these chapters.[1]

I do, however, add this challenge to the volume's theme: rather than "What is a "Slave Society?" (WISS), might we also ask "Why does slavery matter?" (WDSM). This question hit home for me while teaching in the late 1990s at the University of Maryland, where I took on summer

[1] See this version at https://vimeo.com/70437646.

workshops through the (now defunct) Teaching American History program, a brainchild of the late Senator William Byrd. I worked with classroom teachers drawn from the Baltimore Public Schools enrichment programs, which featured 90 percent African American student enrollments. These teachers – also African American – faced impassioned student resistance to units on slavery.

One teacher offered a painfully bitter moment with her own ten-year-old daughter, who, when asked why she did not want to hear about slavery in the United States, rejoined, "It makes me feel bad, mom." I then proposed to the teachers that they try to approach slavery from a different aspect, employing some white captivity narratives from colonial New England and Hispano narratives like that of Marcelina. When we met the following summer, we found that the African American students opened up to a wider "conceptual" approach to talking about slavery. Destigmatizing the racial aspects of slave status somehow erased the shame attendant on their associations and yet did so without lessening the continued importance of recognizing the "tomorrow of slavery" in our own desire for social justice. Herein lies the value, I believe, of volumes like this one, ranging widely across time and space and cultures and race. Pain and guilt become interlocking and mutually understood conditions, born of the past yet available for redress in the present.

In a volume I coedited with Bonnie Martin dedicated to linking the histories of diverse slaveries across the North American continent, we struggled to conceptualize the bricolage of material we had assembled, ranging from work on the precolonial indigenous archaeology of slavery to the nexus of Indian and African slaveries, to the westward expansion of the plantation complex, and finally to post-abolition forms of slave-like oppression like the levied labor and sexual predations associated with Indian boarding schools and modern sex trafficking. We settled on the concept of "linking" diverse slaveries in "actual connections among peoples through networks of trade and migration," as well as "analytical links we ourselves create across time and space," to our readers' appreciation of the "continental epic" of North American slavery.[2]

[2] Martin and Brooks 2015.

An essay in the volume by ethnomusicologist Enrique R. Lamadrid taught us that "La Cautiva Marcelina" continues to echo in the valleys and canyons of New Mexico and southern Colorado among the "Indo-Hispano" descendants of people like Marcelina as the culminating song in the Comanche Nativity Dances performed each December in villages like Alcalde, Antonito, and Ranchos de Taos. By singing her lyrics and remembering her travails, these performers ascribe "value and transcendent meaning to the larger community." Lamadrid argues that such performances of dance and song, embedded in a long history of violence and exploitation, even as they suggest kinship and mutual complicity in a vast regional network of human exchange, aim ultimately toward what Paolo Freire once termed "the great humanistic and historical task of the oppressed: to liberate themselves and their oppressors as well."[3]

With this same object in mind, I turn to another small village in northern New Mexico. On August 23, 2014, I attended the feast day for Santa Rosa de Lima de Abiquiú in the Chama River Valley of northern New Mexico. Following a tradition more than 250 years old, the celebration began with a Catholic mass in the ruined Capilla de Santa Rosa two miles distant from the current village location – Santo Tomás de Abiquiú – after which a procession marched two miles along busy Highway 284/85 with an icon of La Santa toward her installation in a cottonwood-leafed bower in the Santo Tomás de Abiquiú plaza. Led by horseback riders and the community volunteer fire department's red engine, punctuated by arrhythmic explosions from the smooth-bore pistol of sacristan Dexter Trujillo, and viewed by impatient and puzzled motorists who wished only to reach the far more famous Ghost Ranch tours of "O'Keeffe Country," the procession mixed Catholic piety and community pride. Once the villagers completed their personal devotions to La Santa, they formed long lines for a meal in the parish gymnasium; folk dancers entertained, as people enjoyed bowls of red chili and beans or green chili enchiladas. Around the *caliche*-surfaced dusty plaza vendors set up makeshift stands for the sale of religious articles, candy, soda, used books, and locally made *carne seca.*

[3] For an exploration of the depth and breadth of the cultural recognition of Indo-Hispano enmeshment in New Mexico, see Lamadrid 2015.

By mid-afternoon, thunderheads built over nearby Cerro Pedernal, and an audience gathered to witness a performance by a troupe of dancers from Ranchos de Taos, a youth group known as Los Comanches de la Serna. For generations, as long as anyone can remember, the descendants of that village's eighteenth-century founding *genízaros* (janissaries, or military slaves deployed as frontier soldiers) have marked their indigenous ancestry and martial prowess through song and dance. Much like their distant kinfolk who perform "La Cautiva Marcelina," Los Comanches de la Serna specialize in *pasiados*, or the traveling chants of the Comanches, through which they recall a past and simultaneously assert a present as slave and soldier. The performers, ranging in age from little Emeline, age two and a half, to teenage boys like Reyes and Gregorio, danced on the hard-packed plaza while the singer, Francisco "el Cumanche" Gonzales, chanted and his brother accompanied him on a *tombé*, or hand-drum – servitude and soldiering celebrated in song. In an aside to me at the end of the performance, Virgil Trujillo, brother to Dexter and a community leader himself, explained that he had once asked a visitor from Turkey to define what "janissary" meant to him. The visitor replied, "children of war, in all its meanings."

With a population of only some 200 *vecinos* (citizens) today, Abiquiú may seem an unlikely place from which to reflect upon the wide-ranging chapters in this volume. And yet its history also suggests "links" across time and space. Santa Rose de Lima de Abiquiú was initially established by Spanish colonial *pobladores* (settlers) in the 1730s; their original *placita* (settlement) was destroyed in a Comanche raid in 1747, when a band of Comanches and Utes ran off hundreds of head of livestock and took captive twenty-three women and children. Spanish governor Tomás Vélez Cachupín sought their freedom, yet a combination of military and diplomatic efforts would succeed in redeeming only one woman. The other victims apparently found assimilation as kin or slaves (or variations of both) among the widespread Comanche *rancherías* that were forming into what historian Pekka Hämäläinen has termed "the Comanche Empire." Within a few decades, Comanches would create a virtual "raiding industry" preying on people and livestock seized from northern Mexico, and they would hold slaves that numbered perhaps 25 percent of their population. In

Captives and Cousins, I have argued that in the Southwest and across several centuries, interwoven systems of capture, enslavement, forcible incorporation, and explicit exploitation, whether for sex or labor, produced a region-wide "borderlands political economy" predicated on the socially productive value of endemic violence and a system of slavery based in the exploitation of cohorts of producers (of biological, social, or economic value) whose numbers were renewed mainly through capture or purchase.[4]

Yet the Chama River Valley proved too fertile and strategic for the colony to abandon, and in 1754, Governor Vélez Cachupín relocated the settlement upriver to a defensible mesa, where it remains today (and where artist Georgia O'Keeffe would make her home beginning in 1929). The 783 people Vélez Cachupín settled there included fifty-seven *genízaro* families with members numbering 166 and composed of Ute, Comanche, Pawnee, Apache, Kiowa, and Tewa *criados* – women and children "redeemed" from captivity among *los indios bárbaros* by Spaniards and "raised up" in Catholic families. Trained as frontier soldiers, the boys were often multilingual by virtue of origin and were deployed to frontier settlements to protect the colonial core as *genízaro* scouts and fighters and to facilitate trade relations when not combating these same partners. Women and girls would be put to work as household servants or weavers in local *obrajes* (workshops). These *genízaros* joined 104 Spanish families to form a community totaling 617 members grafted from two strains of rootstock into the community that persists today. Those *pobladores* would in turn establish their plaza beneath the eyes of another group of recent immigrants, perhaps a dozen Tewa Puebloan families who had been residing among the Hopis far to the west since the failed 1696 "Second Pueblo Revolt." In the 1740s, Padre Carlos Delgado had brought some of these back to the Chama Valley, where they had created a new pueblo on what today continues to be called "Moque [Hopi] Plaza." The Franciscan mission that has served this mixed-ethnic community for the past 261 years was dedicated to Santo Tomás, whose feast on November 29 now celebrates the indigenous past more than the legacy of Spanish colonialism. An event in that church in May 2015, to which I return later,

[4] Brooks 2002, 64–65; Hämäläinen 2008.

will remind us of the continuing salience of servitude, indigeneity, and colonialism in Abiquiú today.

How can this nexus of unequal statuses, entangled identities, curated memories, and contemporary expression inform a discussion devoted to the classic distinction between "Slave Societies" and "Societies with Slaves" first formulated by Moses Finley? Can the people of Abiquiú, and their many variations across global space and time enrich our inquiry into whether Finley's formulation is "tenable in light of ongoing studies on the practice of slavery in a variety of cultures across global history?" Perhaps if we consider this question from what Peter Hunt terms the "borderlines of slavery," in places like Abiquiú, we can feel our way forward. As Bonnie Martin and I discovered in editing our volume, fundamental to furthering our understanding of human bondage across time and space and within or outside of Finley's two categories is an emphasis on "links" or *intersections* rather than *distinctions.*

A focus on intersections *among* rather than differences *within* Finley's dualism offers an opportunity to discern where *scale* intersects with "experience" and "consequence" in various systems of slavery. Following Fernando Santos-Granero's phenomenological argument, I suggest we are drawn to the study of the slave experience largely in an effort to understand the history and our own relative experiences of "freedom" (or the constraints thereon). We are curious about the consequences of slavery largely due to the long shadow it has cast across historical epochs – its structural implication in the birth of notions of "democracy" in ancient Athens or the Roman Republic, for instance; its role in shaping the discourse and actions of those who drove popular revolutions in eighteenth-century British colonies, France, or Haiti; and the long shadows still cast by slavery in contemporary racial inequalities in the United States, Brazil, Somalia, or Santo Tomás de Abiquiú.

Walter Scheidel and Kyle Harper term this [Orlando] Patterson's paradox: "slavery flourished in those societies which have often been considered to mark the most advanced edge of civilizational progress, like Greece and Rome," and, by implication, the rebelling British colonies that became the United States of America. Certainly, dialing back the analytical lens to bring larger structural shifts into focus around slavery's influences, as does Robert Gudmestad for the

American South, allows us to understand better the growing sectional dissonance that would ultimately lead to civil war and abolition.

Yet, if we foreground slavery's place as a socioeconomic engine of state formation and political evolution in those cases where we find substantial empires and nations, do we miss the perhaps equally important role that "slaveries" played (and play) in small-scale and middle-range societies, past and present? As Christina Snyder prods us to ask, are "Societies with Slaves" any less significant from the standpoint of self-and-other, family, band, tribe, and chiefdom as they are for Greece, Rome, Brazil, and the US South? "A motley patchwork of slaveries extended across North America," she cautions, in which a variety of forms of exploitation, ownership, pathways to incorporation, manumission, and transgenerational stigma intersected with the more formalized systems brought to the Americas by European colonists through their forcible importation of Africans. How are we to treat the fact that the subsequent enslavement of Africans by some members of the five "civilized" tribes of the American Indian Southeast during the colonial era would become an instrument for the exportation of Southern slavery into the American West once Andrew Jackson's Indian Removal Act forced the migration of native slaveholders into Mexican Texas and the Indian Territory?[5]

Are not the cultural transfers and innovations associated with slavery in the non-state societies that Catherine Cameron surveys ultimately as significant as their influences in formal states? Do demographic scale and societal complexity matter to the lived experience of the slave or, for that matter, the master to the degree implied by the Finleyan binary, and, for that matter, do they even affect the ability of non-state units to impact regional and even world affairs? Boko Haram and Daesh [ISIL, ISIS] lead one to wonder. Santos-Granero's notion of "the Amerindian 'political economy of life,' a political economy in which life is the scarcest resource and participant societies are involved in mutual predation with the aim of appropriating as many potentialities of life from their enemies as possible," intersects fruitfully with both Cameron's cases and the argument of Paul Lovejoy. Although some African states qualify as "slave societies"

[5] See Goldberg 2015; Schermerhorn 2015; Torget 2015.

under the Finleyan rubric, the more important question for further research lies in the intersection of those states' demand for slaves and the slave raiding and slave trading that came to characterize virtually all of the "stateless" societies at their margins. This phenomenon doubtless echoed many of the experiential qualities manifested in Kim Bok-Rae's investigation of *nobis* in Korea. Through her close reading of a single legal case, we find ourselves questioning the cross-cultural usefulness of distinctions like "slave" versus "serf" and alerted to the fact that particular experiences may prove more revelatory of the meaning of subordination in social life than the creation of artificial categories of analysis. A similar level of sophistication appears in the Southeast Asian cases addressed by Anthony Reid, where non-absolutist states seem to blend large-scale levies of laborers through warfare or criminalization with much more fluid – even "gentle" – expressions on the individual and family scale. The same could be said of Theresa Singleton's archaeological approach to slavery in the Caribbean, where the first of New World "Slave Societies" were formed, at a much smaller scale and in the absence of the rigid state structures that Finley's formula entails. In the absence of written records that reveal slave experience in the Caribbean, archaeology has the real potential to lift the struggles of sugarcane plantation slaves into the light.

Simple measures of the percentage of slaves present among a given family, village, city, state, nation, or empire seldom reveal experience, since – from the perspective of the slave – enslavement must and always will be considered a personal condition. A house slave in fourth-century Athens experienced her or his bondage in ways that might resonate better with the experiences of nineteen-year-old Celia, a slave in 1850s Missouri who was cruelly and repeatedly raped by her master, Robert Newsome, than with the "barbarian" mine slave of ancient Greece, who was imported from the Black Sea region to labor and perish with little or no knowledge of his distant master. In Celia's case, she would kill her tormenter in self-defense, then ask his grandson to shovel the ashes out of her cabin's fireplace without him having any idea they included those of his grandfather's body, and ultimately be hanged for murder, in a case that established in US law the principle that slave women did not even deserve protection against sexual assault.[6]

Nine months after the Feast Day of Santa Rosa de Lima, I served as facilitator for a daylong community gathering in the village of Abiquiú termed a "Celebration of Our Genízaro Identity." The assembly was a proud display of the ways in which the residents have kept that memory and culture alive through family genealogy, oral history, and the careful curation of a documentary record. Our festival on May 16 celebrated that heritage and saw nearly 200 attendees spend the day in the Santo Tomás de Abiquiú parish gymnasium, sharing memories, songs, dances, and traditional foods like green chili lamb stew, *chicos*, and handmade tortillas. It opened with a reading by Senator Richard C. Martinez of the 2007 "State of New Mexico Memorial," which recognized the *genízaros* as Indigenous Peoples. This represented a key step forward in the local effort to obtain federal recognition as an Indian pueblo. It answered Freire's call, at least for a day, by helping the *genízaro* community "to liberate themselves and their oppressors as well." Distant kinspeople from Indian Pueblos like Santa Clara, Jemez, and Cochiti and even the Comanche nation of Oklahoma also attended to speak of intercultural ties of custom and kinship – born of mutual hostility and intersecting systems of slavery – that had survived the centuries. And all the while these deep patterns of intersection were the center of our discussion, iPhones, Facebook, Twitter, and Instagram posts recorded and disseminated the program to regional, national, and even international audiences. For the people of Abiquiú, the slavery that brought their people together into a single community remains a lived experience and a statement of a willingness to find a way forward as universally recognized and forgiving "children of war."

[6] McLaurin 1991.

Volume Bibliography

Abeyasekere, S. 1983. "Slaves in Batavia: Insights from a Slave Register." In *Slavery, Bondage and Dependency in Southeast Asia*, edited by Anthony Reid, 288–96. St. Lucia: University of Queensland Press.

Acharya, Upendra D. 2013. "Globalization and Hegemony Shift: Are States Merely Agents of Corporate Capitalism?" *Boston College Law Review* 54: 937–69.

Adams, John. 1823. *Remarks on the Country Extending from Cape Palmas to the River Congo*. London: G. and W. B. Whittaker.

Afigbo, A. E. 1981. *Ropes of Sand: Studies in Igbo History and Culture*. Ibadan: Published for University Press in association with Oxford University Press.

Agorsah, Kofi E. 1993. "Archaeology and Resistance History in the Caribbean." *African Archaeology Review* 11: 175–95.

Agorsah, Kofi E. 1994. *Maroon Heritage: Archaeological, Ethnographic and Historical Perspective*. Kingston: Canoe Press, University of the West Indies.

Aimes, Hubert. 1909. "Coartacion: A Spanish Institution for the Advancement of Slaves into Freedmen." *Yale Review* 17: 412–31.

Akrigg, Ben and Rob Tordoff, eds. 2013. *Slaves and Slavery in Ancient Greek Comic Drama*. Cambridge: Cambridge University Press.

Alencastro, L. F. d. 2000. *O trato dos Viventes: formação do Brasil no Atlântico Sul, Séculos XVI e XVII*. São Paulo: Companhia das Letras.

Alexianu, M. 2011. "Lexicographers, Paroemiographers and Slaves-for-Salt Barter in Ancient Thrace." *Phoenix* 65: 389–94.

Alföldy, Geza. 1986. "Die Freilassung von Sklaven und die Struktur der Sklaverei in der römischen Kaiserzeit." In *Die römische Gesellschaft. Ausgewählte Beiträge*, edited by Geza Alföldy, 286–331. First published in *Rivista di Storia Antica* 2 (1972): 97–129.

Algranti, L. M. 1988. *O feitor ausente: estudo sobre a escravidão urbana no Rio de Janeiro*. Petrópolis: Vozes.

Allain, Jean. 2012a. "The Legal Definition of Slavery into the Twenty-First Century." In *The Legal Understanding of Slavery: From the Historical to the Contemporary*, edited by Jean Allain, 199–219. Oxford: Oxford University Press.

Allain, Jean. ed. 2012b. *The Legal Understanding of Slavery: From the Historical to the Contemporary*. Oxford: Oxford University Press.

Allain, Jean and Kevin Bales. 2012. "Slavery and Its Definition." *Global Dialogue* 14: 1–15.

Allain, Jean and Robin Hickey. 2012. "Property and the Definition of Slavery." *International Comparative Law Quarterly* 61: 915–38.

Allen, Calvin. 1978. "Sayyids, Shets and Sultāns: Politics and Trade in Masqat under the Al Bū Sa'īd, 1785–1914." Dissertation, University of Washington.

Allen, Richard B. 1999. *Slaves, Freedmen, and Indentured Laborers in Colonial Mauritius*. Cambridge: Cambridge University Press.

Allen, Richard B. 2008. "The Constant Demand of the French: The Mascarene Slave Trade and the Worlds of the Indian Ocean and Atlantic during the Eighteenth and Nineteenth Centuries." *The Journal of African History* 49.1: 43–72.

Allen, Richard B. 2010. "Satisfying the 'Want of Laboring People': European Slave Trading in the Indian Ocean 1500–1850." *Journal of World History* 21.1: 45–73.

Alpers, Edward A. 1967. *The East African Slave Trade*. Nairobi: Historical Association of Tanzania.

Alpers, Edward A. 1970. "The French Slave Trade in East Africa (1721–1810)." *Cahiers d'Etudes Africaines* 10: Cahier 37: 80–124.

Alpers, Edward A. 1975. *Ivory and Slaves: Changing Pattern of International Trade in East Central Africa to the Later Nineteenth Century*. Berkeley; Los Angeles: University of California Press.

Alpers, Edward A. 2000. "Recollecting Africa: Diasporic Memory in the Indian Ocean World." *African Studies Review* 43.1: 83–99.

Alpers, Edward A. 2008. *East Africa and the Indian Ocean*. Princeton, NJ: Markus Wiener Publishers.

Alvarez Chanca, Diego. 1978. "A letter addressed to the Chapter of Seville by Dr. Chanca..." In *Four Voyages to the New World. Letters and Selected Documents*, edited by R. H. Major, 18–68. Gloucester, MA: Peter Smith.

Ames, Kenneth M. 2008. "Slavery, Household Production, and Demography on the Southern Northwest Coast: Cables, Tacking, and Ropewalks." In *Invisible Citizens: Captives and Their Consequences*, edited by Catherine M. Cameron, 138–58. Salt Lake City: University of Utah Press.

Ames, Kenneth M. and H. D. G. Maschner. 1999. *Peoples of the Northwest Coast: Their Archaeology and Prehistory*. London: Thames and Hudson.

Amselle, Jean-Loup. 1977. *Les négociants de savane*. Paris: Anthropos.

Anderson, Perry. 1974. *Passages from Antiquity to Feudalism*. London: New Left Books.

Andreau, Jean. 1999. *Banking and Business in the Roman World*. Key Themes in Ancient History. Cambridge; New York: Cambridge University Press.

Andreau, Jean and Raymond Descat. 2006. *Esclave en Grèce et à Rome.* Paris: Hachette.

Andreau, Jean and Raymond Descat. 2011. *The Slave in Greece and Rome.* Translated by M. Leopold. Madison: University of Wisconsin Press.

Anghiera, Pietro Martire d'. 1555 [1966]. *The Decades of the New Worlde or West India.* Translated by Rycharde Eden. Ann Arbor, MI: University Microfilms Inc.

Anonymous. 1905. "Descripción de las misiones del río Ucayali." In *Colección de leyes, decretos, resoluciones y otros documentos oficiales referentes al Departamento de Loreto,* compiled by Carlos Larrabure and Correa, 14: 257–65. Lima: Imprenta La Opinión Nacional.

Anonymous. 1988. *Un flibustier français dans la mer des Antilles en 1618–1620.* Clamart: Editions Jean-Pierre Moreau.

Armstrong, Douglas V. 1990. *The Old Village and the Great House: An Archaeological and Historical Examination of Drax Hall.* Urbana: University of Illinois Press.

Armstrong, Douglas V. 2014. "Magens House Compound Kongen Quarters (Charlotte Amalie, St. Thomas)." In *Encyclopedia of Caribbean Archaeology,* edited by Basil A. Reid and R. Grant Gilmore, 3:226–27. Gainesville: University Press of Florida.

Arriaga, Pablo Joseph. 1974 "Carta annua del P. Pablo Joseph de Arriaga, por comisión al P. Claudio Aquaviva, Lima, 3 de abril 1596." In *Monumenta Peruana,* Monumenta Historica Societatis Iesu. Vol. 110, edited by Antonio de Egaña, 6:12–81. Rome: Institutum Historicum Societatis Iesu.

Astor, Aaron. 2012. *Rebels on the Border: Civil War, Emancipation, and the Reconstruction of Kentucky and Missouri.* Baton Rouge: Louisiana State University Press.

Aubert, Jean-Jacques. 1994. *Business Managers in Ancient Rome: A Social and Economic Study of Institores, 200 B.C.–A.D. 250.* Leiden: Brill.

Baade, Hans. 1983. "The Law of Slavery in Spanish Louisiana, 1769–1803." In *Louisiana's Legal Heritage,* edited by Edward Haas, 45–86. Pensacola, FL: Perdido Bay Press.

Bäbler, Balbina. 1998. *Fleissige Thrakerinnen und wehrhafte Skythen: Nichtgriechen im klassischen Athen und ihre archäologische Hinterlassenschaft.* Beiträge zur Altertumskunde, Bd. 108. Stuttgart: B. G. Teubner.

Baier, Stephen and Paul E. Lovejoy. 1977. "The Tuareg of the Central Sudan: Gradations in Servility at the Desert Edge (Niger and Nigeria)." In *Slavery in Africa,* edited by S. Miers and I. Kopytoff, 391–411. Madison: University of Wisconsin Press.

Baird, David W. 1972. *Peter Pitchlynn: Chief of the Choctaws.* Norman: University of Oklahoma Press.

Baker, H. D. 2001. "Degrees of Freedom: Slavery in Mid-First Millennium BC Babylonia." *World Archaeology* 33.1: 18–26.

Bales, Kevin. 2000. *Disposable People: New Slavery in the Global Economy.* Berkeley: University of California Press.

Banaji, Jairus. 2001. *Agrarian Change in Late Antiquity: Gold, Labour, and Aristocratic Dominance.* Oxford Classical Monographs. Oxford; New York: Oxford University Press.

Banaji, Jairus. 2010. *Theory as History: Essays on Modes of Production and Exploitation.* Leiden: Brill.

Bang, Anna K. 2003. *Sufis and Scholars of the Sea: Family Networks in East Africa, 1860–1925.* New York: Routledge-Curzon.

Bang, Peter F. 2008. *The Roman Bazaar: A Comparative Study of Trade and Markets in a Tributary Empire.* Cambridge; New York: Cambridge University Press.

Baptist, Edward E. 2001. "'Cuffy,' 'Fancy Girls,' and 'One-Eyed Men': Rape, Commodification, and the Domestic Slave Trade in the United States." *American Historical Review* 5: 1619–50.

Baptist, Edward E. 2002. *Creating an Old South: Middle Florida's Plantation Frontier before the Civil War.* Chapel Hill: University of North Carolina Press.

Baptist, Edward E. 2014. *The Half Has Never Been Told: Slavery and the Making of American Capitalism.* New York: Basic Books.

Barcia Paz, M. 2014. *West African Warfare in Bahia and Cuba: Soldier Slaves in the Atlantic World, 1807–1844.* Oxford: Oxford University Press.

Barkindo, Bawuro. 1989. *The Sultanate of Mandara to 1902: History of the Evolution, Development and Collapse of a Central Sudanese Kingdom.* Stuttgart: Franz Steiner Verlag.

Barr, Julianna. 2005. "From Captives to Slaves: Commodifying Indian Women in the Borderlands." *Journal of American History* 92: 19–46.

Barr, Julianna. 2007. *Peace Came in the Form of a Woman: Indians and Spaniards in the Texas Borderlands.* Chapel Hill: University of North Carolina Press.

Barrère, Pierre. 1743. *Nouvelle relation de la France équinoxiale.* Paris: Chez Piget, Damonneville et Durand.

Barth, Henry. 1857. *Travels and Discoveries in North and Central Africa: Being a Journal of an Expedition Undertaken under the Auspices of H.B.M.'s Government in the Years 1849–1855.* Vol. 1. New York: Harper and Brothers.

Bashir Salau, Mohammed. 2011. *The West African Slave Plantation: A Case Study.* New York: Palgrave Macmillan.

Baum, Robert. 1999. *Shrines of the Slave Trade: Diola Religion and Society in Precolonial Senegal.* New York: Oxford University Press.

Bay, Edna G. 1998. *Wives of the Leopard: Gender, Politics, and Culture in the Kingdom of Dahomey.* Charlottesville: University of Virginia Press.

Bazin, Jean and E. Terray. 1982. *Guerres de lignages et guerres d'états en Afrique.* Paris: Editions des Archives Contemporaines.

Beard, Mary. 2007. *The Roman Triumph.* Cambridge, MA: Belknap Press of Harvard University Press.

Beaulieu, Augustin de. 1622[1996]. *Mémoires d'un voyage aux Indes Orientales, 1619–1622.* Edited by Denys Lombard. Paris: École française d'Extrême-Orient.

Beckles, Hilary McD. 2011. "Servants and Slaves during the 17th-Century Sugar Revolution." In *The Caribbean: A History of the Region and Its People,* edited by Stephan Palmié and Francisco A. Scarano, 205–16. Chicago: University of Chicago Press.

Beier, Zachery. 2014. "The Cabrits Garrison (Portsmouth, Dominica)." In *Encyclopedia of Caribbean Archaeology*, edited by Basil A Reid and R. Grant Gilmore 3: 83–84. Gainesville: University Press of Florida.

Belaúnde, Luisa Elvira. 2001. *Viviendo bien. Género y fertilidad entre los Airo-Pai de la amazonía peruana*. Lima: Centro Amazónico de Antropología y Aplicación Práctica/ Banco Central de Reserva del Perú.

Belgrave, Charles. 1960. *Personal Column*. London: Hutchinson & Company.

Bellagamba, Alice, Sandra E. Greene, and Martin A. Klein, eds. 2013. *African Voices on Slavery and the Slave Trade, Vol. 1*. Cambridge, Cambridge University Press.

Bellagamba, Alice, Sandra E. Greene, and Martin A. Klein, 2017. *African Slaves African Masters: Politics, Memories and Social Life*. Trenton, NJ: Africa World Press.

Bennett, Charles E. 1968. *Settlement of Florida*. Gainesville: University of Florida Press.

Bennett, Norman Robert. 1965. *New England Merchants in Africa: A History through Documents, 1802 to 1865*. Boston: Boston University Press.

Bentor, Eli. 1990. "Aro Ikeji Festival – Historical Consciousness and Negotiated Identities." In *Repercussions of the Atlantic Slave Trade*, edited by Carolyn Brown and Paul E. Lovejoy, 275–92. Trenton, NJ: Africa World Press.

Bentor, Eli. 1995. "Aro Ikeji Festival: Toward a Historical Interpretation of a Masquerade Festival." Dissertation, Indiana University

Benzoni, M. Girolamo. 1967. *La Historia del Nuevo Mundo*. Biblioteca de la Academia Nacional de la Historia, 86. Caracas: Italgráfica.

Bergad, Laird W. 1990. *Cuban Rural Society in the Nineteenth Century: The Social and Economic History of Monoculture in Matanzas*. Princeton, NJ: Princeton University Press.

Bergad, Laird W. 1999. *Slavery and the Demographic and Economic History of Minas Gerais, Brazil, 1720–1888*. New York: Cambridge University Press.

Bergad, Laird W. 2007. *The Comparative Histories of Slavery in Brazil, Cuba, and the United States*. Cambridge; New York: Cambridge University Press.

Berlin, Ira. 1974. *Slaves without Masters: The Free Negro in the Antebellum South*. Oxford; New York: Oxford University Press.

Berlin, Ira. 1998. *Many Thousands Gone: The First Two Centuries of Slavery in North America*. Cambridge, MA: Belknap Press of Harvard University Press. Paperback edition published 2000.

Berlin, Ira. 2003. *Generations of Captivity: A History of African-American Slaves*. Cambridge: Belknap Press of Harvard University Press.

Bernal, Victoria. 1995. "Cotton and Colonial Order in Sudan: A Social History, with Emphasis on the Gezira Scheme." In *Cotton, Colonialism, and Social History in Sub-Saharan Africa*, edited by Allen Isaacman and Richard Roberts, 96–118. Portsmouth, NH: Heinemann.

Bernus, Edmond and Suzanne Bernus. 1975. "L'Évolution de la condition servile chez les Touregs sahéliens." In *L'Esclavage en Afrique précoloniale*, edited by C. Meillassoux, 27–47. Paris: Maspero.

Berry, Daina Ramey. 2007. *"Swing the Sickle for the Harvest Is Ripe": Gender and Slavery in Antebellum Georgia.* Urbana: University of Illinois Press.

Bhacker, Reda. 1992. *Trade and Empire in Muscat and Zanzibar: Roots of British Domination.* New York: Routledge.

Bicalho, Maria, João Fragoso, and Maria de Fátima Gouvêa, eds. 2001. *O Antigo Regime nos Trópicos: a dinâmica imperial portuguesa.* Rio de Janeiro: Civilização Brasileira.

Bird, Christiane. 2010. *The Sultan's Shadow: One Family's Rule at the Crossroads of East and West.* New York: Random House.

Bishop, Charles A. and Victor Lytwyn. 2007. "Barbarism and Ardour of War from the Tenderest Years: Cree–Inuit Warfare in the Hudson Bay Region." In *North American Indigenous Warfare and Ritual Violence*, edited by R. Chacoan and R. Mendoza, 30–57. Tucson: University of Arizona Press.

Blackburn, Robin. 2010. *The Making of New World Slavery: From the Baroque to the Modern, 1492–1800.* London: Verso.

Blair, W. 1833. *An Inquiry into the State of Slavery amongst the Romans; from the Earliest Period, till the Establishment of the Lombards in Italy.* Edinburgh: Thomas Clark.

Bloch, Marc. 1975. "Personal Liberty and Servitude in the Middle Ages, Particularly in France: Contribution to a Class Study." In *Slavery and Serfdom in the Middle Ages: Selected Essays by Marc Bloch*, edited by Marc Bloch, 33–92. Berkeley: University of California Press.

Bodel, John. 2011. "Slave Labour and Roman Society." In *The Cambridge World History of Slavery. Volume I: The Ancient Mediterranean World*, edited by K. Bradley and P. Cartledge, 311–36. Cambridge: Cambridge University Press.

Bodel, John and Walter Scheidel, eds. 2017. *On Human Bondage: After Slavery and Social Death.* Malden, MA; Oxford: Wiley Blackwell.

Boggiani, Guido. 1945. *Os Caduveo.* São Paulo: Livraria Martins Editôra.

Bolt, Christine. 1987. *American Indian Policy and American Reform: Case Studies of the Campaign to Assimilate the American Indians.* London: Allen & Unwin.

Bonte, Pierre. 1975. "Esclavage et relations de dépendance chez les Touregs Kel Gress." In *L'Esclavage en Afrique précoloniale*, edited by C. Meillassoux, 49–76. Paris: Maspero.

Bourgeot, André. 1975. "Rapports esclavagistes et conditions d'affranchissement chez les Imuhag." In *L'Esclavage en Afrique précoloniale*, edited by C. Meillassoux, 253–80. Paris: Maspero.

Bowne, Eric E. 2005. *The Westos: Slave Traders of the Early Colonial South.* Tuscaloosa: University of Alabama Press.

Bowser, B. J. 2008. "Captives in Amazonia: Becoming Kin in a Predatory Landscape." In *Invisible Citizens: Captives and Their Consequences*, edited by Catherine M. Cameron, 262–82. Salt Lake City: University of Utah Press.

Bradley, Francis. 2013. "Siam's Conquest of Patani and the End of Mandala Relations, 1786–1838." In *Ghosts of the Past in Southern Thailand: Essays on the History and Historiography of Patani*, edited by Patrick Jory, 153–57. Singapore: National University of Singapore Press.

Bradley, Keith. 1989. *Slavery and Rebellion in the Roman World, 140 B.C.–70 B.C.* Bloomington: Indiana University Press.

Bradley, Keith. 1994. *Slavery and Society at Rome.* Cambridge: Cambridge University Press.

Bradley, Keith. 2000. "Animalizing the Slave: The Truth of Fiction." *Journal of Roman Studies* 90: 110–25.

Bradley, Keith. 2010. "Freedom and Slavery." In *The Oxford Handbook of Roman Studies*, edited by A. Barchiesi and W. Scheidel, 624–36. Oxford: Oxford University Press.

Bradley, Keith. 2011. "Slavery in the Roman Republic." In *The Cambridge World History of Slavery. Volume I: The Ancient Mediterranean World*, edited by K. Bradley and P. Cartledge, 241–64. Cambridge: Cambridge University Press.

Bradley, Keith and Paul Cartledge, eds. 2011. *The Cambridge World History of Slavery. Volume I: The Ancient Mediterranean World.* Cambridge: Cambridge University Press.

Brah, Avtar. 1992. "Difference, Diversity, and Differentiation." In *"Race," Culture, and Difference*, edited by J. Donald and A. Rattansi, 126–48. London; Newbury Park, CA: Sage Publications and the Open University.

Brasher, Glenn David. 2012. *The Peninsula Campaign and the Necessity of Emancipation: African Americans and the Fight for Freedom.* Chapel Hill: University of North Carolina Press.

Braund, D. and G. R. Tsetskhladze. 1989. "The Export of Slaves from Colchis." *Classical Quarterly* 39: 114–25.

Bravo, B. 2013. "Un biglietto per la vendita di uno schiavo (Phanagoreia, 500–450 a.c.) e un *katadesmos* pubblicato a torto come una lettera (territorio di Olbia Pontica, ca. 400 a.c.)." *Palamedes* 8: 61–73.

Breen, T. H. and Stephen Innes. 1980. *"Myne Owne Ground": Race and Freedom on Virginia's Eastern Shore, 1640–1676.* New York: Oxford University Press.

Bresson, Alain. 2015. *The Making of the Ancient Greek Economy: Institutions, Markets, and Growth in the City-States.* Translated by Steven Rendall. Princeton, NJ: Princeton University Press.

Breton, Raymond Guillaume. 1665. *Dictionaire Caraibe-François.* Auxerre: Gilles Bouquet.

Brooks, James F. 2002. *Captives & Cousins: Slavery, Kinship, and Community in the Southwest Borderlands.* Chapel Hill: University of North Carolina Press.

Brower, Benjamin Claude. 2009. "The Servile Populations of the Algerian Sahara, 1850–1900." In *Slavery, Islam and Diaspora*, edited by Behnaz A. Mirzai, Ismael Musah Montana, and Paul E. Lovejoy, 169–91. Trenton, NJ: Africa World Press.

Brown, Carolyn and Paul E. Lovejoy, eds., 2010. *Repercussions of the Atlantic Slave Trade: The Interior of the Bight of Biafra and the African Diaspora.* Trenton, NJ: Africa World Press.

Brown, Christopher Leslie. 2006. *Moral Capital: Foundations of British Abolitionism.* Chapel Hill: University of North Carolina.

Brown, Christopher Leslie and Philip D. Morgan. 2006. *Arming Slaves: From Classical Times to the Modern Age.* New Haven, CT: Yale University Press.

Brown, Kathleen M. 1996. *Good Wives, Nasty Wenches, and Anxious Patriarchs: Gender, Race, and Power in Colonial Virginia.* Chapel Hill: University of North Carolina Press.

Brunson, Margaret R. 2002[1991]. *Encyclopedia of Ancient Egypt*, rev. edn. New York: Facts on File, Inc.

Brunt, P. A. 1980. "Free Labour and Public Works at Rome." *Journal of Roman Studies* 70: 81–100.

Buchanan, Thomas C. 2004. *Black Life on the Mississippi: Slaves, Free Blacks, and the Western Steamboat World.* Chapel Hill: University of North Carolina Press.

Bücher, Karl. 1893. *Die Entstehung der Volkswirtschaft: Sechs Vorträge.* Tübingen: Verlag der H. Laupp'schen Buchhandlung.

Buckland, W. W. 1908. *The Roman Law of Slavery: The Condition of the Slave in Private Law from Augustus to Justinian.* Cambridge: Cambridge University Press.

Burdett, A. L. P., ed. 2006. *Slave Trade into Arabia 1820–1973.* 2 vols. Slough: Archive Editions.

Burford, Alison. 1993. *Land and Labor in the Greek World.* Baltimore: Johns Hopkins University Press.

Burke, Diane Mutti. 2010. *On Slavery's Border: Missouri's Small Slaveholding Households, 1815–1865.* Athens: University of Georgia Press.

Burnham, Philip. 1980. "Raiders and Traders in Adamawa: Slavery as a Regional System." In *Asian and African Systems of Slavery*, edited by James L. Watson, 43–72. Oxford: Oxford University Press.

Burton, Richard F. 1872. *Zanzibar: City, Island and Coast.* London: Tinsley Brothers.

Burton, Richard F. 1894. *First Footsteps in East Africa.* London: Tylston and Edwards.

Bush, Michael. 1996. "Serfdom in Medieval and Modern Europe: A Comparison." In *Serfdom and Slavery: Studies in Legal Bondage*, edited by M. Bush, 199–224. New York: Longman.

Cabeza de Vaca, Álvar Núñez. 2003. *The Narrative of Cabeza de Vaca.* Edited by Rolena Adorno and Patrick Charles Pautz. Lincoln: University of Nebraska Press.

Cameron, Catherine M. 2008. "Captives in Prehistory: Agents of Social Change." In *Invisible Citizens: Captives and Their Consequences*, edited by C. M. Cameron, 1–24. Salt Lake City: University of Utah Press.

Cameron, Catherine M. 2011. "Captives and Culture Change: Implications for Archaeologists." *Current Anthropology* 52: 169–209.

Cameron, Catherine M. 2013. "How People Moved among Ancient Societies: Broadening the View." *American Anthropologist* 115: 218–31.

Cameron, Catherine M. 2015 "Commodities or Gifts? Captives/Slaves in Small-Scale Societies." In *The Archaeology of Slavery: A Comparative Approach to Captivity and Coercion*, edited by Lydia Wilson Marshall, 24–40. Carbondale: Center for Archaeological Investigations, Southern Illinois University.

Cameron, Catherine M. 2016a. *Captives: How Stolen People Changed the World.* Lincoln: University of Nebraska Press.

Cameron, Catherine M. 2016b. "The Variability of the Human Experience: Marginal People and the Creation of Power." In *Archaeology of the Human Experience.* Archaeological Papers of the American Anthropological Association No. 27, edited by Michelle Hegmon, 40–53. Washington DC: American Anthropological Association.

Camodeca, Giuseppe. 2000. "La Società Ercolanese." In *Gli antichi Ercolanesi: Antropologia, società, economia,* edited by Mario Pagano, 67–70. Naples: Electa Napoli.

Camp, Stephanie M. H. 2004. *Closer to Freedom: Enslaved Women and Everyday Resistance in the Plantation South.* Chapel Hill: University of North Carolina Press.

Campbell, Gwyn. 2004. "Introduction: Slavery and Other Forms of Unfree Labour in the Indian Ocean World." In *The Structure of Slavery in Indian Ocean Africa and Asia,* edited by G. Campbell, vii–xxxi. London: Frank Cass.

Campbell, Gwyn. 2005. *An Economic History of Imperial Madagascar, 1750–1895: The Rise and Fall of an Island Empire.* Cambridge: Cambridge University Press.

Campbell, Gwyn. 2008. "Islam in Indian Ocean Africa Prior to the Scramble: A New Historical Paradigm." In *Struggling with History: Islam and Cosmopolitanism in the Western Indian Ocean,* edited by Edward Simpson and Kai Kresse, 43–92. New York: Columbia University Press.

Campbell, Gwyn. 2010. "Slavery in the Indian Ocean World." In *The Routledge History of Slavery,* edited by Gad Heuman and Trevor Burnard, 56–61. London: Routledge.

Campbell, Gwyn. 2014. "The Question of Slavery in Indian Ocean World History." In *The Indian Ocean: Oceanic Connections and the Creation of New Societies,* edited by Abdul Sheriff and Engseng Ho, 123–49. London: Hurst & Company.

Campbell, Randolph B. 1989. *An Empire for Slavery: The Peculiar Institution in Texas, 1821–1865.* Baton Rouge: Louisiana State University Press.

Canevaro, Mirko and David Martin Lewis. 2014. "*Khoris Oikountes* and the Obligations of Freedmen in Late Classical and Early Hellenistic Athens." *Incidenza dell'antico* 12: 91–121.

Capogrossi Colognesi, L. 1990. *Economie antiche e capitalismo moderno: la sfida di Max Weber.* Rome: Laterza.

Carandini, Andrea. 1985. *Settefinestre: Una villa schiavistica nell'Etruria Romana.* Modena: Panini.

Carneiro, Robert L. 1991. "The Nature of the Chiefdom as Revealed by Evidence from the Cauca Valley of Colombia." In *Profiles in Cultural Evolution: Papers from a Conference in Honor of Elman R. Service.* Anthropological Papers, Museum of Anthropology, University of Michigan, No. 85, edited by A. Terry Rambo and Kathleen Gillogly, 167–90. Ann Arbor: Anthropological Papers, Museum of Anthropology, University of Michigan.

Carney, Judith Ann. 2001. *Black Rice: The African Origins of Rice Cultivation in America.* Cambridge, MA: Harvard University Press.
Carrié, J.-M. 1982. "Le 'colonat du Bas-Empire': un mythe historiographique?" *Opus* 1: 351–70.
Carrié, J.-M. 1983. "Un roman des origines: les généalogies du 'colonat du Bas-Empire." *Opus* 2: 205–51.
Carter, Robert. 2009. "How Pearls Made the Modern Emirates." In *Proceedings of the International History Conference on New Perspectives on Recording UAE History,* 265–81. Abu Dhabi: International Center for Documentation and Research.
Carter, Robert. 2011. *Sea of Pearls: Seven Thousand Years of the Industry That Shaped the Gulf.* London: Arabian Publishing.
Cartledge, P. A. 1985. "Rebels and *Sambos* in Classical Greece: A Comparative View." In *Crux: Essays in Greek History Presented to G. E. M. de Ste. Croix on His 75th Birthday,* edited by P. A. Cartledge and F. D. Harvey, 16–46. London: Duckworth.
Cartledge, P. A. 2002. *The Greeks: A Portrait of Self and Others.* 2nd edn. Oxford: Oxford University Press.
Cartledge, P. A. 2011. "The Helots: A Contemporary Review." In *The Cambridge World History of Slavery, Volume I: The Ancient Near East and Mediterranean World to AD 500,* edited by K. Bradley and P. Cartledge, 74–90. Cambridge: Cambridge University Press.
Casson, Lionel. 1989. *The Periplus Maris Erythraei: Text with Introduction, Translation, and Commentary.* Princeton, NJ: Princeton University Press.
Castro, H. M. M. d. 1995. *Das cores do silêncio: os significados da liberdade no sudeste escravista, Brasil Século XIX.* Rio de Janeiro: Arquivo Nacional.
Ceccarelli, P. 2013. *Ancient Greek Letter Writing. A Cultural History (600 BC–150 BC).* Oxford: Oxford University Press.
Cecelski, David S. 2001. *The Waterman's Song: Slavery and Freedom in Maritime North Carolina.* Chapel Hill: University of North Carolina Press.
Chacon, R. J. and R. G. Mendoza, eds. 2007a. *North American Indigenous Warfare and Ritual Violence.* Tucson: University of Arizona Press.
Chacon, R. J. and R. G. Mendoza, 2007b. *Latin American Indigenous Warfare and Ritual Violence.* Tucson: University of Arizona Press.
Chagnon, N. A. 1988. "Life Histories, Blood Revenge, and Warfare in a Tribal Population." *Science* 239: 985–92.
Chalhoub, S. 1990. *Visões da liberdade: uma história das últimas décadas da escravidão na corte.* São Paulo: Companhia das Letras.
Chambers, Douglas. 1997. "'My Own Nation': Igbo Exiles in the Diaspora." *Slavery and Abolition* 18: 72–97.
Chambouleyron, Rafael. 2010. *Povoamento, ocupação e agricultura na Amazônia colonial (1640–1706).* Belém: Açaí/Centro de Memória da Amazônia/PPHIST-UFPA.
Chambouleyron, Rafael. 2015. "Indian Freedom and Indian Slavery in the Portuguese Amazon (1640–1755)." In *Building the Atlantic Empires: Unfree*

Labor and Imperial States in the Political Economy of Capitalism, ca. 1500–1914, edited by John Donoghue and Evelyn P. Jennings, 54–71. Leiden: Brill.

Charles-Picard, Gilbert and Colette Charles-Picard. 1961. *Daily Life in Carthage at the Time of Hannibal.* New York: Macmillan.

Chatterjee, I. 2017. "The Locked Box in *Slavery and Social Death*." In *On Human Bondage: After Slavery and Social Death*, edited by J. Bodel and W. Scheidel. 151–66. Malden, MA; Oxford: Wiley Blackwell.

Chevillard, André. 1659. *Les Desseins de son Eminence de Richelieu pour l'Amèrique.* Rennes: Chez Jean Durand.

Chittick, Neville. 1980. "East Africa and the Orient: Ports and Trade before the Arrival of the Portuguese." *Historical Relations across the Indian Ocean.* 13–22. Paris: UNESCO.

Christ, Matthew R. 2007. "Evolution of the *Eisphora* in Classical Athens." *Classical Quarterly* 57.1: 53–69.

Christes, Johannes. 1979. *Sklaven und Freigelassene als Grammatiker und Philologen im antiken Rom.* Forschungen Zur Antiken Sklaverei, Bd. 10. Wiesbaden: Steiner Verlag.

Clarence-Smith, William Gervase. 1989. *The Economics of the Indian Ocean Slave Trade in the Nineteenth Century.* London/Totawa: Frank Cass.

Clarence-Smith, William Gervase. 2006. *Islam and the Abolition of Slavery.* London: Hurst & Company.

Clarkson, Thomas. 1788. *An Essay on the Slavery and Commerce of the Human Species, Particularly the African.* London: J. Phillips.

Claval, Paul. 1993. "Modern Geography and Contemporary Reality." *Geojournal* 31.3, Contemporary French Human Geography: 239–45.

Clayton, Lawrence A., Vernon James Knight Jr., and Edward C. Moore, eds. 1993. *The De Soto Chronicles: The Expedition of Hernando de Soto to North America in 1539–1543*, 2 vols. Tuscaloosa: University of Alabama Press.

Coclanis, Peter A. 2013. "Would Slavery Have Survived without the Civil War?: Economic Factors in the American South during the Antebellum and Postbellum Eras." *Southern Cultures* 19: 67–79.

Cohen, Edward. 1992. *Athenian Economy and Society: A Banking Perspective.* Princeton, NJ: Princeton University Press.

Cole, Shawn. 2005. "Capitalism and Freedom: Manumissions and the Slave Market in Louisiana 1725–1820." *Journal of Economic History* 65: 1008–27.

Collins, Patricia Hill. 1990. *Black Feminist Thought: Knowledge, Consciousness, and the Politics of Empowerment.* Boston: Unwin Hyman Publishers.

Columb, P. H. 1873. *Slave Catching in the Indian Ocean.* London: Longmans, Green & Company.

Columbus, Ferdinand. 1992. *The Life of the Admiral Christopher Columbus by His Son Ferdinand.* New Brunswick, NJ: Rutgers University Press.

Coma, Guglielmo. 1903. "The Syllacio-Coma Letter." In *Christopher Columbus, His Life, His Works, His Remains*, compiled by John Boyd Thacher, 2:223–62. Cleveland, OH: The A.H. Clark Company.

Conrad, Paul Timothy. 2011. "Captive Fates: Displaced American Indians in the Southwest Borderlands, Mexico, and Cuba." Dissertation, University of Texas at Austin.

Cook, Gregory and Amy Rubenstein-Gottschamer. 2011. "Maritime Connections in a Plantation Economy: Archaeological Investigations of a Colonial Sloop in St. Ann's Bay, Jamaica." In *Out of Many, One People: The Historical Archaeology of Colonial Jamaica*, edited by James A. Delle, Mark W. Hauser, and Douglas V. Armstrong, 102–21. Gainesville: University Press of Florida.

Cooper, Frederick. 1977. *Plantation Slavery on the East Coast of Africa*. New Haven, CT; London: Yale University Press.

Cooper, Frederick. 1979. "The Problem of Slavery in African Studies." *Journal of African History* 20.1: 103–25.

Cooper, Frederick. 1980. *From Slaves to Squatters: Plantation Labor and Agriculture in Zanzibar and Coastal Kenya, 1890–1925*. New Haven, CT: Yale University Press.

Coquery-Vidrovitch, Catherine. 1971. "De la traite des esclaves à l'exportation de l'huile de palme et des palmistes a Dahomey: XIXe siècle." In *The Development of Indigenous Trade and Markets in West Africa: Studies Presented and Discussed at the Tenth International African Seminar at Fourah Bay College, Freetown, December 1969*, edited by C. Meillassoux, 107–23. London: International African Institute.

Coquery-Vidrovitch, Catherine. 1975. "Research on an African Mode of Production." *Critique of Anthropology* 4: 38–71.

Coudreau, Henri Anatole. 1887. *La France équinoxiale*. 2 vols. Paris: Challamel ainé.

Coupland, Reginald. 1933[1964]. *The British Anti-slavery Movement, with a New Introduction by J. D. Fage*. London: Frank Cass.

Coupland, Reginald. 1938. *East Africa and Its Invaders, from the Earliest Times to the Death of Seyyid Said in 1856*. Oxford: Clarendon Press.

Coupland, Reginald. 1939. *The Exploitation of East Africa, 1856–1890: The Slave Trade and the Scramble*. London: Faber and Faber.

Crone, Patricia. 1980. *Slaves on Horses: The Evolution of the Islamic Polity*. Cambridge; New York: Cambridge University Press.

Cuvigny, Hélène. 1996. "The Amount of Wages Paid to the Quarry-Workers at Mons Claudianus." *Journal of Roman Studies* 86: 139–45.

Daitz, Stephen G. 1971. "Concepts of Freedom and Slavery in Euripides' *Hecuba*." *Hermes* 99: 217–26.

Dal Lago, Enrico, and Constantina Katsari. 2008a. "The Study of Ancient and Modern Slave Systems." In *Slave Systems: Ancient and Modern*, edited by Enrico Dal Lago and Constantina Katsari, 3–31. Cambridge; New York: Cambridge University Press.

Dal Lago, Enrico, and Constantina Katsari., eds. 2008b. *Slave Systems, Ancient and Modern*. Cambridge: Cambridge University Press.

Daly, John Patrick. 2004. *When Slavery Was Called Freedom: Evangelicalism, Proslavery, and the Causes of the Civil War*. Lexington: University Press of Kentucky.

Dampier, William. 1699 [1931]. *Voyages and Discoveries*, edited by C. Wilkinson. London: Argonaut Press.

Dandamaev, Muhammad. 1984. *Slavery in Babylonia: From Nabopolassar to Alexander the Great (626–331 BC)*. Translated by V. Powell. DeKalb: Northern Illinois University Press.

David, Nicholas. 2012. "A Close Reading of Hamman Yaji's Diary: Slave Raiding and Montagnard Responses in the Mountains around Madagali. Northeast Nigeria and Northern Cameroon." www.sukur.info/MountHammanYaji%20PAPER.pdf.

Davies, John K. 1971. *Athenian Propertied Families, 600–300 BC*. Oxford: Clarendon Press.

Davies, John K. 2007. "Classical Greece: Production." In *The Cambridge Economic History of the Greco-Roman World*, edited by W. Sheidel, I. Morris, and R. Saller, 333–61. Cambridge: Cambridge University Press.

Davis, David Brion. 1966. *The Problem of Slavery in Western Culture*. Ithaca, NY: Cornell University Press.

Davis, David Brion. 2006. *Inhuman Bondage: The Rise and Fall of Slavery in the New World*. Oxford; New York: Oxford University Press. Paperback edition published 2008.

Deagan, Kathleen. 2004. "Reconsidering Taíno Social Dynamics after Spanish Conquest: Gender and Class in Culture Contact Studies." *American Antiquity* 69.4: 597–626.

DeBoer, W. R. 1986. "Pillage and Production in the Amazon: A View through the Conibo of the Ucayali Basin, Eastern Peru." *World Archaeology* 18.2: 231–46.

Degler, Carl. 1959. "Starr on Slavery." *Journal of Economic History* 19: 271–77.

De La Loubère, Simon. 1691 [1969]. *A New Historical Relation of the Kingdom of Siam*. Kuala Lumpur: Oxford University Press.

De las Casas, Bartolomé. 1986. *Historia de las Indias*. 3 vols. Caracas: Biblioteca Ayacucho.

De las Casas, Bartolomé. 1992. "Apologética Historia Sumaria." In *Obras Completas*, Bartolomé de Las Casas, vol. 3. Madrid: Alianza Editorial.

Delle, James A. 1998. *An Archaeology of Social Space: Analyzing Coffee Plantations in Jamaica's Blue Mountains*. New York: Plenum.

Delle, James A. 2014. *The Colonial Caribbean: Landscapes of Power in the Plantation System*. New York: Cambridge University Press.

Delle, James A., Mark W. Hauser, and Douglas V. Armstrong, eds. 2011. *Out of Many, One People: The Historical Archaeology of Colonial Jamaica*. Tuscaloosa: University of Alabama Press.

De Ligt, L. 2012. *Studies in the Demographic History of Roman Italy 225 BC-AD 100*. Cambridge: Cambridge University Press.

De Ligt, L. and P. Garnsey. 2012. "The Album of Herculaneum and a Model of the Town's Demography." *Journal of Roman Archaeology* 25: 69–94.

Descat, R. 2006. "*Argyrônetos*: les transformations de l'echange dans la Grece archaïque." In *Agoranomia: Studies in Money and Exchange Presented to John*

H. Kroll, edited by P. van Alfen, 21–36. New York: American Numismatic Society.

de Vos, Mariette. 2013. "The Rural Landscape of Thugga: Farms, Presses, Mills, and Transport." In *The Roman Agricultural Economy: Organization, Investment, and Production*, edited by Alan Bowman and Roger Wilson, 143–211. Oxford: Oxford University Press.

Dew, Charles B. 1994. *Bond of Iron: Master and Slave at Buffalo Forge.* New York: W. W. Norton.

Deyle, Steven. 2005. *Carry Me Back: The Domestic Slave Trade in American Life.* New York: Oxford University Press.

Díaz de Guzmán, Rui. 1979. "Relación breve y sumaria que haze el governador don Ruiz Diaz de Guzmán." In *Relación de la entrada a los Chiriguanos*, edited by Rui Díaz de Guzmán, 71–80. Santa Cruz de la Sierra: Fundación Cultural "Ramón Darío Gutiérrez."

Domar, Evsey D. 1945. "The Causes of Slavery and Serfdom: A Hypothesis." *Journal of Economic History* 30: 18–32.

Domínguez Gonzáles, Lourdes S. 1986. "Fuentes arqueológicas en el estudio de la esclavitud en Cuba." In *La Esclavitud en Cuba*, edited by Academía de Ciencias de Cuba, 274–78. Havana: Editorial Academia.

Donald, Leland. 1983. "Was Nuu-chah-nulth-aht Society Based on Slave Labor?" in *The Development of Political Organization in Native North America*, edited by Elizabeth Tooker, 108–19. Washington, DC: American Ethnological Society.

Donald, Leland. 1997. *Aboriginal Slavery on the Northwest Coast of North America.* Berkeley: University of California Press.

Doran, Michael. 1975. "Population Statistics of Nineteenth Century Indian Territory." *Chronicles of Oklahoma* 53: 492–515.

Douglass, Frederick. 1845. *Narrative of the Life of Frederick Douglass, an American Slave.* Boston, MA: Anti-slavery Office.

Downey, Tom. 2009. *Planting a Capitalist South: Masters, Merchants, and Manufacturers in the Southern Interior, 1790–1860.* Baton Rouge: Louisiana State University Press.

Drucker, Philip. 1965. *Cultures of the North Pacific Coast.* Scranton, PA: Chandler.

Dubois, Laurent. 2004. *A Colony of Citizens: Revolution & Slave Emancipation in the French Caribbean, 1787–1804.* Chapel Hill: University of North Carolina Press.

Dubois, Laurent. 2012. *A Colony of Citizens: Revolution and Slave Emancipation in the French Caribbean, 1787–1804.* Chapel Hill: University of North Carolina Press.

Ducat, Jean. *Les Hilotes.* 1990. Bulletin de Correspondance Hellénique 20. Athènes: Paris: Ecole française d'Athènes.

Duncan-Jones, Richard. 1994. *Money and Government in the Roman Empire.* Cambridge; New York: Cambridge University Press.

Dunn, Stephen P. 1982. *The Fall and Rise of the Asiatic Mode of Production.* London: Routledge and Kegan Paul.

Dureau de La Malle, A. J. C. A. 1840. *Économie politique des Romains*. Paris: L. Hachette.

Du Tertre, Jean-Baptiste. 1654. *Histoire Generale des Isles de S. Christophe, de la Guadeloupe, de la Martinique, et autres dans l'Amerique*. Paris: Jacques Langlois.

Du Tertre, Jean-Baptiste. 1667. *Histoire Generale des Antilles Habitées par les François*. Paris: Thomas Jolly.

Dyakonov, I. M. 1976–77. "Slaves, Helots, and Serfs in Early Antiquity." *Soviet Anthropology and Archaeology* 15.1–2: 50–102.

Dye, D. 2004. "Art, Ritual, and Chiefly Warfare in the Mississippian World." In *Hero, Hawk, and Open Hand: American Indian Art of the Ancient Midwest and South*, edited by R. F. Townsend and R. V. Sharp, 191–206. New Haven, CT: Yale University Press.

Eaton, Richard Maxwell. 2005. *Social History of the Deccan, 1300–1761*. Cambridge: Cambridge University Press.

Eder, Donald Gray. 1976. "Time under the Southern Cross: The Tannenbaum Thesis Reappraised." *Agricultural History* 50.4: 600–14.

Edmondson, J. 2011. "Slavery and the Roman Family." In *The Cambridge World History of Slavery. Volume I: The Ancient Mediterranean World*, edited by K. Bradley and P. Cartledge, 337–61. Cambridge: Cambridge University Press.

Ehrenberg, Victor. 1974. *The People of Aristophanes*. 3rd edn. New York: Barnes and Noble.

Ekberg, C. J. 2010. *Stealing Indian Women. Native Slavery in the Illinois Country*. Urbana: University of Illinois Press.

Elayi, Josette. 1981. "La révolte des esclaves de Tyr relatée par Justin." *Baghdader Mitteilungen* 12: 139–50.

Eltis, David. 2000. *The Rise of African Slavery in the Americas*. Cambridge: Cambridge University Press.

Eltis, David. 2007. "A Brief Overview of the Trans-Atlantic Slave Trade." www.slavevoyages.org/tast/assessment/essays-intro-01.faces.

Eltis, David and Stanley Engerman. 2011. "Dependence, Servility, and Coerced Labor in Time and Space." In *The Cambridge World History of Slavery, Volume 3: AD 1420–AD 1804*, edited by David Eltis and Stanley L. Engerman, 1–24. Cambridge: Cambridge University Press.

Eltis, David and David Richardson. 2003. "Os mercados de escravos africanos recém-chegados às Américas: padrões de preços, 1673–1865." *Topoi* 4.6: 9–46.

Eltis, David and David Richardson. 2010. *Atlas of the Transatlantic Slave Trade*. New Haven, CT; London: Yale University Press.

Elton, James F. 1879. *Travels and Researches among the Lakes and Mountains of East and Central Africa*. London: Murray.

Elwert, Georg. 1973. *Wirtschaft und Herrschaft von "Daxome" (Dahomey) im 18. Jahrhundert*. Munich: Renner.

Endicott, Kirk. 1983. "The Effects of Slave Raiding on the Aborigines of the Malay Peninsula." In *Slavery, Bondage and Dependency in Southeast Asia*, edited by Anthony Reid, 221–36. St. Lucia: University of Queensland Press.

Engels, Friedrich. 1878[1962]. *Herrn Eugen Dührings Umwalzung der Wissenschaft (Anti-Dühring).* Moscow: Foreign Languages Publishing House.

Emirbayer, Mustafa. 1997. "Manifesto for a Relational Sociology." *American Journal of Sociology* 103.2: 281–317.

Equiano's World website: http://equianosworld.tubmaninstitute.ca.

Erdem, Y. Hakan. 1996. *Slavery in the Ottoman Empire and Its Demise, 1800–1909.* New York: St. Martin's Press.

Erdkamp, Paul. 1999. "Underemployment, and the Cost of Rural Labour in the Roman World." *Classical Quarterly* 49: 556–72.

Erikson, Philippe. 1986. "Altérité, tatouage et anthropophagie chez les Pano: La belliqueuse quête du soi." *Journal de la Société des Américanistes* 72: 185–209.

Espersen, Ryan E. 2017. "'Better than we': Landscapes and Materialities of Race, Class, and Gender in Preemancipation Colonial Saba, Dutch Caribbean." PhD Dissertation. Leiden University, Netherlands.

Ethridge, Robbie. 2006. "Creating the Shatter Zone: Indian Slave Traders and the Collapse of the Southeastern Chiefdoms." In *Light on the Path: The Anthropology and History of the Southeastern Indians,* edited by Thomas J. Pluckhahn and Robbie Ethridge, 207–18. Tuscaloosa: University of Alabama Press.

Ethridge, Robbie. 2009. "Introduction," in *Mapping the Mississippian Shatter Zone: The Colonial Indian Slave Trade and Regional Instability in the American South,* edited by Robbie Ethridge and Sheri M. Shuck-Hall, 1–62. Lincoln: University of Nebraska Press.

Ethridge, Robbie and S. M. Shuck-Hall, eds. 2009. *Mapping the Mississippian Shatter Zone: The Colonial Indian Slave Trade and Regional Instability in the American South.* Lincoln: University of Nebraska Press.

Ewald, Janet J. 2000. "Crossers of the Sea: Slaves, Freedmen, and Other Migrants in the Northwestern Indian Ocean, c. 1750–1914." *The American Historical Review* 105.1: 69–91.

Ewald, Janet J. 2010. "Bondsmen, Freedmen and Maritime Industrial Transportation, c. 1840–1900." *Slavery and Abolition* 31.3: 451–66.

Ewald, Janet J. 2013. "African Bondsmen, Freedmen, and the Maritime Proletariats of the Northwestern Indian Ocean World, c. 1500–1900." In *Indian Ocean Slavery in the Age of Abolition,* edited by Robert Harms, Bernard K. Freamon, and David W. Blight, 200–22. New Haven, CT: Yale University Press.

Faust, Drew Gilpin, ed. 1981. *The Ideology of Slavery: Proslavery Thought in the Antebellum South, 1830–1860.* Baton Rouge: Louisiana State University Press.

Fausto, Carlos. 2001. *Inimigos fiéis. História, Guerra e Xamanismo na Amazônia.* São Paulo: Editora da Universidade de São Paulo.

Ferguson, B. R. and N. L. Whitehead, eds. 1999[1992]. *War in the Tribal Zone: Expanding States and Indigenous Warfare.* 2nd edn. Santa Fe: University of New Mexico Press.

Ferguson, Douglas Edwin. 1973. "Nineteenth Century Hausaland: Being a Description by Imam Imoru of the Land, Economy, and Society of His People." Dissertation, UCLA.

Fernandes, Florestan. 1976. *Circuito Fechado: quatro ensaios sobre o "poder institucional."* São Paulo: HUCITEC.

Fernando, Radin. 2006. *Murder Most Foul: A Panorama of Social Life in Melaka from the 1780s to the 1820s*. Kuala Lumpur: Malaysian Branch of the Royal Asiatic Society.

Ferrer, Ada. 2003. "La société esclavagiste cubaine et la révolution." *Annales. Histoire, Sciences Sociales* 58: 333–56.

Ferrer, Ada. 2014. *Freedom's Mirror: Cuba and Haiti in the Age of Revolution*. New York: Cambridge University Press.

Février, J.-G. 1951–52. "*Vir Sidonius*." *Semitica* 4: 13–18.

Fields, Barbara Jeanne. 1985. *Slavery and Freedom on the Middle Ground: Maryland during the Nineteenth Century*. New Haven, CT: Yale University Press.

Figueroa, Francisco de. 1986. "Ynforme de las missiones del Marañón, Gran Pará ó Río de las Amazonas..." In *Informes de Jesuitas en el Amazonas, 1660–1684*, Monumenta Amazónica B1, 143–307. Iquitos: Instituto de Investigaciones de la Amazonía Peruana/Centro de Estudios Teológicos de la Amazonía.

Filliot, J. M. 1974. *La traite des esclaves vers les Mascareignes au XVIIe siècle*. Paris: l'Office de la recherche scientifique et technique outre-mer.

Findlay, Ronald. 1975. "Slavery, Incentives, and Manumission: A Theoretical Model." *Journal of Political Economy* 83.5: 923–34.

Finley, M. I. 1935. "Review of W. Westermann, 'Sklaverei,' in *Paulys Real-Enzyklopadie der klassischen Altertumswissenschaft*, Supplementband 6, Cols. 894–1068 [1935]." *Zeitschrift für Sozialforschung* 5: 441–42.

Finley, M. I. 1954. *The World of Odysseus*. New York: Viking Press.

Finley, M. I. 1959. "Was Greek Civilization Based on Slave Labour?" *Historia* 8: 145–64. Reprinted in Finley 1960a, 39–72, and Finley 1981, 97–115.

Finley, M. I., ed. 1960a. *Slavery in Classical Antiquity; Views and Controversies*. Cambridge: W. Heffer.

Finley, M. I., 1960b. "The Servile Statuses of Ancient Greece." *Revue Internationale des Droits d'Antiqué* 3. 7: 165–89. Reprinted in Finley 1981, 133–49.

Finley, M. I., 1961. "The Significance of Ancient Slavery (a Brief Reply)." *Acta Antiqua Academiae Scientiarum Hungaricae* 9: 285–86.

Finley, M. I., 1962. "The Black Sea and Danubian Regions and the Slave Trade in Antiquity." *Klio* 40: 51–59.

Finley, M. I., 1964. "Between Slavery and Freedom." *Comparative Studies in Society and History* 6: 233–49. Reprinted in Finley 1981, 116–32, 265.

Finley, M. I., 1965a. "Marx and Asia." *New Statesman*, 20 August edition.

Finley, M. I., 1965b. "La servitude pour dettes." *Revue Historique de Droit Français et Étranger* 43: 159–84. Reprinted in English under the title "Debt Bondage and the Problem of Slavery," in Finley 1981, 150–66, 267–71.

Finley, M. I., 1965c. "Technical Innovation and Economic Progress in the Ancient World." *Economic History Review* 18: 29–45.

Finley, M. I., 1965d. *The World of Odysseus.* Revised edn. New York: Viking Press.
Finley, M. I., 1968. "Slavery." *International Encyclopedia of the Social Sciences*, edited by David L. Sills, 307–13. New York: Macmillan.
Finley, M. I., 1973a. *The Ancient Economy.* London: Chatto & Windus.
Finley, M. I., 1973b. *Democracy Ancient and Modern.* London: Chatto & Windus.
Finley, M. I., 1976a. "Class Struggles." *The Listener*, 78 edition.
Finley, M. I., 1976b. "The Freedom of the Citizen in the Greek World." *Talanta* 7: 1–23.
Finley, M. I., ed. 1979a. *The Bücher-Meyer Controversy.* New York: Arno Press.
Finley, M. I., 1979b. "Slavery and the Historians." *Histoire Sociale* 12: 247–61. Reprinted in Finley 1998, 285–309.
Finley, M. I., 1980. *Ancient Slavery and Modern Ideology.* London: Chatto & Windus.
Finley, M. I., 1981. *Economy and Society in Ancient Greece.* Edited by Brent D. Shaw and Richard P. Saller. London: Chatto & Windus.
Finley, M. I., 1982. "Problems of Slave Society: Some Reflections on the Debate." *Opus* 1: 201–11. Reprinted in Finley 1998, 265–84.
Finley, M. I., ed. 1987. *Classical Slavery.* London: Slavery and Abolition.
Finley, M. I., 1998. *Ancient Slavery and Modern Ideology.* Edited by B. D. Shaw. Expanded edn. Princeton, NJ: Markus Wiener Publishers.
Fisher, Michael H. 2014. *Migration: A World History.* New York: Oxford University Press.
Fisher, N. R. E. 1993. *Slavery in Classical Greece.* London: Bristol Classical Press.
Florentino, Manolo 1997. *Em costas negras: uma história do tráfico de escravos entre a África e o Rio de Janeiro, séculos XVIII e XIX.* São Paulo: Companhia das letras.
Florentino, Manolo 1999. "O outro africano." In *O negro no coração do Império: uma memória a resgatar – Séculos XV–XIX*, edited by D. Lahon, 7–9. Lisbon: Secretario Coordenador dos Programas de Educação Multicultural, Ministério da Educação: Casa do Brasil.
Fogel, Robert W. and Stanley L. Engerman. 1974. *Time on the Cross: The Economics of American Negro Slavery.* Boston, MA: Little, Brown.
Follett, Richard J. 2005. *The Sugar Masters: Planters and Slaves in Louisiana's Cane World, 1820–1860.* Baton Rouge: Louisiana State University Press.
Fonseca, J. 2010. *Escravos e senhores na Lisboa quinhentista.* Lisbon: Edições Colibri.
Ford, Lacy K. 2009. *Deliver Us from Evil: The Slavery Question in the Old South.* New York: Oxford University Press.
Forsdyke, Sara. 2012. *Slaves Tell Tales: And Other Episodes in the Politics of Popular Culture in Ancient Greece.* Princeton, NJ: Princeton University Press.
Foster, H. Thomas, ed. 2003. *The Collected Works of Benjamin Hawkins, 1796–1810.* Tuscaloosa: University of Alabama Press.
Fox, James. 1983. "'For Good and Sufficient Reasons': An Examination of Early Dutch East India Company Ordinances on Slaves and Slavery." In *Slavery, Bondage and Dependency in Southeast Asia*, edited by Anthony Reid, 246–62. St. Lucia: University of Queensland Press.

Fragoso, J. L. R. 1992. *Homens de grossa aventura: acumulação e hierarquia na praça mercantil do Rio de Janeiro, 1790–1830*. Rio de Janeiro: Arquivo Nacional; Arcaísmo como projeto, Nas Encruzilhadas, Homens de Grossa.

Fragoso, J. L. R. and Manolo Florentino. 1993. *O arcaísmo como projeto: mercado atlântico, sociedade agrária e elite mercantil no Rio de Janeiro, c.1790–c.1840*. Rio de Janeiro: Diadorim.

Franklin, John Hope and Loren Schweninger. 1999. *Runaway Slaves: Rebels on the Plantation*. New York: Oxford University Press.

Freamon, Bernard K. 2012. "Islamic Law and Trafficking in Women and Children in the Indian Ocean World." In *Trafficking in Slavery's Wake: Law and the Experience of Women and Children in Africa*, edited by Benjamin N. Lawrance and Richard L. Roberts, 121–41. Athens: Ohio University Press.

Fredrickson, George M. 1981. *White Supremacy: A Comparative Study in American and South African History*. New York: Oxford University Press.

Freehling, Alison Goodyear. 1982. *Drift towards Dissolution: The Virginia Slavery Debate of 1831–1832*. Baton Rouge: Louisiana State University Press.

Freitag, Ulrike. 1997. *Hadhrami Traders, Scholars, and Statesmen in the Indian Ocean*. Leiden; New York: Brill.

Freitag, Ulrike. 2003. *Indian Ocean Migrants and State Formation in Hadhramaut: Reforming the Homeland*. Boston, MA: Brill.

Freu, Christel. 2015. "Labour Status and Economic Stratification in the Roman World: The Hierarchy of Wages in Egypt." *Journal of Roman Archaeology* 28: 161–77.

Frey, Sylvia R. and Betty Wood. 1998. *Come Shouting to Zion: African American Protestantism in the American South and British Caribbean to 1830*. Chapel Hill: University of North Carolina Press.

Fry, Carlos. 1907. "Diario de los viajes y exploración de los ríos Urubamba, Ucayali, Amazonas, Pachitea y Palcazo, 1888." In *Colección de leyes, decretos, resoluciones y otros documentos oficiales referentes al Departamento de Loreto*, compiled by Carlos Larrabure i Correa, 11:369–589. Lima: Imprenta La Opinión Nacional.

Fuente, Alejandro de la. 2008. *Havana and the Atlantic in the Sixteenth Century: Envisioning Cuba*. Chapel Hill: University of North Carolina Press.

Fuente, Alejandro de la and Ariella Gross. 2015. "Manumission and Freedom in the Americas: Cuba, Louisiana, Virginia 1500s–1700s." *Quaderni Storici* 148: 15–48.

Fuhrmann, Christopher J. 2011. *Policing the Roman Empire: Soldiers, Administration, and Public Order*. New York: Oxford University Press.

Furlonge, Nigel D. 1999. "Revisiting the Zanj and Re-visioning Revolt: Complexities of the Zanj Conflict – 868–883 AD." *Negro History Bulletin* 62.4: 7–14.

Furtado, J. F. 1999. *Homens de negócio: a interiorização da metrópole e do comércio nas Minas setecentistas*. São Paulo: Editora HUCITEC.

Fynn-Paul, Jeffrey. 2009. "Empire, Monotheism and Slavery in the Greater Mediterranean Region from Antiquity to the Early Modern Era." *Past & Present* 205: 3–40.

Fynn-Paul, Jeffrey, Damian Pargas, and Karwan Fatah-Black, eds. 2017. *Slaving Zones: Cultural Identities, Ideologies, and Institutions in the Evolution of Global Slavery*. Leiden: Brill.

Gagarin, Michael. 2010. "Serfs and Slaves at Gortyn." *Zeitschrift der Savigny-Stiftung für Rechtsgeschichte, Romanistische Abteilung* 127: 14–31.

Galil, Gershon. 2007. *The Lower Stratum Families in the Neo-Assyrian Period*. Edited by T. Schneider. Vol. 27, *Culture and History of the Ancient Near East*. Leiden: Brill.

Gallay, Alan. 2002. *The Indian Slave Trade: The Rise of English Empire in the American South 1670–1717*. New Haven, CT: Yale University Press.

Gallay, Alan. ed. 2009. *Indian Slavery in Colonial America*. Lincoln: University of Nebraska Press.

Gallego, Julian, and Miriam Valdés Guía. 2010. "Athenian *Zeugitai* and the Solonian Census Classes: New Reflections and Perspectives." *Historia* 59: 257–81.

Gans, Herbert J. 1997. "Toward a Reconciliation of 'Assimilation' and 'Pluralism': The Interplay of Acculturation and Ethnic Retention." *International Migration Review* 31.4: 875–92.

Garcilaso de la Vega, Inca. 1605[1993]. "La Florida by the Inca." In *The De Soto Chronicles: The Expedition of Hernando de Soto to North America in 1539–1543*, edited by Lawrence A. Clayton, Vernon James Knight Jr., and Edward C. Moore. Translated by Charmion Shelby, edition by David Bost, 2:1–559. Tuscaloosa: University of Alabama Press.

Garcilaso de la Vega, Inca. 1963. *Comentarios reales de los Incas*. Montevideo: Ministerio de Instrucción Pública y Previsión Social.

Gardner, J. F. 2011. "Slavery and Roman Law." In *The Cambridge World History of Slavery. Volume I: The Ancient Mediterranean World*, edited by K. Bradley and P. Cartledge, 414–37. Cambridge: Cambridge University Press.

Garlan, Yvon. 1988. *Slavery in Ancient Greece*. Translated by J. Lloyd. Ithaca, NY: Cornell University Press.

Garnsey, Peter. 1970. *Social Status and Legal Privilege in the Roman Empire*. Oxford: Clarendon.

Garnsey, Peter. 1996. *Ideas of Slavery from Aristotle to Augustine*. Cambridge: Cambridge University Press.

Garnsey, Peter. 1998. *Cities, Peasants and Food in Classical Antiquity: Essays in Social and Economic History*. Edited by Walter Scheidel. Cambridge: Cambridge University Press.

Gayarré, Charles. 1866–67. *History of Louisiana*. 2 vols. 2nd edn. New York: W. J. Widdleton.

Gellner, E. 1983. *Nations and Nationalism*. Ithaca, NY: Cornell University Press.

Gelvin, James. 2005. *The Modern Middle East: A History*. New York: Oxford University Press.

Genovese, Eugene D. 1974. *Roll, Jordan, Roll: The World the Slaves Made*. New York: Pantheon Books.

Ghazal, Amal N. 2009. "Debating Slavery and Abolition in the Arab Middle East." In *Slavery, Islam and Diaspora*, edited by Behnaz A. Mirzai, Ismael

Musah Montana, and Paul E. Lovejoy, 139–54. Trenton, NJ: Africa World Press.

Giacone, Antonio. 1949. *Os Tucanos e outras tribus do rio Uaupés, afluente do Negro – Amazonas.* São Paulo: Imprensa Oficial do Estado São Paulo.

Giannecchini, Doroteo. 1996. *Historia natural, etnografía, geografía y lingüística del Chaco Boliviano (1898).* Tarija: Fondo de Inversión Social/Centro Eclesial de Documentación.

Gibbon, E. 1776[1995]. *The History of the Decline and Fall of the Roman Empire.* Vol. 1. Edited by J. B. Bury. New York: Modern Library.

Gibson, Campbell and Kay Jung. 2002. "Historical Census Statistics on Population Totals by Race, 1790 to 1990." U.S. Census Bureau Population Division Working Paper Series No. 56.

Gilbert, Erik. 2004. *Dhows and the Colonial Economy of Zanzibar.* Athens: Ohio University Press.

Girbal y Barceló, Narciso. 1924. "Diario de viaje..." In *Historia de las misiones franciscanas y narración de los progresos de la geografía en el Oriente del Perú,* edited by Bernardino Izaguirre, 8: 101–84. Lima: Talleres Tipográficos de la Penitenciaría.

Glassman, Jonathon. 1995 *Feasts and Riot: Revelry, Rebellion, and Popular Consciousness on the Swahili Coast, 1856–1888.* Portsmouth, NH: Heinemann.

Glatthaar, Joseph T. 1990. *Forged in Battle: The Civil War Alliance of Black Soldiers and White Officers.* Baton Rouge: Louisiana State University Press.

Gledhill, John and Mogens Trolle Larsen. 1982. "The Polanyi Paradigm and a Dynamic Analysis of Archaic States." In *Theory and Explanation in Archaeology: The Southampton Conference,* edited by Colin Renfrew, Michael J. Rowlands, and Barbara Abbott Segraves, 197–229. New York and London: Academic Press.

Goldberg, Mark Allan. 2015. "Linking Chains: Comanche Captivity, Black Chattel Slavery, and Antebellum Central Texas." In *Linking the Histories of Slavery: North America and its Borderlands,* edited by Bonnie M. Martin and James F. Brooks, 197–222. Santa Fe, NM: School for Advanced Research Press.

Goldman, Irving. 1963. *The Cubeo. Indians of the Northwest Amazon.* Urbana, IL: University of Illinois Press.

Gomes, F. 2010. "Indígenas, africanos y comunidades de fugitivos en la Amazonia colonial." *Revista Historia y Espacio* 34: 1–21.

Goody, Jack. 1971. *Technology, Tradition, and the State in Africa.* New York: Oxford University Press.

Gordon-Reed, Annette. 2008. *The Hemingses of Monticello: An American Family.* New York: W. W. Norton.

Goucher, Candice. 1999. "African-Caribbean Metal Technology: Forging Cultural Survivals in the Atlantic World." In *African Sites Archaeology in the Caribbean,* edited by Jay Haviser, 143–56. Princeton, NJ: Markus Wiener Publishers.

Goucher, Candice and Kofi Agorsah. 2011. "Excavating the Roots of Resistance: The Significance of Maroons in Jamaican Archaeology." In

Out of Many, One People: The Historical Archaeology of Colonial Jamaica, edited by James A. Delle, Mark W. Hauser, and Douglas V. Armstrong, 144–60. Gainesville, FL: University Press of Florida.

Goveia, Elsa V. 1965. *Slave Society in the British Leeward Islands at the End of the Eighteenth Century*. New Haven, CT: Yale University Press.

Gow, Peter. 1989. "The Perverse Child: Desire in a Native Amazonian Subsistence Economy." *Man* 24: 299–314.

Gow, Peter. 1991. *Of Mixed Blood: Kinship and History in Peruvian Amazonia.* Oxford: Clarendon Press.

Graeber, David. 2001. *Toward an Anthropological Theory of Value: The False Coin of Our Own Dreams.* New York: Palgrave.

Graeber, David. 2011. *Debt: The First 5,000 Years.* Brooklyn, NY: Melville House.

Graham, A. J. 1992. "Thucydides 7.13.2 and the Crews of Athenian Triremes." *Transactions of the American Philological Association* 122: 257–70.

Graham, A. J. 1998. "Thucydides 7.13.2 and the Crews of Athenian Triremes: An Addendum." *Transactions of the American Philological Association* 128: 89–114.

Greenberg, Kenneth S., ed. 2003. *Nat Turner: A Slave Rebellion in History and Memory.* New York: Oxford University Press.

Greene, Jack P. 1994. "Foundations of Political Power in the Virginia House of Burgesses, 1720–76," in *Negotiated Authorities: Essays in Colonial Politics and Constitutional History*, edited by Jack P. Greene, 238–58. Charlottesville, VA: University of Virginia Press.

Greenwald, David E. 1973. "Durkheim on Society, Thought and Ritual." *Sociological Analysis* 34.3: 157–68.

Gregory, Derek. 1982. "A Realist Construction of the Social." *Transactions of the Institute of British Geographers* 7.2: 254–56.

Gregory, Derek and John Urry. 1985. *Social Relations, Spatial Structures.* New York: Macmillan.

Grey, C. 2011. "Slavery in the Late Roman World." In *The Cambridge World History of Slavery. Volume I: The Ancient Mediterranean World*, edited by K. Bradley and P. Cartledge, 482–509. Cambridge: Cambridge University Press.

Grivno, Max L. 2011. *Gleanings of Freedom: Free and Slave Labor along the Mason-Dixon Line, 1790–1860.* Urbana: University of Illinois Press.

Grubbs, Judith Evans. 1993. " 'Marriage More Shameful than Adultery': Slave–Mistress Relationships, 'Mixed Marriages', and Late Roman Law." *Phoenix* 47: 125–54.

Grumeza, Lavinia. 2014. *Sarmatian Cemeteries from Banat: (Late 1st–Early 5th Centuries AD).* Cluj-Napoca: Mega Publishing House.

Gsell, Stéphane. 1913–28. *Histoire ancienne de l'Afrique du Nord.* 8 vols. Osnabrück: Otto zeller Verlag.

Gudmestad, Robert. 2003. *A Troublesome Commerce: The Transformation of the Interstate Slave Trade.* Baton Rouge: Louisiana State University Press.

Gudmestad, Robert. 2011. *Steamboats and the Rise of the Cotton Kingdom.* Baton Rouge: Louisiana State University Press.

Guitar, Lynne. 2011. "Negotiations of Conquest." In *The Caribbean: A History of the Region and Its People*, edited by Stephan Palmié and Francisco A. Scarano, 115–29. Chicago: University of Chicago Press.

Haas, J. and W. Creamer. 1993. *Stress and Warfare among the Kayenta Anasazi of the Thirteenth Century A.D.* Fieldiana: Anthropology, New Series 21. Chicago: Field Museum of Natural History.

Habicht Mauche, J. 2008. "Captive Wives? The Role and Status of Non-local Women on the Protohistoric Southern High Plains." In *Invisible Citizens: Captives and Their Consequences*, edited by C. M. Cameron, 181–204. Salt Lake City: University of Utah Press.

Hahn, Istvan. 1971. "Die Anfänge der antiken Gesellschaftsformation in Griechenland und das Problem der sogenannten asiatischen Productionsweise." *Jahrbuch für Wirtschaftsgeschichte* 1971, 2: 29–47.

Hahn, Steven. 2003. *A Nation under Our Feet: Black Political Struggles in the Rural South, from Slavery to the Great Migration*. Cambridge, MA: Belknap Press of Harvard University Press.

Hajda, Yvonne P. 2005. "Slavery in the Greater Lower Columbia Region." *Ethnohistory* 52.3: 569–88.

Hall, Edith. 1997. "The Sociology of Athenian Tragedy." In *Cambridge Companion to Greek Tragedy*, edited by P. E. Easterling, 93–126. Cambridge: Cambridge University Press.

Hall, Gwendolyn Midlo. 1992. *Africans in Colonial Louisiana: The Development of Afro-Creole Culture in the Eighteenth Century*. Baton Rouge: Louisiana State University Press.

Hall, Randal L. 2012. *Mountains on the Market: Industry, the Environment, and the South*. Lexington: University Press of Kentucky.

Hall, Richard. 1996. *Empires of the Monsoons: A History of the Indian Ocean and Its Invaders*. London: Harper-Collins.

Hallett, Robin, ed. 1964. *Records of the African Association, 1788–1831*. London: Royal Geographical Society.

Hämäläinen, Pekka. 2008. *The Comanche Empire*. New Haven, CT: Yale University Press.

Hamel, Hendrik. 1994. *Hamel's Journal and a Description of the Kingdom of Korea, 1653–1666*. Seoul: Royal Asiatic Society, Korea Branch.

Hammer, Carl I. 2002. *A Large-Scale Slave Society of the Early Middle Ages. Slaves and their Families in Early Medieval Bavaria*. Aldershot: Ashgate.

Han, Yong-guk. 1977. "朝鮮中葉의 奴婢結婚樣態(上)-1609년의 蔚山戶籍에 나타난 事例를 중심으로." *Yeoksahakbo* 75: 177–97.

Hansen, Mogens. 1991. *The Athenian Democracy in the Age of Demosthenes: Structure, Principles, and Ideology*. Translated by J. A. Crook. Edited by O. Murray. The Ancient World. Oxford: Blackwell.

Hansen, Mogens. 2006. *The Shotgun Method: The Demography of the Ancient City-State Culture*. Columbia: University of Missouri Press.

Hansen, Mogens and Thomas Heine Nielsen. 2004. *An Inventory of Archaic and Classical Poleis: An Investigation Conducted by the Copenhagen*

Polis Centre for the Danish National Research Foundation. Oxford: Oxford University Press.

Hanson, Victor Davis. 1992. "Thucydides and the Desertion of Attic Slaves during the Decelean War." *Classical Antiquity* 11: 210–28.

Hanson, Victor Davis. 1999. *The Other Greeks: The Family Farm and the Agrarian Roots of Western Civilization.* 2nd edn. Berkeley: University of California Press.

Harlow, Vincent T. 1926. *A History of Barbados, 1625–1685.* Oxford: Clarendon Press.

Harmatta, J. 1970. *Studies in the History and Language of the Sarmatians.* Acta Antiqua et Archaeologica, vol. 13. Szeged: Acta Universitatis de Attila József Nominatae.

Harms, Robert, Bernard K. Freamon, and David W. Blight. 2013. *Indian Ocean Slavery in the Age of Abolition.* New Haven, CT: Yale University Press.

Harper, Kyle. 2008. "The Greek Census Inscriptions of Late Antiquity." *Journal of Roman Studies*: 98: 83–119.

Harper, Kyle. 2010. "Slave Prices in Late Antiquity (and in the Very Long Term)." *Historia: Zeitschrift für alte Geschichte* 59.2: 206–38.

Harper, Kyle. 2011. *Slavery in the Late Roman World, AD 275–425: An Economic, Social, and Institutional Study.* Cambridge: Cambridge University Press.

Harper, Kyle. 2012. "The Transformation of Roman Slavery: An Economic Myth?" *Antiquité tardive* 20: 165–72.

Harris, Edward. 2002. "Did Solon Abolish Debt Bondage?" *Classical Quarterly* 52: 415–30.

Harris, Edward. 2012. "Homer, Hesiod and the 'Origins' of Greek Slavery." *Revue des études anciennes* 114: 345–66.

Harris, William V. 1980. "Towards a Study of the Roman Slave Trade." In *The Seaborne Commerce of Ancient Rome,* edited by J. H. D'Arms and E. C. Kopff, 117–40. Rome: American Academy in Rome.

Harris, William V. 1999. "Demography, Geography and the Sources of Roman Slaves." *Journal of Roman Studies* 89: 62–75.

Harris, William V., ed. 2013. *Moses Finley and Politics.* Columbia Studies in the Classical Tradition. Vol. 40. Leiden: Brill.

Harrison, Paul W. 1924. *The Arab at Home.* New York: Thomas Y. Crowell Company.

Hartwig, Gerald W. 1979. "Demographic Considerations in East Africa during the Ninetieth Century." *International Journal of African Historical Studies* 12.4: 653–72.

Hauser, Mark W. 2008. *An Archaeology of Black Markets: Local Ceramics and Economies in Eighteenth-Century Jamaica.* Gainesville: University Press of Florida.

Hauser, Mark W. 2015. "Blind Spots in Empire: Plantation Landscapes in Early Colonial Dominica (1763–1807)." In *The Archaeology of Slavery: A Comparative Approach to Captivity and Coercion.* Center for Archaeological Investigations, Occasional Paper, No. 41, edited by Lydia W. Marshall, 143–65. Carbondale: Southern Illinois University Press.

Hawthorne, Walter. 1999. "The Production of Slaves Where There Was No State: The Guinea Bissau Region, c. 1450–c. 1815." *Slavery and Abolition* 20.2: 97–124.

Hawthorne, Walter. 2001. "Nourishing a Stateless Society during the Slave Trade: The Rise of Balanta Paddy-Rice Production in Guinea-Bissau." *Journal of African History* 42: 1–24.

Hawthorne, Walter. 2003. *Planting Rice and Harvesting Slaves: Transformations along the Guinea-Bissau Coast, 1450–1850*. Portsmouth, NH: Heinemann.

Hawthorne, Walter. 2010. *From Africa to Brazil: Culture, Identity, and an Atlantic Slave Trade, 1600–1800*. Cambridge: Cambridge University Press.

Hayden, Brian. 1996. "Feasting in Prehistoric and Traditional Societies." In *Food and the Status Quest: An Interdisciplinary Perspective*, edited by Polly Wiessner and Wulf Schiefenhovel, 127–48. Providence, RI: Berghahn Books.

Hébrard, Jean M. 2013. "Slavery in Brazil: Brazilian Scholars in the Key Interpretive Debates." *Translating the Americas* 1: 47–95.

Helms, Mary W. 1992. "Political Lords and Political Ideology in Southeastern Chiefdoms. Comments and Observations." In *Lords of the Southeast: Social Inequality and the Native Elites of Southeastern North America*, edited by Alex W. Barker and Timothy R. Pauketat, *Archaeological Papers of the American Anthropological Association*, no. 3, 185–94. Washington, DC: American Anthropological Association.

Herrmann-Otto, Elisabeth. 1994. *Ex Ancilla Natus: Untersuchungen zu den "hausgeborenen" Sklaven und Sklavinnen im Westen des römischen Kaiserreiches*. Forschungen Zur Antiken Sklaverei, Bd. 24. Stuttgart: F. Steiner.

Herrmann-Otto, Elisabeth. 2009. *Sklaverei und Freilassung in der griechisch-römischen Welt*. Hildesheim: Georg Olms.

Hespanha, Antonio Manuel. 2007. "Introdução." In *Conquistadores e negociantes: histórias de elites no Antigo Regime nos trópicos: América lusa, séculos XVI a XVIII*, edited by J. L. R. Fragoso, 13–18. Rio de Janeiro: Civilização Brasileira.

Hickey, Robin. 2012. "Seeking to Understand the Definition of Slavery." In *The Legal Understanding of Slavery: From the Historical to the Contemporary*, edited by Jean Allain, 220–41. Oxford: Oxford University Press.

Higgs, Lauren. 2013. "Report Documents 'Slavery' in Thailand." *Bangkok Post*, 20 June. Accessed July 15, 2013. www.bangkokpost.com/learning/learning-from-news/356294/modern-day-slavery-in-thailand.

Higman, Barry W. 1984. *Slave Populations in the British Caribbean, 1807–1834*. Baltimore, MD: Johns Hopkins University Press.

Higman, Barry W. 1998. *Montpelier Jamaica: A Plantation Community in Slavery and Freedom, 1739–1912*. Kingston: University of the West Indies Press.

Higman, Barry W. 1999. *Writing West Indian Histories*. London: MacMillan.

Higman, Barry W. 2000. "The Sugar Revolution." *Economic History Review* 53.2: 213–36.

Higman, Barry W. 2001. "The Invention of *Slave Society*." *In Slavery, Freedom and Gender: The Dynamics of Caribbean Society*, edited by Brian L. Moore,

Barry W. Higman, Carl Campbell, and Patrick Brian, 57–76. Kingston, Jamaica: University of the West Indies.

Higman, Barry W. 2011. "Demography and Family Structures." In *The Cambridge World History of Slavery, Volume 3: AD 1420–AD 1804*, edited by David Eltis and Stanley L. Engerman. 479–511. Cambridge: Cambridge University Press.

Hin, Saskia. 2013. *The Demography of Roman Italy: Population Dynamics in an Ancient Conquest Society 201 BCE–14 CE.* Cambridge: Cambridge University Press.

Hindess, Barry and Paul Q. Hirst. 1975. *Pre-capitalist Modes of Production.* London: Routledge and Kegan Paul.

Ho, Engseng. 2006. *The Graves of Tarim: Genealogy and Mobility across the Indian Ocean.* Berkeley: University of California Press.

Hobsbawm, E. J. 1971. "From Social History to the History of Society." *Daedalus* 100: 20–45.

Hobsbawm, E. J. 2011. *How to Change the World: Reflections on Marx and Marxism.* New Haven, CT: Yale University Press.

Hodes, Martha Elizabeth. 1997. *White Women, Black Men: Illicit Sex in the Nineteenth-Century South.* New Haven, CT: Yale University Press.

Hodkinson, Stephen. 1992. "Sharecropping and Sparta's Economic Exploitation of the Helots." In *Philolakōn: Lakonian Studies in Honour of Hector Catling*, edited by Jan Motyka Sanders, 123–34. London: British School at Athens.

Hodkinson, Stephen. 2000. *Property and Wealth in Classical Sparta.* London: Duckworth.

Hodkinson, Stephen. 2008. "Spartiates, Helots and the Direction of the Agrarian Economy: Towards an Understanding of Helotage in Comparative Perspective." In *Slave Systems: Ancient and Modern*, edited by E. Dal Lago and C. Katsari, 285–320. Cambridge: Cambridge University Press.

Hoerder, Dirk. 2002. *Cultures in Contact: World Migrations in the Second Millennium.* Durham, NC; London: Duke University Press.

Hogendorn, Jan S. 1999. "The Hideous Trade. Economic Aspects of the 'Manufacture' and Sale of Eunuchs." *Paideuma* 45: 137–60.

Holleran, Claire. 2016. "Labour Mobility in the Roman World: A Case Study of Mines in Iberia." In *Migration and Mobility in the Early Roman Empire*, edited by Luuk de Ligt and Laurens E. Tacoma, 95–137. Leiden: Brill.

Hopkins, Keith. 1967. "Slavery in Classical Antiquity." In *Caste and Race: Comparative Approaches*, edited by Anthony de Reuck and Julie Knight, 66–77. Boston. MA: Little and Brown.

Hopkins, Keith. 1978. *Conquerors and Slaves: Sociological Studies in Roman History, 1.* Cambridge: Cambridge University Press.

Hopper, Matthew S. 2006. "The African Presence in Arabia: Slavery, the World Economy, and the African Diaspora in Eastern Arabia, 1840–1940." Dissertation, UCLA.

Hopper, Matthew S. 2014. "The African Presence in Eastern Arabia." In *The Persian Gulf in Modern Times: People, Ports, and History*, edited by Lawrence G. Potter, 327–49. New York: Palgrave Macmillan.

Hopper, Matthew S. 2015. *Slaves of One Master: Globalization and Slavery in Arabia and in the Age of Empire.* New Haven, CT; London: Yale University Press.

Horsmann, Gerhard. 1998. *Die Wagenlenker der römischen Kaiserzeit: Untersuchungen zu ihrer sozialen Stellung.* Forschungen zur Antiken Sklaverei, Bd. 29. Stuttgart: F. Steiner.

Horton, Robin. 1976. "Stateless Societies in the History of West Africa." In *History of West Africa,* edited by J. F. A. Ajayi and Michael Crowder, 2:72–75. New York: Columbia University Press.

Hourani, George Fadlo. 1995 [1951]. *Arab Seafaring in the Indian Ocean in Ancient and Early Medieval Times,* revised and expanded by John Carswell. Princeton, NJ: Princeton University Press.

Howgego, C. 1994. "Coin Circulation and the Integration of the Roman Economy," *Journal of Roman Archaeology* 7: 5–21.

Howson, Jean. 1995. "Colonial Goods and the Plantation Village: Consumption and the Internal Economy in Montserrat from Slavery to Freedom." Dissertation, New York University.

Hudson, Charles M. 1997. *Knights of Spain, Warriors of the Sun: Hernando de Soto and the South's Ancient Chiefdoms.* Athens: University of Georgia Press.

Hume, David. 1742[1987]. "Of the Populousness of Ancient Nations." In *Essays, Moral, Political, and Literary,* edited by David Hume, edited by Eugene F. Miller, Vol. 2: 381–443. Indianapolis, IN: Liberty Classics.

Hunt, Peter. 1997. "The Helots at the Battle of Plataea." *Historia* 46.2: 129–44.

Hunt, Peter. 1998. *Slaves, Warfare, and Ideology in the Greek Historians.* Cambridge: Cambridge University Press.

Hunt, Peter. 2010. *War, Peace, and Alliance in Demosthenes Athens.* Cambridge: Cambridge University Press.

Hunt, Peter. 2011. "Slaves in Greek Literary Culture." In *The Cambridge World History of Slavery, Volume I: The Ancient Near East and Mediterranean World to AD 500,* edited by K. Bradley and P. Cartledge, 22–47. Cambridge: Cambridge University Press.

Hunt, Peter. 2017. "Slaves or Serfs?: Patterson on the Thetes and Helots of Ancient Greece." In *On Human Bondage: After Slavery and Social Death,* edited by J. Bodel and W. Scheidel, 55–80. Malden, MA; Oxford: Wiley Blackwell.

Ibn Battuta. 2005. *Ibn Battuta in Black Africa.* Translated by Said Hamdun and Noel Quinton King. Princeton, NJ: Markus Weiner Publishers.

I.D.1129. 1919. *A Handbook of Arabia, Vol. I, General, Compiled by the Geographical Section of the Naval Intelligence Division, Naval Staff, Admiralty.* London: H. M. Stationary Office.

Isaacman, B. and A. Isaacman. 1977. "Slavery and Social Stratification among the Sena of Mozambique: A Study of the Kaporo System." In *Slavery in Africa: Historical and Anthropological Perspectives,* edited by S. Miers and I. Kopytoff, 105–20. Madison: University of Wisconsin Press.

Isager, Signe and Mogens Herman Hansen. 1975. *Aspects of Athenian Society in the Fourth Century B.C.* Translated by J. H. Rosenmeier. Odense: Odense University Press.

Issawi, Charles. 1993. "Middle East Economic Development, 1815–1914: The General and the Specific." In *The Modern Middle East*, edited by Albert Hourani, Philip S. Khoury, and Mary C. Wilson, 177–93. Berkeley and Los Angeles, University of California Press.

Jackson, Jean E. 1983. *The Fish People: Linguistic Exogamy and Tukanoan Identity in the Northwest Amazon*. Cambridge: Cambridge University Press.

Jackson, John Andrew. 1862. *The Experience of a Slave in South Carolina*. London: Passmore & Alabaster.

Jackson, R. M. 1934. *Journal of a Residence in Bonny River on Board the Ship Kingston during the Months of January, February and March 1826*. Letchworth: Garden City Press.

Jacob, Oscar. 1928. *Les esclaves publics à Athènes*. Liége: Imp. H. Vaillant-Carmanne.

Jacoby, Karl. 1994. "Slaves by Nature? Domestic Animals and Humans Slaves." *Slavery and Abolition* 15: 89–99.

Jameson, Michael. 1977–78. "Agriculture and Slavery in Classical Athens." *Classical Journal* 73: 122–45.

Jameson, Michael. 1992. "Agricultural Labor in Ancient Greece." In *Agriculture in Ancient Greece*, edited by B. Wells, 135–46. Stockholm: Paul A. Forlag.

Jayakar, A.S.G. "Medical Topography of Muscat by Surgeon A.S.G. Jayakar." In *Administration Report of the Persian Gulf Political Residency and Muscat Political Agency for the Year 1876–77*, p. 96–102. Centre for Documentation and Research, Abu Dhabi, United Arab Emirates (CDR), ND 1/H.

Jenkins, William Sumner. 1935. *Pro-slavery Thought in the Old South*. Chapel Hill: University of North Carolina Press.

Jennings, Evelyn Powell. 2002. "State Enslavement in Colonial Havana, 1763–1790." In *Slavery without Sugar: Diversity in Caribbean Economy and Society since the 17th Century*, edited by Verene A. Shepard, 151–82. Gainesville: University Press of Florida.

Jennings, Jesse D., ed. 1947. "Nutt's Trip to the Chickasaw Country." *Journal of Mississippi History* 9: 34–61.

Jennings, Justin, Kathy L. Antrobus, Sam J. Atencio, Erin Glavich, Rebecca Johnson, German Loffler, and Christine Luu. 2005. "'Drinking Beer in a Blissful Mood': Alcohol Production, Operational Chains and Feasting in the Ancient World." *Current Anthropology* 46.2: 275–303.

Jew, Daniel, Robin Osborne, and Michael Scott, eds. 2016. *M. I. Finley: An Ancient Historian and His Impact*. Cambridge: Cambridge University Press.

Johnson, Walter. 1999. *Soul by Soul: Life inside the Antebellum Slave Market*. Cambridge, MA: Harvard University Press.

Johnson, Walter. 2013. *River of Dark Dreams: Slavery and Empire in the Cotton Kingdom*. Cambridge, MA: Harvard University Press.

Jones, Eric. 2010. *Wives, Slaves and Concubines: A History of the Female Underclass in Dutch Asia*. DeKalb: Northern Illinois University Press.

Jones, Norrece T. 1990. *Born a Child of Freedom, Yet a Slave: Mechanisms of Control and Strategies of Resistance in Antebellum South Carolina*. Middletown, CT: Wesleyan University Press.

Jongman, Willem. 1988. *The Economy and Society of Pompeii*. Amsterdam: J. C. Gieben.

Jongman, Willem. 2003. "Slavery and the Growth of Rome. The Transformation of Italy in the Second and First Centuries BCE." In *Rome the Cosmopolis*, edited by Catherine Edwards and Greg Woolf, 100–22. Cambridge: Cambridge University Press.

Jördens, Andrea. 1990. *Vertragliche Regelungen von Arbeiten im späten griechischen Ägypten.* Heidelberg: Carl Winter Verlag.

Joshel, Sandra R. 1992. *Work, Identity, and Legal Status at Rome: A Study of the Occupational Inscriptions.* Norman, OK: University of Oklahoma Press.

Joshel, Sandra R. 2010. *Slavery in the Roman World.* New York: Cambridge University Press.

Joshel, Sandra R. 2011. "Slavery and Roman Literary Culture." In *The Cambridge World History of Slavery. Volume I: The Ancient Mediterranean World*, edited by K. Bradley and P. Cartledge, 214–40. Cambridge: Cambridge University Press.

Joyner, Charles W. 1984. *Down by the Riverside: A South Carolina Slave Community.* Urbana: University of Illinois Press.

Jung, Yon-sik. 2001. 『일상 으로 본 조선 시대 이야기』. Seoul: Chongnyonsa Publishing Company.

Junker, L. L. 2008. "The Impact of Captured Women on Cultural Transmission in Contact Period Philippine Slave-Raiding Chiefdoms." In *Invisible Citizens: Captives and Their Consequences*, edited by C. Cameron, 110–37. Salt Lake City: University of Utah Press.

Jursa, Michael. 2010. *Aspects of the Economic History of Babylonia in the First Millennium BC: Economic Geography, Economic Mentalities, Agriculture, the Use of Money and the Problem of Economic Growth.* Alter Orient und Altes Testament, Bd. 377. Münster: Ugarit-Verlag.

Jursa, Michael and Sven Tost. Forthcoming. "Greek and Roman Slaving in Comparative Ancient Perspective: The State and Dependent Labour in the Ancient Near East and in the Graeco-Roman World." In *The Oxford Handbook of Greek and Roman Slaveries.* Oxford: Oxford University Press.

Kamen, Deborah. 2013. *Status in Classical Athens.* Princeton, NJ: Princeton University Press.

Kamen, Deborah. 2016. "Manumission and Slave-Allowances in Classical Athens." *Historia* 65: 413–26.

Kan, Sergi. 1989. *Symbolic Immortality: The Tlingit Potlatch of the Nineteenth Century.* Washington, DC: Smithsonian Institution Press.

Karasch, Mary. 1987. *Slave Life in Rio de Janeiro 1808–1850.* Princeton, NJ: Princeton University Press.

Kaye, Anthony. 2007. *Joining Places: Slave Neighborhoods in the Old South.* Chapel Hill: University of North Carolina Press.

Kaye, Anthony. 2014. "The Second Slavery: Modernity in the 19th-Century South and the Atlantic World." In *The Second Slavery: Mass Slaveries and Modernity in the Americas and in the Atlantic Basin*, edited by Javier Laviña and Michael Zeuske, 175–202. Vienna and Berlin: Lit Verlag.

Kazakévich, Emily Grace. 2008[1960]. "Were the *Chōris Oikountes* Slaves?" *Greek Roman and Byzantine Studies* 48: 343–80.

Keeley, L. H. 1996. *War before Civilization: The Myth of the Peaceful Savage.* Oxford: Oxford University Press.

Kehoe, Dennis P. 1988. *The Economics of Agriculture on Roman Imperial Estates in North Africa.* Göttingen: Vandenhoeck & Ruprecht.

Kehoe, Dennis P. 2013. "Contract Labor." In *The Cambridge Companion to the Roman Economy*, edited by W. Scheidel, 114–30. Cambridge: Cambridge University Press.

Kelly, J. B. 1968. *Britain and the Persian Gulf, 1795–1880.* Oxford: Clarendon Press.

Kelly, Kenneth G. 2011. "*La Vie Quotidienne*: Historical Archaeological Approaches to the Plantation Era in Guadeloupe, French West Indies." In *French Colonial Archaeology in the Southeast and Caribbean*, edited by Meredith D. Hardy and Kenneth G. Kelly, 200–02. Gainesville: University Press of Florida.

Kennedy, Hugh. 2016. *The Prophet and the Age of the Caliphates: The Islamic Near East from the Sixth to the Eleventh Century.* 3rd edn. Abingdon; New York: Routledge.

Keppel, George. 1827. *Personal Narrative of a Journey from India to England.* London: H. Colburn.

Kim, Jong-sung. 2013. *조선 노비들-천하지만 특별한*. Seoul: Dawn of History.

Kim, Sung-woo. 2001. *조선 중기 국가 와 사족*. Seoul: Yuksabipyongsa.

Kim, Yong-man. 1996. "노비 생활." In *조선시대 생활사*, edited by the Society of Korean Historical Manuscripts, 315–40. Seoul: Yoksa Bipyong.

Kirschenbaum, Aaron. 1987. *Sons, Slaves, and Freedmen in Roman Commerce.* Washington, DC: Catholic University of America Press.

Klein, Herbert S. 1967. *Slavery in the Americas: A Comparative Study of Virginia and Cuba.* Chicago: University of Chicago Press.

Klein, Herbert S. 1999. *The Atlantic Slave Trade.* Cambridge: Cambridge University Press.

Klein, Herbert S. 2009. "American Slavery in Recent Brazilian Scholarship, with Emphasis on Quantitative Socio-economic Studies." *Slavery & Abolition* 30.1: 111–33.

Klein, Martin A. 1986. "Towards a Theory of Slavery [Note Critique]." *Cahiers d'études africaines* 26.104: 693–97.

Klein, Martin A. 1998. *Slavery and Colonial Rule in French West Africa.* Cambridge: Cambridge University Press.

Klein, Martin A. 2001. "The Slave Trade and Decentralized Societies." *Journal of African History* 42: 49–65.

Knight, Melvin M., Ulrich B. Phillips, Bernhard J. Stern, William Linn Westermann, and Mary Wilhelmine Williams. 1934. "Slavery." *Encyclopaedia of the Social Sciences.* Edited by Edwin Robert Anderson Seligman and Alvin Saunders Johnson, vol. 14:73–93. New York: Macmillan.

Knight, Vernon J. 2010. "La Loma del Convento: Its Centrality to Current Issues in Cuban Archaeology." In *Beyond the Blockade: New Currents in Cuban Archaeology*, edited by L. Antonio Curet, Susan Kepecs, and Gabino La Rosa Corzo, 24–46. Tuscaloosa: University Press of Alabama.

Knobloch, Francis J. 1972. "The Maku Indians and Racial Separation in the Valley of the Rio Negro." *Mankind Quarterly* 13.2: 100–09.

Koch-Grünberg, Theodor. 1906. "Die Makú." *Anthropos* 1.4: 877–99.

Koch-Grünberg, Theodor. 1995. *Dos años entre los indios. Viajes por el noroeste brasileño, 1903–1905*. 2 vols. Bogotá: Editorial Universidad Nacional.

Kok, R. Pedro. 1925–26. "Quelques notices ethnographiques sur les Indiens du Rio Papuri." *Anthropos* 20.3–4: 624–37; 21.5–6: 921–37.

Kolchin, Peter. 1993. *American Slavery, 1619–1877*. New York: Hill and Wang.

Kopytoff, Igor. 1982. "Slavery." *Annual Review of Anthropology* 11: 207–30.

Kopytoff, Igor. 1986. "The Cultural Biography of Things: Commoditization as Process." In *The Social Life of Things: Commodities in Cultural Perspective*, edited by Arjun Appadurai, 64–91. Cambridge: Cambridge University Press.

Kopytoff, Igor and Suzanne Miers, eds. 1977a. *Slavery in Africa: Historical and Anthropological Perspectives*. Madison: University of Wisconsin Press.

Kopytoff, Igor and Suzanne Miers, 1977b. "African 'Slavery' as an Institution of Marginality." In *Slavery in Africa: Historical and Anthropological Perspectives*, edited by Igor Kopytoff and Suzanne Miers, 3–81. Madison: University of Wisconsin Press.

Krieger, Martin. 2008. "Danish Shipping and Trade between Tranquebar on the Coromandel Coast of India and Southeast Asia during the Seventeenth and Eighteenth Centuries." In *The Indian Trade at the Asian Frontier*, edited by S. Jeyaseela Stephen, 117–41. New Delhi: Gyan Publishing House.

Kroeber, A. L. 1923. "American Culture and the Northwest Coast." *American Anthropologist* 25: 1–20.

Kron, Geoffrey. 2011. "The Distribution of Wealth at Athens in Comparative Perspective." *Zeitschrift für Papyrologie und Epigraphik* 179: 129–38.

Krus, Anthony Michal. 2013. *A Chronology for Mississippian Warfare*. Dissertation, Indiana University.

Kudlien, Fridolf. 1986. *Die Stellung des Arztes in der römischen Gesellschaft: Freigeborene Römer, Eingebürgerte, Peregrine, Sklaven, Freigelassene als Ärzte*. Forschungen zur Antiken Sklaverei, Bd. 18. Stuttgart: F. Steiner Verlag.

Kulikoff, Allan. 1986. *Tobacco and Slaves: The Development of Southern Cultures in the Chesapeake*. Chapel Hill: University of North Carolina Press.

Kunz, George Frederick and Charles Hugh Stevenson. 1908. *The Book of the Pearl: The History, Art, Science and Industry of the Queen of Gems*. New York: The Century Company.

Labat, Jean-Baptiste. 1724. *Nouveau Voyage aux Isles de l'Amerique*. 2 vols. Haye: Pierre Husson, Thomas Johnson, Pierre Gosse, Jean Van Duren, Rutgert Alberts, & Charles le Vier.

Lahon, Didier. 1999. *O negro no coração do Império: uma memória a resgatar – Séculos XV–XIX*. Lisbon: Secretario Coordenador dos Programas de Educação Multicultural, Ministério da Educação: Casa do Brasil.

Lahon, Didier. 2007. "O escravo africano na vida económica e social portuguesa do Antigo Regime." *Africana Studia* 7: 73–100.

Lakoff, George. 1987. *Woman, Fire, and Dangerous Things: What Categories Reveal about the Mind*. Chicago: University of Chicago Press.

Lakwete, Angela. 2003. *Inventing the Cotton Gin: Machine and Myth in Antebellum America*. Baltimore, MD: Johns Hopkins University Press.

Lal, Kishori Saran. 1994. *Muslim Slave System in Medieval India.* New Delhi: Aditya Prakashan.

Lamadrid, Enrique R. 2015. "*Cautivos y Criados:* Cultural Memories of Slavery in New Mexico." In *Linking the Histories of Slavery: North American and Its Borderlands,* edited by Bonnie M. Martin and James F. Brooks, 229–56. Santa Fe, NM: SAR Press.

Lambert, Sheila, ed. 1975. *House of Commons Sessional Papers of the Eighteenth Century,* 145 vols. Wilmington, DE: Scholarly Resource.

Landers, Jane. 1999. *Black Society in Spanish Florida.* Urbana: University of Illinois Press.

Langebaek, Carl Henrik. 1992. *Noticias de caciques muy mayores.* Bogotá: Ediciones UniAndes/Editorial Universidad de Antioquia.

Lara, Silvia H. 1988. *Campos da violência: escravos e senhores na Capitania do Rio de Janeiro, 1750–1808.* Rio de Janeiro: Paz e Terra.

Lara, Silvia H. 2005. "Conectando Historiografias: a escravidão africana e o antigo regime na América portuguesa." In *Modos de Governar. Idéias e Práticas Políticas no Império Português (sécs. XVI–XIX),* edited by Maria Fernanda Bicalho, 21–38. São Paulo: Alameda Casa Editorial.

Lara, Silvia H. 2008. "Palmares & Cucaú: o aprendizado da dominação." Dissertation, IFCH/UNICAMP.

Larguèche, Abdelhamid. 1990. *L'abolition de l'esclavage en Tunisie à travers les archives, 1841–1846.* Tunis: Alif, Société tunisienne d'étude du XVIIIème siècle.

Last, Murray. 1967. *The Sokoto Caliphate.* New York: Humanities Press.

Launaro, Alessandro. 2011. *Peasants and Slaves: The Rural Population of Roman Italy (200 BC to AD 100).* Cambridge: Cambridge University Press.

Laviña, Javier and Michael Zeuske, eds. 2014. *The Second Slavery: Mass Slaveries and Modernity in the Americas and in the Atlantic Basin.* Vienna; Berlin: Lit Verlag.

Law, Robin. 1977. *The Oyo Empire, c.1600–c.1836: A West African Imperialism in the Era of the Atlantic Slave Trade.* Oxford: Clarendon Press.

Law, Robin. 1986. "Dahomey and the Slave Trade: Reflections on the Historiography of the Rise of Dahomey." *Journal of African History* 27: 237–67.

Law, Robin. 1991. *The Slave Coast of West Africa, 1550–1750: The Impact of the Atlantic Slave Trade on an African Society.* Oxford: Oxford University Press.

Law, Robin. 2004. *Ouidah: The Social History of a West African Slaving "Port" 1727–1892.* Athens: Ohio University Press.

Law, Robin. 2012. *Dahomey and the Ending of the Trans-Atlantic Slave Trade: The Journals and Correspondence of Vice-Consul Louis Fraser 1851–1852.* Oxford: Oxford University Press.

Lawson, John. 1967. *A New Voyage to Carolina,* edited by Hugh Talmage Lefler. Chapel Hill: University of North Carolina Press.

LeBlanc, S. A. and K. E. Register. 2003. *Constant Battles: Why We Fight.* New York: St. Martin's Press.

Lee, Sung-im. 2007. 「조선시대 양반의 성문화」, 제44차 고전여성문학회, Seoul, June 12.

Legros, D. 1985. "Wealth, Poverty, and Slavery among 19th Century Tutchone Athapaskans." *Research in Economic Anthropology* 7: 37–64.

Lekson, S. H. 2002. "War in the Southwest, War in the World." *American Antiquity* 67: 607–24.

Lemaire, A. 2003. "L'esclave." In *El hombre fenicio: estudios y materiales*, edited by José-Ángel Zamora, 219–22. Roma: Consejo Superior de Investigaciones Científicas.

Lenik, Stephan. 2011. "Mission Plantations, Space, and Social Control: Jesuits as Planters in the Caribbean and Frontiers." *Journal of Social Archaeology* 12.1: 51–71.

Lenski, N. 2008. "Captivity, Slavery, and Cultural Exchange between Rome and the Germans from the First to the Seventh Century CE." In *Invisible Citizens: Captives and Their Consequences*, 80–109. Salt Lake City: University of Utah Press.

Lenski, N. 2011. "Captivity and Slavery among the Saracens in Late Antiquity (ca. 250–630 CE)." *Antiquité Tardive* 19: 237–66.

Lenski, N. 2014. "Captivity among the Barbarians and Its Impact on the Fate of the Roman Empire." In *The Cambridge Companion to the Age of Attila*, edited by Michael Maas, 230–46. New York: Cambridge University Press.

Lenski, N. 2017. "Peasant and Slave in Late Antique North Africa, c. 100–600 CE." In *Late Antiquity in Contemporary Perspective*, 113–55. Cambridge: Cambridge Scholars Press.

Levine, Lawrence W. 1977. *Black Culture and Black Consciousness: Afro-American Thought from Slavery to Freedom.* New York: Oxford University Press.

Levine, Nancy E. 1980. "Perspectives on Nyinba Slavery." In *Asian and African Systems of Slavery*, edited by James L. Watson, 195–222. Berkeley: University of California Press.

Lévy, Edmond. 1974. "Les esclaves chez Aristophane." In *Actes de colloque du Group de recherche sur l'esclavage dans l'antiquité (Besançon 1972)*, 29–46. Besançon: Presses Universitaires de Franche-Comté.

Lévy-Bruhl, Henri. 1931. "Théorie de l'esclavage." *Revue générale du droit* 55: 1–17. Reprinted in M. I. Finley, ed. *Slavery in Classical Antiquity: Views and Controversies*, 151–70. Cambridge: W. Heffer & Sons, 1960.

Lewis, David. 2011. "Near Eastern Slaves in Classical Attica and the Slave Trade with Persian Territories." *Classical Quarterly* 61: 91–113.

Lewis, David. 2013. "Slave Marriages in the Laws of Gortyn: A Matter of Rights?" *Historia* 62: 390–416.

Lewis, David. 2016. "The Market for Slaves in the Fifth and Fourth Century Aegean: Achaemenid Anatolia as a Case Study." In *The Ancient Greek Economy: Markets, Households and City-States*, edited by Edward Monroe Harris, David Martin Lewis, and Mark Woolmer, 316–36. New York: Cambridge University Press.

Lewis, David. 2017. "Orlando Patterson, Property, and Ancient Slavery: The Definitional Problem Revisited." In *On Human Bondage: After Slavery and*

Social Death, edited by J. Bodel and W. Scheidel. 31–54. Malden, MA; Oxford: Wiley Blackwell.

Lim, Sang-hyuk. 2007. "1586 년 이지도·다물사리의 소송으로 본 노비법제와 사회상." *法史學研究 第* 36: 5–38.

Lim, Sang-hyuk. 2010. *나는 노비로소이다*. Seoul: Beyond the Books.

Limbert, Mandana E. 2001. "The Senses of Water in an Omani Town." *Social Text* 68.19.3: 35–55.

Link, Stefan. 1994. *Das griechische Kreta: Untersuchungen zu seiner staatlichen und gesellschaftlichen Entwickung vom 6. bis zum 4. Jahrhundert v. Chr.* Stuttgart: Franz Steiner.

Link, Stefan. 2001. "'Dolos' und 'Woikeus' in Recht von Gortyn." *Dike* 4: 87–112.

Little, L., ed. 2007. *Plague and the End of Antiquity*. Cambridge: Cambridge University Press.

Littlefield, Daniel F. 1980. *The Chickasaw Freedmen: A People without a Country*. Westport, CT: Greenwood Press.

Liverani, Mario. 1982. "Annotazioni di un lettore 'impertinente.'" *Opus* 1: 3–9.

Lloyd, G. E. R. 1966. *Polarity and Analogy*. Cambridge: Cambridge University Press.

Lo Cascio, E. 2002. "Considerazioni sul numero degli schiavi e sulle loro fonti di approvvigionamento in età imperiale." In *Etudes de démographie du monde gréco-romain*. Antiquitas 26, edited by W. Suder, 51–65. Wrocław: Wydawn.

Lo Cascio, E. 2009. *Crescita e declino: studi di storia dell'economia romana*. Rome: "L'Erma" di Bretschneider.

Loomis, William T. 1998. *Wages, Welfare Costs, and Inflation in Classical Athens*. Ann Arbor: University of Michigan Press.

Lorimer, J. G. 1907. *Gazetteer of the Persian Gulf, Oman and Central Arabia*, Vol. 1. Calcutta: Superintendent Government Printing.

Lorimer, J. G. 1908. *Gazetteer of the Persian Gulf*, Vol. 2. Calcutta: Superintendent Government Printing.

Lorimer, J. G. 1915. *Gazetteer of the Persian Gulf, Oman and Central Arabia, Vol. I Historical, Part* 2. Calcutta: Government Printing.

Loth, Vincent. 1995. "Pioneers and *Perkerniers*: The Banda Islands in the Seventeenth Century." *Cakalele* 6: 13–35.

Lotze, Detlef. 1959. *Metaxy eleutheron kai doulon: Studien zur Rechtsstellung unfreier Landbevölkerungen in Griechenland bis zum 4. Jahrhundert v. Chr.* Vol. 17, *Deutsche Akademie der Wissenschaften zu Berlin. Schriften der Sektion für Altertumswissenschaft, 17*. Berlin: Akademie-Verlag.

Love, J. 1986. "Max Weber and the Theory of Ancient Capitalism." *History and Theory* 25: 152–72.

Lovejoy, Paul E. 1979. "Indigenous African Slavery." *Historical Reflection/Réflexions Historiques* 6.1: 19–83.

Lovejoy, Paul E. 1991. "Miller's Vision of Meillassoux." *International Journal of African Historical Studies* 24.1: 133–45.

Lovejoy, Paul E. 2000. "Identifying Enslaved Africans in the African Diaspora," In *Identity in the Shadow of Slavery*, edited by Paul E. Lovejoy, 1–29. London: Continuum.

Lovejoy, Paul E., ed. 2004. *Slavery on the Frontiers of Islam.* Princeton, NJ: Markus Wiener.

Lovejoy, Paul E., 2005. *Slavery, Commerce and Production in the Sokoto Caliphate of West Africa.* Trenton, NJ: Africa World Press.

Lovejoy, Paul E., 2011. "The Autobiography of Oluadah Equiano, the African, and the Life of Gustavus Vassa, Reconsidered." In *Crossing Memories in the African Diaspora*, edited by Ana Lucia Araujo, Mariana Pinho Candido, and Paul E. Lovejoy, 15–34. Trenton, NJ: Africa World Press.

Lovejoy, Paul E., 2012a. *Transformations in Slavery: A History of Slavery in Africa.* 3rd edn. Cambridge: Cambridge University Press.

Lovejoy, Paul E., 2012b. "Olaudah Equiano or Gustavus Vassa – What's in a Name?" *Atlantic Studies* 9.2: 165–84.

Lovejoy, Paul E., 2013a. "Pawnship and Seizure for Debt in Africa during the Era of the Slave Trade." In *Debt and Slavery in the Mediterranean and Atlantic Worlds*, edited by Gwyn Campbell and Alessandro Stanziani, 63–76. London: Pickering and Chatto.

Lovejoy, Paul E., 2013b. "Transformation of the *Ékpè* Masquerade in the African Diaspora." In *Carnival – Theory and Practice*, edited by Christopher Innes, Annabel Rutherford, and Brigitte Bogar, 127–52. Trenton, NJ: Africa World Press.

Lovejoy, Paul E., 2014a. "Jihad na África Ocidental durante a 'Era das Revoluções': em direção a um diálogo com Eric Hobsbawm e Eugene Genovese." *Topoi* 15.28: 22–67.

Lovejoy, Paul E., 2014b. "Pawnship, Debt and 'Freedom' in Atlantic Africa during the Era of the Slave Trade: A Re-assessment," *Journal of African History* 55: 1–24.

Lovejoy, Paul E., 2015. "Les empires d'jihadistes de l'ouest africain aux XVIIIe–XIXe siècle." *Cahiers d'histoire. Revue d'histoire critique* 128: 87–109.

Lovejoy, Paul E., 2016a. *Jihad in West Africa in the Age of Revolutions, 1780–1850.* Athens: Ohio University Press.

Lovejoy, Paul E., 2016b. "*Jihad* and the Era of the Second Slavery." *Journal of Global Slavery* 1.1: 28–43.

Lovejoy, Paul E. and Steven Baier. 1975. "The Desert Side Economy of the Central Sudan." *International Journal of African Historical Studies* 8.4: 551–81.

Lovejoy, Paul E. and Toyin Falola, eds. 2003. *Pawnship, Slavery and Colonialism in Africa.* Trenton, NJ: Africa World Press.

Lovejoy, Paul E. and David Richardson. 2004. "'This Horrid Hole': Royal Authority, Commerce and Credit at Bonny, 1690–1840." *Journal of African History* 45: 363–92.

Lovejoy, Paul E. and David Richardson. 2010. "The Slave Ports of the Bight of Biafra in the Eighteenth Century." In *Repercussions of the Atlantic Slave Trade: The Interior of the Bight of Biafra and the African Diaspora*, edited by Carolyn Brown and Paul E. Lovejoy, 19–56. Trenton, NJ: Africa World Press.

Lovejoy, Paul E. and Suzanne Schwarz, eds. 2013. *Slavery, Abolition and the Transition to Colonialism in Sierra Leone.* Trenton, NJ: Africa World Press.

Lozano, Pedro. 1733. *Descripción chorographica del terreno, ríos, árboles, y animales de las dilatadísimas provincias del Gran Chaco.* Córdoba: Colegio de la Assumpcion, por Joseph Santos Balbàs.

Luna, Francisco Vidal and Iraci del Nero Costa. 1982. *Minas Colonial: economia e sociedade.* São Paulo: FIPE, Pioneira.

Luna, Francisco Vidal and Herbert S. Klein. 2003. *Slavery and the Economy of São Paulo, 1750–1850.* Stanford, CA: Stanford University Press.

Luraghi, Nino. 2002. "Helotic Slavery Reconsidered." In *Sparta: Beyond the Mirage,* edited by A. Powell and S. Hodkinson, 227–48. Swansea: Classical Press of Wales.

Luraghi, Nino. 2003. "The Imaginary Conquest of the Helots." In *Helots and Their Masters in Laconia and Messenia: Histories, Ideologies, Structures,* edited by Nino Luraghi and Susan E. Alcock, 109–41. Cambridge, MA: Center for Hellenic Studies.

Luraghi, Nino. 2009. "The Helots: Comparative Approaches, Ancient and Modern." In *Sparta: Comparative Approaches,* edited by S. Hodkinson, 261–304. Swansea: Classical Press of Wales.

Luraghi, Nino and Susan E. Alcock, eds. 2003. *Helots and Their Masters in Laconia and Messenia: Histories, Ideologies, Structures.* Washington, DC: Center for Hellenic Studies.

Lyne, Robert N. 1905. *Zanzibar in Contemporary Times.* London: Hurst & Blackett.

Mabbett, I. 1983. "Some Remarks on the Present State of Knowledge about Slavery at Angkor." In *Slavery, Bondage and Dependency in Southeast Asia,* edited by Anthony Reid, 44–63. New York: St. Martin's.

MacDowell, Douglas M. 1986. *Spartan Law.* Edinburgh: Scottish Academic Press.

MacEachem, Scott. 2011. "Enslavement and Everyday Life: Living with Slave Raiding in the Northeastern Mandara Mountains of Cameroon." In *Slavery in Africa: Archaeology and Memory,* edited by Paul Lane and Kevin MacDonald, 109–24. London: Oxford University Press.

Maia, M. R. d. C. 2013. "De reino traficante a povo traficado: a diáspora dos courás do Golfo do Benim para as minas de ouro da América Portuguesa (1715–1760)." Dissertation, UFRJ.

Manning, Patrick. 1969. "Slaves, Palm Oil, and Political Power on the West African Coast." *African Historical Studies* 2: 279–288.

Manning, Patrick. 1982. *Slavery, Colonialism and Economic Growth in Dahomey, 1640–1960.* Cambridge: Cambridge University Press.

Manning, Patrick. 1990. *Slavery and African Life: Occidental, Oriental and African Slave Trades.* Cambridge: Cambridge University Press.

Manning, Patrick and Tiffany Trimmer. 2013. *Migration in World History.* 2nd edn. London; New York: Routledge.

Marcílio, Maria Luiza. 2000. *Crescimento demográfico e evolução agrária paulista: 1700–1836.* São Paulo: HUCITEC/EDUSP.

Marcoy, Paul. 1869. *Voyage à travers l'Amérique du Sud de l'Océan Pacifique à l'Océan Atlantique.* 2 vols. Paris: Librairie de L. Hachette et Cie.

Marrs, Aaron. 2009. *Railroads in the Old South: Pursuing Progress in a Slave Society.* Baltimore, MD: Johns Hopkins University Press.

Marquese, R. B. 2004. *Feitores do corpo, missionários da mente. Senhores, letrados e o controle dos escravos nas Américas, 1660–1860.* São Paulo: Companhia das Letras.

Marquese, R. B., T. P. Parron, and M. R. Berbel. 2016. *Slavery and Politics: Brazil and Cuba, 1790–1850.* Albuquerque: University of New Mexico Press.

Marshall, Lydia W., ed. 2015. *The Archaeology of Slavery: A Comparative Approach to Captivity and Coercion.* Center for Archaeological Investigations, Occasional Paper No. 41. Carbondale: Southern Illinois University Press.

Martin, Bonnie and James F. Brooks, eds. 2015. *Linking the Histories of Slavery: North America and Its Borderlands.* Santa Fe, NM: SAR Press.

Martin, D. L. and D. W. Frayer, eds. 1997. *Troubled Times: Violence and Warfare in the Past.* Amsterdam: Gordon and Breach.

Martin, Jack B. and Margaret McKane Mauldin. 2000. *A Dictionary of Creek/Muskogee with Notes on the Florida and Oklahoma Seminole dialects of Creek.* Lincoln: University of Nebraska Press.

Martin, Jonathan D. 2004. *Divided Mastery: Slave Hiring in the American South.* Cambridge, MA: Harvard University Press.

Martin, René. 1971. *Recherches sur les agronomes latins et leurs conceptions économiques et sociales.* Collection d'études anciennes. Paris: Les Belles Lettres.

Marx, Karl. 1859. *Zur Kritik der politischen Ökonomie.* Berlin: Franz Duncker.

Marx, Karl. 1939–41. *Grundrisse der Kritik der politischen Ökonomie.* Fotomechanischer Nachdruck der Ausg. Moskau 1939 und 1941. Frankfurt a. M.: Europäische Verlags Anstalt.

Marx, Karl. 1964. *Pre-capitalist Economic Formations.* Translated by J. Cohen. Edited by E. J. Hobsbawm. London: Lawrence & Wishart.

Marx, Karl and F. Engels. 1977. *Karl Marx, Frederick Engels: Collected Works.* Vol. 9. New York: International Publishers.

Marx, Karl and F. Engels. 1997. *Karl Marx, Frederick Engels: Collected Works.* Vol. 36. New York: International Publishers.

Marx, Karl and F. Engels. 1998. *Karl Marx, Frederick Engels: Collected Works.* Vol. 37. New York: International Publishers.

Marzano, A. 2007. *Roman Villas in Central Italy: A Social and Economic History.* Leiden: Brill.

Maschner, H. D. G. and K. L. Reedy-Maschner. 1998. "Raid, Retreat, Defend (Repeat): The Archaeology and Ethnohistory of Warfare on the North Pacific Rim." *Journal of Anthropological Archaeology* 17.1: 19–51.

Matienzo, Juan de. 1918–22a. "Carta a S.M. del licenciado Matienzo con larga noticia de los indios chiriguanaes, 1564." In *Audiencia de*

Charcas: Correspondencia de presidentes y oidores, edited by Roberto Levillier, 1: 54–60. Madrid: Juan Pueyo.

Matienzo, Juan de. 1918–22b. "Parecer del licenciado Matienzo oydor de Charcas dirigido al virrey del Perú, 16 Mayo, 1573." In *Audiencia de Charcas: Correspondencia de presidentes y oidores*, edited by Roberto Levillier, 1: 271–79. Madrid: Juan Pueyo.

Matilla Vicente, Eduardo. 1977. "Surgimiento y desarrollo de la esclavitude cartiginesa y su continuacion en epoca romana." *Hispania Antiqua* 7: 99–123.

Mattingly, D. J. 1988. "Oil for Export? A Comparison of Libyan, Spanish and Tunisian Olive Oil Production in the Roman Empire." *Journal of Roman Archaeology* 1: 33–56.

Mauss, M. 1925[1990]. *The Gift: The Form and Reason for Exchange in Archaic Societies*. Translated by W. D. Halls. New York: Routledge.

May, Robert E. 2002. *Manifest Destiny's Underworld: Filibustering in Antebellum America*. Chapel Hill: University of North Carolina Press.

Maynard, Mary. 1995. "Beyond the Big Three: The Development of Feminist Theory into the 1990s." *Women's History Review* 4: 259–81.

Maynard, Mary. 2006. "'Race,' Gender and the Concept of 'Difference' in Feminist Thought." In *Feminism in the Study of Religion: A Reader*, edited by Darlene M. Juschka, 434–51. London: Continuum.

McCarthy, Kathleen. 2000. *Slaves, Masters, and the Art of Authority in Plautine Comedy*. Princeton, NJ: Princeton University Press.

McDowell, William L., ed. 1970. *Colonial Records of South Carolina: Documents Relating to Indian Affairs, 1754–1765*. Columbia: University of South Carolina Press.

McGovern, William Montgomery. 1927. *Jungle Paths and Inca Ruins*. New York and London: The Century Company.

McIlwraith, T. F. 1948. *The Bella Coola Indians*. Toronto: University of Toronto Press.

McLaurin, Melton A. 1991. *Celia: A Slave*. New York: Avon Books.

McMahon, Elisabeth. 2013. *Slavery and Emancipation in Islamic East Africa: From Honor to Respectability*. Cambridge: Cambridge University Press.

Meiggs, Russell. 1972. *The Athenian Empire*. Oxford: Clarendon Press.

Meillassoux, Claude. 1960. "Essai d'interprétation du phénomène économique dans les societies traditionelles d'auto subsistence." *Cahiers d'études africaines* 1.4: 38–67.

Meillassoux, Claude., ed. 1975. *L'Esclavage en Afrique précoloniale*. Paris: Maspero.

Meillassoux, Claude. 1978a. "Correspondence on Slavery." *Economy and Society* 7.3: 321–31.

Meillassoux, Claude. 1978b. "Rôle de l'esclavage dans l'histoire de l'Afrique occidentale." *Anthropologie et Sociétés* 2.1: 117–48.

Meillassoux, Claude. 1983. "Female Slavery." In *Women and Slavery in Africa*, edited by Claire C. Robertson and Martin A. Klein, 49–66. Madison: University of Wisconsin Press.

Meillassoux, Claude. 1986. *Anthropologie de l'esclavage. Le ventre de fer et d'argent.* Paris: Presses Universitaires de France.

Meillassoux, Claude. 1991. *The Anthropology of Slavery: The Womb of Iron and Gold.* Translated by Alide Dasnois. Chicago: University of Chicago Press.

Melchisedek, Chetima and Gaïmatakwan Kr Dujok Alexandre. 2015. "Memories of Slavery in the Mandara Mountains: Re-appropriating the Repressive Past." In *Slavery, Memory, Citizenship,* edited by Paul E. Lovejoy and Vanessa Oliveira, 285–99. Trenton, NJ: Africa World Press.

Menard, Russell, R. 2006. *Sweet Negotiations: Sugar, Slavery, and Plantation Agriculture in Early Barbados.* Charlottesville: University of Virginia Press.

Méndez, Francisco. 1969. "Carta do Franciscano Frei Francisco Mendes sôbre os costumes dos Indios Mbaiá e Guaná, no Alto-Paraguai." In *Do Tratado de Madri à conquista dos sete povos (1750–1802),* compiled by Jaime Cortesão, 54–68. Rio de Janeiro: Biblioteca Nacional.

Menget, Patrick. 1988. "Notes sur l'adoption chez les Txicão du Brésil Central." *Anthropologie et Sociétés* 12.2: 63–72.

Mereness, Newton D., ed. 1916. *Travels in the American Colonies.* New York: MacMillan.

Merk, Frederick. 1931. *Fur Trade and Empire: George Simpson's Journal.* Cambridge, MA: Harvard University Press.

Métraux, Alfred. 1930. "Etudes sur la civilisation des Indiens Chiriguano." *Revista del Instituto Etnológico de la Universidad Nacional de Tucumán* 1.3: 295–493.

Meyer, Eduard. 1895[1924]. "Die wirtschaftliche Entwicklung des Altertums." In *Kleine Schriften* 1: 79–168. Halle: Max Niemeyer.

Meyer, Eduard. 1898[1924]. "Die Sklaverei im Altertum. Vortrag gehalten in der Gehe-Stiftung zu Dresden am 15. Januar 1898." In *Kleine Schriften.* 1: 169–212. Halle: Max Niemeyer.

Miers, Suzanne. 2004. "Slavery: A Question of Definition." In *The Structure of Slavery in Indian Ocean Africa and Asia,* edited by Gwyn Campbell, 1–15. London; Portland, OR: Frank Cass.

Mignan, Robert. 1820. *A Winter Journey. Volume II.* London: Richard Bentley.

Miles, Tiya. 2005. *Ties That Bind: The Story of an Afro-Cherokee Family in Slavery and Freedom.* Berkeley: University of California Press.

Millender, Ellen G. 2001. "Spartan Literacy Revisited." *Classical Antiquity* 20.1: 121–64.

Miller, Ivor. 2012. *Voice of the Leopard: African Secret Societies and Cuba.* Jackson: University Press of Mississippi.

Miller, Joseph C. 1989. "The World According to Meillassoux: A Challenging but Limited Vision." *International Journal of African Historical Studies* 22.3: 473–95.

Miller, Joseph C. 2008. "Slaving as Historical Process: Examples from the Ancient Mediterranean and the Modern Atlantic." In *Slave Systems: Ancient and Modern,* edited by Enrico Dal Lago and Constantina Katsari, 70–102. Cambridge: Cambridge University Press.

Miller, Joseph C. 2012. *The Problem of Slavery as History: A Global Approach.* New Haven, CT: Yale University Press.

Millett, Paul. 1989. "Patronage and Its Avoidance in Classical Athens." In *Patronage in Ancient Society,* edited by A. Wallace-Hadrill, 15–47. London: Routledge.

Millett, Paul. 2000. "The Economy." In *Short Oxford History of Europe: Classical Greece,* edited by R. Osborne, 23–51. Oxford: Oxford University Press.

Mingo de la Concepción, Manuel. 1981. *Historia de las misiones franciscanas de Tarija entre chiriguanos.* Tarija: Universidad Boliviana "Juan Misael Caracho."

Mintz, Sidney W. and Richard Price. 1976. *An Anthropological Approach to the Afro-American Past: A Caribbean Perspective.* Philadelphia, PA: Institute for the Study of Human Issues.

Mitchell, D. 1984. "Predatory Warfare, Social Status, and the North Pacific Slave Trade." *Ethnology* 23: 39–48.

Momigliano, Arnaldo. 1987. "Moses Finley on Slavery: A Personal Note." In *Classical Slavery. Slavery and Abolition* 8, edited by M. I. Finley, 1–6.

Monaghan, George William and Chris Peebles. 2010. "The Construction, Use, and Abandonment of Angel Site Mound A: Tracing the History of a Middle Mississippian Town through Its Earthworks." *American Antiquity* 75: 935–53.

Monroe, J. Cameron. 2007. "Dahomey and the Atlantic Slave Trade: Archaeology and Political Order in the Bight of Benin." In *Archaeology of Atlantic Africa and the African Diaspora,* edited by A. Ogundiran and T. Falola, 100–21. Bloomington: Indiana University Press.

Montana, Ismael M. 2013. *The Abolition of Slavery in Ottoman Tunisia.* Gainesville: University Press of Florida.

Monteiro, J. M. 1994. *Negros da terra: Índios e bandeirantes nas origens de São Paulo.* São Paulo: Companhia das Letras.

Montesquieu, Charles-Louis de. 1949. *The Spirit of the Laws.* Translated by T. Nugent. New York: Hafner.

Mooney, James. 1992. *History, Myths, and Sacred Formulas of the Cherokees.* Asheville, NC: Bright Mountain Books.

Moore, Alexander ed. 1988. *Nairne's Muskhogean Journals: The 1708 Expedition to the Mississippi River.* Jackson: University Press of Mississippi.

Morabito, M. 1981. *Les réalités de l'esclavage d'après le Digeste.* Paris: Les Belles Lettres.

Moreno, Alfonso. 2007. *Feeding the Democracy: The Athenian Grain Supply in the Fifth and Fourth Centuries BC.* Oxford: Oxford University Press.

Morga, Antonio de. 1609[1971]. *Sucesos de las Islas Filipinas.* Translated by J. S. Cummins. Cambridge: Hakluyt Society.

Morgan, Edmund S. 1975. *American Slavery, American Freedom: The Ordeal of Colonial Virginia.* New York: Norton.

Morgan, Philip D. 1998. *Slave Counterpoint: Black Culture in the Eighteenth-Century Chesapeake and Lowcountry.* Chapel Hill: University of North Carolina Press.

Morgan, William A. 2013. "Cuban Tobacco Slavery: Life, Labor, and Freedom in Pinar Del Río." Dissertation, University of Texas.

Morilla Critz, José, Alan L. Olmstead, and Paul W. Rhode. 1999. "'Horn of Plenty': The Globalization of Mediterranean Horticulture and the Economic Development of Southern Europe, 1880–1930." *Journal of Economic History* 59.2: 316–52.

Morin, Françoise. 1998. "Los Shipibo-Conibo." In *Guía etnográfica de la alta amazonía, Volumen 3: Cashinahua, Amahuaca, Shipibo-Conibo*, edited by Fernando Santos and Frederica Barclay, 275–435. Quito: Smithsonian Tropical Research/Instituto Francés de Estudios Andinos/Abya-Yala.

Morley, Neville. 1998. "Political Economy and Classical Antiquity." *Journal of the History of Ideas* 59: 95–114.

Morley, Neville. 2007. *Trade in Classical Antiquity*. Cambridge: Cambridge University Press.

Morley, Neville. 2009. *Antiquity and Modernity*. London: Wiley-Blackwell.

Morley, Neville. 2011. "Slavery under the Principate." In *The Cambridge World History of Slavery. Volume I: The Ancient Mediterranean World*, edited by Keith Bradley and P. Cartledge, 265–86. Cambridge: Cambridge University Press.

Morris, Ian. 2005. "Archaeology, Standards of Living, and Greek Economic History." In *The Ancient Economy: Evidence and Models*, edited by Joseph G. Manning and Ian Morris, 91–126. Stanford, CA: Stanford University Press.

Morris, Ian. 2013. *The Measure of Civilization: How Social Development Decides the Fate of Nations*. Princeton, NJ: Princeton University Press.

Morris, Thomas D. 1996. *Southern Slavery and the Law, 1619–1860*. Chapel Hill: University of North Carolina Press.

Mouritsen, Henrik. 2004. "Freedmen and Freeborn in the Necropolis of Imperial Ostia." *Zeitschrift für Papyrologie und Epigraphik* 150: 281–304.

Mouritsen, Henrik. 2005. "Freedmen and Decurions: Epitaphs and Social History in Imperial Italy." *Journal of Roman Studies* 95: 38–63.

Mouritsen, Henrik. 2007. "*CIL X* 1403: The Album from Herculaneum and the Nomenclature of *Latini Iuniani*." *Zeitschrift für Papyrologie und Epigraphik* 161: 288–90.

Mouritsen, Henrik. 2011. *The Freedman in the Roman World*. Cambridge; New York: Cambridge University Press.

Mouritsen, Henrik. 2012. "Slavery and Manumission in the Roman Elite: A Study of the Columbaria of the Volusii and the Statilii." In *Roman Slavery and Roman Material Culture*, edited by Michele G. George, 43–68. Phoenix Supplementary Volumes 52. Toronto: University of Toronto Press.

Mouser, Bruce. 1973. "Trade, Coasters, and Conflict in the Rio Pongo from 1790 to 1808." *Journal of African History* 14.1: 45–64.

Mouser, Bruce. 2010. "A History of the Rio Pongo: Time for a New Appraisal?" *History in Africa* 37: 329–54.

Mouser, Bruce. 2013. *American Colony on the Rio Pongo: The War of 1812, the Slave Trade, and the Proposed Settlement of African Americans, 1810–1830*. Trenton, NJ: Africa World Press.

Mulcahy, Matthew. 2014. *Hubs of Empire: The Southeastern Lowcountry and the British Caribbean, Regional Perspectives of Early America.* Baltimore, MD: Johns Hopkins University Press.

Nadiri, Muhammad Ibrahim Kazaruni. 1367[1988]. *Tarikh-e banadir va jazayir-e Khalij-e Fars dar zaman-e Muhammad Shah Qajar.* Edited by Manuchihr Sutudah. Tehran.

Nafissi, Mohammad. 2005. *Ancient Athens & Modern Ideology: Value, Theory & Evidence in Historical Sciences: Max Weber, Karl Polanyi & Moses Finley.* London: Institute of Classical Studies.

Naiden, F. S. and Richard Talbert, eds. 2014. *Moses Finley in America: The Making of an Ancient Historian.* Special issue of *American Journal of Philology* 135: 167–302.

Nash, Gary B. 1988. *Forging Freedom: The Formation of Philadelphia's Black Community.* Cambridge, MA: Harvard University Press.

Nicholls, Christine Stephanie. 1971. *The Swahili Coast: Politics, Diplomacy and Trade on the East African Littoral, 1798–1856.* London: George Allen and Unwin Ltd.

Nieboer, Herman Jeremias. 1910. *Slavery as an Industrial System: Ethnological Researches.* 2nd edn. The Hague: M. Nijhoff. Reprint, Cambridge: Cambridge University Press 2010.

Nimuendajú, Curt. 1950. "Reconhecimento dos rios Içana, Ayarí e Uaupés." *Journal de la Société des Americanistes* 39: 125–82.

Nino, Bernardino de. 1912. *Etnografía chiriguana.* La Paz: Tipografía Comercial de Ismael Argote.

Nishida, Mieko. 1993. "Manumission and Ethnicity in Urban Slavery, Brazil, 1808–1888." *The Hispanic American Historical Review* 73.3: 361–91.

Northrup, David. 1978. *Trade without Rulers: Pre-colonial Economic Development in South-Eastern Nigeria.* Oxford: Clarendon Press.

Norton, Holly. 2013. "Estate by Estate, the Landscape of the 1733 St. Jan Rebellion." Dissertation, Syracuse University.

Novais, F. A. 1979. *Portugal e Brasil na crise do antigo sistema colonial (1777–1808).* São Paulo: Editora HUCITEC.

Nwokeji, Ugo. 2010. *The Slave Trade and Culture in the Bight of Biafra: An African Society in the Atlantic World.* Cambridge: Cambridge University Press.

Ober, Josiah. 1989. *Mass and Elite in Democratic Athens: Rhetoric, Ideology, and the Power of the People.* Princeton, NJ: Princeton University Press.

Ober, Josiah. 2010. "Wealthy Hellas." *Transactions of the American Philological Association* 140: 241–86.

Ober, Josiah. 2015. *The Rise and Fall of Classical Greece.* Princeton, NJ: Princeton University Press.

Oberg, Kalervo, 1973. *The Social Economy of the Tlingit Indians.* Seattle: University of Washington Press.

Ogot, Bethwell A. 1979. "Population Movements between East Africa, the Horn of Africa and the Neighboring Countries." In *The African Slave Trade from the Fifteenth to the Nineteenth Century,* 175–82. Paris: UNESCO.

Ogundiran, Akinwumi. 2013. "The End of Prehistory? An Africanist Comment." *American Historical Review* 118: 788–801.

O'Kane, J., trans. 1688[1972]. *The Ship of Sulaiman.* London: Routledge.

Ordinaire, Olivier. 1887. "Les sauvages du Pérou." *Revue d'Ethnographie* 6: 265–322.

Ortiz, Fernando 1995. *Cuban Counterpoint: Tobacco and Sugar.* Edited with introduction by Fernando Coronil. Durham, NC: Duke University Press.

Osborne, Robin. 1991. "Pride and Prejudice, Sense and Subsistence: Exchange and Society in the Greek City." In *City and Country in the Ancient World,* edited by J. Rich and A. Wallace-Hadrill, 119–45. London: Routledge.

Osborne, Robin. 1995. "The Economics and Politics of Slavery at Athens." In *The Greek World,* edited by Anton Powell, 27–43. London; New York: Routledge. Reprinted in *Athens and Athenian Democracy,* edited by R. Osborne, 85–108. Cambridge: Cambridge University Press, 2010.

Osborne, Robin. 1996. *Greece in the Making, 1200–479 BC.* London: Routledge.

Oudin-Bastide, Caroline. 2005. *Travail, capitalisme et société esclavagiste: Guadeloupe, Martinique (XVIIe–XIXe siècle).* Paris: Editions la decouverte.

Owen, Roger. 1969. *Cotton and the Egyptian Economy, 1820–1914: A Study in Trade and Development.* Oxford: Clarendon Press.

Owen, Roger. 1993. *The Middle East in the World Economy, 1800–1914.* New York: I. B. Tauris.

Owen, W. F. W. 1833. *Narrative of Voyages to Explore the Shores of Africa, Arabia, and Madagascar.* New York: J & J Harper.

Palais, James B. 1996. *Confucian Statecraft and Korean Institutions: Yu Hyŏngwŏn and the Late Chosŏn Dynasty.* Seattle: University of Washington Press.

Palais, James B. 1998. *Views on Korean Social History.* Seoul: Yonsei.

Palgrave, William Gifford. 1883. *Personal Narrative of a Year's Journey through Central and Eastern Arabia, 1862–63.* London: Macmillan & Company.

Palmié, Stephan. 2011. "Toward Sugar and Slavery." In *The Caribbean: A History of the Region and Its People,* edited by Stephan Palmié and Francisco A. Scarano, 131–62. Chicago: University of Chicago Press.

Palmié, Stephan and Francisco A. Scarano, eds. 2011. *The Caribbean: A History of the Region and Its People.* Chicago: University of Chicago Press.

Parsons and Abbott. 1832. "Census of Creek Indians Taken by Office of Indian Affairs," Microcopy T-275, roll 1, frame 112, 194, National Archives, Washington, DC.

Patault, A.-M. 1989. *Introduction historique au droit des biens.* Paris: Presses universitaires de France.

Paterson, David E. 2009. "Slavery, Slaves, and Cash in a Georgia Village, 1825–1865." *Journal of Southern History* 75: 879–930.

Patterson, Orlando. 1982. *Slavery and Social Death.* Cambridge, MA: Harvard University Press.

Patterson, Orlando. 1991. *Freedom in the Making of Western Culture.* New York: Basic Books.

Patterson, Orlando. 2003. "Reflections on Helotic Slavery and Freedom." In *Helots and Their Masters in Laconia and Messenia: Histories, Ideologies, Structures,* edited by N. Luraghi and S. E. Alcock, 289–310. Cambridge, MA: Harvard University Press.

Patterson, Orlando. 2008. "Slavery, Gender, and Work in the Pre-modern World and Early Greece: A Cross-Cultural Analysis." In *Slave Systems: Ancient and Modern,* edited by Enrico Dal Lago and Constantina Katsari, 32–69. Cambridge: Cambridge University Press.

Patterson, Orlando. 2012. "Trafficking, Gender and Slavery: Past and Present." In *The Legal Understanding of Slavery: From the Historical to the Contemporary,* edited by Jean Allain, 323–59. Oxford: Oxford University Press.

Patterson, Orlando. 2017. "Revisiting Slavery, Property, and Social Death." In *On Human Bondage: After Slavery and Social Death,* edited by J. Bodel and W. Scheidel, 265–96. Malden, MA; Oxford: Wiley Blackwell.

Pearson, Michael N. 2003. *The Indian Ocean.* New York: Routledge.

Penningroth, Dylan C. 2003. *Claims of Kinfolk: African American Property and Community in the Nineteenth-Century South.* Chapel Hill: University of North Carolina Press.

Perdue, Theda. 1979. *Slavery and Evolution of Cherokee Society, 1540–1866.* Knoxville: University of Tennessee Press.

Perry, Jonathan S. 2014. "From Frankfurt to Westermann: Forced Labor and the Early Development of Finley's Thought." *American Journal of Philology* 135: 221–41.

Person, Yves. 1992. "The Coastal Peoples: From Casamance to the Ivory Coast Lagoons." In *General History of Africa,* edited by D. T. Niane, 301–23. London.

Petersen, Lauren Hackworth. 2006. *The Freedman in Roman Art and Art History.* New York; Cambridge: Cambridge University Press.

Peterson, J. E. 2014. "Muscat as a Port City." In *The Persian Gulf in Modern Times: People, Ports, and History,* edited by Lawrence G. Potter, 153–72. New York: Palgrave Macmillan.

Peukert, Werner. 1978. *Der atlantische Sklavenhandel von Dahomey, 1750–1797: Wirtschaftsanthropologie und Sozialgeschichte.* Wiesbaden: Steiner Verlag.

Pfaffenberger, Bryan. 2008. "Society." In *International Encyclopedia of the Social Sciences,* edited by William A. Darity Jr., 2nd edn., 7: 650–53. Detroit, MI: Macmillan Reference.

Phelan, J. L. 1959. *The Hispanization of the Philippines: Spanish Aims and Filipino Responses, 1565–1700.* Madison: University of Wisconsin Press.

Phillips, William D., Jr. 1985. *Slavery from Roman Times to the Early Transatlantic Trade.* Minneapolis: University of Minnesota Press.

Piker, Joshua. 2004. *Okfuskee: A Creek Indian Town in Colonial America.* Cambridge, MA: Harvard University Press.

Pipes, Daniel. 1981. *Slave Soldiers and Islam: The Genesis of a Military System.* New Haven, CT: Yale University Press.

Plass, Paul. 1995. *The Game of Death in Ancient Rome: Arena Sport and Political Suicide.* Madison: University of Wisconsin Press.

Polanyi, Karl. 1944. *The Great Transformation.* New York: Rinehart & Company.

Polanyi, Karl. 1966. *Dahomey and the Slave Trade: An Analysis of an Archaic Economy.* Seattle: University of Washington Press.

Polo de Ondegardo, Juan. 1991. "Relation du Licencié Polo au vice-roi Toledo." In *Alter ego: naissance de l'identité Chiriguano,* edited by Isabelle Combès and Thierry Saignes, 195–42. Paris: Editions de l'Ecole des Hautes Etudes en Sciences Sociales.

Popenoe, Paul. 1926. "The Distribution of the Date Palm." *The Geographical Review* 16.1: 117–21.

Popović, Alexandre. 1998. *The Revolt of African Slaves in Iraq in the 3rd/9th Century.* Princeton, NJ: Markus Wiener Publishers.

Powell, Lawrence N. 2012. *The Accidental City: Improvising New Orleans.* Cambridge, MA: Harvard University Press.

Prado, Francisco Rodrigues do. 1839. "Historia dos Indios Cavalleiros ou da nação Guaycurú." *Revista do Instituto Histórico e Geográfico Brasileiro* 1.1: 25–57.

Prado Júnior, C. 1942. *Formação do Brasil contemporâneo.* São Paulo: Livraria Martins Editora.

Pred, Allan. 1984. "Place as Historically Contingent Process: Structuration and the Time-Geography of Becoming Places." *Annals of the Association of American Geographers* 74.2: 279–97.

Prestholdt, Jeremy. 2004. "On the Global Repercussions of East African Consumerism." *The American Historical Review* 109.3: 755–82.

Prince, Mary. 1831. *The History of Mary Prince, a West Indian Slave.* London: F. Westley and A. H. Davis.

Pritchett, W. Kendrick and Anne Pippin. 1956. "The Attic Stelai, Part II." *Hesperia* 25: 178–317.

Prus, Robert. 1996. *Symbolic Interaction and Ethnographic Research: Intersubjectivity and the Study of Human Lived Experience.* Albany: State University of New York Press.

Quarles, Benjamin. 1961. *The Negro in the American Revolution.* Chapel Hill: University of North Carolina Press.

Quinn, David B., ed. 1979. *New American World: A Documentary History of North America to 1612,* 5 vols. New York: Arno.

Raaflaub, Kurt. 2004[1985]. *The Discovery of Freedom in Ancient Greece.* 2nd edn. Translated by Renate Franciscono. Chicago: University of Chicago Press.

Raben, Remco. 1962. "Batavia and Colombo: The Ethnic and Spatial Order of Two Colonial Cities, 1600–1800." Dissertation, University of Leiden.

Raboteau, Albert J. 1978. *Slave Religion: The "Invisible Institution" in the Antebellum South.* New York: Oxford University Press.

Ragatz, Lowell J. 1928. *The Fall of the Planter Class in the British Caribbean, 1763–1833.* New York, London: The Century Company.

Raimondi, Antonio. 1905. "Informe sobre la provincia litoral de Loreto." In *Colección de documentos oficiales referentes a Loreto,* compiled by Carlos Larrabure y Correa, 7:118–278. Lima: Imprenta de La Opinión Nacional.

Raleigh, Walter. 1596. *The Discoverie of the Large, Rich, and Bewtiful Empyre of Guiana*. London: Imprinted by Robert Robinson.

Ramelli, Ilaria. 2016. *Social Justice and the Legitimacy of Slavery: The Role of Philosophical Asceticism from Ancient Judaism to Late Antiquity*. Oxford Early Christian Studies. Oxford: Oxford University Press.

Ramos, Alcida Rita, Peter Silverwood-Cope, and Ana Gita de Oliveira. 1980. "Patrões e clientes: Relações intertribais no alto Rio Negro." In *Hierarquia e simbiose. Relações intertribais no Brasil*, edited by Alcida Rita Ramos, 135–82. São Paulo: Editora HUCITEC.

Randall, R. H. 1953. "The Erechtheum Workmen." *American Journal of Archaeology* 57: 199–210.

Rathbone, Dominic. 1991. *Economic Rationalism and Rural Society in Third-Century A.D. Egypt: The Heroninos Archive and the Appianus Estate*. Cambridge: Cambridge University Press.

Rawick, George P. 1972. *From Sundown to Sunup: The Making of the Black Community*. Westport, CT: Greenwood Publishing.

Redmond, E. 1994. "Tribal and Chiefly Warfare in South America." *Memoirs of the Museum of Anthropology, University of Michigan* 28. Ann Arbor: University of Michigan Press.

Reeves, Matthew B. 2014. "Mundane or Spiritual? – the Interpretation of Glass Bottle Containers Found on Two African Diaspora Sites." In *Materialities of Rituals in the Black Atlantic*, edited by Paula Saunders and Akinwumi Ogundiran, 176–96. Bloomington: Indiana University Press.

Reginaldo, L. 2009. "África em Portugal?: devoções, irmandades e escravidão no Reino de Portugal, século XVIII." *História (UNESP)* 28: 239–320.

Reid, Anthony. 1983a. "Introduction: Slavery and Bondage in Southeast Asian History." In *Slavery, Bondage and Dependency in Southeast Asia*, edited by Anthony Reid, 1–43. New York: St. Martin's.

Reid, Anthony. 1983b. "'Closed' and 'Open' Slave Systems in Pre-colonial Southeast Asia." In *Slavery, Bondage and Dependency in Southeast Asia*, edited by Anthony Reid, 156–81. New York: St. Martin's.

Reid, Anthony. 1988–93. *Southeast Asia in the Age of Commerce*. 2 vols. New Haven, CT: Yale University Press.

Reid, Anthony. 1993. "The Decline of Slavery in Nineteenth Century Indonesia." In *Breaking the Chains: Slavery, Bondage and Emancipation in Modern Africa and Asia*, edited by Martin Klein, 64–82. Madison: University of Wisconsin Press.

Reid, Anthony. 2006. *Verandah of Violence: The Background to the Aceh Problem*. Singapore: NUS Press.

Reilly, Benjamin. 2015. *Slavery, Agriculture, and Malaria in the Arabian Peninsula*. Athens: Ohio University Press.

Reis, J. J. 1993. *Slave Rebellion in Brazil: The Muslim Uprising of 1835 in Bahia*. Baltimore, MD: Johns Hopkins University Press.

Reitmeyer, J. F. 1789. *Geschichte und Zustand der Sklaverey und Leibeigenschaft in Griechenland*. Berlin: August Mylius.

Reséndez, Andrés. 2016. *The Other Slavery: The Uncovered Story of Indian Enslavement in America*. Boston, MA: Houghton Mifflin.

Reute, Emily (Salma binti Sa'id). 1907. *Memoirs of an Arabian Princess*. Translated by Lionel Strachey. New York: Doubleday, Page & Company.

Rhee, Young-hoon. 1998. "한국사에 있어서 노비제의 추이와 성격." In *노비 농노 노예*, edited by Yoksahakhoe, 304–422. Seoul: Ilchogak.

Rhee, Young-hoon. 2000. "노비의 결혼과 부부생활." In *조선시대생활사 2*, edited by the Society of Korean Historical Manuscripts, 102–17. Seoul: Yoksa Bipyong.

Rhee, Young-hoon. 2006. "11~16 세기 한국의 노비와 일본의 게닌(下人), 『경제사학." *Review of Economic History* 36: 3–40.

Rhee, Young-hoon. 2007. "한국사 연구에서 노비제가 던지는 몇 가지 문제." In *한국사시민강좌 4*, edited by the Committee of the Citizens' Forum on Korean History, 141–50. Seoul: Ilchogak.

Ribeiro, Alexandre Vieira. 2009. "A cidade de Salvador: estrutura econômica, comércio de escravos, grupo mercantil (c.1750–c.1800)." Dissertation, IFCS-UFRJ.

Richter, Daniel K. 1992. *The Ordeal of the Longhouse: The Peoples of the Iroquois League in the Era of European Colonization*. Chapel Hill: University of North Carolina Press.

Richter, Daniel K. 2011. *Before the Revolution: America's Ancient Pasts*. Cambridge, MA: Harvard University Press.

Riggs, Oscar Willoughby. 1886. "The Fruit-Ships at New York." *Frank Leslie's Popular Monthly* 21.5: 599–611.

Rihll, Tracey. 1996. "The Origin and Establishment of Ancient Greek Slavery." In *Serfdom and Slavery: Studies in Legal Bondage*, edited by M. L Bush, 89–111. London: Longman.

Rihll, Tracey. 2011. "Classical Athens." In *The Cambridge World History of Slavery. Volume I: The Ancient Mediterranean World*, edited by K. Bradley and P. Cartledge, 48–73. Cambridge: Cambridge University Press.

Rippon, John, ed. 1793. "An Account of the Life of Mr. David George, from Sierra Leone to Africa, given by himself in a conversation with Brother Rippon of London, and Brother Pearce of Birmingham." In *The Baptist Annual Register for 1790, 1791, 1792, & part of 1793, including Sketches of the State of Religion Among Different Denominations of Good Men at Home and Abroad*, 473–84. London: Dilly, Button, and Thomas.

Rivaya-Martínez, J. 2012. "Becoming Comanches: Patterns of Captive Incorporation into Kinship Networks, 1820–1875." In *On the Borders of Love and Power: Families and Kinship in the American West*, edited by D. W. Adams and C. DeLuzio, 47–70. Berkeley: University of California Press.

Rivers, Larry E. 2012. *Rebels and Runaways: Slave Resistance in Nineteenth-Century Florida*. Urbana: University of Illinois Press.

Roberts, John W. 1989. *From Trickster to Badman: The Black Folk Hero in Slavery and Freedom*. Philadelphia: University of Pennsylvania Press.

Robertshaw, P. 1999. "Women, Labor, and State Formation in Western Uganda." In *Complex Polities in the Ancient Tropical World*. Archaeological

Papers of the American Anthropological Association, No. 9., edited by E. A. Bacus and L. J. Lucero, 51–66. Arlington, VA: American Anthropological Association.

Robertson, C. C. and M. A. Klein, eds. 1983a. *Women and Slavery in Africa.* Madison: University of Wisconsin Press.

Robertson, C. C. and M. A. Klein, 1983b. "Women's Importance in African Slave Systems." In *Women and Slavery in Africa,* edited by C. C. Robertson and M. A. Klein, 3–25. Madison: University of Wisconsin Press.

Rochefort, Charles de. 1666. *The History of the Caribby-Islands.* London: Printed by J. M. for Thomas Dring and John Starkey.

Rockman, Seth. 2009. *Scraping By: Wage Labor, Slavery, and Survival in Early Baltimore.* Baltimore, MD: Johns Hopkins University Press.

Rodrigues, A. C. 2009. "Homens de negócio: vocabulário social, distinção e atividades mercantis nas Minas setecentistas." *História* 28.1: 191–214.

Rodrigues Neves, Maria de Fátima. 1990. "Ampliando a família escrava: compadrio de escravos em São Paulo do século XIX." In *História e população: estudos sobre a América Latina,* edited by Sérgio Nadalin et al., 242–43. Belo Horizonte: SEADE/ABEP/IUSPP.

Roe, Peter G. 1982. *The Cosmic Zygote. Cosmology in the Amazon Basin.* New Brunswick, NJ: Rutgers University Press.

Romans, Bernard. 1999. *A Concise Natural History of East and West Florida.* Edited by Kathryn E. Holland Braund. Tuscaloosa: University of Alabama Press.

Romera, Lugo, Karen Mahé, and Sonia Menéndez Castro. 2003. *Barrio De Compeche: Tres Estudios Arqueológicos,* La Fuente Viva, 27. Havana: Fundación Fernando Ortíz.

Roper, Moses. 1848. *Narrative of the Adventures and Escape of Moses Roper, from American Slavery.* Berwick-upon-Tweed: Published for the author and printed at the Warder Office.

Röschenthaler, Ute. 2011. *Purchasing Culture in the Cross River Region of Cameroon and Nigeria.* Trenton, NJ: Africa World Press.

Rosivach, Vincent J. 1999. "Enslaving *Barbaroi* and the Athenian Ideology of Slavery." *Historia* 48: 129–57.

Rossi, Benedetta. 2015. *From Slavery to Aid: Power, Labour, and Ecology in the Nigerien Sahel, 1800–2000.* Cambridge: Cambridge University Press.

Rothman, Joshua C. 2003. *Notorious in the Neighborhood: Sex and Families across the Color Line in Virginia, 1787–1861.* Chapel Hill: University of North Carolina Press.

Rugemer, Edward Bartlett. 2008. *The Problem of Emancipation: The Caribbean Roots of the American Civil War.* Baton Rouge: Louisiana State University Press.

Rushforth, Brett. 2003. "'A Little Flesh We Offer You': The Origins of Indian Slavery in New France." *William and Mary Quarterly,* 3rd series, 60: 777–808.

Rushforth, Brett. 2012. *Bonds of Alliance: Indigenous and Atlantic Slaveries in New France.* Chapel Hill: University of North Carolina Press.

Salau, Mohammed Bashir 2006. "Ribats and the Development of Plantations in the Sokoto Caliphate: A Case Study of Fanisau." *African Economic History* 34: 23–43.

Salem, Ellen. 1978. “Slavery in Medieval Korea.” Dissertation, Columbia University.

Sallares, Robert. 1991. *The Ecology of the Ancient Greek World.* Ithaca, NY: Cornell University Press.

Salman, Michael. 2001. *The Embarrassment of Slavery: Controversies over Bondage and Nationalism in the American Colonial Philippines.* Berkeley: University of California Press.

Samuel, A. E. 1965. “The Role of *Paramone* Clauses in Ancient Documents.” *Journal of Juristic Papyrology* 15: 221–311.

Sánchez Labrador, José. 1910–17. *El Paraguay Católico.* Buenos Aires: Imprenta de Coni Hermanos.

Santos-Granero, F. 2009. *Vital Enemies: Slavery, Predation, and the Amerindian Political Economy of Life.* Austin: University of Texas Press.

Saunders, Paula. 2014. “Charms and Spiritual Practitioners: Negotiating Power Dynamics in an Enslaved African Community in Jamaica.” In *Materialities of Rituals in the Black Atlantic*, edited by Paula Saunders and Akinwumi Ogundiran, 159–75. Bloomington: Indiana University Press.

Saunders, Paula. 2015. “Analysis of an African Burial Ground in Nineteenth-Century Jamaica.” *Journal of African Diaspora Archaeology and Heritage* 4.2: 143–71.

Scheidel, Walter. 1994. *Grundpacht und Lohnarbeit in der Landwirtschaft des römischen Italien.* Frankfurt: Peter Lang.

Scheidel, Walter. 1997. “Quantifying the Sources of Slaves in the Early Roman Empire.” *Journal of Roman Studies* 87: 157–69.

Scheidel, Walter. 2003. “Helot Numbers: A Simplified Model.” In *Helots and Their Masters in Laconia and Messenia: Histories, Ideologies, Structures*, edited by N. Luraghi and S. E. Alcock, 240–47. Cambridge, MA: Harvard University Press.

Scheidel, Walter. 2005a. “Human Mobility in Roman Italy, II: The Slave Population.” *Journal of Roman Studies* 95: 64–79.

Scheidel, Walter. 2005b. “Real Slave Prices and the Relative Cost of Slave Labor in the Greco-Roman World.” *Ancient Society* 23: 1–17.

Scheidel, Walter. 2008. “The Comparative Economics of Slavery in the Greco-Roman World.” In *Slave Systems: Ancient and Modern*, edited by Enrico Dal Lago and Constantina Katsari, 106–26. Cambridge; New York: Cambridge University Press.

Scheidel, Walter. 2011. “The Roman Slave Supply.” In *The Cambridge World History of Slavery. Volume I: The Ancient Mediterranean World*, edited by K. Bradley and P. Cartledge, 287–310. Cambridge: Cambridge University Press.

Scheidel, Walter. 2012. “Slavery.” In *The Cambridge Companion to the Roman Economy*, edited by Walter Scheidel, 89–113. Cambridge: Cambridge University Press.

Scheidel, Walter, Ian Morris, and Richard P. Saller, eds. 2007. *The Cambridge Economic History of the Greco-Roman World.* Cambridge: Cambridge University Press.

Schermerhorn, Calvin. 2015. "'The Time Is Now Just Arriving When Many Capitalists Will Make Fortunes': Indian Removal, Finance, and Slavery in the Making of the American Cotton South." In *Linking the Histories of Slavery: North American and Its Borderlands*, edited by Bonnie M. Martin and James F. Brooks, 151–70. Santa Fe, NM: SAR Press.

Schiffmann, I. 1976. "Zur Interpretation der Inschriften IFPCO Sard. 26 und 39 aus Sardinien." *Rivista di Studi Fenici* 4: 49–52.

Schoen, Brian. 2009. *The Fragile Fabric of Union: Cotton, Federal Politics, and the Global Origins of the Civil War.* Baltimore, MD: Johns Hopkins University Press.

Schumacher, Leonhard. 2001. *Sklaverei in der Antike: Alltag und Schicksal der Unfreien.* Munich: C. H. Beck.

Schumacher, Leonhard. 2011 "Slaves in Roman Society." In *The Oxford Handbook of Social Relations in the Roman World*, edited by M. Peachin, 589–608. Oxford: Oxford University Press.

Schütrumpf, Eckart. 1993. "Aristotle's Theory of Slavery – a Platonic Dilemma." *Ancient Philosophy* 13: 111–23.

Schwartz, Stuart B. 1970. "The 'Mocambo': Slave Resistance in Colonial Bahia." *Journal of Social History* 3.4: 313–33.

Schwartz, Stuart B. 1985. *Sugar Plantations in the Formation of Brazilian Society: Bahia, 1550–1835.* Cambridge; New York: Cambridge University Press.

Schwartz, Stuart B. 1988. "Recent Trends in the Study of Slavery in Brazil." *Luso-Brazilian Review* 25.1: 1–25.

Schwartz, Stuart B. 2001. "Repensando Palmares: resistência escrava na colônia." In: *Escravos, roceiros e rebeldes*, edited by Stuart B. Schwartz, 213–55. Bauru: Edusc.

Schwartz, Stuart B. and Stephen F. Gudeman. 1984. "Cleansing Original Sin: Godparenthood and the Baptism of Slaves in Eighteenth-Century Bahia." In *Kinship Ideology and Practice in Latin America*, edited by R. T. Smith, 35–58. Chapel Hill: University of North Carolina Press.

Schwarz, Philip J. 1988. *Twice Condemned: Slaves and the Criminal Laws of Virginia, 1705–1865.* Baton Rouge: Louisiana State University Press.

Schwitalla, Al W., Terry L. Jones, Marin A. Pilloud, Brian F. Codding, and Randy S. Wiberg. 2014. "Violence among Foragers: The Bioarchaeological Record from Central California." *Journal of Anthropological Archaeology* 33: 66–83.

Scott, James C. 1972. "Patron-Client Politics and Political Change in Southeast Asia." *American Political Science Review* 66: 91–113.

Seddon, David, ed. 1978. *Relations of Production: Marxist Approaches to Economic Anthropology.* London: Frank Cass.

Séhou, Ahmadou. 2010. "L'esclavage dans les Lamidats de l'Adamaoua (Nord-Cameroun), du début du XIXe siècle." Dissertation, Université de Yaoundé.

Sela-Sheffy, Rakefet. 2006. "Integration through Distinction: German-Jewish Immigrants, the Legal Profession and Patterns of Bourgeois Culture in British-Ruled Jewish Palestine." *Journal of Historical Sociology* 19.1: 34–59.

Serra, Ricardo Franco de Almeida. 1845. "Parecer sobre o aldeamento dos Indios Uaicurús e Guanás, com a descripção dos seus usos, religião, estabilidade, e costumes." *Revista do Instituto Histórico e Geográfico Brasileiro* 7.26: 204–12.

Serra, Ricardo Franco de Almeida. 1850. "Continuação do parecer sobre os índios Uaicurus e Guanás." *Revista do Instituto Histórico e Geográfiico Brasileiro (Segunda Serie)* 6.19: 348–95.

Shaw, Brent D. 1993. "The Early Development of M. I. Finley's Thought: The Heichelheim Dossier." *Athenaeum* 81: 177–99.

Shaw, Brent D. 1998. "'A Wolf by the Ears': M. I. Finley's Ancient Slavery and Modern Ideology in Historical Context." In *Ancient Slavery and Modern Ideology*, edited by Brent D. Shaw. Expanded edn., 3–74. Princeton, NJ: Markus Wiener Publishers.

Shaw, Brent D. 2013. *Bringing in the Sheaves: Economy and Metaphor in the Roman World*. Toronto; Buffalo: University of Toronto Press.

Shaw, Brent D. and Richard P. Saller. 1981. "Editor's Introduction." In M. I. Finley, *Economy and Society in Ancient Greece*, edited by Brent D. Shaw and Richard P. Saller, ix–xxvi. London: Chatto & Windus.

Shaw, Rosalind. 2002. *Memories of the Slave Trade: Ritual and the Historical Imagination in Sierra Leone*. Chicago: University of Chicago Press.

Shephard, Verene A. 2002. "Introduction." In *Slavery without Sugar: Diversity in Caribbean Economy and Society since the 17th Century*, edited by Verene A. Shepard, 1–18. Gainesville: University Press of Florida.

Shepherd, Gill. 1980. "The Comorians and the East African Slave Trade." In *Asian and African Systems of Slavery*, edited by J. L. Watson, 73–99. Oxford: Basil Blackwell.

Sheriff, Abdul. 1981. "The East African Coast and Its Role in Maritime Trade." In *General History of Africa, Vol. II, Ancient Civilizations of Africa*, edited by G. Mokhtar, 551–67. Paris: UNESCO and London: Heinemann Educational Books.

Sheriff, Abdul. 1987. *Slaves, Spices, and Ivory in Zanzibar: Integration of an East African Commercial Empire into the World Economy, 1770–1873*. Athens: Ohio University Press.

Sheriff, Abdul. 2001. *Afro–Arab Interaction in the Indian Ocean: Social Consequences of the Dhow Trade*. Cape Town: Centre for Advanced Studies of African Society.

Sheriff, Abdul. 2005. "The Slave Trade and Its Fallout in the Persian Gulf." In *Abolition and Its Aftermath in Indian Ocean Africa and Asia*, edited by Gwyn Campbell, 103–19. London and New York: Routledge.

Sheriff, Abdul. 2010. *Dhow Cultures of the Indian Ocean: Cosmopolitanism, Commerce and Islam*. New York: Columbia University Press.

Sheriff, Abdul. 2013. "Social Mobility in Indian Ocean Slavery: The Strange Career of Sultan bin Aman." In *Indian Ocean Slavery in the Age of Abolition*, edited by Robert Harms, Bernard K. Freamon, and David W. Blight, 143–59. New Haven, CT: Yale University Press.

Shoemaker, Nancy. 2004. *A Strange Likeness: Becoming Red and White in Eighteenth-Century North America.* New York: Oxford University Press.

Shrimpton, Gordon S. 1991. *Theopompus the Historian.* Montreal: McGill-Queen's University Press.

Shtaerman, E. M. 1964. *Die Krise der Sklavenhalterordnung im Westen des Römischen Reiches.* Translated by W. Seyfarth. Berlin: Akademie-Verlag.

Silva, Alcionilio Brüzzi Alves da. 1962. *A civilização indigena do Uaupés.* São Paulo: Missão Salesiana do Rio Negro.

Silverwood-Cope, Peter. 1990. *Os Makú: povo caçador do noroeste da Amazônia.* Brasília: Editora Universidade de Brasília.

Simpson, George. 1847. *Narrative of an Overland Journey round the World.* Philadelphia, PA: Lea and Blanchard.

Singleton, Theresa A. 2015. *Slavery behind the Wall: An Archaeology of a Cuban Coffee Plantation.* Gainesville: University Press of Florida.

Sirks, A. J. B. 1993. "Did the Late Roman Government Tie People to Their Status or Profession?" *Tyche* 8: 159–75.

Sirks, A. J. B. 2008. "The Colonate in Justinian's Reign." *Journal of Roman Studies* 98: 120–43.

Slenes, R. W. 1999. *Na senzala, uma flor: esperanças e recordações na formação da família escrava: Brasil Sudeste, século XIX.* Rio de Janeiro: Editora Nova Fronteira.

Smail, D. and A. Shryock. 2013. "History and the 'Pre.'" *American Historical Review* 118: 709–37.

Smalligan, Laura M. 2011. "Cross River Creoles: Skin-Covered Art from the Era of the Slave Trade." Dissertation, Yale University.

Smith, Frederick and Karl Watson. 2009. "Urbanity, Sociability, and Commercial Exchange in the Barbados Sugar Trade: A Comparative Colonial Archaeological Perspective on Bridgetown, Barbados in the Seventeenth Century." *International Journal of Historical Archaeology* 13.1: 63–79.

Smith, John David, ed. 2002. *Black Soldiers in Blue: African American Troops in the Civil War Era.* Chapel Hill: University of North Carolina Press.

Smith, Katherine A. 2012. "Economy, Politics and the Early Formation of a Cultural Identity in the British Virgin Islands' Slave Society." In *Slavery in Africa and the Caribbean: A History of Enslavement and Identity since the 18th Century*, edited by Olatunji Ojo and Nadine Hunt, 144–74. London: I. B. Tauris.

Smith, Margaret. 2008. "Working for a Living: A Study of Working Men and Work Practices in Classical Athens." Doctoral Dissertation, Macquerie University.

Smith, Michael Garfield. 1960. *Government in Zazzau, 1800–1950.* London: Oxford University Press.

Snell, William Robert. 1972. "Indian Slavery in Colonial South Carolina." Dissertation, University of Alabama.

Snyder, Christina. 2010. *Slavery in Indian Country: The Changing Face of Captivity in Early America.* Cambridge, MA: Harvard University Press.

Snyder, Christina. 2013. "The Long History of American Slavery." *OAH Magazine of History* 27: 23.

Solin, Heikki. 1971. *Beiträge zur Kenntnis der griechischen Personennamen in Rom.* Commentationes Humanarum Litterarum 48. Helsinki: Societas Scientiarum Fennica.

Sosin, Joshua D. 2015. "Manumission with *Paramone*: Conditional Freedom?" *Transactions of the American Philological Association* 145: 325–81.

Soucek, Svatopluk. 2008. *The Persian Gulf. Its Past and Present.* Costa Mesa, CA: Mazda Publishers, Inc.

Souza, L. d. M. e. 2006. *O sol e a sombra: política e administração na América portuguesa do século XVIII.* São Paulo: Companhia das Letras.

Speelman, Cornelis. 1670. *Notitie dienende voor eened Korten Tijd en tot nader last van de Hooge Regering op Batavia voor den ondercoopman Jan van Oppijnen.* Leiden: Typescript held in KITLV collection.

Stahl, Eurico G. 1928. "La tribu de los Cunibos en la región de los lagos del Ucayali." *Boletín de la Sociedad Geográfica de Lima* 45.2: 139–66.

Starna, William A. and Ralph Watkins. 1991. "Northern Iroquoian Slavery." *Ethnohistory* 381: 34–57.

Stavorinus, J. S. 1798[1969]. *Voyages to the East Indies.* Translated by S. H. Wilcocke. 3 vols. London: Dawsons of Pall Mall.

Ste. Croix, G. E. M. de. 1981. *The Class Struggle in the Ancient Greek World: From the Archaic Age to the Arab Conquests.* Ithaca, NY: Cornell University Press.

Steinberg, Philip E. 2009. "Sovereignty, Territory, and the Mapping of Mobility: A View from the Outside." *Annals of the Association of American Geographers* 99.3: 467–95.

Steward, Julian Haynes and others. 1956. *The People of Puerto Rico: A Study in Social Anthropology.* Urbana: University of Illinois Press.

Stilwell, Sean. 2014. *Slavery and Slaving in African History.* Cambridge: Cambridge University Press.

Stolberg, Sheryl Gay. 2012. "Obama Has Ties to Slavery not by His Father but His Mother, Research Suggests," *New York Times*, July 30, accessed at www.nytimes.com/2012/07/30/us/obamas-mother-had-african-forebear-study-suggests.html?pagewanted=all&_r=0.

Stradelli, Ermanno. 1890. "L'Uaupés e gli Uaupés." *Bolletino della Società Geografica Italiana* 3.5: 425–53.

Strauss, Barry S. 1986. *Athens after the Peloponnesian War: Class, Faction and Policy 403–386 B.C.* Ithaca, NY: Cornell University Press.

Strickland, S. 1831. *Negro Slavery Described by a Negro: Being the Narrative of Ashton Warner, a Native of St. Vincent's.* London: Samuel Maunder, Newgate Street.

Suárez de Figueroa, Lorenzo. 1965. "Relación de la ciudad de Santa Cruz de la Sierra, 1586." In *Relaciones Geográficas de Indias.* Biblioteca de Autores Españoles 183, edited by Marcos Jiménez de la Espada, 402–06. Madrid: Ediciones Atlas.

Sued-Badillo, Jalil. 2011. "From Taínos to Africans in the Caribbean: Labor, Migration, and Resistance." In *The Caribbean: A History of the Region and*

Its People, edited by Stephan Palmié and Francisco A. Scarano, 97–113. Chicago: University of Chicago Press.

Sullivan, George Lydiard. 1873. *Dhow Chasing in Zanzibar Waters*. London: Sampson Low, Marston, Low & Searle.

Susnik, Branislava. 1968. *Chiriguanos: dimensiones etnosociales*, vol. 1. Asunción: Museo Etnográfico Andrés Barbero.

Sutherland, H. 1983. "Slavery and the Slave Trade in South Sulawesi, 1660s–1800s." In *Slavery, Bondage and Dependency in Southeast Asia*, edited by Anthony Reid, 263–85. St. Lucia: University of Queensland Press.

Sutter, John D. 2013. "Slavery's Last Stronghold." *CNN Story*. Accessed July 15, 2013. www.cnn.com/interactive/2012/03/world/mauritania.slaverys.last.stronghold/index.html.

Swan, Caleb. 1855. "Position and State of Manners and Arts in the Creek, or Muscogee Nation in 1791." In *Information Respecting the History, Condition and Prospects of the Indian Tribes of the United States*, edited by Henry Rowe Schoolcraft, 5:251–83. New York: Paladin Press.

Swanton, John R. 1911. *Indian Tribes of the Lower Mississippi Valley and Adjacent Coast of the Gulf of Mexico*. Washington, DC: Government Printing Office.

Swanton, John R. 1995. *Myths and Tales of the Southeastern Indians*. Norman: University of Oklahoma Press.

Tadman, Michael. 1989. *Speculators and Slaves: Masters, Traders, and Slaves in the Old South*. Madison: University of Wisconsin Press.

Tannenbaum, Frank. 1947. *Slave and Citizen, the Negro in the Americas*. New York: A. A. Knopf.

Taylor, Anne Christine. 1999. "The Western Margins of Amazonia from the Early Sixteenth to the Early Nineteenth Century." In *The Cambridge History of the Native Peoples of the Americas*, edited by Frank Salomon and Stuart B. Schwartz, 3.2:204–56. Cambridge: Cambridge University Press.

Taylor, Timothy. 2001. "Believing the Ancients: Quantitative and Qualitative Dimensions of Slavery and the Slave Trade in Later Prehistoric Eurasia." *World Archaeology* 33.1: 27–43.

Tchernia, André. 1983. "Italian Wine in Gaul at the End of the Republic." In *Trade in the Ancient Economy*, edited by Peter Garnsey, Keith Hopkins, and C. R. Whittaker, 87–104. Berkeley: University of California Press.

Tchernia, André. 1986. *Le vin de l'Italie romaine: Essai d'histoire économique d'après les amphores*. Bibliothèque des écoles françaises d'Athènes et de Rome. 261. Roma: Ecole française de Rome.

Temin, Peter. 2013. *The Roman Market Economy*. Princeton, NJ: Princeton University Press.

Terray, Emmanuel. 1974. "Long Distance Exchange and the Formation of the State: The Case of the Abron Kingdom of Gyaman." *Economy and Society* 3: 315–45.

Terray, Emmanuel. 1975. "Classes and Class Consciousness in the Abron Kingdom of Gyaman." In *Marxist Analyses and Social Anthropology*, edited by Maurice Bloch, 85–134. London: Malaby Press.

Terribilini, Mario and Michel Terribilini. 1961. "Resultats d'une enquête faite chez les Maku (Brésil)." *Bulletin Annuel Musée e Institut d'Ethnographie de la Ville de Genève* 4.4: 39.

Testart, Alain. 1998. "L'esclavage comme institution." *L'Homme* 145: 31–69.

Testart, Alain. 2001. *L'esclave, la dette et le pouvoir: Études de sociologie comparative.* Paris: Errance.

Testart, Alain, Christian Jeunesse, Luc Baray, and Bruno Boulestin. 2012. "Les esclaves des tombes néolithiques." *Pour la Science* 76: 106–11.

Thomas, Bertram. 1931. *Alarms and Excursions.* London: George Allen & Unwin, Ltd.

Thompson, D. J. 2011. "Slavery in the Hellenistic World." In *The Cambridge World History of Slavery. Volume I: The Ancient Mediterranean World,* edited by K. Bradley and P. Cartledge, 194–213. Cambridge: Cambridge University Press.

Thornton, John K. 1991. "African Dimensions of the Stono Rebellion." *American Historical Review* 96: 1101–13.

Thornton, John K. 1998. *Africa and Africans in the Making of the Atlantic World, 1400–1800.* Cambridge: Cambridge University Press.

Thornton, John K. 1999. *Warfare in Atlantic Africa 1500–1800.* London: Routledge.

Thornton, Russell. 1987. *American Indian Holocaust and Survival: A Population History since 1492.* Norman: University of Oklahoma Press.

Todd, Stephen. 2007. "Lady Chatterley's Lover and the Attic Orators: The Social Composition of the Athenian Jury." In *The Attic Orators,* edited by E. Carawan, 312–58. Oxford: Oxford University Press.

Toledano, Ehud R. 1982. *The Ottoman Slave Trade and Its Suppression, 1840–1890.* Princeton, NJ: Princeton University Press.

Toledano, Ehud R. 1998. *Slavery and Abolition in the Ottoman Middle East.* Seattle: University of Washington Press.

Toledano, Ehud R. 2000. "The Concept of Slavery in Ottoman and Other Muslim Societies: Dichotomy or Continuum." In *Slave Elites in the Middle East and Africa: A Comparative Study,* edited by Miura Toru and John Edwards Philips, 159–75. London: Kegan Paul International.

Toledano, Ehud R. 2007a. *As If Silent and Absent: Bonds of Enslavement in the Islamic Middle East.* New Haven, CT: Yale University Press.

Toledano, Ehud R. 2007b. "Enslavement and Abolition in Muslim Societies." *Journal of African History* 48: 481–85.

Toledano, Ehud R., ed. 2011a. *African Communities in Asia and the Mediterranean: Identities between Integration and Conflict.* Halle, Germany: Max Planck Institute and Trenton, NJ; Asmara, Eritrea: Africa World Press.

Toledano, Ehud R. 2011b. "Review: *Women and Slavery in the Late Ottoman Empire: The Design of Difference* by Madeline C. Zilfi." *Insight Turkey* 13.3: 208–11.

Toledano, Ehud R. 2012. "The Arabic-Speaking World in the Ottoman Period: A Socio-political Analysis." In *The Ottoman World,* edited by Christine Woodhead, 453–66. Abingdon: Routledge.

Toledano, Ehud R. 2013a. "Turkish Nationalism and Islamic Faith-Based Politics: Historical and Contemporary Perspectives." In *Nation-State and Religion: The Resurgence of Faith*, edited by Anita Shapira, Yedidia Z. Stern, and Alexander Yakobson, 2:101–18. Eastbourne: Sussex Academic Press.

Toledano, Ehud R. 2013b. "Abolition and Anti-slavery in the Ottoman Empire: A Case to Answer?" In *A Global History of Anti-slavery Politics in the Nineteenth Century*, edited by William Mulligan and Maurice Bric, 117–36. Houndsmills, Basingstokes, Hampshire: Palgrave Macmillan.

Toledano, Ehud R. 2015. "Muhammad Farid: Between Nationalism and the Egyptian-Ottoman Diaspora." In *Contextualising Community: Diasporas of the Modern Middle East*, edited by Anthony Gorman and Sossie Kasbarian, 70–102. Edinburgh: Edinburgh University Press.

Toledano, Ehud R. 2017. "Ottoman Elite Enslavement and 'Social Death.'" In *On Human Bondage: After Slavery and Social Death*, edited by John Bodel and Walter Scheidel, 136–50. Malden, MA; Oxford: Wiley Blackwell.

Tomich, Dale. 2014. "Commodity Frontiers, Conjuncture and Crisis: The Remaking of the Caribbean Sugar Industry, 1783–1866." In *The Second Slavery: Mass Slaveries and Modernity in the Americas and in the Atlantic Basin*, edited by Javier Laviña and Michael Zeuske, 143–64. Vienna and Berlin: Lit Verlag.

Tomich, Dale and Michael Zeuske, 2008. "Introduction, the Second Slavery: Mass Slavery, World-Economy, and Comparative Microhistories: Part I." *Review (Fernand Braudel Center)* 31.2: 91–100.

Tompkins, Daniel P. 2008. "Weber, Polanyi, and Finley. Review of *Ancient Athens and Modern Ideology: Value, Theory and Evidence in Historical Sciences*, by Mohammad Nafissi." *History and Theory* 47.1: 123–36.

Tompkins, Daniel P. 2013a. "Moses Finkelstein and the American Scene." In *Moses Finley and Politics*, edited by William V. Harris, 5–30. Leiden: Brill.

Tompkins, Daniel P. 2013b. "The World of Moses Finkelstein: The Year 1939 in M. I. Finley's Development as a Historian." In *Moses Finley and Politics*, edited by William V. Harris, 95–125, 197–207. Columbia Studies in the Classical Tradition. Vol. 40. Leiden: Brill.

Tompkins, Daniel P. 2014. "What Happened in Stockholm? Moses Finley, the Mainz Akademie, and East Bloc Historians." In ΧΑΡΑΚΤΗΡ ΑΡΕΤΑΣ: *Donum Natalicium Bernardo Seidensticker ab Amicis Oblatum.* Hyperboreus 20: 436–52. Munich: C. H. Beck.

Tompkins, Daniel P. 2016. "The Making of Moses Finley." In *M. I. Finley: An Ancient Historian and His Impact*, edited by Daniel Jew, Robin Osborne, and Michael Scott, 13–30. Cambridge: Cambridge University Press.

Torget, Andrew J. 2015. "The Saltillo Slavery Debates: Mexicans, Anglo-Americans, and Slavery's Future in Nineteenth-Century North America." In *Linking the Histories of Slavery: North American and Its Borderlands*, edited by Bonnie M. Martin and James F. Brooks, 171–96. Santa Fe, NM: SAR Press.

Townsend, Joan B. 1983. "Pre-contact Political Organization and Slavery in Aleut Societies." In *The Development of Political Organization in Native*

North America, edited by Elizabeth Tooker. Washington, DC: American Ethnological Society.

Treggiari, Susan. 1973. "Domestic Staff at Rome in the Julio Claudian Period." *Histoire Sociale* 6: 241–55.

Treggiari, Susan. 1975. "Jobs in the Household of Livia." *Papers of the British School at Rome* 43: 48–77.

Troutt Powell, Eve M. 2006. "Will That Subaltern Ever Speak? Finding African Slaves in the Historiography of the Middle East." In *Middle East Historiographies: Narrating the Twentieth Century*, edited by I. Gershoni, A. Singer and Y. H. Erdem, 242–61. Seattle: University of Washington Press.

Turley, David. 2000. *Slavery*. Malden, MA: Blackwell.

United Nations Office on Drugs and Crimes (UNODC). 2009. Global Report on Trafficking in Persons. Accessed July 15, 2013. www.unodc.org/documents/Global_Report_on_TIP.pdf.

Van der Kraan, Alfons. 1983. "Bali: Slavery and Slave Trade." In *Slavery, Bondage and Dependency in Southeast Asia*, edited by Anthony Reid, 315–40. St. Lucia: University of Queensland Press.

Van Norman, William C. 2013. *Shade-Grown Slavery: The Lives of Slaves on Coffee Plantations in Cuba*. Nashville, TN: Vanderbilt University Press.

Van Wees, Hans. 2001. "The Myth of the Middle-Class Army: Military and Social Status in Ancient Athens." In *War as a Cultural and Social Force: Essays on Warfare in Antiquity*, edited by T. Bekker-Nielsen and L. Hannestad, 45–71. Selskab, Denmark: Det kongelige Danske Videnskabernes.

Van Wees, Hans. 2003. "Conquerors and Serfs: Wars of Conquest and Forced Labour in Archaic Greece." In *Helots and Their Masters in Laconia and Messenia: Histories, Ideologies, Structures*, edited by N. Luraghi and S. E. Alcock, 33–80. Cambridge, MA: Harvard University Press.

Van Wees, Hans. 2011. "Demetrius and Draco: Athens' Property Classes and Population in and before 317." *Journal of Hellenic Studies* 131: 95–114.

Vassa, Gustavus. 1789. *The Interesting Narrative of the Life of Olaudah Equiano, or Gustavus Vassa, the African, Written by Himself*. London: Self-published.

Vaughan, J. H. and A. H. M. Kirk-Greene, eds. 1995. *The Diary of Hamman Yaji: Chronicle of a West African Ruler*. Bloomington: Indiana University Press.

Vera, D. 1995. "Dalla 'villa perfecta' alla villa di Palladio: sulle trasformazioni del sistema agrario in Italia fra principato e dominato." *Athenaeum* 83: 189–211, 331–56.

Vera, D. 2007. "Essere 'schiavi della terra' nell'Italia tardoantica: le razionalità di una dipendenza." *Studia historica* 25: 489–505.

Vernet, Thomas. 2003. "Le Commerce." *Azania* 28: 69–97.

Villiers, Alan. 1940. *Sons of Sinbad*. New York: Charles Schribner's Sons.

Villiers, John. 1981. "Trade and Society in the Banda Islands in the Sixteenth Century." *Modern Asian Studies* 15.4: 723–50.

Vlassopoulos, Kostas. 2007. *Unthinking the Greek Polis: Ancient Greek History beyond Eurocentrism*. Cambridge: Cambridge University Press.

Vlassopoulos, Kostas. 2011. "Greek Slavery: From Domination to Property and Back Again." *Journal of Hellenic Studies* 131: 115–30.

Vlassopoulos, Kostas. 2016. "Finley's Slavery." In *M. I. Finley: An Ancient Historian and His Impact*, edited by Daniel Jew, Robin Osborne, and Michael Scott, 76–99. Cambridge: Cambridge University Press.

Vlastos, G. 1968. "Slavery in Plato's Thought." In *Slavery in Classical Antiquity: Views and Controversies*, edited by M. I. Finley, 133–49. Cambridge: Heffer.

Vogt, J. 1953. *Sklaverei und Humanität im klassischen Griechentum.* Wiesbaden: Steiner.

von Dassow, Eva. 2011. "Freedom in Ancient Near Eastern Societies." In *The Oxford Handbook of Cuneiform Culture*, edited by Karen Radner and Eleanor Robson, 205–24. Oxford; New York: Oxford University Press.

Wade, Richard C. 1964. *Slavery in the Cities: The South, 1820–1860.* New York: Oxford University Press.

Wagner, Carlos G., and Luis Alberto Ruiz Cabrero. 2015. "La mano de obra rural en los asentamientos fenicios de Occidente." In *La main-d'oeuvre agricole en Méditerranée archaïque: statuts et dynamiques économiques: actes des journées "Travail de la terre et statuts de la main d'oeuvre en Grèce et en Méditerranée archaïques," Athènes, 15 et 16 décembre 2008*, edited by Julien Zurbach, 85–108. Bordeaux: Ausonius.

Wallace, Alfred R. 1853. *A Narrative of the Travels on the Amazon and Rio Negro.* London: Reeve and Company.

Wallerstein, Immanuel, Hale Decdeli, and Resat Kasaba. 1987. "The Incorporation of the Ottoman Empire into the World Economy." In *The Ottoman Empire and the World Economy*, edited by Huri Islamoglu-Inan, 88–97. New York: Cambridge University Press.

Walz, Terence and Cuno, Kenneth M., eds. 2010. *Race and Slavery in the Middle East: Histories of Trans-Saharan Africans in Nineteenth-Century Egypt, Sudan, and the Ottoman Mediterranean.* Cairo: American University in Cairo Press.

Ward, Kerry. 2009. *Networks of Empire: Forced Migration in the Dutch East India Company.* New York: Cambridge University Press.

Ward-Perkins, B. 2005. *The Fall of Rome: And the End of Civilization.* Oxford: Oxford University Press.

Warren, James. 1981. *The Sulu Zone 1768–1898: The Dynamics of External Trade, Slavery and Ethnicity in the Transformation of a Southeast Asian Maritime State.* Singapore: Singapore University Press.

Waselkov, Gregory A. and Kathryn E. Holland Braund, eds. 1995. *William Bartram on the Southeastern Indians.* Lincoln: University of Nebraska Press.

Watson, Alan. 1987. *Roman Slave Law.* Baltimore, MD: Johns Hopkins University Press.

Watson, George. 2004. "The Man from Syracuse: Moses Finley (1912–1986)." *Sewanee Review* 112: 131–37.

Watson, James L. 1980. "Slavery as an Institution: Open and Closed Systems." In *Asian and African Systems of Slavery*, edited by James L. Watson, 1–15. Berkeley: University of California Press.

Weaver, P. R. C. 1972. *Familia Caesaris: A Social Study of the Emperor's Freedmen and Slaves.* Cambridge: Cambridge University Press.

Weber, Max. 1891[2008]. *Die römische Agrargeschichte in ihrer Bedeutung für das Staats- und Privatrecht = Roman Agrarian History in Its Relation to Roman Public and Civil Law.* Translated by Robert I. Frank. Claremont: Regina Books.

Weber, Max. 1896[1988]. "Die sozialen Gründe des Untergangs der antiken Kultur" = "The Social Causes of the Decline of Ancient Civilization." In *The Agrarian Sociology of Ancient Civilizations*, translated by Robert I. Frank, 389–411. London: J. C. B. Mohr.

Weber, Max. 1909[1988]. *Agrarverhältnisse im* Altertum = "The Agrarian History of the Major Centres of Ancient Civilization." In *The Agrarian Sociology of Ancient Civilizations*, translated by Robert I. Frank, 81–386. London: J. C. B. Mohr.

Weiss, A. 2004. *Sklave der Stadt: Untersuchungen zur öffentlichen Slaverei in den Städten des Römischen Reiches.* Steiner: Stuttgart.

Welskopf, Elisabeth Charlotte. 1957. *Die Produktionsverhältnisse im alten Orient und in der griechisch-römischen Antike, ein Diskussionsbeitrag.* Berlin: Akademie-Verlag.

Westermann, William. 1955. *The Slave Systems of Greek and Roman Antiquity.* Memoirs of the American Philosophical Society, Vol. 40. Philadelphia, PA: American Philosophical Society

Westermarck, Edward. 1906. *The Origin and Development of the Moral Ideas.* Vol. 1. London: Macmillan and Co.

Whitehead, Neil L. 1988. *Lords of the Tiger Spirit. A History of the Caribs in Colonial Venezuela and Guyana, 1498–1820.* Dordrecht; Providence, RI: Foris Publications.

Whitehead Consulting Group. 1972. *Sultanate of Oman Economic Survey, 1972.* Windsor: Harold Whitehead & Partners, Ltd.

Wicker, F. D. P. 1998. "The Road to Punt." *The Geographical Journal* 164.2: 155–67.

Wickham, C. 2005. *Framing the Early Middle Ages: Europe and the Mediterranean, 400 800.* Oxford: Oxford University Press.

Wiencek. 2012. "Master of Monticello." *Smithsonian* October: 40–49.

Wiggermann, F. A. 2000. "Agriculture in the Northern Balikh Valley: The Case of Middle Assyrian Tell Sabi Abyad." In *Rainfall and Agriculture in Northern Mesopotamia: Proceedings of the Third MOS Symposium (Leiden 1999)*, 171–231. Leiden: Nederlands Instituut voor het Nabije Oosten.

Wilbur, Clarence Martin. 1943. *Slavery in China during the Former Han Dynasty, 206 B.C.–A.D. 25.* Vol. 34, Anthropological Series, Field Museum of Natural History. Chicago: Field Museum of Natural History.

Wilder, Craig Steven. 2013. *Ebony & Ivy: Race, Slavery, and the Troubled History of America's Universities.* New York: Bloomsbury.

Wilk, Richard R. and Lisa C. Cliggett. 2007. *Economies and Cultures: Foundations of Economic Anthropology.* 2nd edn. Boulder, CO: Westview Press.

Wilkie, Laurie A. and Paul Farnsworth. 2005. *Sampling Many Pots: An Archaeology of Memory and Tradition at a Bahamian Plantation.* Gainesville: University Press of Florida.

Wilkinson, J. C. 1977. *Water and Tribal Settlement in South-East Arabia: A Study of the Aflaj of Oman*. Oxford: Clarendon Press.

Willetts, Ronald F. 1967. *The Law Code of Gortyn*. Berlin: De Gruyter.

Williams, Eric E. 1944. *Capitalism and Slavery*. Chapel Hill: University of North Carolina Press.

Williams, Gomer. 1897. *History of the Liverpool Privateers and Letters of Marque, with an Account of the Liverpool Slave Trade, 1744–1812*. London: W. Heinemann.

Winton, Richard. 2007. "Thucydides 2.13.6–7: Oldest, Youngest, Hoplites, Metics." *Classical Quarterly* 57.1: 298–301.

Wolf, Eric R. 1966. *Peasants*. Edited by M. Sahlins. *Foundations of Modern Anthropology*. Englewood Cliffs, NJ: Prentice-Hall.

Wolf, Eric R. 1982. *Europe and the People without History*. Berkeley: University of California Press.

Wondji, Christophe. 1992. "The States and Cultures of the Upper Guinea Coast." In *General History of Africa: Africa from the Sixteenth Century to the Eighteenth Century*, edited by B. A. Ogot, 368–98. London: Heinemann.

Wood, Betty. 1995. *Women's Work, Men's Work: The Informal Slave Economies of Lowcountry Georgia*. Athens: University of Georgia Press.

Wood, Betty. 1997. *The Origins of American Slavery: Freedom and Bondage in the English Colonies*. New York: Hill and Wang.

Wood, Ellen Meiksins. 1988. *Peasant-Citizen and Slave: The Foundations of Athenian Democracy*. London; New York: Verso.

Wood, Peter H. 1974. *Black Majority: Negroes in Colonial South Carolina from 1670 through the Stono Rebellion*. New York: Knopf.

Woodward, Robyn. 2010. "Feudalism or Agrarian Capitalism? The Archaeology of the Early Sixteenth-Century Spanish Sugar Industry." In *Out of Many, One People: The Historical Archaeology of Colonial Jamaica*, edited by James A. Delle, Mark W. Hauser, and Douglas V. Armstrong: 22–40. Tuscaloosa: University of Alabama Press.

Woolf, G. 1998. *Becoming Roman: The Origins of Provincial Civilization in Gaul*. Cambridge: Cambridge University Press.

Wright, Donald R. 2000. *African Americans in the Colonial Era: From African Origins through the American Revolution*. 2nd edn. Wheeling, IL: Harlan Davidson.

Wright, Leitch, Jr. 1986. *Creeks & Seminoles: The Destruction and Regeneration of the Muscogee People*. Lincoln: University of Nebraska Press.

Yearbook of the United States Department of Agriculture, 1894–1935.

Yelvington, Kevin A. 2006. "The Invention of Africa in Latin America and the Caribbean: Political Discourse and Anthropological Praxis, 1920–1940." In *Afro-Atlantic Dialogues: Anthropology and the Diaspora*, edited by Kevin A. Yelvington, 45–52. Santa Fe, NM: School of American Research Press.

Yeo, Cedric A. 1952. "The Economics of Roman and American Slavery." *Finanzarchiv* 13.3: 445–85.

Yu, Hee-chun. 1936. *眉巖日記*. Vol. 5. Seoul: Korean History Compilation Society.

Zelin, K. K. 1968. "Principles of Morphological Classification of Forms of Dependence." *Soviet Anthropology and Archaeology* 6.4: 3–24.
Zelnick-Abrahmovitz, Rachel. 2000. "Did Patronage Exist in Classical Athens?" *L'antiquité classique* 69: 65–80.
Zeuske, Michael. 2013. *Handbuch Geschichte der Sklaverei: eine Globalgeschichte von den Anfängen bis zur Gegenwart.* Berlin: Walter de Gruyter.
Zeuske, Michael. 2014. "The Second Slavery: Modernity, Mobility, and Identity of Captives in Nineteenth-Century Cuba and the Atlantic World." In *The Second Slavery: Mass Slaveries and Modernity in the Americas and in the Atlantic Basin,* edited by Javier Laviña and Michael Zeuske, 113–42. Vienna; Berlin: Lit Verlag.
Zhou, Daguan. 1297[2007]. *A Record of Cambodia: The Land and its People.* Translated by Peter Harris. Chiang Mai: Silkworm Books.
Zilfi, Madeline C. 2010. *Women and Slavery in the Late Ottoman Empire: The Design of Difference.* New York: Cambridge University Press.
Zilversmit, Arthur. 1967. *The First Emancipation: The Abolition of Slavery in the North.* Chicago: University of Chicago Press.
Zimmern, A. 1909. "Was Greek Civilization Based on Slave Labour?" *Sociological Review* 2.1: 1–19, 159–76.

Index

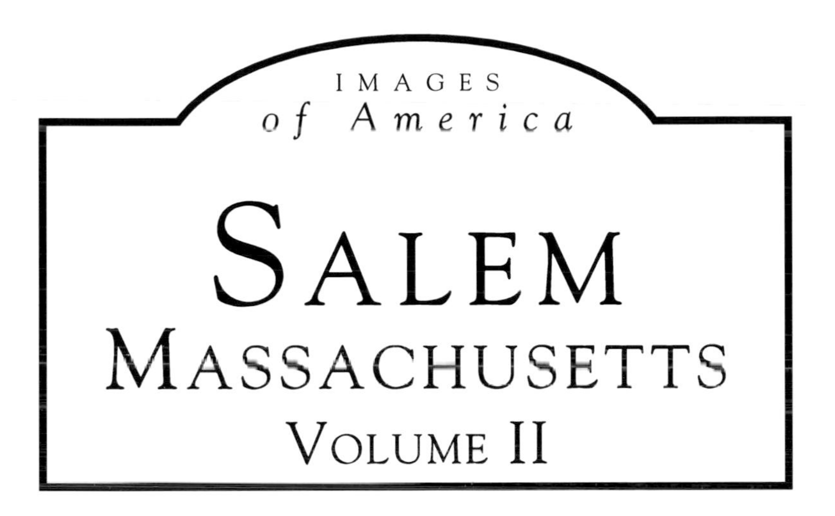

Stephen J. Schier and Kenneth C. Turino

ISBN 978-0-7385-6418-0

Published by Arcadia Publishing
Charleston, South Carolina

Printed in the United States of America

Library of Congress Catalog Card Number: 2004100628

For all general information contact Arcadia Publishing at:
Telephone 843-853-2070
Fax 843-853-0044
E-mail sales@arcadiapublishing.com
For customer service and orders:
Toll-Free 1-888-313-2665

Visit us on the Internet at www.arcadiapublishing.com

Depicted here is the official City of Salem seal. The dove holding the olive branch in its beak stands for peace. The image within the shield shows a full-rigged Salem vessel sailing to a distant port, probably the East Indies. On the shore is a full-length, standing, oriental figure holding a parasol, surrounded by tropical vegetation. The Latin motto on the scroll banner translates as, "To the farthermost parts of the rich East." Around the circumference are the dates of Salem's founding and incorporation as a city.

Contents

WITCH PINS.
Preserved among the files of the County Court
at Salem; the accused were charged with
using them to torment their victims with.

This popular, 19th-century image contains some truth and a great amount of imagination. The pins were indeed preserved with the files of the witch trials in Essex County, but in no way could be associated directly with people involved in the hysteria. The pins are commonly found in 17th- and 18th-century court records throughout the colony and act to hold associated pieces of paper together, much as a modern-day staple. The paper conservators working in the Massachusetts Supreme Judicial Court Archives routinely remove them when repairing historic records. (Courtesy Weston Collection.)

INTRODUCTION

The history of Salem is today too often associated with the witchcraft trials of the 17th century, but its history is so much more. The purpose of this publication is to focus on the city of Salem during the age of photography—its residents, neighborhoods, places of work, and recreation. Much of early Salem does survive, and its citizens are surrounded by it daily, while visitors come from all over the world to see and learn about its rich history. Its architecture is a testament to the great artistic heritage which can be seen in the magnificent buildings designed by Samuel McIntire (1757–1811), and those that are to be found in the historic McIntire District and other areas. The McIntire District includes some of Salem's most famous streets, including Chestnut, Federal, Essex, Warren, Pickering, Cambridge, and Flint Streets. The photographs included in this book are a further testament to the city's artistic heritage. Salem is fortunate to have the Salem Maritime National Historic site—the nation's first national historic site under the National Park System—as well as the House of the Seven Gables and several other museums. The Peabody Essex Museum is filled with artistic treasures, among them furniture, paintings, and china—produced in Salem as well as brought back from the Far East. Much of this material was created during Salem's heyday as one of America's leading ports in the early Republic. Its library is also one of the great repositories for Essex County printed materials, original documents, and photographs.

Soon after the invention of photography, both in England by William Henry Fox Talbot (1800–1877) and France by Jacques Louis Mande Daguerre (1789–1851) in 1839, enterprising individuals brought the relatively inexpensive technique to America. The first known Salem photographers, or daguerreotypists as they were called, appear in 1843. At that time, three photographers advertised in the *Salem Gazette*. Samuel Masury's advertisement stated, "the public can rely on having a first rate likeness set in superior style." These early daguerreotypes or photographs were made of a sheet of silver-plated copper. A total of 13 photographers worked in the city before 1860, but much of this early work, mainly portraiture, does not survive. By this time, the art of photography was rapidly growing and changing with the development of a wet-plate process in the mid-1850s, which produced a negative and allowed for numerous copies to be made. The images included in this publication date from the 1860s, by which time photography had become an established profession. Two prominent photographic studios whose work is included in this book are Guy and Brothers (1868–1878), and J.W. and J.S. Moulton (1873–1881). These studios published many of their photographs as stereographs which, when viewed through stereoscopes, would blend two almost identical images to create a single, three-dimensional effect. By the late 1870s, further improvements had been made in photography, including the use of glass-plate negatives, which were used to produce many of the images included in this book.

Many of these early artists came to photography from the fine arts, and others seemed to possess a wide variety of enterprising skills. One example of the latter is Elijah R. Perkins of Salem, who was listed in the Salem Directories in 1869–1872 as a "Photographic Artist, Dealer in Fancy Fowles and Eggs, Sole Agent for Glines Slate Roofing Paint." Unquestionably the preeminent Salem photographer is Frank Cousins (1851–1925). Originally an amateur, he turned professional, specializing in photography of architecture and street scenes, producing some of the finest images of the city by capturing the real feeling it possessed. Mr. Cousins, who was active as a photographer from 1888 to 1920, was also a dealer in dry and fancy goods. The authors are fortunate to be able to include several examples of his early work.

Photography is a window to the past that truly is a democratic medium. Over two hundred photographic images have been selected for this publication. These images help document our cultural heritage, landscape, citizens, work, and play. They have been chosen to supplement those in *Images of America: Salem*, and include expanded chapters on Salem's waterfront and public safety. Many of the images have never been published before and are taken from several private albums and informal collections. A large number of the images compromising this book were taken by professionals. The authors have also included many candid photographs of families and neighborhoods to round off the selection.

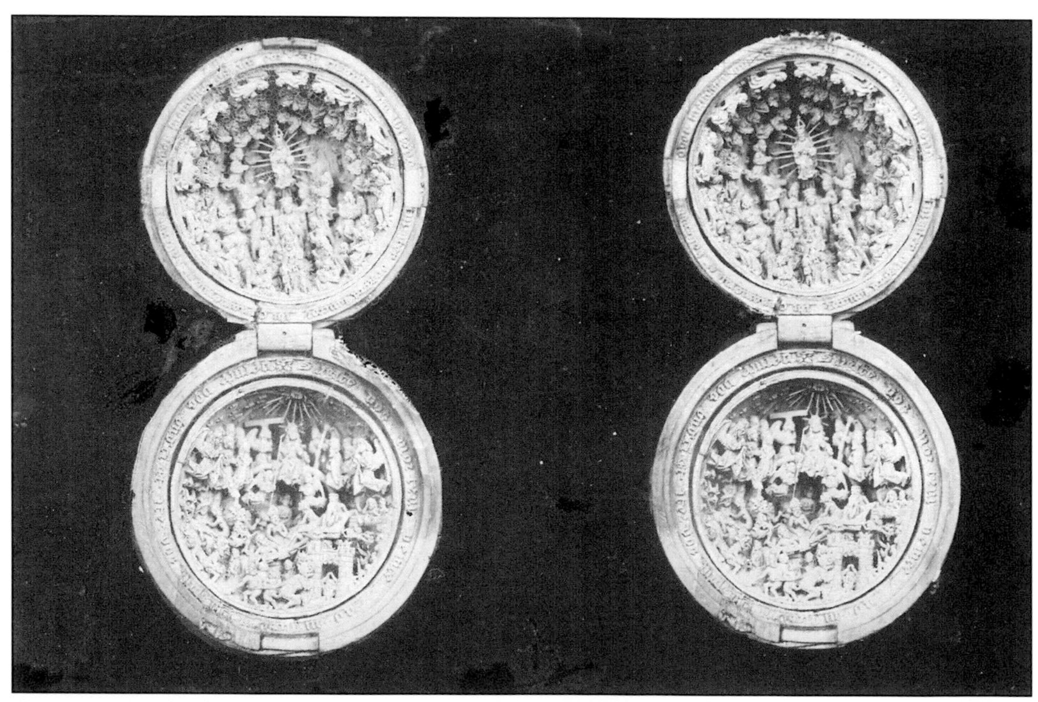

Generations of Salem children remember looking into the carved mahogany case with the large magnifying glass to view the European Boxwood carving depicting Heaven and the Day of Judgment. This late-15th century carving is a terminal ornament of the rosary. There are over one hundred full-length figures and heads carved into the two hemispheres. Each half measures 1.5 inches in diameter. The artifact was given to the East India Marine Society in 1806 by General Elias Hasket Derby. (Courtesy of the Estate of Borinous Schier.)

One

The McIntire Historic District

Beautiful, Elm-lined Chestnut Street, depicted in this c. 1910 photograph, is in the heart of the McIntire Historic District. Chestnut Street was laid out in 1796, a time when shipmasters and merchants were accumulating vast wealth. They chose to construct palatial residences away from the bustle and noise of Salem Harbor. Chestnut Street was planned to be 40 feet wide, but influential planners and original builders, such as John Pickering VI (1777–1846) and Pickering Dodge (1778–1833), changed all this, and the street was widened to 80 feet. (Courtesy of Mrs. Henry P. Binney Jr.)

This grand, Greek Revival, two-story, wooden home was built in 1834–35 for John C. Lee at 14 Chestnut Street. The Lee family lived here for 90 years. In 1925, celebrated artist Frank W. Benson (1862–1951) purchased this fine dwelling as a residence for his family. The home remained in the Benson family until 1957. (Courtesy Weston Collection.)

Hamilton Hall, at 9 Chestnut Street and 7 Cambridge Street, was built between 1805 and 1807 and designed by architect Samuel McIntire of Salem. The building was named for Alexander Hamilton (1757–1804), an American statesman and the first secretary of the United States Treasury. He visited Salem on June 20, 1800, and was entertained at the Essex Street home of Benjamin Pickman. Hamilton Hall is the gathering place of Salem's elite, where many social activities are held, including lectures, dinners, concerts, and other celebrations. (Courtesy Weston Collection.)

This view of the South Congregational Church at the corner of Cambridge and Chestnut Streets was taken c. 1891 by photographer Frank Cousins. The church, designed by Samuel McIntire, was erected in 1804 and dedicated January 1, 1805. McIntire designed the structure after models by Sir Christopher Wren of England. In 1903, a spectacular conflagration completely destroyed this architectural gem. (Courtesy Weston Collection.)

Pictured here is a view of Essex Street, taken in the early spring of 1891 by Frank Cousins, showing the Buffington-Goodhue-Wheatland house at 374 Essex Street. The substantial, gambrel-roof dwelling, with its many chimneys, was probably built by 1785. The imposing brick-and-brownstone building on the right has been the headquarters of the Salem Public Library since 1887, when the heirs of Captain John Bertram donated the building to the city. (Courtesy Weston Collection.)

The Sprague-Waite house was located at 376 Essex Street. The two-and-a-half-story house, with its hipped roof and widows walk, was built *c.* 1796 and demolished almost one hundred years later in 1893. (Courtesy Weston Collection.)

Here is a Frank Cousins photograph, showing the elaborate porte cochere and carriage house of the Loring-Emmerton house at 328 Essex Street. This was the home of the Honorable George Bailey Loring (1817–1891), a statesman, diplomat, member of Congress, agricultural commissioner, and minister to Portugal. President Franklin Pierce (1804–1869) was entertained here on several occasions. The three-storied brick house was built in 1818 in the Federal style. In 1885, the new owner of the house, Miss Caroline O. Emmerton, commissioned Boston architect Arthur Little (1852–1925) to remodel her mansion in the fashionable Colonial Revival style. (Courtesy Weston Collection.)

The building next to the William T. Pickering house, at 343 Essex Street, at the corner of Botts Court, is the Swedenborgian Church. The building was removed prior to 1906, when the Salem Athenaeum was built. (Courtesy Weston Collection.)

John Pickering IX (1897–1978), of 18 Broad Street, seems quite content riding down Pickering Street with his pet goat. In the background is Harlan Kelsey of Pickering Street. (Courtesy Pickering Collection.)

The dignified Edward P. Cassell stands in front of the Peirce-Nichols house, at 80 Federal Street. He was a well-known and respected caterer in Salem for almost 50 years, operating out of Hamilton Hall on Chestnut Street. Mr. Cassell hand-delivered invitations to various social events, carrying the coveted invitations in the double-handled straw basket he is holding. (Courtesy of Miss Eleanor Broadhead.)

Mary Orne Pickering stands in the backyard of her ancestral home at 18 Broad Street, c. 1910, on a beautiful spring day. The elaborate Victorian verandah was removed when the house was restored and updated under the direction of Boston architect Gordon Robb in 1947. (Courtesy Pickering Collection.)

A wooden ramp was built by the side of the Pickering family barn, at 18 Broad Street, so that the young children could have a safe and convenient place to enjoy winter sledding. This photograph was taken *c.* 1907. (Courtesy Pickering Collection.)

Tea time at the Benson home, at 7 Hamilton Street, was always a memorable occasion. Pictured from left to right are Henry P. Benson, his wife, Rebecca, and Mrs. Baker. Tea is served on lacquered Chinese tables in this tastefully decorated parlor. The large painting of the Benson children above the sofa was painted by Frank Benson. (Courtesy Pickering Collection.)

The grand staircase and foyer of the Benson home was decorated with hand-painted murals and a well-proportioned, tall case clock. The house was built in 1898 in the Colonial Revival style. The architect was the owner's brother, John P. Benson (1865–1947). Henry P. Benson, the owner, lived there until his death in 1957. This photograph was taken in 1940. (Courtesy Pickering Collection.)

The photographer catches Rebecca Benson's image in the mirror attached to her vanity, in the bedroom of her Hamilton-Street home. Henry and Rebecca Benson had three daughters: Rosamon Whitmore Storrow, Ruth Benson Pickering, and Rebecca Benson Haskell. The photograph was taken in 1941. (Courtesy Pickering Collection.)

The formal dining room of the Benson home had a matching set of Hepplewhite shieldback chairs, a corner cupboard displaying a Paris porcelain tea set, and a Hepplewhite sideboard laden with family silver. The photograph is from 1941. (Courtesy Pickering Collection.)

From an etching by Samuel Chamberlain

Chestnut Street, Salem, "the finest street, architecturally, in New England. . . . The spoil accumulated through twenty years' voyaging to the uttermost limits of the Far East, produced at Salem the fairest flowers of American domestic architecture." *Samuel Eliot Morison in Maritime History of Massachusetts.*

Old Salem, Mass., welcomes you to Chestnut Street Day

**Wednesday, June 28, 1939.*

For the day, the atmosphere of Salem's GREAT SHIPPING ERA will be recreated. Men and women will be dressed in costumes of the first half of the Nineteenth Century, many of them heirlooms from trunks and sea chests long stored in the attics of old Salem families.

Thirty of the FINEST MANSIONS on the street will be open to you.

There will be OLD FASHIONED DANCING, CROQUET, BOWLING ON THE GREEN and other features. And for the children, PUNCH AND JUDY.

Luncheon will be served in famed HAMILTON HALL, the Calvary Baptist Church (formerly the South Church) and in two private houses; and Tea in a garden.

The TIME

Ten o'clock in the morning until Seven in the evening

The ADMISSION FEES

To the STREET	$1.00
To the HOUSES	1.00
To any SINGLE HOUSE	.50
Children under twelve	.25

Further information may be had by applying to Chestnut Street Associates, 34 Chestnut St., Salem.

*In case of rain Chestnut Street Day will be held the next day.

Chestnut Street Days started almost 75 years ago, in 1926. It is not a yearly event, but has occurred sporadically over the years. Homeowners proudly open their elegant homes for tours, displaying family heirlooms, including paintings, furniture, export porcelain, and rare and exotic items brought back by sea captains on their many trips to foreign ports.

The lovely Mrs. John Pickering and her daughter Katharine, dressed for Chestnut Street Days, June 25, 1947, make their curtsy to the past in the interesting old Java Head House, at 26 Chestnut Street. The Pickerings were the tenth generation to live in the famed Pickering house, built in 1651. (Courtesy Pickering Collection.)

The young Timothy Pickering, resplendent in his top hat and tails, holds the reins of the pony. Rides in the fancy, diminutive, covered carriage down Chestnut Street cost 10¢. (Courtesy Pickering Collection.)

The stagecoach, crowded with passengers, accompanied by liverymen and drawn by two pairs of matched horses, strikes a dramatic picture on Salem's most famous street. (Courtesy Pickering Collection.)

During Chestnut Street Days, many of the fine homes were opened for tours. In addition to the tours, demonstrations of Colonial-era crafts were held. The unidentified woman is busily spinning at her flax wheel. (Courtesy Pickering Collection.)

A young boy masquerades as an Italian emigrant as he cranks his hurdy-gurdy, giving Chestnut Street melodious tones. The photograph is from June 1947. (Courtesy Pickering Collection.)

The old-time atmosphere on Chestnut Street would not be complete without a town crier ringing his large brass bell. (Courtesy Pickering Collection.)

Margaret Franks of Hamilton Street and Francis Tuckerman Parker of Botts Court strike a fashionable pose in front of the Allen-Osgood-Huntington triple house, numbers 31, 33, and 35 Chestnut Street, during Chestnut Street Days, in June 1947. (Courtesy Pickering Collection.)

On a beautiful June day, elegantly dressed ladies, accompanied by children, stroll along a brick sidewalk on Chestnut Street. Pictured from left to right are Katharine and Sarah Pickering, an unknown child, Ginny Potter, Lee Benson, Nora Lawson, and Ann Benson. (Courtesy Pickering Collection.)

Dressed to perfection by their caring parents, these young ladies and gentlemen pose for the photographer during Chestnut Street Days, June 25, 1947. Pictured from left to right are brothers Warren and Benjamin Shreve, Warren Potter, Lee Sprague, Marcia Gardner, and Katharine Pickering. The children seem to enjoy the excitement and festivities taking place around them. (Courtesy Pickering Collection.)

Employees of Eaton's Apothecary, on Essex Street, dress up for Chestnut Street Days, in June 1947. Barbara A. Doucette, in her beautiful blue gown, is fifth from the left. (Courtesy Doucette Collection.)

Young society women, when they came of age, were introduced into the community with a debutante ball, held at historic Hamilton Hall on Chestnut Street. The polished hardwood floor was ideal for dancing because of the spring action built beneath the surface. The photograph is c. 1964. (Courtesy Pickering Collection.)

Noted Lynn photographer Joseph Noel photographed the Dodge-Shreve house, *c.* 1970. The house has been owned by many distinguished Salemites, including members of the Phillips, Pierce, Allen, Cabot, and Shreve families. Built between 1822 and 1825 for merchant Pickering Dodge, the house is one of the best examples of Federal architecture in the city. (Courtesy Lynn Historical Society Collection.)

The Assembly House, on 138 Federal Street, was built in 1782, and is currently owned by the Peabody-Essex Museum. Today it is used for the purpose it was originally built for—lectures, receptions, and other social and cultural events. Among the prominent guests to be entertained here were the Marquis de Lafayette (1784) and President George Washington (1789). Noted architect Samuel McIntire remodeled the building into a private home in the late 1700s. It was between 1833 and 1856 that the second owner, Benjamin Chamberlain, added the elaborate front porch shown here. (Courtesy Lynn Historical Society Collection.)

Two

Along the Waterfront

The boatyard of Andrew J. Frisbee was located on White Street. Mr. Frisbee was a shipwright, yacht builder, spar marker, and a dealer in all kinds of vessel fittings. He lived at 12 Mall Street and had a second job as superintendent of the Essex Marine Railroad. The Salem vessel on the right is named *Three Brothers*. The ferryboat was owned and operated by the Upton brothers, and was the first boat to transport passengers to the Winne-Egan Hotel on Bakers Island. The house on the left is known as the Jonathan Whipple house, located at 49 Turner Street. (Courtesy Weston Collection.)

The *Agnes May* was among the fleet of 20 vessels that sought safety in Salem Harbor during a hurricane in late November 1898. Out of Saint John, New Brunswick, the schooner of 91 tons was anchored nearest the wharf, and on Sunday morning her anchors began to drag and, "despite the efforts of the Captain and crew of four men she was blown to the shore." The vessel was one of nine to be damaged while the ferocious storm wrecked havoc all along the coast. (Courtesy Buczko Collection.)

By the second half of the 19th century, Salem's wharves were home to many coal yards. On Derby Wharf, Smith and Parker, coopers, could be seen in 1884. By 1886, they had expanded to include coal and oil. When Charles H. Parker left the business in 1887–88, he and his family founded Parker Brothers. Winchester Smith carried on the business for a few more years, but by 1893–94, the site was vacant. (Courtesy Weston Collection.)

A busy Phillips Wharf, looking towards Salem Harbor, shows railroad tracks and a freight car, while across the harbor the beautiful shore of Marblehead can be seen.

Pictured here is a water view of the rambling brick super-structure of the mills of the Naumkeag Steam Cotton Company. At one time, this was the principal industry in Salem, employing 1,300 people. The company was incorporated in 1839, and was destroyed in the great Salem fire of 1914. The company stayed in Salem and quickly rebuilt its sprawling complex.

This view of Derby Wharf shows the ravages of repeated storms and erosion. The wharf extends nearly 2,000 feet into Salem Harbor, and was constructed after 1762 by Captain Richard Derby. The white-painted, brick lighthouse, built in 1871, was restored in recent times by a group of dedicated volunteers. (Courtesy Theriault Collection.)

A low-tide view of Philadelphia Wharf, jetting out into Salem Harbor, is pictured here. The large building on the right is the Pennsylvania and Reading Coal and Iron Company. (Courtesy Theriault Collection.)

The shore of Baker's Island was photographed here on August 16, 1896. Located at the entrance to Salem Harbor, the island was known as Baker's Island as early as 1630. Over the years, the island has been home to a hotel, lighthouses, and cottages. In the late 19th century, access to the island was by ferry service. (Courtesy Buczko Collection.)

Baker's Island, located in Salem Bay, has a land mass of over 58 acres. It is a privately owned island, except for 10 acres containing a lighthouse and other buildings that are owned and controlled by the federal government. By the turn of the century, the island had a hotel (the Winne-Egan), 26 summer cottages, and an icehouse. Ice was harvested from one of three larger ponds in the winter months and stored for the summer season. The simple, wood-frame cottages, built high above the rocky shore, offered commanding vistas of Salem Sound. Many of the cottages had distinctive names, such as The Barnacle, Driftwood, Old Pilots Retreat, The Shanty, Maplewood, and Montressa. (Courtesy Michaud Collection.)

Misery Island, in Salem Bay, is owned and maintained by the Trustees of Reservations. The island is said to have received its name in the 1600s, when Captain Moulton was shipwrecked there and forced to spend several days and nights on the desolate island. The episode was referred to as Moulton's Misery. During the early days of this century, the island had a hotel called the Casino, a nine-hole golf course, and many summer cottages, The hotel closed in 1918, and a fire in the 1920s swept across the island destroying the hotel and many of the cottages. (Courtesy Michaud Collection.)

A view of the Winter Island Lighthouse, near Fort Pickering, shows the iron bridge used to reach the white-painted iron structure. For many years, this section of Winter Island was taken over by the federal government for use as an airport and base for the United States Coast Guard Service. (Courtesy Theriault Collection.)

Praising the city, the book *Salem and the Willows* stated Salem "can boast of one of the finest parks, The Willows, on the entire North Shore." With the arrival of the Eastern Railroad branch line to Salem Willows in the 1870s, the resort developed. In this 1891 photograph, visitors repose in the shade. The old steamboat wharf can be seen in the distance, with the steamboat launch wharf and pavilion in the foreground. (Courtesy Weston Collection.)

Salem Willows needed numerous hotels and restaurants to support the throngs of people coming in season. Central House, 8 High Street, at Jupiter Point, began in the early 1800s as a hotel and dining room. Mrs. C.B. Bacheller operated the hotel in the summer only. (Courtesy Weston Collection.)

The Salem Willows Yacht Club was established in 1932, and is located on the banks of Salem Willows Park. Shown here is the private pier for the members, complete with a convenient gasoline pump. (Courtesy Theriault Collection.)

This photographic postcard depicts low tide at the beach at Salem Willows. The peaceful nature of the Willows can be appreciated before the throngs of summer bathers arrive. (Courtesy Michaud Collection.)

The J.C.B. Smith Memorial Swimming Pool was the outgrowth of a bequest of $20,000 to the City of Salem for a memorial to the late J.C.B. Smith, retired real estate operator of Salem Willows. This memorial consists of 20 acres of shore property and 8 acres of pool. The work started on December 16, 1933, and was carried on under the direction of the Honorable George J. Bates (mayor), the Honorable Robert W. Hill (trustee of the J.C.B. Smith bequest), Harlan P. Kelsey, Inc. (landscape architects), the J.R. Worcester Company (construction engineers), and Ambrose Walker (bathhouse and pavilion architect). (Courtesy Michaud Collection.)

AERIAL VIEW OF THE J. C. B. SMITH SWIMMING POOL. E. R. A. PROJECT

The Salem Almshouse was located on Salem Neck. Originally built in 1815–16 from the plans of Boston architect Charles Bulfinch (1763–1844), it was enlarged in 1884 and included several outbuildings. The building originally served the needs of the many seafaring men who came in and out of the port. The almshouse was demolished in 1954. (Courtesy Michaud Collection.)

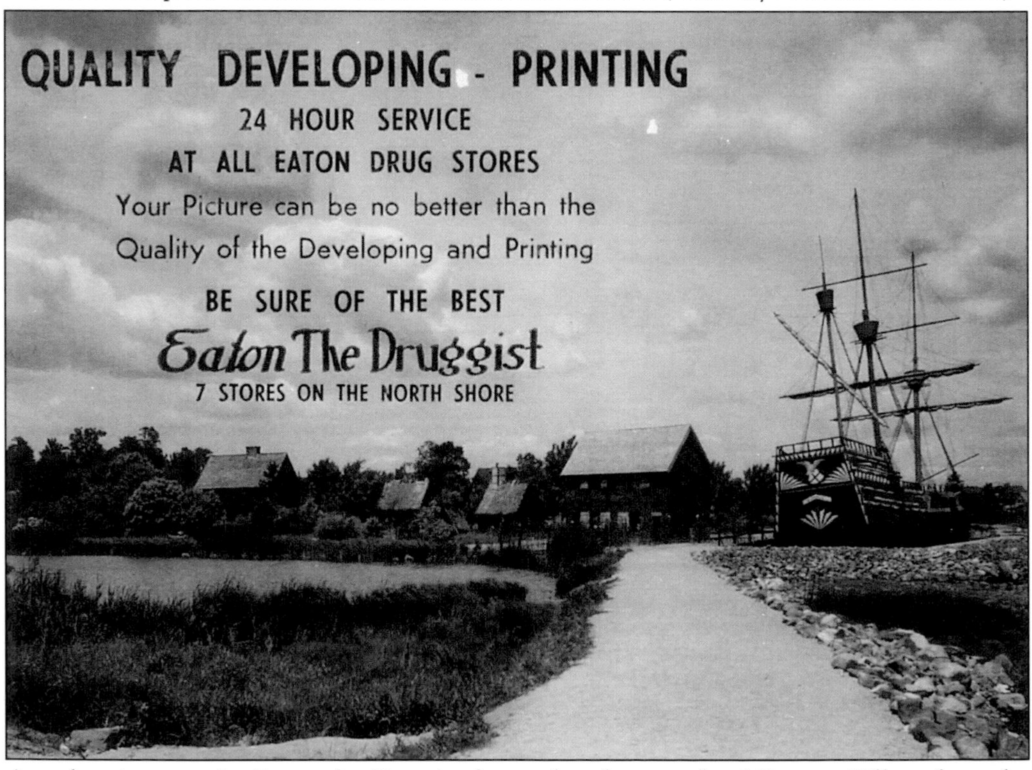

An advertisement for Eaton the Druggist featured a photograph of Pioneer Village from the 1940s or '50s. By this time, Eaton's had grown, as the ad says, to "7 stores on the North Shore." (Courtesy Blodgett Collection.)

It is a busy summer day at the Forest River Pool, on the banks of Salem Harbor, where the saltwater pool provided ideal refreshment on hot and humid summer days. The water could be changed daily with each high tide. The bathhouse contained showers, changing rooms, and a concession stand. (Courtesy Theriault Collection.)

A 1924 view of the tourist camp at Forest River Park shows several families enjoying the lovely seaside park. The park, consisting of 29 acres, was purchased by the city and opened to the public in 1907. (Courtesy Theriault Collection.)

Over the course of six days in 1926, Salem celebrated the 300th anniversary of its founding with a full schedule of programs. Here, looking toward Beverly across the Essex Bridge, is a sign announcing the event. The festivities began on Sunday, July 4, with the ringing of church bells, and over the course of the event included several parades, including a horrible and grotesque, a floral and historical, and a military parade. Dory racing off Salem Willows, concerts on the common, a grand ball, and a woman making a balloon ascension and triple-parachute jump at the Willows were all part of the program. (Courtesy Theriault Collection.)

At the old North Bridge that spans the North River, Lieutenant Colonel Leslie, on February 26, 1775, along with a portion of the 64th Regiment of British regulars sent from Boston to seize cannon and ammunition stored in Salem, was confronted by the Essex Regiment under command, it is said, of Colonel Timothy Pickering (1745–1829). Leslie was compelled to retreat without accomplishing his objective. This was the scene of the first armed resistance to Great Britain in the Revolutionary War. (Courtesy Michaud Collection.)

Three

THE HEART OF THE COMMUNITY

Mary Harrod Northend was a well-known Salem author and antiquarian, whose books included *Historic Names of New England* and *Colonial Homes and their Furnishings*. Her books, written in the 1910s and '20s, were well illustrated. Here, Catherine Muriel Schultz models for a series of illustrations on canning and kitchen work. (Courtesy Soper Collection.)

The Hunt house, at the corner of Washington and Lynde Streets, was built *c.* 1698, and razed in 1863. This was one of the many gabled houses in existence during Nathaniel Hawthorne's time, which might have provided inspiration for *The House of the Seven Gables.* (Courtesy Weston Collection.)

Pictured here is an interior view of the first meetinghouse of the Salem Society of Friends, now located on the grounds of the Peabody-Essex Museum. The building was erected *c.* 1688 by Thomas Maule, a Quaker. Later the structure was incorporated into a dwelling. For many years the Essex Institute used the meetinghouse to display Mrs. Henry Goodwin Vaughan's collection of dolls and toys, which she had graciously donated to the museum. (Courtesy Weston Collection.)

The Narborne house, located at 71 Essex Street, was built in 1672 and still retains its ancient charm. Shown in the back yard is the well head, a boardwalk, a garden protected by pickets, and probably a dry sink. (Courtesy Weston Collection.)

A rear view of the John Ward house, on its original site at 38 St. Peter Street, shows a 19th-century addition that was removed before 1905. The dwelling was built *c.* 1684 for John Ward (*c.* 1653–1732), and was the home of three generations of Wards until 1816. The house was used as a bakery for 40 years during the 19th century. Miss Sarah W. Symonds, an artist and sculptor, had her studio in the house from 1903 through 1909. In 1910, the 17th-century structure was moved to the grounds of the Essex Institute and restored under the direction of George Francis Dow. The house was officially opened to the public in 1912. (Courtesy Weston Collection.)

The Derby-Ward house is located at 27 Herbert Street, at the corner of Derby Street. The substantial, gambrel-roofed dwelling was built for Captain Richard Derby. His three sons were born and raised here (Elias Hasket (1739–1799), Richard, and John). The Derby family sold the property to the Ward family in the late 18th century. Nathaniel Hawthorne was a frequent visitor to this home when he lived on Herbert Street. In the garden, shaded by an ancient apple tree and surrounded by fragrant flowers, he would find inspiration and write stories in the summer garden house. (Courtesy Theriault Collection.)

The John Hodges house is situated on the corner of 81 Essex Street and 1 Orange Street. The fine Georgian, colonial dwelling was built for the merchant John Hodges, *c.* 1788. The dwelling has a gambrel roof with three formal, closed-gable dormers, a symmetrical facade, corner quoins, and an elegant central entryway. In the basement of this dwelling is a tunnel, now blocked up, which runs down Orange Street to the wharves at Salem Harbor. Goods from the vessels could be delivered directly from the ships to the Hodges cellar. (Courtesy Weston Collection.)

St. John the Baptist Church (Roman Catholic), located at 28 St. Peter Street, opposite Federal Street, was originally built in 1826, for the Second Baptist Society. The building was remodeled in 1867, 1877, and 1909. In 1910, the newly organized Polish Catholic Society purchased the edifice when the First and Second Baptist Society reunited. (Courtesy Weston Collection.)

The Cavalry Baptist Church, at the corner of Herbert and Essex Streets, was built in 1873. In 1903, the society sold the building to the Sons of Jacob for use as a synagogue. The site is today used for parking by the Hawthorne Hotel. (Courtesy Weston Collection.)

The original wooden structure of St. James Church (Roman Catholic), located at 160 Federal Street, was situated near the present-day church at 152 Federal Street. The wood-frame church was built c. 1849, and was demolished in 1892. It was replaced by the present, massive, Gothic-Revival, brick-and-granite edifice. (Courtesy Weston Collection.)

This Frank Cousins photograph depicts an exterior view of the Independent Congregational Church, at Barton Square, *c.* 1892. The architect was Thomas Waldron Sumner (1768–1849) of Boston. The church was begun in June 1824, and completed a year later in 1825. Mr. Sumner was paid $396.52 for his designs and supervision during the construction process. The church was later converted into a theater and was destroyed in the early 20th century. (Courtesy Weston Collection.)

The interior of the First Baptist Church, at 56 Federal Street, was illuminated by gas chandeliers. The motto painted above the altar reads, "Glory to God in the Highest and on Earth Peace Good Will Toward Men." The church was built in 1806 and remodeled in the prevailing Victorian style in 1868. (Courtesy Weston Collection.)

The Protestant Seaman's Bethel Church was located on Herbert Street and was built in 1827. The building on the right was the former Lynde School—later the Polish School. The Herbert Street Seaman's Bethel Church became part of the Polish School property, having earlier served as the Ward One Kindergarten. (Courtesy Weston Collection.)

The Captain Thomas Poynton house, built *c.* 1750, was located at 7 Brown Street Court. The carved pineapple over the doorway is said to have come from England. Captain Poynton took meticulous care of this finial, keeping the symbol of hospitality brightly gilded and the leaves painted green. The doorway was preserved and installed in Plummer Hall by the Essex Institute in 1911. (Courtesy Weston Collection.)

The Ezekiel H. Derby estate, on Lafayette Street, contained vast amounts of land in South Salem. It was said that a thousand live oaks flourished on the many acres. In the old manor house lived three elderly maiden sisters, the Misses Marianne B., Caroline R., and H. Matilda Derby. In 1867, they sold their ancestral estate to James F. Almy, Charles S. Clark, and Nathaniel Wiggin. The developers broke up the property, razed the old dwelling, and laid out house lots and streets. Within a short period of time, many fine Victorian homes were built in this area. (Courtesy Weston Collection.)

The Pickman-Derby-Brookhouse Mansion was located at the corner of Washington and Lynde Streets. The house was built in 1764 by Colonel Benjamin Pickman as a gift to his son, Clarke Gayton Pickman. Later, the mansion was the residence of Elias Hasket Derby (1739–1799). The dwelling was razed before 1915 to make way for the Masonic Temple. The domed cupola was removed to the grounds of the Essex institute, where it eventually deteriorated. The ceiling fresco, painted by the Michel Felice Corné (*c.* 1752–1845), was preserved and installed at the Peabody Museum.

This impressive, Colonial-Revival home at 320 Lafayette Street was built for Albert E. Cole, of Briggs and Cole in Boston, around 1905. Mr. Cole lived at this address until 1962. The building was torn down and replaced by the Park Towers Apartments, which opened in 1965. (Courtesy Michaud Collection.)

The boyhood home of Nathaniel Hawthorne (1804–1864), at 10 1/2 and 12 Herbert Street, was owned by Hawthorne's grandfather, Richard Manning. Hawthorne's room was on the third floor in the southwest corner. The view from the window was that of his birthplace on Union Street. Hawthorne stated in 1840, "Here I sit in my old accustomed chamber where I used to sit in days gone by. Here I have written many tales. Should I have a biographer, he ought to make great mention of this chamber in my memoirs, because so much of my lonely youth was wasted here." (Courtesy Weston Collection.)

Young, impeccably dressed students at the Prescott School, on Howard Street, gather together for a class photograph. Beyond the wooden board fence is the Howard Street Cemetery, where, in 1801, the first burials took place. The photographer of this *c.* 1897–1899 group portrait was Mrs. Lizzie M. Mitchell of Beverly, Massachusetts. (Courtesy Gentile Collection.)

The three-storied mansard-roofed school, known as old St. Mary's, was completed in 1855. The street at that time was called Walnut Street. In 1915, the name was changed to Hawthorne Boulevard. The Sisters of Notre Dame staffed the school and taught only girls until 1891, when the sisters resigned. In that same year, the Sisters of Charity took over the teaching responsibilities for the Immaculate Conception Parish. The devout sisters opened the school to both sexes. In 1892, they established a four-year high school, later replaced by a two-year commercial school. The old, wooden-frame building was replaced in 1941 with a modern brick building. The school closed in 1971. (Courtesy Gentile Collection.)

A 1905 group photograph, by Ames Studio of Salem, shows the graduation class at old St. Mary's School. In the center of the first row is Sarah F. McKeever Kilhouley. (Courtesy Gentile Collection.)

UNDEFEATED WITCHES

In December 1944, the Salem High School Witches played the Peabody Tanners. Both teams were undefeated and, according to the *Salem Evening News*, played "before an estimated 18,000 congealed fans. . . the long-heralded Salem-Peabody battle for the State Championship was held. . . at the end of 40 minutes of bruising play both teams remained in the undefeated class, the final score being 0 to 0." Peabody's Tanners became the state champs by one-fifth of a point. Pictured from left to right are as follows: (front row) Steve Rizzotti, Lytel Smith, Arthur Sarkishian, Stanley Froncki, Captain Joe Tassinari, Henry Briggs, and Cliff Roby; (back row) Norman Dion, Don Poitras, Don Chalifour, Emilio Belleau, Louis Mroz, and Armand Longvall. (Courtesy Soper Collection.)

Only female students appear in this 1947 photograph of the typing class of Saint Joseph's Academy. Even at this late date, typing could lead to what was considered an appropriate position for young women. Saint Joseph's Academy was located on Harbor Street and consisted mainly of descendants of French Canadians. (Courtesy Mathias Collection.)

The Simon Forrester house is situated at the corner of 188 Derby Street and Hodges Court. Captain Simon Forrester (1748–1817) purchased this three-story, hipped-roof residence in 1791. At that time the dwelling was under construction, and Samuel McIntire completed the finish work on the east parlor. (Courtesy Weston Collection.)

Nathaniel Hawthorne and his family moved into this Federal-style home at 14 Mall Street in September of 1847. Hawthorne wrote one of his greatest romantic novels in his third-floor, front-room study, next to the street. It is here that Hawthorne gave the manuscript of *The Scarlet Letter* to his publisher, Henry Fields. The book turned out to be a huge literary and financial success for Hawthorne. In 1850, Hawthorne moved out of this dwelling to Lenox, Massachusetts, never returning to Salem again. (Courtesy of the Estate of Borinous Schier.)

The John Crowninshield house was originally located at 2 Brown Street. The house was built *c.* 1755 and later moved to the end of Kimball Court, where it still stands today. On March 26, 1773, famed mathematician, author, and astronomer Nathaniel Bowditch was born in this dwelling. In 1802, Bowditch wrote the *New American Practical Navigator*, which is still in use today. (Courtesy Weston Collection.)

The Ropes Memorial, at 318 Essex Street, was established as an educational memorial. It was set up by the last will and testament of the maiden Ropes sisters, Mary Pickman and Eliza Orne, who died in 1907. The house, built in 1719, was acquired in 1768 by Judge Nathaniel Ropes from the descendants of the original owner, Samuel Bernard. In 1894, the Misses Ropes moved the mansion house back from the street and added the McIntire-style fence. On June 25, 1913, the house and formal gardens were officially opened to the public. The Trustees of the Ropes Memorial owned the complex, but it is now managed by the Peabody-Essex Museum.

This oddly shaped wood-frame dwelling was located at the corner of 2 Williams Street and 25 Washington Square North. During the last half of the 19th century, the home was owned by William C. Barton and his heirs. In the 1890s, Joseph M. Parsons, a mason and contractor, purchased the structure. He had it razed, and in 1897 built a very fashionable house in the Queen Anne style. (Courtesy Weston Collection.)

Noted Salem photographer Frank Cousins was born in this house at 26 English Street. The house itself had a colorful history, having been originally built as Major William Browne's mansion house in 1698. Merchant William "Billy" Gray purchased the house in 1783, and from 1805 until 1828 it was the Sun Tavern. At that time, the building was dismantled and parts removed to St. Peter, English, and Webb Streets. The Cousins' owned the house from 1846 to 1879. The building was razed after 1918. (Courtesy Michaud Collection.)

The city's first street railway, the Salem Street Railroad Company, began in 1862 with horse-drawn vehicles. The Salem and Danvers Street Railway was incorporated in 1840. According to the *Municipal History of Essex County*, "This was the start of what has come to be a great far-reaching system of electric street cars." (Top photograph courtesy of Theriault Collection; bottom photograph courtesy of Michaud Collection.)

Mager Page built this substantial house and barn between 1879 and 1881, on what was then 1 Lynn Road—shortly afterward it was changed to Loring Avenue, named after Dr. George B. Loring, who owned most of the land in the area. The Page family can be seen, in 1888, with Mrs. Augusta Page, Cora, Fred, Edgar, and Frank. Originally a sole cutter, Mager Page later worked for W. Page & Company, on 8 Dodge Street, which made heels and soles. (Courtesy Doucette Collection.)

Here the home of Paul and Celanire (Caron) Fontaine can be seen at 331 Jefferson Avenue, around 1914. On the porch, from left to right, are Eva (Lefebvre) Fontaine and Celanire Fontaine. On the lawn, from left to right, are Eva, Alice, and George (children of Paul and Celanire), and Henry and Teddy Mellon. (Courtesy Michaud Collection.)

Gallows Hill was the execution site of 19 people condemned to die for witchcraft. Executions by hanging took place on June 10, July 19, August 19, and September 22, 1692. This photograph, probably taken *c.* 1895, shows the crest of the famous, craggy, grass-covered hill. The executions probably took place at the base of the hill, near the Proctor Street area. (Courtesy Weston Collection.)

In the Salem fire of June 25, 1914, many homes were destroyed, including 225 Lafayette Street. The Second Empire-style home was built in the mid-1890s for Alonzo P. Weeks, a cashier at the Merchant's National Bank of Boston. Reverend James L. Hill lived here from 1897 until the fire. He replaced the building and continued to live on the site until 1931. (Courtesy Michaud Collection.)

Janice Burbeck and her pet Spitz "Patchy" relax on the stairs to their 1 Mall Street home in 1941. Miss Burbeck, a Myrna Loy look-a-like, was the only family member who could handle "Patchy." (Courtesy Soper Collection.)

Standing under a 48-star American flag, 17-year-old Richard Thornton Soper can be seen at his 7 Boardman Street home in August 1942. A graduate of Salem High School, Richard Soper enlisted in the Maritime Service and became a captain by the age of 20. (Courtesy Soper Collection.)

Relaxing after a hard day's work and enjoying a refreshing cocktail in the Main Brace Lounge at the Hawthorne Hotel are, from left to right, Jonathan Butler, his sister, Harriet Shreve, and John Pickering X. The mural in the background depicts Salem's heyday as a shipping port, and was painted by Larry O'Toole. The photograph was taken c. 1942.

Four

Salem at Work

This dilapidated brick building was located at 206 and 208 Essex Street. It was razed, probably around 1891, to make way for the Salem Five Cents Savings Bank building, constructed in 1892. The sign in James G. Ryan's Tailor Shop window reads, "Final reduction before building is taken down, every article must be sold." (Courtesy Weston Collection.)

This early photograph, actually a stereopticon slide, shows Zina Goodell's building, located at 18 Lafayette Street. The building was constructed between 1857 and 1859, and the photograph was taken between 1874 and 1881. Several companies had space in the building, including G.D. Choate Machine Stitching, Smith & Smart Brass Founders and Finishers, and W.S. Brookhouse and Company Boot and Shoe Manufacturers. (Courtesy Michaud Collection.)

C.A. Wentworth was listed as a shoemaker in the Salem Directories between 1874 and 1878. The shop at 174 Essex Street shows the styles of the day. In 1876, there were 59 boot and shoe makers and manufacturers, as well as those that specialized in stock such as innersoles and heels, all attesting to the importance of this industry in Essex County. Wentworth's was one of 19 boot and shoe dealers. Perhaps the stiff competition caused his shop to survive only a short time. Frank Cousins Dry Goods can be seen to the right. This building is now the site of the Museum Place Mall. (Courtesy Michaud Collection.)

The Salem photographic studio of J.W. and J.S. Moulton, at 206 Essex Street, produced this stereopticon in 1878. The ice industry was wide-spread throughout New England. Salem had several companies, such as the one shown here, a number of which harvested ice from Wenham Lake. (Courtesy Michaud Collection.)

This handsome brick-and-granite commercial building was located at 170–174 Essex Street, at the corner of St. Peter Street. In the 1890s it housed Frank Cousins' store, known as the "Bee Hive." The store carried a line of dry and fancy goods, millinery, hosiery for ladies, gents, and children, bustles, hoop skirts, laces, jewelry, and other small wares. (Courtesy Weston Collection.)

The stately Ionic column of Mechanic Hall stands like a sentry at the corner of Essex and Crombie Streets. The brick, Greek Revival structure, built in 1839, was destroyed by a devastating fire on February 4, 1905. The Walter C. Packard Furniture & Carpet Company was established in 1872. The original building burned in January 1881, and for a time business was conducted at neighboring Mechanic Hall, until the store was rebuilt. Packards carried a magnificent and costly stock, consisting of furniture, carpets, draperies, stoves, ranges, lamps, bric-a-brac, and even high-grade bicycles. (Courtesy Weston Collection.)

The Essex Bank building, at 11 Central Street, was designed by renowned Boston architect Charles Bulfinch in 1811. The former Essex Bank, established in 1792, was the first bank in Essex County. The Salem Fraternity, organized in 1864, purchased this commercial brick building as their headquarters in 1899. The fraternity is the oldest boy's club in America, and was established primarily for Salem boys without friend and family influences. At the Central Street headquarters, there was a gymnasium, industrial classes, reading rooms, music classes, and various games. (Courtesy Weston Collection.)

Pictured here is an 1891 exterior view of the lumber yard of J.P. Langmaid and Sons, located at 195–205 Derby Street for many decades. In 1910, Langmaid Lumber provided hard-to-find stock to George Francis Dow for use during the restoration of the John Ward house on the grounds of the Essex Institute. (Courtesy Weston Collection.)

The Witch City Ice Company, owned by Joseph F. Lynah, was located at 71 Beaver Street. This photograph was taken at the corner of 68 Beaver Street and Silver Street. (Courtesy Theriault Collection.)

Calixte Rousseau (1863–1909) operated a variety store at 47 Harbor Street sometime after 1894. Mr. Rousseau is shown here in the center, and to his right is Adelard Fraser. The sign above Mr. Rousseau, and the one in the window, show that he catered to the French community. The building burned in the 1914 Salem fire. (Courtesy Michaud Collection.)

The three-story brick building at 266 Derby Street was built after the Salem fire in 1914. The ground floor served commercial interests, including the Polish Industrial Bankers, while the upper two floors provided housing. (Courtesy Theriault Collection.)

These employees appear to be very busy at work in the office of the Dinsmore Manufacturing Company, located at 288 Derby Street. The company was founded in 1870 by Alfred D. Dinsmore to manufacture piece and sewing machines for the textile industry. Harry Duke, inventor and founder of the Duke Machine Company, purchased the Dinsmore Manufacturing Company in 1934, improving the machines and obtaining additional patents. The tradition was continued by his son Lewis, who added improvements to the equipment. Lewis Duke's widow, Charlotte, continues to direct the Dinsmore product line in its tradition of excellence. (Courtesy Duke Collection.)

These interior views of the Dinsmore Manufacturing Company, at 288 Derby Street, show various aspects of manufacturing. Today the building interior has changed drastically, and is now the home of the Salem Wax Museum, with thousands of tourists frequenting this site annually. (Courtesy Duke Collection.)

Louis A. Blood poses in front of his grocery shop at 391 Essex Street, at the corner of Flint Street. The brick store was built for Stephen Fogg in 1826. The connected residential structure at 391 1/2 Essex Street was added in 1840. (Courtesy Blodgett Collection.)

Louis Blood, *c.* 1940, is preparing to grind freshly roasted coffee beans for one of his long-time customers, Rebecca Brodhead Benson of Hamilton Street. Mr. Blood owned the store at 391 Essex Street and lived next door in the attached brick home, at 391 1/2 Essex Street. (Courtesy Blodgett Collection.)

A *c.* 1940 interior scene at Louis A. Blood's grocery store is shown here. Pictured from left to right are Elmer Eaton, Henry P. Benson, Frederick Hussey, and the proprietor. Mr. Eaton and Mr. Benson appear to be playing checkers on top of a hogshead. The other two gentlemen are warming themselves by the big potbellied stove. (Courtesy Blodgett Collection.)

The Marblehead Water Pumping Station at Legge's Hill, Salem, was built in 1893. After Marblehead's great fire of 1877, the town required a complete system of waterworks. No water in sufficient quantity could be found for fire and domestic purposes in the town, but permission was obtained from the state legislature and the City of Salem to take the land at Legge's Hill. Water from the town's supply at Legge's Hill entered the pipes for the first time on October 1, 1889, and the station was built subsequently. (Courtesy Michaud Collection.)

This Essex Street scene in the mid-1920s shows, from left to right, (186) Lefavour's Music House, (184) the Walk-Over Boot Shop, (180–182) the Charles Hudson Department Store, and (178) Dan. A. Donahue Men's Clothing Store. Next door to Donahues was the entrance to the New Essex House, which had offices on the second floor and rooms at the rear. Beyond the entrance was W.T. Grant's Company, and at the end of the block, on the corner of St. Peter Street, was Eaton the Druggist. (Courtesy Blodgett Collection.)

Eaton's Drug Store, at the corner of Essex and St. Peter Streets, was a familiar sight. The drug store, occupied by F. Elmer Eaton for many years, boasted the finest ice cream sodas in town, made by the best "sodajerker," Albert J. Perkins. (Courtesy Blodgett Collection.)

F. Elmer Eaton, formerly manager at the Ropes Drug Company, established Eaton the Druggist in 1921—this interior photograph dates from around that period. The store, besides dispensing medicines, was well known for its soda fountain, and also featured cigars and confections. (Courtesy Blodgett Collection.)

Photographed in the mid-1920s, Eaton the Druggist, at 120 Essex Street, often featured elaborate displays, such as this one for A.P.W. Paper Company. (Courtesy Blodgett Collection.)

Five

Public Safety

The old Salem Police Station is still standing at 15 Front Street. The structure, built in 1859–60, was restored during Salem's redevelopment programs in the early 1970s by well-known local architect James Ballou, who was in charge of the project. The granite "Police Station" sign has since been removed, as well as the iron bars on the windows that face Klop Alley. This building served the police department and police court until 1913, when a larger facility was built at 17 Central Street. (Courtesy of Salem Police Department Collection.)

This image shows a rear view of the old Salem Police Station, as seen from Klop Alley. The brick, two-story structure, with its hip roof and ventilation chimney, was built in 1859–60. Behind the station is a dilapidated wooden addition and storage shed. (Courtesy Theriault Collection.)

The brick-and-cement police station at 17 Central Street was erected in 1913, under the supervision of Salem architect John M. Gray (1887–1977). Mr. Gray also designed the St. Thomas the Apostle Church on North Street in Peabody, and the 1927–28 addition to Salem High School on Highland Avenue. The Colonial Revival-style building housed not only the police department, but also the First District Court of Essex County and the city marshall's office.

After 31 years of service with the Salem Police Department, Thomas J. Morrow, who lived at 9 Boston Street, retired. He began his career with an appointment on April 25, 1906, and became a regular officer July 19, 1910. His granddaughter, Mrs. James A. Soper, remembers him as "a big man" and "rather intimidating." (Courtesy Soper Collection.)

Four high-ranking Salem police officials strike an authoritative pose in a photographer's studio during the early 1890s. Pictured from left to right are City Marshall J.W. Hart, Deputy Marshall John B. Skinner, Police Captain George H. Blinn, and Sergeant John H. Bickford. (Courtesy of Salem Police Department Collection.)

Mounted Salem police officers lead a parade as it passes the store window of Sam Charlie Laundry at 37 Essex Street. The billboard on the boy's back (left foreground) announces a minstrel show and dance at the Now and Then Hall, probably in the early teens. (Courtesy Michaud Collection.)

Salem policemen in dress uniform pose in front of the granite-and-iron gates of the main entrance of Greenlawn Cemetery on Memorial Day, 1918. Pictured from left to right are Lieutenant John Barrett, John Haskin, Thomas Garstand, Martin Doyle, John O'Hara, Richard Butler, Robert Connors, Robert Coblints, Charles Burkinshaw, Fred Sargent, Thomas Cooper, John O'Day, Charles Kellet, Dennis Barry, John Brennan, George Rehal, Walter Huntersa, Joseph Coffey, and Captain Edwin Dennis. (Courtesy of Detective James Gauthier.)

Traffic boxes were at one time a common site in cities. Pedestrians are shown here hurrying across Washington Street in 1928. Officer Joseph Vincent McDonough stares straight ahead as he stands in the traffic box in front of Webber's Department Store. (Courtesy Dionne Collection.)

Patrolman Edward C. Brennan and his father, Captain John D. Brennan, are in the back yard of their Salem home during the summer of 1938. (Courtesy of Patrolman Thomas J. Brennan.)

In this late-1940s photograph, a well-dressed Salem policeman, "Moxie" Murphy, seems very happy with his newly installed loud speaker. Perhaps he is getting ready for a classic Salem snow emergency, where the police cruise the congested, snow-covered streets, broadcasting the message, "Get your vehicles off the road or they will be towed." (Courtesy of Salem Police Department Collection.)

On a beautiful summer day in 1949, shaded by a towering Elm tree, police officer William Michaud stands next to the new Chrysler DeSoto four-door sedan police cruisers. The three-story brick building on the right housed the Central Street garage. (Courtesy of Salem Police Department Collection.)

An elaborate, oak, late-Victorian, police-and-fire-alarm system was used at the Central Street police station until the early 1950s. In the past, all alarms that emanated from call boxes came into the police station first. The massive desk is supported by reeded and turned legs, terminating in castors. Thick, beveled glass, upper doors, and a labyrinth of tools and equipment were used for communication. (Courtesy of Salem Police Department Collection.)

On December 12, 1960, police officials proudly stood among their new Plymouth station wagon cruisers. The station house and the first district court are decked out for the holidays with glittering Christmas garlands festooned across Central Street. Pictured from left to right are Joseph Carbone, Marshall McDonough, unknown, Mayor Francis X. Collins, unknown, and Albert Michaud. (Courtesy of Salem Police Department Collection.)

During the 1935 season some members of the Salem Police Department played on a local team known as "Les Canadians." The wooden bats are arranged in a pyramid form and are crowned with a hide-covered baseball. (Courtesy of Salem Police Department Collection.)

This group photograph was taken at the Policemen's Ball on October 8, 1958. Pictured from left to right are Officer and Mrs. George Brackett, Officer and Mrs. Jeremiah Cronin, Lieutenant and Mrs. Marshall McDonough, Mayor Francis X. Collins and guest, and Officer and Mrs. Murray Greenlaw. (Courtesy of Salem Police Department Collection.)

The Policemen's Ball, held at the State Armory at 136 Essex Street on October 8, 1958, was a very formal affair. Music was provided by the Lou Ames Orchestra. The festivities were held in the huge drill shed which was 170 feet long and 86 feet wide. The drill shed was built in 1890, while the head house, with its crenellated-top, octagonal towers, was built in 1908. Fire struck the massive brick-and-stone landmark in February of 1982. The drill shed has been restored as a visitor center, managed by the National Park Service. (Courtesy of Salem Police Department Collection.)

In large police departments such as Salem, where they use a number of various kinds of vehicles—including cars, trucks, and motorcycles—a full-time mechanic is essential for keeping the vehicles in good operating order. Here, at the repair garage at 17 Central Street, a police mechanic uses a chain fall to hoist a large engine into a vehicle. (Courtesy of Salem Police Department Collection.)

On June 17, 1957, over two dozen uniformed Salem police officers posed before boarding a bus owned by Michaud Bus Lines, Inc. The officers were participating in a Communion breakfast in Lynn, followed by a parade down Market Street in Lynn. (Courtesy of Salem Police Department Collection.)

Officer William Dansreau mans the new police communication desk, installed in January of 1952. The system appears streamlined compared to the Victorian fire alarm system. The reels and tapes in the background, known as tappers, are part of that old system. (Courtesy of Salem Police Department Collection.)

A group of 13 young men reluctantly pose for the police photographer inside the police station on Central Street. As the saying goes, "boys will be boys," and these boys were detained for, "causing trouble on Swampscott Road," during the middle of August, 1962. (Courtesy of Salem Police Department Collection.)

Chief Engineer William O. Arnold and his driver pose in front of the fire department headquarters at 34 Church Street. Chief Arnold ran the department from 1888 to 1914. The brick-and-granite structure was built in 1861, remodeled in 1887, and converted into retail and other business uses in 1975–76. (Courtesy Dionne Collection.)

An Amoskeag Pumper fuming smoke is seen in action by the North River at Commercial Street. (Courtesy Dionne Collection.)

The Salem fire of June 25, 1914, caused huge devastation to the city. Here furniture is strewn on a lawn, awaiting rescue before the approaching fire. (Courtesy Dionne Collection.)

Box 48 sounded a general alarm on June 25, 1914, for a fire which began at Blubber Hollow. The great Salem fire burned 252 acres. This scene shows the area where the fire originated, shortly after the blaze was put out. (Courtesy Dionne Collection.)

The conflagration of 1914 was the major disaster to happen to Salem in the 20th century. Here two views show the devastation. The top photograph shows two burnt-out apartment buildings, the Florence and the Montcalm on Harbor Street. In the bottom photograph, Saint Joseph's French Roman Catholic Church stands as a destroyed hulk on Lafayette Street. (Courtesy Michaud Collection.)

The militia set up a kitchen on Broad Street to serve the numerous volunteers after the fire. The militia was called out to protect and secure the vast area destroyed by the June 1914 conflagration. (Courtesy Dionne Collection.)

During the disastrous Salem fire of June 25 and 26, 1914, the militia was called in to keep the peace. With 252 acres devastated and 3,500 families homeless, open space was at a premium. John Pickering VII (1857–1919) graciously allowed the militia men to camp out on the grounds of his ancient home at 18 Broad Street.

The crew of Ladder Number Two from Bridge Street are shown on their American LaFrance Aerial Ladder, around 1921. The city's scalehouse on Bridge Street can be seen in the background. (Courtesy Dionne Collection.)

Members of Chemical Number One pose by their American LaFrance Auto/Chemical car, around 1912. The photograph was taken by Hagar. (Courtesy Dionne Collection.)

A city service ladder truck is shown in front of the fire station at 415 Essex Street in 1921. (Courtesy Dionne Collection.)

This police photograph was taken in April 1952 at 8:15 a.m. The fire, which took place early Saturday morning, gutted a first-floor office and scalehouse at the New England Coke Company on Canal Street. (Courtesy Michaud Collection.)

Six

Street Scenes

Town House Square, at the intersection of Essex and Washington Streets, has always been busy with all kinds of traffic. The sign on the corner building reads, "Salem Five Cents Savings Bank." (Courtesy Weston Collection.)

An early stereopticon view taken of Washington Street at Front Street shows a busy street scene. The building seen here is on the site of the Salem News offices, between Front and New Derby Streets. The fence in the foreground stood in front of the Ward house, now the Higginson Book Company, located at 148 Washington Street. (Courtesy Michaud Collection.)

This stereopticon view of Front Street from Washington Street was published expressly for Guy and Brothers at 163 Essex Street by photographers Cook and Friend. (Courtesy Michaud Collection.)

J.W. and J.S. Moulton, photographers at 256 Essex Street, sold a series of stereopticon views of Salem between 1873 and 1881. This image of Washington Street from city hall was taken before 1878. (Courtesy Michaud Collection.)

This is an early albumen photograph of Washington Street, as seen from Essex Street. The building in the center of the photograph housed the Salem National Bank on the first floor, and the YMCA on the third floor. The building in the foreground at the left was the First Church, later the Daniel Low building. (Courtesy Michaud Collection.)

Gas street lights were lit for the first time on Christmas Day in 1850. Electricity was introduced to the city in 1881. By 1891, when this photograph of Town House Square was taken, electric wires and wood poles having several tiers of crossbars marred the streetscape. (Courtesy Weston Collection.)

Taken from a stereopticon view, an open car trolley moves along the cobblestone-paved Essex Street toward Washington Street. Horse-drawn trolleys began operating in 1862, when a line was built from Salem to South Danvers (Peabody). Soon after, cars ran between Salem and Beverly. (Courtesy Michaud Collection.)

Salem's Market Square, or Derby Square, was photographed by the Moulton & Erickson Photo Company in the late 1880s. A number of peddlers have brought their various wares to market, with the center cart advertising, "Fresh Fish of all kinds. Oysters and Clams." The building on the right is the Market House, built as the town hall in 1816 and opened on July 8, 1817, on the occasion of President Monroe's visit. The building was abandoned on March 23, 1836, when Salem became a city. Signs in the window advertise the City Lunch and Dining Rooms owned by Otis A. Eldridge, which occupied the basement and first floor. A hall on the second floor was kept for meetings and public events. At the far left is Abbott and Reynolds Country Produce on Front Street. In the same building was the dining room of Thomas F. Hurley. (Courtesy Michaud Collection.)

Depicted in the center of this Frank Cousins photograph is the Ward house at 148 Washington Street, built c. 1784–1788 for the merchant Joshua Ward. George Washington was a guest here on October 29, 1789, having spent the night on the second floor, northeast chamber. The home of Sheriff George Corwin, who executed the people condemned for witchcraft in 1692, originally stood on this site. In 1978 and 1979, the building was restored under the direction of Staley B. McDermet of Salem. (Courtesy Michaud Collection.)

The Joseph Story house, at 26 Winter Street, was built in 1811 by the Marblehead native Judge Joseph Story (1779–1845). Judge Story was an Associate Justice of the United States Supreme Court, a United States congressman, and one of the founders of Harvard Law School. At his Winter Street residence he entertained many dignitaries, including the fifth president of the United States, James Monroe (1758–1831), in 1824, and French general and statesman Marquis de Lafayette (1757–1834) on August 31, 1824. Judge Story's son, William Wetmore Story (1819–1895), a noted sculptor, author, and poet, was born here. (Courtesy of the Estate of Borinous Schier.)

The 23rd Regiment Memorial is located at the end of Winter Street by Salem Common. The huge, 58-ton, granite boulder was moved from Salem Neck in 1905. The memorial's bronze plaque lists the 13 engagements the 23rd Regiment Massachusetts Volunteer Infantry was engaged in during the Civil War. On the back of the boulder is a bronze corps. badge of the 18th Army Corps.

This *c.* 1891 spring view of Essex Street shows, from left to right, Plummer Hall, the home of the Salem Athenaeum, the Tucker-Daland house, headquarters of the Essex Institute, the home of David Pingree, the George Creamer building, and Franklin Hall. (Courtesy Weston Collection.)

The large, impressive, brick Franklin Building was built in the Italianate Revival style in 1863–64. It replaced an earlier building by the same name which was destroyed by fire in 1860. The multi-use structure, owned by the Salem Marine Society, was located at 18 Washington Square West, at the corner of Essex Street. The society was formed in 1766, and is the oldest charitable organization in the city of Salem. In addition to the meeting hall and reading rooms, the building was used for business offices, retail stores, and apartments. It was razed to make way for construction of the Hawthorne Hotel in 1924–25. (Courtesy Weston Collection.)

The second Lynde Block was built after a disastrous fire completely consumed the original Lynde Block on May 14, 1866, at the corner of Essex Street and Liberty Street. The Lynde Block depicted here was built a year later. The commercial building survived until 1973, when the Peabody Museum razed the structure for its expansion program. (Courtesy Weston Collection.)

A view from the North Bridge, looking down North Street, shows a varied streetscape with factories and houses. The three-story, wooden factory on the right housed two manufacturing concerns. The Locke Brothers, Nathaniel C., Albert N., and Mark C., ran a manufacturing company that made pressure and damper regulators for water and steam. The other business was owned by Joseph F. Pitman, a shoe manufacturer. (Courtesy Weston Collection.)

It is hard to believe today that the scene depicted in this c. 1890 photograph is the intersection of Essex, Summer, and North Streets. The wooden building on the corner was owned by David Pingree and is the present-day site of Jerry's Army & Navy Store. The brick building is the present-day location of Michael Roberts Hair Fashions. In the 1890s, the brick store at 299 Essex Street was the shop of Timothy O'Connell, a boot maker and an agent for the Cunard Line of steamships. The bicycle store on the left is Whitten Bicycles, at 295 Essex Street. (Courtesy Weston Collection.)

Washington Street in the 1890s was cobblestone-paved with inset iron trolley tracks. The buildings on the left are the Pickman-Derby-Brookhouse Mansion, the Odell Block, and the spire of the Tabernacle Congregational Church. Shown on the right is the large, imposing commercial building known as the Kinsman Block, built in 1882. (Courtesy Weston Collection.)

According to Bryant F. Tolles Jr., in *Architecture in Salem*, the Essex County courthouse buildings, "form a visually exciting as well as historically significant streetscape." Richard Bond (1797–1861) designed the granite, Greek Revival-style building on Federal Street, which was built between 1839 and 1841. The two Egyptian Revival columns are its most impressive feature. Enoch Fuller (1828–1861) designed the building to the left in 1861–62. This photograph shows the alterations made between 1887 and 1889, including the added tower, which gave it its present, Richardsonian-Romanesque appearance. The tower at the far left graced the First Baptist Church, but was removed in 1926. (Courtesy Weston Collection.)

General Frederick Townsend Ward (1831–1862) was born in this brick home at 96 Derby Street, at the corner of Carlton Street. His exploits during the Tai Ping rebellion brought him great fame and success in China. He died in battle and is buried there. A temple was dedicated to his memory, where he was worshipped as a god. The Peabody-Essex Museum houses a memorial library relating to China in Ward's memory, as well as personal effects of General Ward and his Asian wife. (Courtesy Weston Collection.)

The marble Father Mathew statue was moved to Hawthorne Boulevard in 1916. It was erected in 1887, over a fresh-water spring on Central Street. The water provided refreshment for those who wanted to imbibe. Father Mathew, the "Apostle of Temperance," founded the Father Mathew Catholic Total Abstinence Society. He visited Salem only once, on September 19, 1849. The society, organized in Salem on November 14, 1875, had headquarters at 129 Essex Street, the former Tucker estate, which they purchased in 1896. (Courtesy Michaud Collection.)

Pictured here is a rear view of the Father Mathew statue on Central Street looking toward Essex Street. (Courtesy Dionne Collection.)

This view of Winter Street looking toward Bridge Street was photographed by Frank Cousins, *c.* 1892. The triangular grassy area is known as the Merritt Triangle, and is centered by a fanciful, circular, wrought-and-cast-iron fence. Towering trees provide shade in summer to the elegant brick- and wood-framed, three-story residences, all of which are enhanced by window shutters. (Courtesy Weston Collection.)

The Roger Conant statue is situated at the intersection of Brown Street and Washington Square, overlooking the Salem Common. The granite boulder is from the wooded area near Buchanan Bridge in nearby Lynn. The bronze statue of Conant was designed by Henry Hudson Kitson for the Conant Family Association. The dedication took place on June 17, 1913. In 1626, Roger Conant and his companions were the first to settle in Salem, then called Naumkeag.

The Nathaniel Hawthorne (1804–1864) monument was erected on Hawthorne Boulevard in 1925. The bronze statue was designed a few years earlier by Bela Lyon Pratt (1867–1917). The Rockport Granite Company cut and erected the granite pedestal according to designs submitted by Wenham and Boston architects Philip Horton Smith (1890–1960) and Edgar Walker. (Courtesy Michaud Collection.)

The dedication of the Hawthorne Monument, in 1925, completed the Hawthorne Boulevard project. The boulevard replaced two streets, Walnut and Elm Streets. Many houses were moved to other locations within the city—others were torn down. On the right is the Church of the Immaculate Conception, at 15 Hawthorne Boulevard, built in the Romanesque Revival style in 1857 by Salem architect Enoch Fuller (1828–1861). The steeple was remodeled and replaced in 1880, and it houses in its belfry the largest bell in Salem, weighing 3,250 pounds. (Courtesy Theriault Collection.)

On April 30, 1915, the Salem City Council passed a bill to establish Hawthorne Boulevard. Shown here is the nearly completed thoroughfare. The three-story brick building in the center of the photograph is Franklin Hall. (Courtesy Theriault Collection.)

This gambrel-roof dwelling with a rear lean-to addition was located at 66 Boston Street. The pitched-roof structure at 64 Boston Street was positioned at the junction of Goodhue, Bridge, and Boston Streets. The commercial building in the background is the Hygrade Lamp Company, manufacturers of Tungsten incandescent lamps. Today all these buildings are gone. The factory was razed in recent years and is now a vacant lot. (Courtesy Theriault Collection.)

In the mid-1950s, this building, located at the corner of Federal and Ash Streets, was removed to make way for the New England Telephone & Telegraph Company sales accounting office. In the 1890s, the stone building at 12 Federal Street was owned by the Frothingham family. The brick home at 2 Ash Street was owned by the Haskell family. (Courtesy Theriault Collection.)

Seen here is a wintry view of Brown Street, looking toward Salem Common. Behind the iron-and-brick fence is a partial view of the John Ward house, owned by the Essex Institute. The wood-framed houses on the right, at 3 and 5 Brown Street, were razed in the late 1960s to provide parking for the Essex Institute. (Courtesy Theriault Collection.)

This view of the cobblestone-paved Norman Street looks toward the train station, with its fortress-like, Norman-style towers. The house on the right was the home of Benjamin and Elizabeth Cox. (Courtesy Dionne Collection.)

Depicted in this 1920s photograph is the corner of Margin and Norman Streets, the present-day site of the United States post office building. A whole city block of houses and businesses were removed to build the federal building, at the cost of 51 buildings and over one million dollars in restitution. The construction of the post office also included the widening of streets, including Gedney, Crombie Street Extension, Norman, and Margin Streets in the surrounding area. The post office opened for business on July 31, 1933. (Courtesy Theriault Collection.)

The cobbler shop of T.A. Corson, located at the present-day site of Red's Sandwich Shop, is barely visible in this Central Street image. Thomas A. Corson (1841-1944) was the last surviving Civil War veteran of the General Lander Post Five Grand Army of the Republic, located at 58 Andrew Street, Lynn, Massachusetts. (Courtesy Theriault Collection.)

The Reverend James P. Franks, rector at the Grace Episcopal Church, poses for a photograph with his Model T Ford. He and his family lived at 6 Hamilton Street. (Courtesy Soper Collection.)

A Salem Trolley car turns the corner onto Essex Street from Washington Square East. The house on the left, at 70 Essex Street, was owned at one time by Elizabeth Chambers. The house next to it, at 70 Washington Square East, was owned by Zina Goodell of Goodell's Hardware. (Courtesy Dionne Collection.)

This view of Salem Common was taken after the devastating hurricane known as "Carol" hit New England on August 31, 1954. The once-beautiful common is littered with debris from uprooted trees and broken branches. The Victorian structure on the right is the Now and Then Club, followed by the Oakes-Gray-Perkins house and O'Donnell Funeral Home. (Courtesy Soper Collection.)

The children in this photograph, Rita Fontaine, Leon Fontaine, and Hector Jalbert Jr., do not appear to be interested in being photographed. Grandmother Celanire (Caron) Fontaine stands on the lawn in front of her 331 Jefferson Avenue house in 1927. (Courtesy Michaud Collection.)

Huntt's Lunch offices were located in Lynn, where they ran several restaurants. In 1944, the company operated restaurants in Boston, Brookline, Brighton, and Salem. This stylish, Art-Deco, Salem branch served customers at 99 Washington Street and was photographed in the 1930s. (Courtesy Dionne Collection.)

This aerial photograph was taken of downtown Salem in August of 1974. In the foreground is Derby Street, and in the center is Central Street. At this time, East India Square, now Museum Place Mall, was under construction. In the distance is the North River. (Courtesy of the *Lynn Daily Evening Item* Collection.)

Seen here, in an aerial view taken on August 6, 1974, is Salem State College from Canal Street, with Marblehead in the distance. The tall buildings, both classroom space and dormitories, can be clearly seen at the time of this photograph. Construction was underway on the O'Keefe Sports Center (to the right of the center). (Courtesy of *Lynn Daily Evening Item* Collection.)

Seven

Celebrations and Civic Events

This photograph of the American Legion Band, Post 23, may have been taken at the dedication of the present bandstand on Salem Common during the tercentenary celebration in 1926. Originally a memorial to the soldiers of all wars, the bandstand was rededicated to Jean Marie Missud during the bicentennial on July 4, 1976. Missud (1852–1941) was called "the prince of musicians" and was the leader of the famous Salem Cadet Band from 1879 to 1939. (Courtesy Theriault Collection.)

This Frank Cousins photograph shows the John Tucker Daland house, at 132 Essex Street, decorated for the 400th anniversary celebration of Columbus Day on October 12, 1892. John T. Daland (1795–1858), a wealthy Salem merchant, commissioned well-known Boston architect Gridley J.F. Bryant (1816–1899) to design a palatial residence for his family. The Italianate brownstone-and-brick home was built between 1851 and 1852. The Daland family and their heirs lived here until 1885, when it was purchased by the Essex Institute for use as its headquarters. (Courtesy Weston Collection.)

A Frank Cousins photograph shows East India Marine Hall decorated for the 400th anniversary celebration of Columbus's discovery of America, on October 12, 1892. For many years the first-floor rooms of the East India Marine Hall provided income-producing rents for the society. Some of the notable tenants were the Asiatic Bank, the Naumkeag Bank, the Salem Marine Insurance Company, and the Gas Light Company. (Courtesy Weston Collection.)

Dressed in their finery on a beautiful summer day, *c.* 1880, from left to right, Mary Pickering, Sally Cox, Margaret Rantoul, Minnia Phillips, Edith Rantoul, John Pickering, Arthur Clarke, and Benjamin Cox posed for the photographer in a tranquil sylvan knoll. (Courtesy Pickering Collection.)

The Gallows Hill Bonfire Association, organized on June 1, 1890, spent two months in 1897 piling 7,000–8,000 barrels. The structure collapsed due to a poor foundation and inclement weather on June 29. Within five days a "mammoth" bonfire was created with 24 tiers, made up of eight tiers of hogsheads, three of pork barrels, and 13 of lime barrels. The base measured 175 feet in circumference with a height just over 100 feet. On July 4, 1897, a flag from the Sheridan Club, organized November 13, 1887, was raised as the Salem Brass Band played "The Star Spangled Banner." The fire was lit a few minutes before midnight, and it took nearly 15 minutes for the fire to reach each barrel. Thousands of people watched what the *Salem News* called, "the largest bonfire ever seen in this vicinity, probably in New England, perhaps in the country." This photograph was taken by Albert C. McIntire. (Courtesy Michaud Collection.)

Pageants became popular in the early part of the 20th century to educate people about "colonial history." A product of the Colonial Revival movement, these pageants usually ran over several days and included large casts made up of local residents. A souvenir program shows Native Americans viewing what may be the *Arabella*—the ship that brought Governor Winthrop and the charter of the settlement in 1630. (Courtesy of the Estate of Borinous Schier.)

"Salem Pageant is a gorgeous spectacle," reported the *Salem News* on June 14, 1913. "With an almost perfect night, an attendance of about 2000 persons, and the participants (numbering 1200, exclusive of orchestra and mixed chorus of 150 voices), entering into their work with a delightful enthusiasm, the Pageant of Salem has given its initial presentation at Kernwood." This photograph postcard shows part of the cast for the episode on the persecution of the Quakers. (Courtesy Michaud Collection.)

The Pageant of Salem was held on June 13, 14, 15, and 17, 1913, at Kernwood, the estate of the late S. Endicott Peabody. The Gothic-style mansion was built in 1840 by Francis Peabody. The pageant featured highlights of Salem's history and was presented under the management of the board of directors of the House of the Seven Gables Settlement Association. The cast included hundreds of actors and actresses from the Salem community—many from the most prominent families. Depicted here are John and Rebecca Pickering in the garden of their home at 18 Broad Street. John played the role of Colonel Timothy Pickering in the episode of Leslie's Retreat at the North Bridge.

Academy Hall at the Peabody Museum opened February 12, 1886. The hall included a three hundred-seat auditorium, complete with a raised stage and sloping floor. Depicted in this 1898 photograph are, from left to right, Mrs. W.P. Andrews, Mrs. Pickering, and F.P. Fabens. Academy Hall was razed in 1974 to make way for the Ernest S. Dodge wing. (Courtesy Pickering Collection.)

Salem ladies, dressed in old family garments, pose in front of the Derby house during the Salem tercentennial in 1926. Pictured from left to right are as follows: (front row) Miss Margaret Rantoul, Mrs. Oscar Ives, Mrs. Alden P. White, Mrs. Christian Lantz, and Mrs. Thomas Sanders; (middle row) Miss Katherine Fabens, Mrs. Benjamin Shreve, Mrs. Charles Allen, and Miss Charlotte Rantoul; (back row) Miss Eleanor Broadhead and Mrs. Alfred Putnam. (Courtesy Pickering Collection.)

A bird's-eye view of Salem Common shows the old wooden bandstand surrounded by hordes of people. The spire at the far left belongs to the Bentley School on Essex Street. The massive brick building on the right is the Phillips School. (Courtesy Theriault Collection.)

Officials and invited guests gather on the rooftop of the Hawthorne Hotel to watch the flag-raising ceremony during the opening festivities of the newly completed edifice. The six-story-tall, brick, Colonial Revival hotel, at 18 Washington Square West, was built in 1924–25. Philip Horton Smith of Boston and Wenham was the architect. The builder and contractor was the H.C. Stephens Company of New York, New York. (Courtesy Theriault Collection.)

An Eastern Massachusetts Electric Company truck, probably at its 197A Washington Street location in Salem, was photographed in the 1920s, all decked out, possibly for a Fourth of July celebration competition. The truck includes Father Time, with an hourglass and scythe, as well as a skull—unusual imagery for a patriotic celebration. (Courtesy Theriault Collection.)

A parade passes by the chamber of commerce building at the corner of Washington and New Derby Streets in the 1920s. The main store and offices of the Ropes Drug Company were located in this building, along with the chamber of commerce. Ropes also had stores in Beverly and Danvers. Hats certainly had to be in style, for nearly every man is wearing a cap or straw bowler. (Courtesy Theriault Collection.)

A bird's-eye view of the 1926 Salem Tercentenary Parade shows floats progressing up Washington Street. (Courtesy Dionne Collection.)

The American Legion Post 34 was organized in 1919, and could boast of several musical groups, such as the Scottish Bag Pipe Band. The band is pictured here in front of the Tabernacle Church at 58 Washington Street. The post held its meetings at the Legion hall at 329 Essex Street, the former home of Frank and Elizabeth Balch. (Courtesy Theriault Collection.)

Patriotic celebrations have been a part of Salem's civic life for years. This image, taken in front of Moustakis Confectionery at 220 Essex Street, was taken some time in the 1930s and shows the Second Corp. Cadets of the 102 Field Artillery. (Courtesy Joseph F. Schier Collection.)

The centennial of Salem as a city was a gala event held in 1936. The leading politicians of the day can be seen standing on a reviewing stand in front of city hall. (Courtesy Michaud Collection.)

With the defeat of Japan at the end of World War II, Salem celebrated V-J Day with parades and other events, as did many other communities. This photograph was taken September 2, 1945, on Washington Street. A large "V" is visible in front of the Salem Depot. One feature, now long-gone, was the police traffic box. (Courtesy Michaud Collection.)

As part of the 1936 centennial celebrations of the 100th year as a city, a parade marches down Mill Hill (Washington Street). On the left, the Mill Hill Garage and Mill Hill Motor Company are visible. (Courtesy Michaud Collection.)

On May 25, 1946, Martial Michaud and his wife, Philomene (pictured in the center), hosted a wedding reception for their daughter in their 47 Leavitt Street home. The bride and groom, Marie-Laure Michaud and Leo Momeau, are to the right of the clock. (Courtesy Michaud Collection.)

These children, who grew up off Salem Common, played football as the Salem Steam Rollers in 1938. They are, from left to right, as follows: (front row) Arthur Nagle, Jim Soper, John Adams, Joey Perkins (the water boy), unidentified, Mike Liebsch, and Herman Stromberg; (back row) unidentified, Paul Chase, unidentified, Dick Soper, Bill Burns, unidentified, and unidentified. (Courtesy Soper Collection.)

In the late 1940s, employees of Reid and Hughes Department Store, at 182 Essex Street, held a "Girls Club Party." The lovely ladies consisted of, from left to right, Assistant Manager Bob Burnett, Manager David Brown, unidentified, attorney for the store Bill Welch, Vice President Ivan Martin, William Kulakowski, buyer Ed Coffill, and unidentified. (Courtesy Shay Collection.)

Salem's French Canadian community has traditionally been strong, and their lives were often centered around their churches, Saint Anne's and Saint Joseph's, and schools such as Saint Joseph Academy. Here, at the Canadian Klondike Club, at 96 Lafayette Street, the community came to socialize at the 25th wedding anniversary of Blanche Moreau and Thomas Bois (front left and right) on June 26, 1945. Several hundred friends and relatives attended the event hosted by Martial Michaud, one of the club's officers and stepson of Thomas Bois. He is pictured behind Thomas. (Courtesy Michaud Collection.)

Festivities at the Salem Willows on the Fourth of July for many years have included a horribles parade. Here residents in outlandish costumes parade in the 1950s. (Courtesy Mathias Collection.)

Most students are happy to complete their academic studies, and here the graduation class of 1960 at St. Mary's School on Hawthorne Boulevard smiles broadly. (Courtesy Gentile Collection.)

A view of the Broad Street Cemetery shows the tomb of Colonel Timothy Pickering (1745–1829) in the foreground, and the tomb of John Pickering VI (1777–1846) in the background. (Courtesy Pickering Collection.)

ACKNOWLEDGMENTS

The authors wish to express their thanks and gratitude to the following people and organizations that graciously loaned photographs and illustrations for publication in *Salem, Volume Two*. We would like to thank the collector and antiquarian H. Russell Weston for the use of his extensive photographic collection on North Shore images. Expressions of gratitude go to D. Michel Michaud, who once again lent us images from his vast collection. To Henry R. Theriault, who probably has the greatest Salem postcard collection, we give thanks and appreciation for his knowledge of Salem history and the use of his voluminous collection. We thank Nelson Dionne, another great Salem collector, who helped us fill in missing gaps in many of the book's chapters. To the former Salemites Mr. and Mrs. James A. Soper, we thank them for the use of many precious family photographs. The authors wish to especially thank Sarah C. Pickering for the many wonderful images she provided for this second Salem volume. The Salem Police Department was instrumental in procuring long-hidden photographs from their archives. We thank Chief Robert M. St. Pierre for allowing us to publish these images. Kudos go to Captain Harold Blake, who was able to identify the officers in the photographs. The utmost respect goes to Sergeant Conrad Prosniewski, who was a liaison between the department and the authors. Thanks to Detective Gauthier and his photographic skills, who copied the photographs and provided an image of his own. Other people and organizations who provided images and deserve our thanks are Joseph F. Schier; Officer Thomas J. Brennan; the Lynn Historical Society; the estate of Borinous Schier; Christopher, Ben, and Sally Mathias; Barromee Dube; Cynthia and William Q. Gentile; Stephen Buczko; Eleanor Shay; Mrs. Henry P. Binney Jr.; Barbara A. Doucette; Edward W. Carberg; Charlotte R. Duke; and Miss Eleanor Broadhead. A special thanks goes to author and antiquarian John Hardy Wright and Christopher Mathias for proof-reading the manuscript, and to our typist and proof-reader Fay Greenleaf, who has helped with our previous books, and provided us with support.